FOURTH EDITION

THEORIES AND STRATEGIES
IN COUNSELING
AND PSYCHOTHERAPY

Burl E. Gilliland
The University of Memphis

Richard K. James
The University of Memphis

Allyn and Bacon
Boston • London • Toronto • Sydney • Tokyo • Singapore

Vice President, Education: Nancy Forsyth
Series Editor: Ray Short
Editorial Assistant: Christine Svitila
Marketing Manager: Kris Farnsworth
Sr. Editorial Production Administrator: Susan McIntyre
Editorial Production Service: Ruttle, Shaw & Wetherill, Inc.
Composition Buyer: Linda Cox
Manufacturing Buyer: Megan Cochran
Cover Administrator: Linda Knowles

Library of Congress Cataloging-in-Publication Data

Gilliland, Burl E.
   Theories and strategies in counseling and psychotherapy / Burl E.
Gilliland, Richard K. James. — 4th ed.
     p.   cm.
   Includes bibliographical references and index.
   ISBN 0-205-26832-3
   1. Psychotherapy.   2. Counseling.   I. James, Richard K.
   II. Title.
RC480.G53   1998
616.89'14—dc21   97-20362
                                          CIP

Printed in the United States of America

10 9 8 7 6 5 4 3 2   RRD 04 03 02 01 00 99 98

CONTENTS

PREFACE

Writing a textbook on counseling and psychotherapy as we move to the twenty-first century is a daring venture. This is true for three reasons. First, the number and complexity of theories has grown exponentially in the last three decades. The popularity of traditional therapies such as the psychoanalytic and client-centered approaches has declined while other emergent modalities, such as the cognitive-behavioral approaches, have rapidly increased in popularity. However, for all therapies, the central axiom is *change*. The recent emphasis on accountability, the lack of demonstrated superiority of one approach over another, and the trend toward integration and eclecticism have made it difficult to write a text that clearly distinguishes approaches, yet treats them from a contemporary perspective.

The second reason is that therapy has moved from the Freudian couch into the community. The people we train work in businesses as big as Federal Express and as small as locally owned real estate agencies. Customer relations personnel at South Central Bell, personnel managers at Dobbs House, chaplains at hospitals, officers and NCOs in the armed services, ministers in churches, recruiters for a wide range of organizations, nurses in a variety of health-care settings, and salespersons from car dealers to clothiers all find utility in the practice and use of the theories and techniques found in this book. Such people use these approaches not only with others, but also for themselves. None of these people would label themselves *therapists* or *counselors*. Yet all of them have found worth, both personally and professionally, in the ideas promoted in this book.

When we move to the helping professions themselves, we find the same diversity in the field. Employee assistance counselors, marriage and family therapists, preretirement counselors, rehabilitation therapists, drug and alcohol counselors, psychiatrists, high school counselors, clinical psychologists, vocational and employment counselors, counseling psychologists, elementary school counselors, student personnel workers in higher education, gerontological counselors, crisis interventionists, mental health agency therapists, social workers, educational psychologists, pastoral counselors, psychiatric nurses, teachers, and corrections counselors all find some utility in the theories and techniques in this book. The list of occupations that are indirectly and directly allied with counseling and psychotherapy is staggering and continues to grow.

The third reason is the profession itself. Since the first edition of this book was published in 1984, we have seen a dramatic increase in the influence of both professional and state accrediting bodies on what constitutes a comprehensive program of study in the field and what a person must do to achieve certification or licensure for mental health work. National legislation has also affected programs and delivery of services. As an example, the 1992 Americans with Disabilities Act ushered in dramatic shifts in the way business and industry must deal with work barriers and disabling conditions of physically and mentally challenged clients. Clearly, mental health plays a major role in what services will be provided to this group and how they will be delivered.

The advent of managed care has had an extraordinary influence on the provision of mental health services. Cost containment has pushed all professionals in the mental health field to be diagnostically clear and behaviorally specific, and to supply the briefest and most efficacious treatment possible. As a result, managed care certainly has an impact on the kind of theoretical modalities used in treatment.

Finally, increased awareness by professional organizations that service providers need to recognize the pluralism of their clientele has resulted in a tremendous amount of discussion and research on the way services should be delivered to populations that do not fit the ethnocentric Western European mold that has long held sway in psychotherapy.

We have opted to approach the several different theories from a practical point of view, to slant them toward entry-level professionals whatever their field, and to include many of our own cases and experiences to reflect the wide and ever-expanding clientele that depicts the current human dilemma. We use the words *counselor* and *therapist* in different places as generic representations of all helping professions. We use other terms to represent the helping professions sparingly, if at all. We hope that other professionals who call themselves by other names will not be offended.

In this fourth edition we have added what we believe are significant new therapeutic techniques and deleted some that seem not to have held up under the demands of practice. First, we have added a brief section in Chapter 4 (Jungian therapy) on chaos theory. This theory, which has its origins in a highly theoretical mathematics field, has started to emerge in the field of psychotherapy. Second, because of the continued expansion of cognitive-based therapies, we have again enlarged Chapter 11. In particular, Eye Movement Desensitization and Reprocessing (EMD/R), a rather mystifying technique but one that is backed by solid research, has been added. Third, due to the resurgence of personal construct theory, we have added the constructivist approach to the eclectic chapter (13). Finally, we end this book with a somewhat controversial therapeutic approach: computer-assisted therapy. We believe that enough progress has now been made in the use of the computer as therapist that it should be introduced to prospective therapists of the twenty-first century, who will undoubtedly work with it in the years ahead.

To do all of the foregoing, we have closely edited each chapter. We have continued to give case studies a good deal of space because we believe that written examples of what we do and why we do it are as close to real life as a textbook can get. While this approach may be at the expense of more detailed theoretical discussion, our hope is that this book will demonstrate for beginners in the field how theory *goes into practice,* thus we give somewhat more emphasis to the latter. We hope the result is clear and concise, flows smoothly, and covers theory adequately.

Finally, our different styles of therapy show through in our writing, despite our best efforts to standardize the text. Therapists are not clones, nor are writers of books on therapy. We trust that our different styles, both in techniques and in writing, give an eclectic flavor to this book, which we think represents us. Our choices of theoretical systems, our organization of chapter topics and content, and our depth of coverage are the result of our eclectic view, our experience in teaching beginning students, our formal and informal discussions with colleagues, and our work with clients. We hope the product will help you help your clients. If it does, we will have done our job.

Burl and Dick

1

INTRODUCTION

PURPOSES OF THE BOOK

Our objective in writing this book is to integrate the theory and application of the major current systems of counseling and psychotherapy. Programs in counselor and therapist education are frequently criticized for being too theoretical. Theories and strategies are often dealt with separately, and helper trainees sometimes have difficulty making the transition. We attempt to bridge this theory/application gap.

Our specific goals for the book are: (1) to provide beginning graduate or undergraduate students in counseling and psychotherapy with a survey of current theories applied to real counseling situations similar to what they themselves may encounter; (2) to present the material systematically and in language that is as nontechnical as possible; and (3) to encourage each learner to incorporate the "best" of each theory into his or her personal style and repertory of helping skills.

OVERVIEW

We put a good deal of thought and discussion into the selection of the thirteen theoretical positions we discuss in the book. We used three criteria—*applicability* to a broad spectrum of practitioners, a recognized sound *theoretical foundation,* and *current* usage—and selected the thirteen theories that in our judgment best met those criteria.

We considered several criteria for sequencing the thirteen approaches in the text—historical development, process similarities, philosophical kinship, and so on. Table 1.1 on pages 2–3 shows some of the key contributors and characteristics we used in ordering the chapters. Psychoanalytic therapy comes first because of its historical prominence, its body of clinical and scientific knowledge, and its influence on the various therapies that followed. All the major approaches to counseling and psychotherapy either flowed from or were developed in reaction to psychoanalytic theory.

TABLE 1.1   Theoretical Approaches to Counseling and Psychotherapy

General Approach	Chapter and Theoretical System	Personality Theory Base and Founder and/or Major Contributors	Key Characteristics
Psychodynamic	2. Psychoanalytic therapy	Psychoanalysis *Founder:* Sigmund Freud	Deterministic, topographic, dynamic, genetic, analytic, developmental, historical, insightful, unconscious-motivational
Social-Psychodynamic	3. Adlerian therapy	Individual psychology *Founder:* Alfred Adler *Major contributors:* R. Dreikurs D. Dinkmeyer, Sr. H. Mosak	Holistic, phenomenological, socially oriented, teleological, field-theoretical, functionalistic
Transcendental-Psychodynamic	4. Jungian therapy	Analytical *Founder:* Carl Jung	Deterministic, teleological, symbolic, unconscious-motivational, transpersonal, individuational
Humanistic, Experiential, Existential	5. Person-centered counseling	Person-centered theory *Founder:* Carl Rogers	Humanistic, experiential, existential, organismic, self-theoretical, phenomenological, person-centered, here-and-now-oriented
	6. Gestalt therapy	Gestalt therapy theory *Founder:* Frederick Perls	Existential, experiential, humanistic, organismic, awareness-evocative, here-and-now-oriented, client-centered, confrontive
Cognitive, Behavioral, Action-Oriented	7. Transactional analysis	Transactional analysis theory *Founder:* Eric Berne *Major contributors:* R. Goulding M. Goulding	Cognitive, analytic, redecisional, contractual, interpretational, confrontational, action-oriented, awareness-evocative, social-interactive
	8. Behavioral counseling, therapy, and modification	Behavior theory and conditioning theory *Major contributors:* B. F. Skinner J. Wolpe	Behavioristic, pragmatic, scientific, learning-theoretical, cognitive, action-oriented, experimental, goal-oriented, contractual

TABLE 1.1   *Continued*

General Approach	Chapter and Theoretical System	Personality Theory Base and Founder and/or Major Contributors	Key Characteristics
	9. Rational-emotive behavior therapy (REBT)	Rational-emotive theory *Founder:* Albert Ellis *Major contributors:* W. Dryden R. A. DiGiuseppe R. Grieger	Rational, cognitive, scientific, philosophic, action-oriented, relativistic, didactic, here-and-now-oriented, decisional, contractual, humanistic
	10. Control theory/reality therapy	Reality theory *Founder:* William Glasser	Reality-based, rational, anti-deterministic, cognitive, action-oriented, scientific, directive, didactic, contractual, supportive, non-punitive, positivistic, here-and-now-oriented
	11. Cognitive therapy	Cognitive theory *Major contributors:* A. Beck, A. Ellis, D. Meichenbaum, A. Lazarus, J. Wolpe	Cognitive, rational, scientific, goal-directed, systematic, logical, mental and emotive, imaginal, perceptual, stress-, thought-, and belief-managerial
Trait, Factor, Decisional, Actuarial	12. Trait-factor counseling/ Person & Environment Fit	Trait-factor theory *Contributors:* E. G. Williamson D. Paterson J. Darley, D. Biggs	Scientific, empirical, decisional, informational, educational, vocational, evaluative, data-based, past-present-future-oriented, action-oriented, technological, personal-environment-interactive, problem-solving, objective, systematic, didactic, interpretative
Integrative	13. Eclectic counseling and psychotherapy	Eclecticism *Contributors:* F. C. Thorne S. Garfield J. Palmer A. Ivey R. Carkhuff	Integrative, systematic, scientific, comprehensive, organismic-environmental, cognitive, past-present-future-oriented, behavioral, educational, developmental, humanistic, analytic, decisional
	14. Computer-assisted therapy	*Major contributors:* K. M. Colby J. H. Greist M. Wagman	Integrative, systemic, pro-grammed, systematic, inter-active, electronic, eclectic

We placed Adlerian therapy second because it originated as a direct alternative to Freud's formulations, because it is to this day one of the most comprehensive of the social-psychological theories, and because it has had a long and sustained history of research and application to mental health.

Jungian therapy comes third because, although it too is dynamic, it is also a direct reaction to Freudian formulations. Its emphasis on humankind's transcendent, spiritual nature is radically different from Freud's sexual emphasis or Adler's socialization approach.

We included two representative systems from the humanistic-experiential-existential category—the person-centered and Gestalt approaches. Two of the best-known humanistic theories, both have contributed heavily to other therapies. Rogers's person-centered theory has been influential in making the personal relationship between client and counselor an essential part of practically all theories. Perls's Gestalt therapy has shown practitioners of the other therapies how to use awareness-evoking techniques to help clients integrate conflicting feelings.

Transactional analysis (TA) follows Gestalt therapy because of the process similarities of the two systems. But TA is more action-oriented, making it the logical lead-in to four other cognitive, behavioral, action-oriented approaches: behavioral counseling, rational-emotive therapy, control/reality therapy, and cognitive therapy. This cluster of approaches represents a wide diversity of philosophies, tenets, and strategies for helping clients. It is eclectic in many ways, though the characteristics of the five therapies are essentially compatible. The strongest commonality in this cluster is that each therapy assumes that client perception alone is not a sufficient therapeutic outcome; purposeful action by the client is also required. All of the cognitive, behavioral, action-oriented approaches purport to integrate the client's thinking and doing in ways that produce satisfactory coping behavior.

We placed trait-factor counseling next because it is also decisional, directive, and psychoeducational. We believe this therapy's original theses of helping clients make informed choices based on strong assessment and actuarial methods will be resurgent in an increasingly technological society. Psychotherapy in this society will rely more and more on computer assistance as an inexpensive and efficient way to provide mental health service. We conclude this book with a new chapter on the computer as counselor. A computer that can beat the world's champion chessmaster is a small presage of computers that will think, adapt, and interact with humans. This chapter will undoubtedly cause much controversy and discussion. However, it is our belief that the computer will play an ever increasing role in counseling theory and practice in the future, and that future is very near at hand if we can believe the artificial intelligence scientists.

In keeping with what we perceive to be a trend toward an integrated theory of counseling, we believe there is greater value in focusing on the similarities and mutually sustaining aspects of each therapy than in pitting one theory against another. We believe that each theory has valuable dimensions to offer the prospective counselor. But we also hold that each learner must become personally involved in each approach to experience permanent and optimum gains from studying it. We ask our students to apply each approach to their present concerns and lives. We try to serve as living models for students by applying the approaches to our own lives. Continual learning enhances each of us personally and professionally. We hope that each learner emerges with a wide array of skills incorporated into his or her natural talents and style. We believe it would be a fundamental mistake to rely exclusively on one theory. Counselors need an integrated philosophy of counseling and of life, a broad world view, and mastery of several diverse helping strategies.

Our treatment of each theoretical system contains sections on (1) fundamental tenets, (2) the counseling process, (3) strategies for helping clients, (4) a sample case or cases, (5) contributions of the system, (6) shortcomings of the system, and (7) therapy with diverse populations, as well as (8) a summary, (9) suggestions for further reading, and (10) references. None of the sections attempt in-depth coverage. This book is a *survey* emphasizing theory and strategy. Readers who wish to study an approach in greater depth are encouraged to begin with our suggestions for further reading.

SUGGESTIONS FOR USING THE BOOK

Based on our combined experience as learners, teachers, and practitioners, we have a few suggestions we believe will enhance the usability of this book and the skills prospective counselors will acquire from it and from classroom instruction:

1. *Continue to learn.* Use this book as a catalyst. Let it be a launching pad for reading, exploration, volunteer counseling in agencies where you can practice the skills described in these pages, and continual personal and professional development. There is no such thing as finishing one's education. We encourage our students to supplement the text and classroom instruction by doing prepracticum counseling in an agency as part of the course grade contract. We also encourage you to read, read, read. The list of suggested readings at the end of each chapter is a start to comprehensive understanding and mastery of the theory presented.

2. *Use video- and audiotape techniques.* Constructive feedback over an extended period enhances one's counseling skills. Readings alone may not be of sufficient instructional value. Hearing and/or seeing oneself deal with different problems at different times is valuable, and observing other members of the group in their counseling practice is doubly so. The value of reproductive media, whether sophisticated video equipment or simple audiotape recorders, in maintaining or improving one's own counseling skills is substantial.

3. *Use the case studies.* We have tried to provide you with "pure" cases that exemplify the major components of the approach being discussed. All of these were "real McCoy" counseling cases, which fortunately had positive outcomes. That has not been true of every case we have encountered. Sometimes we fail. We don't like that. It makes us more determined to find something that will work. As a result, we grow. We learn new techniques. We combine old techniques in different ways. Although we have presented "pure" cases, we don't often operate that way. We are not opposed to, and in fact encourage, combinations of approaches. Therefore we are probably more eclectic than anything else. Being eclectic does not necessarily mean taking a shotgun approach to client problems. We think a great deal before we act. We would ask you to do the same. Look at the case studies as examples. Think about them, discuss them, and try them out. Then form your own counseling Gestalt.

4. *Take risks.* We understand how scary it is to put oneself on display, especially in front of a class with an instructor present—and especially with a grade on the line! We don't like to be seen as incompetent any more than you do. If we didn't take risks, though, nothing would ever happen, and both we and our clients would stay immobilized. Therefore, we urge you to take a risk by trying the techniques in this book. There is no better place than a classroom for doing this. Mistakes can be remediated a lot more easily here than in the trenches with real clients. Solicit your instructor for feedback on how you are doing. Criticism is never fun to hear, but it is a must if you are to become skillful.

We encourage our students to take such risks and try out combinations of approaches. However, this does not mean "shotgunning." Gauge carefully what you believe will work, and then give it your best effort. Who knows—you and your instructor may both be pleasantly surprised!

5. *Cultivate a pluralistic viewpoint.* Each chapter in this book includes a section on that theory's applicability to a diverse clientele. One of the major issues in counseling today is the multicultural aspect of counseling and the training of therapists to become culturally sensitive to their clientele. (Burn, 1992; Sue, 1992; Sue, Arredondo, & McDavis, 1992). There are both universal and focused views of multicultural counseling. A universal view considers not only racial and ethnic minorities, but other minority or special populations as well. A focused view looks at multicultural counseling in relation to "visible and racial ethnic minorities" (Sue, Arredondo, & McDavis, 1992). While both views have merit, the sections on diversity in this book take a more universal view of multiculturalism and what it means in practice.

Therefore, when we speak of diversity of clientele, we are painting as broad a picture as possible, to include race, culture, religion, ethnic background, sexual orientation, disabling conditions, and other characteristics that make clients somehow "different" from the therapist. We do so because we are pretty sure that our own unconscious biases tend to run deeper than skin color, difference in race, or distinctive ethnicity. While we would like to believe we are clearly aware of our biases toward individuals who may think, feel, look, and behave differently than we, or at least are working hard to uncover and come to grips with them, the task is anything but easy. Morrow and Deidan (1992) have looked at a number of ways that inferential bias subtly creeps into counseling and may have the potential insidiously to influence how we perceive and work with the client. Thus, anytime we have clients who do not fit our own ethnocentric, social, religious, or psychological viewpoint, the chance for bias arises.

In summary, different theories have strengths and weaknesses not only in dealing with different problems, but also in dealing with different populations. We urge you to think about not only what theory best addresses a particular problem and feels right for you, but also what theory fits best with the diverse characteristics of the client in front of you. We urge you to discuss these issues with your classmates, particularly those who may have different perspectives than yours.

No therapy is ever static (see Figure 1.1). Notice that the triangle in Figure 1.1 has a component at each corner: the therapist, the client, and, at the apex, the diverse backgrounds they bring unbidden to therapy. Figure 1.1 demonstrates that not only is there a dynamic interactive effect between therapist and client, as rep-

CULTURE, ECOSYSTEM, ENVIRONMENT

**FIGURE 1.1   Reciprocal Interaction
in Psychotherapy and
Counseling.**

resented by the bidirectional arrows, there is also a more subtle but profound effect from each individual's culture, ecosystem, and environment. These arrows indicate a mutual and dynamic interactive effect as constantly occurring between all of the possible factors that affect both therapist and client: family, geographic region, race, religion, locale, physical ability, gender, economic situation, vocation, physical needs, social affiliations, and so on. Thus cultural, ecological, and environmental dynamics are a two-way street. No therapy is done in a sterile vacuum chamber free from the multiple effects of these factors on both therapist and client. The wise therapist understands the foregoing, and also understands how these factors may consciously or unconsciously influence therapy and how they are critical to the selection and use of theory and technique. We urge you not only to think about which theories and techniques seem "right" for you, but also to think about what seems "right" for the client.

   6. *Be a discerning consumer.* All too often, a beginning student is easily proselytized. Whether by reading a theory that has some intrinsic appeal, listening to a dynamic teacher who espouses a particular approach, or attending seminars by proponents of a therapy who extol it as the cure for everything from a broken heart to a stressful situation, many students injudiciously sponge up an approach and attempt to apply it to all clients in all situations. Such efforts are sophomoric.

   The field of counseling and psychotherapy is approximately one hundred years old. Many of the theories you will read about in this book are less than forty years old. The field is thus a babe in arms compared with other disciplines. Although the theories in this book have been well researched, they rest on mainly untestable philosophical assumptions rather than on empirically refutable propositions. In physics, an object will always fall at a constant rate of acceleration in the earth's gravitational field. In counseling and psychotherapy, the approach taken with a person who anesthetizes him- or herself in front of the afternoon soaps with a pitcher of martinis may be quite different from that taken with a sixteen-year-old doing street drugs with his or her peer group. Yet in neither case is there a formula such as $V = \frac{1}{2}gt^2$ that applies to the problem. The best developed of contemporary theories might better be termed *process models,* that are prescriptive in a "best bet" sense for actions counselors and therapists might take in specific settings with specific clients for specific reasons (Blocher, 1987).

In that sense, the field is probably in a preparadigmatic stage of development: legitimate methods, problems, and standards of solution serve to define competing schools of thought rather than facilitate agreement among constituencies. Without a clear framework for defining what counselors and therapists need to do, all of the facts that could pertain to the development of theory into practice are likely to seem equally relevant (Kuhn, 1962, p. 15). Does this mean that no approach has utility, that the field is no better than "witch doctoring"? We think not. We do think the research to date has opened doors for further exploration into the multifold reasons people get ensnared in problems and how counselors and therapists help people resolve those problems.

Thus, we would propose that the beginning reader not take an all-or-none perspective in reading this book. We didn't write it in that manner. Even the eclectic approach, which demonstrates how a number of theories can be combined for specific problems, is not a panacea. We are still in the dawn of the field, and as beginning travelers all, we urge you to consider each approach with an open mind. Consider how it fits you yourself and what it may represent for particular clients under particular conditions. Realize that no one approach is *the* way to treat all problems, and that much research still needs to be done.

PERSONAL QUALITIES OF THE COUNSELOR

We believe this book contains much essential information for the prospective counselor. But we also believe that the most important element in counseling is the personhood of the counselor. The most powerful impact on the client may be that of observing what the counselor *is* and *does*. Counseling is collaborative. It is something two people do together. The counselor must be willing to invite the client to interact with a person (the counselor) who is also struggling, evolving, risking, evaluating self, problem solving, and experiencing all the normal human emotions, from severe grief to ecstasy. It is important for clients to view counselors as people who are competent (but not perfect), mature, stable, persevering, and continually learning and growing. It is also important for them to understand that counselors are fallible and can experience *ambivalence, failure, frustration,* and *change.* Unless counselors can work vigorously and systematically on self-evaluation and the solution of their own problems, much of the therapeutic value of their contact with clients will be lost. Above all else, research study after research study has found that therapist effectiveness has much more to do with the client's trust and belief in the therapist than with the therapist's adherence to a particular theory of psychotherapy.

Humans are not static. We all have our peaks as well as our valleys. We all need someone to help us at times. We believe that *learning to be effective clients enhances our effectiveness as counselors*. As counselors ourselves, we do not feel disparaged to get help when we need it. We also believe that counselors cannot help clients when they themselves are anxious or depressed. Effective counseling cannot be separated from effective living. *Effectiveness training should be a primary goal* of every helper, because *effective living is the most valuable and powerful technique any counselor can offer in a helping relationship.*

We hope that reading this book and practicing the various approaches to counseling will help you live more effectively.

SUGGESTIONS FOR FURTHER READING

Cormier, L. S., & Hackney, H. (1987). *The professional counselor: A process guide to helping.* Englewood Cliffs, NJ: Prentice-Hall.

Egan, G. (1990). *The skilled helper: Model, skills, and methods for effective helping* (4th ed.). Pacific Grove, CA: Brooks/Cole.

Ivey, A. E. (1988). *Intentional interviewing and counseling: Facilitating client development* (2nd ed.). Pacific Grove, CA: Brooks/Cole.

REFERENCES

Blocher, D. H. (1987). On the uses and misuses of the term theory. *Journal of Counseling and Development, 66,* 67–68.

Burn, D. (1992). Ethical implications in cross-cultural counseling and training. *Journal of Counseling and Development, 70,* 571–577.

Kuhn, T. S. (1962). *The structure of scientific revolutions.* Chicago: University of Chicago Press.

Morrow, K. A., & Deidan, C. T. (1992). Bias in the counseling process: How to recognize and avoid it. *Journal of Counseling and Development, 70,* 584–587.

Sue, D. W. (1992). The challenge of multiculturalism. *American Counselor, 1,* 6–14.

Sue, D. W., Arrendondo, P., & McDavis, R. J. (1992). Multicultural counseling competencies and standards: A call to the profession. *Journal of Counseling and Development, 70,* 477–486.

2

PSYCHOANALYTIC THERAPY

FUNDAMENTAL TENETS

History

Psychologists in the United States virtually ignored psychoanalysis from the 1890s to the 1920s and then vigorously opposed it from the 1920s until about the 1950s. By the middle of the twentieth century, psychologists were subjecting psychoanalytic concepts to rigorous experimental tests (Shakow & Rapaport, 1964), and subsequently many of the psychoanalytic principles were incorporated into mainstream psychology (Hornstein, 1992, p. 254). By the 1990s, psychoanalytic theory was considered a cornerstone of modern counseling and psychotherapy (Fine, 1990; Hornstein, 1992). Of the several hundred therapies in use from the 1970s to the 1990s, most derived some fundamental formulation, technique, or impetus from the psychoanalytic system (Fine, 1979; 1990; Goldman & Milman, 1978). Let's begin with a brief overview of psychoanalytic theory from its founder, Sigmund Freud, to current practitioners.

Freud was born in Freiberg, Czechoslovakia, in 1856, and died in London in 1939 (Jones, 1961, p. 3). He grew up in a time of great scientific progress, which influenced the development of his psychological theories. For example, one of the most important scientific works of that time was the *Origin of the Species* by Charles Darwin. Darwin's idea that a human was an animal among other animals and thus could be studied naturalistically was a foundation for Freud's study of the workings of the human mind. A second major influence came from the field of physics. Hermann von Helmholtz proposed that a human was an energy system that obeys the same physical laws as other matter. This conception of people led to Freud's idea that human motivation was influenced by unconscious sources of energy (Arlow, 1995, pp. 18–19; Fine, 1973, pp. 1–5).

At seventeen Freud entered medical school, where he was strongly influenced by Ernst Brücke, a prominent physiologist. Brücke's influence ultimately led Freud to create a dynamic psychology involving transformations and exchanges of energy within the personality (Jones, 1961, p. 9). After medical school Freud studied the nervous system and earned a reputation as a promising young neurologist. He began to specialize in the treatment of nervous disorders. He first studied in France with Jean Charcot, who used hypnosis to treat hysteria and other disorders. Hypnosis became a key component of Freud's practice as well. He then studied with Joseph Breuer, who had developed a cathartic method of therapy to treat hysteria (Arlow, 1979, pp. 5–9; Jones, 1961, pp. 38–65).

While scientifically exploring underlying causes of behavior, Freud formulated the idea of unconscious forces. In the 1890s he began analyzing his own unconscious forces, and during this time he wrote the *Interpretation of Dreams*. This work contained his views on the dynamics of the mind as well. In 1901 he published the *Psychopathology of Everyday Life,* which proposed that slips of the tongue, errors, accidents, and faulty memory are the results of unconscious motives. In 1905 he published three other important works: *A Case of Hysteria,* which described the treatment of hysterical disorders; *Three Essays on Sexuality,* which showed how sexual conflicts can produce neurosis; and *Wit and Its Relation to the Unconscious,* which proposed that much humor was a covert form of communicating hostility (Fancher, 1973).

All of these works led to the psychoanalytic system of psychology (Fine, 1973, p. 2). However, it was not Freud or his writings alone that made the psychoanalytic system so powerful and widespread. Equally important were the men who gravitated to him in what came to be known as the Vienna circle. Otto Rank, Alfred Adler, Carl Jung, Karl Abraham, Max Eitingon, Sandor Ferenczi, Hans Sachs, and Ernest Jones all started out as confederates and disciples of Freud but later developed, extended, and reformulated his theories, often in bitter disagreement with their mentor. In particular, Jung and Adler moved away from the "pure" psychoanalytics of Freud and developed their own theories and following. In 1909 Freud was invited to America by G. Stanley Hall to speak at Clark University. Following this initial visit, prominent psychologists in America such as Hall and William James became receptive to the components of psychoanalytics (Abeles, 1979, p. 136). While Freud's ideas were taking root, he continued to refine the psychoanalytic system, and from 1914 until his death in 1939 he extended his ideas into an ego psychology through which he attempted to understand the total personality (Fine, 1973, p. 4).

The Nazi rise to power prompted numerous adherents of Freud to leave continental Europe for America in the 1930s. America thereon became the world center for psychoanalysis (Arlow, 1995, p. 22). From the 1930s to the 1950s, theorists and therapists such as Karen Horney, Erik Erikson, Harry Stack Sullivan, and Erich Fromm broadened basic Freudian psychoanalytics. These theorists, characterized as Neo-Freudians, included cultural and social determiners and the development of interpersonal relationships as necessary extensions of the psychoanalytic view (Fine, 1962, pp. 257–259; Fine, 1973, pp. 4–6; Giovacchini, 1977, pp. 19–20).

A number of contemporary psychoanalytically oriented therapists have developed innovations to Freudian and Neo-Freudian formulations. Some of these newer approaches to psychoanalytic therapy are described in the section on strategies for helping clients.

Overview of Freudian Psychoanalytic Therapy

Freudian psychology has been tagged with several names: psychoanalysis, psycho-analytic theory, psychodynamic theory, psychodynamic therapy, psychodynamics, psychoanalytic psychotherapy, dynamic psychiatry, dynamic psychology, and depth psychology. By whatever name, it is a psychology of the conflicting forces inherent in the dualistic nature of humankind. The conflicting dualism of the mind may be dichotomized into *conscious* and *unconscious*. The dualism of humans in society may be dichotomized into the person as a biological animal and the person as a social being (Arlow, 1979, p. 1). It is through conflicts between the conscious and the unconscious and between the biological motivating forces in people and the social tempering forces in the environment that the personality develops, acculturation occurs, and values are acquired. Freud described this human motivation as being governed by the tendency to seek pleasure (a biological drive) and to avoid pain. He called this tension-reducing force the *pleasure principle* (Arlow, 1995, p. 16; Freud, 1958, pp. 213–227).

Freud's conception of the development of neurosis grew from his studies of hysteria and hypnosis. In these studies he found that certain unacceptable events and thoughts people had consciously experienced were sometimes repressed into an area of the mind he called the *unconscious*. These experiences, which were of a sexual nature, directly influenced the person's behavior and caused hysterical symptoms. These ideas were the basis of Freud's theory of the development of neurosis (Fancher, 1973). Thus, the hysterical neurotic became the accepted prototype for the early Freudians' understanding, diagnosis, and treatment of maladjusted patients.

The methods of psychoanalysis grew from the early studies of hysteria and hypnosis. Hypnosis was found to be useful for relieving hysterical symptoms in some cases, but not all of Freud's clients responded equally well to this method. Freud thereupon began to use an open-ended, gently guided discovery technique to bring to light childhood sexual fantasies. This technique evolved into the *free association* method, one of the cornerstones of classic psychoanalysis. The primary goal of this method is to make unconscious material conscious and thereby promote insight and understanding. Interpretation is then applied to the unconscious material, as it is applied to dreams, facilitating the client's understanding of the influence of unconscious motives on present behavior. Finally, the client uses transference, an emotional response to the therapist that represents a repetition of the individual's fantasies about a past relationship (such as with a parent), to gain insight and eventually to resolve the neurotic conflict (Arlow, 1995, p. 32; Goldman & Milman, 1978, pp. 2–19).

Auld and Hyman (1991, p. 17), citing Rapaport (1967), identified seven postulates or assumptions that have driven psychoanalytic therapy from the middle of the twentieth century to the 1990s:

1. Access to unconscious functioning comes through the *associative process*.
2. Later mental structures have to be explained by earlier experiences, by turning back to the past.
3. Psychic continuity is a lifelong process.
4. Mental life has meaning.
5. Determinism, the conviction that nothing that happens is accidental, is an accepted principle.

6. Instinct, that is, as the source of motivation in bodily processes, is an accepted concept.
7. The assumption of the concept of the unconscious is necessary because conscious experiences leave gaps in mental life that unconscious processes bridge.

Auld and Hyman hold that postulate one (which they added to the other six assumptions developed by Rapaport), is the guiding rationale for psychoanalytic technique. Thus, their view of psychoanalytic therapy is built on the premise that insofar as the psychodynamics of the patient "can be elucidated by pursuing his or her associations, the therapist and the patient, working together, can understand the patient and have a constructive effect on the patient's life." Therapists use all of the powerful tools that the psychoanalytic system has to offer. But in modern practice therapists do not simply instruct clients to talk at length about their childhood experiences and fantasies. Rather, psychoanalytic therapists are committed to discovering what clients are experiencing and discovering in the moment—collaboratively with their therapists in the therapy room. Auld and Hyman (1991, p. 6) contend that "more than any other kind of therapy, psychoanalytic therapy deals with the here-and-now."

According to Arlow (1989, 1995), effective psychoanalytic treatment can best be understood by examining *empathy, intuition,* and *introspection* (1989, pp. 39–40). Arlow explains that empathy is a form of "emotional knowing," central to the psychotherapeutic process, whereby a therapist exercises the ability to identify with and share the client's experiences both affectively and cognitively. He describes intuition as the organization, in the therapist's mind, of the myriad of data communicated by the client "into meaningful configurations outside the scope of consciousness" of the therapist (1989, p. 40), yet made conscious through unconscious mental operations. The therapist becomes aware of such unconscious material through introspection, a process using mental free association, whereby the therapist consciously synthesizes the client's accumulated communications. These introspections are not communicated to the client but rather are used to understand and help the client finally to attain the insight and ego strength needed to cope with whatever emotional traumas or dilemmas brought him or her to therapy in the first place. The communication of *empathy* directly to the client has been recognized and recommended by many modern psychoanalysts as a prerequisite to effective psychotherapy (Bacal, 1995; Feiner & Kiersky, 1994; Josephs, 1994; Kohut, 1995; Warren, 1994).

Theory of Personality

According to Arlow (1995), personality "evolves out of the interaction between inherent biological factors and the vicissitudes of experience." Psychoanalytic personality theory is based on several fundamental principles cited by Arlow (pp. 23–24):

1. *Determinism.* Mental events are not random, haphazard, accidental, unrelated phenomena. They are causally related chains of events.
2. *Topography.* All mental elements are judged according to accessibility to consciousness.

3. *Dynamic viewpoint.* The interaction of libidinal and aggressive impulses is biologically based and is more correctly defined by the term *drives* than by the
more common but acceptable term *instincts.*

4. *Genetic viewpoint.* Psychoanalysts have empirically linked later conflicts, character traits, neurotic symptoms, and psychological structures to childhood
events, wishes, and fantasies.

Freud proposed that the personality consists of three major parts—the id, the ego,
and the superego (Hall, 1954).

The Id

The id exists at birth and is the source of psychic energy and the instincts, the
most important of which are sex and aggression. Energy in the id is mobile and
can be readily discharged through action and wish fulfillment. One function of
the id is to fulfill the pleasure principle, which, as we have seen, is a basic motivating force that serves to reduce tension by seeking pleasure and avoiding pain
(Arlow, 1995, pp. 21–22; Fine, 1973, p. 14).

The id is the newborn's reservoir of emotional energy. A basic function of the
id is to maintain the organism in a state of tension-free comfort. When the infant
is hungry, the id seeks immediate gratification to restore the infant to a state of
comfort (Hansen, Stevic, & Warner, 1982, pp. 28–29). Frustration occurs when the
infant's oral erotic wishes are not immediately satisfied. The experience of overcoming early frustration initiates learning and development. The sucking instinct
serves some important purposes. It satisfies the oral erotic need for stimulation
and satisfaction. Because of this a *cathexis*—the concentration of one's psychic energy on some person, thing, idea, or aspect of self—develops between the infant's
need for protection and satisfaction and the mother, the mother's breasts, or the
bottle. The infant's early experience of locking the mouth onto the nipple may
serve as the first "click" of insight and thereby the root of all later learning (Belkin,
1980, pp. 56–57). Thus the id is the energizer and the starting point of the organism's personality.

The Ego

The ego is a complex psychological organization that acts as an intermediary between the id and the external world. It has both defensive and autonomous functions. It is not present at birth but is developed as the person interacts with the
environment. To function as this intermediary, the ego operates by the *reality principle.* The reality principle postpones the discharge of energy until an object that
will satisfy the need, or reduce tension, is found. Unlike the id, the ego is able to
tolerate tension and thus delay gratification. The reality principle is served by the
secondary process, which consists of discovering or producing reality through a
plan developed by thought and reason. The secondary process interacts with the
environment and develops the ego. These lines of development are also influenced by heredity and maturational processes. The ego has been called the executive of the personality because it controls and governs the id and the superego
and maintains interaction with the external world (Fine, 1973, p. 15; Giovacchini,
1977, p. 21; Hansen, Stevic & Warner, 1982, p. 29).

The Superego

The superego is the moral, social, and judicial branch of the personality; it represents the ideal rather than the real. The superego strives for perfection rather than pleasure or reality. It develops as a result of the need to control the aggression that results when needs are not immediately satisfied. The superego develops from the ego by assimilating parental standards and eventually substitutes parental authority with its own inner authority. It takes over the governance of the psyche and mediates between the person and the environment. It acts as the moral and social gatekeeper and keeps the person's baser instincts from running rampant (Fine, 1973, pp. 15–16; Giovacchini, 1977, p. 21).

The superego has two subsystems—the ego ideal and the conscience. The ego ideal is composed of the child's conceptions of what the parents consider to be perfection, or the perfect person. These conceptions are established through experiencing parental acceptance. The conscience is composed of the child's conceptions of what is considered to be morally bad and is established through experiencing admonitions, punishment, or lack of acceptance (Giovacchini, 1977, p. 21).

In summary, the id is the reservoir of the psychic energy that operates the three systems of personality. Since the id can receive gratification only through reflex and wish fulfillment, the ego rationally satisfies the impulses of the id by selecting objects in the environment that will reduce tension and bring pleasure. The ego eventually obtains control of most of the id's psychic energy. The superego serves as the moral arm of this personality structure, using the prohibitions of conscience to block discharge of energy or directing the discharge of energy through the ego ideal. A person who is dominated by the id will tend to be impulsive; one who is dominated by the superego will be overly moralistic and perfectionistic. The ego functions to keep the individual from these two extremes (Hansen, Stevic, & Warner, 1982, pp. 28–30). Where the ego is working well, the personality is a unified blend of the three systems (Giovacchini, 1977, p. 21).

The Development of Personality

Childhood sexuality plays an important role in the development of the personality (Freud, 1961a, pp. 141–149). The infant is capable of receiving sexual gratification from rhythmic stimulation of any part of the body; Freud termed this *polymorphous perversity.* As the infant matures, the generalized ability to receive sexual gratification decreases as certain parts of the body become preferred sites for gratification. In other words, the possibilities for gratification of the sexual instinct narrow as the infant develops. Freud postulated a series of developmental stages that describe this narrowing process of sexual gratification. These stages, now referred to as the stages of psychosexual development, are as follows.

Oral Stage

This stage occurs during the first year of life and develops from the act of feeding in which the mouth and lips naturally come to receive more stimulation than other parts of the body. Because oral responses had been demonstrated to have strong sexual connotations in perversions, neuroses, and latent dream content, Freud thought that the nonnutritive components of an infant's oral behavior were sexual. Conscious and unconscious memories of oral experiences have a central position in the psychological life of the infant, and new experiences are organized around these memories (Arlow, 1995, p. 25; Wolman, 1968, pp. 67–69).

Freud proposed that the mouth has five functions: (1) taking in, (2) holding on, (3) biting, (4) spitting out, and (5) closing. Each is a prototype for certain personality traits. These functions take on symbolic meaning in the adaptations the individual makes in coping with the anxieties and stresses of life. For example, taking in through the mouth is the prototype for acquisitiveness, holding for tenacity, and spitting out for rejection. Whether these traits become part of one's personality depends on the amount of anxiety and frustration experienced in the oral stage. For example, an infant who was weaned too soon or too abruptly may develop a strong tendency to be possessive in order to avoid repetition of the anxiety and frustration of the weaning experience (Fine, 1979, pp. 150–171; Hall, 1954).

Anal Stage

The anal stage develops during the second and third years of life as the anal area begins to assume a central position in the child's sexual development. This area becomes more strongly associated with sexual gratification than the mouth. As children become capable of voluntary muscle control and eventual bowel control, they discover that sexual stimulation occurs from voluntarily retaining and expelling feces. Anal ideas and memories involve such activities as elimination, retention, smearing, or cleaning. Just as with the oral stage, the prototypes of later personality characteristics develop during the anal stage. Expulsive elimination is the prototype for emotional outbursts and temper tantrums in later life. Toilet training, which usually occurs during this time, can have the effect of establishing prototypes for later conflicts with authority figures, meticulous cleanliness and orderliness, or even generosity and philanthropy (Arlow, 1995, p. 25; Fine, 1979, pp. 177–188).

Phallic Stage

This stage occurs after mastery of the tasks of toilet training. At approximately age three or four the child discovers the pleasures of genital manipulation and another shift of the zone of sexual stimulation occurs. Because of increased dexterity, the child can now have regular and intense pleasure by stimulating the genitals. It is during this stage that the Oedipus complex develops. Freud named this stage for its parallels with the Greek play *Oedipus Rex,* in which Oedipus kills his father and marries his mother. The Oedipus complex develops when the child has intense sexual feelings for the parent of the opposite sex. The male child fears castration by the powerful father and subsequently represses his desires for the mother and identifies with the father. The female child thinks she has already been castrated and thus suffers from penis envy and is not as fearful of her mother as the male is of his father. Difficulties in the resolution of the Oedipus complex may lead to problems of sexual identity (Arlow, 1995, pp. 25–27; Wolman, 1968, pp. 71–72).

Latency Period

The first stages constitute the *pregenital* stages. Fixation at any one of these stages may produce oral, anal, or phallic character types in later life. These stages are precursors to the fourth stage of psychosexual development, the latency period, which extends from age five or six to puberty. At about age six, the sexual instinct diminishes and the child enters a stage of sexual quiescence. During this stage, children enter school and apply themselves to the tasks of learning. Although the sexual instinct is repressed, the sexually charged memories of the previous stages are still intact and will influence personality development (Arlow, 1995, pp. 27–28; Freud, 1961a, pp. 141–149).

Genital Stage

This fifth stage of psychosexual development occurs at puberty and is characterized by nonnarcissistic behavior that develops in the direction of biological reproduction. Characteristics of this stage are an attraction for the opposite sex, socialization and group activities, marriage and the establishment of a family, and vocational development. The genital stage becomes fused with the pregenital stages as kissing, caressing, and sexual intercourse satisfy pregenital impulses. This stage lasts from puberty to death or senility, whichever comes first (Babcock, 1983, pp. 37–44; Wolman, 1968, pp. 81–82).

In summary, Freud emphasized the role of sexuality in the development of personality. The narrowing manifestations of sexuality proceed through five psychosexual stages of development. As the person proceeds through these stages, propelled by inherent forces and molded by the environment, he or she acquires various components of personality. Fixation at any of the first three stages may produce certain personality types, such as the oral, anal, or phallic character. Although there are two further stages of psychosexual development, the basis for the individual's personality in later life is determined during the first three stages.

Nature of Maladjustment

A basic theme of Freudian psychology is that human development requires the suppression of "impure" childish impulses. Adults continue to fight these antisocial and disruptive impulses. In Freud's time a common manifestation of the attempt to repress these "loathsome" childhood wishes was hysteria. It was through Freud's work with hysterical clients that he discovered the relationship between sexual fantasies and impulses and hysterical symptoms. He first thought that childhood seduction and sexual trauma were the cause of hysterical symptoms, but he eventually proposed that his client's "memories" were the products of wish fulfillment rather than actual traumatic events. He found traces of childhood sexuality in himself, and from these observations concluded that the unsuccessful resolution of the Oedipus complex was responsible for neurotic symptoms (Freud, 1961b, pp. 173–183).

Basically, what precipitates the neurosis is that the impulses of the Oedipus complex have a strong need for satisfaction. Most people can satisfactorily resolve these impulses. The most common and significant conflicts arise from wishes during the Oedipal phase. Childhood neuroses are usually manifested through nightmares, phobias, tics, mannerisms, ritualistic behaviors, and general apprehensiveness. Childhood behavior disorders are generally related to repressed neuroses. Adult neurosis is generally interpreted as a resurfacing of childhood neurosis (Arlow, 1995, pp. 29–30).

Freud proposed that the psychic processes in neurosis and psychosis had a fundamental unity. The symptoms of the psychotic are explainable by the same unconscious mental processes that give rise to the symptoms of the neurotic client and the dreams of a normal person. The principal difference between psychosis and neurosis is the change in the psychotic's relationships with people and the environment: the psychotic withdraws from the world and people, often thinking that the world has changed and that people are unreal. Thus the psychotic, unlike the neurotic and the normal person, has a break with reality (Arlow & Brenner, 1964).

Major Concepts

Psychoanalytic theory embodies a host of formulations, assumptions, and concepts. The major Freudian concepts that we will mention are the unconscious, instincts, identification, displacement, the Freudian symbol, defense mechanisms, transference, and free association.

The Unconscious

The unconscious is an actual entity of the mind, the lowest of its three layers. The preconscious is the middle layer and the conscious is the upper layer (Wolman, 1968, pp. 6–11). The contents of these three layers of the mind vary in their degree of availability to conscious awareness. Some are readily accessible, because resistance to their expression is weak; others are not available except through psychoanalysis. What seems most important about unconscious content is the influence it exerts on the behavior of the consciously unaware individual. Its effects range from forgetfulness, slips of the tongue, and accidents to neurosis manifested in hysterical symptoms. Freud explained that the unconscious stores material that is unavailable to awareness because of incompatibility. The incompatibility is between certain unacceptable ideas and the ego, which represses those ideas (Wollheim, 1971).

Wolman (1989) introduced the concept of the *protoconscious* rather than the preconscious. The protoconscious is described as a bridge between conscious and unconscious phenomena. For example, many altered states of consciousness such as lucid dreams, posthypnotic states, meditation, and parapsychological phenomena are observed on the protoconscious level when individuals are neither totally conscious nor totally unconscious. Fluctuating modes and shifts from the unconscious to protoconscious states of mind, and vice versa, may be observed in schizophrenics and autistic children.

Instincts

Instincts are organic motivational forces, or *drives* (Wolman, 1968, pp. 39–40). Freud recognized two classes of instincts—the life instincts, which he labeled *libido,* and the death instincts, or *thanatos.* The seat of the instincts is the id. Instincts direct psychological processes and function as the motivational forces in people. Each instinct has a source (energy), an aim (removal of a need), an object (such as food), and an impetus (strength) (Hall, 1954).

Identification

Identification is an ego mechanism that is important in personality development (Wolman, 1968, p. 68). One form of identification is the incorporation of the qualities of another person into one's personality. According to Hall (1954), there are four types of identification:

1. *Narcissistic identification* is identification with others who possess the same trait as the identifier, such as athletic ability.
2. *Goal-oriented identification* is identification with someone who has a trait the identifier hopes to acquire. A male child wanting to be strong like his father is an example.
3. *Object-loss identification* occurs when someone attempts to regain a lost object by identifying with it. The child who tries to regain parental love through attempts to please his or her parents by adopting their values and standards is an example.
4. *Authority identification* is identification with the prohibitions set down by parents and other authority figures. This type of identification leads to the development of the conscience.

Displacement

This is the process by which psychic energy from the instincts can be rechanneled from one object to another. Only the object of the instinct varies; the source and the aim of the instinct remain the same. Through this process a major portion of the personality is formed. The development of the personality through displacement is a complex process by which multiple tensions can be reduced, and the object chosen may be far removed from the drive that started the process. For example, the original drive for oral gratification, which is first satisfied by sucking the nipple, will undergo several displacements—thumb sucking, candy sucking, cigarette smoking, beer drinking, eating, talking, oratory, and so forth (Hall, 1954; Wolman, 1968, pp. 147–152).

The Freudian Symbol

The Freudian symbol is a socially acceptable representation, usually in dreams, of an unconscious and objectionable thought, wish, or object. For example, the penis may appear in dreams as an elongated object or an object capable of penetration, such as a knife, gun, snake, statue, spire, or cigar. The vagina is represented by objects capable of being receptacles, such as a cave, box, tunnel, or pocket. In psychoanalytic treatment, the symbols in dreams, which may represent a wide range of unconscious thoughts, are analyzed as a means to make unconscious material conscious (Hall, 1954).

Defense Mechanisms

Defense mechanisms are used by the ego to reduce anxiety associated with threatening situations and feelings. Anxiety is generated by the instinctual demands of the id and the pressures of the superego. In contrast with realistic measures for dealing directly with the source of the threat, defense mechanisms distort, deny, or falsify the reality of the anxiety-producing situation. These protective mechanisms are used by most people, and at times, particularly when the ego is developing, may prevent the person from being overwhelmed by parental and societal demands. Such demands may become so excessive that the defense mechanisms employed thwart the natural development of the person and thereby become unhealthy. Some of the more important defense mechanisms are as follows (Wolman, 1968).

1. *Repression.* Repression forces a threatening memory, thought, or perception out of consciousness and prevents it from returning. Repression may prevent a person from seeing an object that is actually in view, or it may allow distortion of objective reality in order to protect the ego from the danger associated with the perception. Freud attributed hysterical disorders to repression. Repression may contribute to a conversion reaction resulting in so-called psychosomatic disorders such as asthma, arthritis, and ulcers (Wolman, 1968).

2. *Projection.* When forces from the id or the superego threaten a person, the ego sometimes attributes those forces to an external source. The ego is attempting to convert internal anxiety into an objective external anxiety that is easier to handle. Thus, projection is the attribution of one's feelings or characteristics to people in general. One who is unhappily married may reduce the anxiety associated with that condition by concluding that all marriages are unhappy (Wolman, 1968, p. 146).

3. *Reaction formation.* Reaction formation occurs when the ego sidetracks the expression of a threatening impulse by prompting the person to behave in the opposite way. A person who crusades against vice and corruption may be doing so (unconsciously) to deny an urge to participate in these same activities. The principal features of reaction formation are an exaggerated demonstration of the opposite feeling and an inflexibility of expression of that feeling. Reaction formations are also employed against external threats, as in the case of exaggerated friendliness toward or obedience to someone or something that is feared (Wolman, 1968, p. 146).

4. *Fixation.* Fixation is a psychological stunting whereby the person fails to proceed from one developmental stage to another. People generally experience anxiety when faced with the prospect of engaging in a new behavior; they worry about performing adequately, are afraid of being ridiculed for failure, or fear punishment. Most people will take the risk in order to grow. However, some people feel such great anxiety at the thought of the anticipated situation that they refuse to engage in the new behavior and thus remain fixated at an earlier developmental level. This fixation, a fear of leaving the old for the new, is called separation anxiety (Wolman, 1968, pp. 140–141).

5. *Regression.* Regression is a retreat to a previous stage of development. Some forms of regressive behavior are so common they are viewed as childish. The college freshman regresses when he or she returns to the security of the parental home every weekend or drops out of school rather than face the anxiety of confronting the world "alone." A more severe expression of regressive behavior is withdrawal into a world of daydreams and fantasies to the exclusion of independent functioning in society (Hall, 1954).

Transference

Transference is a key concept in psychoanalytic therapy. It occurs when the client's feelings are directed toward the therapist as though the therapist were the source of the feelings. The therapist's analysis helps the client distinguish between the fantasy and the reality of the feelings transferred from some previous significant person to the therapist (Arlow, 1995). Also, the client is helped to gain an understanding of how he or she "misperceives, misinterprets, and relates to the present in terms of the past" (p. 32). Since most transferee's feelings are unconscious, the skill of the therapist is needed to help the client realign these distorted relationships.

Free Association

Free association is a technique that encourages the client to report to the therapist without bias or criticism whatever enters his or her mind. Such reports enable the therapist to uncover repressed material. The analysis of hidden conflicts helps the client gain the insight that is the core of growth (Fine, 1973, p. 21). According to Auld and Hyman (1991, p. 243), *"free association is the primary method (perhaps the only one) by which the therapist and the patient gain access to unconscious conflict* [emphasis added]. Thus, free association becomes the defining element of psychoanalytic therapy."

THE COUNSELING PROCESS

Central Focuses

According to Arlow (1995) the principles and techniques of psychoanalysis are based on the psychoanalytic theory of neurosis. Those techniques and principles that evolved through Freud's study of clients' nervous disorders are employed to make the contents of the unconscious conscious. Two basic focuses for bringing unconscious material into awareness are *free association* and *transference*. The standard technique for studying the functioning of the mind is called the psychoanalytic situation (Arlow, 1995). The client lies on a couch looking away from the therapist and expresses whatever comes to mind. The client looks away from the therapist so that the latter's nonverbal behavior will not influence the production of whatever comes to the client's mind. The therapist's role is to observe and occasionally interpret the content of the client's free associations; the client, in turn, reflects and comments on the interpretation. The purpose of this situation is to allow repressed material to come to conscious, verbal awareness so that the psychic conflict can be examined, interpreted, and eventually resolved (pp. 28–31).

Therapy

According to Arlow (1995, pp. 31–33) treatment is composed of four phases: the opening phase and the development, working through, and resolution of the transference.

The Opening Phase

This phase has two parts. The first consists of a set of interviews during which the client's problem is determined and a decision is made as to the appropriateness of analysis. The structure of the analytic situation is explained, particularly the delineation of the responsibilities of the therapist and the client. If the therapy proceeds after the first few sessions, then the second part of the opening phase begins. The client continues to assume the position on the couch, and everything he or she says and does is observed and recorded (Arlow, 1995, pp. 31–32). The therapist thereby compiles a comprehensive file of conscious and unconscious material. The therapist uses these dreams, fantasies, projections, free associations, and early memories, as well as emergent life themes, to facilitate client insight during subsequent phases of therapy.

The Development of Transference

The development and analysis of transference constitute an important therapeutic phase. The client's feelings for the therapist, who has become a significant figure in the client's life, are used to demonstrate how the client perceives, interprets, and responds to the present in the same ways he or she responded to significant persons in the past. By understanding how this past behavior influences and determines present behavior, the client can learn to make more appropriate decisions. Concomitant to the analysis of transference, the therapist must be aware of the possibility of countertransference: the therapist's unresolved feelings for significant others may be transferred to the client. Any countertransferences must be analyzed and worked through. This step in the analysis is necessary so that the therapist's unresolved feelings will not interfere with the analysis of the client's transference (Arlow, 1995, p. 32). The analytic process is enhanced by both the therapist and the client gaining a conscious awareness into the emergent transference and countertransference aspects of their ongoing relationship.

Working through Transference

This phase overlaps with the previous phase. The working through of one transference usually precipitates the recall of a significant event that in turn leads to further insights. Working through the transference is an evolving process, and with each working through there is further clarification and understanding (Arlow, 1995, pp. 32–33). Many clients manifest *resistance* during therapy. Resistance is either the active or the passive opposition of the client to the therapist's attainment of the therapeutic objectives. Even though at the conscious level the client wants help, he or she uses defense mechanisms to avoid bringing to the surface unconscious, usually repressed, material such as painful memories or guilt feelings. Working through client resistance is an important aspect of the therapist's role in the psychoanalytic process.

The Resolution of Transference

When the client and the therapist believe that the client's major conflicts have been worked through, a date is set for termination of the therapy. The purpose of this phase is to resolve the client's neurotic attachment to the therapist. Several aspects of this phase are common. One is that the client may be reluctant to give up the relationship and may maintain dependency on the therapist. The resolution of this aspect of therapy represents the finishing touches to the client's therapy. Sometimes further memories related to the interpretations made earlier in the treatment emerge. It is important to work through any grandiose fantasies or wishes the client may have regarding his or her condition after therapy is terminated (Arlow, 1995, p. 33).

Finally, psychoanalytic therapy focuses exclusively on how the client's mind works (Giovacchini, 1977). The therapist's views are not imposed on the client. The therapy is centered in interpretation within the context of transference (p. 19). A unique and powerful characteristic of psychoanalysis is the therapist's ability and willingness to allow transference to develop with the objective of increasing the client's autonomy by extending his or her control over inner, primitive forces (p. 39).

STRATEGIES FOR HELPING CLIENTS

Psychoanalysis focuses on the workings of the client's mind. The attainment of the Socratic motto "Know thyself" is the essential goal of the therapy (Giovacchini, 1977, p. 36). The therapist may use a variety of strategies to enhance the analysis of transference. *Assessment* of the client's emotional, situational, and medical readiness to participate in and profit from therapy is essential. Not all clients or problem situations lend themselves to the psychoanalytic approach. The early sessions are typically devoted to *free association, dream interpretation, fantasizing, hypnotic techniques,* or other ways of gaining access to the client's unconscious.

Modern psychoanalytic therapists have developed a variety of treatment strategies. Based on Freudian formulations, these strategies have broadened the client population served and represent innovative refinements of classical psychoanalytic practice (Belkin, 1980, pp. 23–24). Other innovations depart from traditional psychoanalysis. Several of the latter are identified here.

Written Facilitation of Free Association

Keeping a diary is another way for the client to facilitate free association (Pearsons, 1965). The case of Mary in Chapter 13 (eclectic counseling and psychotherapy) is an example of the use of a written diary to encourage a resistant client to engage in free association and self-examination (Progoff, 1977).

BRIEF PSYCHOTHERAPIES

The advent of managed care and the work of psychotherapy outcome researchers such as Strupp (1986, 1992, 1993), Strupp and Binder (1984), Ellis (1995), and Small (1972) have brought credibility and widespread application of different forms of *brief psychotherapy.* In terms of brief psychotherapy's impact on psychoanalytic therapy, a number of studies have consistently shown that the clients' length of stay has far less influence on outcome scores than does the quality of the therapist–client relationship (Alpher, Henry, & Strupp, 1990; Binder, 1993; Demos & Prout, 1993; Harrist, Quintana, Strupp, & Henry, 1994; Henry, Butler,

Strupp, & Schacht, 1993; Henry, Schacht, Strupp, & Butler, 1993; Najavits & Strupp, 1994; Strupp, 1992, 1993). The gist of all these studies is that although severe cases of mental disturbance may require long-term treatment, many individuals with situational problems can be served effectively in one to ten sessions (Ellis, 1995, pp. 187–189; Strupp & Binder, 1984).

Psychoanalytic Therapy

Small and Bellak developed a six-step model for *brief psychotherapies* (Small, 1972, pp. 27–35). First, the problem is identified. Second, a detailed history is taken to secure data that will reveal the client's personal experiences and lead to a diagnosis. Third, causal relationships are established. Fourth, methods of intervention are chosen. The fifth step incorporates the working-through phase. The sixth and final step is to leave the client with a positive transference. In step four Small and Bellak recommend *environmental manipulation* strategies, similar, to those suggested by Ellis's (1995) rational-emotive behavior therapy (REBT), which depart from and greatly augment the procedures used in traditional psychoanalytic therapy. Examples might include the therapist telephoning family members or friends; job placement referrals for the client; teaching clients cognitive skills to use when problems beset them; and even providing clients with audiotaped cassettes of therapy sessions to listen to in their homes, cars, or offices to enhance their ego coping strength during periods of crisis or stressful situations.

Autonomous Psychotherapy

Auld and Hyman (1991, p. 3) brought Freudian psychotherapy into contemporary usage through what Szasz (1974) termed *autonomous psychotherapy*. They employ some of the basic formulations of both Szasz and Freud and apply modern psychodynamic techniques based on empirical research findings of the past fifty years.

In autonomous psychotherapy the therapist and client develop a working alliance, built on mutual trust and a supportive and empathic relationship, that facilitates both parties in bringing the client's unconscious conflicts to light. The supportive, caring, and empathic relationship, similar to what we would construe to be a person-centered modality, operates to elicit free association to uncover unconscious material needed for the therapy to move forward. Unlike the person-centered approach, which uses basic facilitative conditions to help clients become more self-actualized, *autonomous* psychotherapy practitioners use these basic facilitative techniques to effect therapy while providing optimum client autonomy. Thus the autonomous psychotherapist uses fewer artificial means, such as hypnosis or word association, than do traditional psychoanalytically oriented therapists in assisting their clients to uncover therapeutically important material from the unconscious.

The therapist must be knowledgeable and skilled in facilitating the associative process, working through transference issues, dealing with the client's repression, handling resistance, and performing other psychoanalytic techniques. But the curative factors lie in the associative process, the therapist's ability to make appropriate interpretations within the working alliance, and the capability and motivation of the client and therapist to experience autonomy, work through defenses, and deal with issues of transference and other impediments to resolving unconscious conflicts.

Time-Limited Dynamic Psychotherapy

Strupp and Binder's (1984) time-limited dynamic psychotherapy integrates important elements of both traditional and modern psychoanalytic therapy. Although the time limitation of the therapy is not as clear-cut as in transactional analysis or REBT, it is an important dynamic because it motivates both client and therapist to work toward attainment of some degree of clarity or progress during each session. Time is of greater essence than in more traditional forms of psychoanalytic therapy.

Theoretical Tenets

Time-limited dynamic psychotherapy is an interpersonal model in that the source of the client's disturbance is viewed as being rooted in difficulties in interpersonal relationships. The major purpose of psychotherapy is to assist the client to form new, healthy relationships. The therapist-client relationship plays an important part in enabling the client to gain insight as well as to develop and strengthen relationship skills. Conceptually, the therapist may focus on the past, present, or future, thus helping the client to understand and root out damaging attitudes of the past, mitigate against emotional deficits of the present, and prepare for improved relationships in the future (Strupp, 1986).

Three major tasks of therapy are: (1) to identify cyclical maladaptive patterns; (2) to bring to the client's attention those patterns; and (3) to help the client explore how those patterns affect behavior and relationships (Strupp, 1986). The therapist has an opportunity to be both a participant and an observer and is able to step aside as an objective mentor and point out patterns to the client. The therapist is also observant of his or her own reactions and uses these reactions to help clients discover their own thoughts, emotions, and relationship needs. Thus, time-limited dynamic psychotherapy may be conceptualized as having balance among emotional, cognitive, and experiential components and typically focusing on past, present, and future factors that affect clients (Strupp, 1986).

Techniques and Strategies

Time-limited dynamic psychotherapy strategies and techniques operate on a personal and trustful level. Yet the element of connecting present dilemmas to past traumas and patterns is pervasive in time-limited therapy. Objective interpretation, action-oriented problem solving, and effective mentoring are continually evident. Both the client and the therapist remain aware of the need to make therapeutic progress within the constraints of time, which is a limited and valued therapeutic commodity.

Ego Psychology

Ego psychology, founded on Erikson's (1963; 1968; 1982) principles of psychosocial development throughout the life span and promoted by theorists such as A. Freud (1936) and Hartmann (1939), sought to broaden and extend S. Freud's earlier formulations into a more complete theory of human behavior. The main thrust was the study of the ego and its functions. Hartmann (1939) viewed the ego as the guiding factor in an individual's adaptation to an "average expectable environment." Later, Beres (1956) and Blanck and Blanck (1968; 1974; 1986) redirected ego psychology away from psychic conflict and focused instead on the deficiencies and arrests accrued during development of the person's ego functions. Thus, in therapeutic application, ego psychotherapy becomes a task of promoting undeveloped or underdeveloped ego strengths and skills.

Typically, the ego therapist serves as a model or a sort of auxiliary ego for the client while the client is in the process of developing a stronger ego. Caper (1995) emphasizes that current ego analysts are concerned mainly with real and contemporary events affecting the client, whereas Britton (1995) describes the ego as a creature of the frontier between the internal and external worlds of the client. Britton suggests that belief is to psychic reality what perception is to material reality. Belief gives the force of reality to that which is psychic, just as perception does to that which is physical. Consequently, compared with a traditional psychoanalytic practitioner, the ego therapist pays less attention to uncovering unconscious conflict and analysis of transference and more attention to here-and-now reality testing. The therapist is quite active in assessing the client's ego status, guiding the client toward goal attainment, asking open questions, directing the client to focus on the realities of life such as deficits in psychosocial functioning, praising the client for achieving successes, and tending to take the client's presenting problems or conflicts at face value and emphasizing the integration of his or her current interpersonal and sociocultural adjustment into the ego or self-concept (Altman, 1995; Levine, Jakubowski, & Cote, 1992).

The therapist's role is similar to that of a mentor or coach and represents a model or pattern that the patient may emulate to form a psychic attachment or object identification that is realistic and appropriate. Because a major goal of ego therapy is strengthening the ego so the client may develop healthy psychosocial functioning, therapeutic strategy deals more with remediation and correction than with unconscious conflict resolution.

Object-Relations Psychology

Object-relations therapy, similar to ego psychotherapy, emphasizes the importance of the client's intrapsychic relationships with others more than do the traditional psychoanalytic therapies. According to Hamilton (1988) and St. Clair (1986), Freud used the term *object* with reference to that external person, target, or thing that satisfies the individual's needs. The word *other,* used synonymously with *object,* might typically denote the intrapsychic relationship with a significant other person with whom the client forms a psychic attachment. That other person might also be the therapist.

Object-relations therapists may focus on any number of "object" relationship conflicts: experiences of attachment and separation, boundaries between self and others, interpersonal relations as dominant elements in personality development, and identity diffusion and identity coherence (Auld & Hyman, 1991, p. 245). In the therapeutic setting the client's stories may be taken at face value, not to be considered as either verifiable or refutable but rather to be regarded as associations. Auld and Hyman contend that "one should focus on what these associations of the patient tell us about the patient's unconscious conflicts: They are representations of this latent material" (p. 246).

Object-relations therapists seek to establish personal, empathic, trusting relationships with clients. Transference and countertransference are handled as object relations in the therapeutic setting. Analysis and interpretation are oriented less on uncovering unconscious conflicts and more on the client and therapist collaboratively examining the nature of the client's interpersonal and psychosocial relationships (Stricker & Healey, 1990). The therapist typically focuses on those "object" relationships that drive the patient's current interactions with people. McCathy (1995) underscores the analytic task of facilitating individuation from internal objects and recommends that analysts form an alliance with the client's development process. Object-relations theorists emphasize relatedness, dissociative processes, and disruptive anxieties in self–object dialogues. Warren (1994) emphasizes the importance of the appropriate use of empathy in conducting object-relations therapy as one psychoanalytic approach. The primary goals of object-relations therapy are to make clients aware of relationship deficits and to help them discover ways to improve interpersonal functioning.

Self Psychology

Self psychology (Kohut, 1971; 1977; Wolf, 1988) is the study of that aspect of mental functioning in which the person as self is the central focus. Therapy deals with the deficits and pathologies of the client's mental life. Self psychology is closely aligned with object-relations psychology. The development of the self is conceptualized as initially (during infancy) requiring a "self" object outside of oneself to provide life-sustaining functions. As a person normally matures he or she develops the "self" object through a process that Kohut (1977; 1984) termed *transmuting internalizations*. That process facilitates the person's growth and enhancement of the self (Pires & Pedro, 1994). The ideal self is empathic. If the developing "self" object is missing, stunted, or distorted, an ideal self is not attained and the person develops deficits in mental and relationship functioning that may lead to debilitating disorders (Lachmann, 1993).

Therapy is based on providing empathic experiences wherein the client confronts—through transference relationships with the therapist, who the client has idealized—failures that replicate his or her original failure to develop an ideal, cohesive self (Bacal, 1995; Butz, 1992; Lachmann & Beebe, 1995; Wolf, 1994). By working through such failures of empathy in the safety of the therapeutic situation, the client overcomes the crippling lack of development of an earlier ideal self and achieves a transmuting internalization (Kohut, 1977, 1984; Leach, 1995; Stolorow, 1995; Wallerstein, 1995). The most important aspect of self psychology therapy is for the client to experience the utmost empathy from the therapist, which in turn helps the client to discover who he or she really is (Pauchant & Dumas, 1991; Tobin, 1991; Warren, 1994). Such transmuting internalization or self-discovery diminishes the need for the interpretation of unconscious conflict (Auld & Hyman, 1991, p. 247).

SAMPLE CASE

The case of Carla illustrates some of the contemporary psychoanalytic techniques used with an adolescent female client.

Dream Work

Carla, sixteen years old, was given up by her biological parents at age four. She was adopted at age seven. Her adoptive home was stable and religious. At fourteen she began having dreams that her adoptive father was making sexual advances toward her. Carla's ability to distinguish between fantasy and reality was uncertain, and she developed a love–fear attitude toward her adoptive father. At age fifteen she exhibited chronic delinquent behavior, which included running away from home on numerous occasions, experimenting with drugs, and engaging in sex with a wide variety of males. Carla's behavior produced a great deal of guilt, anxiety, helplessness, and fear that she was losing her mind. Initial therapy focused on her dream. She reported that in one of her dreams her adoptive father fondled her and attempted to engage in intercourse with her, whereupon she awakened in terror. A brief segment of a therapy session about that dream follows:

TH: How did you react to the dream?

CL: I know it was a dream, but I've had funny feelings about it. I guess I'm a little afraid of him now. I find myself avoiding him.

TH: So now you're not sure about how much of your imagery and fears of sexual relations with your father comes from your dream or how much is projected from your conscious thoughts.

The main dilemma, from a psychoanalytic viewpoint, was the confusion between the dream content and Carla's conscious thoughts. After a period of striving to do so, Carla learned to fantasize having normal daughter–father relations.

TH: Carla, can you free-associate this idea of a healthy relationship with your father?

CL: (*thoughtful silence*) Okay, what I want to see is myself being in the room with him, without having any sexual thoughts—to just be normal—to enjoy being with him and to trust him. I want to be able to embrace him or be embraced—to have him kiss me on the cheek, without my pulling back and thinking awful things. I guess I'm still having trouble getting away from all the stuff in the dreams.

TH: It sounds like you're trying to separate all the images in your dreams and fantasies from your conscious experiences and desires, but there's a blockage. Can you free-associate around that blockage?

CL: (*thoughtful silence*) I'm feeling kind of torn . . . between two feelings. I have an image of a desire to be this little girl again—to be touched and caressed and hugged and loved. Another picture—the one that bothers me most—is of a more mature love relationship with him. It's like . . . he's not really my father, but he's someone like my father. Like he's my boyfriend with all the qualities of my father. I guess what I want is to have a boyfriend like my father.

In this segment Carla verbalized the desire to have a love relationship with someone with her father's qualities. In the interviews that followed she was able to work through her fantasies and clarify her distinctions between father–child and father–adolescent daughter relationships. She was also able to fantasize having appropriate heterosexual relationships.

Object-Relations Psychology

Object-relations theory had a substantive influence on the therapist's early conceptualization and case management with Carla. Carla's impaired psychosocial development was manifested in several areas, such as attachment and separation, identity diffusion, and maintenance of boundaries between self and others—none of which she seemed to be consciously aware. During therapy sessions at the beginning of Carla's treatment she disclosed a number of her life events, memories, fantasies, and judgments that provided significant information about her personality and unconscious conflicts.

CL: I guess it didn't take my real mother long to get tired of me!

The therapist considered such material not in terms of narrative or verifiable truth but as associations revealing Carla's object-relations distortions and unconscious conflicts (Auld & Hyman, 1991, pp. 245–246). These important associations, judged to be representations of latent material, provided valuable and powerful background knowledge. No "techniques" were immediately employed with Carla to attempt to remediate her unconscious distortions and conflicts or to "rush" her into gaining insight. Much of the value of object-relations psychology rests in the education of the therapist early in the therapeutic relationship (Hamilton, 1988). Without such "education" the therapist cannot make helpful responses later on.

Psychoimagination Techniques

When Carla was seventeen, the therapist employed psychoimagination techniques (Shorr, 1972) to help Carla rehearse steps she could take to establish normal relations with her father.

TH: You've said you wish to be able to openly be with your father, carry on both serious and casual conversations, and feel no threat at all. Can you get in touch with your fantasies, project yourself into your desired encounter, and describe your actions and feelings?

CL: (*moment of thoughtfulness*) I'm at home with my mother. We're talking and enjoying each other. I'm helping prepare dinner. I see Dad drive into the carport. He comes in the kitchen door and kisses my mom . . . then he kisses me . . . I feel faint for a moment, then I remember exactly what I planned to do . . . I planned to put my mind on enjoying being with my parents instead of thinking about what had happened in my dreams.

TH: Can you project yourself into the emotions you want to experience while, at the same time, holding to that view of the family situation as vividly and realistically as possible?

CL: (*moment of thoughtfulness*) I'm surprised at how comfortable I'm feeling compared to a few months ago. I'm relaxed. I'm thinking how different it is now. I see me talking, laughing, and listening to both parents . . . not putting ulterior motives into his voice and actions . . . I'm seeing him as the dad he really is, and always has been . . . and I guess I'm pleased with me too . . . pleased that I can see myself as valuable and lovable. Even with my faults, I'm still a good daughter.

TH: You seem to be fully owning your dreams and fantasies. You're also painting a very positive picture. What are the words you're saying to your dad, mom, and yourself? And what emotions do you want to feel and project for them to receive?

CL: Okay, I'm talking about things that interest them . . . asking Mom about her day at the office . . . asking Dad about his visit to the ETV studio. I'm feeling good about having such interesting parents. I'm feeling comfortable with Dad, but I'm also aware of my desire to enjoy and pay attention to both parents equally (*thoughtful silence*).

TH: It sounds to me that you're rehearsing a "perfect" situation. I wonder if we can check out whether you are retreating to a previous stage in your earlier childhood or substituting a "hoped for" family scene to keep from dealing with problems and anxieties that are too painful to face.

CL: I've thought about that too. I don't want to be defensive. But I really think I've progressed beyond that point. I do have some concerns . . . that I may wake up and discover that I'm back like I was before . . . and that frightens me. What I want to do is maintain what I've got and go on from there. I don't see myself as going backwards or deluding myself.

Supportive and Cathartic Techniques
Langs (1973), Small (1972), and Stricker (1978) have described modern applications of psychoanalytic therapy, such as supportive and cathartic techniques. *Supportive* techniques are used when the client's anxiety level is assessed as ego-threatening to the client.

CL: My life seems to be crumbling all around me. My parents have been out of town for a week. Our dog, Ginger, got killed, and last night I kept having visions of seeing my wrists cut and bleeding, like when I slashed them when I was fourteen.

TH: Carla, I hear your desperation, and I'm concerned right now about your physical and emotional safety. I want us to talk about your suicidal fantasies. I cannot ignore these fantasies, and I want to tell you that there may be direct relationships among your background experiences, your present loneliness, your parents being out of town, your grief and loss of Ginger, and your regressing to thoughts of slashing your wrists. I want you to know that we're going to work on these together, and that I'll continue to work with you, be with you, and be available to you until this crisis situation is over. I can assure you that the crisis will pass! Now, let's go back and start by your telling me about all those events that led to your feeling like your life is crumbling.

The therapist was attending to Carla's need for support while considering her unique background and present circumstances. The therapist continued to take a very directive and active stance in the session, as recommended by Stricker (1978). The therapist kept three considerations in mind: (1) the support and safety of Carla were paramount; (2) even in this crisis, Carla's age and need for independence and responsibility were important; and (3) it was primarily Carla's *ego* that was being supported.

   Cathartic techniques help clients recognize and express emotions verbally without having to act on them impulsively. A segment from a later session with Carla illustrates a cathartic technique.

TH: Carla, I want you to know it is safe for you to talk about your vulnerable feelings here.

CL: Like I said, I suddenly felt like I wanted some cocaine last night, but I knew I'd end up back out on the streets again and I didn't want that! I'm scared I'm not strong enough to resist it forever. I feel so stupid and weak and helpless when I'm feeling like this. I nearly blew it.

TH: It's okay to feel like that. But it's not okay to act on it impulsively. One reason we're meeting together is to look at and help you strengthen your inner resources and choices. The first step is to talk about it right here. This is where you're going to begin to overcome your fears and to be able to do whatever you choose to do. Carla, I'm really glad you're here today.

The therapist was setting the stage for the cathartic opportunity for Carla to express her feelings verbally and bring them under ego control. Stricker (1978) stresses the modern cathartic strategy of immediacy of client expression of fears in a safe, protected, and supportive therapeutic atmosphere (p. 143). Carla's therapist used cathartic techniques to show her that she could gain insight and ego control over her negative emotions such as fear.

Short-Term Counseling Techniques

Tilley (1984) has demonstrated how a great number of psychoanalytically oriented approaches can be used with efficiency and immediacy in short-term counseling. Carla's therapist used many such techniques during their work together, one of which is illustrated here.

RECEPTIONIST: (*speaking to the therapist*) Carla is on the phone. She wishes to speak directly with you. Shall I take a number?

TH: No, thank you. I'll take it now. Please transfer it to the phone next door. Thank you. (*goes to adjoining room*) Hello, Carla, Dr. G. here. How may I help you?

CL: I'm sorry about calling you while you're busy, but I have an emergency. It's about my mother being in the hospital and my needing to go stay with her this afternoon until my daddy can get there, and I'll probably be twenty minutes late getting to your office for my appointment. My mother's got cancer and I wanted to talk to you before I leave for the hospital, so I can decide what I want to say to her when I see her.

TH: Carla, I'm very glad you called. I'm in the middle of something right now. Are you at a number where I can reach you eight or ten minutes from now?

CL: Yes.

TH: Good! Give me the number and I'll call you right back just as soon as I'm free. This is very important. Please keep your line free so I can get right back with you. Thank you.

Whether or not to accept phone calls from specific clients is a controversial issue among traditional psychoanalytically oriented therapists. According to Tilley (1984, p. 191), there are compelling reasons that therapists should do so. Depressed clients may need to hear the therapist's voice; the therapist may want to hear and assess the client's level of stress; and usually a therapist, not a receptionist, should make judgments about cancellations.

Direct-Decision Techniques

The psychoanalytic applications of direct-decision therapy (Greenwald, 1973) are many. They draw on several other systems of therapy, such as Adler's individual psychology, rational-emotive behavior therapy, behavior modification, and trait-factor counseling.

TH: Carla, you say that you are disappointed because your commitment to the religious group is losing its meaning to you.

CL: That's right. I thought it would be a lasting cure for my previous sinful life. Now, I don't want to go back to the street life, but I'm beginning to believe the religious life, like that of this group, is not the way I want to live either.

TH: Let's examine the circumstances and the time in which you originally chose to join the group—that is, what your goals were at the time.

Here the therapist makes a typical response based on the direct-decision tenet that all decisions have validity to the person at the time they were made. The therapist senses that even though Carla's original decision may have been vital to her psychic economy at that time, the payoffs she is currently receiving from the group affiliation may not be providing sufficient ego supports for her. Having explored in depth the original context of Carla's joining the group, the therapist asks a direct-decision question.

TH: Carla, what goal do you have right now? In terms of your needs today?

CL: Well, what I want most right now is to start getting my education in order. I want to go to the university and prepare for a career.

Carla's answer to that question provided the direction needed for the therapist to pursue a variety of options available to her.

Summary

Carla's therapist used traditional Freudian methods plus several innovative techniques, all within a modern psychoanalytic context, to help Carla open up action alternatives. These techniques included Hamilton's (1988) object-relations psychology; Shorr's (1972; 1980) psychoimagination; Greenwald's (1973) direct-decision techniques; and short-term counseling and psychotherapy strategies (Demos & Prout, 1993; Sifneos, 1987; Strupp, 1993; Tilley, 1984). Many modern psychoanalytic procedures (Alexander & French, 1980; Auld & Hyman, 1991; Goldman & Milman, 1978; Greenberg & Mitchell, 1983; Hamilton, 1988; Kohut, 1977; Sifneos, 1987; Strupp, 1993; Strupp & Binder, 1984; Tilley, 1984; Wolf, 1988) enable the contemporary therapist to extend Freudian formulations far beyond classical psychoanalysis. Even so, Carla's therapist worked through the traditional transference, resistance, and countertransference stages of therapy with her. Contemporary analytic therapists allow the client to "experiment with and integrate fantasy and reality, reality and potentiality, self and not self, and choices of action all within the context of a cooperative therapeutic alliance and encounter" (Shorr, 1980, p. 522). Carla's case was fairly typical. To gain control of her life, her ego had to gain control of her psychic energy by mediating the struggle between her id and her superego. Her id impulsively demanded immediate gratification and attention by impelling her to act out her instincts. Her superego demanded perfection in her behavior by imposing parental, societal, and religious standards and heaped large doses of guilt on her for her failure to attain perfection. Through therapy, she was finally able to integrate fantasy and reality and bring her id and her superego into a rational balance.

For the reader who seeks a diversity of case studies by both classical and modern psychoanalytic practitioners, Goldman and Milman (1978) have provided a rich array of cases. Belkin (1980) has supplied several excellent case histories depicting both classical and modern psychoanalytic procedures with clients of several different types and from several age groups. Sifneos (1987), Tilley (1984), and Strupp and Binder (1984) have demonstrated how psychoanalytic techniques can be used effectively with many different kinds of clients in short-term dynamic psychotherapy and counseling.

CONTRIBUTIONS OF THE PSYCHOANALYTIC SYSTEM

Freud (1958) is considered one of the founders of psychotherapy and psychiatry. His ideas influenced literature, art, religion, social science, and education during his time and continue to do so to some extent. It is difficult to be aware of Freudian psychology and not see some of his concepts manifested in human behavior—unconscious motivation, the symbolism in dreams, defense mechanisms, and the sexual origins of conflicts, to mention a few. The practice of "talking therapy" has been carried forth in every major model of psychotherapy. *Anxiety, resistance, transference,* and *interpretation* are familiar terms to therapists. Therapy models directly influenced by Freudian and psychoanalytic thought include ego counseling, Adlerian therapy, Gestalt therapy, and transactional analysis. The most unique and valuable feature of the psychoanalytic approach is the nurturance, within the transference relationship, of client autonomy and self-control (Alpher, Henry, & Strupp, 1990; Arlow, 1995; Auld & Human, 1991, pp. 5–22; Giovacchini, 1977, p. 40; Warren, 1994).

SHORTCOMINGS OF THE PSYCHOANALYTIC SYSTEM

Traditional psychoanalysis has several limitations. This is not surprising when we consider that the method was first developed a century ago in a Victorian society whose values were much different from those of today. One of the major drawbacks of the Freudian approach is that the completion of analysis may require several years. This inordinate time requirement seems ill-suited to today's fast lifestyle. Lengthy analysis also costs more, which may make it prohibitive to almost everyone except the affluent. Another limitation is that there are simply not enough trained analysts to provide therapy and counseling for the many people who seek it. Finally, some problems are not ideally suited to psychoanalytic therapy because of the time required for analysis. People go to therapy with many kinds of problems. Although Freudian analysis has long been known for its applicability to marital, vocational, parenting, sexual, assertiveness, shyness, divorce, grief, and loneliness problems, many of these contemporary areas are now viewed as being much more suited to therapeutic approaches that can provide help more efficiently than traditional psychoanalysis can.

Auld and Hyman (1991) list several types of client situations that they believe are not appropriate for psychoanalytic therapy. Among these are distresses that arise from other than psychological causes, such as biologically based disorders (p. 4). They are unenthusiastic about using psychoanalytic techniques with clients who are addicted to alcohol or other drugs or who have committed sexual offenses or other crimes (p. 5). They also raise questions and cite controversies and criticisms regarding the use of psychoanalytic therapy with women (pp. 219–238).

PSYCHOANALYTIC THERAPY WITH DIVERSE POPULATIONS

Several psychoanalytic therapies are appropriate for use with diverse populations. Arlow (1995) characterizes psychoanalysis as the most inclusive and most comprehensive system of psychology. It extends to clients with diverse cultures, ages, life styles, races, ethnicities, and physical abilities.

Self psychology (Feiner & Kiersky, 1994; Josephs, 1994; Kohut, 1971, 1995; Wolf, 1988) is particularly appropriate for use with diverse populations because one of its primary strategies is to establish and maintain an optimally empathic relationship with the client. Though the self psychologist as therapist may deal with many different types of clients and presenting disturbances, the strong and pervasive empathic case handling nurtures positive psychotherapeutic movement. Attention is given to the development of the client's self-esteem, which, in turn, enables the therapist to focus on the client's disturbance (Auld & Hyman, 1991, p. 247). The condition of optimal empathy enables client and therapist to focus on the client's current inner core of concerns, rendering any differences (cultural or other) tangential to the therapeutic condition (Feiner & Kiersky, 1994; Josephs, 1994; Kohut, 1995).

Many clients from backgrounds "different" from the prevailing majority population suffer from identity and/or developmental deficits, and *object-relations* therapy (Greenberg & Mitchell, 1983; Hamilton, 1988; McCathy, 1995; Stricker & Healey, 1990) can be appropriate for such clients. For example, borderline clients from ethnic minorities who have a diffused sense of identity may be assisted in working through their identity diffusion by exploring the meaning of their ethnicity as an emergent part of their therapy (Comas-Diaz & Minrath, 1985). Because object-relations therapy focuses strongly on the client's interpersonal relationships, attachments, and boundaries between self and others (Auld & Hyman, 1991, p. 245), object-relations therapists may address clients' strengths and assets and emphasize a psychosocial approach in facilitating the development of a sense of identity and self-esteem. According to Auld and Hyman (1991, p. 230), citing Grier and Cobbs (1968, pp. 157–160), in addition to receiving culturally sensitive training, the therapist must also combine an understanding of the unique conditions that shape minority clients' lives and provide a framework wherein clients can resolve their inner conflicts as well as respond appropriately to prejudices in the environment.

Training for psychoanalytic therapy has long included intensive self-analysis and introspection to promote a full understanding of self on the part of the therapist and how one's selfhood affects the therapeutic relationship. Contemporary psychoanalytic approaches have broadened the perspective of therapist self-analysis to include environmental and cultural factors to sensitize the practitioner to diverse clientele (Riskin, 1993).

The past thirty years have been a time of exponential growth, expansion, and change in therapist training and philosophy (Hornstein, 1992, p. 261). The development of a keen awareness of cultural, gender, and other diversities is now considered an essential component of training and practice (Auld & Hyman, 1991, pp. 221–238). Self-perception (Hornstein, 1992, p. 261) and the ability to handle the wide array of reciprocal impact issues (Kell & Mueller, 1966) that arise in working with diverse clientele are major assets of the psychoanalytic therapist.

Ego and object-relations psychology are not the only subsystems in the psychoanalytic family equipped by education and philosophy to work effectively with diversity. Time-limited dynamic therapists (Strupp, 1993; Strupp & Binder, 1984), autonomous psychotherapists (Auld & Hyman, 1991), short-term or brief therapists (Sifneos, 1987; Tilley, 1984), and many other modern psychoanalytically oriented therapists understand and work empathically and successfully with people of various colors, cultures, genders, sexual orientations, and other lifestyles and backgrounds (Feiner & Kiersky, 1994; Josephs, 1994; Kohut, 1995).

Livneh and Sherwood (1991, pp. 526–527) have documented several psychoanalytic constructs that are applicable to counseling clients with physical disabilities. Among those relevant to understanding the psychosocial implications of physical disability are the ego's defense mechanisms, body image and self-concept, mourning and grief, and the centrality of early developmental stages.

Livneh and Sherwood (1991) consider the psychoanalytic approach appropriate for counseling clients with disabilities because of its dynamic and developmental aspects. Because physical disability is never a static condition, psychoanalysis accommodates the differential and developmental strategies needed to facilitate client movement and fluctuation through the usually progressive adaptational phases such as shock, anxiety, denial, depression, internalized anger, externalized hostility, acknowledgment, and adjustment (p. 525).

Psychoanalytic therapy has several deficits to working with diverse populations. One is *cost-effectiveness:* many clients do not wish to expend the money, time, motivation, effort, or commitment required to make efficient use of therapy. For others, the psychoanalytic approach is simply out of sync with their sociocultural and/or socioeconomic backgrounds. Clearly, it is out of step with the fast pace of many people's lives.

A second and related deficit of psychoanalytic therapy is its *time-datedness.* Modern health-care systems are largely driven by funding from government, insurance-related, and health maintenance organization (HMO) sources unknown in the past. Though many proponents of the psychoanalytic approach have turned to brief, time-limited therapies as a remedy, the perception persists that psychoanalytic therapy may go on and on for unspecified lengths of time. Funding agencies are not prone to support time-unlimited treatment systems.

An age of *elitism* is a third problem for the psychoanalytic approach. The context in which it was founded and practiced for many years led to charges and the widely held belief that it is elitist and not pertinent to most people. This has spawned many alternative therapies. Its elitist image leads people to believe that psychoanalytic therapy is not applicable to those in lower socioeconomic classes and that the therapeutic system is bound to a narrow, nineteenth-century culture. We have concerns about applying the psychoanalytic approach to peoples whose origins and cultures differ significantly from those of the founding European analysts and patients.

A fourth deficit of the psychoanalytic approach is its relevancy to modern *family systems.* The patriarchal families in existence during the early development of psychoanalytic therapy are all but extinct. Treatment concepts that were appropriate for an 1890s patriarchal family do not apply to family structures at the turn of the twenty-first century (such as blended, commuter, single parent, and so on). The unique and complex problems inherent in the cultures of modern family systems require approaches that are far different from treatments that were appropriate for the nuclear families of a former era.

SUMMARY

Freud grew up in a time of scientific progress that influenced the development of psychotherapy and set the stage for the scientific study of human behavior. In his study of human behavior, Freud postulated a basic biological force that motivates people to seek pleasure and avoid pain. He called this motivating force the pleasure principle. He also postulated the theory that much individual behavior is influenced by experiences, thoughts, and feelings that are not in conscious awareness. It was through the idea of material repressed into the unconscious that Freud's theory of neurosis was developed. For example, hysteria grew from repression of unacceptable impulses and wishes.

Freud viewed the human personality as an interworking energy system composed of the id, the ego, and the superego. The id is the original source of psychic energy, the ego is the executive of the personality, and the superego is the conscience and ego ideal. The development of the personality is influenced by childhood sexuality and follows a sequence known as the stages of psychosexual development.

The techniques of psychoanalysis developed from Freud's work with hysterical clients. The purpose of these techniques was to make the contents of the unconscious conscious so that the client could understand the reasons for his or her neurotic behavior and thus behave differently. To this end, Freud developed the free-association method, in which the client tells the therapist, without any super-ego censorship of thoughts, whatever comes to mind. The therapist interprets the client's free associations to foster client understanding and uncover additional unconscious material. The final phase of therapy involves the working through of the client's transference to the therapist of conflicts and wishes with significant others in the client's life.

During the latter years of Freud's life and immediately after his death, the work of Neo-Freudians such as Horney, Erikson, Sullivan, and Fromm broadened psychoanalysis. Many contemporary theorists and therapists have developed and extended psychoanalytic techniques that are appropriate and effective with the complex problems of clients in modern, fast-paced society (Arlow, 1995; Auld & Hyman, 1991; Goldman & Milman, 1978; Strupp, 1993; Strupp & Binder, 1984).

SUGGESTIONS FOR FURTHER READING

Alexander, F. M., & French, T. M. (1980). *Psychoanalytic therapy: Principles and applications.* Lincoln: University of Nebraska Press, Bison Paper Edition.

Arlow, J. A. (1995). Psychoanalysis. In R. J. Corsini & D. Wedding (Eds.), *Current psychotherapies* (5th ed., pp. 15–50). Itasca, IL: F. E. Peacock.

Auld, F., & Hyman, M. (1991). *Resolution of inner conflict: An introduction to psychoanalytic therapy.* Washington, DC: American Psychological Association.

Demos, V. C., & Prout, M. F. (1993). A comparison of seven approaches to brief psychotherapy. *International Journal of Short-Term Psychotherapy, 8*(1), 3–22.

Fine, R. (1979). *A history of psychoanalysis.* New York: Columbia University Press.

Freud, S. (1938). *The basic writings of Sigmund Freud* (A. A. Brill, Ed. and Trans.). New York: Random House.

Goldman, G. D., & Milman, D. S. (Eds.). (1978). *Psychoanalytic psychotherapy.* Reading, MA: Addison-Wesley.

Hornstein, G. A. (1992). The return of the repressed: Psychology's problematic relations with psychoanalysis, 1909–1960. *American Psychologist, 47,* 254–263.

Sifneos, P. E. (1982). *Short-term dynamic psychotherapy: Evaluation and technique* (2nd ed.). New York: Plenum.

Strupp, H. H. (1992). The future of psychodynamic therapy. [Special issue: The future of psychotherapy.] *Psychotherapy 29*(1), 21–27.

Strupp, H. H., & Binder, J. L. (1984). *Psychotherapy in a new key: A guide to time-limited dynamic psychotherapy.* New York: Basic Books.

Tilley, B. W. (1984). *Short term counseling: A psychoanalytic approach.* New York: International Universities Press.

REFERENCES

Abeles, N. (1979). Psychodynamic theory. In H. M. Burks & B. Stefflre (Eds.), *Theories of counseling* (pp. 132–171). New York: McGraw-Hill.

Alexander, F. M., & French, T. M. (1980). *Psychoanalytic therapy: Principles and applications.* Lincoln: University of Nebraska Press, Bison Paper Edition.

Alpher, V. S., Henry, W. P., & Strupp, H. H. (1990). Dynamic factors in patient assessment and prediction of change in short-term dynamic psychotherapy. *Psychotherapy, 27*(3), 350–361.

Altman, N. (1995). Theoretical integration and personal commitment: Commentary
on Seligman and Shanok. *Psychoanalytic Dialogues, 5*(4), 595–604.

Arlow, J. A. (1979). Psychoanalysis. In R. Corsini (Ed.), *Current psychotherapies* (2nd ed.,
pp. 1–43). Itasca, IL: F. E. Peacock.

Arlow, J. A. (1989). Psychoanalysis. In R. J. Corsini & D. Wedding (Eds.), *Current psychotherapies* (4th ed.) (pp. 18–62). Itasca, IL: F. E. Peacock.

Arlow, J. A. (1995). Psychoanalysis. In R. J. Corsini & D. Wedding (Eds.), *Current psychotherapies* (5th ed., pp. 15–50). Itasca, IL: F. E. Peacock.

Arlow, J. A. & Brenner, C. (1964). *Psychoanalytic concepts and the structural theory.* New
York: International Universities Press.

Auld, F., & Hyman, M. (1991). *Resolution of inner conflict: An introduction to psychoanalytic therapy.* Washington, DC: American Psychological Association.

Babcock, R. (1983). *Sigmund Freud.* New York: Tavistock Publications, in association
with Methuen, Inc.

Bacal, H. A. (1995). The essence of Kohut's work and the progress of self psychology.
Psychoanalytic Dialogues, 5(3), 353–366.

Belkin, G. S. (Ed.). (1980). *Contemporary psychotherapies.* Skokie, IL: Rand McNally.

Beres, D. (1956). Ego deviation and the concept of schizophrenia. *The Psychoanalytic
Study of the Child, 11,* 164–235.

Binder, J. L. (1993). Observations on the training of therapists in time-limited dynamic
psychotherapy. *Psychotherapy, 30*(4), 592–598.

Blanck, G., & Blanck, R. (1974). *Ego psychology: Theory and practice.* New York: Columbia
University Press.

Blanck, R., & Blanck, G. (1968). *Marriage and personal development.* New York: Columbia
University Press.

Blanck, R., & Blanck, G. (1986). *Beyond ego psychology: Developmental object relations theory.* New York: Columbia University Press.

Britton, R. (1995). Psychic reality and unconscious belief. *International Journal of Psycho-
Analysis, 76*(1), 19–23.

Butz, M. R. (1992). The fractal nature of the development of the self. *Psychological Reports,
71*(3), 1043–1063.

Caper, R. (1995). On the difficulty of making a mutative interpretation. *International
Journal of Psycho-Analysis, 76*(1), 91–101.

Comas-Diaz, L., & Minrath, M. (1985). Psychotherapy with ethnic minority borderline
clients. *Psychotherapy, 22,* 418—426.

Demos, V. C., & Prout, M. F. (1993). A comparison of seven approaches to brief psychotherapy. *International Journal of Short-Term Psychotherapy, 8*(1), 3–22.

Ellis, A. (1995). Rational-emotive behavior therapy. In R. J. Corsini & D. Wedding
(Eds.), *Current psychotherapies* (5th ed., pp. 162–196). Itasca, IL: F. E. Peacock.

Erikson, E. H. (1963). *Childhood and society* (2nd ed.). New York: W. W. Norton.

Erikson, E. H. (1968). *Identity: Youth and crisis.* New York: W. W. Norton.

Erikson, E. H. (1982). *The life cycle completed.* New York: W. W. Norton.

Fancher, R. E. (1973). *Psychoanalytic psychology: The development of Freud's thought.* New
York: W. W. Norton.

Feiner, K., & Kiersky, S. (1994). Empathy: A common ground. *Psychoanalytic Dialogues,
4*(3), 425–440.

Fine, R. (1962). *Freud: A critical re-evaluation of his theories*. New York: D. McKay.

Fine, R. (1973). Psychoanalysis. In R. Corsini (Ed.), *Current psychotherapies* (pp. 1–33). Itasca, IL: F. E. Peacock.

Fine, R. (1979). *A history of psychoanalysis*. New York: Columbia University Press.

Fine, R. (1990). *The history of psychoanalysis*. New York: Jason Aronson.

Freud, A. (1936). *The ego and the mechanisms of defense* (C. Baines, Trans.). New York: International Universities Press. (Translated work published 1946)

Freud, S. (1958). Formulations on the two principles of mental functioning. In J. Strachey (Ed. and Trans.), *The standard edition of the complete psychological works of Sigmund Freud* (Vol. 12, pp. 213–227). London: Hogarth Press. (Original work published 1911)

Freud, S. (1961a). The infantile genital organization: An interpolation into the theory of sexuality. In J. Strachey (Ed. and Trans.), *The standard edition of the complete psychological works of Sigmund Freud* (Vol. 19, pp. 141–149). London: Hogarth Press. (Original work published 1923)

Freud, S. (1961b). The dissolution of the Oedipus complex. In J. Strachey (Ed. and Trans.), *The standard edition of the complete psychological works of Sigmund Freud* (Vol. 19, pp. 173–183). London: Hogarth Press. (Original work published 1924)

Giovacchini, P. L. (1977). Psychoanalysis. In R. J. Corsini (Ed.), *Current personality theories* (pp. 15–43). Itasca, IL: F. E. Peacock.

Goldman, G. D., & Milman, D. S. (Eds.). (1978). *Psychoanalytic psychotherapy*. Reading, MA: Addison-Wesley.

Greenberg, J., & Mitchell, S. (1983). *Object relations in psychoanalytic theory*. Cambridge, MA: Harvard University Press.

Greenwald, H. (1973). *Direct decision theory*. San Diego: EDITS.

Grier, W. H., & Cobbs, P. M. (1968). *Black rage*. New York: Basic Books.

Hall, C. S. (1954). *A primer of Freudian psychology*. New York: World Publishing.

Hamilton, N. G. (1988). *Self and others: Object relations theory in practice*. Northvale, NY: Jason Aronson.

Hansen, J. C., Stevic, R. R., & Warner, R. W., Jr. (1982). *Counseling theory and process* (3rd ed.). Boston: Allyn & Bacon.

Harrist, R. S., Quintana, S. M., Strupp, H. H., & Henry, W. P. (1994). Internalization of interpersonal process in time-limited dynamic psychotherapy. *Psychotherapy, 31*(1), 49–57.

Hartmann, H. (1939). *Ego psychology and the problem of adaptation* (D. Rapaport, Trans.). New York: International Universities Press.

Henry, W. P., Butler, S. F., Strupp, H. H., & Schacht, T. E. (1993). Effects of training in time-limited dynamic psychotherapy: Changes in therapist behavior. *Journal of Consulting and Clinical Psychology, 61*(3), 434–440.

Henry, W. P., Schacht, T. E., Strupp, H. H., & Butler, S. F. (1993). Effects of training in time-limited dynamic psychotherapy: Mediators of therapists' responses to training. *Journal of Consulting and Clinical Psychology, 61*(3), 441–447.

Hornstein, G. A. (1992). The return of the repressed: Psychology's problematic relations with psychoanalysis, 1909–1960. *American Psychologist, 47*, 254–263.

Jones, E. (1961). *The life and works of Sigmund Freud*. New York: Doubleday.

Josephs, L. (1994). Empathic character analysis. *American Journal of Psychoanalysis, 54*(1), 41–54.

Kell, B. L., & Mueller, W. J. (1966). *Impact and change: A study of counseling relationships*. New York: Appleton-Century-Crofts.

Kohut, H. (1971). *The analysis of the self*. New York: International Universities Press.

Kohut, H. (1977). *The restoration of the self.* New York: International Universities Press.

Kohut, H. (1984). *How does analysis cure?* Chicago: University of Chicago Press.

Kohut, H. (1995). Introspection, empathy, and psychoanalysis: An examination of the relationship between mode of observation and theory. *Journal of Psychotherapy Practice and Research, 4*(2), 163–177.

Lachmann, F. M. (1993). Self psychology: Origins and overview, *British Journal of Psychotherapy, 10*(2), 226–231.

Lachmann, F. M., & Beebe, B. (1995). Self psychology: Today. *Psychoanalytic Dialogues, 5*(3), 375–384.

Langs, R. (1973). *The technique of psychoanalytic psychotherapy.* New York: Jason Aronson.

Leach, D. (1995). Sexual conflict and self disintegration in the work of J. K. Huysmans. *Literature and Psychology, 41*(1–2), 37–51.

Levine, C., Jakubowski, L., & Cote, J. (1992). Linking ego and moral development: The value consistency thesis. *Human Development, 35*(5), 286–301.

Livneh, H., & Sherwood, A. (1991). Application of personality theories and counseling strategies to clients with physical disabilities. *Journal of Counseling and Development, 69,* 525–538.

McCathy, J. B. (1995). Adolescent character formation and psychoanalytic theory. *American Journal of Psychoanalysis, 55*(3), 245–267.

Najavits, L. M., & Strupp, H. H. (1994). Differences in the effectiveness of psychodynamic therapists: A process outcome study. *Psychotherapy, 31*(1), 114–123.

Pauchant, T. C., & Dumas, C. A. (1991). Abraham Maslow and Heinz Kohut: A comparison. *Journal of Humanistic Psychology, 31*(2), 49–71.

Pearsons, L. (1965). *The use of written communications in psychotherapy.* Springfield, IL: Chas. C. Thomas.

Pires, U., & Pedro, M. (1994). 0 problema da mudança: Kohut e São Tomás de Aquino (paralelismos possíveis). [The problem of change: Kohut and St. Thomas Aquinas: Possible parallels.]. *Revista Portuguesa de Psicanálise, 13,* 91–103.

Progoff, I. (1977). *At a journal workshop: The basic text and guide for using the intensive journal process.* New York: Dialogue House Library.

Rapaport, D. (1967). The scientific methodology of psychoanalysis. In M. M. Gill (Ed.), *The collected papers of David Rapaport* (pp. 165–220). New York: Basic Books.

Riskin, J. D. (1993). STAPP: Cross-cultural application. *International Journal of Short Term Psychotherapy, 8*(4), 217–224.

Shakow, D., & Rapaport, D. (1964). *The influence of Freud on American psychology.* New York: International Universities Press.

Shorr, J. E. (1972). *Psycho-imagination therapy: The integration of phenomenology and imagination.* New York: Intercontinental Medical Book Corp.

Shorr, J. E. (1980). Psycho-imagination therapy. In R. Herink (Ed.), *The psychotherapy handbook* (pp. 522–523). New York: New American Library.

Sifneos, P. E. (1987). *Short-term dynamic psychotherapy: Evaluation and technique* (2nd ed.). New York: Plenum.

Small, L. (1972). Crisis therapy: Theory and method. In G. D. Goldman & D. S. Milman (Eds.), *Innovations in psychotherapy* (pp. 21–38). Springfield, IL: Chas. C. Thomas.

St. Clair, M. (1986). *Object relations and self psychology: An introduction.* Pacific Grove, CA: Brooks/Cole.

Stolorow, R. D. (1995). An intersubjective view of self psychology. *Psychoanalytic Dialogues, 5*(3), 393–399.

Stricker, G. (1978). Therapeutic crisis. In G. D. Goldman & D. S. Milman (Eds.), *Psychoanalytic psychotherapy* (pp. 129–148). Reading, MA: Addison-Wesley.

Stricker, G., & Healey, B. J. (1990). Projective assessment of object relations: A review of the empirical literature. *Psychological Assessment, 2*(3), 219–230.

Strupp, H. H. (1986). Time-limited dynamic psychotherapy (Videotape No. 1, client named Richard). In E. L. Shostrom (Executive Producer), S. K. Shostrom (Producer), & H. Ratner (Director), *Three approaches to psychotherapy III* (three VHS videotapes). Corona Del Mar, CA: Psychological and Educational Film.

Strupp, H. H. (1992). The future of psychodynamic psychotherapy. [Special issue: The future of psychotherapy.] *Psychotherapy, 29*(1), 21–27.

Strupp, H. H. (1993). The Vanderbilt psychotherapy studies: Synopsis. *Journal of Consulting and Clinical Psychology, 61*(3), 431–433.

Strupp, H. H., & Binder, J. L. (1984). *Psychotherapy in a new key: A guide to time-limited dynamic psychotherapy.* New York: Basic Books.

Szasz, T. (1974). *The ethics of psychoanalysis.* New York: Basic Books.

Tilley, B. W. (1984). *Short term counseling: A psychoanalytic approach.* New York: International Universities Press.

Tobin, S. A. (1991). A comparison of psychoanalytic self psychology and Carl Rogers's person-centered therapy. *Journal of Humanistic Psychology, 31*(1), 9–33.

Wallerstein, R. S. (1995). Locating Erikson in contemporary psychoanalysis: Commentary on Seligman and Shanok. *Psychoanalytic Dialogues, 5*(4), 567–577.

Warren, M. P. (1994). The missing link: The role of empathy in communicative psychoanalysis. *International Journal of Communicative Psychoanalysis and Psychotherapy, 9*(2), 35–39.

Wolf, E. S. (1988). *Treating the self: Elements of clinical self psychology.* New York: Guilford.

Wolf, E. S. (1994). Varieties of disorders of the self. *British Journal of Psychotherapy, 11*(2), 198–208.

Wollheim, R. (1971). *Sigmund Freud.* New York: Viking.

Wolman, B. B. (1968). *The unconscious mind: The meaning of Freudian psychology.* Englewood Cliffs, NJ: Prentice-Hall.

Wolman, B. B. (1989). The protoconscious. *Dynamische Psychiatrie, 22*(1–2), 22–30.

3

ADLERIAN THERAPY

History

The history of Adlerian counseling can be divided into three eras: (1) its origin in Europe, where it split off from Freudian psychoanalytics in the early 1900s under its namesake, Alfred Adler; (2) its rooting and fledgling growth in America through the advocacy of Rudolf Dreikurs—writer, therapist, and editor; and (3) the growth and dissemination of Adlerian concepts and techniques in the elementary school guidance movement through the work of Don Dinkmeyer.

In 1902, Alfred Adler was invited to join Freud's inner circle, probably because of articles he had written in defense of Freud. However, it was not long before theoretical divisions started to separate the two men. The schism widened, and in 1912 Adler and others of Freud's circle split to form the Society for Free Psychoanalytic Thought and started publishing the *Journal for Individual Psychology*.

More than any other early psychologist, Adler envisioned a social psychology that reached out into the community. The most notable example of such outreach programs was the child guidance centers he started in the Vienna public schools in 1922.

One of the major precepts of Adlerian psychology, that of inferiority and superiority, may be traced to Adler's own early life. His childhood was marked by sickness, accidents, and failure in school, all of which contributed to a compensatory drive to become superior. Adler's determination culminated in a medical degree, publication of over three hundred books and articles, worldwide lecture tours, and the naming of a therapeutic modality after himself by the time of his death in 1937.

If not for Rudolf Dreikurs, the fledgling Adlerian movement might have ceased to exist. Dreikurs pushed hard for the adoption of child guidance centers in America. His prolific writing about Adlerian psychology and his own innovations, such as group therapy, the modeling of real-life counseling sessions before audiences (Dreikurs, 1959), multiple therapist procedures, and a comprehensive counseling approach to children (Dinkmeyer, Pew, & Dinkmeyer, 1979, p. 3), did much to bring Adlerian psychology to the attention of the general public. Dreikur's editorship of the *Journal of Individual Psychology* and the *Individual Psychology Bulletin* and his founding of the Alfred Adler Institute in Chicago and the North American Society of Adlerian Psychology have played a crucial part in revealing Adlerian therapy as a comprehensive therapy for humankind and not merely an approach good for "talking to kids." Dreikurs died in 1972.

However, it was not until the emergence of Don Dinkmeyer, an acolyte of Dreikurs, that Adlerian concepts became widespread. Two excellent commercial enterprises, *Developing Understanding of Self and Others* (DUSO) (Dinkmeyer & Dinkmeyer, 1982) and *Systematic Training for Effective Parenting* (STEP) (Dinkmeyer & McKay, 1976), have enabled thousands of children, parents, and human service workers to profit from the basic tenets of Adler and Dreikurs. Through his prolific writing and directorship of the Communication and Motivation Training Institute in Coral Springs, Florida, Dinkmeyer disseminated his version of Adlerian psychology to America.

The "common-sense" basis of the approach has resulted in many of Adler's ideas being appropriated by other theorists without due credit to Adler (Ansbacher, 1977, pp. 77–78). Such concepts as inferiority and superiority complexes, goal orientation, lifestyle, the will to power, dependency, and overprotection have become so widespread that few realize they were originated by Adler. The logotherapy of Frankl (1970), the humanism of Maslow (1970), the existentialism of May (1970), and the rational-emotive approach of Ellis (1971) all owe much to Adler. A number of other approaches, such as Glasser's reality therapy, Satir's family therapy, Berne's transactional analysis, and Perls's Gestalt therapy, have borrowed from Adlerian counseling techniques (Mosak, 1989; Sweeney, 1989).

Adlerian theory, practice, and research have expanded greatly through the journal and the many university programs and individual courses in Adlerian psychotherapy. The Adler Institute itself offers clinical practitioners a master's degree and a doctoral degree in clinical psychology (Mosak, 1989, p. 76).

Overview of Adlerian Therapy

Humans are constantly "becoming"—moving toward fictional goals that they think lead to superiority. At times such behavior is self-defeating. The pursuit of unrealistic and unattainable goals—the result of inferiority feelings—leads to discouragement. In its most severe forms such discouragement fosters neurosis, psychosis, substance abuse, perversions, problems in children, criminal behavior, and suicide (Adler, 1956, p. 158).

To combat such problems, the Adlerian counselor seeks to help the client lead a socially useful lifestyle. Such a lifestyle involves a mentally healthy individual becoming part of the mainstream by meeting the challenge of the primary Adlerian life tasks of work, love, and friendship (Dreikurs, 1981, pp. 34–41). Such tasks are woven into the fabric of society, and the goal of counseling thus becomes realigning individual interests with those of society.

The role of the counselor is to apprise the client of mistaken goals that lead to self-defeating behavior and to help the client broaden his or her social interest so that self-centeredness, egotism, and isolation are expunged in favor of sincere, meaningful, and positive interpersonal relationships. A holistic view of the client is taken by the counselor, and the concept of discrete traits, factors, attributes, typologies, indexes, and so forth, becomes secondary to the unity of the individual (Mosak, 1989, p. 73).

However, no person is merely a clone of some perfect human model that exists in society. Personhood is perceived to be phenomenological, which means that each individual is unique. Society is viewed as teleological, meaning that humans exist for a definite purpose or design in the natural scheme of things. Adlerian theory holds that people are not pushed by the objective past or controlled by mechanistic or external forces (although they may think they are), but rather, they are pulled by the future and controlled by themselves (even though they may occasionally need help from a counselor).

The counselor pulls the client into this future world of positive interpersonal relationships and provides an internal frame of reference that aids the client's attempt to live purposively in the commonweal. The counselor's main tasks are to model and promote social feeling in the client and to reorient an inappropriate lifestyle so that the individual not only reacts to society, but also is inextricably woven into society's fabric as an equal and contributing thread. The counselor creates such a climate for change by actively collaborating with the client to uncover the unique rules and purposes of behavior that govern the client. Confrontation, encouragement, interpretation, and self-disclosure couched in empathy, warmth, unconditional positive regard, and concreteness are all used to help clients understand their beliefs and feelings and gain insight into their mistaken goals and self-defeating behaviors (Dinkmeyer, Dinkmeyer, & Sperry, 1987).

Theory of Personality

Adlerian psychology is both an individual and a social psychology—individual in the sense that the person is viewed as a unified organism (Mosak, 1989, p. 73); social in the sense that humans are seen as being motivated primarily by social interest. Because individual psychology was developed in reaction to Freudian psychoanalytic psychology, the Adlerian position on personality differs from the psychoanalytic view in several important ways. First, social urges take precedence over sexual urges in personality development. Second, consciousness rather than unconsciousness is the primary source of ideas and values. Third, the determinants of behavior consist of more than just one's genetic endowment or early sexual impressions. Fourth, normal psychological development is the model of choice rather than varying degrees (or the lack thereof) of mental illness (Dinkmeyer, Dinkmeyer, & Sperry, 1987).

From birth, when we are utterly dependent on others for our survival, to adulthood, when to be fully functional we must learn to cooperate with others, all behaviors may be construed to have social meaning (Dinkmeyer, Pew, & Dinkmeyer, 1979, p. 7). *Social meaning* may be defined as "wanting to belong." Whether belonging is in terms of family, significant others, or professional or social groups, "no man is an island unto himself."

Life Tasks

The goals of belonging are embedded in life tasks. There are three major life tasks—friendship, occupation, and love (Dreikurs, 1981). Life tasks are aimed at the development of a feeling of responsibility to the commonweal. If one of the tasks is evaded, difficulties in fulfilling the others will be expressed sooner or later (Dreikurs, 1981, p. 34).

The life task of friendship is probably the best indicator of a person's social interest because one's relationships with significant friends express one's attitude toward the whole community. The individual is free to decide whether friendships will be formed, and if so, to what extent, and whether he or she will adapt to others and cooperate with them or choose solitude and detachment from society (Dreikurs, 1981, p. 40).

Because work consumes the greater portion of our waking moments, occupation is a prime life task. Only the most discouraged people evade work, which is why the inability to work is often regarded as a serious illness and why nonfulfillment of this task threatens the very maintenance of one's life (Dreikurs, 1981, p. 34). Satisfaction in and a willingness to assume an occupational role are crucial in a technocracy because of the interdependence of humankind. Ultimately, the willingness to work depends on the individual's sense of duty to oneself and to society. If resistance to duty develops in childhood, it invariably persists throughout one's working life. The importance of the occupational task weighs most heavily on those who have failed in the life tasks of love and friendship, because these individuals have no other effective way of keeping in touch with society (Dreikurs, 1981, pp. 35–36).

Love is seen by Adlerians not in terms of libidinal drives but rather as a matter of role. The major task of love is understanding and relating to the opposite sex. Fulfillment of this task demands a maximum of social interest because it involves the closest of all contacts between two humans. It tests to the limit their capacity for cooperation and eliminates the distance that can be maintained in occupational and social relationships (Dreikurs, 1981, p. 40). To achieve such a capacity, fully functioning individuals do not see men or women in stereotypical or antagonistic roles, but rather as equal and contributing partners. Adlerians, then, have much to say about equal rights between the sexes.

Two other life tasks have been added to the first three. Humankind needs to deal with its relationship to the spiritual (Mosak & Dreikurs, 1967). People do not live by bread alone and must define a spiritual self in relation to the cosmos, God, and universal values and how to relate to these concepts to obtain a spiritual centeredness such that the other life tasks all take on meaning (Mosak, 1989, p. 68; Witmer, 1989, pp. 33–46).

Finally, humans need to understand their individual selves, the "I" and the "me" (Dreikurs & Mosak, 1967). Being able to define and affirm ourselves means that it is imperative that good relations exist between the "I" and the "me" as between "I" and other people (Mosak, 1989, p. 68; Witmer, 1989, p. 33).

None of these life tasks stands apart from the others. A solution to one helps provide a solution to the others. All of the life tasks deal with the same problem—the necessity for humankind to persevere in the contemporary environment. Social interest is not just welded to the individual by external forces, but is part of the individual's psychological equipment and is used in striving for perfection (Adler, 1956, pp. 132–133).

Nomothetic Principles

Yet, basic questions remain. Why are people different? Why do some become law-abiding citizens and others criminals? Why do some become neurotics, others psychotics, and the rest, by degrees, well-adjusted? In essence, what makes us what we are? For Adler, the answer to this question lies in four parts. Three of the parts are *nomothetic* (they apply generally to humankind) but include many exceptions:

1. The basic dynamic force is the striving for a fictional goal—one of superiority.
2. Successful adaptation to life depends on the degree of social interest in goal striving.
3. Goal striving may be considered more or less active and can be considered according to type (Ansbacher & Ansbacher, 1956, p. 172).

Fictional Goals

Fictional goals are the outcome of unconscious notions that have no counterpart in reality. Fictions, then, are generated in an unreal world, but this makes them no less important than the objective facts of the real world. This "as if" world becomes the individual's real world of values (Vaihinger, 1956, p. 77). Fictional goals are concerned with the future. However, this future is not objective but subjective because it is expressed and wished for by the individual in the present. According to Adler, because individuals are seldom, if ever, aware of their fictional goals, such hidden goals make up the essential content of the unconscious (Vaihinger, 1956, p. 89).

Fictions start early in life. A newborn child enters an environment that is by no means neutral. That environment is represented by the family constellation. Through observation, exploration, trial and error, and feedback from this primary environment, the child quickly learns what will and will not work (Dinkmeyer, Dinkmeyer, & Sperry, 1987, p. 34). As children attempt to carve out a territory in the family constellation, they generate goals that they hope will lead to a feeling of self-worth. Problems arise because children make erroneous judgments and do not always think logically. This makes no difference, for they accept such judgments and thoughts "as if" they are true, even though they have no basis in fact (Mosak, 1979, pp. 56–57). Adler called this way of thinking the individual's *private logic*. Private logic is the hidden reason that people do not do what the situation normally calls for. In the young child, fictional conceptualizations form the first far-reaching goals of what is to become the lifestyle. These fictions happen at such a young age that they are submerged by the individual (Dinkmeyer, Pew, & Dinkmeyer, 1979, p. 26). Nevertheless, they survive, carrying the individual forward into his or her fictional future. Fictions may be divided into (1) convictions about who one is, (2) convictions about who one should be, (3) convictions about what the rest of the world should be, and (4) convictions about what is ethically right or wrong (Mosak & Dreikurs, 1973).

Fictional goals are not necessarily bad, evil, or debilitating. They are merely an attempt at "somebodyness," at belonging and striving for a piece of significance in the eyes of others (Rule, 1985). If people did not have such goals, there would be no striving for perfection and society would not progress.

Most often severe errors in lifestyle are seen in those children who are pampered or rejected by significant others. If not compensated for or corrected, such errors continue to build and block progress into useful social living. Later problems of occupation, love, and I-to-you relationships have little likelihood of being overcome without therapeutic intervention. The individual who learns to deal in socially acceptable compensatory ways with life's problems will strive for the commonly acceptable individual goal of perfection. However, the individual who cannot navigate life's shoals is likely to seek an exaggerated goal of personal superiority. Taken to the extreme, these private, dysfunctional goal fictions lead to neurosis, psychosis, substance abuse, perversions, suicide, and criminal behavior (Ansbacher & Ansbacher, 1956, pp. 165–166). It is from individuals with such fictions that all human failures come; this is the human "flotsam and jetsam" the counselor is most likely to encounter.

Striving for fictional goals can be considered according to the degree and type of activity. Individuals tackle their problems with varying degrees of activity, and the degree of activity acquired in childhood becomes a thread that runs true into adulthood. Because of their belief that individuals should be seen in light of their particular development, Adlerians are reticent to classify people. However, to demonstrate people's attitudes and behavior toward external problems, Adlerians have proposed the following types:

1. *Ruling.* The individual is dominant in relationships. Much activity but little social interest is shown.
2. *Getting.* The individual expects things from others and is dependent on them. Little activity and little social interest are demonstrated.
3. *Avoiding.* The individual shies away from problems. Again, little activity and social interest are shown.
4. *Driving.* The individual wants to achieve. Total success or nothingness are the only alternatives. Much activity and little social interest are shown.
5. *Controlling.* The individual likes order, but it must be his or her order. A great deal of activity is expended in keeping the unexpected to a bare minimum. Social interest is minimal because others in the system are constantly disrupting the individual's plans.
6. *Being victimized or martyred.* Both types are similar in their suffering. However, victims have diminished activity and interest, whereas martyrs have increased activity and interest.
7. *Being good.* The individual satisfies his or her sense of superiority by being more competent, more useful, more right, and "holier than thou." Only by excelling in whatever area of moral perfection they undertake can such people truly belong. Heightened activity and interest characterize this club, to which very few can belong.
8. *Being socially useful.* The individual cooperates with others and contributes to their social well-being without self-aggrandizement. Activity and social interest are both great and positive (Adler, 1956, pp. 126–162; Mosak, 1971).

None of the foregoing types is inherently bad. The behavioral outcome of each will depend on what the individual does with his or her convictions. Very seldom will the counselor see these pure types; a blend is much more common (Dinkmeyer, Dinkmeyer, & Sperry, 1987, p. 39).

Idiographic Principles

The fourth part of Adler's answer to why people are different is *idiographic* (it applies to the individual and no one else). It is the wholeness and uniqueness of the individual in implementing the three nomothetic laws discussed earlier (Ansbacher & Ansbacher, 1956, p. 172). In simple terms, it is the style of life. One's lifestyle is the overall pattern that influences one's feeling, thinking, and behaving (Rule, 1985). An individual's lifestyle is based on private logic, develops out of his or her life plan, and is powered by fictional goals (Dinkmeyer, Dinkmeyer, & Sperry, 1987, p. 31). It is the consistent movement toward the goal of belonging as that goal is interpreted by the individual and the rest of society. Counselors who understand the individual's lifestyle are provided with a map that shows where the individual is going, even if he or she has no clear idea what route to take.

Therefore, it matters not so much what the individual is born with or into but rather how the individual perceives his or her genetic and environmental endowment and what he or she does with it. Constitutional traits are not causative. For example, superior intellectual ability does not guarantee great academic performance. An individual so endowed who perceives other smart people as nerds may be an academic underachiever to appear cool (Dinkmeyer, Dinkmeyer, & Sperry, 1987, pp. 24–25). Behavior, then, is clearly a function of perception. We tend to behave according to how things appear to us, and when our perception changes our behavior changes accordingly. Thus, *perception* of the situation often determines behavior and belief more than the *reality* of the situation (Dinkmeyer, Dinkmeyer, & Sperry, 1987, p. 18). Individual psychology, then, draws its conclusions not from a person's possessions but from his or her use of those possessions. These applications and, more important, the manner in which the individual "experiences" them are the bricks and mortar with which an attitude toward life is built (Adler, 1956, pp. 250–256).

Nature of Maladjustment

Adler's approach to maladjustment can be best explained by his approach to neurosis. All the behavior disorders, mental and physical incapacities, delinquent and criminal acts, and psychoses are directly related to what Adler has to say about the neurotic. For Adler, the obsessive-compulsive person is the prototype of all neurosis. The obsessive-compulsive's indecisiveness and doubt, deprecation of others, godlike strivings, and focus on minutiae are all routine safeguards that exclude him or her from the social mainstream (Dinkmeyer, Dinkmeyer, & Sperry, 1987, p. 47).

Adler (1956, p. 239) depicted neurosis as follows:

1. An individual has a mistaken opinion of self and the world.
2. The individual will resort to various forms of abnormal behavior aimed at safeguarding his or her opinion of self.
3. Such safeguarding occurs when the individual is confronted with situations he or she feels will be met unsuccessfully.
4. The mistake consists of being self-centered rather than taking humankind into account.
5. The individual is not consciously aware of these processes.

Inferiority Complex

These five components of neurosis issue from the wellspring of maladjustment—the inferiority complex. Inferiority feelings should be distinguished from an inferiority complex. All of us have inferiority feelings, since we all find situations we wish to improve (Adler, 1958, p. 51). However, inferiority becomes pathological (a complex) only when the individual is overwhelmed by a sense of inadequacy and becomes incapable of development (Adler, 1929, pp. 78–79).

Inferiority is one horn of a dilemma. The person with an inferiority complex seeks escape through a compensatory move toward superiority. However, such compensation is aimed no longer at solving problems but rather at preserving the useless side of life (Adler, 1958, p. 52).

Neurotics vacillate between inferiority and superiority. They are highly ambitious but lack courage. Avoidance, displacement, projection, retreat, helplessness, and detouring all describe how they save face when confronted with the ultimate threat—being seen as a failure. The symptoms they display have great social significance. Such symptoms are ways of avoiding responsibility in the environment or attempts to control the behavior of those with whom they relate (Dinkmeyer, Pew, & Dinkmeyer, 1979, p. 37). Neurotics are constantly putting psychological distance between themselves and people, environments, and tasks. They can be characterized as "Yes, but" personalities. They know what should be changed but cannot or, more likely, will not change (Dinkmeyer, Dinkmeyer, & Sperry, 1987, p. 44).

Family Constellation

Whence does the twisted logic of the neurotic come? For the Adlerians, the family constellation and atmosphere are the axes on which most other factors in the development of the child turn. The family constellation mediates the genetic and constitutional factors the child brings into it and the cultural factors the child learns from it. The personality characteristics of each family member, the birth order of the child, the sex of siblings, and family size all influence how the child finds his or her niche. Depending on the prevailing family atmosphere, the child can develop in the direction of accepting attitudes shared by the family, in the direction of rejecting them, or somewhere in between (Dinkmeyer, Pew, & Dinkmeyer, 1979, p. 24). As long as the family shares trust, confidence, mutuality, love, work, and social interest in equitable ways, the child will likely find a wholesome niche for potential growth.

However, there are a variety of family atmospheres that are anything but equitable. Those that reject, suppress, overprotect, and disparage the child (Dewey, 1971) are breeding grounds for discouragement, and the discouraged child becomes the maladjusted child (Mosak, 1979, p. 57). Such children find their place in the family constellation by striving for the mistaken goals of attention, power, revenge, and inadequacy (Dreikurs, 1953). Shulman (1973) has noted three common mistakes of adaptation in the growing child: (1) distorted attitudes of self, people, and the world ("I, others, and the world are all rotten"); (2) distorted goals and operating methods ("I must be perfect, and I will ignore, reject, or fight anything that interferes with belonging"); and (3) distorted ideas and conclusions ("I must be the best, so I'll look out for number one"). These distorted ideas may be a small part of every normal child's passage into adulthood, but if they become concrete, serious problems can occur in later life.

Safeguarding

The adult neurotic is a veritable draft horse in creating ways of safeguarding the fictional goal. Safeguarding becomes so consuming that the task the neurotic is threatened by is almost forgotten. No problem can be solved because neurotics become so skilled at safeguarding that they generate symptoms that they use to delude themselves and divert others from focusing on the core of the neurosis. These symptoms become obstacles the neurotic can hide behind, feeling secure from the horrible life tasks that are "out there just waiting" to terrorize him or her.

Although the symptoms may relieve the neurotic of responsibility or help him or her gain power over others, safeguarding calls for more and more maladaptive responses. Excuses channel the maladjusted individual into even narrower behavior modes. The neurotic vows to do anything to get rid of the symptoms that hinder and debilitate life at every turn. But this is a lie because the fictional cost—loss of prestige—is too high. Depreciation, accusation, guilt, martyrdom, anxiety attacks, psychosomatic illness, and restriction of physical perimeters are but a few of the items on the smorgasbord of maladaptive safeguarding behaviors the neurotic relishes.

Neurotics and Psychotics

Neurotic symptoms and behaviors provide ideal examples for understanding Adlerian concepts of maladjustment. Further, one who understands the operating mode and the reasons for being of the neurotic can also understand other pathological individuals. Psychotics, for example, move from the neurotic's "Yes, but" approach to involvement to a "No" approach to life tasks (Dinkmeyer, Dinkmeyer, & Sperry, 1987, p. 44).

Paradoxically, Adlerians propose that the psychotic is engaged in problem solving, as opposed to the neurotic's avoidance of problems. However, the psychotic's solutions are on the useless side of life. Their fictional goals have grown so large that they are irrational, nonconstructive, nonconsensual, inferior, and highly ineffective (Mosak & Goldman, 1995).

The superiority goals of psychotics place them beyond the reach of mere humans. These inordinate superiority goals allow psychotics to believe, among other things, that "Everybody is out to get me," "I am Christ, Muhammad, Buddha," or "I am the worst sinner of all time." They have lost social interest to the degree that they have finally abandoned their own reason and understanding (Mosak, 1989, p. 80).

Addicts

For addicts, life normally revolves around the abused substance rather than people. Ironically, feeling "normal" means that the substance abuser becomes more lonely and isolated as the addiction progresses. For the substance abuser who has an inferiority complex, the beginning of addiction is based on acute feelings of shyness, isolation, impatience, anxiety, and depression. For the substance abuser who has a superiority complex, addiction fulfills a need for power (Dinkmeyer, Dinkmeyer, & Sperry, 1987, p. 57).

Criminals

Criminals believe that everyone else exists for their benefit. They believe they have the right to seize the goods, health, or life of others and set their own interests above the common good (Adler, 1970, p. 257). They generally have failed to obtain attention in socially acceptable ways and thus resort to socially unacceptable but personally enhancing behavior (Eckstein, 1981, p. 64). Most criminal behavior can be traced back to a childhood filled with attempts to fit into a dysfunctional family constellation. All three of these pathological types have mistaken goals of belonging (Dinkmeyer, Pew, & Dinkmeyer, 1979, p. 52), and their problem-solving devices propel them away from, rather than into, the mainstream.

Basic Propositions

A number of basic propositions about the human condition undergird Adlerian theory (Ansbacher & Ansbacher, 1956, pp. 1–2; Sweeney, 1989, pp. 5–9, 28).

1. The basic force behind human activity is a striving from a perceived negative situation to a hoped-for positive situation, from inferiority to superiority.
2. Each individual strives in a particular direction for a unique goal or an ideal self. Although influenced by biological and environmental factors, the goal is the unique creation of the person. Because it is an ideal, the goal is also fictional.
3. Aspiring to high social interest is the key to human productivity and happiness. Social interest must be nurtured or the individual's faulty perceptions of him- or herself can result in discouraged, self-defeating behaviors.
4. The goal is the key to understanding the individual.
5. There is no inconsistency in the individual. All psychological processes are consistently directed toward the goal. The goal is the individual's *lifestyle* and is firmly established at an early age.
6. Drives are not discrete, nor are divisions between the conscious and unconscious. They are only components of a unified system.
7. The individual's perceptions of self and the world and the subsequent interpretation of those perceptions are all aspects of the lifestyle, which is the cognitive map he or she uses to guide him- or herself in approaching basic life tasks.
8. The individual cannot be seen as separate from the social situation. The two are integral.
9. All important life problems are social problems. All values become social values.
10. Socialization is not gained by external duress but is an innate human ability that needs to be developed.
11. Maladjustment is characterized by increased inferiority feelings.
12. Unsuccessful coping with basic life tasks is a sign of discouragement. It can be overcome anytime in life if the individual chooses to do so.

THE COUNSELING PROCESS

Adlerian counseling has four phases: establishment of the relationship, investigation of the lifestyle, interpretation of the lifestyle, and reorientation (Rule, 1985). Overarching these phases is a cooperative effort by counselor and client to ferret out the client's goals and faulty beliefs about life tasks and reeducate him or her. Mosak (1979, p. 64) has described the objectives of this reeducation as follows: (1) fostering social interest; (2) decreasing inferiority feelings and overcoming discouragement; (3) changing the person's lifestyle; (4) changing faulty motivation or values that underlie even acceptable behavior; (5) encouraging the individual to recognize his or her equality among fellow humans; and (6) helping the client to become a contributing human being. Incorporating these objectives, psychotherapy deals with the changing of one's lifestyle and counseling deals with behavior change within the existing lifestyle. Adlerians, although interested in changing behavior, have as their major goal not behavior modification but motivation modification (Mosak, 1989, pp. 66, 79, 82).

The Client-Counselor Relationship

Because therapy is a cooperative venture, a contract should be forged between the counselor and the client that spells out the therapeutic goals of each. Such a contract is necessary because the client, though hurting enough to seek therapy, perceives both therapy and the counselor as dangerous. As a result, the client is less than likely to be open and honest or to follow prescribed treatment (Shulman, 1973, p. 105), even if he or she avows just the opposite. The client may see dangers such as these in the counselor and the therapeutic situation (Shulman, 1973, pp. 106–109):

1. *Being defective.* The client will not be able to live up to the counselor's expectations and requirements.
2. *Being exposed.* The client cannot allow the counselor to see his or her faults.
3. *Being disapproved of.* The client is dependent on the good will of the counselor.
4. *Being ridiculed.* The client will not report symptoms for fear of this.
5. *Being taken advantage of.* The client distrusts the counselor.
6. *Not being able to get help.* The client cannot have confidence in the counselor.
7. *Submitting to order.* The client is determined to have his or her own way and will not submit to any order except his or her own.
8. *Facing responsibility.* Courage fails the client, who is appalled at the task the counselor requires of him or her.
9. *Unpleasant consequences.* The client is excessively fearful and habitually anticipates dire results from counseling.

The dangers clients see in the counselor and therapy are microcosms of how they live their total lives. The counselor's foreknowledge of these perceived dangers and the understanding that they are dynamics of the inferiority-superiority continuum are the opening wedge in the counselor's attempt to understand the client's defenses. If the counselor understands that the client brings all of these safeguarding behaviors into counseling, fully armed and prepared to fight, and if the counselor can accept this, one of the basic conditions for accepting and understanding the client has been met.

Understanding the Client

To gain a true understanding of the client's lifestyle and communicate that understanding to the client, the counselor listens to and observes the client closely, trying to identify the client's beliefs, perceptions, and feelings and the movement and pattern of his or her life (Dinkmeyer, Dinkmeyer, & Sperry, 1987, p. 66). Everything the client says and does—how he or she relates with significant others, including the counselor, what symptoms he or she presents, and what action or inaction he or she has taken to alleviate these symptoms—has social as well as therapeutic significance. As Adler (1956) has indicated, we can start wherever we choose. Every expression, word, thought, or feeling leads to the motives and goals around which the individual's lifestyle is built. Nonverbal behaviors—the way people stand, sit, walk, and sleep—are all indicative of the way people approach their goals (p. 220). Even physical symptoms—the client's *organ dialect,* whereby the client speaks with his or her bladder, head, stomach, and so on—emphasize the goal (pp. 222–223).

Assessment and Analysis

Adlerians are divided on psychological testing. Because Adlerians are concerned with process, little diagnosis is done in terms of nomenclature (Mosak, 1989, p. 68). Most avoid diagnosis except for nontherapeutic purposes, such as filling out insurance labels. Labels are static descriptions and ignore the movement of the individual. They describe what the individual has, but not how he or she moves through life. Whereas older Adlerians tend to stick with lifestyle assessment, early recollections, and psychological birth order, many younger Adlerians may employ a variety of assessment devices for differential diagnosis and treatment purposes (Mosak, 1989, pp. 98–99).

Reliable and valid standardized lifestyle inventory measures can be collected and used as quick screening devices (Kern, 1982; Wheeler, Kern, & Curlette, 1991). The Nystul Turning Point Survey (NTPS) is such an instrument. The five tasks of life are incorporated into a semantic differential scale that rates happiness and meaning of life. The NTPS helps clients gain insight into past turning points in their lives and further helps them identify therapeutic goals in regard to future turning points they would like to experience (Nystul, 1993).

When combined with other intake data, such as family atmosphere and constellation, birth order, earliest childhood memories, dreams, and therapist observations, lifestyle inventories yield a comprehensive profile of the family lifestyle and the client's role in it (Sweeney, 1989, p. 211). Combined with past and present ecological factors, these are all important data for understanding the client's present condition and future course of action in regard to basic mistakes and self-defeating behaviors (Dinkmeyer, Pew, & Dinkmeyer, 1979, pp. 31–32).

Family Atmosphere and Constellation

Another facet of the client's lifestyle is obtained using a family-constellation questionnaire (Dinkmeyer, Pew, & Dinkmeyer, 1979). The client is asked to describe, among other things, his or her parents' personalities, their ambitions and relationships with their children, and their marital relationship. Detailed information is obtained on the client's siblings including birth order; who was most different or most like the client; and who had unusual talents, sickness, or physical, sexual, or social development. Finally, a variety of attributes are listed, and the client is asked to write the names of the siblings who (in the client's judgment) rate the highest and lowest for each attribute (pp. 265–267) (Harold Mosak [personal communication, August 4, 1992] believes this method is an unfortunate shortcut that allows the therapist to know something about all of the siblings but very little about the client!). Retrieval of this information allows the client to relive deeply emotional moments in his or her first contact with society—contact with the family. Of all the questions on the form, probably none has caught the public's attention more than birth order.

Birth Order

Adlerians believe that psychological position in the family (rather than chronological position) is probably as important as the parents' method of child rearing (Dinkmeyer, Pew, & Dinkmeyer, 1979, p. 87). Even so, Adlerians such as Mosak (1979, p. 57; 1989, p. 77) qualify their use of the child's psychological position with words like "most likely" and "perhaps" and do not recognize causal, one-to-one relationships between family position and sibling traits. Whatever relationship exists between ordinal position and traits is idiosyncratic to the atmosphere, stability, and total configuration of factors in the family constellation. Further, not only birth order but also gender plays a part in each sibling's psychological position in the family (Singh, 1990).

Birth order by itself is meaningless, since it does not reflect the child's attitude and movements, the formation of alliances within the family, or the unique ways in which the child approaches the family system (Dinkmeyer, Dinkmeyer, & Sperry, 1987, pp. 26–27). No two children are ever born into the same family situation, because the family environment changes: parents become older, wiser, and wealthier or poorer; move and change jobs; divorce, remarry, and die (Pepper, 1971). At best, birth order by itself denotes general traits that are only statistical probabilities.

Early Recollections

Another major component of the lifestyle inventory is early recollections. These are used as an index of social interest and provide a great deal of diagnostic data about the client (Allers, White, & Hornbuckle, 1990; Slavik, 1991). First memories show the individual's fundamental view of life. Clients will usually discuss first memories because they appear to be innocuous. Yet no memories are chosen by chance. The client, however unconscious the choice may be, remembers only those memories that bear on his or her goal and lifestyle and are significant to the individual in understanding, managing, and controlling life experiences (Dinkmeyer, Dinkmeyer, & Sperry, 1987, p. 36; Sweeney, 1989, pp. 217–218). Thus, early recollections are the story of the client's life and permit the derivation of the client's "basic mistakes" (Mosak, 1989, p. 87). These early memories are much like other projective techniques in that they allow the client to relate affective perceptions to what he or she believes is an objective event (Ansbacher & Ansbacher, 1956, p. 350).

Recording the age of the recollection can be helpful, especially if the client had no recollections until a significant family event occurred, such as the birth or death of a sibling or a move.

Important components of early recollections that the counselor should typically take note of are: Is the client active or passive? Is he or she an observer or a participant? Is the client giving or taking, approaching or avoiding? Who else is in the scene, and does that person or gender continuously reappear in the same manner? Is the client alone or with others? Is a person who should typically be in the scene left out? What items or things are in the scene? Where does it typically take place? What relationship does the client have with others? What feeling, tones, and states are conveyed? Are the recollections positive or negative? Is there a great deal of color, detail, and embellishment or is the scene barren and devoid of everything except the bare essentials? What themes appear again and again to form an overall pattern of striving? How does the family constellation support the early recollections? How are the early recollections currently played out? No standard set of questions exists for the lifestyle inventory. Rather, most practitioners modify questions such as these to gain as panoramic a view as possible of the client's current functioning and fictional goal striving (Sweeney, 1989, pp. 217–218).

Dreams

Dreams are much like early memories in that they help the counselor understand and define problem areas, predict the near-future direction of the client's lifestyle, alert the counselor to the client's therapeutic movement in the counseling relationship, and teach the client to understand his or her own personality dynamics (Shulman, 1973, p. 71). Dreams may be seen as a short-term problem-solving process that serves as a "stop-or-go" function in regard to immediate dilemmas, whereas early recollections serve as a "stop-or-go" function for lifestyle and long-range issues (Mosak, 1992).

Current Life Tasks

All of the foregoing data are analyzed, synthesized, and related to contemporary life tasks. The primary life tasks of social relationships, work, sexuality, feelings about self—the counselor covers all of these in an open-ended, systematic manner to ascertain how well the client is coping with life (Dinkmeyer, Pew, & Dinkmeyer, 1979, pp. 81–82). The data provided should portray the client's degree of social interest. People who have low social interest are continuously posing the question "How am I doing?" Whether they are doing well or faring badly, their successes and failures are predicated on self-involvement. In contrast, people with a high social interest continuously ask themselves the question "What am I doing?" This "what" question indicates the quality rather than the quantity (or lack thereof) of their endeavor and is predicated on creating, sharing, enjoying, and taking satisfaction in their efforts (Sweeney, 1989, p. 22).

Priorities

The objective in the counselor's lengthy assessment is to establish the number-one priority in the client's lifestyle. Priorities are listed in the lifestyle interview under two headings: "Important to my belonging" and "To be avoided at all costs." "Important to my belonging" is divided into four categories by Kefir (1972):

1. *Superiority*—Being competent, right, useful, victimized, martyred. The price paid is overinvolvement, overresponsibility, fatigue, stress, and uncertainty about one's relationship with others.
2. *Control*—Either of others or oneself. Controllers constantly work on their goals. Controllers of others pay the price of distancing themselves from others. Self-controllers pay a price of diminished spontaneity and creativity.
3. *Comfort*—Pleasures without waiting. People with this priority get what they want but hurt others in the process. The price paid is diminished productivity and reduced positive social interaction.
4. *Pleasing*—Without respect for oneself or for others. If relationships continue any length of time, rejection, disgust, frustration, despair, and exasperation are the outcomes. The price paid is stunted growth, alienation, and retribution.

According to Dinkmeyer, Pew, and Dinkmeyer (1979, p. 82), stress for the comforter, rejection for the pleaser, humiliation for the controller, and meaninglessness for the superiority type are to be avoided at all costs. Two basic questions are generated from the establishment of the number-one priority: "How do I use my number-one priority to belong?" and "What must I avoid at all cost when using my number-one priority?" (Dinkmeyer, Dinkmeyer, & Sperry, 1987, p. 99). The answers to these questions apprise the counselor of the client's mistaken beliefs and goals and allow more viable alternatives to be considered.

Insight and Interpretation

Adlerians do not believe in delaying action on problems while the client becomes intellectually insightful about them. People who come for therapy have no intention of giving up their number-one priorities. The only reason they come is that the price they pay behaviorally has gotten too steep. Therefore, a major goal of counseling is to help the client see his or her number-one priority, accept it for what it is, and decide whether the price is really worth paying (Dinkmeyer, Pew, & Dinkmeyer, 1979, p. 83).

The client gains insight through the counselor's interpretation of his or her ordinary communications, dreams, fantasies, behavior, symptoms, transactions with the counselor, and other interpersonal transactions. The emphasis in interpretation is on purpose rather than cause, on movement rather than description, on use rather than possession. Past to present is related only to indicate the continuity of the maladaptive lifestyle, not to demonstrate causal connection (Mosak, 1989, p. 89).

Yet initial interpretations, however accurate, are rarely accepted by the client. On-target interpretations are invariably resisted. Adlerians see resistance only as a lack of courage by the client to return to useful living and a discrepancy between the goals of the client and the counselor (Dreikurs, 1967, p. 65). Such a lack of courage and goal disparity may be manifested by the client's expression of doubt and criticism, special requests, forgetfulness, tardiness, silence, and persistent symptoms. Whatever form the resistance takes, the counselor can be sure that it is the way the client generally acts toward people he or she sees as important, influential, and possibly dangerous (Ansbacher & Ansbacher, 1956, pp. 336–337).

Reorientation

Reorientation is the final action-oriented stage of counseling. The counselor offers alternative ideas or beliefs for the client's consideration (Dinkmeyer, Dinkmeyer, & Sperry, 1987, p. 70). Reorientation is the attempt to persuade the client, by means that range from gentle to forceful, that change is in his or her best interest.

The first step in reorienting the client is to clarify what he or she wants and determine whether it is realistic. The second step involves realigning inappropriate and self-defeating beliefs, perceptions, feelings, and goals with common sense. The counselor continually mirrors the idea that the client and no one else chooses his or her mistaken goals. The third step is to move from insight to outsight—to take what is learned in counseling and move it into the world at large. The fourth step involves dealing with lack of progress. Any failure to progress is seen in terms of the mistaken purpose and payoff of continuing the self-defeating behavior. The counselor has the client evaluate alternative behaviors by asking, "What is the worst thing that could happen if I changed?" Reorientation is primarily a motivation-modification rather than a behavior-modification approach. The Adlerian thesis is that if client beliefs, attitudes, and perceptions are changed, then behavior will soon follow (Dinkmeyer, Dinkmeyer, & Sperry, 1987, pp. 119–121).

STRATEGIES FOR HELPING CLIENTS

Adlerian techniques for helping clients are many and have certainly become more eclectic since Adler started individual psychology.

Basic Listening and Responding Skills

Adlerians use basic listening and responding skills in much the same way that person-centered counselors do.

Restatement

CL: I heard you were the best, and since I'm getting out of the joint in a little while, thought you'd be the guy to help me get my act together. I'm a little hinky about this

CO: The yard talk is that I've helped some people out—particularly short-timers You're also a little nervous—about what, though, I'm not sure.

Reflection

CL: I'm fed up with being controlled by her, but I do love her!

CO: You're angry with her, yet your deep feelings for her make you want to stick with the relationship. Perhaps under the anger you're afraid you might lose her.

Guesses, Hunches, Hypotheses

CL: I really get angry, but then she can make me feel so damn good!

CO: Sounds as if she can really get to you with those conflicting feelings.

Interpretation

Interpretation takes guesses, hunches, and hypotheses a step further. Through interpretation the counselor tries to tease out the reasons for a person's behavior. The counselor's response is tentatively phrased so that the client will not become resistant. Interpretation focuses more on the "whys" of behavior than other counseling techniques. Interpretation must be timed appropriately—when the client is ready for it, can accept it as congruent with his or her fictional goals, and can use it to consider new ways of behaving (Dinkmeyer, Dinkmeyer, & Sperry, 1987, p. 102).

CL: I dunno, I really get confused about the anger and the love.

CO: Seems like it's not so much confusion, rather that "I want her to love me but I must be in control . . . I must be *the man*."

Nonverbal Behavior

Adlerians may not interpret nonverbal behavior to the extent that Gestalt therapists do, but they are well aware of it and are willing at least to bring it to the client's conscious awareness and at most to interpret it. Further, Adlerians may suggest that the client use nonverbal behavior as a fail-safe mechanism (Dinkmeyer, Dinkmeyer, & Sperry, 1987, pp. 90–91).

CL: I thought to myself, "If I can't have her, nobody will."

CO: As you say that, I notice that you're wiping your hands on your pants. My guess is that they're sweating and you're starting to feel tense, kinda like a guitar string. I wonder if you can monitor that, kinda use it as a checkpoint about your emotions. My guess is when those physical kinds of things happen your emotions are starting to take over . . . that old superiority stuff and all of the problems that go with it.

Immediacy

Immediacy means dealing with what is going on right here and right now. It is helpful in pointing out to the client how his or her verbalizations may run counter to his or her behavior, and how what happens in counseling is a microcosm of the larger, real world (Dinkmeyer, Dinkmeyer, & Sperry, 1987, p. 123).

CL: I'd really like to take that drafting course, but the warden, the unit counselor, and my case manager all have to approve it. What's the use!

CO: The way you say it, it's like you can't fight all that authority. Sounds kinda like those excuses you use on the outside and kinda like you want me to know this is already gonna fail before you start.

Confrontation
The counselor catches discrepancies between what the client says and what the client does and nonpunitively challenges the client on them. Dinkmeyer, Pew, and Dinkmeyer (1979, pp. 110–111) have gleaned four areas of confrontation from Adlerian literature.

Confronting Subjective Views
The client is confronted with the private logic he or she used to make a certain behavior acceptable in his or her own mind. The confrontation technique used here pins the client down on what was going on at the moment of that behavior.

CL: Well, I only tried dope once and this guy talked me into it. I'm really against it.

CO: So what was going on with you at that time? What were you saying to yourself to make taking the dope okay?

Confronting Mistaken Beliefs and Attitudes
The client is confronted with those mistaken beliefs and attitudes that poison his or her attempts at positive social adaptations.

CL: I don't know about women. They gripe when the man takes over and gripe when he doesn't.

CO: It's not the women so much, but you who doesn't know how to respond. At times it seems like you issue them an invitation to get on you so you can show them who's really in control.

Confronting Private Goals
The client is confronted with his or her denial of feelings that the counselor suspects are being hidden.

CL: Maybe, but women really do confuse me.

CO: Confused . . . or could it be that "if I don't show them I'm in control, they'll see me for a real wimp!"

Confronting Destructive Behavior
Clients may become self-destructive by avoiding the issue (passive aggression) or by acting out (active aggression) toward the counselor.

CL: Hey, haven't you ever felt like if you didn't stand up to a woman, she'd run all over you?

CO: When you start attacking my manhood, it makes me wonder if what I just said doesn't strike pretty close to home.

Paradoxical Intention

Adlerian therapy is an effective framework for using paradox to resolve impasses in therapy (Kopp & Kivel, 1990). Paradoxical intention involves having the client attempt to increase his or her debilitating thoughts and behaviors. The client practices, enlarging the symptoms out of proportion to the reality of the situation. By becoming acutely aware of how ridiculous such behavior is in terms of a satisfying lifestyle, the client will either change or give up the behavior. The technique is used for a specific period and is treated as an experiment (Dinkmeyer, Dinkmeyer, & Sperry, 1987, pp. 124–125).

CL: Every time I get with her, things go okay as long as I'm in control, but when she starts to take control I can really fly into a rage in a hurry.

CO: Why not work on that anger? How about nurturing that rage and practicing those behaviors when you're in control? I mean really work at getting angry when everything is going your way.

Creating Images

Images of the neurotic defenses may be extremely helpful in clarifying for clients how absurd their behavior can be. Closely allied to paradoxical intention, imaging involves the client imagining a farcical scene as he or she enters a threatening social situation (James & Myer, 1985).

CL: If I could just get off this inferiority-superiority merry-go-round.

CO: Let's try an experiment. Every time you're about to see Karen, I'd like you to stand in front of the mirror, flex your muscles, and repeat the words "Macho Man!" three times. Then when you're with her and you start to feel the need to control things, flex, and repeat the words to yourself. Do that every time you feel yourself getting into that situation.

Techniques Specific to Adlerians

Asking "The Question"

Asking "the question" is generally regarded as a tool for determining whether a client's problem is physical or psychological. But it also has therapeutic value, in that the client's response can be reflected or interpreted. Here are two examples, one that would indicate a physiological basis for the symptom, the other a psychological basis (Dinkmeyer, Dinkmeyer, & Sperry, 1987, pp. 102–103):

CO: If I had a pill that would make the headaches go away, how would things be different in your life?

CL: (*physical basis*) I would feel better, like I wouldn't want to drive a railroad spike through my forehead to release the pressure.

CL: (*psychological basis*) I would feel better and wouldn't wind up making my visiting time with Karen a real bummer!

CO: (response to psychological basis) Hmm! The headaches really knock you for a loop, but what you just said didn't emphasize headaches so much as time with Karen. I wonder about that.

Catching Oneself

When the client understands the fictional goals he or she pursues and wants to do something about them, the counselor provides a checklist of mental "stop signs." Such "stop signs" allow the client to catch him- or herself in the irrational behavior and, without guilt or recrimination, stop. The technique takes practice, because at first clients generally catch themselves too late (Dinkmeyer, Dinkmeyer, & Sperry, 1987, pp. 126–127).

CL: When I start to work up to that uncontrollable rage, I notice my hands sweat and I get really confused.

CO: Yes, and I notice you actually use the word *confused.* So why not use those as stop signs? When you first notice your hands sweating or you say to the person, "I'm confused," *Stop!* Think to yourself, "I know what's about to happen; I've got to go to the alternate game plan."

Acting As If

Many clients use the ploy "If only I could. . . ." At such times the client is instructed to act out the role as if he or she could do it. By trying out the role, clients often find they not only can act out a part but also become a different person in the process (Dinkmeyer, Dinkmeyer, & Sperry, 1987, p. 126).

CL: If only I could deal straight up with the lieutenant every time he stops by my home [cell].

CO: For the next week, I'd like you to try this out. Treat anybody, particularly staff personnel, that stops by your home as if they were your guests that you invited in for a cup of coffee and they are there at your invitation.

Spitting in the Soup

By unveiling the hidden motivation for the client's self-defeating behavior the counselor sets up an approach-avoidance situation. By "spitting in the soup" of the client's behavior, the counselor makes it extremely unpalatable. The client may still try to eat the soup (practice the behavior), but there will never be quite the relish there was before. In short, the counselor spoils the soup (game) of the client (Dinkmeyer, Dinkmeyer, & Sperry, 1987, p. 126).

CL: I don't know, so many years in here, I just feel like giving up.

CO: You certainly have the choice of doing that.

CL: What? You're supposed to be supportive.

CO: Right now you'd like me to say something like, "You've got to keep at it; you'll prevail." Yet, I believe that's kind of a game you play so you can be dependent on others and then blame them when things go wrong. If you want to play that, okay!

Pushing the Button

Mosak (1979, p. 73) describes this technique as being effective with people who believe their emotions control them. Pushing the button involves having the client alternately picture pleasant and unpleasant experiences and note the feelings that accompany the experiences. By alternating experiences and feelings the clients become aware that they control their emotions, and not vice-versa.

CO: Just imagine standing in the surf fishing and the pleasant feeling of calmness that brings. Now compare that with sabotaging Karen's car and those feelings of rage. Notice the difference; notice how as you create the picture, the feelings get created along with it. So you have the choice of which button you want to push.

Encouragement

This is a primary technique throughout the counseling process. The basic Adlerian notion that clients are not sick but rather discouraged means that the counselor's primary task is one of encouragement. However, encouragement does not mean rewarding the client materially. It means investing in clients a feeling of self-worth and accepting clients for what they are and not for what they should or could be (Dinkmeyer, Dinkmeyer, & Sperry, 1987, p. 214).

Use of encouragement as a therapeutic tool should be judicious and with clear forethought about what the counselor is encouraging and the reasons for doing it. Care should be taken to ensure that encouragement does not become misconstrued as sympathy, appeasement, bribery, or rewarding or invite other forms of dependency or manipulation from the client. To provide encouragement, the following points should be considered (Sweeney, 1989, p. 110):

1. *What* one is doing is more important than *how* one is doing.
2. The present is more the focus than the past or the future.
3. The deed is what is important, rather than the doer.
4. The effort, rather than the outcome, is to be emphasized.
5. Intrinsic motivation, such as satisfaction, enjoyment, and challenge, is more worthwhile than extrinsic payoffs.
6. What is being learned is more important than what is not being learned.
7. What is being done correctly is more important that what is being done incorrectly.

CL: How could I have done that . . . killed that woman . . . what a loser I am. (*Cries*)

CO: It really hurts as you think back on it and experience those feelings now, and you wonder whether I see you as that same person who did that. What I see is a person who has worked hard in therapy, who can start to catch himself when he feels put down and not act out in violent ways. Right now I see a person trying to get his life together by going to school and learning, by practicing what you have learned in therapy. You are thinking straighter and staying out of trouble a lot more than when you started counseling two years ago.

Midas Technique

This involves exaggerating the client's neurotic demands. Originated by Shulman (1973, p. 191), the technique is based on King Midas, who discovered that his consuming desire for gold and his ability to have all he wanted soon became a curse rather than a blessing. Like Midas, the client gets what he wants from the counselor. The counselor treats the client in overbearingly sympathetic ways by catering to his or her demands. Such a confrontive approach should be carried out with humor so that the behavior, not the client, is held up for satire.

CO: That's terrible! That's catastrophic! The phone company is criminal for not putting your call through to Karen, and we all know the meaning of the word *criminal.* Let's make a list of all those terrible injustices like that. Hey! How dare they take away your precious time. What right do they have to control your life like that!

Pleasing Someone
Since loss of social interest is one of the main factors in client discouragement, the counselor enjoins the client to go out and do something nice for someone. The client is thereby propelled back into the social mainstream (James & Myer, 1985).

CL: I just want to be left alone. I don't even wanna talk to my best friend, Joe . . . and I'm afraid he's gonna get bent out of shape.

CO: I wonder if you could catch Joe and tell him some of the things that are going on for you now and tell him you really appreciate his support and friendship.

Avoiding the Tar Baby
Dinkmeyer, Pew, & Dinkmeyer (1979, p. 118) describe the tar baby as the perceptions on life the client carries into counseling and attempts to fit into the counselor. Anger, discouragement, seductiveness, martyrdom, and a host of other traps are set for the unwary counselor as the client resists change. To avoid those traps the counselor must respond in ways that are contrary to what the person expects.

CL: It's up and down. I've been at this twelve weeks and I don't see us any further than where we were when I started.

CO: You'd like me to get discouraged and give up. The work has been getting tougher lately and you'd really like to have an excuse for not getting into some of those treacherous waters.

Homework

Insight alone is not sufficient to reorient the client. The client is expected to take what is learned in therapy and put it to work in the real world through task assignments, report back on successes and failures, and modify assignments conjointly as needed with the therapist. Task assignments can be used in all phases of therapy including relationship building, data collection and assessment, lifestyle analysis, and behavioral change (Carach, 1990).

Summary

As may be seen from the foregoing sample of Adlerian techniques, the counselor is not passive, but highly active in encouraging the client. Throughout therapy the Adlerian counselor remains free to have feelings and opinions and to express them.

The therapist is not a blank slate as in the Freudian sense. Such a stance would promote social distance. In the egalitarian and human relationship of counseling, Adlerians seek to help a client regain or increase social interest through a close and personal interactive approach (Mosak, 1989, pp. 99–100).

SAMPLE CASE

Initial Interview to Establish Lifestyle[1]

Al is a twenty-eight-year-old white man who is serving a life sentence for murdering his girlfriend when he was twenty years old. He has come to counseling because he has realized that something is wrong with the way he thinks and behaves. Al has become especially concerned with his lifestyle for two reasons. The first is a woman, Karen, whom he met through the prison volunteer program. Though at first he was deeply in love with her, he now has questions about the relationship. The second reason is that Al's court case was reopened and he won a reduction in sentence. He will be up for parole in three years and is extremely concerned that once free he will become violent again.

On a scale of satisfaction with current life tasks ranging from 1 (things are going very well) to 5 (things are very dissatisfying) Al rates himself as follows:

occupation—2	meaning—3
friendship—4	leisure—2
opposite sex—5	parenting—3
self—3	

In terms of occupation, Al has taken numerous prison courses in engineering technology and is now certified to be an engineering technologist. He hopes to continue his education and receive a B.S. in civil engineering.

In terms of relationships, Al has only one fairly close friend inside the prison and no friends outside except for Karen. His relationship with the opposite sex, in his own words, is poor. The woman he murdered was his first love. She was rather controlling and demanding, but initially he saw her actions as manifesting concern and love. However, as the relationship progressed, it also deteriorated. He felt himself losing control of the situation and became suspicious and paranoid about her actions toward him. This stormy relationship lasted eight months and was punctuated by verbal battles, threats of suicide on Al's part, all-night vigils outside her house, sabotage of her car, an aborted murder attempt, and finally a calmly planned and carried out murder.

Al's present concern with Karen is that he sees their relationship moving in the same direction. He has started to experience the same kinds of thoughts that occurred in the first relationship, which culminated in murder. In regard to himself and the meaning he obtains from life, Al vacillates between optimism and extreme pessimism. He stated that he has been like this for as long as he can remember. Al related feeling

---

[1]The interview format is based on Don Dinkmeyer, W. L. Pew, and Don Dinkmeyer, Jr., "Appendix A: Guide for Initial Interview for Establishing the Life Style," *Adlerian Counseling and Psychotherapy* (Monterey, CA: Brooks/Cole, 1979), pp. 265–274.

good about his leisure time, which he uses for self-study through reading. He also takes every extension course he can obtain through the university prison program. Al would very much like to have a family. In fact, one of the things he found attractive about the woman he murdered was that she had a two-year-old daughter: "A ready-made family and the girl was calling me Daddy." Al had a poor family life as a child. He has no brothers or sisters. His parents were divorced when he was eight. There were many verbal and physical battles between his parents. His mother was an alcoholic. He stated that after the divorce he never saw his mother again and did not miss her. He and his father lived with his father's sister and mother. Al hated his aunt, who ridiculed both him and his father. He loved his grandmother and indicated that the last time he cried was at her funeral. He was eleven at the time. He and his father have never been close. As a child he was afraid of him because of the beatings he received from him. Al now feels that his father cared about him but is still not able to communicate with him.

Al described himself as a loner who had few relationships—even casual ones—during grade and high school. He reported very little difficulty with school, but generally he did little work, was often truant, and barely obtained his high school diploma. His sexual life was minimal until he graduated from high school. Although his sexual fantasies were rather exotic, he felt intimidated by women his own age. Upon graduation from high school he started forming casual relationships with women, invariably older ones. He stated he "just felt secure with an older woman who knew her way around." He further related that he feared nothing as a child or a teenager and could hold his own in any fight. This has held true to the present. Al is pretty much left alone by some very tough people in a very tough prison. Al's work experience before incarceration was erratic. He held a variety of menial jobs and usually quit or was fired after a short time because he "lost interest" or the work was "beneath him." Al's earliest recollection was going to his grandmother's house, sitting in a chair stacked with telephone books so he could reach up to the table like a grown-up, and eating ginger cookies she had made. He recalled this as being very pleasant and loved being spoiled by his grandmother.

Al's number-one priority appears to be control flavored with superiority. He fights very hard to deny his feelings and emotions. Although Al is attracted to women and idealizes a family life, he invariably chooses women who are themselves controlling. At first, Al mistakes control for caring and falls deeply in love with "the perfect woman." Over time, Al's own fictional goal of control distorts any chance of a meaningful relationship occurring. The result is a breakdown in the relationship and humiliation, which Al cannot tolerate because of his need to be superior. To rectify this dilemma, Al acts out, defending his fictional goals with catastrophic results. Al's assets are his intelligence and his desire to understand himself. He is energetic both in the jobs he is assigned in the prison and in his college coursework. He has voluntarily sought counseling and has contracted to work hard at rearranging his life.

Excerpts from Al's Counseling Interviews

Session 1

CL: I don't get hurt or feel insecure. You, nobody can hurt me.

CO: Is that true? I feel hurt and insecure at times.

CL: (*Smiles nervously*) No, it's a crock. I put up a front.

CO: So what you're giving me is an image you show the world. My guess is you defend yourself with those images. In the short run they seem to meet your needs, but in the long run they leave you vulnerable and stressed. . . . The work we'll be doing in here will mostly be probing at and attacking those defenses. You can accept or reject my guesses, but I want you to know they're gonna keep coming. It's going to be hard work and scary at times, and that's the last lecture you get from me, okay?

CL: Okay! That's what I came for—to get straightened out. Let's go!

Session 3

CL: She was running around on me, very immature, so I'd follow her around, mess up her car . . . cut her brake line.

CO: You wanted to hurt her . . . show her who was boss.

CL: No . . . I . . . uh . . . wanted her attention. I'd sleep in the car in front of her house. For what reason I don't know. Maybe to protect her.

CO: You protected her by cutting her brake lines. What was your purpose in that? To show her your love? See how you delude yourself?

CL: I do? (*Long silence*)

CO: One of the reasons you were fighting was because she was possessive of you and then the roles changed, she wanted out, you lost control, became insecure, more possessive, kinda like a whirlpool.

CL: I guess I wanted to be sure she couldn't control me.

CO: Guess?

CL: Yeah, I know.

CO: See how you fool yourself?

CL: (*Silence, deep in thought, hand tremors*) I was confused.

CO: Your image of you was confused.

Session 5

CO: Listening to the tapes, anything you want to go over?

CL: I was fine until I came to you. Now I'm depressed.

CO: See what I'm doing for you. (*Both laugh*)

CL: Reviewing things I feel real depressed. Don't do that to me again!

CO: I don't do anything. You do those things. When those hurtful feelings come out there's going to be some depression.

CL: It's tough, not like I thought it'd be in therapy. Scary.

CO: When you feel that way, what happens?

CL: I get moody . . . short with people . . . confused . . . don't know what I want. Although I felt good after I got some of that stuff out in the open with you.

CO: That was one of your goals in coming here, but you avoid those upsetting feelings. Those feelings you avoid come out in moods and actions.

CL: It really got to me Saturday night when my girl came down. She's an only child and her parents wanted her to do something. She didn't know if she could come. I feel like I'm competing for her attention. I got really uptight and so did she. Then we had an argument.

CO: You've got to be the center of attention.

CL: Yeah, I want attention, to feel good, accepted. I mean like Jean waited on me hand and foot. I felt like a king. Real caring.

CO: What extremes do you go to to get people to feel the way you want them to about you? Like your girlfriend you murdered, the lies about your age, sexual experience, all making you feel important when you first met.

CL: I wasn't feeling important.

CO: Right. That's why you lied.

CL: I was confused. I mean I wasn't real sure of myself, about sex, especially, like I was a fag or something.

CO: Okay! When you felt that way what thoughts went through your head?

CL: I really blew it, but then Jean said a little later that I'd make a good father for her daughter. *Wow,* did that blow my mind.

CO: So it wasn't the way she looked that made her attractive. Nineteen and a father, pretty heavy stuff, feeling important. Sounds like some needs your own family never met.

CL: (*Silence, avoids interpretation*) I got into a routine, calling her, seeing her, started losing sleep, no time, no money. She started getting more and more demanding, and I started lying . . . car broke down, couldn't get to a phone. She started throwing other guys up to me. She knew how to get to me.

CO: You talk a lot about how you behaved, not how you felt.

CL: I felt like a lost sheep. My whole life got boiled down to six months. I couldn't live with her or without her. Jealousy.

CO: My guess is that everything you do has something to do with that goal of control, being top dog. Can you start checking those feelings, those behaviors that lead to that?

Session 8

CL: I realize those lies I make up to cover my feelings. I think I should impress somebody. My thoughts get me in trouble.

CO: The way I interpret things is the way I make myself feel and act.

CL: I won't admit what I did to the other cons.

CO: What is the reason you won't admit it?

CL: I said I killed a man in a fight. To kill a woman you're not much of a man. I couldn't admit I was irrational or lost control.

Session 12

CL: She was taking advantage of me and I loved her and it hurt that she'd do that.

CO: Hurt, insecure.

CL: I didn't want to deal with those feelings so I killed her . . . . She played with dynamite and it blew up.

CO: Sounds like a real nice way of not being responsible. Being vulnerable and not owning it. See! You still make it her fault!

CL: Yeah, it's a defense. I was trying to be a lot of things I couldn't be. I think I understand what went on. I've grown up some emotionally. All those years I couldn't let it out, wanted to cry but couldn't. (*Sobs*)

CO: That fits an image.

CL: Yeah, real men don't cry! What a crock! Stupid!

Session 13

CL: I'm kinda testing Karen.

CO: Why do you test her, and isn't that what you did with Jean?

CL: Yeah, I did do that. I don't want to let her know I need her.

CO: Sounds like you set yourself up to be let down. You're bright, good-looking, sensitive when you want to be.

CL: Everybody says that, but I can't believe it.

CO: Is it possible to be perfect?

CL: No way! I play the game.

CO: That game worked so well for you, it helped you murder, and it still goes on. So if you get rejected, will you die on the spot?

CL: I don't think I put Karen up on a pedestal like Jean. If she were to go, I'd feel bad, but I'm starting to believe there'd be other fish in the sea.

CO: What makes you think you can handle it better now than then?

CL: Because the games scare the hell out of me now.

CO: The games are part of your insecurity. Do you still feel insecure?

CL: I don't know, it's confusing to narrow it down.

CO: You use the word *confused* a lot. Every time you seem to start to feel insecure you use that word. Do you realize that?

CL: Maybe it's a habit.

CO: A habit that needs to be broken. That word, *confused,* is a checkpoint. When you use it, notice how you feel. It may be a warning that you're feeling stress.

CL: Kinda like a stop sign. If I hear it, before I react I'm gonna check myself out . . . see what's going on inside me.

Session 16

CL: In the past I couldn't handle the rejection. I was afraid. Now, you either accept me or you don't. I'm not in competition. I don't have to put on an act. It's okay to be imperfect.

CO: With Karen?

CL: If I'm feeling apprehensive with her I work it out. It's funny, she's a lot more scared of me, the human being, than Al, the manipulator. She said she was a lot more secure with Al, the "man." That didn't bother me. I didn't need to go back to that. If she needs that, she doesn't need me.

CO: Is this another delusion, this new way of thinking? Are you just fooling yourself?

CL: It's not a delusion. Hard to explain. I'm really at peace. I can see problems a lot clearer. A lot of other guys in here say I'm different.

Summary

In the beginning, Al personified the fictitious goals of control and superiority. Those goals are extremely crystallized, though Al comes to therapy seeking to change. His words in the opening session say it all: "My girl is a counselor and tries that stuff on me and it doesn't work, but with you it's okay." The counselor is a retired professional football player and is the essence of the macho man, so at least on the surface he meets Al's need to deal with "real men."

The counselor tenaciously attacks Al's mistaken attitudes, fictitious goals, and defended feelings. The counselor catches Al safeguarding and points it out both by interpretation and confrontation. The going is slow. At times Al denies the interpretations, but later he accepts them.The insight gained from the counselor and from playbacks of the counseling sessions move Al slowly but surely toward awareness of the way he deludes himself. The checkpoints he establishes with the counselor allow him to start recognizing his emotions and controlling them rather than vice versa. The excerpts from the sessions demonstrate Al's progress from a highly defensive client who admits to little feeling to a person able to look at the past, make sense of its psychological meaning, and use the insight he has gained to deal in more congruent ways with his present self.

You may wonder if Al's progress was really just another con, a distorted way of achieving control and superiority over the counselor, the institution, and society. A subsequent report leads us to believe Al's therapeutic gains were real. He had been on extremely good behavior for the nine months preceding the report and had been permitted to move to a prison where he could complete his degree. He had established a number of checkpoints that he monitored both with the counselor and with a counseling group he had joined. Feedback from other inmates indicated he was no longer a loner. He had become involved in a number of positive relationships. The counselor also worked with Al's girlfriend, Karen, helping her change some of her attempts to control the relationship. Although much work remained to be done by both Al and Karen, they were continuing, with several starts and stops, to explore their new relationship. Finally, the counselor's gut feeling was that Al had changed, and that with continued group therapy and careful monitoring of his checkpoints, he would not murder again.

CONTRIBUTIONS OF THE ADLERIAN SYSTEM

Adlerian therapy, as it is promoted and practiced, is a therapy for all society. Its emphasis on human perfectibility through increased social interest makes it a unique counseling theory.

Because Adlerian theory views people as being pulled by the future, its practitioners care what generations to come will inherit in a comprehensive ecological sense. A keystone of Adlerian therapy is encouragement, and because of their inherent belief in the perfectibility of humankind Adlerians do not hesitate to be encouraging. The approach, then, focuses on mental health rather than mental illness.

Because it is phenomenological, the Adlerian view does not consider humans predestined by their genetic or environmental endowment. Each individual has the distinctive qualities to be whatever he or she chooses to be. The Adlerian approach is, indeed, a psychology of use and not of possession.

The Adlerian approach has extended therapy from the patient on the couch to a variety of procedures in the real world. Group counseling, parent education, and family-system procedures can all be traced to Adlerians.

Because it has been an outreaching system, the Adlerian approach has had great impact on the public domain. Nowhere has this been more apparent than in education. From Adler's work in the Vienna school system in the 1920s to the advent of Dinkmeyer's DUSO program in the 1970s, individual psychology stands above all other therapeutic modalities in its attempts to humanize education. Finally, perhaps the greatest contribution of individual psychology has been its integration into so many other modalities—and, indeed, into the mainstream of America—that many of its concepts have come to be understood as what Adler would have called "common sense" (Dinkmeyer, Dinkmeyer, & Sperry, 1987).

SHORTCOMINGS OF THE ADLERIAN SYSTEM

A major problem has been the rather awesome amount of family constellation and lifestyle information typically collected by Adlerians. Although Adlerians vigorously promote collection of this information as fluid and flexible, persistent stereotypes exist among counselors that these protocols are inscribed in stone. Perhaps the most abused and confused of these stereotypes, especially for the neophyte counselor, is birth order. "If you're born first, so who's on second, and what's that mean anyway?" This parody of the old Abbot and Costello comedy dialogue about baseball runners typifies the business of birth order. Although Adlerians maintain that they do not stereotype by birth order, this perception still exists and is difficult to put to rest.

If the beginning counselor can wade through these difficulties, there is still the problem of interpretation of early recollections and dreams. The notion of interpretation has long been vigorously debated in therapeutic circles. We have no hope of resolving that issue here.

We wonder if Adlerian theory, like all approaches that rely heavily on verbal erudition, logic, and insight, is not limited to clients who are a cut above those of normal intellect. Sadly, not all of our clients fit into that intellectual category.

ADLERIAN THERAPY WITH DIVERSE POPULATIONS

Adlerians believe that individuals who are high on social interest will think of themselves and others as equals and behave accordingly. Five decades ago, Dreikurs (1946) predicted that women, African Americans, children, and other minorities would progressively demand equality in society. Since the beginning of organized society there has been a pressing need to replace "demand" personality characteristics such as ambition, righteousness, obligation, conformity, and individualism with enthusiasm, understanding, participation, self-respect, and cooperation (Dreikurs, 1971).

Adlerian therapy's emphasis on building equitable relationships, cooperation and responsibility skills, empathy for others, and encouragement makes it one of the preeminent therapies of choice for elementary school counselors and others who work with groups of children in multicultural settings (Herring & Runion, 1994).

Because perceived or actual inferiority status plays such a central part in how persons acclimate to primary socializing agents such as families, neighborhoods, schools, cities, and countries, Adlerians understand clearly the general dynamics of disenfranchised individuals and groups who see little opportunity for a productive lifestyle and are alienated and discouraged. Thus, their major therapeutic tools are weighted heavily in favor of gaining insight into reasons for having a positive social interest and encouraging broad and equal participation in society. Particularly in regard to their longstanding emphasis on sexual equality, Adlerians have much to offer feminist therapy (Rigby-Weinberg, 1986).

Although Adler's writings proposed that homosexuality was a neurotic lifestyle, many contemporary Adlerians see utility in using the approach to help gays and lesbians gain self-acceptance and broadened social interest. The Adlerian view of egalitarianism crosscuts all populations and is uniquely suited to help gays and lesbians combat stigmatization, feelings of inferiority, and discouragement (Chandler, 1995; Chernin & Holden, 1995; Fisher, 1993; Kottman, Lingg, & Tisdell, 1995).

Further in the Adlerians' favor, their approach should make a great deal of sense and have credibility to those cultures that highly value the family system and honor one's parents. Unlike Freudians or transactional analysts, Adlerians do not specifically vilify parents.

Although one of the primary focuses of Adlerian therapy is on gaining dynamic insight and understanding as applied to one's lifestyle, it does not do so esoterically or to the exclusion of other very pragmatic, confrontive, and action-oriented techniques. From that standpoint it may be somewhat surprising that the case study in this chapter comes from a prison setting. However, many prison inmates have come to gain a different perspective on what their lifestyles are about and have changed their lifestyles dramatically through Adlerian therapy.

Conversely, the speed of this approach, which, like its psychoanalytic cohorts, tends to be slow in comparison to other therapies, may be too slow in its payoffs for those who operate on short time frames and immediate reinforcement schedules. There is some movement underway to convert it to brief therapy formats (Shulman, 1989a; 1989b; Sperry, 1989). While straightforward and more universal in comparison to other analytic, dynamic therapies, it does take creative brainwork and insight to understand what is going on. For many individuals who are used to operating on and looking for concrete outcomes, this may not be acceptable. For those clients who are alienated from society, Adlerian therapy is probably perceived as one of the bigger scams in therapy: Why would anyone want to attempt to gain a greater social interest in society when that society is not worth much to begin with?

Although social inferiority has replaced organ inferiority as the cornerstone of Adlerian personality theory (Mosak, 1989, p. 81), Adlerians still have much to say to physically disabled clients. The concepts of lifestyle, compensation, and striving for superiority are primary in understanding the impact of physically disabled populations. Organ inferiority feelings may result from either congenital or early acquired physical or mental abnormalities. Thus, the defense mechanism of compensation acts to overcome these real or imagined deficits by strengthening one's ability in the deficit area of indirectly compensating by obtaining mastery in another area (Livneh & Sherwood, 1991).

Due to its person-in-the-environment model of counseling and the educational and developmental models that undergird practice, it is tailor-made for use with diverse populations (Corey, 1991). While it might be questioned as having the most broad-based therapeutic approaches for a culturally varied clientele because of its analytic basis, quite clearly it has far and away the widest philosophical appeal of any theory.

SUMMARY

Individual psychology was developed by Alfred Adler as a denial of Freud. Adler forged a psychotherapy that directly related the individual's mental health to degree of social interest. The life tasks of social, occupational, and sexual relationships are primary to the development of a wholesome and fulfilling lifestyle. Through Rudolf Dreikurs, the Adlerian approach took root in America. Group therapy, child guidance centers, and parent training programs are among its major contributions to society. The modality is marked by its great concerns for the individual's relationship with his or her total environment. Adlerians are optimistic about humankind and value the well-being of the individual and society over that of organizations and institutions. Adlerian theory is, then, a functional and operational social psychology.

Adlerians believe the original socializing agent, the family, plays a large part in the adjustment or maladjustment of the individual. Thus, they spend a great deal of time trying to make sense of the client's family constellation and childhood in attempting to assess what his or her present fictional goals are and how those goals are translated into feelings of inferiority and superiority.

Practitioners of the approach use a variety of counseling techniques, from basic restatement and reflection skills to specific Adlerian techniques such as "spitting in the soup" and "avoiding the tar baby." All techniques provide encouragement as clients work to realign their goals with those of society and attempt to find more satisfying lifestyles.

Although individual psychology has been criticized as being just "common sense," its practicality in everyday living would seem to be just what Adler wanted. Although its identity may be obscure, its theoretical concepts, such as inferiority and superiority complexes, birth order, lifestyle, and acting "as if," have become so ingrained in contemporary vocabulary that it is indeed a psychology of social usefulness both in theory and practice.

SUGGESTIONS FOR FURTHER READING

Adler, A. (1958). *What life should mean to you.* A. Porter (Ed.). New York: Putnam's Capricorn Books.

Ansbacher, H. L., & Ansbacher, R. R. (Eds.). (1956). *The individual psychology of Alfred Adler: A systematic presentation in selections from his writings.* New York: Harper & Row, Harper Torchbooks.

Dinkmeyer, D. C., Dinkmeyer, D. C., Jr., & Sperry, L. (1987) *Adlerian counseling and psychotherapy* (2nd ed.). Columbus, OH: Chas. E. Merrill.

Dinkmeyer, D. C., Pew, W. L., & Dinkmeyer, D. C., Jr. (1979). *Adlerian counseling and psychotherapy.* Monterey, CA: Brooks/Cole.

Dreikurs, R. (1953). *Fundamentals of Adlerian psychology.* Chicago: Alfred Adler Institute.

Nikelly, A. G. (ed.). (1971). *Techniques for behavior change.* Springfield, IL: Chas. C. Thomas.

Sweeney, T. J. (1989). *Adlerian counseling: A practical approach for a new decade* (3rd ed.). Muncie, IN: Accelerated Development Inc.

REFERENCES

Adler, A. (1929). *The science of living.* New York: Greenberg.

Adler, A. (1956). (1) The neurotic disposition; (2) Psychology of use; (3) Social interest. In H. L. Ansbacher & R. R. Ansbacher (Eds.), *The individual psychology of Alfred Adler: A systematic presentation in selections from his writings* (pp. 126–162; 205–262). New York: Basic Books.

Adler, A. (1958). *What life should mean to you.* New York: Putnam's Capricorn Books.

Adler, A. (1970). Superiority. In H. L. Ansbacher & R. R. Ansbacher (Eds.), *Superiority and social interest* (p. 257). Evanston, IL: Northwestern University Press.

Allers, C. T., White, J., & Hornbuckle, D. (1990). Early recollections, detecting depression in the elderly. *Individual Psychology: Journal of Adlerian Theory, Research, and Practice, 46,* 61–66.

Ansbacher, H. L. (1977). Individual psychology. In R. J. Corsini (Ed.), *Current personality theories* (pp. 45–82). Itasca, IL: F. E. Peacock.

Ansbacher, H. L., & Ansbacher, R. R. (1956). (1) Degree of activity; (2) Early reflections and dreams; (3) Individual psychology in its larger setting; (4) The style of life; and (5) Understanding and treating the patient. In H. L. Ansbacher & R. R. Ansbacher (Eds.), *The individual psychology of Alfred Adler: A systematic presentation in selections from his writings* (pp. 1–18; 163–203; 326–365). New York: Basic Books.

Carach, M. S. (1990). Utilizing task assignments within Adlerian therapy. *Individual Psychology: Journal of Adlerian Theory, Research, and Practice, 46,* 217–224.

Chandler, C. K. (1995). Guest editorial: Contemporary Adlerian reflections on homosexuality and bisexuality. *Individual Psychology: Journal of Adlerian Theory, Research, and Practice, 51,* 82–89.

Chernin, J., & Holden, J. M. (1995). Toward an understanding of homosexuality: Origins, status, and relationship to individual psychology. *Individual Psychology: Journal of Adlerian Theory, Research, and Practice, 51,* 90–101.

Corey, G. (1991). Invited commentary on macrostrategies for delivery of mental health counseling services. *Journal of Mental Health Counseling, 13,* 51–57.

Dewey, J. (1971). Family atmosphere. In A. G. Nikelly (Ed.), *Techniques for behavior change* (pp. 41–48). Springfield, IL: Chas. C. Thomas.

Dinkmeyer, D. C., & Dinkmeyer, D. C., Jr. (1982). *Developing understanding of self and others, DUSO-1 revised, DUSO-2 revised.* Circle Pines, MN: American Guidance Service.

Dinkmeyer, D. C., Dinkmeyer, D. C., Jr., & Sperry, L. (1987). *Adlerian counseling and psychotherapy* (2nd ed.). Columbus, OH: Chas. E. Merrill.

Dinkmeyer, D. C., & McKay, G. D. (1976). *Systematic training for effective parenting.* Circle Pines, MN: American Guidance Service.

Dinkmeyer, D. C., Pew, W. L., & Dinkmeyer, D. C., Jr. (1979). *Adlerian counseling and psychotherapy.* Monterey, CA: Brooks/Cole.

Dreikurs, R. (1946). *The challenge of marriage.* New York: Hawthorn Books.

Dreikurs, R. (1953). *Fundamentals of Adlerian psychology.* Chicago: Alfred Adler Institute.

Dreikurs, R. (1959). Early experiments with group psychotherapy. *American Journal of Psychotherapy, 13,* 882–891.

Dreikurs, R. (1967). *Psychodynamics, psychotherapy, and counseling.* Chicago: Alfred Adler Institute.

Dreikurs, R. (1971). *Social equality: The challenge of today.* Chicago: Henry Regnery.

Dreikurs, R. (1981). The three life tasks. In L. Baruth & D. Eckstein (Eds.), *Lifestyle: Theory, practice and research* (2nd ed., pp. 34–41). Dubuque, IA: Kendall/Hunt.

Dreikurs, R., & Mosak, H. H. (1967). The tasks of life II. The fourth life task. *Individual Psychologist, 4,* 51–55.

Eckstein, D. G. (1981). Lifestyle concepts applied to correctional counseling. In L. Baruth & D. Eckstein (Eds.), *Lifestyle: Theory, practice and research* (2nd ed; pp. 63–67). Dubuque, IA: Kendall/Hunt.

Ellis, A. (1971). Reason and emotion in the individual psychology of Adler. *Journal of Individual Psychology, 27,* 50–64.

Fisher, S. K. (1993). A proposed Adlerian theoretical framework and intervention techniques for gay and lesbian couples. [Special issue: Marriage and couples counseling.] *Individual Psychology: Journal of Adlerian Theory, Research, and Practice, 49,* 438–449.

Frankl, V. E. (1970). Fore-runner of existential psychiatry. *Journal of Individual Psychology, 26,* 38.

Herring, R. D., & Runion, K. O. (1994). Counseling ethnic children and youth from an Adlerian perspective. *Journal of Multicultural Counseling, and Development, 22,* 215–226.

James, R., & Myer, R. (1985). Using Adlerian confrontation with children. Paper presented at the National/Elementary Middle School Guidance Conference, Normal, IL.

Kefir, N. (1972). Priorities. Manuscript.

Kern, R. (1982). *Lifestyle scale.* Coral Springs, FL: CMTI Press.

Kopp, R. R., & Kivel, C. (1990). Traps and escapes: An Adlerian approach to understanding resistance and resolving impasses in psychotherapy. *Individual Psychology: Journal of Adlerian Theory, Research, and Practice, 46,* 139–147.

Kottman, T., Lingg, M., & Tisdell, T. (1995). Gay and lesbian adolescents: Implications for therapists. *Individual Psychology: Journal of Adlerian Theory, Research, and Practice, 51,* 114–128.

Livneh, H., & Sherwood, A. (1991). Application of personality theories and counseling strategies to clients with physical disabilities. *Journal of Counseling and Development, 69,* 525–538.

Maslow, A. H. (1970). Holistic emphasis. *Journal of Individual Psychology, 26,* 39.

May, R. (1970). Myth and guiding fiction. *Journal of Individual Psychology, 26,* 39.

Mosak, H. H. (1971). Lifestyle. In A. G. Nikelly (Ed.), *Techniques for behavior change* (pp. 77–84). Springfield, IL: Chas. C. Thomas.

Mosak, H. H. (1979). Adlerian psychotherapy. In R. J. Corsini (Ed.), *Current psychotherapies* (2nd ed., pp. 44–94). Itasca, IL: F. E. Peacock.

Mosak, H. H. (1989). Adlerian psychotherapy. In R. J. Corsini & D. Wedding (Eds.), *Current psychotherapies* (4th ed., pp. 65–116). Itasca, IL: F. E. Peacock.

Mosak, H. H. (1992). The "traffic cop" function of dreams and early recollections. *Individual Psychology: Journal of Adlerian Theory, Research, and Practice, 48,* 319–323.

Mosak, H. H., & Dreikurs, R. (1967). The life tasks III. The fifth life task. *Individual Psychologist, 5,* 16–22.

Mosak, H. H., & Dreikurs, R. (1973). Adlerian psychotherapy. In R. J. Corsini (Ed.), *Current psychotherapies* (pp. 35–84). Itasca, IL: F. E. Peacock.

Mosak, H. H., & Goldman, S. E. (1995). An alternative view of the purpose of psychosis. *Individual Psychology: Journal of Adlerian Theory, Research, and Practice, 51,* 46–49.

Nystul, M. S. (1993). The Nystul Turning Point Survey: An assessment instrument to analyze Adlerian tasks of life. *Individual Psychology: Journal of Adlerian Theory, Research, and Practice, 49,* 185–198.

Pepper, F. C. (1971). Birth order. In A. G. Nikelly (Ed.), *Techniques for behavior change* (pp. 49–54). Springfield, IL: Chas. C. Thomas.

Rigby-Weinberg, D. N. (1986). A future direction for radical feminist therapy. *Women and Therapy, 5,* 191–205.

Rule, W. R. (1985). An Adlerian perspective. *Journal of Applied Rehabilitation Counseling, 16,* 9–14.

Shulman, B. H. (1973). *Contributions to individual psychology.* Chicago: Alfred Adler Institute.

Shulman, B. H. (1989a). Single-session psychotherapy: A didactic demonstration. *Individual Psychology: Journal of Adlerian Theory, Research, and Practice, 45,* 82–89.

Shulman, B. H. (1989b). Some remarks on brief psychotherapy. *Individual Psychology: Journal of Adlerian Theory, Research, and Practice, 45,* 34–37.

Singh, A. (1990). Toughmindedness in relation to birth order, family size, and sex. *Individual Psychology: Journal of Adlerian Theory, Research, and Practice, 46,* 82–87.

Slavik, S. (1991). Early memories as a guide to client movement through life. *Canadian Journal of Counseling, 25,* 331–337.

Sperry, L. (1989). Contemporary approaches to brief psychotherapy: A comparative analysis. *Individual Psychology: Journal of Adlerian Theory, Research, and Practice, 45,* 3–25.

Sweeney, T. J. (Ed.). (1989). *Adlerian counseling: A practical approach for a new decade* (3rd ed.). Muncie, IN: Accelerated Development Inc.

Vaihinger, H. (1956). Fictionalism. In H. L. Ansbacher and R. R. Ansbacher (Eds.), *The individual psychology of Alfred Adler: A systematic presentation in selections from his writings* (pp. 77–100). New York: Basic Books.

Wheeler, M. S., Kern, R. M., & Curlette, W. L. (1991). Life style can be measured. *Individual Psychology: Journal of Adlerian Theory, Research, and Practice, 47,* 229–240.

Willhite, R. G. (1981). "The Willhite": A creative extension of the early recollection process. In L. Baruth & D. Eckstein (Eds.), *Lifestyle: Theory, practice and research* (2nd ed., pp. 84–94). Dubuque, IA: Kendall/Hunt.

Witmer, J. M. (1989). Reaching toward wholeness. In T. J. Sweeney (Ed.), *Adlerian counseling: A practical approach for a new decade* (3rd ed., pp. 31–80). Muncie, IN: Accelerated Development Inc.

4

JUNGIAN THERAPY

FUNDAMENTAL TENETS

History

Carl Gustav Jung was born in Kesswil, Switzerland, in 1875, the only child of a Swiss clergyman. Jung's early family life undoubtedly influenced his theory. On one side was his worldly and outgoing mother, on the other a staid and pious father. He also had eight uncles, all of whom were clergymen in the Swiss Reformed church. Certainly, the heavy emphasis placed on religion by his family influenced the spiritual aspects of his theory, although Jung stated that for a great portion of his youth he was bored by it. Jung was taught to read Latin at an early age by his father; this along with his mother's reading to him about exotic religions would seem to account for his early and abiding interest in history and his facility with ancient languages (Smith & Vetter, 1991, p. 96).

As a young man he was intrigued by spirituality and the occult and was struck by the repetitious themes, symbols, anecdotes, and occurrences of spiritualistic phenomena that he found in a variety of writings and reported experiences. These repetitious themes came from all over the world and throughout recorded history. They were so similar that they defied rational explanation. Jung's experiences with the supernatural in his own home caused him to attend seances for more than two years and culminated in the writing of his doctoral dissertation in 1902. His dissertation "On the Psychology and Pathology of So-Called Occult Phenomena" laid the groundwork for a number of major themes in his later work (Campbell, 1971, pp. ix–xiii).

After graduation from medical school he became an assistant at the Burgholzi Mental Hospital and Psychiatric Clinic in Zurich. During this time he worked with Bleuler and Janet, two giants in the early twentieth-century frontiers of mental illness. In 1906 he struck up a correspondence with Freud. It appeared his close working relationship with Freud would make him the heir apparent as the chief theoretician of psychoanalysis. Indeed, he was the first president of the International Psychoanalytic Society. However, like Adler, he became disenchanted with

Freudian theory. Basic disagreements over emphasis on sexuality and the importance of psychoses as opposed to neuroses and different views on the structure of personality culminated in 1913 with Jung's breaking away from Freud and starting his own analytic school (Nystul, 1993, p. 137). In 1913 he gave up his instructorship in psychiatry at the University of Zurich to go into private practice. From 1933 to 1942 he was professor of psychology at the Federal Polytechnical College in Zurich.

Like Freud and Adler, Jung was a prolific writer. His collected works comprise twenty volumes (Read, Fordham, & Adler, 1953–1978). His writing covers a wide range of topics and illuminates his most famous contributions of the extrovert and the introvert, the four functions of thinking, feeling, sensation, and intuition, and primordial archetypes (Sahakian, 1969, p. 82). Jung's interests were widely varied, with religion, mythology, literature, philosophy, and archaeology holding important places in his intellectual life. These interests are clearly reflected in his travels, writing, research, and practice (Nystul, 1993, p. 137). Jung continued to write and conduct research until his death in 1961 at the age of eighty-five. Jung was much more than a psychologist or a psychiatrist—he was a classical scholar in the truest sense of the word (Rychlak, 1973, p. 132).

Until the 1960s, Jungian analytical psychology was practically nonexistent in America (Kaufmann, 1989, p. 126). However, two disparate movements have caused it to take root and begin to grow. First was the emergence of the Myers-Briggs Type Indicator (MBTI), which measures personality according to Jungian function (Myers & McCaulley, 1985). Interest in the MBTI has grown to the extent that the Center for Application of Psychological Type in Gainesville, Florida, conducts nationwide conferences on the study and use of the MBTI. True to their calling, in the workshop literature of the Center, teaching staff typically list their MBTI type after their professional degrees! Indeed, it is not uncommon for avid followers of the MBTI to have their typology printed on T-shirts, stationery, and desk plates!

Second, since the "psychedelic" seventies, considerable interest in altered states of consciousness, the metaphysical and spiritual aspects of human growth and development, and transpersonal psychology as a legitimate field has developed. Jungian therapy is the only major contemporary therapy to actively embrace and use theology in its work. Thus, it has special appeal for those who feel that spirituality and the need to achieve a transcendent state are necessary ingredients in the therapeutic process.

Today, Jungian training institutes are found throughout the world and are part of the International Association for Analytical Psychology (IAAP). Because of the interdisciplinary nature of the therapy, Jungians offer training to people from a wide variety of academic backgrounds. Among the more interesting requirements for admission to training is that an individual must have had at least one hundred hours of personal analysis with an IAAP analyst (Training Institute of the Interregional Society of Jungian Analysts)!

Overview of Jungian Analytic Therapy

Jungians view humans in a positive sense and believe they are inherently predisposed to make their individual mark in the world. However, this individuation process is not accomplished by merely obtaining fame and glory through material achievement or notoriety (Jung, 1971d, p. 8). Rather, to become truly individual-ized, human beings must become transcendent and come to grips with the un-conscious part of their personalities. Individuals who fail to integrate fully the many oppositional forces of conscious and unconscious components of their per-sonality will never fully develop to optimal capacity or achieve self-realization.

Individuation is the process through which people move toward self-realization and is the penultimate goal of living and of therapy. It is a complex and difficult process that calls for reconciliation and integration of a variety of forces, traits, and attitudes, and it may be beyond the scope of many individuals. Therefore, the process of therapy may be twofold. In a minimal sense, it may be enough for the client to experience affective catharsis of a problem, gain insight into it, and then learn new ways of coping or solving the problem. At a far deeper level, some clients may go beyond the immediate problems of their lives and plunge into a transformation of their psychic processes and their total being. If successful, they may emerge as very different and changed individuals who have achieved a higher consciousness and a clearer picture of their distinctiveness and separateness from the rest of humanity.

To become individuated, clients must come to grips with powerful, uncon-scious archetypical complexes that are in constant, submerged flux. The complexes of the shadow and the anima/animus are two of the principal oppositional and tumultuous unconscious forces that must be reconciled. The therapeutic modality most commonly used to bring these and other archetypes to conscious awareness is dream work. Thus, analytical psychotherapy attempts to create a communicative link between the conscious and unconscious and make understandable through debate and interpretation what may appear to the individual as very illogical and completely undecipherable (Kaufmann, 1989, p. 119).

Theory of Personality

Analytic psychology does not have a comprehensive topographic, genetic, eco-nomic, dynamic, structural view of personality, as does Freudian psychoanalytic theory (Kaufmann, 1989, p. 127), nor does it view socialization as the critical com-ponent of personality development, as does Adlerian psychology. Its personality basis is a very dynamic, fluid, and complex view of the psyche. The psyche is com-posed of numerous subsystems and functions within those systems that are con-stantly active and oppositional to one another and at the same time inter- and independent.

Jung believed that the psyche is composed of interdependent systems com-prised of the *conscious,* which provides consistency and direction and handles per-ceptions, memories, thoughts, and feelings; the *personal unconscious,* which contains forgotten or repressed material that has been lost to conscious thought but is still retrievable; and the *collective unconscious,* which is the transpersonal or nonpersonal conscious that is not concerned with any personal experiences (Jung, 1971a). The personality is composed of these parts in an integrative, wholistic way (Smith & Vetter, 1991, p. 97).

The Jungian view of the personality may be depicted as an upright, somewhat flexible and fluctuating cylinder (Rychlak, 1973; Smith & Vetter, 1991).

Ego

At the top of the cylinder is the Jungian conscious, with the ego at its center. It rests on the total field of both conscious and unconscious contents of the personality and is the central complex and point of reference in the field of consciousness (Hall, 1989, p. 31; Jung, 1971a, p. 141). The ego consists of thoughts, feelings, evaluations, sensations, perceptions, and active memories. It has both an internal and an external frame of reference, provides the framework for one's self-perception and identity, and is the reality base for interaction with the environment (Smith & Vetter, 1991, p. 98).

Persona

The persona is the thick shield that covers the ego. It develops during childhood and is the public image that the individual allows others to see. It is the compromise that one must make between personal desires and those of society (Smith & Vetter, 1991, p. 98). Persona is the conscious everyday component of the self and is reflected in various roles, such as work, family, leisure, and social settings. For Jung, the goal of individuation is inversely related to one's persona. That is, the more one is aware of the social, personal self and operates on it, the less one is able to understand and act on the private, personal self (Nystul, 1993, pp. 139–140).

Self

Sandwiched in the middle of the cylinder is the personal unconscious. At the center core of this layer is the self, which is the unifying and stabilizing agent of the personality. The self is the regulating center of personality and mediates between the conscious, unconscious, and collective unconscious (Hall, 1989, p. 32). The self cannot emerge until other systems of the personality have fully developed, which seldom occurs before middle age. The self begins to develop when the individual moves from sole reliance on the conscious ego to a middle ground between the conscious and the unconscious. The emergence of a more spiritual, philosophical self is the result of an optimal blending of conscious and unconscious (Nystul, 1993, p. 140).

Surrounding the self are three highly evolved archetypes: the shadow, anima/animus, and a host of supporting complexes.

Shadow

The shadow comes from both the personal and the collective unconscious and contains the primitive, uncivilized elements within us that are unacceptable to society and are generally repressed (Smith & Vetter, 1991, p. 103). Generally, the shadow represents traits and attitudes that are the negative or evil side of the personality that people either fail to recognize or deny exists (Hall, 1989, p. 33). It is conjectured that these negative thoughts and actions occur from animal instincts that were inherited through the evolutionary process (Nystul, 1993, p. 139).

The shadow is the antithesis of the persona. It is the reservoir of those characteristics we find most repugnant in ourselves and attempt to disavow. While one's personal shadow is relatively easy to identify and handle, the archetypical shadow is far deeper and wider in its evil nature (Harris, 1996, pp. 43–44). It is Freddy Kruger, the creature from the Black Lagoon, the devil, all of Stephen King's characters, and every nasty alien conjured up by science fiction writers rolled into one Evil. The shadow is manifested by the defense mechanism of projection. That is, another person, who will always be of the same sex, will be projected as causing the client's lousy feelings, crazy thinking, and rotten behavior (Jung, 1971a, p. 146).

Acknowledgment of the shadow as an integral part of the individual's personality development requires considerable moral effort because it challenges the positive image the individual wishes to present to the world. Integration of the shadow marks the first stage in the analytic process (Jung, 1971a, p. 145).

Anima and Animus

These are masculine and feminine archetypes that are present in varying degrees in all individuals and are roughly equivalent to the concept of yin and yang. Anima is the feminine side archetype in men and animus is the masculine side archetype in women (Hall, 1989, p. 32). Each is responsible for certain characteristics stereotypically associated with the opposite sex. That is, the anima may behaviorally manifest itself as tenderness in the man and the animus as aggressive behavior in the woman. These opposite sex characteristics allow each sex to understand and react appropriately to the other (Jung, 1971a, p. 153). Jung believed that these archetypes come from millennia of generations of men and women living together and slowly picking up parts of each other's personalities (Hall & Lindzey, 1978).

Complexes

More commonly known in Adlerian theory, complexes were originated by Jung and are a major component of the personal unconscious. They are an emotionally charged group of ideas or images. At the center of a complex is an archetype or archetypal image (Hall, 1989, p. 30). As the individual interacts with the environment, repeated exposure to specific objects of importance and key concepts results in a coalescing of these experiences around the object or experience and adhesion to it (Rychlak, 1973, p. 139). A complex has constellating power in that it may increase its potency by attracting other supporting experiences to it. Such power, if left unchecked, may cause a splitting of the complex into a splinter personality, which may cause severe maladjustment (Smith & Vetter, 1991, pp. 100–101). Whenever there is a strong emotional reaction to a person or a situation, a complex is constellated or activated (Hall, 1989, p. 31). Because complexes reside in the personal unconscious, knowledge or awareness of them is generally unknown to and repressed by the individual (Jung, 1910).

Personal Unconscious

Jung believed that the personal unconscious holds those pieces of information that are unacceptable to the ego (Harris, 1996, p. 31). He identified three categories of the personal unconscious: First are those things we forget: "Where in the world are my research notes for this chapter?"; second, thoughts that are repressed and brought back to memory: "I'll be darned—the name of that girl I took to the homecoming dance in 1963 was Karen. Now why did that pop into my head?"; third, elements that have never reached consciousness (the unknown archetypes that nevertheless influence and guide us).

Collective Unconscious
At times called the objective psyche or transpersonal conscious (Kaufmann, 1989, p. 131), the collective unconscious is both the most intriguing central aspect of Jung's theory and the most controversial. Resting at the bottom of the cylinder and far below conscious awareness, the collective unconscious is composed of a culturally universal unity at its core with an infinite number of culturally universal archetypes surrounding the core (Smith & Vetter, 1991, p. 99). Jung believed that all humans have generic images, myths, and symbols that deal with concepts such as mother and father, earth and heaven, and birth and death. Not only are these images present in the world around us, they are also biologically transmitted by what Jung called *memory traces* in the cortex. They are transmitted down though the generations and are an integral and guiding part of our thinking, feeling, and acting. While the collective unconscious is not directly retrievable to consciousness, it is nevertheless universal and functions as the major undergirding component of the personality (Hall & Lindzey, 1978; Kaufmann, 1989). Its concrete representation in the individual's present reality is in the form of what Jung calls primordial images or archetypes.

Archetypes
Jung named these culturally and generationally transmitted and inherited personality building blocks of the unconscious *archetypes*. Because they emanate from the deepest regions of the collective unconscious and are so ancient, they are also called primordial images. Specific archetypes have evolved so completely that they now stand as separate but interlocking systems in the personality. These are the anima and animus, the shadow, and the self (Hall & Lindzey, 1978). Supporting these major systems are a host of different, commonly held archetypes that are universal patterns or motifs and are the basic content of religions, mythologies, legends, and fairy tales. They emerge in individuals in the form of dreams and visions (Hall, 1989, p. 30).

The Dynamic Personality
The Jungian personality is restless. It has an instinctual need to seek what Jung has variously called *individuation, transcendence,* and *self-realization* (Jung, 1954b, p. 81). Being active and mobile, the cylinder is ever-changing. Now lopsided, now depressed on one end or the other, now stretched wasp-waisted, the perfect figure would be close to a cylinder, with equal parts of conscious, unconscious, and collective unconscious. However, this cylinder is not fixed and immobile, but fluid and dynamic. For Jung, even at the hypothetical endpoint of self-realization, the personality is still energized, still seeking its personal holy grail (Jung, 1954a; 1971e; 1971f).

Nature of Maladjustment
Pathology is not seen in Jungian psychology as a diseased or abnormal state. Rather, symptoms associated with psychopathology could be instructive for both the client and the analyst in providing clues to the function of the personality and also serve as warning signals when something is wrong in the personality system (Nystul, 1993, p. 140). The extent of disturbance we eventually suffer will be a function of the number and one-sidedness of incompatible opposites we generate in living and how soon we attempt to compensate for our lack of balance (Rychlak, 1973, p. 169).

Neurosis versus Psychosis

The fundamental difference between a neurosis and a psychosis, such as schizophrenia, is the split between the ego and some of the complexes. In a neurotic, the split is relative. Even in a multiple personality there is cooperation between the different persons who generally keep to their respective roles and, if possible, do not bother each other. Personality disassociation in schizophrenia is quite different. The personality is almost completely split off in schizophrenia (Hall & Lindzey, 1978; Kaufmann, 1989). Its concrete representation in the individual's present reality is in the form of what Jung calls primordial images or archetypes.

Insanity is thus an invasion from the unconscious of contents that are flatly incompatible with the aspirations and intentions of the ego (Rychlak, 1973, p. 169). For most of his career, Jung (1960a, p. 253) believed that psychoses were so intractable to therapy because they had some sort of metabolic toxin as their cause. Thus, talking could do little to rein in the unbridled complexes that came stampeding into conscious.

Conversely, the full-blown neurotic fights furiously for the maintenance and supremacy of ego-consciousness and relentlessly subjugates the unconscious. By attempting to maintain ever more rigid ego control, the neurotic approaches the morass of psychosis, yet somehow manages to remain on a relatively safe but teetering precipice (Jung, 1960a, pp. 234–238).

However, neuroses also serve a positive purpose. First, they start a holding action against unconscious complexes that would inundate the conscious if allowed to do so. Second, they send a message that has a purpose for our mental health and teach us something if we are willing to experience it. In Jung's words, "We do not cure it, it cures us" (Jung, 1964a, pp. 169–170).

Morals and Conscience

There is a component in maladjustment that has to do with morals and conscience. People develop a neurosis for want of a conscience (Jung, 1960a, pp. 355–356). Continual denial of the collective body of ethical beliefs and moral standards designed to compensate for selfish behavior will invariably result in a neurotic outcome (Jung, 1954b, p. 120). Therefore, when the client's conscience talks, he or she had better listen, or some very negative behavioral outcomes are likely to occur (Jung, 1960a, pp. 355–356).

Thus, denial assumes a prominent role in the analyst's attempt to ferret out the client's evasion of a task. The analytical therapist asks, "What is the task which the client does not want to fulfill at this time? What difficulty is the client trying to avoid now?" (Jung, 1961, p. 182). The client attempts to flee into the known and idyllic past and remain there, supposedly safely in control in preference to confronting life in the present with all of its unknowns and risks (Jung, 1961, p. 166).

Major Concepts

Power of the Unconscious

Humankind's heredity is psychic as well as physical in nature. The unconscious is an intuiting agent that far exceeds the capacity of the conscious mind. Unlimited power resides in its collective aspect, and the archetypes are carriers of this tremendous energy or libido. The libido is fueled by the energizing forces of diametrically opposed force fields of the personality that are constantly under tension and generate tremendous amounts of energy (Harris, 1996, p. 22). It should be clearly understood that Jungian libido is not just Freudian sexual energy, but psychic energy in any manifestation. Release of this energy causes emotional reactions that stimulate feeling toned thoughts, which in turn form clusters of ideas called complexes. Finally, from a positive viewpoint, the unconscious is not merely composed of repressed material but is a fountainhead of creativity, guidance, and meaning.

Symbols
All products of the unconscious that come to awareness do so as symbolic messages. Archetypes are the birthing agents for symbols. The most common symbols occur as dreams. Dreams are the avenue of egress for the unconscious to gain awareness and, as such, are the axis on which therapy revolves.

Jung's symbols are different from Freud's symbols. For Jung, symbols are intuitive ideas that have not yet formed, as opposed to Freud's view that symbols are symptomatic signs released into conscious awareness (Jung, 1966).

Environment and Conditioning
According to Jungian theory, environment and conditioning play a critical part in the personality by interacting with archetypes (Kaufmann, 1989, p. 131). Thus, behavior is both consciously and unconsciously motivated by environmental and psychic stimuli.

Motivation
The individual is both pushed by inherited archetypes and developed complexes from the past and pulled toward the future by the need for self-actualization, individuation, transcendent functioning, and selfhood (Smith & Vetter, 1991, p. 107). Although the past determines a good deal of the present, human movement is focused on the future.

Polarity and Oppositional Balancing
There are four functions of consciousness: thinking, feeling, sensing, and intuiting. These functions along with other functions and archetypes are polar opposites to one another. Opposites are the driving principle of all psychic energy and have a counterbalancing relationship. In the mentally healthy individual, conscious and unconscious components of the personality are balanced. The Jungian personality is always in a state of psychic flux through a transfer of psychic energy that invariably oscillates in a bipolar manner.

Any systems, attitudes, or functions may interact with one another in any of three ways: compensation, unification, or opposition. Compensation most often occurs when parts of the unconscious attempt to countervail parts of the conscious. Thus, the person who is consciously dominated by feeling and thinking may be unconsciously motivated by intuition and sensation. Oppositionally polar tendencies are in constant struggle with one another and are key in energizing one for effective living. Because polarities also have the power to attract, there is also the possibility of unification (Smith & Vetter, 1991, p. 108).

Transcendence and Spirituality

Technology and scientific knowledge are but one way to solve psychological problems. Transcendence and spirituality are another. Conscious rationality forms but one small aspect of the human experience. Unconscious archetypes form an even larger realm. As a result, self-realization can come only through transcendence and individuation, which is as instinctual as the drives of sex, hunger, aggression, and thirst (Kaufmann, 1989, p. 120).

No other theory begins to approach the breadth and scope of Jung's when it comes to views of the spirit, spirituality, and whatever passes for each person's immortal diety. Jung ranged across such arcane religions as Mithraism and Gnosticism to Christianity, Buddhism, and Judaism to the Great Spirit of the American Indian and tarot cards (Harris, 1996, pp. 172–178). In the Jungian quest to reach out and touch the transcendental nature of humankind, there is probably no known religion that is not of interest—particularly if it includes a heavy dose of mysticism.

Individuation

Individuation is the attempt at realization of the self (Kaufmann, 1989, p. 130). It is the hypothetically attainable endpoint of our existence and also the hypothetical culmination of the transformation stage in therapy. It is an instinctual force that continuously pushes us toward wholeness and realization of our own particular meaning in life (Kaufmann, 1989, p. 120). The important factor in individuation is not the amount of achievement one attains, but whether the personality is being truer to its own deeper potentialities rather than identifying in egocentric or narcissistic ways with cultural roles. The process, both in theory and as applied in therapy, involves a continuing dialogue between the ego and the self. Thus, successful movement toward individuation is both intimate and transpersonal, because both conscious and unconscious must be called into play and melded together for the possibility of individuation to occur (Hall, 1989, p. 4; Jung, 1971e, p. 279).

THE COUNSELING PROCESS

To allow an integration of the conscious and unconscious selves and the emergence of the true self, much of therapy involves the slow, methodical detective work of exploring the symbolic, often obtuse, and at times seemingly incomprehensible components of the unconscious. Currently, there are three major schools of thought on how this might be achieved. The classical school focuses on integration of self. The developmental or genetic school focuses on transference phenomena and dynamic interpretation of childhood experiences. The archetypal school focuses on the primordial images derived from the collective unconscious (Dehing, 1992; Samuels, 1985; 1989; Spiegelman, 1989; Walker, 1992).

Unlike the cause-and-effect systems of Freud or the behaviorists, Jungian psychology is symbolic and multidimensional in its interpretations. Probably the only law in Jungian psychology is that there is no law. Jungian psychology is paradoxical in that there are no simple yes and no answers. Therapy, like life, depends on the situation. Any action or trait taken to an extreme will become a counteracting force, and it is this force that is the essence of both therapy and living fruitfully. Jung had little use for a theory of personality that defined itself by a law of averages and measures of central tendency. He saw a workable theory of personality as primarily *paradoxical* and characterized by its *irregularity* (Jung 1964a). The Jungian personality is made up of many subpersonalities, which constantly replace one another in taking the driver's seat down life's rocky road while the others sit in the back of the bus—some patiently waiting and others noisily demanding to drive. In full bloom, analytic therapy is concerned with all of these passengers and their ancestral ghosts!

Analytical therapy typically involves four stages of treatment: confession and catharsis, elucidation, education, and transformation. While each stage seems final and may be sufficient for a return to mental health, none is complete in itself. Even transformation is not an endpoint (Jung, 1966, pp. 68–75).

Confession and Catharsis

Confession is the emotional side of mental distress and affirms that intellectual insights alone are rarely sufficient to effect change. By beginning to own feelings, the client establishes contact with the feeling tone of the unconscious complexes that cause maladjustment. This form of catharsis functions in much the same manner as the religious confessional (Rychlak, 1973, p. 176).

Elucidation

Rarely is confession and its subsequent catharsis sufficient. Elucidation is the dynamic interpretation by the therapist of the client's past and also the projection or transfer of important complexes to the therapist (Jung, 1954b, pp. 61–62). Therefore, for elucidation to be effective, the therapeutic dynamics of transference and countertransference need to occur and be dealt with by client and therapist.

Transference and Countertransference

Transference/countertransference is one of the keystones around which analytic therapy is built, and may be both personal and archetypal. It can be positive or negative and invariably has the oppositional forces of attraction and repulsion at work (Harris, 1996, pp. 116–119). Transference is a special instance of the more general phenomenon of projection and needs to be analyzed. For Jung, the therapist is not just a sexual transference object, but rather a symbol of the social bond that holds society together (Jung, 1961, p. 199).

However, in attempting to establish this bond, the client becomes dependent and regressive, with an outpouring of feeling toned projections, typically concretized by acting out behaviors. Once the client realizes he or she has been projecting on the therapist, the transference is resolved (Rychlak, 1973, p. 177). Before this can happen, any countertransferences that may exist must also be resolved and recognized as such by the therapist.

Countertransference is the analyst's projection on the client and is a necessary happening that may be used by the therapist as a guide during the course of therapy. It is inevitable that countertransference will arise in the relationship because all projections provoke counterprojections (Jung, 1960b, p. 237).

Thus, both transference and countertransference may be expected and even invited. From that standpoint, the therapist is as much in analysis as the client, and if the therapist believes the client must work through a narcissistic personality, then the therapist should look to his or her own narcissism.

Education

The therapist must now help clients to educate themselves in all aspects of life that have been found lacking. Jung proposes no particular way of doing this, except to say that whatever needs doing will be made plain by this stage of therapy, and the therapist will need to act as would any friend, by lending moral support and encouragement to the client's efforts (Rychlak, 1973, pp. 177–178).

For many clients, the first three stages will be enough, and therapy will be terminated by clients who are armed with the necessary knowledge and insight to attain some semblance of balance to their lives (Rychlak, 1973, p. 178). Yet some individuals have potential beyond the average; for these people, to educate them to normality would be their worst nightmare because their deepest need is to march to the tune of a different drummer (Jung, 1954b, p. 70). Understanding their "abnormal" lives calls for therapists and clients to plunge into the fourth and most complex stage of therapy.

Transformation

The final stage of transformation is unlike any other in psychotherapy and is necessary for self-realization or individuation. It is the shadow complex, which triggers the individuation process. Clients do not relish this stage because of their fears that it may overwhelm them (Jung, 1967, pp. 197–198). The shadow provides a fearsome but necessary contrast to the conscious realm of personality. It is necessary to the extent that it allows for the tension of opposites from which psychic energy is generated (Jung, 1963b, p. 497). Character is actually enriched through this constant interplay between the shadow's intrusion and the compensating measures we take to control it. Thus clients must see it, confront it, and learn to live with it.

However, it is not the shadow that is directly confronted, but rather the anima or animus that directs the shadow's actions in the unconscious and serves as a bridge to the conscious world (Jung, 1967, p. 42). Once out in open conscious, the anima/animus is quite likely to have very decided opinions about a number of things, and very lively internal dialogues are likely to ensue between the personified anima/animus and the client. Thus is the coming-out party of the polar opposite of the client's conscious ego. Yet victory of the ego over the anima/animus or vice versa is not the goal of therapy, for in the former case that would be a return to a complete state of consciousness with no self-realization and in the latter case to a complete state of unconsciousness, again with no self-realization (Rychlak, 1973, pp. 179–180).

What is needed is a balancing act between the two. This process is not easily done and requires a great deal of time and concentrated effort from both client and therapist in the quest for the emergence of the self.

Finally, the emergence of the self has some far-reaching consequences for the ego, which is usurped by the arrival of a new focal point of the personality (Jung, 1967, p. 45). This is all very upsetting to the ego, which does not always give up its position without a fight (Rychlak, 1973, p. 182). The ego is a very short-sighted, biased psychic complex that lives on extrinsic concrete reinforcement, while the self has a much larger catholic character that thrives on intrinsic, abstract reinforcers. Balancing the two forces balances the transformation equation.

STRATEGIES FOR HELPING CLIENTS

Counseling Goals

The aim of therapy is to help the client move toward greater self-realization. For this to occur, the client needs to develop other major systems that may be arrested or achieve a better balance between subsystems of the personality (Nystul, 1993, p. 140). Most people who come for therapy have lost touch with their inner world and are barely aware of its existence. One of the major goals of therapy is rebridging the gap between these inner and outer worlds. Some clients must be reminded again and again to pay attention to their inner world. Others are flooded by their inner world and pay too much attention to it. There is no bridge because the two worlds are commingled. The therapist's job, then, is to separate these two worlds and build a bridge between the two (Kaufmann, 1989).

The Counseling Relationship

Jungians do not perceive therapy as a typical client–therapist relationship wherein the client is *treated*. Acceptance is the *sine qua non* of analytic therapy (Kaufmann, 1989, p. 139). Jungians see themselves more as guides to help another person delve into the unconscious. They can function as expert guides because they have traveled the territory and know it from their own analysis (Nystul, 1993). Depending on the client's development, the therapist may exchange feelings, experiences, and even dreams. The analyst may teach, cajole, give advice, reflect feelings, or give support. Much like Gestalt therapy, major emphasis is placed on conscious assimilation of immediate experience (Kaufmann, 1989, p. 135).

Jungian therapy hinges on an equitable relationship between client and therapist. To instigate such a relationship, the therapist must give up all pretense to superior knowledge and all authority and desire to influence the therapeutic process. The therapist must give the client the opportunity to be free to say, feel, and think what he or she wishes. In that regard, the therapist's reaction is the only thing with which he or she can legitimately confront the client (Jung, 1966, pp. 5–10). Thus, a major axiom for analytic therapy is that the therapist follows religiously the direction of the unconscious and abandons all fixed notions and preconceptions about the client (Kaufmann, 1989, p. 134).

Counseling Techniques

Jung was skeptical of mandating techniques because he felt they could be restrictive to the individuation process (Nystul, 1993, p. 141). Jung as a therapist was unorthodox and pragmatic in his approach and would use whatever worked (Kaufmann, 1989, p. 132). However, knowing the client's background and how it is linked to present functioning is mandatory, not only for the insight it provides into conscious dynamics but also as the opening move in discovering the complexes that contribute to maladjustment.

Assessment

Two forms of assessment are closely allied with Jungian therapy. First and foremost are personality types. Within the Jungian personality schema there are two major types of attitudes—the outgoing, gregarious, or extroverted personality and the introspective, shy, or introverted personality. Each individual has some combination of the foregoing with the dominant attitude represented in the conscious and the nondominant in the unconscious. Complimentary to extroversion and introversion are four functions that allow for further differentiation of personality type: thinking, feeling, sensation, and intuition (Jung, 1971b).

These are divided into two pairs: sensation is paired and contrasted with intuition and thinking is paired and contrasted with feeling (Jung, 1971b). Sensation is the perceptual function that allows the individual contact with the real world through the five physical senses. Intuition perceives the world via the unconscious. While it has no basis in rational thought, it provides flashes of insight and impressions that do have some basis in reality (Hall, 1989, p. 31). Thinking and feeling classify the functions of sensation and intuition. Thinking classifies data into logical and discrete categories while feeling classifies input into pleasant or unpleasant categories and arranges it into a value structure. Thus, the two counterbalance each other: feeling gives full play to emotions, and thinking attempts to suppress emotion by reliance on factual data. Gradually, one function will assume a superior role and the other assumes an inferior role in the personality (Smith & Vetter, 1991, pp. 104–105). It is from these attitudes and functions that the MBTI was developed (Nystul, 1993, p. 140).

The other major component of Jungian assessment is the word association method that Jung modified and adapted to determine types of complexes. The client is asked to respond as quickly as possible to one hundred stimulus words that, as Jung stated, "are chosen in such a manner as to strike easily all complexes which occur in practice." Hesitation, stumbling responses, lengthy response times, repetition of the stimulus words, and repetition of inappropriate responses to a variety of stimulus words are indications of constellating complexes (Jung, 1910). Jung measured these responses with various biofeedback devices and found distinct physiological differences in words that were troublesome to respond to and those that were not. Once these complexes were uncovered, they could then be brought to the attention of the client and thus bring unconscious material into awareness (Smith & Vetter, 1991).

Exploration

The process of therapy starts with a thorough investigation of the client's current functioning in the environment. Particularly since the unconscious is compensatory to the conscious, the only way to get at it is to know the client's present reality. The investigation includes the past history of the client, various important influences in the client's life, attitudes, values, and ideas. The analyst is then able to point out inconsistencies and contradictions, peculiar reactions and odd behavior patterns. Many of the client's tacit assumptions are challenged and questioned (Kaufmann, 1989, p. 133).

There are three schools of thought in how therapy occurs. The classicists emphasize the journey into the self. The archetypals emphasize archetypal imagery exploration. The developmental Jungians journey across the life span. Dream interpretation, regression to childhood, relational emphasis between therapist and client, sandplay, art, dance, and body sensation (as in a sweatlodge experience) may be primary operating procedures for Jungians (Harris, 1996, pp. 129–130).

DREAM INTERPRETATION

Dreams, the purest form from which to draw on the vast storehouse of the unconscious, often emerge as the most fruitful source of therapeutic material; therefore, dream work is a fundamental core of therapy (Jung, 1933; 1963a). Jungian therapy treats essentially all unconscious sources—dreams, fantasies, paintings, daydreams—in the same manner. We will use dream interpretation as the foundation of our exploration of therapy.

Jungian dream interpretation differs from Freudian dream analysis. Freudian dream analysis is based on repression; that is, dreams are viewed as the emergence of repressed material from the unconscious. Jungians take the phenomenological view that the drama of the dream represents the unconscious message to the dreamer expressed in symbolic terms (Jung, 1964b). The dream message is not necessarily hidden; it may appear to be trying to reveal itself to the dreamer. The dreamer may have preconceptions that either make the dream message seem illusive or impel the dreamer to resist following the wisdom of the unconscious. The dream force may appear to provide a simple solution to a complicated problem or point to a complication of a situation that the dreamer had assumed to be simple. The ego may have real difficulty associating to the dream because the dreamer is not yet ready to accept an obvious solution that appears self-evident to the strong (unconscious) dream force or the dream message presents an understanding of the situation that is too threatening or scary for the dreamer to face readily (Kaufmann, 1989, pp. 133–136).

Just as one does not automatically speak a foreign language, one cannot see the meaning in the dream automatically. This does not mean there is no meaning, but that one does not currently understand the significance of the dream. Dreams are often looked at long and hard with no meaning apparently gleaned from them, and sometimes the meaning is realized months or even years after the fact (Gilliland & High, 1985; Kaufmann, 1989).

Assumptions in Dream Interpretation

Primacy of the Unconscious

A fundamental assumption in dream interpretation is the existence of the unconscious. Making sense of dream material stands or falls with the hypothesis of the unconscious. If one does not accept the hypothesis, he or she will simply say the dream is a negligible byproduct of the psyche. Obviously dreams would then hold no value in therapy. However, if dreams are from the unconscious, then interpretation is an attempt to get at the meaning of the dream in such a way as to improve the dilemmas of the client and reduce projections from the unconscious (Jung, 1933).

Dreams Bear Messages

Another primary assumption in dream interpretation is that there is *meaning* in the dreams. Neither the client nor the therapist may necessarily know the meaning of the client's dreams. They may discover the meaning by working together in a collaborative manner. That calls for a relationship of mutual respect and trust and a commitment to working on the common objective of bringing the client's unconscious attitudes, motives, and choices to conscious awareness (Jung, 1933; 1963a).

Archetypal Images

A third basic assumption in dream interpretation is that dream contents contain personal and/or archetypal images (Hall, 1977). The personal images that are remnants of one's own history are best interpreted by the client making associations to those images because, in the final analysis, the client is the expert judge of the authenticity of the images. Archetypal images not recognized by the dreamer as a part of the personal past are usually interpreted with the therapist assisting the client in acquiring a collective view of such images.

Dreams reflect the tendency of the psyche to heal itself, perform a compensatory function by indicating discrepancies between our conscious and unconscious, and provide clues for goals for future development (Harris, 1996, p. 154). Just as the inner workings of the body are always seeking balance, so also the dream seeks to balance the contents of the psyche. This can be seen most clearly in a person holding a one-sided conscious view. The psyche produces a dream that will show the other side of whatever attitude the person has (Hall, 1977).

A final assumption is that dreams are symbolic. To interpret dreams literally is a mistake. The interpretation is only a hypothesis, not a statement of "truth" (Harris, 1996, p. 159).

Process of Interpretation

Homework

Often the dream analysis process entails the therapist and the client designing appropriate homework. Even clients who rarely remember dream content can quickly and effectively begin to remember and record their dreams. Therefore, a typical homework assignment might be writing detailed, chronological, and specific descriptions of their dreams, together with pertinent associations that are directly connected with particular images in the dreams. By consistently writing thorough dream descriptions, clients soon learn to record and recognize sequences of dreams or recurrent dreams and to judge the power or valence of their dreams. Structured homework and instruction by the therapist can teach clients to recall, recognize, and record dream maxims, thus enhancing their amplifications as well as the quality of their dream interpretations (Hall, 1977).

Dream Maxims

A *dream maxim* is an expression of a general truth, principle, concept, or rule that helps to describe or explain dream phenomena. Hall (1977, pp. 276–278) has identified eleven dream maxims that provide therapists and clients with vital information to assist in analyzing, interpreting, discovering, and unlocking the mysteries dreams seem to hold. These maxims can readily be given to clients as written guidelines pertaining to their homework.

1. *What is something unique about the dream?* Assume that the dream can reveal something unique—some new understanding that contributes to the dreamer's wholeness.

2. *What are the form and structure of the dream?* What is the visual dramatic form that moves from problem to development, to climax, to outcome in the dream?

3. *Where is the dream ego in the dream?* Is the dreamer a spectator, a bystander, or an active participant? Is the dreamer passive, proactive, assertive, or aggressive? Sometimes the dream ego shifts in the dream.

4. *Is each motif in the dream described as carefully as the dreamer's memory permits?* Take special care to push to the limit details of each motif. If a "woman" is described by the dreamer, specify whether she is young or old, attractive or unattractive, positive or negative, active or passive. No question is too absurd to ask about a dream's motif.

5. *What feelings does the dream ego experience?* Does the dream ego feeling correspond to what it should in everyday life? Is there an absence of feeling? Is the feeling exaggerated?

6. *Are the motifs of the dream, particularly persons in the dream who are known to the dreamer in waking life, better taken as objective or subjective figures?* Because dreamers sometimes project unconscious complexes onto persons known to them, it is important to help the dreamer distinguish between dream images that are taken subjectively and those taken objectively.

7. *Where does the dream fit in the ongoing series of dreams from the dreamer?* Does the dream represent a recurring dream or dream theme? Is it exact? Is there a new or a different theme?

8. *Is it a "big" dream or a "little" dream?* Some dreams are "fine-tuning" of previous dreams; some dreams represent themes that indicate a new direction. The latter are "big" dreams.

9. *Don't treat the dream concretely or as direct advice.* To ask the dream what to do in an objective situation ignores the responsibility of the waking ego. To take the dream as direct advice does not take into account the compensatory nature of dreams.

10. *Don't reduce the dream to interpersonal terms alone.* To deal with the dream as elements of interpersonal relationships exclusively does not adequately communicate the intrapsychic quality or power of the dream.

11. *Does the dreamer have any private unspoken interpretations that he or she has not subjected to the analytic process?* It is necessary to inquire into the dreamer's feelings as to the thoughts, ideas, or interpretations that have not been spoken to, so as to allow interpretations from both the therapist and client viewpoints.

It is important that clients bring to the dream interpretation session written responses to as many of the maxims as possible. However, these maxims should be used as guidelines, because we cannot expect to be able to apply every maxim to every dream.

Dreamwork

A very important aspect of the association and amplification processes is to make clients aware of "obvious" symbolic dream images. An *association* is a mental connection between a concrete dream image and its symbolic meaning, not necessarily causal, by virtue of contiguity. For example, a client might vividly dream about a flower. The association could be the sequence of events in the client's life leading up to his or her wedding. An *amplification* is what a dream object or image really *is*. For example, a client may associate a friend to a lamp appearing in his or her dream, but basically the lamp is something that provides light in the darkness (Kaufmann, 1989, p. 136). Many clients have to be taught to recognize these images because they have no "conscious" awareness of the "obviously" big picture.

Dream interpretation is not easy or simple. Every dream is different. There are many leads, diversions, ambiguities, possibilities, and contradictions. Solving the mystery of a dream can often be equated to solving a mathematical equation. A series of dreams presents multiple unknowns and interpretations and must sometimes be approached on a trial-and-error basis. Often the dream may be interpreted in different, even contradictory contexts. A dream may be interpreted on either the objective or the subjective level. The *objective level* pertains to people or events outside the dreamer. For example, if one dreams about his or her mother, the dream may be interpreted as expressing something about the reality of the actual relationship between the person and the mother. The *subjective level* refers to people or events pertaining to the dreamer's "inner" psyche, such as one's inner parent, spouse, dilemma, supervisor, and so on. An example of a subjective level interpretation might be a young woman engaged to be married even though she is ambivalent about her commitment to her fiancé. She dreams he is about to take her out dancing when the guys from his workplace suddenly appear with their hunting gear, and her fiancé departs with them to go hunting, leaving her feeling betrayed and hurt. On the objective level, this dream may mean that the stability of the young woman's relationship with her future husband may be questionable. On the subjective level, the dream may be saying to her that her inner (animus) side is not up to the stresses of the masculine competition that she intuitively knows would be required to make such a marriage work (Kaufmann, 1989, p. 137).

Major Steps in Dream Interpretation

Step One

The dreamer writes the details of the dream(s) as quickly as possible after awakening (Jung, 1933, p. 12). This provides a clear understanding of the exact details of the dream before the memory of the specifics becomes convoluted, commingled, or distorted.

In writing the dream content in specific detail the client attempts to describe and clarify the context of the dreams. Context specification is important because it keeps the therapist from injecting premature associations and attempting to interpret the dreams too early. In step one the therapist questions the client incisively to make sure that both client and therapist understand the exact content; sequence of dream events; dreamer feelings about dream images; whether the dream is a repetition of a previous dream or is one in a series of dreams; and the power, strength, or valence of the dream. A series of dreams gives more confidence in interpretations than does one isolated dream. Also, a series of dreams provides a clearer perspective of basic or developing themes (Jung, 1933, p. 14). The more powerful the dream, the more important the message the dream is attempting to reveal to the dreamer's conscious ego and psychic system.

Step Two

The dream is reassembled with amplifications in mind. The gathering of associations and amplifications in progressive order on one or more of three levels—personal, cultural, and archetypal—helps to identify the core maxims of the dream images (Hall, 1977).

   Amplification of a dream is analogous to "peeling" the three layers of a complex: (1) personal associations; (2) images of a more cultural or transpersonal nature; (3) the archetypal level of amplification—that is, in the context of snakes, houses, automobiles, incest, mourning, alcohol and drugs, death, and so on (Hall, 1989). In many dreams the order of events holds much of the secret of the dream. Questions are open-ended and not focused on specific questions found in step one. Instead, amplifying questions help the client to discover the larger picture and set the stage for expanded understanding of the dream. Therapist questions during the reassembly/amplification step could be: "What do you think the dream wants to tell you?" "How do you see the dream now?" "How do you feel about the dream?" To further amplify the dream, the therapist may use a fairy tale or anecdote that parallels or explains something related to it. Amplification does not involve interpretation, but rather adds information to the client's story or reframes it. The purpose is to help the client recognize similarities between his or her personal experience and its archetypal configuration (Harris, 1996, pp. 149–150).

Step Three

In essence, the assimilation step is where the therapist and the client make conscious sense of the dream. An important aspect of step three is for the client to come to the point where he or she can answer the therapist's question: "What *conscious* attitude does the dream compensate?" "What *symbolic attitude* in the client's *unconscious* does the dream compensate?" (Jung, 1933, p. 17).

SAMPLE CASE

Theo, a forty-four-year-old man, has a masters degree and is a guidance counselor in a public middle school in a large city. He has been divorced four years. His ex-wife works as a secretary for the city's utility company. Theo's three children, ages seven, ten, and twelve, live with their mother. At the time of the divorce it was decided that his ex-wife would keep the house because of its location in a stable neighborhood and desirable school district for the children. Theo lives in an apartment across town from his ex-wife and children. The expenses of keeping up the family, paying child support, and maintaining two places has been a heavy burden and strain on Theo's resources. He is not displeased with his teaching job, but neither is he very happy. He has thought about resigning and going to California or Hawaii. But he cannot bring himself to abandon his responsibilities to his children, and he knows that if he quit his job they would surely suffer.

Theo has been going to the same Jungian analyst for almost four years, having started analysis shortly after the divorce. His analysis was difficult for about a year. Finally, he and the analyst worked through the transference and countertransference issues and now the therapeutic relationship is stable. Theo does not think about quitting analysis or changing analysts the way he did previously. On a Friday in early December of the school year, Theo was offered a job as principal of a different middle school, starting the first of January, in the middle of the academic term. The superintendent's office wanted an answer from Theo by the following Wednesday. That night, Friday, Theo had one of the most vivid and clear dreams he had had since he began Jungian analysis.

Step One: Written Details

Theo's dream, verbatim, as written and delivered to the analyst, follows.

Friday night I had a most unusual dream. It was really a sequence of three dreams in a row, three scenarios, or three acts, as if in a play.

Scene One

Driving with someone on a curvy two-lane highway in the high hills of California. Some mountainous scenery; some desertlike slopes. I was noticing the floral life. One place we stopped. Got out of the car. Saw lots of purple violets growing everywhere—blooming profusely. Lots of wiry grasses and arid desert plants everywhere. It was obvious to me that there was a scarcity of moisture here. Some small evergreen trees were noticed. Lots of rocks everywhere, scattered all over the slopes. At that time I suddenly noticed that the person I was with was one of my students at the Sunday school where I teach. We began planting pine seedlings all over the open landscape. I took great pains to instruct the student where to plant the evergreen seedlings. I pointed out that, since rainfall is scarce here, the best place for the roots of the seedlings to be placed to survive is near the base or watershed of sloping flat-sided rocks. We then set about planting seedlings as fast as we could, looking for good, loose soil, near watershed slopes of as many flat rocks as possible. We were working very fast. I was feeling a sense of urgency to get as many seedlings planted as we could. I wanted to get this barren land covered with young trees, and I was afraid that we would not get it covered. (That scene trailed off and ended there.)

Scene Two

The same California mountains, except at a higher elevation—among densely wooded alpine forests and exceedingly steep terrain. Corlew, my brother just younger than myself, was with me and my youngest daughter, Rethia, was there. In the dream Rethia was only three years old. She was quite small. We got out of the car and were walking through the dense forest. I was carrying Rethia. Corlew and I were walking some distance apart and I lost sight of him, but I could still hear him.

I came upon a very steep slope, still carrying Rethia. I couldn't turn back, and the slope got so steep I was beginning to lose footing. I was trying to hold on to bushes and to Rethia and to keep from sliding down the precipice. My boots were digging into the soft earth as I tried to maintain my footing. I could see that I could not manage much longer. I was telling Rethia to hang on to me, in case I slipped and started plunging down the ever steeper precipice—almost vertical by now. I was fearful of losing my grip on Rethia in case we fell. I was most concerned about both of us getting seriously injured in the dense woods and steep mountains with nobody knowing where we were and rescue virtually impossible. (That segment [scene] faded out just about the time our plunge down the steep mountainous slope seemed imminent.)

Scene Three
Rethia and I were injured in the fall (even though I do not recall the actual fall, itself), I more seriously than she. We were coming from the dense forest on the opposite side of the escarpment from which we had apparently fallen. We came upon a barbed wire fence and a paved road was on the other side of the fence. I was crawling; Rethia was walking. Rethia was saying, to a man in the road, that I was hurt and couldn't walk, and she was asking him to help us. Rethia and the man held up the lower strand of the barbed wire while I crawled under it into the road. The man said he was a physician and would attend to us—for us to come on to his house.

I could not see any houses anywhere—only woods and the road and fence. He said, "Come on." He and Rethia started walking out to the road, supposedly toward a house. I told them them I would come on in a moment; that I wanted to contact Corlew, because I feared he was lost in the forest. I struggled to get up on my feet, and finally did with some difficulty. I yelled, as loudly as I could, Corlew's name, cupping my hands to my mouth toward the direction I thought Corlew might be. I yelled some more and thought I heard him faintly reply, but the breeze in the tree branches and the noises of the forest and the echo of my voice muffled the sound, and I couldn't make voice contact with Corlew. I was quite worried about him, and became very frustrated and frightened for him. I went on out the road and spotted two houses, fine-looking mansions, way off the road, among many, many trees.

I didn't get to the houses. The physician, Rethia, and now the Sunday school student met me. The doctor said he examined Rethia and that she was OK. He said I was OK too—apparently, I assumed, he gave me a clean bill of health without even examining me other than observing me as I crawled under the barbed wire fence. I accepted his diagnosis. He said, "Here's your clothes." At that moment, I realized I had on only my shorts. I took my clothes and was looking for a place to put them on when the dream began to fade away. The physician, Rethia, and the student seemed to fade out of the picture. I was urgently trying to find a place to put my clothes on and go looking for Corlew. I just could not find a place to get dressed and was frustrated over that when the dream completely trailed off, finally into oblivion—but not from my memory. (This was the most powerful dream I have had in several years!)

Step Two: Reassembly with Amplifications

TH: Let's first try to identify the emotional tone the dream has for you.

CL: I guess I get nervous, scared, and curious when I think about it.

TH: Let's focus on the sequencing of the dream. In the first scene you were vividly seeing things growing. What specific feelings do you associate with that scene?

CL: Well, two feelings: one was elation at the tranquility and the beauty of the plants in the landscape; the other was frustration over the fact that the one variety of pine was scarce and might have trouble growing in that semi-arid location.

TH: I gather that your frustration got translated into action on your part when you started furiously planting the seedlings like you were racing against time.

CL: That's right. I don't know where that was coming from, but I was feeling a strong sense of urgency to get those young pine plants in the ground and get that barren landscape thriving.

Here the therapist was assisting Theo to get a clear mental picture of the dream contexts: keeping the sequence of dream events intact; clarifying emotional responses to the dream images; and ensuring that Theo did not lose the true dream images by commingling them with waking events that had occurred since the dream. Clarifying dream context is very important prior to proceeding to further amplification (Hall, 1977, pp. 276–277).

A session was devoted to the amplification of the three scenes of Theo's dream. The therapist and Theo carefully, step by step, verbally sorted through and audiotaped the images, order of events, symbols, motifs and Theo's emotional associations with people, activities, and scenes in the dream. Then they used the tape recording of Theo's dream amplification to study, reflect, and collaboratively dissect certain dream components. Theo wrote down as many amplifications as they could identify. A limited sampling of the amplifications for each scene serves to illustrate the product of step two.

Scene One
1. I was not driving the car on the curvy two-lane highway. Someone else was, but it was not clear whether or not it was the Sunday school student. I'm sure the driver was a female. Maybe that represents the anima side of my personality driving me.
2. The environment of the place was starved for moisture. In what way is my present existence starved for nurturance?
3. I was feeling singularly responsible for nurturing the environment to health as well as for instructing the feminine archetype in myself. In what ways am I attempting to assume total responsibility for creating and cultivating my current life and surroundings?
4. At the start of the scene, I was passive (being driven); later in the scene, I was active and emotionally involved, feeling a sense of frustration and even urgency to get a vital task completed. What urgent tasks or events in my everyday living constitute a frantic personal drive to control, influence, or attain?

Scene Two
1. Corlew represents the "younger brother" side of my Self that I am in great fear of losing; Rethia may be that feminine (anima) part of my personality that is young, dependent, precious. In what ways am I attempting to preserve and protect those precious parts of my personality?
2. The steep slope, loss of footing, vulnerable trek through the dangerous and unknown forest, and inability to turn back or protect the tender feminine (anima) side of my personality may represent a pervasive feeling of loss of control in some essential part of my life. In what ways am I losing or fearful of losing some vital part of my existence?

Scene Three

1. In the dream I was injured. How, in my current waking life, am I injured or debilitated?
2. Following my "accident" and pseudo rescue, the Sunday school student reappeared; Rethia never left me. Both anima representations in my personality were vividly present. What conscious attitude(s) regarding my anima does my waking ego wish to keep me from facing?
3. Near the end of the scene. I found myself virtually without clothing. In what ways am I, in my everyday life, feeling naked and vulnerable?
4. Throughout scene two, I was upset because I could not make contact with my younger brother, and at the very last I was in a hurry to put on my clothes and go look for him. How am I losing or in danger of losing contact with the inner "younger brother" of my existence?
5. The whole dream was unusually powerful and memorable. What message does that power and totality of the dream have for my waking conscious? What obvious conscious attitude(s), if any, is my ego resisting?

Step Three: Assimilation

Theo's dream amplification provided the springboard for assimilation and a good deal of analysis that was a collaborative enterprise between the therapist and Theo, who, at that stage in his individuation process, was conversant with the process of dream interpretation.

CL: Now that we've been going over the details of the dream, I do see some real relevancy to my present life.

TH: What seems to be the strongest symbolic and emotional message the dream is trying to convey?

CL: Well, that some aspects of my life have been unraveling lately, and that's scary. I need to get hold of them before they get hold of me. I mean, at first I had no notion that the urgent hurrying depicted in the dream images might be a conscious compensation. Sure, I have been under stress lately. The regional ten-year accreditation visiting team is coming in next week. Would you believe the evaluation was scheduled for December 9 through 12? I'm the coordinator of that! Semester exams begin the day they leave. The Christmas holiday crunch is upon us. I don't have the money I need for all my obligations and my kids' Christmas. No wonder I hadn't thought about all that, much less face it!

TH: So, Theo, now that you connect all the pieces, some of the dream components make pretty good sense.

CL: I can think of some other implications too. Like, what is the barren landscape of my present life that may cause me to have an urgent need to get it started growing? It's not yet clear to me what the urgency of the dream image of planting those trees symbolizes or compensates.

TH: For right now, what does the magnitude of the dream series have to tell you? This was a BIG dream. [The therapist was referring to the fact that Jungians and their clients commonly agree that a "big" dream symbolizes or compensates in the "big picture" in one's life.] What does that mean for your overall life? Also, what did you learn about yourself? And what more do you feel the need to learn about yourself? And what do you want to do about this dream?

Here the therapist is working with Theo on the process of assimilation, defined by Jung (1933, p. 16) as "a mutual interpretation of conscious and unconscious contents, and not—as is too commonly thought—a one-sided valuation, interpretation and deformation of unconscious contents by the conscious mind." The focus of assimilation of Theo's dreams is to decipher the message contained therein so that he can both understand and act on those messages.

The application of dream analysis learnings can now begin in the client's life. The therapist will be right there to guide and assist him. Jungian therapy is about the big pictures in life, about the total human existence and enterprise. As Kaufmann (1989, p. 135) has indicated, the most profitable way to use a dream is to view it as a metaphorical drama unfolding before our eyes. That is what the therapist was attempting to facilitate with Theo.

In the brief encounter with Theo we did not get into the intricate workings of the *subjective* level versus the *objective* level interpretations. Nor did we deal with the many complex ramifications of the emergence of Theo's shadow (Sanford, 1984) in the dream. These dimensions are always present in dream material and are a rich source of information for the therapist and the client who have the will and the stamina to stick with it.

Because much of Jungian theory rests on paradox, it should come as no surprise that not only do Jungians take their religions seriously, they also take science (nonlinear quantum mechanics theory in particular) quite seriously and fractals, strange attractors, and chaos and complexity theory extremely seriously. The parallel between analytic theory and these exotic fields in physics and mathematics is that in what looks like absolute disorder there may be, in fact, an evolving order that is quite elegant in both nature and the self (Butz, 1992). For analytic therapists, such fields offer support for the slow, methodical waiting of analytic psychology's nonlinear therapy to unfold (Harris, 1996, pp. 179–188). From that standpoint, we now offer a brief introduction to the cutting edge and controversial field of chaos and complexity theory.

CHAOS AND COMPLEXITY THEORY

Background

Chaos and complexity theory, popularized by such theorists as Prigogine (1984) and Gleick (1987) in the 1980s, has recently received a great deal of attention in the scientific community (Briggs, 1992; Briggs & Peat, 1989; DeAngelis, 1993; Eiser, 1994; Hall, 1991; Schroeder, 1991). Initially, chaos theory was principally examined by and applied to the so-called "hard sciences" such as physics. More recently, a body of literature has begun to emerge regarding chaos theory's relevancy to behavioral science disciplines. It is now accepted that certain elements of chaos theory contain important implications for counseling and psychotherapy (Barton, 1994; Brack, 1993; Brack, Brack, & Zucker, 1995; Brennan, 1995; Butz, 1993, 1995; Chamberlain, 1993; 1994; 1995; Gleatt, 1995; McCown & Johnson, 1993; Peca, 1992; Wilbur, Kulikowich, Roberts-Wilbur, & Torres-Rivera, 1995).

Overview

Chaos and complexity theory is not a substitute or a replacement for other systems of counseling. To the contrary, it serves as a viable adjunctive and alternative paradigm that enriches other therapeutic perspectives. The essence of chaos theory, according to Gleick (1987), is that there is an underlying order in all systems, but that systems are so complex that long-term predictability is not feasible. Waldrop (1992) noted that complexity theory deals with the self-organization that emerges from the unpredictable. Thus, "chaos and complexity theory challenge our presuppositions that reality is always linear, predictable, and controllable" (Brack, Brack, & Zucker, 1995, p. 200).

Ford (1994) speaks of "complexity" in terms of "organized complexity" and the concept of "system." There is organization in all living systems, but it is the pattern of complexity of relatedness of the parts that defines a specific organization. "If parts are related in such a way that together they produce a property that none may manifest by itself, then organization exists" (p. 36). What we may view as chaos in a person, a system, or an organization may then be what Ford calls "organized complexity," even though we might not recognize it as such viewed through a traditional concept of linearity or cause-and-effect thinking.

Applied to counseling practice, a linear view of a case study may indicate that a person's life might appear to be in total disarray and dysfunction and that the person's behavior and thinking are unpredictable, dangerous, chaotic, and without order. But what may seem at one level to be erratic and unpredictable, when viewed from a more global and holistic vantage point may actually turn out to be ordered.

Chaos Theory, Counseling, and Psychotherapy

An oversimplified version of chaos theory in regard to counseling and psychotherapy is that (1) the universe, the world, and nature are inherently chaotic or in a continual state of random disequilibrium, but there appear to emerge random and cyclical periods of nonchaos, equilibrium, or order in human functioning just as there are in nature; (2) the chaos or disequilibrium that occurs in the lives of human beings appears to emerge randomly, but there are periods of cyclical and systematic order and homeostasis; (3) in the lives of clients, the periods of disequilibrium are equated with chaos, whereas the periods of equilibrium are equated with nonchaos or order; (4) infrequently, but importantly, a seemingly insignificant and perhaps unexplainable event occurs during a stressful situation that appears to exert a dramatic and positive effect on the client's ability to attain equilibrium and clarity amid the perceived chaos; (5) isolated events in human life, like isolated events in nature, cannot be studied and defined as well as they can be studied and defined in a global or holistic frame of reference; and (6) in any given dilemma or chaotic system there is an underlying order in that system; even when it may appear to be totally disordered to the client or a casual observer (Butz, 1993; 1995; Chamberlain, 1993; 1994).

Chamberlain (1995, pp. 118–120) provided a case example of chaos and complexity that applies the theory to therapeutic intervention in a family dealing with suicidal ideation and threat. Amid family turmoil, dysfunction, and long-term family therapy, the father found the daughter making plans to kill herself, having already made several attempts. The father, wanting to spontaneously create a reframe of the situation from "I must keep her from committing suicide," to "I want to make her want to live," began choking the daughter. By exerting great effort, the daughter broke the father's grip. Although the choking event did not even begin to resolve all the family's serious systemic problems, it did stop the suicide attempts. During a six-year follow-up period, the daughter was never known to become suicidal again. This example illustrates how a one-time brief event, done out of frustration and desperation, may change the course of a suicidal person's life where years of professional time, medication, and money have failed.

One such example can be found in the case of "Larry" (Harding, 1992), a man in his fifties who once lived what people considered to be the American dream. He had a well-paying civil service job, a comfortable suburban home, a caring wife, and three bright children. But it all went sour for Larry when he fell victim to bipolar disorder, or manic depression. A conventional linear view of Larry's chaos could render it unexplainable. All manner of conventional linear thinking, assessment, medication, and psychotherapy went for naught. But a broader, global view of his situation may make more sense when considering the many dynamic pressures, demands, expectations, seemingly random dilemmas, and complex interactions that his whole family encountered over an extended period of many years.

For instance, Larry attributed his bipolar disorder to recent job stress and family pressures. Chaos and complexity theory, however, would likely examine concomitantly, from Larry's internal perspective as well as from a global external assessment, his current and total past internal and environmental physical, social, familial, vocational, economic, spiritual, and educational lives. Whereas Larry, his family, physicians, therapists, employer, and coworkers might view his apparently chaotic dilemma condition as having come about as a result of recent and specific work, family, or social events, chaos theory would likely hold that his condition is not necessarily chaotic. Rather, chaos theory would characterize Larry's total life history as a system with an underlying order—as any other system in nature has an underlying quality of order.

As counselors we cannot control the ebb and flow of the chaotic external or internal environments of our clients. We can study the patterns of chaotic development in the lives of our clients and perhaps learn to intervene at opportune times and in appropriate ways that will take advantage of the twists and turns in the cycles of chaos that continually assail our clients. We cannot create homeostasis or equilibrium in our clients, but we may be able to recognize the cyclical changes that emerge and we may even be able, on occasion, to generate interventions that turn the tide of chaos. If counselors can recognize and act on those occasional insignificant and unexplainable events that occur during a crisis situation (and that appear to exert a dramatic and positive effect on the client's ability to attain equilibrium and clarity amid the chaos), then we may find that chaos theory offers a new and helpful perspective on our work. In Larry's case, the so-called chaotic situation has two opposing and ambivalent qualities: on the one hand, at any given moment his behavior and thinking make perfect sense when viewed exclusively from Larry's internal perspective. On the other hand, when Larry externalizes his situation as helpless, and perhaps even hopeless, his dilemma becomes one of both danger and opportunity. That is the point at which the counselor might be of the greatest help to Larry. It may be the only point at which Larry himself may have an opportunity to understand the underlying systemic order that drives his "chaos" and a chance to grasp the opportunity to shift from a state of disequilibrium to one of equilibrium or homeostasis.

CONTRIBUTIONS OF THE JUNGIAN SYSTEM

Hall and Lindzey (1978, p. 149) contend that second only to Freud, Jung's formulations opened more conceptual windows into the "soul of man" than any other person. Sahakian (1969, p. 83) observed that Jung integrated the vital function of religion into the individuation process and, thus, into the world of psychology and therapy.

Jung's (1958) psychological formulations had a major impact on modern religious thought. He also made formidable contributions toward bridging the gaps between Eastern and Western therapies by the infusion of new meaning to such concepts as self-transcendence, altered states of consciousness, meditation, and mysticism (Nystul, 1993, p. 142). Clearly, Jungian theory is a therapy of the "soul." It provides something that much of humankind quests for—something transcendent and larger than the self that takes care of the "soul" and nurtures the person (Jung, 1971f).

Jungian theory is not reductionistic (that is, it does not seek to define therapeutic success structurally). Therapists and clients are therefore not bound by strict rules and mechanistic formulations. In Jungian terms, the transcendent influence, not the environment, drives and gives human intuition legitimacy, thus keeping mechanism/reductionism at bay. The approach has also been the proving ground for developing and using the MBTI as an understandable and positive way of viewing and examining the personality.

While many critics debunk Jungian psychology and therapy as a lot of "hocus-pocus" and "mumbo-jumbo," no other therapuetic modality's adherents are as willing to explore the outer limits of theory. Their romance with exotic physics and mathematics is the very way that new theory is built and turned into practice. In short, if psychotherapy is to progress, we need dreamers like the Jungians.

SHORTCOMINGS OF THE JUNGIAN SYSTEM

Probably the most notable shortcoming in the Jungian system of therapy lies in the difficulty of validating the concept of the collective unconscious. It is very difficult, if possible at all, to prove the existence and workings of the archetypes. Nystul (1993, p. 142) summarized several criticisms, noting that the metaphysical components of Jungian theory are incapable of proof and that the theory lacks the developmental concepts necessary to explain the growth of the mind.

In addition to the therapy being difficult for therapists to learn, another criticism pertains to the issue of efficiency. The therapy may be prohibitive for some clients who simply cannot afford the time and money required for attainment of therapeutic outcomes. Even the Freudians have developed brief or time-limited therapies. Also, some Jungians appear to cater to clients who have the intellect and talent to deal in symbolisms and are prone to ignore or not accept clients who are of lesser intellect or who simply need to make situational changes or behavioral adjustments. At least among some non-Jungians there are those who perceive that Jungian therapists revel in unraveling the symbols and unconscious mechanisms as an end in itself.

A major shortcoming of Jungian theory lies in the tendency of therapists to stay locked into the "big picture" with the client. They are not so much concerned with the pressing problems of the day. That is, they are not *product*-oriented but rather so *process*-oriented that everyday problems and "product" may get short shrift.

Jung got in political hot water for his alleged sympathies with National Socialism (the Nazis) and anti-Semitism in pre-World War II Europe. Although he later vilified Hitler, Jung's reluctance to speak out against the Nazis has caused much dialogue over the years—not much of it supportive of his stance (Neuman, 1991).

Jung also gets in contemporary hot-water with feminists for his rather demeaning view of women. As a result, contemporary Jungians have been kept busy doing a lot of repair work on gender differences (Hooke & Hooke, 1994).

Because of the sacrosanct nature of therapy in analytic psychology, Jungians are reluctant to give details or diagnoses to third-party insurers (Harris, 1996, p. 109). Beyond indicating the severity of the client's symptoms, the use of diagnosis is not a key component of analytic therapy (Harris, 1996, p. 137). In the current managed care climate, analytic therapy runs the risk of becoming marginalized because of its refusal to adhere to third-party insurer guidelines (Frey-Wherlin, 1993).

JUNGIAN THERAPY WITH DIVERSE POPULATIONS

The transcendent qualities engendered by the Jungian approach appeal to a wide range of clients from different cultural and ethnic backgrounds because a common thread throughout most of humanity is a need for identification with a power greater than themselves. The theory does not view psychopathology as a disease or as being deviant from some culturally derived "norm." Rather, symptoms are considered messages from the person's unconscious that something is awry and that something different is needed to bring fulfillment to the individual (Kaufmann, 1989, p. 132). According to Walker (1992) the Jungian analyst of the 1990s is fully aware of the changing nature of society and culture and, perhaps more than any other professional working in the realm of the human dilemma, is able to understand the unique psychic feelings, pressures, and needs of clients, regardless of their cultural or ethnic origins. Estes (1992) has formulated unique ways of describing the female psyche in Jungian terms. She uses multicultural myths, fairy tales, and stories in creative ways to help women and minorities reconnect with lost or unfulfilled instinctual and visionary attributes.

Jung in the original can certainly be considered sexist, but it must be remembered that what he said and felt, and how he acted toward women certainly echoed contemporary thought during the early twentieth century. Where Jung was ahead of his time is in the androgynous view he takes of the anima/animus—the male and female parts that exist within each of us.

Although Jung had little to say in regard to homosexual relationships, contemporary Jungians believe that since both sexes contain aspects of one another (anima/animus), to stereotype by gender or condemn such relationships is spurious (Schwartz-Salant & Stein, 1992).

Jungian therapy represents a kind of "tie that binds" for people who cannot conceptualize any kind of counseling devoid of a religious bent—those who need a rock of spirituality for a firm foundation; people whose religious beliefs are pre-eminent in their lives (Jung, 1958). Also, the system should have a great appeal for people who have an Eastern philosophical outlook—a need for a "yin/yang" harmony of opposing forces. Another diverse group for whom Jungian therapy should have a special appeal are those who profoundly believe in the transmission of cultural influences of ancestors. For people whose living mythology constitutes a vital and functional part of their society, Jungian analysis rings true—unlike other therapies that would dismiss mythology as "shamanism." Jungians may welcome and validate shamanism as an important component of therapy for people whose belief systems include diverse religions or mythological values (Walker, 1992).

Jungians look beyond achievement on a worldly basis and are more interested in the person's spiritual assets. In that regard, Jungians see spiritual equality in all people—due to the commonalities of their symbols and ways of approaching solutions to problems (Jung, 1971f).

Jungian therapy is not the therapy of choice for most people from lower socio-economic groups, especially those who have immediate, pressing, concrete, physical concerns. It is also not a preferred therapy among those who require solid, concrete symbols for their thinking and feeling or those whose total identification is based on defining themselves in terms of external events and environmental reinforcement.

SUMMARY

Jungian therapy, usually called analytical psychotherapy, emerged as a response and alternative to Freudian psychoanalytic psychology. Because of Jung's disenchantment with Freud's theories, Jung developed an approach that creates, by means of a symbolic approach, a dialectical relationship between consciousness and the unconscious. A prolific writer, Jung conceptualized unique formulations and workings of the conscious, personal unconscious, collective unconscious, ego, persona, self, shadow, anima/animus, complexes, and archetypes (Hall, 1977; 1989; Jung, 1954a; 1963a). The major goal of therapy is for the client to attain individuation, which is the ultimate state of reaching self-realization or personal potential. The importance of transcendence and spirituality is recognized as a part of the individuation process.

Counseling and psychotherapy is a methodical and complex process that focuses on integration of the conscious and unconscious through therapist–client collaborative exploration of the symbolic messages the unconscious may reveal to the conscious. Dream work, the core of therapy, is among the most powerful and often-used strategies for making the unconscious known to the conscious (Jung, 1963a). An important aspect of therapist–client work entails working through transference and countertransference relationships that invariably arise during the course of therapy or, as Jungians prefer to call it, "analysis."

By helping the waking (conscious) ego to integrate the total personality (unconscious + conscious), the individual can be empowered to move toward personal fulfillment. In the absence of such integration, the process of individuation is severely inhibited. Given successful analysis and integration, the person's prospects for individuation and even personal transcendence are greatly enhanced.

The inquisitive spirit of the Jungians has resulted in a somewhat unlikely marriage between analytic psychology's transcendental bent and the chaos theory of mathematics.

SUGGESTIONS FOR FURTHER READING

Campbell, J. (Ed.). (1971). *The portable Jung* (R. F. C. Hull, Trans.). New York: Penguin Books.
Harris, A. S. (1996). *Living with paradox: An introduction to Jungian psychology.* Pacific Grove, CA: Brooks-Cole.
Jung, C. G. (1933). *Modern man in search of a soul.* New York: Harcourt, Brace & World.
Jung, C. G. (1964). *Man and his symbols.* New York: Doubleday.

REFERENCES

Barton, S. (1994). Chaos, self-organization, and psychology. *American Psychologist, 49,* 5–14.
Brack, C. J., Brack, G., & Zucker, A. (1995). How chaos and complexity theory can help counselors to be more effective. *Counseling and Values, 39,* 200–208.
Brack, G. (1993, August). *Chaos theory: A critical new dimension in consultation.* Paper presented at the Annual Convention of the American Psychological Association, Toronto, Canada.
Brennan, C. (1995). Beyond theory and practice: A postmodern perspective. *Counseling and Values, 39,* 99–107.
Briggs, J. (1992). *Fractals: The patterns of chaos.* New York: Simon & Schuster.
Briggs, J., & Peat, F. D. (1989). *Turbulent mirror: An illustrated guide to chaos theory and the science of wholeness.* New York: Harper & Row.
Butz, M. R. (1992). The fractal nature of the development of the self. *Psychological Reports, 3,* (2), 1043–1063.
Butz, M. R. (1993, August). *Chaos theory and familial dynamics: What does it look like?* Paper presented at the Annual Convention of the American Psychological Association, Toronto, Canada.
Butz, M. R. (1995). Chaos theory, philosophically old, scientifically new. *Counseling and Values, 39,* 84–98.
Campbell, J. (Ed.). (1971). *The portable Jung* (R. F. C. Hull, Trans.). New York: Penguin Books.
Chamberlain, L. (1993, August). *Strange attractors in patterns of family interactions.* Paper presented at the Annual Convention of the American Psychological Association, Toronto, Canada.
Chamberlain, L. (1994, August). *Is there a chaotician in the house? Chaos and family therapy.* Paper presented at the Annual Convention of the American Psychological Association, Los Angeles, CA.
Chamberlain, L. (1995). Chaos and change in a suicidal family. *Counseling and Values, 39,* 117–128.

DeAngelis, T. (1993). Chaos, chaos everywhere is what the theorists think. *The APA Monitor, 24*(1), 1, 41.

Dehing, J. (1992). The therapist's interventions in Jungian analysis. *Journal of Analytical Psychology, 37,* 29–47.

Eiser, J. R. (1994). *Attitudes, chaos, and the connectionist mind.* Oxford, UK: Blackwell Publishers.

Estes, C. P. (1992). *Women who run with the wolves: Myths and stories of the wild woman archetype.* New York: Ballantine Books.

Ford, D. H. (1994). Humans as self-constructing living systems: A developmental perspective, behavior, and personality. (2nd ed.). State College, PA: IDEALS, Inc.

Frey-Wherlin, T. C. (1993). Widerstand und Anpassung: Die Analytische Psychologie und die Institutionen. *Analytische Psychologie, 24,* (4), 288–301.

Gilliland, B. E., & High, H. (1985, February). *Dream analysis via small peer groups.* Paper presented at the Annual Convention of the Tennessee Association for Counseling and Development. Memphis, TN.

Gleick, J. (1987). *Chaos: Making a new science.* New York: Viking Penguin.

Gleatt, H. B. (1995). Chaos and compassion. *Counseling and Values, 39,* 108–116.

Hall, C. S., & Lindzey, G. (1978). *Theories of personality* (3rd ed.). New York: John Wiley & Sons.

Hall, J. A. (1977). *Clinical uses of dreams: Jungian interpretations and enactments.* New York: Grune & Stratton.

Hall, J. A. (1989). *Jung: Interpreting your dreams—A guidebook to Jungian dream philosophy and psychology.* New York: St. Martin's Press (Cassette/booklet accompanying Audio Renaissance Tapes, Inc., Los Angeles, CA, entitled, *Jung: Interpreting your dreams*).

Hall, N. (1991). *Chaos: A guide to the new science of disorder.* New York: W. W. Norton.

Harding, W. (Producer). (1992). *LARRY.* (26-minute videotape documentary of Dr. Larry Gladwin Harding's life of chaos as a bipolar or manic depressive person.) Arvada, CO: Walking Eagle Productions, 670 West 84th Way, No. 17, Arvada, CO 80003.

Harris, A. S. (1996). *Living with paradox: An introduction to Jungian psychology.* Pacific Grove, CA: Brooks-Cole.

Hooke, W. D., & Hooke, S. L. (1994). The orthodox Jungian perspective on gender differences in consciousness: A reexamination: Erratum. *Journal of Analytical Psychology, 39*(1), 3.

Jung, C. G. (1910). The association method. *American Journal of Psychology, 21,* 219–240.

Jung, C. G. (1933). *Modern man in search of a soul.* New York: Harcourt, Brace & World.

Jung, C. G. (1954a). *The development of personality. Collected works* (Vol. 17), *Bollingen Series XX,* G. Adler, M. Fordham, & H. Read (Eds.) (R. F. C. Hull, Trans.). New York: Pantheon Books.

Jung, C. G. (1954b). *The practice of psychotherapy. Collected works* (Vol. 16), *Bollingen Series XX,* G. Adler, M. Fordham, & H. Read (Eds.) (R. F. C. Hull, Trans.). New York: Pantheon Books.

Jung, C. G. (1958). *Psychology and religion. Collected works* (Vol. 11), *Bollingen Series XX,* G. Adler, M. Fordham, & H. Read (Eds.) (R. F. C. Hull, Trans.). New York: Pantheon Books.

Jung, C. G. (1960a). *The psychogenesis of mental disease. Collected works* (Vol. 3), *Bollingen Series XX,* G. Adler, M. Fordham, & H. Read (Eds.) (R. F. C. Hull, Trans.). New York: Pantheon Books.

Jung, C. G. (1960b). *The structure and dynamics of the psyche. Collected works* (Vol. 8), *Bollingen Series XX,* G. Adler, M. Fordham, & H. Read (Eds.) (R. F. C. Hull, Trans.). New York: Pantheon Books.

Jung, C. G. (1961). *Freud and psychoanalysis. Collected works* (Vol. 4). *Bollingen Series XX*, G. Adler, M. Fordham, & H. Read (Eds.) (R. F. C. Hull, Trans.). New York: Pantheon Books.

Jung, C. G. (1963a). *Memories, dreams, reflections.* Recorded and edited by Aniela Jaffé. New York: Pantheon Books.

Jung, C. G. (1963b). *Mysterium coniunctionis. Collected works* (Vol. 4), *Bollingen Series XX*, G. Adler, M. Fordham, & H. Read (Eds.) (R. F. C. Hull, Trans.). New York: Pantheon Books.

Jung, C. G. (1964a). *Civilization in transition. Collected works* (Vol. 10), *Bollingen Series XX*, G. Adler, M. Fordham, & H. Read (Eds.) (R. F. C. Hull, Trans.). New York: Pantheon Books.

Jung, C. G. (1964b). *Man and his symbols.* New York: Doubleday.

Jung, C. G. (1966). *The spirit in man, art, and literature. Collected works* (Vol. 15), *Bollingen Series XX*, G. Adler, M. Fordham, & H. Read (Eds.) (R. F. C. Hull, Trans.). New York: Pantheon Books.

Jung, C. G. (1967). *Alchemical studies. Collected works* (Vol. 13). *Bollingen Series XX*, G. Adler, M. Fordham, & H. Read (Eds.) (R. F. C. Hull, Trans.). New York: Pantheon Books.

Jung, C. G. (1971a). Aion. In J. Campbell (Ed.), *The portable Jung* (R. F. C. Hull, Trans.) (pp. 139–162). New York: Penguin Books.

Jung, C. G. (1971b). Personality types. In J. Campbell (Ed.), *The portable Jung* (R. F. C. Hull, Trans.) (pp. 178–272). New York: Penguin Books.

Jung, C. G. (1971c). *Psychological types.* Princeton, NJ: Princeton University Press.

Jung, C. G. (1971d). The stages in life. In J. Campbell (Ed.), *The portable Jung* (R. F. C. Hull, Trans.) (pp. 3–22). New York: Penguin Books.

Jung, C. G. (1971e). The structure of the psyche. In J. Campbell (Ed.), *The portable Jung* (R. F. C. Hull, Trans.) (pp. 23–46). New York: Penguin Books.

Jung, C. G. (1971f). The transcendent function. In J. Campbell (Ed.), *The portable Jung* (R. F. C. Hull, Trans.) (pp. 273–300). New York: Penguin Books.

Kaufmann, Y. (1989). Analytical psychotherapy. In R. J. Corsini & D. Wedding (Eds.), *Current psychotherapies* (4th ed.; pp. 118–125). Itasca, IL: F. E. Peacock.

McCown, W., & Johnson, J. (1993, August). *Chaos in response to changes in family systems: Empirical findings.* Paper presented at the Annual Convention of the American Psychological Association, Toronto, Canada.

Myers, I. B., & McCaulley, M. H. (1985). *Manual: A guide to the development and use of the Myers-Briggs Type Indicator.* Palo Alto, CA: Consulting Psychologists Press.

Neuman, M. (1991). Was Jung anti-semite? *Israel Journal of Psychotherapy, 5,* 201–208.

Nystul, M. S. (1993). *The art and science of counseling and psychotherapy.* New York: Macmillan.

Peca, K. (1992, April). *Chaos theory: A scientific basis for alternative research methods in educational administration.* Paper presented at the Annual Convention of the American Educational Research Association, San Francisco, CA.

Prigogine, I. (1984). *Order out of chaos: Man's dialogue with nature.* Toronto: Bantam Books.

Read, H., Fordham, M., & Adler, G. (Eds.). (1953–1978). *Jung's collected works.* Princeton, NJ: Princeton University Press.

Rychlak, J. F. (1973). *Introduction to personality and psychotherapy: A theory construction approach.* Boston: Houghton Mifflin.

Sahakian, W. S. (Ed.). (1969). *Psychotherapy and counseling: Studies in technique.* Chicago: Rand McNally.

Samuels, A. (1985). *Jung and the post-Jungians.* London: Routledge & Kegan Paul.

Samuels, A. (1989). Analysis and pluralism: The politics of psyche. *Journal of Analytic Psychology, 34,* 33–51.

Sanford, J. S. (1984). *Evil: The shadow side of reality.* New York: Crossroad.

Schroeder, M. (1991). *Fractals, chaos, and power laws: Minutes from an infinite paradise.* New York: W. H. Freeman.

Schwartz-Salant, N., & Stein, M. (Eds.). (1992). *Chiron: Gender and soul in psychotherapy.* Wilmette, IL: Chiron.

Smith, B. D., & Vetter, H. J (1991). *Theories of personality* (2nd ed.). Englewood Cliffs, NJ: Prentice-Hall.

Spiegelman, J. M. (1989). The one and the many: Jung and the post-Jungians. *Journal of Analytic Psychology, 34,* 53–71.

Waldrop, M. (1992). *Complexity: The emerging science at the edge of order and chaos.* New York: Simon & Schuster.

Walker, W. (1992, November 16). *Jungian analysis.* (Audio Cassette Recording, 4-92). Memphis, TN: Center for Counseling and Education.

Wilbur, M. P., Kulikowich, J. M., Roberts-Wilbur, J., & Torres-Rivera, E. (1995). Chaos theory and counselor training. *Counseling and Values, 39,* 129–144.

5

PERSON-CENTERED COUNSELING

FUNDAMENTAL TENETS

History

Person-centered counseling was formulated in 1940 by Carl R. Rogers (Raskin & Rogers, 1995, p. 128.) It is an amalgam whose composition may be traced to several aspects of Rogers's life. His years growing up in a hardworking Protestant family in the rural Midwest undoubtedly had much to do with his belief in the individual's ability to be self-reliant and thereby overcome adversity. His educational background in agriculture, science, philosophy, theology, education, and psychology formed a cosmopolitan Gestalt that coalesced around the free thinking and philosophical inquiry of Union Theological Seminary; the Eastern philosophies he came in contact with in the World Federation of Christian Students in Peking; the pragmatic and phenomenological philosophy of Dewey; the scientific emphasis on precise measurement and control in psychology; and the human and common-sense approach to clinical psychology of Leta Hollingsworth at Columbia University. Rogers's wide-ranging academic background was buttressed by exposure to Freudian psychoanalytics during his year of internship at the Institute for Child Guidance (Meador & Rogers, 1979, pp. 136–140).

After receiving his doctorate at Columbia in 1931, Rogers took a position in the Child Study Department of the University of Rochester in Rochester, New York. There he came into contact with a number of Otto Rank's disciples, who confirmed and embellished many of Rogers's ideas about the relationship being the focal point of therapy. However, the fruition of what came to be known as client-centered therapy occurred when Rogers moved to Ohio State University in 1940. With the publication of *Counseling and Psychotherapy* (Rogers, 1942), Rogers's new method of psychotherapy went public (Meador & Rogers, 1979, p. 138).

Rogers's book was a benchmark in therapy. Until the 1940s the prevalent therapeutic views could be divided into two camps—those who adhered to the esoterics of the psychoanalytic view and those who ascribed to the rigor of a trait-factor approach. Rogers's ideas deviated sharply from these two camps and brought many disillusioned therapists into the new arena of nondirective therapy (Meador & Rogers, 1979, pp. 138–139).

Client-Centered Therapy (Rogers, 1951) marked the second stage of Rogers's evolution as a theorist. This book developed in depth his theory of personality, particularly in regard to self-concept and its relationship to organismic experience. Rogers also expanded his therapeutic approach from one in which the therapist only mirrored the content of the client to one in which the therapist also attempted to reflect the underlying affect of the client's words. This shift gave new and deeper meaning to accurate, empathic understanding of the client's phenomenological world (Meador & Rogers, 1979, pp. 139–140).

The third, or experiential, stage (Holdstock & Rogers, 1977, p. 128) in the evolution of the person-centered approach occurred when Rogers decided to subject his process theory to a rigorous test. In 1957 Rogers moved from the University of Chicago, where he had been working with fairly normal individuals at the university counseling center, to the University of Wisconsin, where he field-tested his ideas with hospitalized schizophrenics. The outcome of this stage brought the therapist into full partnership with the client. The counselor's feelings and self-experiencing during therapy and his or her communication of those feelings and experiences to the client added new and positive dimensions to therapeutic outcomes (Holdstock & Rogers, 1977, p. 128; Meador & Rogers, 1973, p. 123). The fourth, or person-centered stage, has been characterized by a broadening of Rogers's ideas into a variety of settings far beyond therapy (Rogers, 1969; 1970; 1972). This stage has also focused on the locus of power in the client as having implications for institutions such as schools, government agencies, and businesses (Meador & Rogers, 1973, p. 124). Also in this fourth stage, Rogers increasingly stressed the importance of counselor genuineness and the use of self in therapy (Bozarth, 1990). Renewed attention has been given to realizing the full potential of each individual and to seeing the individual not as an assemblage of discrete roles but as a holistic person, one who is greater than the sum of his or her parts (Holdstock & Rogers, 1977, p. 124). This fourth stage has continued an evolution toward greater therapist freedom to be an active partner in the relationship as long as this behavior meets the functional conditions for promoting client growth.

The current person-centered approach represents a transformation from a helper-to-client to a person-to-person relationship (Cain, 1987; Grant, 1990; Sims, 1989). The person-centered system is no longer simply a method of psychotherapy. It is a "point of view, a philosophy, an approach to life, a way of being, which fits any situation in which growth—of a person, a group, or a community—is part of the goal" (Rogers, 1980, p. ix).

Rogers has had several profound effects on the helping professions. First, his theories have been linked to improved discovery learning in education as well as self-actualization in therapy (Herlihy, 1985). Second, the person-centered approach has been largely responsible for helpers becoming more open and tending to perceive individuals as their own best experts on their feelings and their lives (Bozarth, 1985; Brent, 1984; Rogers, 1985). Third, in-service training and continuing education programs for counselors and therapists have drawn heavily on Rogerian methods (Slack, 1985). Fourth, Rogerian philosophy has taken on an eclectic flavor, encompassing such diverse applications as rehabilitation counseling (See, 1985); primary prevention in mental health (Cowen, 1985); therapy with children, adolescents, and families (Ginsberg, 1984); and enhancement of group therapy and sensitivity groups (Bozarth, 1989; Lewis, 1985; Willis, 1985).

Thus, by Rogers's death in 1987, the person-centered approach had moved from the counselor's office into the mainstream of society. It was indeed a lasting legacy to a person who had lived his philosophy in the most self-actualized way (Cain, 1987; Zimring, 1988).

Person-centered counseling constructs have evolved and somewhat expanded beyond Rogers's basic facilitative conditions of empathy, genuineness, acceptance, the self, and experience. Three examples of such evolutionary progression are that the current person-centered practice has: (1) expanded the concept of acceptance to include active and overt affirmation of the individual's uniqueness and value (Zimring, 1992)—an attribute that we believe is especially important in helping the disadvantaged and other people from diverse national, racial, cultural, socioeconomic, and lifestyle backgrounds, as well as those with disabling conditions; (2) revolutionized scientific and applied psychology's approach to the helping process (Raskin, 1992); and (3) infused a new energy into the group movement whereby person-centered concepts exert positive influences on community groups far wider than was formerly possible through strategies confined to individual counseling (Bozarth, 1992). Even so, the fundamental person-centered framework remains essentially intact. Every theory or system of helping that we know has benefited from the thoughts and works of Carl R. Rogers (Kirschenbaum & Henderson, 1989; Patterson, 1989).

Overview of Person-Centered Counseling

Person-centered counseling is an approach to helping individuals and groups based on the philosophy that a self-directed growth process follows the provision and reception of a special kind of relationship characterized by *genuineness, nonjudgmental caring,* and *empathy* (Raskin & Rogers, 1995, 1995, p. 128). *Trust* is the fundamental and pervasive concept of person-centered counseling. The foundation of Rogerian counseling is an *actualizing tendency* that is perceived to be present in every living organism. In people this actualizing tendency impels each individual to move toward the realization of his or her full potential. The focus of this chapter is on those conditions, strategies, and attitudes that encourage and promote growth in all people. The sample cases depict the important elements of empathic understanding, genuineness, respect, and caring. These attributes sound deceptively simple. In reality, they are both complex and difficult to attain.

Theory of Personality

Personality theory has not been of major concern to person-centered therapists (Meador & Rogers, 1979, p. 142); rather, the manner in which change comes about in the human personality has been the focus. Therapists have concentrated on the process of personality change instead of the causes of the person's present personality characteristics (Rogers, 1959, p. 194). However, because of the clinical application of the person-centered approach, a field theory of personality change has developed (Meador & Rogers, 1979, p. 143).

According to Rogers, each person is unique and has the ability to reach his or her full potential. Such ability and potential are seated in an innate wisdom of the organism. This inherent wisdom has been termed the *organismic valuing process*. It is through this process that an infant can evaluate what feels good (actualizing) and what does not (nonactualizing) at any given moment. Also present from birth is the actualizing tendency, which develops the individual's capabilities to maintain and enhance his or her life. This uniquely human tendency is referred to as *striving toward self-actualization* (Holdstock & Rogers, 1977, p. 132; Kirschenbaum & Henderson, 1989, p. 244; Raskin & Rogers, 1995, pp. 136–139).

As the child's awareness of his or her own being and functioning develops, the *self* and *self-concept* are formed from experiences, values, meanings, and beliefs that maintain and enhance the child and from which he or she derives a sense of "me" or "I." Included in this sense of self are the child's perceptions of relationships with others and the values he or she attaches to these perceptions (Harren, 1977). If, for example, a child constantly receives approval and affection for behaving in an assertive manner, these experiences will gradually become components of his or her self-concept. Once the self-concept is formed, the individual acquires two additional needs, which are social manifestations of the actualizing tendency— the need for positive regard from others (Holdstock & Rogers, 1977, p. 133) and the need for positive self-regard (Meador & Rogers, 1979, p. 143). Although it is initially important that the individual be liked by others, it is also eventually important that the self-worth of the individual cease to depend on consistent and continual positive regard from others (Kirschenbaum & Henderson, 1989, pp. 245–246).

Parents need to achieve a delicate balance between focusing positive attention on children but not overprotecting them or depriving them of significant relationships and allowing them to become more and more independent as maturation occurs (Holdstock & Rogers, 1977, pp. 132–133). As children grow older, experiencing hinges on their ability to both integrate and differentiate experiences— integrate in the sense that they combine external experiences with information from their own bodies, differentiate in the sense that their processing of these experiences and information into behavior leads to actualization. Such actualization can be obtained only through positive self-regard, which in turn occurs only to the extent that significant others have positive regard for them and they are cognizant of and affect that regard (Holdstock & Rogers, 1977, p. 133.) A dilemma occurs when behaviors experienced as satisfying by the child are not experienced as satisfying by others, and vice versa. Until congruence is achieved between the child and the significant others, the child cannot regard him- or herself as positive or worthwhile. When the child perceives that he or she is being valued only when behaving or feeling a certain way, what is known as a *condition of worth* becomes internalized in his or her self-concept (Holdstock & Rogers, 1977, p. 135).

As the child internalizes conditions of worth into the self-concept, he or she begins to deny or distort organismic experiences in order to continue to regard him- or herself as worthwhile. For example, Mary's parents label her as "bad" when she becomes angry, so Mary tries to suppress her anger in order to feel good about herself. She may even distort or deny her experiences so that she perceives herself as being at fault rather than letting herself experience anger. Thus, by denying and distorting experiences, children increasingly lose touch with the organismic valuing process. Their need to protect themselves from experiences that are inconsistent with their self-concept leads to a state of incongruence between self-concept and experience. This incongruence is the major concept in the person-centered view of maladjustment (Harren, 1977).

Nature of Maladjustment

Whenever an individual's perception of his or her experience is distorted or denied, a state of psychological maladjustment and vulnerability exists (Rogers, 1959, p. 226). Distortion or denial occurs when an experience is held to be incongruent with one's self-structure (Meador & Rogers, 1979, p. 148). If a young woman's concept of self includes "I am not popular with guys," she can distort the experience of obtaining a date to make it congruent with the self by stating, "He must really be terrible, awful, ugly to ask me out" or deny it by stating, "He can't really like me, and once he sees me he'll leave, vomit, tell everybody what a loser I am." The incongruence between self-concept and experience is never accurately identified by the individual (Kirschenbaum & Henderson, 1989, p. 248).

The Rogerian concept of congruence applies to the person's acting, thinking, and feeling as these states relate not only to self-concept and experience but also to perceived self and actual self. The young woman's incongruence related to her dating difficulty is an example of the first. Her incongruence between her perceived self and her actual self is exemplified in the following example.

The young woman seeking a date may believe she is gentle, homely, and socially inept and have commensurate feelings of shyness, fear, and loneliness. She might, in truth, be gentle, but not homely or socially inept. Instead of these last two characteristics she might be graceful and beautiful, which she disowns. And she might, indeed, feel lonely but not shy or fearful. These last two feelings may actually be caring and empathy, which she also disowns. When such a discrepancy exists between the actual and the perceived selves, the result is tension and internal confusion (Kirschenbaum & Henderson, 1989, pp. 248–249).

Characteristics and feelings get so commingled that "neurotic behavior" occurs. Such behavior becomes incomprehensible because it is at cross purposes with the individual's need to reduce tension. Yet the individual continues to distort the actual self in order to eliminate incongruence with experience, and as a result defenses start to break down (Meador & Rogers, 1979, pp. 145–148).

When the individual's defenses are rent asunder and the behavioral response can no longer maintain the current structure of self, then he or she becomes vulnerable to anxiety, threat, and disorganization. This debilitating state happens because the person perceives the experience with such intenseness that he or she generalizes the situation in absolute and unconditional terms, relies on vague abstractions rather than concrete reality, and is dominated by belief rather than fact (Meador & Rogers, 1979, pp. 147–149). In the case of the apprehensive woman, absolutes ("all men are threatening"), overgeneralizations ("past dates have been bad, so this one will be too"), and beliefs ("I'm a loser and always will be") get translated into anxiety ("oh, my God—it's just got to go right"), threat ("it's an hour before the date, and I'm already starting to feel a headache"), and disorganization ("I want to go out, but I already wish it was over").

Such incongruence between self-concept and experience leads to rigidity in perception and behavior and generates defenses that include rationalization, fantasy, compensation, projection, and paranoid ideation (Holdstock & Rogers, 1977, p. 136). The young woman's date becomes a self-fulfilling prophecy: it winds up being the catastrophe she expected, reinforces her experiences so that all future engagements are likely to turn out the same way, and culminates in her having even less trust in her worth than before.

In person-centered counseling there are no discrete entities such as neurosis or psychosis. Behaviors occur along a continuum and differ not in kind but only in degree of incongruence between one's self-concept and one's experience. When defensive behaviors prove less and less successful, denied aspects of experience that contradict the self-concept become more and more overwhelming. At the extreme end of this continuum is what is commonly called psychosis (Holdstock & Rogers, 1977, pp. 138–139). Attempts at adaptation and maintenance by the individual can lead to loss of the potential to develop and subsequent self-alienation. Persons may deny or change their values to fit the perceptions of others and thereby cease to function as themselves. One outcome may be that role definitions of significant others or groups are assumed to such an extent that the individual's identity is lost. The core of the individual is no longer "I am" but rather "I am an Alpha Beta Chi," "I am a woman," or "I am a professor in a prestigious university." Although such relationships allow for contact with others, taken to extremes they deny meaningful relationships with all other people and diminish the "I am." By denying experiencing in order to be accepted by others, the individual cheats him- or herself, for striving to be accepted does not guarantee acceptance. When self-concept is defined in terms of others, incongruence exists between social experience and self-concept (Holdstock & Rogers, 1977, pp. 134–136), especially when the individual is confronted by new events and the input of significant others. As a result, person-centered therapy is aimed at the incongruence individuals develop between their experiences and their self-concept (Meador & Rogers, 1979, p. 144; Raskin & Rogers, 1995, pp. 129–130).

Major Concepts

Several unique concepts exemplify the person-centered approach. The conceptual core of the approach is that human beings are essentially rational, constructive, positive, independent, realistic, cooperative, trustworthy, accepting, forward-moving, and full of potential (Rogers, 1961, pp. 90–92, 194–195). Undergirding this positive view of humankind are several major constructs (Rogers, 1959, pp. 194–212), which we have abridged for clarity:

1. *Actualizing tendency.* This is the inherent tendency of the person to develop in ways that serve to maintain or promote growth.
2. *Conditions of worth.* A person's worth is conditional when his or her self-esteem is based on significant others' valuation of experience. Experience so valued may have positive or negative connotations to the person.

3. *Congruence.* The person is congruent when there is no dissonance among his or her acting, thinking, and feeling states. Experiences are wholly integrated into the self-concept.

4. *Empathic understanding.* When a person knows, not only at a cognitive level but also at a deeper affective level, how it feels to be another person while retaining one's own autonomy, he or she has achieved empathic understanding. One perceives as if one were the other person but without ever losing the "as if" condition.

5. *Experience* (noun). Experience consists of all the cognitive and affective events within the person that are available or potentially available to his or her awareness.

6. *Experience* (verb). To experience is to receive the impact of all the sensory or physiological events happening at the present moment.

7. *Genuineness.* When a person is being genuine, there is no difference between the real and the perceived selves; the person is transparent in that there are no facades of affect or behavior.

8. *Organismic valuing process.* This is the process whereby experiences are accurately perceived, constantly updated, and valued in terms of the satisfaction experienced by the person. In this process, the person's values are never fixed or rigid. The actualizing tendency is the criterion for the person's development and maintenance of positive values.

9. *Positive regard.* Positive regard is the perception of the self-experience of another person that leads the individual to feel warmth, liking, and respect for the acceptance of that person.

10. *Positive self-regard.* Positive self-regard is a positive attitude toward the self that is not dependent on the perceptions of significant others.

11. *Self-actualization tendency.* This is the tendency toward actualization of that part of the person represented in the self. In a positive sense it is the tendency of the person to move toward achieving his or her full potential.

12. *Self-concept.* The self-concept is the person's total internal view of self in relation to the experiences of being and functioning within the environment. It includes values attached to such a view.

13. *Self-experience.* A self-experience is any event in the individual's perceptual field that he or she sees as relating to "self," "me," or "I."

14. *Unconditional positive regard.* This is the individual's perception of another person without ascription of greater or lesser worthiness to that person. It is characterized by a total rather than a conditional acceptance of the other person.

15. *Unconditional self-regard.* This is the perception of the self in such a way that no self-experience can be discriminated as being more or less worthy of positive regard than any other self-experience.

These positive constructs and the person's tendency to strive toward them are the necessary and sufficient condition for the freeing of the individual's capacity to move toward self-actualization (Bozarth, 1991a; Patterson, 1986, pp. 389–393; Raskin & Rogers, 1995, p. 137). Only in the absence of such conditions is it necessary to provide external control of the individual (Rogers, 1959, p. 221).

THE COUNSELING PROCESS

The central focus of counseling is the client's experiencing of feelings (Kirschenbaum & Henderson, 1989, pp. 239–240). Because the process is not problem-centered, goal-centered, or behavior-centered, many individuals have difficulty understanding its values, rationale, or operational focus. Students of counseling sometimes demonstrate this difficulty by asking questions such as "How can I help this person if I don't even know what the problem is?" "What can I do for this client if he doesn't know what he wants to do?" or "What do I do when the client doesn't even state a problem?" These questions may be clarified by viewing person-centered counseling from the perspective of the client as well as that of the counselor.

The Client's Perspective

In the initial phases of counseling, clients typically exhibit a variety of attitudes, feelings, and characteristics: (1) they are apprehensive about the counselor, the counseling itself, and/or the wisdom of participating in counseling; (2) their feelings about much of their life experiences are often either unrecognized or unexpressed; (3) they are often unaware of their manner of experiencing and are distant from the meanings of their experiences; (4) their evaluation of their behaviors, attitudes, and feelings may be oriented toward societal codes, moral admonitions, and other people's values; (5) they may exhibit overt or covert negativism, anxiety, self-doubt, and blaming of others; (6) they may have difficulty accepting responsibility for themselves but, paradoxically, may be striving to assume responsibility for others; (7) they frequently view the world in a somewhat mechanical fashion, making it difficult to separate objects from experiences, feelings from facts, and external situations from beliefs about such situations; (8) they may find expressing ownership of difficulties and emotions particularly threatening.

As clients successfully move through counseling, their attitudes, feelings, and perceptions move forward along a continuum. This movement is characterized by (1) feeling less apprehensive about the counseling, the counselor, and their own participation; (2) beginning to recognize and express previously denied feelings and moving toward a more open, honest mode of communication; (3) gradually gaining awareness of inner experiencing and eventually being able to live freely and to accept the process of experiencing; (4) moving from a locus of evaluation and valuing outside themselves toward evaluation and valuing that is consistently owned and internalized; (5) diminishing negativism, anxiety, self-doubt, and blaming of others in favor of optimism, calmness, self-acceptance, and constructive or realistic responses to what others say or do; (6) accepting responsibility for behaviors or choices and, with increasing comfort, ceasing to feel responsible for the acts and choices of others; (7) making sharper distinctions between objects and experiences and becoming more able to separate feelings from facts and external situations from beliefs; and (8) expressing ownership of difficulties and emotions with greater ease, openness, and assurance (Rogers, 1965).

The Counselor's Perspective

Person-centered counselors strive to approach the client's world without preconceived notions. They know in advance that their clients are more likely to experience and make positive gains if the client–counselor relationship is one of mutual trust, acceptance, and spontaneity. If counseling is to be of optimum value to clients, counselors will (1) experience inner freedom and congruence and exhibit a willingness for clients to do the same; (2) impose no external values or standards on clients; (3) endeavor to be genuine in their relationships with clients; (4) listen and respond to clients and communicate empathy; (5) communicate through their words, voice, and nonverbal behavior their acceptance, understanding, respect, and prizing of the clients as people; (6) see a new, exciting, positive venture in each new client relationship; (7) endeavor to communicate unconditional positive regard toward clients; (8) trust that their congruence shows; (9) communicate to clients that they are *accurately* and *fully* hearing their verbal messages as well as their nonverbal cues and messages; (10) ensure that their own verbal and nonverbal responses reflect an accurate understanding of clients' feelings and messages; (11) communicate to clients that they trust them to be responsible, self-directing persons; and (12) nurture the conditions (the climate) wherein clients can experiment with new behaviors (Kirschenbaum & Henderson, 1989, pp. 239–240).

The Conditions of Growth

There are three main conditions for promoting psychological growth: *genuineness, unconditional positive regard,* and *empathic understanding* (Raskin & Rogers, 1995, pp. 128–138).

Genuineness

For Rogers, a key component to genuineness is being *transparent.* Transparency means that there are no pretensions about what the counselor is or does. There is no hiding behind a professional demeanor or a false front of personal superiority. What the client sees is what the client gets, with no hidden innuendos, no retreat into psychological jargon, and no defenses to hide counselor inadequacies. The counselor presents him- or herself as he or she is at that moment, with all of the flux and flow of feeling, thought, and behavior that transpires in the relationship. Thus, being transparent means being *congruent.* Counselors who are congruent are clearly cognizant of what they are experiencing between their gut (feeling) and their head (thinking), how the two blend together in awareness, and how that awareness is expressed to the client as a presentation of their total personhood and investment in the therapeutic moment (Rogers, 1977, pp. 9–10). As Rogers (1969) states, "When I can accept the fact that I have deficiencies, many faults, make lots of mistakes, and am often ignorant when I should be knowledgeable, often prejudiced when I should be open-minded, often have feelings which are not justified by the circumstances, then I can be much more real" (p. 228).

Genuineness means that the counselor opens him- or herself to the emotive experience that takes place in the counseling relationship. Warmth and compassion when the client is in distress, anger when the client is assailed by overpowering forces, boredom when the client is mired down, and fear when the client re-acts destructively toward the counselor or others—these are some of the emotional hallmarks that describe the counselor who acts genuinely. The more the counselor can be aware of and give voice to these feelings, whether positive or negative, the more likely it is that therapy will move forward (Rogers, 1977, pp. 9–10).

Owning such feelings is the height of genuineness and takes a special kind of courage and tenacity of purpose not easily attained. It would be far easier for the counselor to pronounce judgments that would put the client on the defensive than to own feelings that might make him- or herself vulnerable. Yet any judgments about the client are immediately debatable, no matter how "expert," and mark the counselor as incongruent with the client's needs in the therapeutic moment. Owning feelings needs to be tempered by judicious use. The therapeutic encounter is the client's time, and not a platform for the counselor to vent his or her frustrations, inadequacies, and irritation over unjust treatment the client has encountered and life in general. Through temperate and well-timed and targeted owning statements, the counselor provides a living model for the client to take a risk by responding in more congruent and genuine ways and to feel safe in doing so. The extent to which the counselor is deeply in touch with his or her own feelings and attitudes and expresses them in deeply felt ways to the client is the extent to which therapy will be facilitated (Rogers, 1977, pp. 11–12).

Unconditional Positive Regard

Words such as *prizing, acceptance,* and *caring* are synonymous with an attitude that is positive toward the client. Easily said, unconditional positive regard is far more difficult to demonstrate. At any given time, the counselor needs to be willing to accept the confusion, fear, anger, resentment, courage, sorrow, and multiplicity of other feelings the client may have. Such caring is total and nonpossessive and lacks prior conditions of rightness or appropriateness of the client's feelings. It conveys to the client that the counselor is willing for him or her to legitimately be whatever he or she is at that time. Unconditional positive regard is not an all-encompassing, all-loving approach to the client, nor is it something the counselor "should" do. No one, including the counselor, feels such unconditional caring for everyone all the time. Tempered with genuineness, unconditional positive regard needs to be reasonably frequent in therapy. Research indicates that the more it is present, the more likely therapy will be successful, and the less it is present, the less likely there will be constructive change in the client (Rogers, 1977, pp. 10–11).

Empathic Understanding

Seeing through the client's eyes, walking in the client's shoes, and feeling both the agony and the ecstasy of the client describe empathic understanding. Empathy is realized by the counselor's ability accurately and sensitively to enter into the inner, private world of the client and experience at the deepest levels what the client is feeling. Moment by moment the counselor adapts, comprehends, encounters, and mirrors the client's feeling state.

To be empathic, the counselor must walk an emotional tightrope, moving delicately within the client's realm of experiencing without being *judgmental* or *sympathetic*. Empathy becomes judgmental when the counselor not only reflects the client's feeling state but also applies his or her own emotional yardstick in measuring its appropriateness for the client. Such evaluations do little to convey empathic understanding and a lot to put the client in a closed, defensive posture. Sympathy is equally problematic. Sympathy goes beyond empathy in that the counselor not only feels the emotional state of the client but also assumes that state! Whether consumed with the client's depression or indignant at the way significant others have dealt with the client, the counselor who shows sympathy presents only a facade of understanding. What sympathy really demonstrates is the inability of the counselor to come to grips with the emotion-laden content the client presents and probably says more about the counselor's feelings of inadequacy than the client's.

To be empathic, the counselor must not only sense meanings of which the client may scarcely be aware, but also must not precipitously confront such unconscious feelings, since to do so would be extremely threatening and convey the exact opposite of what empathy means. Empathic understanding means checking frequently with the client to validate perceptions and not being paralyzed by the content the client presents or the meaning of that content for the client. To engage in this balancing act, the counselor needs to be able to look with unfrightened eyes at the fearful things the client sometimes sees. In a sense it means laying aside oneself for the moment, and to do this the counselor must be very secure in stepping out of him- or herself into the sometimes frightening world of the client (Rogers, 1980, pp. 142–143).

By pointing out to the client in tentative terms the possible meaning in what he or she may be experiencing, the counselor provides linchpins to anchor the client's feelings more firmly, bring those feelings to awareness, and allow the client to experience them more fully. Empathic understanding, then, is a complex, strong, and demanding attribute but is also a subtle and gentle way of being in the therapeutic moment (Rogers, 1980, pp. 142–143).

From the 1940s until his death, Rogers articulated the importance of empathy in all human endeavors. Today this fundamental condition of therapeutic movement—indeed of all human relationships—is just as important.

Reciprocity

Encompassing all three of these conditions of psychological growth is reciprocity in the therapeutic relationship. As clients experience genuineness, unconditional positive regard, and empathy in response to even the most hideous aspects of their lives, they begin to experience prizing, caring, and acceptance of themselves; are able to drop defensive facades; and more openly experience themselves as individuals with self-actualizing abilities and unconditional self-regard (Patterson, 1990a; Rogers, 1977, p. 12; Rogers, 1986).

STRATEGIES FOR HELPING CLIENTS

In person-centered counseling the relationship is of the essence: it is the beginning, the main event, and the end. It is important that the client–counselor relationship be one of safety and mutual trust. Even difficult (involuntary) clients who are alienated and highly resistant can be successfully helped by the person-centered counselor. Patterson's (1990a) research demonstrated that such resistive clients—who experience the persistent offering of the core conditions (of empathy, genuineness, and acceptance) by a skilled person-centered counselor—can profit from counseling and make positive change. Once an atmosphere of safety and trust exists, the probability that a facilitative relationship can be developed is greatly enhanced (Bozarth, 1990; Rogers, 1965; 1977; 1980; 1986).

Since person-centered counseling is essentially a "being" and relationship-oriented approach, it is important to note than Rogerian strategies for helping people are devoid of techniques that involve doing something to or for the client. There are no steps, techniques, or tools for inducing the client to make measured progress toward some goal; instead, the strategies are geared to experiential relationships. They occur in the here and now and permit both client and counselor to "live" and experience an ongoing process (Kirschenbaum & Henderson, 1989, pp. 60–152). Rather than intellectualize about the client's concerns, the counselor deals directly with the client's deep concerns of the moment. Person-centered strategies mainly emphasize the three conditions for psychological growth, which are initiated by the counselor. These strategies may be described as follows.

Facilitating Empathic Understanding

As we have seen, empathic understanding means perceiving the world from the client's point of view and communicating these perceptions to the client. Some major counseling strategies that facilitate empathic understanding include attending, verbally communicating empathic understanding, nonverbally communicating empathic understanding, and using silence (Cormier & Cormier, 1991, pp. 74–78; Raskin & Rogers, 1995, pp. 142–143).

Attending

The counselor cannot achieve empathic understanding without attending to the client in a way that can be sensed by the client from the beginning. Counselor attention to the client involves both an attitude and a skill. Effective counselors put aside their own concerns while focusing fully on the concerns of the client—without sacrificing their own identity and uniqueness.

Facial expressions and body posture tell the client whether the counselor's mind is attuned to what the client is saying and feeling. An appropriate amount of nodding (of agreement or encouragement), eye contact, smiling, mirroring the client's mood, seriousness of expression, genuine interest in the client, and deep concern communicates the counselor's attentiveness. The posture of the counselor communicates whether he or she is relaxed, respectful, uneasy, bored, acceptant, anxious, puzzled, tired, or receptive regarding the client's concerns. Appropriate facial attentiveness and body posture can instill in the client a sense of the counselor's degree of involvement, sincerity, commitment, and trust. On the other hand, too much eye contact, smiling, mirroring, and nodding are as negative as the absence of, or too little of, these behaviors. Too much nodding or constant eye contact, to the point of a "stare-down" gaze, may increase the client's uneasiness with the relationship, especially if the client feels distrustful or threatened to begin with.

The physical distance between client and counselor is important. Many clients feel out of contact with a counselor who insists on sitting behind a desk. The client may interpret the desk as the counselor's way of keeping the client a safe distance away or as a condescending gesture (Hall, 1966). Generally, clients and counselors feel better about the interview if they are in comfortable, informal surroundings with no furniture between them. Attentiveness is enhanced when the counselor is facing the client at the distance that is most comfortable to the client. Some clients feel uneasy, threatened, and "hovered over" if the counselor sits too close. The counselor must be sensitive to the personal and cultural variances of clients so that the distance will facilitate rather than distract from the interview.

Voice qualities—modulation, tone, pitch, smoothness, diction, enunciation, and variation (absence of monotone)—tell the client an enormous amount about the attentiveness of the counselor. Choosing words that reflect the client's cultural background and value system helps communicate understanding, as well as acceptance, to the client. To the visually handicapped or the vision-impaired client, voice quality is the major criterion for judging the counselor's attention.

Many clients come to counseling with feelings of vulnerability, apprehension, fear, caution, or uncertainty. The counselor who cultivates the attitude and the skill of attending can allay these negative feelings. The counselor who focuses totally on the client enters the client's world quickly and empathically and thereby increases the chances of freeing the client to be genuine in the relationship. Effective attending is unobtrusive. The counselor who attends naturally does not call attention to that skill.

Verbally Communicating Empathic Understanding

Empathic understanding means understanding the client's affective and cognitive messages and then letting him or her know that these feelings and thoughts have been accurately understood at the surface level and at a deeper level. At the surface level the counselor limits verbal communication to restating or reflecting what the client has communicated. For example:

CL: I am pretty low after that test. I didn't think I'd do that badly.

CO: You're feeling disappointed about the test. (restatement)

At a deeper level of empathic responding, the counselor understands and communicates the inferred, implied, or deeper meaning. For example:

CO: You're feeling surprised and disappointed about how you did on the test, especially since you were expecting more of yourself. (reflection of a deeper meaning)

The first response is considered minimally helpful; the latter response is considered more facilitative because it makes the client aware of a wider perspective and a deeper personal meaning. Whereas the first response leaves the client at the "disappointed" or "victim" state of awareness, the latter places self-expectation—something the client was barely aware of and initially only implied—at the forefront, where the client can now grasp and deal with it. The counselor used what Egan (1975, pp. 134–135) describes as *advanced accurate empathy*. This is not to imply that the counselor should pursue a "fishing expedition" responsiveness, hoping to hit upon the client's hidden motives. Rather, it implies that the counselor attends to the total client, that he or she is fully attuned to all the verbal and nonverbal cues and subtle messages of the client.

Facilitative verbal communication must focus on the client's current affective and cognitive content. Thus the counselor deals *directly with* the client's concerns and is not lured into talking *about* the client's situation. The following dialogue illustrates this important distinction:

CL: My parents just don't trust me. I can never do anything right, according to them!

CO: Your parents don't have any confidence in you—there are many parents like that. (*talking about the situation*)

CO: You're feeling hurt and angry with your parents because you really would like for your parents to show confidence in you—you really would like to prove to them and to yourself that you can do things right. (*dealing with the client's concerns*)

The latter response is better because it focuses right where it should—on the client, facilitating self-exploration—rather than on the parents, who are not present. Also, the second response leaves the next communication squarely up to the client.

Nonverbally Communicating Empathic Understanding

Empathic understanding involves accurately interpreting both nonverbal and verbal messages and cues, which the client and counselor continuously emit. Nonverbal messages may be transmitted through a number of recognizable ways— posture, body movement, body position, facial expression, smiles, frowns, wrinkled forehead, biting of the lip, rate of body movement (quick or slow), gestures, voice quality (tone, pitch, volume, rate), use of hands, use of legs and feet, eye contact, eyebrow gestures, and so on. Omissions, unspoken messages, and the observed energy level of the body also transmit cues. Even the placement of furniture affects social and personal distance and understanding. A client who chooses the seat farthest from the counselor, for example, may be communicating discomfort or distrust. It is important for counselors to observe and be sensitive to clients' nonverbal cues as well as their own nonverbal messages to clients. We can transmit and interpret nonverbal cues such as puzzlement, fear, anger, joy, exhaustion, doubt, avoidance, rejection, and embarrassment through many different body messages. Although the interpretation of nonverbal cues is by no means perfect, attentiveness to those cues in the context of the words being spoken does contribute enormously to our understanding of the affective and cognitive messages of the client (Cormier & Cormier, 1991, pp. 21–24; Cormier & Hackney, 1987, pp. 35–64; Hall, 1966: Knapp, 1978).

Silence as a Way of Communicating Empathic Understanding

In many instances in counseling "silence is golden." There comes a time when both counselor and client are busy thinking about what has been said and observed. No words are needed (Raskin & Rogers, 1995, p. 142). Indeed, words might be intrusive at that moment. The observant counselor senses when the client is meaningfully processing feelings or information. Therefore, silence as a strategy can be a deeply empathic response. It communicates to the client, "I see and sense that we need time to deal with this; I respect your ability to handle it, and I'm right here to support you whenever you're ready to continue." Here is an example of the use of silence to communicate empathic understanding:

CL: It's just like he told me—that he can count on one hand the number of times I've told him that I love him.

CO: You feel badly because you perceive that he is hurt because you don't often use the words "I love you."

CL: Yes, but . . . (*three minutes of thoughtful silence*) All right, I don't want to hurt him. But I don't know that I love him—he insists, "It's got to be love." (*Thirty seconds of silence*) Sometimes it's like he's no different from my mother. I feel like I've just got to get away—out on my own for a while.

CO: You don't know what you want, but you believe that what you've got now is not what you want.

CL: (*Two minutes of thoughtful silence*) It all goes back to when I was a child. I was a spoiled brat. I got everything I wanted. I wanted this—I got it; I wanted to date that guy—I dated him. I don't want to date him any more! (*Thirty seconds of silence*) I always did what my mother wanted. I even married when she wanted me to. (*Thirty seconds of silence*) That's just immaturity! I guess I'm just a thirty-two-year-old kid who never grew up!

The periods of silence were not uncomfortable to either client or counselor. The two were deeply in contact with each other—fully sensitive to the nonverbal cues, which were perhaps more powerful than the verbal ones.

Once the client understands that the counselor is comfortable with and accepts the silence, he or she is encouraged to explore more openly. The client senses that the counselor has no need or desire to direct the topic, tone, or focus. Some silent behavior tends to give more emphasis to what the counselor communicates verbally. Also, the modeling effect of empathic silence by the counselor may be to prompt the client to take more time to reflect.

Communicating Genuineness

Egan's (1975) system of helping skills was derived from Rogerian theory. According to Egan, the communication of genuineness includes:

1. *Freedom from roles.* Being role-free means that the counselor is genuine in life as well as in the therapeutic relationship, that he or she is professional without hiding behind a professional role, and is congruent in experiencing and communicating feelings (p. 91).
2. *Spontaneity.* The spontaneous person communicates freely, with tact and without constantly weighing what to say. Counselors who are spontaneous behave freely, without being impulsive or inhibited, and are not rule or technique bound. Their verbal expression and behavior are based in self-confidence (p. 92).

3. *Nondefensiveness.* The genuine person is also nondefensive. Counselors who behave nondefensively know about their strong and weak areas and how they feel about them. Therefore, they can be open to negative client expressions without feeling attacked. They try to understand this negative expression and facilitate the exploration of it rather than defending themselves (pp. 92–93).
4. *Consistency.* Genuine people have few discrepancies between what they think, feel, and espouse and how they actually behave. For example, counselors behaving genuinely would not think one thing about a client and tell him or her something else, nor would they espouse one value and then act contrary to this value (pp. 93–94).
5. *Sharing of self.* The genuine person willingly self-discloses when appropriate. Thus, counselors behaving genuinely will allow clients and others to know them through open verbal and nonverbal expression of their feelings (p. 94).

A segment from an interview illustrates genuineness in the counseling relationship. The setting was a class in counseling techniques. The client, in a modeling situation, was angry at the professor (who was the counselor). The client readily volunteered to be counseled in the fishbowl.

CL: You cut me off the other day, before I even had a chance to ask you to be my chairman. You threw up the excuse of having too many advisees already. I resented that! You're supposed to be warm, accepting, and understanding!

CO: I can see that you are angry at me because my behavior didn't fit your idea of how I should respond to you.

CL: How can you explain acting like such a caring person here in class and being so callous toward me before I even got a chance to explain my situation?

CO: You see my behavior as inconsistent and maybe hypocritical.

CL: That's right. And at this point I wouldn't ask you to serve as my chairman even if you were the last person in this department.

CO: I'm sorry you feel that way. It seems to me that I'd be in a double bind—and perhaps you would be too—if I tried to chair your committee at this point.

The counselor refused to accept the gauntlet thrown down or to engage in excuses or defenses. By being nondefensive, consistent between thoughts and actions, and owning feelings, he was able to remain free from the manipulative ploys of the client. By owning feelings in a nonthreatening way the counselor let the client know that while the situation may not have been resolvable, the client was still valued as a person and could trust the counselor to be congruent and genuine.

Communicating Unconditional Positive Regard

The third fundamental condition of counselor behavior is the communication of unconditional positive regard to the client. As we have seen, this condition has been variously termed *acceptance, respect, caring,* and *prizing.* Egan (1975) refers to unconditional positive regards as *respect* and states that it is an active value of the high-functioning helper. According to Egan, respect can be communicated in several ways by the counselor's perceived orientation to the client: being "for" a client because of the client's basic humanity and potential for growth; committing oneself to work with the client; supporting the client as a unique individual and helping to develop this uniqueness; believing in the client's potential for self-direction; and assuming the client is committed to change (pp. 95–96). These five attitudes can become operational in the counseling relationship if the counselor engages in the following four behaviors (pp. 97–98):

1. Giving quality attention to the client's concerns and feelings;
2. Communicating a nonevaluative attitude toward the client as a person worthy of genuine care;
3. Responding to the client with accurate empathy and, as a result, communicating an understanding of the client's frame of reference;
4. Cultivating the client's resources and thus demonstrating to the client his or her own potential and capabilities for action.

The following counseling segment provides an example of acceptance. The client's presenting problem was her loss of an extended lesbian relationship.

CL: I've debated, inside of me, a long time—whether to share this with you. I have some apprehension—as to how you'll view my love life with my girlfriend.

CO: You're feeling some anxiety over whether I can fully accept your style of love life.

CL: Yes. (*pause*) Even now, I'm wondering if you think I'm strange or abnormal—I'm wondering whether I should be discussing this with you.

CO: I sense the great risk you're taking with me. My real concern is helping you deal with your inner feelings and choices—my esteem of you isn't based on your sexual orientation or lifestyle.

The counselor's words and body language communicated an openness to accepting and valuing the client as a person and were a catalyst for moving the counseling relationship forward. The counselor's accepting response focused on the client's real concerns rather than on the counselor's attitudes about her sexual orientation. The segment reminds us that the act of communicating acceptance must be free from any form of judgment or condescension. The counselor should accept and affirm the client as a person of worth, regardless of the client's personal orientation or lifestyle (Kirschenbaum & Henderson, 1989, pp. 20–23).

SAMPLE CASES

Case of Jackie, Age Thirty

Even though the following transcript cannot convey voice tones, facial expressions, gestures, and other nonverbal dimensions, it illustrates the style, technique, and process that the typical person-centered counselor displays.

CL: Sometimes I think I must be crazy to put up with what I've gone through. I lived through hell. I could tell you some tales. Nobody would believe it! It would make a good book if anyone would believe it! (laughter) I've paid my dues—still paying for it.

CO: You're kind of amazed that you got through it. And now, you're ready to put the frightful mess behind you.

CL: Yeah. I must have been some kind of nut to stay in it that long. (*pause*) You know, I lived with that man twelve years—and all the time him treating me like shit. He didn't care about me. He didn't know me—not really . . . I knew him though. When they made him, they threw the mold away. He had a brilliant mind—about some things. But he was sure dumb about me. (*pause*) I had three kids by him and he didn't even know who I was. Have you ever heard of such a crazy thing? (*laughter*) I don't know why I put up with it. (*pause*) Yeah I do. Religion! Family! My mother! I was just as stubborn as a mule. For a long time, I thought I'd rather die than get divorced.

CO: Even though it's over, you're still feeling an awful lot of emotion—you'd even like to know why you did what you did. I gather from your tone of voice that you are rather pleased with yourself for having the strength to do what you felt you had to do.

CL: It was do or die. You never know what you can do until put to the test. (*laughter*) Well, something had to give. Things kept getting progressively worse. His drinking was getting worse and worse. It was always bad. But I knew I had done all I could do. He couldn't accept help, and the kids were beginning to suffer, I knew it would be rough. I didn't have a job. (*laughter*) To think I was such a kid when I married him—I was just sixteen. I didn't have a dab of sense. (*laughter*)

CO: Your voice communicates anger and regret. But I'm feeling confused about all the laughter that's coming out.

CL: Hmm . . . I guess it's to keep from crying. I guess I've felt like crying for so many years that I've just learned to cover it up with laughter. (*tears; very long pause*) I just hope I can get over it. I've got these three kids to raise all by myself, and I've got to finish the LPN course. I've come this far. It's not easy, but my God! All I've got to do is look back at where I've been. I've got my job at the supermarket—and I've got a roof over my head—and I'm doing okay in school—and I'm rid of the S.O.B. I guess I don't have much time to feel sorry for myself.

CO: It sounds like you're realizing what a great responsibility rests on your shoulders and that, even though you're not very happy, you're betting on yourself to pull through.

CL: Uh-hmm. (*long pause*) We had our first test on clinical nursing practice today! I was scared to death. I knew I had studied. But I was scared! (*pause*) When we got our evaluations in staffing this afternoon my instructor looked at me and said, "Jackie, you did well!" I liked to have fainted. I made ninety-two.

In the case of Jackie, a divorced mother, the person-centered counselor was attending to the verbal and nonverbal messages—including what appeared to be laughter at inappropriate times. This client was a prolific talker and was also silent for periods of time. These silences were perceived by the counselor to be periods of fruitful processing. Therefore, the counselor did not interrupt or vocally call attention to the silence.

The counselor's response to the laughter ("Your voice communicates anger and regret. But I'm feeling confused about all the laughter that's coming out") demonstrated that the counselor owned the feeling of confusion and also allowed the client to explore herself at a deeper level of understanding. This was a typical person-centered response. A response such as "Why are you laughing at such unfunny things?" could have been perceived as judgmental and might have damaged the relationship.

Case of Vernon, Age Twelve

The case of Vernon, a very obese sixth grader who was addicted to candy, depicts person-centered counseling with a different kind of client.

CL: (*sits down in chair; slumps; hangs head; looks at floor; doesn't look at counselor or speak*)

CO: Hi, Vernon. I'd like to know what's troubling you.

CL: (*doesn't speak; doesn't look up; shrugs*)

CO: I'd like to understand what that means—what you're really saying to me when you shrug your shoulders.

CL: (*doesn't look up; doesn't move*) Don't matter. Don't nobody care anyhow. (*low, mumbled voice*)

CO: You're feeling alone, that there's just no use going into it—no one can or will do anything that shows they care.

CL: (*glances up, briefly makes eye contact, then resumes looking down; remains slumped*) I didn't want to come in here anyhow. Why don't they just leave me alone? (*low, mumbled voice*)

CO: You don't want to be here. You'd like for people to get off your case—to just forget all about you.

CL: (*glances up again, briefly makes eye contact; then looks down again; remains slumped*) Ain't no use bothering about me. Nobody cares about me.

CO: You feel isolated, that no one cares about you. You believe that things would be better if there was just *one person* in the world who sincerely cared about Vernon.

CL: (*glances up, longer this time, then lowers head*) Ain't got no friends. Everybody hates me.

CO: You're really feeling lonely and abandoned. You wish you had *some* friends.

CL: (*not looking up; eyes getting teary; very long silence*)

CO: It's just so unpleasant to be all alone—to have no friends at all—and to wish that someone would treat you right.

CL: (*glances up briefly; looks down*) Everybody just laughs and pokes fun at me.

CO: And that just makes you feel negative toward yourself. But what you really want, down deep inside, is someone who cares about you—someone who will accept you as the person you are—without putting you down or judging you in any way.

CL: (*looks up, makes eye contact, looks away, but does not look down this time*) They keep calling me names. They all call me names. Some of them call me "Fatso," some call me "Blimp"; some call me "Hippo." They do it in the bathroom; they do it in the halls; they do it in the lunchroom. They all laugh. That's what burns me up.

CO: It sounds like you're feeling angry at others because of the names they call you, and maybe you're a little dissatisfied with yourself for putting up with it. Frankly, it makes me a little angry to discover that you're being treated this way, too. Let's you and me look at some things you and I can do to improve on the way people are speaking to you.

Here we see the counselor dealing with an unwilling and, at first, noncommunicative client. There is also evidence that the counselor is attempting to nurture a growth-promoting climate. The genuine and accepting statement "Frankly, it makes me a little angry to discover that you're being treated this way, too" does not judge the client, his tormentors, or the school. It communicates to the client that the counselor is involved. Also, the counselor's anger at the disrespectful treatment of the client was a real part of the relationship and deserved to be openly admitted. That the counselor was genuine and empathic and communicated these qualities served as a model for the client and probably represented a growth-promoting factor for Vernon. As we have noted, we make a sharp distinction between empathy and sympathy. Sympathy is rarely helpful to a client. If the counselor had said "That's terrible! They shouldn't be treating you this way!" such a sympathetic statement might have encouraged Vernon to continue to feel sorry for himself and to ruminate, and it might have distracted him from examining viable alternatives for himself.

CONTRIBUTIONS OF THE PERSON-CENTERED SYSTEM

The person-centered system has made several notable contributions to counseling and psychotherapy. For one thing, it is applicable to a wide variety of helping situations and settings—individual counseling, group counseling, family counseling, classroom learning, and supervision in education, business, hospitals, clinics, and government. Another strength is that the person-centered counselor consciously avoids taking responsibility for decision making by clients. Therefore, clients come to realize that they are responsible for making their decisions and consequently may develop a feeling of personal power. As Rogers (1977) noted, power "is politically centered in the client" (p. 14). This is a crucial point in facilitating the development of independence in the client.

Person-centered counseling has a history of encouraging inquiry, hypothesis testing, and investigation of its tenets and its outcomes (Bozarth, 1991b; Patterson, 1990b). As a result, the system is supported by a large body of research conducted over a long period. The theory is healthy today because of this research. Person-centered researchers have overcome criticism from detractors by developing effective ways to assessing client progress.

The person-centered approach has done much to remove the helping process from the exclusive control of highly trained professionals and make it understandable and usable to all people. The fundamental conditions of genuineness, empathic understanding, and unconditional positive regard can be understood and used successfully at some level by any person. The simplicity and under-standability of the person-centered approach do not diminish its effectiveness or validity. It is a system that is strengthened by both public and professional use and is therefore a highly "democratic" system of helping. Power, authority, or control over the client is missing; the personal power, autonomy, responsibility, and inner strength of the client are seen as curative outcomes in themselves (Kirschenbaum & Henderson, 1989; Raskin & Rogers, 1995; Raskin, 1992).

Another contribution of the person-centered approach has been to elevate the importance of *listening, caring* and *understanding* in counseling and in the training of counselors, psychologists, social workers, and other professionals. Listening, responding, and relating skills are part of most helping endeavors and the train-ing of helpers largely because of the influence of Rogerian principles. In short, the core skills of helping (Carkhuff, 1969a; 1969b; Cormier & Cormier, 1979; 1985; 1991; Cormier & Hackney, 1987; Egan, 1975; 1982; 1986; Hackney & Cormier, 1979; Ivey, 1988) have roots in the person-centered movement.

SHORTCOMINGS OF THE PERSON-CENTERED SYSTEM

One of the principal shortcomings of the person-centered approach is a deficiency not of the theory itself but rather in the way it is sometimes applied. Some coun-selors misunderstand or misuse the theory at the practical level. Many practition-ers who understand the principles (or think they understand) and philosophically agree with them (or think they agree) have difficulty in effectively applying them. As a result, one frequently hears statements such as "It's a good theory, but it won't work with clients in our setting." Even though the individuals who make such statements are speaking in earnest, their difficulty may lie in a subtle need on their part to control clients, a desire to manage or do for clients, or some insti-tutional practice that limits person-centered relating. Even with much training and modeling, some counselors and therapists find that the system is not con-gruent with their own beliefs of behavior. In other words, they may find that it is not a part of their being to experience the process, even though they have a thor-ough knowledge of the principles involved.

Another possible drawback is that the counselor's own identity may become obscured through deep involvement with clients. This is particularly true of helpers who have strong feelings for their clients. They may tend to submerge their own feelings and concerns into those of their clients and thereby lose some of their own identity and objectivity. Such counselors may become overinvolved with clients and their problems—a situation that is detrimental to their clients as well as to themselves.

A frequent criticism of the person-centered approach is that the counselor is too easily manipulated. This criticism relates to both of the shortcomings just dis-cussed. If the practitioner limits interaction to listening and reflecting, some clients will either manipulate or discount him or her. Some clients may be helped simply by experiencing a relationship with a listening and reflective helper; others may not. The counselor who has a total grasp of the system and brings to the encounter the necessary experiential background and personal qualities is more likely to be helpful. Otherwise, manipulation and ineffectiveness in facilitating client growth may be valid concerns.

Another criticism of the person-centered approach is that it may be adequate for "healthy" clients, but what about the more severely disturbed clients or clients with less-than-normal intelligence? Although Rogers (1967) and others have reported the use of person-centered counseling with schizophrenic clients, we believe that the approach is least effective with those clients whose contact with reality, ability to communicate, and intellectual functioning are at the lower end of the scale.

Another shortcoming of the person-centered system is the possible tendency of the counselor—especially the inexperienced counselor or the one who does not fully understand the system—selectively to attend to and reflect the client's self-defeating statements. Though not a flaw in the system itself, it is a vulnerable point. After accurate reflection of the client's dilemmas—what then? Do clients simply leave with the understanding that their dilemmas are genuine? This perceived lack of technique to get clients moving out of their negative feelings—the perceived lack of concrete steps for them to take—is one of the most frequent criticisms of the person-centered system.

PERSON-CENTERED COUNSELING WITH DIVERSE POPULATIONS

The person-centered system adheres to several conceptual formulations (Patterson, 1996; Zimring, 1992) that promote understanding, accepting, and valuing diversity (Cain, 1987; Natiello, 1990; Rogers, 1980; 1987a; 1987b; Sims, 1989; Zimring, 1990). Unconditional positive regard for each individual and belief in the inherent positive growth tendency of the person are only two such formulations. The person-centered approach is recognized worldwide for its contributions to human relations, cross-cultural empathy, facilitating communication among disparate groups, and nurturing diversity among people who are distinctly different in dimensions such as race, ethnicity, religion, life style, age, sex, sexual orientation, physical disabilities, and societal status (Kirschenbaum & Henderson, 1989, pp. 433–477).

In his later years, Rogers devoted a substantial amount of energy and influence to the resolution of intercultural concerns (Kirschenbaum & Henderson, 1989, pp. 438–445). He sincerely believed that person-centered concepts could be applied to governments, nations, and community groups as well as to individuals and that the quest for world peace would be enhanced when people come to use these concepts in their normal interactions (Bozarth, 1992; Raskin & Rogers, 1989, p.183; Rogers, 1987b). Rogers (1987c) facilitated human relations training workshops, consulted with institutions and international groups, and contributed to the literature regarding the reduction of tension among differing groups, including diverse cultural groups. Clearly, a major strength of the person-centered approach is found in the practical application of acceptance, genuineness, and empathic understanding to ameliorate adversities and misunderstandings among diverse national, cultural, or racial groups (Boy, 1990; Bozarth, 1992; Kirschenbaum & Henderson, 1989; Natiello, 1990; Patterson, 1996; Raskin, 1992; Raskin & Rogers, 1989; Rogers, 1977; 1980).

For helping individuals, particularly from cultural backgrounds different from that of the counselor, the person-centered approach is notably effective in initially opening the client-counselor dialogue. Person-centered formulations facilitate the establishment of trust by the client (who may have seldom, if ever, consulted a counselor) and credibility of the counselor in the eyes of the client. The person-centered system is also an excellent modality for highly motivated clients who enter counseling with the objective to fulfill their lives and who are ready and capable of understanding, acting, and using the counseling experience as a departure point to start taking responsibility for themselves.

According to Livneh and Sherwood (1991), the central constructs of person-centered theory that apply to understanding the psychological implications of physical disability include "(a) the salience of the phenomenological field, (b) the self-concept, and (c) the denial and distortion of threatening experiences" (p. 529). Person-centered proponents argue that it is not so much the physical disability that psychologically affects clients but rather the subjective meanings, attitudes, and beliefs associated with the personal perception.

Person-centered strategies have definite merits for helping people with physical disabilities, including:

1. Facilitating clients' insight into their perceptions and feelings, especially during the period immediately following injury or disabling condition and the early phase of rehabilitative treatment;
2. Accepting the disability emotionally without devaluing themselves or resorting to defensive behaviors concerning the existence of their condition;
3. Moving toward becoming more open to experience and acceptance of the disability;
4. Perceiving of themselves with disabilities more realistically and less anxiously;
5. Viewing themselves as a process characterized by change and fluidity, as opposed to rigidity and immobility;
6. Developing an increased trust in themselves with their disabilities as opposed to themselves as disabled;
7. Acting with confidence and assertiveness, as opposed to being nonconfident and passive (Livneh & Sherwood, 1991, pp. 529–530).

For physically disabled clients, Livneh and Sherwood (1991), cite See (1985), and identify several limitations in person-centered strategies in rehabilitation counseling. Among these deficiencies are the person-centered system's aversion to:

1. Setting goals other than self-actualization;
2. Diagnosing and evaluating;
3. Giving advice;
4. Focusing on the external environment;
5. Facilitating process rather than outcome goals;
6. Avoiding task-oriented needs, such as facilitating constructive client behavior and skill development.

There are some distinct deficiencies in the person-centered approach in working with certain other categories of clients. Some people have limited experience in dealing with their feelings. For those clients whose lifestyles, family mores, cultural heritage, and vocations predispose them to respond to environmental, behavioral, parental, or authoritation advice or influence, person-centered counseling may seem ineffective or even unsuitable. Some clients may need goal-directedness, short-term reinforcement, short-term concrete results, and structured guidance that the person-centered counselor may not be prepared for or comfortable in providing. Clients with severely disadvantaged educational and social experience or limited intellectual capacity may be more responsive to a product-oriented therapy than to the process orientation of person-centered counseling.

In addition to the strengths discussed above, person-centered counseling is specially suited to helping several other unique groups of people. For clients whose primary presenting concern is loneliness, person-centered counseling can often serve as the connecting link, the anchor, the bridge over troubled waters that they need. The conditions of acceptance, genuineness, empathy, and caring are sufficient to facilitate—in lonely clients of all ages—a sense of hope, belonging, and affirmation needed to catalyze them into formulating their inner choices and direction. For the lonely person, empathic interaction with another person is of the essence, the balm that no technology or passive media and few content-centered counselors can provide.

Another unique population that is appropriately served by the person-centered approach is people who have suffered loss. Most clients who are in a state of bereavement and grief fare better with an empathic, acceptant, genuine, caring support person rather than a product-oriented helper. Still another population that responds to the techniques of person-centered counseling is the elderly. Reminiscence, validation, and anchoring strategies (Gilliland & James, 1997, pp. 499–500) are especially appropriate for gerontology work. These strategies, based on person-centered principles, operate to get clients in touch with their meaningful past, restore them psychologically to more therapeutic periods in their lives, and serve as connecting anchors for recovery of lost emotional security.

Finally, a major strength of the person-centered approach of *all diverse populations* has emerged through the intensive group work developed by Rogers during the 1960s and 1970s (Raskin & Rogers, 1995, p. 153). Such groups can facilitate the basic encounter of nontherapist peers in a group, responding to each other with undivided empathy in mutual understanding, sharing, and not holding back in their quest for personal growth.

SUMMARY

Person-centered counseling is a continually growing, evolving, and changing theoretical system. Its founder, Carl R. Rogers, was in the forefront of its development from its beginning in the 1940s until his death in 1987. As the approach has evolved, it has been called *nondirective, client-centered, experiential,* and *person-centered.* Although it is now evolving toward a more eclectic system, certain fundamental tenets remain. Among these tenets is the assumption that there are three necessary and sufficient conditions that promote positive growth in clients: genuineness, unconditional positive regard, and empathic understanding. Recent applications of the theory emphasize more active participation by the counselor. The theory has long been vulnerable to misuse and misinterpretation by practitioners. Despite this shortcoming, the person-centered counselor is seen as a genuine, caring, empathic person who is fully involved with the client in an ongoing and vital way.

SUGGESTIONS FOR FURTHER READING

Combs, A. W. (1989). *A theory of therapy: Guidelines for counseling practice.* Newbury Park, CA: Sage Publications.
Kirschenbaum, H., & Henderson, V. L. (Eds.). (1989). *The Carl Rogers reader.* Boston: Houghton Mifflin.
Raskin, N.J., & Rogers, C. R. (1995). Person-centered therapy. In R. J. Corsini & D. Wedding (Eds). *Current psychotherapies* (5th ed., pp. 155–194). Itasca, IL: F. E. Peacock.
Rogers, C. R. (1951). *Client-centered therapy.* Boston: Houghton Mifflin.
Rogers, C. R. (1961). *On becoming a person.* Boston: Houghton Mifflin.
Rogers, C. R. (1969). *Freedom to learn: A view of what education might become.* Columbus, OH: Chas. E. Merrill.
Rogers, C. R. (1970). *Carl Rogers on encounter groups.* New York: Harper & Row.
Rogers, C. R. (1972). *On becoming partners: Marriage and its alternatives.* New York: Delacorte Press.
Rogers, C. R. (1977). *Carl Rogers on personal power: Inner strength and its revolutionary impact.* New York: Delacorte Press.
Rogers, C. R. (1980). *A way of being.* Boston: Houghton Mifflin.

REFERENCES

Boy, A. V. (1990). The therapist in person-centered groups. *Person-Centered Review, 5,* 308–315.
Bozarth, J. D. (1985). Quantum theory and the person-centered approach. *Journal of Counseling and Development, 64,* 179–182.
Bozarth, J. D. (1989). Person-centered therapy with couples. [Special issue: Person-centered approaches with families.] *Person-Centered Review, 4*(3). 280–294.
Bozarth, J. D. (1990). The evolution of Carl Rogers as a therapist. [Special issue: Fiftieth anniversary of the person-centered approach.] *Person-Centered Review, 5*(4), 387–393.
Bozarth, J. D. (1991a). Actualization: A fundamental concept in client-centered therapy. [Special issue: Handbook of self-actualization.] *Journal of Social Behavior and Personality, 6*(5), 45–59.
Bozarth, J. D. (1991b). Person-centered assessment. *Journal of Counseling and Development, 69*(5), 458–461.
Bozarth, J. D. (1992, August). *The person-centered community group.* Paper presented at the symposium on Contributions of Client-Centered Therapy to American Psychology's 100 Years, presented at the Centennial Convention of the American Psychological Association, Washington, DC.
Brent, J. S. (1984). Person-centered apologetics: An empathic approach. *Journal of Psychology and Christianity, 3,* 18–26.
Cain, D. J. (1987). Carl R. Rogers: The man, his vision, his impact. *Person-Centered Review, 2,* 283–288.
Carkhuff, R. (1969a). *Helping and human relations. Vol. 1: Selection and training.* New York: Holt, Rinehart & Winston.
Carkhuff, R. (1969b). *Helping and human relations. Vol. 2: Practice and research.* New York: Holt, Rinehart & Winston.

Cormier, L. S., & Hackney, H. (1987). *The professional counselor: A process guide to helping.* Englewood Cliffs, NJ: Prentice-Hall.

Cormier, W. H., & Cormier, L. S. (1979). *Interviewing strategies for helpers: A guide to assessment, treatment, and evaluation.* Pacific Grove, CA: Brooks/Cole.

Cormier, W. H., & Cormier, L. S. (1985). *Interviewing strategies for helpers: Fundamental skills and cognitive-behavioral interventions* (2nd ed.). Pacific Grove, CA: Brooks/Cole.

Cormier, W. H., & Cormier. L. S. (1991). *Interviewing strategies for helpers: Fundamental skills and cognitive behavioral interventions* (3rd ed.). Pacific Grove: CA, Brooks/Cole.

Cowen, E. L. (1985). Person-centered approaches to primary prevention and mental health: Situation-focused and competence-enhancement. *American Journal of Community Psychology, 13,* 31–48.

Egan, G. (1975). *The skilled helper: A model for systematic helping and inter-personal relating.* Pacific Grove, CA: Brooks/Cole.

Egan, G. (1982). *The skilled helper: Model, skills, and methods for effective helping* (2nd ed.). Pacific Grove, CA: Brooks/Cole.

Egan, G. (1986). *The skilled helper: A systematic approach to effective helping* (3rd ed.). Pacific Grove, CA: Brooks/Cole.

Gilliland, B. E., & James, R. K. (1997). *Crisis intervention strategies* (3rd ed.). Pacific Grove, CA: Brooks/Cole.

Ginsberg, B. G. (1984). Beyond behavior modification: Client-centered play therapy with the retarded. *Academic Psychology Bulletin, 6,* 321–334.

Grant, B. (1990). Principled and instrumental nondirectiveness in person-centered therapy. *Person-Centered Review, 5,* 77–88.

Hackney, H., & Cormier, L. S. (1979). *Counseling strategies and objectives* (2nd ed.). Englewood Cliffs, NJ: Prentice-Hall.

Hall, E. T. (1966). *The hidden dimension.* Garden City, NY: Doubleday.

Harren, V. A. (1977). Client-centered theory of personality and psychotherapy. In D. C. Rimm & J. W. Somerville (Eds.), *Abnormal psychology* (Chapter 17). New York: Academic Press.

Herlihy, B. (1985). Person-centered Gestalt therapy: A synthesis. *Journal of Humanistic Education and Development, 24,* 16–24.

Holdstock, T. L., & Rogers, C. R. (1977). Person-centered theory. In R. J. Corsini (Ed.), *Current personality theories* (pp. 125–151). Itasca, IL: F. E. Peacock.

Ivey, A. E. (1988). *Intentional interviewing and counseling: Facilitating client development* (2nd ed.). Pacific Grove, CA: Brooks/Cole.

Kirschenbaum, H., & Henderson, V. L., (Eds.). (1989). *The Carl Rogers reader.* Boston: Houghton Mifflin.

Knapp, M. L. (1978). *Nonverbal communication in human interaction* (2nd ed.). New York: Holt, Rinehart & Winston.

Lewis, C. M. (1985). Symbolization of experience in the process of group development. *Group, 9,* 29–35.

Livneh, H., & Sherwood, A. (1991). Application of personality theories and counseling strategies to clients with physical disabilities. *Journal of Counseling and Development, 69,* 525–538.

Meador, B. D., & Rogers, C. R. (1973). Client-centered therapy. In R. J. Corsini (Ed.), *Current psychotherapies* (pp. 119–165). Itasca, IL: F. E. Peacock.

Meador, B. D., & Rogers, C. R. (1979). Person-centered therapy. In R. J. Corsini (Ed.), *Current psychotherapies* (2nd ed., pp. 131–184). Itasca, IL: F. E. Peacock.

Natiello, P. (1990). The person-centered approach: Collaborative power and cultural transformation. *Person-Centered Review, 5,* 268–286.

Patterson, C. H. (1986). *Theories of counseling and psychotherapy* (4th ed.). New York: Harper & Row.

Patterson, C. H. (1989). Foundations for a systematic eclectic psychotherapy. *Psychotherapy, 26*(4), 427–435.

Patterson, C. H. (1990a). Involuntary clients: A person-centered view. *Person-Centered Review, 5*(3), 316–320.

Patterson, C. H. (1990b). On being client-centered. [Special issue: Fiftieth anniversary of the person-centered approach.] *Person-Centered Review, 5*(4), 425–432.

Patterson, C. H. (1996). Multicultural counseling: From diversity to universality. *Journal of Counseling and Development, 74*(3), 227–231.

Raskin, N. J. (1992, August). *A revolutionary approach to counseling and psychotherapy.* Paper presented at the symposium on Contributions of Client-Centered Therapy to American Psychology's 100 Years, presented at the Centennial Convention of the American Psychological Association, Washington, DC.

Raskin, N. J., & Rogers, C. R. (1989). Person-centered therapy. In R. J. Corsini & D. Wedding (Eds.). *Current psychotherapies* (4th ed., pp. 155–194). Itasca, IL: F. E. Peacock.

Raskin, N. J., & Rogers, C. R. (1995). Person-centered therapy. In R. J. Corsini & D. Wedding (Eds.). *Current psychotherapies* (5th ed.: pp. 128–161). Itasca, IL: F. E. Peacock.

Rogers, C. R. (1942). *Counseling and psychotherapy.* Boston: Houghton Mifflin.

Rogers, C. R. (1951). *Client-centered therapy.* Boston: Houghton Mifflin.

Rogers, C. R. (1959). A theory of therapy, personality, and interpersonal relationships as developed in the client-centered framework. In S. Koch (Ed.), *Psychology: A study of science, formulations of the person and the social context* (Vol. 3, pp. 184–256). New York: McGraw-Hill.

Rogers, C. R. (1961). *On becoming a person.* Boston: Houghton Mifflin.

Rogers, C. R. (1965). Client-centered therapy (Film no. 1, client named Gloria). In E. L. Shostrom (Ed.), *Three approaches to psychotherapy* (three 16 mm color motion pictures). Orange, CA: Psychological Films, Inc.

Rogers, C. R. (1967). *The therapeutic relationship and its impact: A study of psychotherapy with schizophrenics.* With E. T. Gendlin, D. J. Kielser, & C. Lomax. Madison: University of Wisconsin Press.

Rogers, C. R. (1969). *Freedom to learn: A view of what education might become.* Columbus, OH: Chas. E. Merrill.

Rogers, C. R. (1970). *Carl Rogers on encounter groups.* New York: Harper & Row.

Rogers, C. R. (1972). *On becoming partners: Marriage and its alternatives.* New York: Delacorte Press.

Rogers, C. R. (1977). *Carl Rogers on personal power: Inner strength and its revolutionary impact.* New York: Delacorte Press.

Rogers, C. R. (1980). *A way of being.* Boston: Houghton Mifflin.

Rogers, C. R. (1985). Reaction to Gunnisons' article on the similarities between Erikson and Rogers. *Journal of Counseling and Development, 63,* 565–566.

Rogers, C. R. (1986). Person-centered therapy (videotape no. 1, client named Kathy). In E. L. Shostrom (Executive Producer), S. K. Shostrom (Producer), & H. Ratner (Director), *Three approaches to psychotherapy II* (three VHS videotapes). Corona Del Mar, CA: Psychological and Educational Film.

Rogers, C. R. (1987a). Inside the world of the Soviet professional. *Counseling and Values, 32,* 46–66.

Rogers, C. R. (1987b). Our international family. *Person-Centered Review, 2,* 139–149.

Rogers, C. R. (1987c). Steps toward world peace, 1948–1986: Tension reduction in theory and practice. *Counseling and Values, 32,* 38–45.

See, J. D. (1985). Person-centered perspective. *Journal of Applied Rehabilitation Counseling, 16,* 15–20.

Sims, J. M. (1989). Client-centered therapy: The art of knowing. *Person-Centered Review, 4,* 27–41.

Slack, S. (1985). Reflections on a workshop with Carl Rogers. *Journal of Humanistic Psychology, 25,* 35–42.

Willis, R. J. (1985). "The life of therapy": An exploration of therapeutic method. *Psychotherapy in Private Practice, 3,* 63–70.

Zimring, F. M. (1988). Attaining mastery: The shift from the "me" to the "I". *Person-Centered Review, 3,* 165–175.

Zimring, F. M. (1990). A characteristic to Rogers's response to clients. *Person-Centered Review, 5,* 433–448.

Zimring, F. M. (1992, August). *Contributions to the constructs of self, empathy, and experience.* Paper presented at the symposium on Contributions of Client-Centered Therapy to American Psychology's 100 Years, presented at the Centennial Convention of the American Psychological Association, Washington, DC.

6

GESTALT THERAPY

FUNDAMENTAL TENETS

History

Frederick S. (Fritz) Perls is credited with the formulation of Gestalt therapy. Psychoanalysis, which he studied and practiced between 1924 and 1936, provided the theoretical framework for his understanding of human behavior, a framework whose similarities and differences with Gestalt therapy he continually pointed out. Perls first became acquainted with Gestalt psychology through Kurt Goldstein, with whom he worked in 1926, but it was not until the early 1940s that Perls actually incorporated principles of Gestalt psychology into his writing. His *Ego, Hunger and Aggression* (1947) marked his break from psychoanalysis and a bridge to Gestalt therapy.

Goldstein's theory of holism, with its emphasis on figure-ground formulation, is the basis of one of the major concepts of Gestalt therapy. Sigmund Friedlander, a German philosopher described by Perls as one of his three gurus, provided what Perls later developed into the concept of "working toward the awareness and integration of polarities." Perls was also influenced by the semanticists I. A. Richard and Alfred Korzybski, who were concerned with the effect of language on thought and behavior (Kogan, 1976, pp. 241–242). Perls also seems to have been strongly influenced by the psychodramatic methods of Jacob Moreno, as evidenced by the parallels in the practice of psychodrama and Gestalt therapy. Perls credited his wife, Laura, who was his coworker for about twenty-five years, with having made valuable contributions to his work.

In the early 1930s, as Hitler came to power in Germany, Fritz and Laura moved to South Africa, where he was engaged in training psychoanalysts from 1934 to 1942 (Kogan, 1976, pp. 237–243). From 1947 until his death, Perls lived in North America, where his work influenced and was influenced by the human potential movement. He and Laura founded the Gestalt Institute of America in New York City in 1951. Until then they were still calling themselves psychoanalysts (Rosenfeld, 1978), and Perls was still working from behind a reclining patient (Resnick, 1984). The term *Gestalt therapy* was first used as the title of a book by Perls, Hefferline, and Goodman. However, Gestalt therapy remained relatively unknown until Perls went to the Esalen Institute in California in 1963. During his six years at Esalen, Perls presented workshops using the hot seat format. (The hot seat is a workshop technique in which one individual at a time sits in "the hot seat," where his or her problems are publicly confronted, first by the therapist, then by peer group members.) Ironically, the hot seat work at Esalen that so firmly established Gestalt therapy and Perls as the foremost practitioner represented only a small segment of the approach and of Perls's work as a therapist. Perls died in 1970 (Kogan, 1976, pp. 246–253).

Since Perls's death, Gestalt therapy has continued to grow, first through the generation of students trained by Laura and Fritz and then through a second generation of therapists trained by Laura. Other therapists continue to be trained at major Gestalt centers in San Francisco, Cleveland, New York, Los Angeles, and San Diego. The *Gestalt Journal* is the literary organ that disseminates research, theory, and innovative techniques of the approach.

Overview of Gestalt Therapy

"*Gestalt* is a German word meaning whole or configuration" (Simkin, 1976, p. 225). Perls used it to mean a unique kind of patterning in which parts are integrated into perceptual wholes. This integration is a basic function of human organisms. For the individual, the organization of the world is defined by the subjective reality of his or her perceptions. Thus, the Gestalt approach is said to be phenomenological. That is, it does not attempt to define an absolute reality. The Gestalt approach is also existential, in that it deals with what is currently happening to the individual. In that sense it focuses on the sources of experiences, such as what an individual is thinking and doing and how he or she is feeling. Understanding of the self and others is based on the totality of experience as expressed in gestures, voice, posture, and breathing as well as unspoken words (Passons, 1975, pp. 47–58; Polster, 1992).

Another basic function of the organism is a constant striving to maintain equilibrium, which is continually disturbed by the organism's needs and regained by the gratification or elimination of these needs. This innate biological process provides a basis for subsequent conceptual activity and behavior. For example, when we are thirsty we conceive of various choices (water, milk, juice) and act on one of them to gratify or eliminate our need for liquids. This process also operates on a variety of other levels as the organism develops psychologically, socially, and spiritually. The restoration of balance is termed *organismic self-regulation*. This inevitable drive to maintain balance is the process necessary for human growth. Gestalt therapy is similar to this basic biological growth process. The therapist helps the individual become aware of a need, suggests an experiment to illuminate various aspects of the need, and promotes behavior that leads to resolution of the need.

Therapy focuses on heightening the individual's awareness of responsibility for his or her behavior, feelings, and thoughts, including those he or she may be unaware of. To achieve this, Gestalt therapists reject searching for causes of behavior, feelings, and thoughts. Instead they suggest that the individual try specific activities (experiments) that they have designed to increase awareness (Yontef, 1976, pp. 216–218; 1995).

Although Gestalt therapists believe awareness to be curative, a certain amount of frustration arising from the person's needs must exist if the person is to grow and learn self-support. Therefore, the therapist will not allow the individual to manipulate him or her into taking responsibility for satisfying these needs. Instead, the therapist frustrates the individual's attempt to give up responsibility for self in order that the person may learn to be independent.

Theory of Personality

Gestalt psychology is based on the notion that the whole is greater than the sum of its parts. That is, an individual cannot be reduced to discrete psychological parts and still maintain the essence of the whole person. Likewise, for Gestalt therapists, understanding the integration of the total person (the self) in his or her own phenomenological field is the core of the Gestalt theory of personality. Motivation, holism, and the development of a capacity for aggression provide the primary structural components for viewing the personality.

Homeostasis

People are motivated by a continual striving for *homeostasis* (balance). This striving is instinctual: it flows from the natural self-regulating rhythm of the organism between the states of equilibrium and disequilibrium (Walker, 1971, pp. 72–74). This homeostatic principle serves to order individual perceptions. We may think of the perception of a need in terms of a figure emerging from a background (Polster & Polster, 1973, pp. 28–32). When a person perceives a need, such as the need to satisfy a sex urge, hunger, or thirst, he or she is said to be in a state of disequilibrium, and a figure (the need) has emerged from the background. Equilibrium is restored when the person can assimilate something from the environment to satisfy the need. With equilibrium restored, the way is clear for the emergence into awareness of a new figure (need). Thus, the person exists in a constant state of flux as a need emerges into the foreground, a way to satisfy the need is selected, the need recedes into the background, and a new need emerges (Walker, 1971, p. 77).

Holism

Holism entails two relationships important to Gestalt theory. The first is the interdependent, inseparable unity of the human body and spirit; the human is a psychological and physical totality. The second relationship is the unity of human beings and environment through their interdependence (Walker, 1971, pp. 77–79).

Aggression

Human interaction in growthful and creative ways in the environment requires the full development of a capacity for aggression (Walker, 1971, pp. 109–111). Aggression can be understood by referring to Perls's explanation of the child's development of this quality. Perls related the development of aggression to teething, which enables the child to attack his or her solid environment by ingesting solid food (Perls, 1969, pp. 108–111). Here, eating is a destructive process (the taking apart of food) that results in the assimilation of food and causes growth. Likewise, the person can "de-structure" other aspects of the environment, assimilate these aspects, and grow as a result.

The relationship among homeostasis, holism, and aggression presupposes that the person and his or her environment coexist (Perls, 1973, pp. 15–18). Although the individual and the environment are separate, the interaction between them cannot be split; the two are a whole. The *ego boundary* defines this interaction. It is both the person's internal and external definitions of him- or herself when engaged in interactions with the environment. In an ideal sense, the ego boundary is not carved in stone but is fluid and elastic to meet the demand of changing conditions (Perls, 1969, p. 7). Human aggression comes into play between the person and the environment by means of contact or withdrawal at a point called the *contact boundary.* More specifically, when an object has been contacted or withdrawn from in a way satisfying to the individual, both the object and the need associated with it disappear into the background. The situation is finished; another Gestalt is completed. A frightened person runs (withdraws) from a dangerous animal, and the situation is finished. Withdrawal may leave some situations unfinished and thus precipitate further avoidance, but at the time of withdrawal, anxiety is reduced and homeostasis is restored.

Problems occur when boundaries become fused. Fusion occurs when the person's own self-identity becomes lost as he or she tries to fit into the environment. Somewhat paradoxically, then, although Gestalt therapy promotes productive living as a continuing, changing, experiencing of one's world, it does not do so at the expense of maintaining one's separateness from that world. From that standpoint, its theory base is clearly existential.

Nature of Maladjustment

Perls (1969, pp. 59–61) viewed neurosis as the major manifestation of maladjusted behavior. The development of neurotic behavior is related to the three concepts just discussed: the development of aggression, the maintenance of homeostasis, and the interaction of a person and the environment.

When the aggressive process of assimilating food is wholesomely developed, then the basis for a wholesomely aggressive approach to the rest of the individual's life is established. However, if this initial aggressive process is thwarted, then the individual's capacity aggressively to create a personal life is also thwarted.

When a need is perceived, the individual selects from the environment an appropriate object or means to restore homeostasis. However, the neurotic's rhythm of contact and withdrawal (the striving for homeostasis) is itself out of balance. Neurotics do not know when to participate (contact) and when to withdraw because the many unfinished situations of their lives interfere with their sense of orientation. Therefore, they cannot tell which objects in the environment will satisfy their needs. They have lost the freedom of choice because they cannot see the choices that are available (Perls, 1973, pp. 20–24).

Because a person is both an individual and a social creature, the person's life is an interaction between him or her and the environment, which is constantly changing. The individual must be able to change his or her techniques of manipulation and interaction in response. Neurosis arises when the individual becomes incapable of doing this. His or her behavior becomes the same regardless of the demands of the situation. People are neurotic when their attempts to maintain equilibrium lead them to withdraw farther and farther from society (Perls, 1973, pp. 25–32).

Although some neuroses are caused by traumatic events, most are caused by day-to-day interference with growth. The neurosis is born as a defense designed to maintain the integrity of the organism, and the neurotic behavior is an attempt to maintain equilibrium within a defensive system.

There are five major boundary disturbances that lead to neurosis: introjection, projection, retroflection, deflection, and confluence (Perls, 1973, pp. 25–32).

Introjection

Psychologically swallowing whole concepts is called *introjection*. Perls compares it to the biological process of eating, digesting, and assimilating nourishment so that the body will grow. Individuals also accept, digest, and assimilate concepts, facts, ethics, and standards from the environment. When these learnings become part of the person, he or she changes and grows. However, if swallowed whole, without digestion and assimilation, they become foreign bodies within the individual. If enough of these concepts and ideas that are not owned by the person are swallowed intact, the person cannot develop a unique personality (Perls, 1973, pp. 32–35).

Introjectors have difficulty knowing what they believe and what they do not believe. They report seeing themselves as phony, superficial, and distant from others. In therapy, the habit of introjection often makes them compliant clients who swallow what the therapist says without assimilating it. The therapist must therefore be careful not to compound an existing problem by mistaking easy compliance for true change (Harman, 1982). Introjectors are exemplified by the dependent client, who willingly does everything the therapist asks but never quite seems to succeed at the task at hand.

Projection

To project is to make someone or something in the environment responsible for what originates in oneself. The person with a healthy personality is aware of owning assumptions and hunches he or she makes about the world; the person who projects is not. Extreme projection results in paranoia. The projector cannot accept his or her feelings and thus attaches them to others. For example, a man may deplore the sexy way a woman is acting when in actuality he cannot accept his own feelings of sexuality. The result is a split between the individual's actual characteristics and his or her awareness of them (Polster & Polster, 1973, pp. 78–82). Words often used in the projector's speech are *they, them, he, she,* and *you.* This third-person approach to contact with the environment means that such individuals are always looking outside themselves for the sources of their problems. The projector needs to experience ownership of his or her feelings and attitudes or, in Gestalt terminology, the "I" of his or her existence (Harman, 1982).

Retroflection

Retroflection is doing to self what one would like to do to others. The retroflector redirects behavior inward and substitutes the self for the environment as a target for it. For instance, the retroflector turns anger inward rather than expressing it toward others. This behavior creates stress and a rigid and blocked personality. Energy once available for spontaneous behavior and growth is now used to block the release of the retroflected feelings (Polster & Polster, 1973, pp. 82–89). Retroflection in the extreme is the depressed client who turns his or her rage at the world inward and decides to commit suicide as a way of dealing with his or her repressed feelings of anger and rage. Retroflection can also be doing things for ourselves that we would want others to do for us (Sharf, 1996, p. 258). The self-reliant, self-sufficient, rugged individualism personified by the Hank Williams, Jr., ballad *A Country Boy Can Survive* may in fact be what the survivalist wistfully hopes others would do for him or her.

Deflection

Deflection is a subtle maneuver to avoid contact with the environment. The deflector avoids intense emotions; deals mainly in polite civilities; talks about things rather than people; relates problems from an abstract, intellectual, third-person perspective; talks constantly to avoid experiencing interaction; speaks of the there-and-then rather than the here-and-now; and avoids physical contact (Sharf, 1996, p. 258). From a therapeutic standpoint the deflector is passive-aggressive. The deflector is like cotton candy—there is the appearance of a lot of stuff, but there is little emotional substance for the therapist to sink his or her teeth into because the client seeks to avoid contact in the present therapeutic moment.

Confluence

Confluence is the absence of a boundary between self and the environment. Examples of this state are found in the infant at birth and the adult in a moment of ecstasy. Neither is aware of a separation between the self and the environment. People who are pathologically confluent are unaware of the boundary between themselves and others. Thus they cannot make good contact; nor can they withdraw. In less extreme confluence, the person cannot tolerate differences in others from him- or herself and may instead demand likeness from them. An example of this type of confluent behavior is the parent who considers the child an extension of him- or herself (Perls, 1973, pp. 38–40). The parent becomes so fused with the child that all contact boundaries are lost. The child must act, sleep, breathe, and do what the parent demands. At a minimum, the backstage mom or the grandstand dad both depict a confluent approach. Both are frustrated in missing out on their fantasy career goals and thus project them through their offspring. At a more lethal level, the spurned lover who becomes a stalker, the jealous spouse who becomes a batterer, and the borderline personality disorder who blatantly disregards socially sanctioned boundaries are all individuals with confluence issues. The foregoing boundary disturbances and resulting adjustment/maladjustment hinge on how well individuals are able to deal with, or have the therapist help them deal with, the following concepts of Gestalt therapy.

Major Concepts

1. Here-and-now orientation
2. Awareness
3. Responsibility
4. Polarities
5. Top dog/underdog
6. Environmental contact
7. Figure-ground
8. Unfinished business

Here-and-Now Orientation

Interventions in Gestalt therapy are built on actual present behavior. Present behavior is not just defined as what the client is talking about, but rather as how congruent or incongruent the body language of the client is with what he or she is saying. For Gestalt therapy, becoming aware of what is going on with one's body is directly related with what is going on with one's self (Clance, Thompson, & Simerly, 1994). Talking about what happened "way back when," whether twenty years or five minutes ago, is a safe way of avoiding contact with the emotionality of the moment and particularly contact with the therapist in the therapeutic environment. While the therapist may build the therapeutic environment to be imposing, confirming, or competing to bring the client into contact (Frew, 1992), emphasis is always on the "now."

The therapist calls attention to the individual's posture, breathing, mannerisms, gestures, voice, and facial expressions. For example, clients are asked to experience their posture and then to put into words the existential meaning of the posture. A man who speaks with his jaw and chest thrust forward may live his life as a battle. His existence is reflected in his posture. Interventions are almost exclusively in the form of "what" and "how" questions, such as "What are you doing?" and "How are you feeling?" These questions keep awareness centered in the present. The therapist prevents the individual from escaping experience by focusing on present awareness. To this end, he or she instructs the client to complete the basic sentence. "Now I am aware . . . . " The word *I* is emphasized, for it symbolizes ownership of what is going on with the person (Walker, 1971, pp. 76–93).

Awareness

In Gestalt therapy, awareness is everything. Awareness is the ability of the client to be in full mental and sensory awareness of experiencing the now. As such, it is viewed as curative. As previously indicated, however, clients will do their best to avoid experiencing their awareness in the "now" because or the threatening nature of the emotions that are elicited. Therefore, one of the major tasks of the Gestalt therapist is to aggressively frustrate the client's attempts to break out of the awareness of the "here-and-now" and retreat to the "there-and-then." Gestalt therapists are not opposed to using humor, sarcasm, dramatics, confrontation, and shock to create awareness, as Perls in particular was not. Little time is spent by the therapist rehashing the client's history of problems in an attempt to gain insight. Rather, the experimental nature of the therapeutic encounter is to aid the client in becoming aware of present behavior and developing and experimenting with new behaviors (Thompson & Rudolph, 1996, p. 144).

The individual achieves awareness of the meaning of his or her day-to-day existence by acting out in therapy whatever life situations are not completed. An unresolved conflict with a significant person in the client's life is worked through as if it were happening in that moment. The individual also acts out in therapy the repetitive behaviors of everyday life. These behaviors, without therapy, cannot be brought to a satisfactory conclusion because the individual interrupts them. Interruption may occur in the following way. A man wants to make closer contact with a woman he knows, but each time he has an opportunity to do so, he does not take advantage of it. He may prevent himself from following through by worrying about how he would feel if she rejects him. In therapy, situations are designed to uncover the moment at which he interrupts the flow of experience and prevents himself from achieving a creative solution (Perls, 1973, pp. 63–64).

Responsibility

Gestalt therapy views the existential meaning of the word *responsibility* as one of its basic concepts. Responsibility means that each individual, and no one else, determines the essence of his or her existence. Further, it means owning one's projections instead of blaming others for one's thoughts, feelings, impulses, and behaviors. Responsibility is also "response-ability," or the ability to respond. Whenever a person acts, decides, or chooses, he or she is exercising response-ability (Perls, 1973, p. 68).

Accepting responsibility for one's life is characteristic of a person with a healthy personality. Denying this responsibility means giving up power and control over one's life. For example, a married woman completes her graduate degree and is offered a job she has always dreamed about, but in a city several hundred miles from her husband's place of employment. Her husband will not change jobs to accommodate her wish to accept the offer and says that their marriage will not survive separate living arrangements. The woman chooses to accept a less desirable position in the city in which her husband is employed and then blames him for her lack of fulfillment and her unhappiness. However, the ultimate responsibility for her decisions and subsequent feelings lies with her. Had she decided to accept the dream job, she also would have been responsible for this choice and her subsequent feelings.

Current theorists and practitioners of Gestalt therapy have modified the Perlsian conception of responsibility from the 1970s "me" generation conception to one that now more fully appreciates the interdependent nature of people (Hendlin, 1987; Hycner, 1987; Saner, 1989; Wheeler, 1991; Zinker, 1987). These authors have modified the extreme position of Perls on individual autonomy as the hallmark of maturity and health. They instead describe the healthy, mature person as one who can successfully balance contact and withdrawal in interpersonal relationships. Being responsible is to consider both the effects of one's behavior on others and one's intrapersonal needs.

Polarities

When organismic self-regulation is interfered with, the person may experience internal or interpersonal conflicts. These conflicts occur between thoughts, traits, values, and actions that are polar opposites. Generosity and stinginess, for example, are opposite poles of a "giving" continuum.

Integrating these polarities is a primary therapeutic goal. Whenever an individual recognizes an aspect of him- or herself, the antithesis (the polar opposite) of this characteristic can become powerful enough to emerge from the background as a figure.

Assagioli (1965) has identified five generic polarities that include physical, emotional, mental, spiritual, and interindividual issues. The bipolar dilemmas that generate out of these generic issues are infinite in number and a great deal of time is spent by most of us in figuring out how to get off the horns of these everyday dilemmas. Indeed, a variation of one of the most famous of the Gestalt techniques is the "empty chair," which is used to let clients literally sit on either side of the dilemma and have a dialogue with the empty chair on the other side. At a deeper level these polarities may be longstanding and deeply embedded in the individual and are part of an unfinished gestalt or business the client needs to complete. Thus, integrating polarities involves facilitating full awareness of them by experiencing them in contact during therapy (Simkin, 1975, pp. 9–10).

Top dog/Underdog

Gestalt therapists frequently use the term *top dog/underdog* when they refer to polar opposites. The top dog takes the role of the parental authoritarian who says, "I know what is best for you." The underdog sabotages the top dog by playing helpless: "I don't know how to do that. Will you help me?" The top dog is a righteous, moralist authoritarian. It is the "should" and "should not" part of the person and in transactional analysis therapy would clearly be the critical parent. The underdog is the wheedling, excuse-making, defensive, cunning, pleasure-seeking "I want it" part of the person. In transactional analysis terms underdog would be a blend of the adaptive child and the free child. This polarity is a major player in the person's life and each of its sides is constantly vying for control of the individual. A typical empty chair exercise involving these polarities will have a dialogue between "I should" and "I want" parts of the person (Sharf, 1996, p. 268; Thompson & Rudolph, 1996, p. 146).

Environmental Contact

"The function that synthesizes the human need for union and separation is contact" (Polster & Polster, 1973, p. 99). Contact is necessary for growth. It is the means for changing oneself and one's experience of the world. When one makes contact with the environment, change is inescapable because of one's assimilation or rejection of what was contacted. Learning that one likes the taste of alcohol upon having one's first mixed drink and embracing a religious belief after hearing a charismatic speaker are examples of change with contact.

Contact is made through seven functions: looking, listening, touching, talking, moving, smelling, and tasting (Polster & Polster, 1973, pp. 129–138). The failure to make contact has been described as the gap between what one ultimately wants to do and what one actually refuses to do. When one is afraid to be physically close to another person but wants to be close, one is creating a gap between what one is and what one could be.

The problem is that much of our contacts are not assimilated in positive ways and wind up fragmenting our lives so that we become stuck and immobilized and are able to only make neurotic contact with the environment. According to Perls (1969; 1971) there are five levels or stages of neurotic contact that represent psychological growth:

1. The *phony* layer. Attempting to be somebody one is not, reacting in stereotypical patterns, doling out meaningless platitudes, being insincere, and lying for self-enhancement or gain are some of the activities that make people phony. A great deal or time is spent by many clients building and maintaining these facades.

2. The *phobic* layer. Phobias are set in place as a way to avoid feared psychological pain. As people become more aware of their phoniness, they become more frightened about their own vulnerability and set in place a variety of defense mechanisms to keep them from imagined harm.
3. The *impasse* layer. When the games people play during the first two layers are no longer effective and are dropped or extinguished, they are likely to become stuck because the individuals know of no better way to cope with their fears and inadequacies.
4. The *implosive* layer. When all the previous roles are stripped away, people begin to be aware of how they limit themselves and commence experimenting with new behaviors. In essence, they pull themselves together, contracting, compressing, and imploding as they reintegrate into different people.
5. The *explosive* layer. As reintegration occurs and new behaviors are learned, a great deal of pent-up energy becomes available. This energy mushrooms out with a new, more authentic person who is now capable of experiencing and expressing emotions.

Polster and Polster (1973, pp. 115–116) distinguish between four frames of reference when viewing contact boundaries:

1. *Familiarity boundaries* are constantly repeated events that are never considered until they are disrupted. One thinks little of a job or a relationship until one is fired or divorced, and then the boundary loss is devastating.
2. *Body boundaries* may restrict general sensations or make various parts of the body be completely off limits to sensations. Psychological frigidity and impotence are classic examples.
3. *Expressive boundaries* are learned at an early age and set the limits for the amount and kinds of feelings we are allowed to display. Display of feelings is a risky business; thus many people have constricted expressive boundaries. Typically, Gestalt therapy will be given the task of the expansion of expressive boundaries.
4. *Value boundaries* are values we hold that are resistant to change. These values are so rigidly held that they represent some of the most difficult and confrontive work the Gestalt therapist must do if these boundaries are to change.

Figure-Ground

The concept of figure-ground is best understood through the dynamics of perceiving. The perceiver orders perceptions of incoming stimuli into an experience of a figure against a background. The figure is comparable to what the eye is drawn to in a picture or what the ear hears in a song. Another important characteristic of perception is *closure:* the figure is seen as a complete, bounded image. This natural movement toward closure also operates in social situations. However, it is frequently interrupted or left unfinished, and the situation is forced into the background, where it continues to influence present behavior.

Magic eye prints are an excellent, if not maddening, example of visual figure-ground Gestalts. For many people the background of squiggle lines is meaningless until the perceptual area of their brains can pierce through the lines and have the submerged figure suddenly pop into awareness. Emotional figure-ground configurations are analogous to magic eye prints. A past unresolved incident (an argument with one's first love that leads to a broken engagement) gets pushed into a mental file drawer due to the emergence of other pressing matters. As time passes, the squiggle lines of history cover it up, but it is not gone—merely covered! Wheeler (1991, pp. 53–54) cautions that Gestalt therapy is much more than exclusive attention to the emerging figure. To adhere to the holistic nature of Gestalt therapy, therapeutic attention should also focus on the relational context from which the figure emerges. This relational context is the ground of the client's existence and provides the backdrop for the client's behavior. To ignore the ground is to become figure-bound. To attend to the interplay between figure and ground provides a holistic rather than an episodic approach to Gestalt therapy.

Unfinished Business

People have the capacity to tolerate a great number of unfinished situations. These remain in the background, influencing behavior and perceptions. For instance, a hungry person may perceive an ambiguous stimulus as food. A person with an unresolved conflict with a parent will play out this conflict with a spouse or a supervisor. People perceive in the present what was unfinished in the past. The figure that emerges from the background is the material for the Gestalt therapeutic encounter. This figure may change as new aspects of it come into awareness.

Unfinished business, then, has to do with unfulfilled needs, unexpressed feelings, and uncompleted situations (Thompson & Rudolph, 1996, p. 142) that may be submerged from conscious awareness but are continuously recycled and demand attention. Unfinished business puts the client in an endless feedback emotional loop in which the old problem continuously reemerges, sometimes in the same form and with the same situation (an attempt to rekindle a broken romance), sometimes camouflaged in a slightly altered situation (new person but same doomed romantic tactics as before). The individual may attempt to "get it right" over and over but even if successful (she finally hits the romance lottery and comes up with the grand prize) may still somehow feel unresolved and unfulfilled because the past business (the old romance with all its traps and snares) has not been "finished." As a result, unfinished business deals mainly with negative feelings, fantasies, and memories such as abandonment, estrangement, guilt, fear, anger, hatred, remorse, and sorrow (Sharf, 1996, p. 260). One of the major goals of Gestalt therapy is to create awareness of the unfinished business, bring closure to it—in short, "finish" it.

THE COUNSELING PROCESS

Central Focus

During the years since Perls's death, the focus of Gestalt therapy has shifted toward a style that is more relational in nature. In this shift, the therapeutic power of the relationship is acknowledged; a trend toward support for and less frustration of the client is advised; a balance between here-and-now emphasis and historical perspective is allowed; and attention to rational thought as well as feeling and sensation is permitted (Hendlin, 1987). This shift in focus has resulted in a more balanced integration of mind/body, emotion/intellect, and individual/relational aspects of therapy.

Within this more integrative brand of Gestalt practice, the therapist will facilitate the individual's awareness of self and all the feelings, behaviors, experiences, and unfinished situations that make up the self. This facilitation is accomplished through the therapist's creative use of experiments. These experiments—actions suggested by the therapist—enable the individual actually to experience various aspects of self during the present moment of therapy. They also help the individual to accept and assume responsibility for the various aspects of self that he or she may have been previously denied. These aspects of self are then reintegrated more completely into a more fully functioning individual (Polster & Polster, 1973, pp. 213–232). Four aspects of human experience on which awareness can be focused are discussed next.

Sensation and Action

Sensation refers to physical experience, such as hunger, itching, heart palpitation, pain, warmth, tingling, and relaxation; *action* refers to behavior. Often sensation and action are related minimally if at all. This means that the individual may be unaware of sensation and not act on it, or feel sensation but still not act on it. At times of union between sensation and action, profound feelings of integration are present. This union, which the Polsters call the *synaptic experience,* is the matrix of creativity. "In this state of aliveness, wholeness, and spontaneous expression, [the individual] is dancing on the edge of awareness" (Polster & Polster, 1973, p. 215).

The Gestalt therapist explores sensation by asking what the person is experiencing while he or she is talking about a concern. Exploring sensation enhances the awareness of the moment and has the potential to restore the past awareness of the child, whom Gestalt therapists describe as having purity of awareness and sensation. The role of Gestalt therapy is to bring back the spontaneity and imagination of the child through concentration on sensation. When the person concentrates on internal sensation, events may occur that are remarkably comparable to events arising out of hypnosis, drugs, and sensory deprivation. When the individual is taken out of his or her customary frame of reference, away from the cognitive and logical to the experience of sensation, he or she can act spontaneously (Polster & Polster, 1973, pp. 216–217).

A major component of Gestalt therapy in general, and sensation in particular, is the creation of awareness of nonverbal behavior. Gestalt therapy takes much more interest in body language than most therapies. It does so because it believes that individuals whose body language and verbal language are congruent with one another are much more integrated in their functioning. Witness the mother who talks of her daughter's drug addiction, how it is tearing the family apart, utters a nervous laugh, states that she and her husband are now together on how to approach the problem, and things will now be better; as she does so, she changes her body position, crosses her arms tightly against her body, and tucks her legs up to her chest. Clearly the verbal messages of the family's togetherness are not congruent with what her body says about the problem.

Passons (1975, pp. 101–102) believes there are four important reasons for closely monitoring the body language of a client. First, each physical behavior is an expression of a person at that particular instant. Rarely are physical movements in the intensity of a therapeutic situation random events. Second, nonverbal behaviors seldom are preconceived or planned. In that regard, they are a better indicator of the true emotional state of the client. Third, clients are usually far more attuned to what they are saying as opposed to what their bodies are doing. Pointing out what a person's body is doing in relation to what is being said is a powerful way of creating awareness. Fourth, becoming aware of and getting body language congruent with verbal language is a powerful tool in creating awareness and changing behavior, particularly in males (Clance, Thompson, & Simerly, 1994).

Feelings
Feelings, such as fear, sadness, happiness, joy, and guilt, are perceived by Gestalt therapists as qualitatively different from sensation and physical response. This qualitative difference is found in the individual's personal assessment of a feeling versus that of a sensation or physical response. Gestalt therapy aims to make room for feelings so that the unfinished situations they are attached to can be integrated into life. This integration is accomplished through awareness in much the same way that sensation is integrated into life. As the client talks, the therapist artfully moves him or her back and forth between awareness and feelings, actions, and verbal expression to emphasize the substance and drama in the story and to fill in gaps in experience. The therapist must rely on the evolution of his or her observations and suggestions to the client. If this rhythm is achieved, then a new experience is created that will match the feeling state of the individual. To achieve a feeling state in the client, the therapist emphasizes what exists—the primary way of dealing with feelings. For example, the therapist may ask the client, "What are your feelings now?" or may tell the client, "Stay with that feeling and see where it leads you" or "Get into the feeling of anger as if you were angry" (Polster & Polster, 1973, pp. 222–227).

Wants
Awareness of wants directs, mobilizes, and channels the individual's actualizing tendencies. Wants link present experience and future gratification. Only by becoming aware of what he or she wants now can the individual become responsible for forging the experiences that make up his or her life. Knowing what one wants motivates action. The Gestalt therapist asks the client, "What do you want?" The goal of this question is to get the individual to define wants so that they emerge as figures in a figure-ground configuration. Then the individual can decide how to attain them (Polster & Polster, 1973, pp. 227–230).

Values and Assessments
Values and assessments are larger units of experience than sensation, feelings, and wants. One goal of Gestalt therapy is to sort out values and assessments so that actions can be rooted in current needs rather than in evaluations based on behavior that was required in the past. When dealing with values and assessments, the therapist may be tapping a whole range of judgments and internal contradictions that are no longer appropriate to the current situation. Part of the therapeutic process is to help the individual rebuild new values by integrating the person he or she was with the person he or she is now. This may involve focusing awareness on the past by bringing it into present experience. The person is then free to respond differently to old situations because current responses can be based on current evaluations rather than on past evaluations (Polster & Polster, 1973, pp. 230–232).

In summary, sensory awareness of past, present, and future events, feelings, cognitions, beliefs, and perceptions is experienced in the here and now of therapy. A major assumption of Gestalt therapy is that such awareness will bring the unfinished situation into the foreground of the individual's perception. In other words, the therapist, creatively and intuitively, helps bring to the client's awareness the existential meaning of his or her symptoms or disguised expression. Through active participation in therapy, the client experiences and assimilates experience rather than interrupting it, and thereby reowns alienated parts of his or her personality and reintegrates them into a new conception of self. This part of therapy is called *closure* or *completing the unfinished Gestalt.*

Conditions of Growth

Many clients who come to therapy function in a chronic state of low-grade emergency, operate from a viewpoint of fixed perceptions, and lack fluidity of figure-ground formation. They have not learned to deal growthfully with the excitement of contact, and consequently they interrupt rather than initiate and maintain contact. Such people often develop a system of permissible contact that serves to reduce excitement. This system minimizes surprise and limits contact to what is familiar. This approach can result in inhibited, rigid behavior that limits growth. The therapist's job is to introduce a new situation in which excitement exists, contact can be made, and growth can occur. The key to the therapeutic endeavor is to keep the level of excitement within manageable limits.

Polster (1985) describes a three-phrase integration sequence in which the therapist uses support to keep the client's excitement within manageable limits. The first phase of this sequence is *discovery*. Discovery involves bringing an issue into the foreground so that it becomes a figure and the client achieves awareness of it. *Accommodation,* the second phase, involves adjusting to the excitement of discovery. This phase has implications for action outside therapy and mobilizes the client's own resources to deal with this excitement. *Assimilation* is the third phase; it involves making a new behavior part of oneself. For a while during this phase, the new behavior will be situation-bound, but later it can become a natural part of the person's behavior.

STRATEGIES FOR HELPING CLIENTS

The experiment is the means by which much of Gestalt therapy is conducted. By playing out feelings and actions in the relative safety of therapy, the individual is mobilized to confront difficulties and emergencies in life (Polster & Polster, 1973, pp. 237–244). Several forms of the experiment are described: (1) enactment, (2) directed behavior, (3) fantasy, (4) dream work, and (5) homework.

Enactment

Enactment is based on the idea that learning requires action. In Gestalt therapy, enactment involves dramatizing some aspect of the individual's existence. Examples of material suited to enactment are unfinished business from the recent past, a characteristic, and polarities. As an example of both a characteristic and a polarity, an individual may view any signs of dependent behavior as indications of weakness.

The following dialogue illustrates the use of enactment with a twenty-five-year-old university student struggling to accept his impending blindness. His rehabilitation counselor has recommended preparing for his blindness by participating in mobility training with either a cane or a guide dog. The student is extremely resistant to engaging in any behavior that will call attention to his visual impairment. One of the issues that clearly emerges from this struggle is his strong desire to be viewed as an independent person. His therapist suggests the experiment of engaging in a dialogue between two aspects of himself, the side that is currently functioning independently and the side that will one day require considerable accommodation and assistance in his daily living. In an attempt to concretize the feelings about the bipolar dilemma the therapist proposes that the client give character names to the feeling states. Polster (1995) proposes that the therapeutic aim of synthesizing alienated aspects of ourselves can be done by construction of heterogeneous characters, each with its own place and voice because within each of us reside a host of characters that, depending on conditions, may be more or less prominent at any given time.

TH: Can you give names to those two feelings, just as if they were real people, but components of yourself?

CL: The independent one would be Iron Mike, the dependent one would be Wimp.

TH: Start out by talking to Wimp.

CL: You won't be able to do anything by yourself. You'll have to rely on other people all the time. You'll have to ask people to help you. You won't be able to read. Somebody will have to drive you to school. You won't be able to take care of yourself, and you'll be a burden to everyone. (*pauses*) You're nothing but a wimp! Useless!

TH: Is there anything else you want to say? (*Shakes head no*) Okay, then, switch chairs and answer from Wimp's side.

CL: Well, I don't know what to say. It seems pretty bad to me too. (*Thinks a while, then speaks from dependent side*) When it comes right down to it, you're either going to have to make some adjustments or just give up.

TH: Change sides and answer from Iron Mike's side.

CL: It just isn't that simple. (*angry tone and fist clinched*) I hate to have to ask anybody for anything. I've always been able to get by on my own. Never needed anyone. I don't want to start now. You can have your adjusting.

TH: Okay. Answer him.

CL: (*long pause and without much energy*) It doesn't seem to me that adjusting is always asking for help. Like the rehab counselor said, you can still do a lot of things on your own even when you can't see. You could learn to use a cane and you could go through that rehab place.

TH: How do you feel as you take Wimp's side?

CL: Sad and frightened. But maybe if I can get Iron Mike to come around we can whip this.

TH: Ask him for help.

CL: Look, if you're so tough then I need your help. I don't know whether I can handle this. (*starts to shake*)

TH: Switch sides. What do you want to say to him?

CL: You can't handle it, what do you think I feel?

TH: What do you feel?

CL: (*jaw clenched*) I feel like I've got to carry the whole load and always have, now I'm not so sure I can. It really makes me angry and scared too.

TH: So what do you want to do with that anger and fear, Mike? If that clenched jaw could talk, what would it say?

CL: By God! Make it work somehow. Get my courage back, but I'm not so sure I can.

TH: Get up from the chairs. (*Client steps out and away from the chairs*) I'm wondering if one of these sides seems more preferable. Which chair would you choose?

CL: Neither one really, and both. Wimp is reasonable and Iron Mike is strong, but they're both afraid of going blind. Somehow I need to get the strong and reasonable together so they can both handle the fear.

Although the enactment did not provide an integration of the polarities, there does seem to have been some movement in the client's thinking about his dilemma. There was also considerable awareness that there is more than one side to the argument. As this awareness is internalized and affects feelings, some integration will occur.

By concretizing the independent/dependent feeling states through character names, the client is able to bring abstract feeling states into more realistic terms that can be identified and addressed. As more feelings surface, more names may be added to the character repertoire and their strengths and weaknesses examined for the parts they play in helping or hindering the client as he attempts to come to grips with his approaching disability. The empty chair is not a cure-all. What it will do is resolve the split between the client's top dog and underdog and allow the polarity to come into awareness so that the client can confront his ambivalent feelings and take responsibility for both sides. After this awareness occurs, then the therapist can move the client past the first two neurotic stages of phoniness and phobic responses to the impasse stage where the client is now stuck (Friedman, 1993). At this point the therapist will stay with the experience and not return to the empty chair technique. A homework assignment that will give the client an opportunity to use his strengths will be jointly formulated by the therapist and the client.

The therapist also uses two techniques that are standard with Gestalt work. She allows the client to experience the polarity and then uses a processing question: "How do you feel?" The continuous use of this question throughout the exercise is designed to keep the client continuously attuned to his feeling state as he moves back and forth. By pointing out to the client his clenched jaw, the therapist also seeks to make the client aware of his body language and how congruent it is with his verbal responses.

Directed Behavior

This strategy involves instructing or guiding the person in something that uncovers or highlights some aspect of behavior that may have been blocked from awareness. This allows the person to discover a new way of looking at previous behavior. Although directed behavior may be similar to enactment, it differs in its focus on specific behavior; it is also more instructional (Polster & Polster, 1973, pp. 252–255). For example, a directed behavior experiment may instruct the person to practice behaviors that the person does not recognize as his or her own. A woman who has a little girl's voice but does not realize this may be asked deliberately to talk like a little girl. Another example would be to direct a shy and unassuming person to speak with assertiveness and authority to the group. Both of these experiments can lead to deeper self-awareness in the directed person and can open the way to new and creative behavior.

The following directed behavior was used to help a male client achieve some closure after hot seat work revolving around the issue of unconditional versus conditional acceptance, particularly by his mother. He thought her love was conditional on his achievements. The therapist directed the client to approach each group member, stand in from of him or her, make eye contact, and say "I don't have to do anything for you to like me. I am good enough for you to like me for myself."

CL: I get the idea. It doesn't seem necessary to say it to everyone.

TH: Go ahead. Just try it for an experiment. Put it in your own words.

CL: (*reluctantly agrees and begins awkwardly with the first group member*) I don't have to do anything for you to like me. I'm okay just as I am.

(*The client stands rather meekly, with shoulders hunched over and arms hanging loosely at his sides*)

TH: Notice how you're standing and your voice tone. (*The therapist goes over to the client and pulls his shoulders back and puts both hands on his hips*)

TH: How does that feel?

CL: Weird! Like it's not me.

TH: I'd like you to experiment with that weird feeling a bit, because what you're doing verbally isn't "you" yet either. Perhaps by taking that "weird not you" posture, that can serve as a kind of cue for the new "you" you're trying to build.

As the client proceeded around the group, his tone became more assertive and he received hugs and other nonverbal support from the group.

TH: How was that for you? What was your experience?

CL: I really felt like I didn't have to do anything for them to like me. It's the first time I can remember feeling that way. I hope I can hang on to it.

Fantasy

Fantasy can be used to make contact with a resisted event, feeling, or personal characteristic, an unavailable person, an unfinished situation, or the unknown (Polster & Polster, 1973, pp. 255–265). As in enactment, there is often a tremendous release of emotional energy during the fantasy. One example of fantasy is contacting a parent or significant other who has died. Repressed emotion, unfinished business, and resistance to thinking and talking about the death are likely to be evident. In this experiment the therapist instructs the person to imagine the deceased sitting and facing him or her (an empty chair is often placed in front of the person) and to engage in dialogue with the deceased. During the dialogue the therapist may instruct the client to tell the dead person what he or she resented and appreciated about him or her and to express guilt for past actions. The person can also be directed to take the role of the deceased and to project what the deceased would say to him or her about resentments, appreciations, and guilts. Then the person and the deceased say "goodbye," symbolizing a letting go of each other. This farewell, usually accompanied by a release of emotion, may bring a sense of relief or peace with the closure of the unfinished situation.

The following excerpt depicts a client who has been verbally abusive with his wife and daughter. He has a great deal of trouble expressing his own feelings. The course of therapy has revealed that his father was a cold, emotionally distant parent who was verbally abusive to the client both as a child and an adult. The father died five years ago. The following scenario depicts the use of guided imagery to help the client get in touch with feelings he has for his father and complete some unfinished business with him.

CL: I don't know what to say about my old man. He never beat me but he was pretty cold.

TH: Could you just close your eyes and imagine what that feeling of "cold" would be?

CL: Like his tombstone. Grayish, black granite, hard, and in January with the snow blowing. It sends a chill down my spine.

TH: Where are you in the scene?

CL: Standing off to the side looking at it. Wanting to say or do something, but not sure what.

TH: What would you like to do?

CL: Get rid of it. I hate that thing.

TH: Do that.

CL: I don't know how, it's granite. I need some tools, like a jackhammer.

TH: Put an air hammer and compressor into your image. What's happening?

CL: I start in on it, chipping at it, but it's really hard.

TH: How are you feeling?

CL: Frustrated. Like I always was with him cause he was immobile and wouldn't crack.

TH: What would help you out?

CL: Like, a crane with a wrecking ball and a rock crusher.

TH: They're now in your image, so go ahead and use them. Tell me what's happening.

CL: Man, I knocked a big chunk out of it. How does that feel, not so tough now. (*Smile crosses face*) Now I'll grind that up. There, it's dust. (*Continues to work on breaking up tombstone*)

TH: How are you feeling?

CL: (*Perspiration on client's face, hands clenched*) Better, but not happy. Really, kind of sad. Like I wished he wouldn't have been that way, but he needed to have that hard rock shell busted off of him.

TH: What would you like to say to your father now that you have busted away the hard rock?

CL: That I miss the times we fished together and I loved him for those times, but despised him for not being there when I needed his emotional support.

TH: Say that to him?

CL: (*Says that to father's gravesite in image and continues talking out his positive and negative feelings toward the deceased parent*)

TH: Can he hear you?

CL: Yes, now that I've got the rock busted away.

TH: Anything else you'd like to do with that image?

CL: Yes, I don't even want that rock dust around, it's gritty and nasty.

TH: How do you want to get rid of it?

CL: Load it up in a dump truck and dump it in the river.

TH: Do that. How do you feel?

CL: Like it's finished, relieved maybe.

TH: Open your eyes and tell me what this experience has meant.

CL: I guess the thing that strikes me the most is I'd not like to have my daughter sitting in an office like this in twenty years doing the same thing I just did, but to me. That scares me, and I'm gonna need to make some changes with her so that it doesn't.

The guided imagery is used as a way of getting the client in touch with his feelings. Note that it is not the father but the feeling of "cold" that is operationalized in the image, because it is the feeling about the relationship that needs to be finished, not the parent. When the client is at an impasse, the "guided" part of the imagery occurs. The therapist provides the client with the necessary equipment to move the image forward. The therapist also stops periodically and processes how the client is feeling. Indeed, as new feelings emerge, it is not uncommon to symbolize those feelings and bring them out into the foreground. At times, if the image is stuck, the therapist may physically move the client around in the scene so that he can achieve a different perspective. The therapist may have the client assume the role of the tombstone because there is a good deal of evidence that the tombstone is an integral part of the client as well. Finally, the therapist brings the image into real time by asking the client to process the experience. The "aha" experience he has in seeing his daughter in his place is typical of the insights clients gain through this procedure.

Dream Work

A dream can serve as the basis for an experiment that brings the dream material to life in therapy. According to Perls (1973, pp. 73–76), dreams are projections of the person; various parts of a dream represent various aspects of the person's existence. In dream work, the person is instructed to recount a dream or a fragment of a dream, speaking in the present tense as if the dream were happening at that moment. After the dream, or a portion of it, is recounted, the person is instructed to play out the parts of the dream, usually by engaging in a dialogue with those parts. Some therapists, such as Zinker (1977, pp. 170–174) use psychodramatic techniques in which group members follow the dreamer's direction and act out the dream. The purposes of dream work include exploring contact possibilities available to the dreamer, such as becoming aware of, owning, and assimilating parts of the self; generating power for unfolding the dreamer's potential for interacting with other people; and recognizing existential meanings that bear on the person's life. Also, some Gestalt therapists explore the dream as a message about the client–therapist relationship (Wheeler, 1991, pp. 99–100). Working with the dream from this perspective provides an opportunity to explore here-and-now aspects of the therapeutic relationship.

Homework

One aim of therapy is to educate an individual to a sense of personal readiness for action (Polster & Polster, 1973, pp. 278–281). Homework is the means by which the insights, possibilities, and meanings brought to awareness in therapy can be implemented in the individual's day-to-day existence. Homework must apply to the client's conflict area, building on the therapy experience to develop possibilities for new and creative behavior. Homework should be tailored to the person's willingness and present ability to try the new behavior. For example, a man who has extreme difficulty in striking up a conversation with women may start out by greeting several women each day, experiencing his awareness of this behavior, perhaps modifying his approach, and gradually working up to longer and more personal conversations. The possibilities for homework are as numerous as the conflicts clients encounter in therapy. The therapist and the client have to generate tasks for behaviors that are suitable to the conflict and appropriate to the individual's risk-taking potential.

SAMPLE CASE

This case study consists of an individual Gestalt therapy session that was part of a demon-stration of Gestalt techniques to a group of students studying counseling. The material for the individual session grew out of a group exercise in which participants were first relaxed and then instructed to imagine themselves as animals. A guided fantasy exer-cise followed these instructions. Subsequently, one of the participants volunteered to be a client in a demonstration of individual Gestalt work. The volunteer—Carol, age thirty-three—had become a lamb in her fantasy. The therapist directed her to engage in a dialogue with the lamb. Portions of a transcript of the session follow.

TH: So why don't we start out by being Carol and talking to the lamb.

CL: I don't like to talk to something that can't answer me back, but . . . (*pause*)

TH: Develop that a little.

CL: I'd like to talk to you if you could talk back to me. I think you are kind of cute, fuzzy. I hate to think that you are going to have to grow up because I think you're hav-ing more fun right now than when you are grown. Maybe you don't feel like that, but you can't tell me. I see you wanting to get out of the chair and run. You don't seem to have any patience. So just go and run. You don't have to stay here with me because I can still like you when you're way off in the distance and that's kind of nice.

TH: Okay, switch chairs. Now you're the lamb talking back to Carol.

CL: (*voice becomes childlike*) I'm kind of glad you think I'm so cute because I think I'm kind of nice. I like to be fuzzy because when I rub up against a stone it doesn't hurt because I have so much protection. But I really would rather run. I don't like to stay in one place too long. Just let me go and play by myself and then come back and play with all the other lambs.

TH: What is that? (*no answer*) Who is that?

CL: I suppose it's Carol.

TH: Uh . . . (*client begins to cry*) What's happening? (*pause*) Go ahead and stay with that. (*client cries with more intensity*) Just keep breathing. (*pause*) Can you give voice to your tears?

CL: (*voice wavering and tears in eyes*) I suppose it's because I feel too much responsi-bility right now, and I don't want it. I'm in the middle of two generations and most of the time it's very lonely. Right now, I just want to leave it. But if I left it, there would be misunderstanding and sadness. There would be an unsympathetic attitude.

The two sides of this client's existential dilemma have emerged—the part of the client that wants to be free and the part that is trapped by her sense of responsibility for her family. A dialogue is set up between these parts.

TH: What I'd like you to do is put Carol over there (*pointing to the empty chair desig-nated "overly responsible Carol," located opposite from another empty chair designated* "responsible Carol"), the side of Carol who would like to be free, who has too much responsibility. And tell her what the consequences would be if she did what she wanted to do.

CL: (*client takes responsible role instead*) Huh!—you can't believe what would happen—well, if you just took off now, you know how your family would feel. Your daughter would be upset because she wouldn't understand. Your mother would be upset because she would think you had to be there when your daughter needed you or when your son needed you. And if your other son comes down and doesn't find you here, he probably wouldn't stay.

TH: You'd let a lot of people down.

CL: Yeah—obviously—I couldn't do it. You could do it, *but* after you had been gone a day or so, you would be miserable. It would be much better to go when everyone understood why you are going. Until you can reach this understanding, I don't think you should (*pauses and laughs*), but anyway . . . (*trails off and seems to realize she is talking to herself*).

TH: Go ahead and give it to her. She's irresponsible.

CL: You can't go until they *understand,* because you *should* care enough about their feelings not to hurt them. When everything is fine, then you can leave.

TH: Talk to the real responsible person who is going to take care of all those people—solid-as-a-rock Carol. And you (*indicating other chair*) are Carol who wants to run in pastures and be free.

CL: (*laughs*) I understand what you are telling me, but right now I think it's a lot of bull (*rapid, firm speech with seemingly decisive tone*). If I want to go and do, I should be able to do so. I have stayed patient for a long enough period of time, and if I want to go away and do something I should be able to do it. I'm old enough to know what to do, and I don't think it's going to upset anyone if I just take off. When I come back I would be easier to live with, feel better, and have a different frame of mind. So you telling me I have to be responsible doesn't sit too well with me. I'm upset with you telling me this. I don't think it's your place to tell me what I have to do. Because if I want to go, that should be my own decision.

TH: What do you resent about Carol over there?

CL: I resent her saying I should be more responsible.

TH: Say that again.

CL: (*stronger tone*) I resent you saying I should be more responsible for my children, for my mother, but you don't say (*cries*) I should be more responsible for me.

TH: Stay with that. Just let me be me. (*pause*) I want to be me.

CL: (*in tears*) I feel I could be more me if I didn't keep hearing how I should be feeling all the time. (*words measured and slower*) I could be more myself if everyone wasn't so demanding of my time.

TH: Plus the family is too demanding.

When the therapist proposed, "*You* are too demanding of my time," Carol responded by bringing her family into focus. She was then instructed to engage in a dialogue with her family because her energy had seemed to switch toward them and away from herself.

TH: Okay. Let's just do this. Put Grandma and the kids over there and give them hell. They deserve it.

CL: (*bursts out laughing*) But maybe they don't. Becky, you expect too much of me economically. You expect too much of my time, and I think you expect me to accept whatever mood you're in without caring how I feel.

TH: Tell her what you don't like about that.

CL: I think you should understand from a point of view of economics why some things are not feasible, like a new pair of designer jeans. When you have six pairs, you don't need a seventh pair. I also don't always have time to take you where you want to go, and there are some places that I don't think you should go. Because you upset me this way, that interferes with my time to be myself because I worry about you and whether you're happy and whether you are going to be able to live with yourself.

TH: I want a lot for you. (*feeds Carol a line to say to her daughter*)

CL: Mm-hm. I do want a lot for you, but there are limitations.

TH: I want you to respect me. (*feeds another line*)

CL: No. Not so much that. I know it's difficult to live with someone else. There are times when you can like someone and can't love them and times when you love someone but can't like them. I think you should understand that. And Mama (*angrily switches to mother*), I wish you would stop telling me how the children should behave. If I can live with it, then you should be able to live with it. I think it's unfair to always take it out on me when you think the children don't behave the way you think they should. They have a right to like me, love me, or not, and that is their decision.

At this point it seemed appropriate for the therapist to instruct Carol to talk with her son rather than having Mama engage in dialogue with her, because her last sentence to Mama was said with finality.

TH: What do you want to say to Jack?

CL: Jack, I think you know I wish you were a little neater. I think sometimes you are too much alone, but there's nothing I can do for you. If that's how you are comfortable, then that's fine. Other than cut your hair. (*laughs*)

TH: Tell Jack what you appreciate about him.

CL: I like your care, your concern. I appreciate your doing what I ask you to do. I appreciate that you care enough for me to be concerned about different things. That you don't cause any waves between Becky and you. I enjoy you because I can talk to you like an adult. I think the times we have together are fun. I appreciate your sense of humor that's so much like mine that I feel I'm not your mother but somebody you enjoy. I know sometimes you hurt inside, and I know you've been able to take care of that and not let it depress or upset you. I really (*voice breaks*) love you. (*cries, pauses*)

In this session Carol's awareness of her existence emerged sharply, as did some self-discovery and some clarification of her feelings toward family members. She also showed awareness of her responsibility for her existence, but seemed barely able to acknowledge any choice in her life. There seemed to be no integration of the polarities of freedom and responsibility during the session. However, the session may have led Carol to work further on her own regarding her feelings of responsibility and her feelings toward the members of her family.

CONTRIBUTIONS OF GESTALT THERAPY

One of the major contributions of Gestalt therapy is its experiential nature. Talk about the problem, conflict, or issue is minimized and actual experiencing of its existential meaning for the individual is maximized. Most other therapies tend to emphasize talking about the problem and cognitively understanding it, often to the exclusion of feeling and experiencing its meaning to the individual's existence. Whereas some therapies attempt to change behavior directly without changing the person, Gestalt therapy uses clients' behavior to make them aware of their creative potential to discover for themselves and to facilitate their own change.

Another contribution is the Gestalt approach to working with dreams. Rather than interpreting a dream for a client, the Gestalt therapist helps him or her discover the existential message of the dream. Working with parts of a dream as projections of the self rather than as symbolic representations of hidden meaning removes much of the mystery associated with psychoanalytic interpretation. This approach allows clients to take responsibility for the content of their dreams and find their meaning for themselves. A third contribution of Gestalt therapy is its practice of using body and other nonverbal language to help clients become aware of their conflicts and choices. Other therapists do recognize the importance of attending to the client's nonverbal behavior for the purpose of adding nuance to what the client is saying. But Gestalt therapy acknowledges nonverbal behavior as one of the keys to discovering meaning.

The creative stance of Gestalt therapy is a major contribution to the therapy field in general. Most therapies, with the exception of Gestalt and person-centered, are technique rather than process oriented. And even person-centered counseling, which emphasizes process, is oriented around the technique of reflection. In theory, Gestalt therapists approach each therapeutic session as an existential encounter.

Probably the greatest compliment an approach can receive is from those who use it to build their own theories. Self-psychology, object relations, transactional analysis, and neurolinguistics have all borrowed heavily from Gestalt to enhance their own approaches (Jacobs, 1992; Polster & Polster, 1993).

SHORTCOMINGS OF GESTALT THERAPY

The Gestalt approach is not without limitations (Fagan & Shepherd, 1970, pp. 238–243). Some of these limitations have to do with the training, experience, skills, and personality of the therapist. The techniques of Gestalt therapy often lead to the intense expression of emotion. The therapist must have the experience and emotional presence to guide the individual through the expression of this affect and through the cognitive and affective integration of what he or she experienced during the therapy session. Otherwise the individual can be left feeling unfinished and less integrated than before the experience.

The therapist must also be aware of his or her needs for approval, admiration, or, perhaps, guru-like status. Because of the dramatic nature of Gestalt therapy and the frequent presence of an audience, the therapist must avoid the temptation to play to the audience and to push the individual too fast just to produce a dramatic effect. Also, therapist impatience with the individual will be communicated and possibly taken as another rejection or a further confirmation of ineffectiveness.

Gestalt therapy is often practiced as individual therapy in a group setting. Although there may be some benefit from spectator therapy, unless a person gets in the hot seat the experience can be a passive one. This aspect of some Gestalt groups ignores many of the group-interaction processes that ultimately lead the individual to feelings of personal worth, power, and responsibility (Kepner, 1980). When the Gestalt therapist directs the proceedings so much that the group remains passive, opportunities to develop responsibility and self-support are not available.

A final limitation of traditional Gestalt therapy is its emphasis on the individual as sole master of his or her fate without regard to the functioning of society or the day-to-day influences of other people. The individual who takes on the philosophy of individual responsibility wholeheartedly will experience considerable frustration and even intolerance of the way things are in the real world. Rather than being an isolated incident in a group situation or the therapist's office, Gestalt therapy, and its underlying concepts, should be integrated into the individual's daily life.

GESTALT THERAPY WITH DIVERSE POPULATIONS

Gestalt therapy's primary focus on process (what is happening to the person internally) rather than on content (verbal material and external events being discussed) is an advantage for its use in multicultural counseling. According to Yontef and Simkin (1989, p. 347), the process-oriented Gestalt therapist can work effectively with people in crisis, adults in poverty programs, interaction groups, psychotics, and almost any group imaginable.

Some of the gender issues that people bring to counseling are feelings of powerlessness, lack of trust in their capacity to find self-direction, difficulties in maintaining firm interpersonal boundaries, reluctance to express bottled-up feelings, and meeting others' needs to the exclusion of their own (Enns, 1987). Gestalt techniques can be empowering to both women and men who present gender issues such as these by focusing on self-awareness, providing avenues for acknowledging feelings, identifying and integrating disowned aspects of the personality, and finding ways of exercising autonomy and power.

Tannen (1986; 1990) has documented notable differences in how women and men use language in conversational styles and the misunderstandings those different styles generate in cross-gender communication. The Gestalt approach's precise use of language can enhance awareness of those difficulties and empower people with gender issues to achieve self-definition. Tannen's (1990) model of cross-gender communication also applies to cross-cultural understanding: "So when speakers from different parts of the country, or of different ethnic or class backgrounds, talk to each other, it is likely that their words will not be understood exactly as they were meant" (p. 13). Gestalt therapy offers a variety of strategies, in addition to precise language, for bridging these communications gaps between disparate people. Gestalt groups, for instance, are well suited to providing supportive interaction, sharing of experience, validation of feelings, acceptance of people, strengthening of attachments, and bonding with others who have similar issues.

Livneh and Sherwood (1991, pp. 530–531) report that Gestalt therapy strategies provide rich opportunities for helping clients with disabilities. Prototypical examples of appropriate use of Gestalt techniques in rehabilitation settings are enhancing self-awareness, encouragement of client responsibility for self, and enabling clients to deal with impasse and attain closure of unfinished needs and concerns. The Gestalt concepts considered most critical for understanding the psychosocial adaptation to physical disability are the holistic view of the person, the emphasis on self-awareness and the here and now, personal responsibility, and the principles of polarities and closure.

The emphasis of Gestalt therapy on existential living, aggression, and conflict makes it well suited for clients who who have AIDS (Klepner, 1992; Siemens, 1993) or other terminal diseases. Not only can Gestalt deal with the many loss issues of hurt, grief, and anger that undergird the psychological foundations of these diseases, it also can provide a format for transcending them and living life in full contact with the world.

While many clients may deny the role that affect plays in their lives and may need to come to grips with their feelings, they may be highly resistant to the artificiality of some Gestalt techniques, such as talking to an empty chair; speaking to one's hand or other body parts; or engaging in imagery, fantasy, and/or projection. These concerns would apply to any client whose cultural mores are in opposition to such tactics. Gestalt techniques may be viewed as contrived, "weird," and uncomfortable to people from many cultural and socioeconomic backgrounds. For people who deny emotions as an integral part of their lives, the confrontive style of Gestalt therapy can be extremely threatening and may drive them away from both individual and group therapy.

Finally, clients who cannot or have not developed the ability to use symbols, images, dreams, projections, or fantasies tend to experience minimal benefit from Gestalt therapy. Since the goals of Gestalt therapy include awareness and inner integration of conflicts and opposing polarities, the clients who benefit the most from therapy are those who have a well-developed sense of symbolizing, imaging, and fantasizing in their personal lives. Clients who have difficulty symbolizing or articulating in symbolic terms may not fare well with a purely Gestalt therapist.

SUMMARY

Gestalt therapy was developed by Frederick Perls from a background of training and experience that included psychoanalysis, Gestalt psychology, semantics, psychodrama, and the human potential movement. The therapy is based on a personality theory that stresses the organism's innate striving toward homeostasis; the holistic nature of the person and the environment; and the organism's development of a capacity for aggression that facilitates contact with the environment. It is the failure to develop this aggression in a wholesome and complete manner that leads to maladaptive behavior, or what Perls termed *neurosis*. During therapy, the client's maladaptive behavior is directly dealt with through the creative utilization of experiments that facilitate the development of awareness. Several key concepts govern the nature of the therapeutic encounter, and their embodiment in therapy contributes to the development of the client's awareness. These concepts are the experiential nature of Gestalt therapy, here-and-now orientation, awareness, responsibility, polarities, top dog/underdog, environmental contact, figure-ground, and unfinished business. Specific Gestalt therapeutic strategies include enactment, directed behavior, fantasy, and dream work. These strategies enable clients to experience the meaning of their existence during the therapeutic encounter. Homework, another strategy, is sometimes assigned to help the client integrate insights and learning from therapy with day-to-day existence.

Gestalt therapy's most potent contribution is that it brings aspects of the client's existence into the therapy room, where therapist and client work with them experimentally. The resulting experiences not only enable the client to achieve a degree of inner integration through self-discovery now, but provide him or her with insights that may contribute to the experiencing of new Gestalts or "aha" moments long after the therapy session ends.

SUGGESTIONS FOR FURTHER READING

Harmon, R. L. (Ed.). (1990). *Gestalt therapy discussions with the masters.* Springfield, IL: Charles C. Thomas.
O'Leary, E. (1992). *Gestalt therapy: Theory, practice and research.* London: Chapman & Hall.
Perls, F. (1969). *Gestalt therapy verbatim.* New York: Bantam.
Perls, F., Hefferline, R., & Goodman, P. (1951). *Gestalt therapy: Excitement and growth in the human personality.* New York: Dell.
Polster, E., & Polster, M. (1973). *Gestalt therapy integrated.* New York: Brunner/Mazel.
Wheeler, G. (1991). *Gestalt reconsidered: A new approach to contact and resistance.* New York: Gardner Press.

REFERENCES

Assagioli, R. (1965). *Psychosynthesis.* New York: Viking Press.
Clance, P. R., Thompson, M. B., & Simerly, E. D. (1994). The effects of the Gestalt approach on body image. *Gestalt Journal, 17*(1), 95–114.
Enns, C. Z. (1987). Gestalt therapy and feminist therapy: A proposed integration. *Journal of Counseling and Development, 66,* 93–95.
Fagan, J., & Shepherd, I. (Eds.). (1970). *Gestalt therapy now: Theory/techniques/applications.* New York: Harper & Row.

Friedman, N. (1993). Fritz Perls's layers and the empty chair: A reconsideration. *Gestalt Journal, 16*(2), 95–119.

Frew, J. (1992). From the perspective of the environment. *Gestalt Journal, 15*(1), 39–60.

Harman, R. L. (1982). Gestalt therapy theory: Working at the contact boundaries. *Gestalt Journal, 5*, 39–48.

Hendlin, S. J. (1987). Gestalt therapy: Aspects of evolving theory and practice. *Humanistic Psychologist, 15*, 184–196.

Hycner, R. H. (1987). An interview with Erving and Miriam Polster: The dialogical dimension in Gestalt therapy. *Gestalt Journal, 10*, 27–66.

Jacobs, L. (1992). Insights from psychoanalytic self-psychology and intersubjectivity theory for Gestalt therapists. *Gestalt Journal, 15*(2), 25–60.

Kepner, E. (1980). Gestalt group process. In B. Feder & R. Ronall (Eds.), *Beyond the hot seat: Gestalt approaches to group* (pp. 5–24). New York: Brunner/Mazel.

Klepner, P. (1992). AIDS/HIV and Gestalt therapy. *Gestalt Journal, 15*(2), 5–24.

Kogan, G. (1976). The genesis of Gestalt therapy. In C. Hatcher & P. Himmelstein (Eds.). *The handbook of Gestalt therapy* (pp. 235–257). New York: Jason Aronson.

Livneh, H., & Sherwood, A. (1991). Application of personality theories and counseling strategies to clients with physical disabilities. *Journal of Counseling and Development, 69*, 525–538.

Passons, W. R. (1975). *Gestalt approaches in counseling.* New York: Holt, Rinehart & Winston.

Perls, F. (1969). *Gestalt therapy verbatim.* New York: Bantam.

Perls, F. (1971). *In and out of the garbage pail.* New York: Bantam Books.

Perls, F. (1973). *The Gestalt approach and eyewitness to therapy.* New York: Bantam.

Polster, E. (1992). The self in action: A Gestalt outlook. In J. K. Zeig (Ed.), *The evolution of psychotherapy: The second conference* (pp. 143–154). New York: Bruner-Mazel.

Polster, E. (1995). *A population of selves: A therapeutic exploration of personal diversity.* San Francisco, CA: Jossey-Bass.

Polster, E., & Polster, M. (1973). *Gestalt therapy integrated.* New York: Brunner/Mazel.

Polster, E., & Polster M. (1993). Frederick Perls: Legacy and invitation. *Gestalt Journal, 16*(2), 23–25.

Polster, M. (1985). Gestalt therapy: Evolution and application. Paper presented at the Evolution of Psychotherapy Conference, Phoenix, AZ.

Resnick, R. W. (1984). Gestalt therapy East and West: Bicoastal dialogue, debate, or debacle? *Gestalt Journal, 7*, 13–22.

Rosenfeld, E. (1978). An oral history of Gestalt therapy, Part I: A conversation with Laura Perls. *Gestalt Journal, 1*, 8–31.

Saner, R. (1989). Cultural bias of Gestalt therapy: Made-in-USA. *Gestalt Journal, 12*, 57–71.

Sharf, R. S. (1996). *Theories of psychotherapy and counseling: Concepts and cases.* Pacific Grove, CA: Brooks/Cole.

Siemens, H. (1993). A Gestalt approach in the care of persons with HIV. *Gestalt Journal, 16*(1), 91–104.

Simkin, J, (1975). An introduction to Gestalt therapy. In F. D. Stephenson (Ed.), *Gestalt therapy primer* (pp. 9–10). Springfield, IL: Chas. C. Thomas.

Simkin, J. (1976). The development of Gestalt therapy. In C. Hatcher & P. Himmelstein (Eds.), *The handbook of Gestalt therapy* (p. 225). New York: Jason Aronson.

Tannen, D. (1986). *That's not what I meant! How conversational style makes or breaks your relations with others.* New York: William Morrow.

Tannen, D. (1990). *You just don't understand: Women and men in conversation.* New York: Ballantine Books.

Thompson, C. L., & Rudolph, L. B. (1996). *Counseling children.* Pacific Grove, CA: Brooks/Cole.

Walker, J. (1971). *Body and soul: Gestalt therapy and religious experience.* Nashville: Abingdon.

Wheeler, G. (1991). *Gestalt reconsidered: A new approach to contact resistance.* New York: Gardner Press.

Yontef, G. M. (1976). Theory of Gestalt therapy. In C. Hatcher & P. Himmelstein (Eds.), *The handbook of Gestalt therapy* (pp. 216–218). New York: Jason Aronson.

Yontef, G. M. (1995). Gestalt therapy. In A. S. Gurman &. S. B. Messner (Eds.), *Essential psychotherapies: Theory and practice* (pp. 261–303). New York: Guilford Press.

Yontef, G. M., & Simkin, J. S. (1989). Gestalt therapy. In R. J. Corsini & D. Wedding (Eds.), *Current psychotherapies* (4th ed., pp. 323–361). Itasca, IL: F. E. Peacock.

Zinker, J. (1977). *Creative process in Gestalt therapy.* New York: Brunner/Mazel.

Zinker, J. (1987). Gestalt values: Maturing of Gestalt therapy. *Gestalt Journal, 10,* 69–89.

7

TRANSACTIONAL ANALYSIS

FUNDAMENTAL TENETS

History

Eric Berne (1910–1970), trained as a psychiatrist and psychoanalyst, began developing the essence of transactional analysis (TA) theory in the 1950s. Berne's discovery of the ego states (1955–1962) is considered to be the first phase in the development of TA. This discovery was based on neurological experiments that suggested that different *ego states* are reexperienced by persons upon direct stimulation of the brain. Berne recognized the importance of this discovery and identified three distinct ego states—Parent, Adult, and Child—which constitute a coherent system of thinking, feeling, and behaving.

As a theory, TA began to gain notoriety in the 1960s with the publication of two widely read books: *Games People Play* (Berne, 1964) and *I'm OK—You're OK* (Harris, 1969). With the advent of the *OK* book, which sold over 15 million copies in eighteen different languages, TA became *the* self-help psychological approach of the 1970s.

In the second phase of its development (1962–1966), TA focused mainly on games. Berne's interest in communication theory helped him to understand that in many instances, two types of messages (social and psychological) were originating at the same time from one communication source. Berne observed that the covert psychological meaning of such messages differed from the overt social meaning. This finding resulted in his concept of games—a series of these two-level transactions leading to a predictable outcome or payoff. In this period of development, TA remained primarily an intellectual approach emphasizing the concept of insight.

The dominant force in TA during the third developmental phase (1966–1970) was script analysis. The concept of scripts emerged concurrently with Berne's (1966) book on group treatment and in response to the question "Why do different people play the same games over and over?" Techniques for analyzing and understanding scripts (Berne, 1966; 1972; Steiner, 1967; 1974) were developed and put to use in treatment (Goulding & Goulding, 1978; Schiff, 1970). Thus, TA began to shift away from a passive, intellectual–insight approach to a more proactive regimen in which the therapist intervenes and changes client scripts.

In the 1970s, TA gained additional prominence through such popular publications as *Born to Win* (James & Jongeward, 1971) and *What Do You Say After You Say Hello?* (Berne, 1972), published two years after Berne's death in 1970. After Berne's death, TA continued to incorporate new if somewhat idiosyncratic treatment techniques, such as Dusay's (1972; 1977; Dusay & Dusay, 1989, p. 416) "energy distribution and action" and "egogram" and Schiff's (1970) "reparenting" approach.

The fourth influence on TA was the hybridization by the Gouldings (1978; 1979) of TA and Gestalt into *redecision therapy*. Redecision therapy ferrets out the affect that links past to present and allows the client to challenge his or her beliefs about the self in the past. In challenging those beliefs comes the opportunity to reconsider old scripts and replace them with newer, more functional ones (McClendon & Kadis, 1995). According to Clarkson (1992), TA has shifted and evolved so that currently it clearly embraces all three main streams of psychology—behavioral, analytic, and humanistic.

Overview of Transactional Analysis

Transactional analysis has several identifying characteristics. First, it is *contractual:* the therapist is guided by a therapeutic contract in working with clients.

Second, TA is *decisional* and views *responsibility* as a key issue in therapy. Clients are assisted in tracing here-and-now behavior and feelings back to some basic decisions they made regarding how to get along in the world. Often, it is this decision process that is the essence of TA.

A third major characteristic of TA is that its practitioners share a *common vocabulary* of well-defined terms easily understood by clients. *Education* of clients in the essential concepts of TA is viewed as a necessary component of counseling. Books explaining TA theory, such as *Born to Win* (James & Jongeward, 1971), are often assigned to clients as an adjunct to therapy.

Finally, Woollams and Brown (1979) have pointed out two other distinguishing characteristics of TA. All TA therapists apply concepts of *ego states* and life *scripts* and follow a treatment approach based on the assumption "I'm OK—You're OK."

TA's theory of personality and its therapeutic principles are operationalized by collecting and analyzing four different types of information:

1. *Transactions*—what people say and do to one another
2. *Scripts*—endless feedback loops of behavior generated in early childhood and continuing to the present
3. *Games and cons*—transactions (often maladaptive) that are played with others and that lead to payoffs (also often maladaptive)
4. *Structures*—the differential composition of ego states specific to each individual.

Theory of Personality

Transactional analysis theorists understand personality development in terms of several key concepts: ego states, strokes, injunctions, decisions, script formation, games, transactions, and life positions (Berne, 1964; Goulding, 1989; Goulding & Goulding, 1979; Woollams & Brown, 1979). Given Berne's psychoanalytic roots, all of these concepts have a distinct Freudian flavor (Novellino & Moiso, 1990). However, whereas the Freudian constructs of the superego, ego, and id exist in the unconscious, the constructs of TA are behavioral realities (Goldhaber & Goldhaber, 1976, p. 9). The basic personality premise of TA is that all of us are three people in one—a child, an adult, and a parent (Harris & Harris, 1985, p. 12). These constructs are shown in Figure 7.1.

The Child Ego State

The Child ego state consists of "impulses, feelings, and spontaneous acts." It contains the "recordings of the child's early experiences, responses, and the 'positions' taken about self and others" (James & Jongeward, 1971, p. 18). The Child ego state has two basic functional states—the Free Child and the Adapted Child. The Free Child is spontaneous, playful, eager, joyful, and curious. However, individuals who stay in their Free Child state too long may be considered "out of control" or "irresponsible." In contrast, individuals in their Adapted Child ego state may be described as compliant, compromising, rebellious, or industrious and act as if a parent may be watching or listening. The important distinction between Free Child and Adapted Child behavior is that the Adapted Child state is an adaptation to others whereas the Free Child state is a spontaneous expression of feelings and behavior without regard to the reactions of others (Dusay & Dusay, 1989, p. 438).

Throughout one's life, the Child ego state is both an influence and a state of being that is internally derived. It provides the "want to" of the personality and is the force that motivates the individual (Harris & Harris, 1985, p. 17).

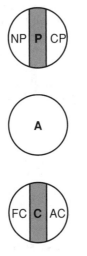

FIGURE 7.1   Ego States

The Parent Ego State

In terms of function, the Parent ego state may be divided into the Nurturing Parent and the Critical Parent. In most cases, someone functioning as a Nurturing Parent behaves in a caring, concerned, and protective manner but may sometimes appear overprotective. Someone functioning as a Critical Parent is experienced as an oppressive, prejudiced, powerful, intimidating, and controlling person who demands "yes" and "no" answers. Trusting neither self nor others, the Critical Parent calls on external authority to enforce his or her demands (Harris & Harris, 1985, pp. 223–224).

Too much of a Critical Parent results in aggression, while too little results in passivity. Too much Nurturing Parent results in an overbearing and inhibiting personality, while too little means an inconsiderate and uncaring personality (Dusay & Dusay, 1989, p. 408).

In the Parent ego state is recorded a modeled and taught concept of life. This unerasable concept is composed of events that actually happened in childhood. Traditions and values reside in the concept, although values as well as other information may need updating later in life by the person's Adult ego state. The problem is that the individual internalizes this tape in a distorted fashion, recording both the distorted and the objective realities of what one's parents were. Because the child is dependent on its parents, it is unable to comprehend that they were not God, but human, and thus made mistakes. As a result, the child grows to adulthood with a commingled but "ultimately right" Parent ego state that is filled with demands, directions, and dogmatic decisions. The Parent ego state, then, is the externally derived "have to" of the personality (Harris & Harris, 1985, pp. 14–18).

The Adult Ego State

The Adult ego state is the referee between the demands of the Parent ego state and the wants of the Child ego state. The Adult ego state adds the thought concept to the taught concept of the Parent ego state and the felt concept of the Child ego state. It provides the "how to" for the personality by asking "why" questions and considering consequences. The Adult ego state is not only a functioning part of the personality but also an observable state, and it is internally derived. One of its major functions is to update the Parent ego state (Harris & Harris, 1985, pp. 17–18).

The Adult ego state is not divided because it is unemotional and functions solely as a computer (Dusay & Dusay, 1989, p. 409). Therefore, too much adult results in a technically rational but boring individual not unlike Mr. Spock of *Star Trek* fame, while too little adult results in an illogical and irrational individual (Dusay & Dusay, 1989, p. 437).

Strokes

In TA theory, the need for strokes is considered the basic motivation for any human social interaction and necessary to an individual's healthy functioning (Dusay & Dusay, 1979, p. 377).

The most positive strokes come from parents who unconditionally accept their children. However, even if acceptance of children is conditional, the Child ego state will be happy if promised strokes are delivered (Harris & Harris, 1985, p. 45). As children grow, they receive strokes that may be either positive—"I love you!"—or negative—"I hate you!" Although naturally preferring positive strokes, children consider negative strokes better than no strokes at all (Woollams & Brown, 1979, p. 43). On the basis of parental messages and in order to obtain strokes, children may decide to adapt to what they perceive their parents desire, even though such behavior may be detrimental to their long-term health and overall well-being. Although parental strokes are probably the strongest and most enduring for the child, strokes in adulthood may also be obtained from peers, bosses, spouses, and children and from our own realization that we did a good job (Harris & Harris, 1985, pp. 47, 87). When straightforward, direct strokes are not available, people may opt to play games and rackets to obtain them (Woollams, 1978). In summary, the strokes one receives or gives to others reinforce one's life position and furthers his or her script, ego functions, transactions, rackets, and games (Cassius, 1980, p. 216).

Life Positions

Life position is a result of decisions made in response to how parent figures react to the child's initial expressions of his or her feelings and needs (Woollams & Brown, 1979, p. 108) and is a major component of an individual's life script. There are four basic life positions an individual may adopt (Cassius, 1980; Harris, 1969; Woollams & Brown, 1979):

1. *I'm OK—You're OK.* This is probably the position reflecting how the child entered the world. As long as the child's emotional and physical needs are met in a loving, accepting way (given "permissions"), the infant retains this position and maintains a "winner's" script.
2. *I'm OK—You're not OK.* If a child is mistreated, he or she may decide others are not OK, which is essentially a defense against a more basic feeling of being "not OK." People in this position often blame and distrust others and react to the world with frustration or anger (sometimes called the "paranoid" position).
3. *I'm not OK—You're OK.* If the child's needs are not met, the child may decide that it is his or her fault for being "lacking" in some fundamental way. This is the most common position and is sometimes called the "depressive" position. People who are frequently in this position commonly experience guilt, depression, inadequacy, and fear.
4. *I'm not OK—You're not OK.* If stroking is lacking or extremely negative, the child may decide, "I'm not OK—You're not OK." Since there is no source of positive stroking, the infant may give up and feel hopeless. Persons who adopt this position are more likely to end up in mental institutions, jail, or the morgue.

Script Formation

Berne (1972, p. 31) stated that in early life, individuals decide how they will live and how they will die, and this plan, "ever-present" in their heads, is called a script. Scripts have a variety of components, including decisions, life positions, fantasy characters, games, payoffs, physiological attributes (body language), and parental injunctions (Cassius, 1980, p. 214; Steiner, 1967, pp. 38–39). Scripts often incorporate specific elements from fairy tales and myths in which the person may be seen as playing different dramatic roles (Karpman, 1968).

Parents may send children two types of messages that influence the formation of their life position: permissions and script messages. Permissions—positive strokes given unconditionally—are growth-promoting messages. In contrast, script messages are negative, growth-restricting, and destructive injunctions.

After the child incorporates early messages from the parents, a script develops into a strong belief system, which is staunchly defended as an adult (Dusay &

Dusay, 1989, p. 409). Negative, long-term, global injunctions and attributions do little for the child's physical and mental health. There are two types of such messages. First are those messages that come from the Critical Parent, a pseudoparent who is in reality operating in the Child ego state. The Critical Parent may give several injunctions phrased in a variety of "Don't" messages: "Don't do (be, love). . . ." Stated in all-inclusive, nonspecific terms, these messages stultify discrimination between growth-promoting and growth-restricting activities and lead to a pathological Child ego state that carries into adulthood (Steiner, 1974, p. 60).

Another component of the Critical Parent is the use of attributions to form script messages in the child (Laing, 1971). These are "Do" messages that may be set from birth through myths such as "You were born on Martin Luther King's birthday, so do be a great man." Even names subtly suggest attributional states: Cliff, Jr., will follow in his father's footsteps, Biff will raise hell, Lydia will be elegant, and Billie Jean will be the boy her father never had. Attributions or counterinjunctions are "driver" statements that set what the child must, should, or will do, whereas injunctions tell the child what he or she must, should, or will not do in order to gain the parents' favor (Steiner, 1974, pp. 62–64).

Counterscripts

To complicate matters, the nurturing parent also contributes contradictory "Do" messages that may have problematic consequences for the child. Called a *counterscript,* these parental messages demand acquiescence to the social and cultural expectations of society. The Nurturing Parent makes a positive verbal demand— "Be a caring person"—which is contradicted by the hypocritical action of the Critical Parent who says, "I won't give any money to that charity; they're just a bunch of welfare parasites." In other words, "Do as I say, not as I do!"

Transactions

A transaction is the basic unit of behavior in TA theory. It is the actual line of communication among the Parent, Adult, and Child ego states of two people and determines whether communication is likely to continue, stop, or be dishonest.

A transaction is "an exchange of strokes between two persons, consisting of a stimulus and a response between specific ego states" (Woollams & Brown, 1979, p. 65). A conversation involves a series of linked transactions. There are three kinds of transactions—complementary, crossed, and ulterior. The vectors of these transactions are illustrated in Figure 7.2. In a *complementary transaction* the response comes from the same ego state to which the stimulus was directed and is directed back to the same ego state that sent the stimulus. Thus, it is a parallel transaction. For example, Bob asks (from his Adult ego state), "How much does this cost?" and Joan (from her Adult) responds, "Five dollars." Or Bob says (from his Child), "I can't find my tie!" and Mary responds (from her Parent), "I'll help you find it; don't worry." In complementary transactions, communication may continue without breaking down (Woollams & Brown, 1979, pp. 66–68) as long as the vectors stay in parallel, as demonstrated by the lines in Figure 7.2.

A *crossed transaction* occurs when communication lines are not parallel and the receiver responds to the sender in an ego state different from the one to which the message was directed. For example, Bob asks (from his Adult) "How much does this cost?" and Joan responds (from her Free Child), "None of your beeswax, nosy!" This crossed adult–defiant child transaction is illustrated by the vectors in

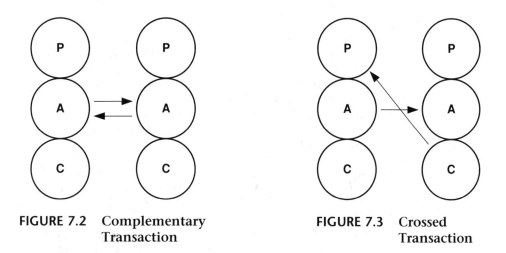

FIGURE 7.2   Complementary
Transaction

FIGURE 7.3   Crossed
Transaction

Figure 7.3. Whenever a crossed transaction occurs, a breakdown in communication is likely to follow (Woollams & Brown, 1979, pp. 66–68).

An *ulterior transaction* is one that contains two levels of communication—a social level and a psychological level—and always involves more than two ego states. The psychological message is the ulterior message; it is aimed at an ego state different from the one the social message is aimed at. For example, Leona, a real estate saleswoman, sends a psychological message to the customer's Child: "You're not big enough to play with us!" although ostensibly it is sent as a social Adult-to-Adult transaction: "While this is a really fine home, its payment schedule may be a little rough to handle on your salary; we'll have to really work to make this deal go!" The psychological response may trigger the customer's Child into thinking, "Oh, yeah, well I'll show you I'm big enough to make payments. I want this house, so gimme it NOW!" Such an ulterior transaction is demonstrated by the dotted vectors in Figure 7.4, where the double message from the salesperson is transmitted to both the Adult and the Child of the purchaser, and the purchaser's response comes back as a defiant Child to the Parent of the salesperson.

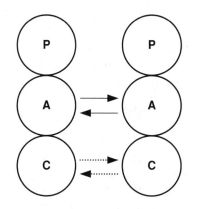

FIGURE 7.4   **Ulterior Transaction**

Games

Games are a recurring set of transactions, often repetitious, superficially plausible, but with a concealed motive (Berne, 1964, pp. 48–50). Games may be played at a variety of levels and intensities: some are socially acceptable; in others feelings are hurt without any permanent damage; and still others are played for keeps (Goldhaber & Goldhaber, 1976, p. 139).

Structurally, a game is a series of duplex (social–psychological) transactions that lead to a well-defined predictable payoff that justifies a not-OK, or discounted, position (Woollams & Brown, 1979, p. 117). A game begins with an outwardly straight stimulus; contains a covert or ulterior message that is responded to overtly; and ends with a payoff in which at least one person may be hurt (Goulding & Goulding, 1979, p. 30). Games are defense mechanisms as well as transactions, and everyone plays them 60 to 70 percent of the time (Cassius, 1980, p. 215).

The general advantage of a game is that it is a stabilizing influence. Homeostasis is promoted by the stroking one receives, and psychological stability is reinforced by the confirmation of one's position (Berne, 1964, p. 56.) Whatever their product—self-castigation, justification, reassurance, absolution, revenge, alleviation of guilt, sexual gratification, vindication, and so on—games are a way of saying from the Child ego state, "I too am OK!" (Harris & Harris, 1985, p. 210).

Berne (1964) delineated six general reasons people play games (biological, existential, internal psychological, external psychological, internal social, and external social). Understanding these reasons can provide the therapist with important information about issues the client brings to therapy, and each reason (to a greater or a lesser extent) reinforces the others to keep the client in homeostasis (Bary & Hufford, 1990).

Rackets

The payoff in which individuals have some favorite negative feeling that they use to confirm their life position is termed a *racket*. This collection of bad feelings is usually learned from a parent figure to whom the Child ego state has become accustomed (Cassius, 1980, p. 215; Goldhaber & Goldhaber, 1976, p. 138).

Stamps

People prefer to collect their own brand of racket feelings, such as guilt, anger, inadequacy, or depression, that reinforce their script. These feelings are called *trading stamps,* and they represent the kind of emotional reaction that marks the end of a game. When enough stamps are collected, they may be turned in for psychological prizes. Some prizes are minor, such as hitting, screaming, crying, and laughing; some are much bigger, such as murder, suicide, divorce, and job loss (Cassius, 1980, p. 215; Goldhaber & Goldhaber, 1976, p. 138).

Drama Triangle

Karpman's (1968) drama triangle is an enclosed system with a *persecutor* (I am better than you; you are inferior), a *rescuer* (I know more than you; you are inferior), and a *victim* (I am helpless) at its corners. In terms of strokes, the persecutor discounts others with negative strokes, the rescuer discounts others with conditional positive strokes, and the victim discounts him- or herself with negative strokes. An individual may move into a game or racket from any of the three basic positions by "exaggerating or devaluating the worth of himself or herself or the other person" (Woollams & Brown, 1979, p. 122). Individuals switch positions as the game or racket progresses.

When the other person refuses to continue to play, such individuals switch drama triangle positions and play games in order to continue receiving strokes. Thus, a person may begin as a victim, complaining about "how unfair life is," and as long as he or she has a sympathetic audience—"Yeah, life is rotten" (a complementary transaction)—the racket can continue. However, if the "rescuer" responds by switching to the victim position—for example, "I'm stupid—I've run out of suggestions"—the original victim may switch to the persecutor role and respond, "You selfish clod. You're just like all the others. You care only about yourself!" By switching positions, each person can collect a stroke payoff—the racket feeling—and justify his or her life position. Summerton (1992) extends Karpman's triangle into a pentagon for use with organizational and cultural dimensions of games. Organizational games are not just extensions of individual games; they have a new set of interesting characters such as the sniper, savior, and stage manager.

Discounting

Discounting occurs at the following four levels of severity (Mellor & Schiff, 1975; Woollams & Brown, 1979, p. 103):

1. A person may discount the *existence* of a problem. A woman may deny that her family is sick even though her spouse is having an affair, a child has attempted suicide, and she is anesthetizing herself with martinis and tranquilizers.
2. One may discount the *significance* of the problem. The family may be sick, but it is not important to do anything about it. Things always work out, so the person may invest no energy in solving it.
3. One may discount the *change possibilities* of the problem. Operating out of this external locus of control, the person may believe, "It is out of my hands and only God can deal with it."
4. One may discount his or her *ability* to solve the problem but acknowledge that others may have the ability to do so. The person may decide that Dr. Cassius, who runs that radio show for people with marital problems, should be called.

Nature of Maladjustment

Overview

According to TA theory, emotional disturbance reflects learned behaviors based on early decisions children make. One aspect of the script decision involves adopting a life position. One possible choice is an "I'm OK—You're OK" life position, in which case the child has chosen a "winner's" script. On the other hand, the child may decide "I'm OK—You're not OK," "I'm not OK—You're OK," or "I'm not OK—

You're not OK," all of which are unhealthy life positions leading to "loser" scripts. Such "loser" script decisions commonly take three general forms, according to Dusay and Dusay (1979, p. 405):

1. "I'm sad"—a depressive decision by persons who believe they are "not OK" in relation to others;
2. "I'm mad"—a paranoid decision by persons who have decided they will be "OK" at the expense of others being "not OK";
3. "I'm scared"—a schizophrenic decision by persons who have decided that they are "not OK," nor is anyone else.

Thus, one way of viewing pathology is to consider the maladjusted individual as having opted for a "loser's" script.

Origin
Most humans live in a state of stroke scarcity, and thus spend much of their waking hours seeking to obtain strokes—if not in positive then in negative ways. Besides social taboos that militate against the indiscriminate obtaining and giving of strokes, a variety of parental "Don't" and "Do" tapes keep people from getting strokes from significant others. If these strokes are not obtained from humans, then they may be obtained from alcohol, drugs, fast cars, gambling, work, or any other of a variety of negatively addicting substances or objects (Steiner, 1971).

Injunctions come to the Child ego state in a number of formats; culled by the Gouldings (1976; 1979), the Harrises (1969; 1985), and Kahler and Capers (1974), they form a recipe book for maladaptive behavior. Here are the major "don'ts" and "dos" of maladjustment and some typical decisions the child makes in response to them:

1. *"Don't."* This injunction may be given by frightened parents who send the message "Don't do anything risky—the world is a dangerous place." As a result, the child may come to believe that no possible course of action is right or safe.
2. *"Don't be"* or *"Don't exist."* This message is considered the most lethal of any. Often parents send this message in a subtle manner by suggesting "If it weren't for you, our lives would be better." Children who interpret messages as "Don't be" messages may make very different decisions in response. One child may decide, "You're wrong; I'm valuable"; another may create a fantasy parent who really cares. However, if the child totally accepts this injunction, he or she may decide, "If things get too bad, I'll kill myself" or "I'll show you even if it kills me."
3. *"Don't be close."* If a parent figure discourages physical closeness or positive stroking, a child may interpret this as a "Don't be close" message. Children may also give themselves this injunction upon losing a parent through death or divorce, concluding, "What's the use of getting close; I just lose them in the end" or "I'll never trust anyone again."
4. *"Don't be important."* If children are discounted in some way, they may experience this message as "Don't be important." In response, a child may decide, "Everyone else counts first around here," "I'll never amount to anything," or "I may become important but I can never let anyone know."

5. *"Don't be a child."* This script message is given most often to the eldest child, who is expected to be responsible for younger siblings. Some decisions that children may make in response to this injunction are to deny their needs; to grow up always to take care of others; or to "go crazy" in order to get their needs met.

6. *"Don't grow."* Parents may say, "Don't grow beyond infancy," "Don't grow beyond a certain age," "Don't be sexual," and/or "Don't leave me." It is most often the youngest child who is given these injunctions. Two common responses are deciding to remain in the "cared for" position and deciding to fight back and prove themselves.

7. *"Don't succeed."* The parent may communicate "If you are more successful than I am, I will not love you" or "You can't do anything right," which may be translated as "Don't succeed" by the child. Some typical decisions children make in response to this message are to work extra hard to succeed; to succeed and yet not enjoy success; or to accept the injunction totally and fail.

8. *"Don't be you"* (the sex you are). Parents or others may send a child messages that they value the opposite sex more highly. In response, children may decide not to listen; to accept other people's evaluations; or to do sex-appropriate activities but feel bad about themselves.

9. *"Don't be sane"* or *"Don't be well."* Parents may give children strokes for being sick and withhold them when they are well. If the parents reward, tolerate, or model "crazy" behavior, the child may receive a "Don't be sane" message. If children accept these injunctions, they may remain sick or "crazy" to keep getting strokes.

10. *"Don't belong."* If parents communicate that they should be somewhere else, such as in another country, a child may interpret this as a "Don't belong" message. In response, the child may decide, "I'll never belong to anyone" (or "any group" or "any country") or "Nobody will ever like me, because I don't belong."

To obtain strokes, the child believes that he or she will be "OK" if one or more of the following "Do" messages can be accomplished (Harris & Harris, 1985, p. 36). These counterinjunctions, however, are also restrictive and, like injunctions, also prevent growth (Goulding & Goulding, 1979, p. 38).

1. *"Do be perfect."* If a B grade is obtained, an A is better. If an A grade is obtained, then an A+ is better. Obtaining a medical degree is not as good as getting a specialty in neurosurgery. No defects are allowed.

2. *"Do be the best."* Winning isn't everything, it's the only thing. No strokes are given for effort or accomplishment.

3. *"Do try hard."* "You are not living up to your potential" is the broken record the child hears over and over. "Idle hands are the devil's workshop," but superhuman efforts will still not get the job done.

4. *"Do hurry up."* Taking time to process events and "smell the daisies" is unacceptable. If one hurries, a multitude of activities can be accomplished. It doesn't matter if the efforts are slipshod.

5. *"Do be strong."* "Bearing up under the load" without complaining or feeling is the mark of an emotionally strong individual who is able to take the world on in equal terms and give and ask it no quarter.

These "driver" messages are all impossible to evaluate or accomplish and thus are open-ended, one-way contracts that may never be brought to successful closure. Following counterinjunctions to overcome injunctions has two results. First, injunctions are much more likely to prevail and remain firmly in place, culminating in a no-win situation. Second, many counterinjunctions are the direct antitheses of injunctions, are impossible to follow, and put the individual in a double bind (Goulding & Goulding, 1979, pp. 38–39).

Driver statements given by parents, such as "Be perfect" "Hurry up," "Please," "Try hard," and "Be strong," each generate specific kinds of fears, which lead to compensatory defensive responding in the form of a specific type of righteous behavior. Righteous behavior in turn leads to "Not OK" behavior with "Not OK" roles that move around Karpman's triangle with payoffs that are invariably bad. For example, "Be perfect" people are besieged by guilt and worry. In a vengeful child state they are anything but perfect and make a mess of things. Their script consists of "I am worthless/shameful" and their neurotic and psychotic tendencies range from being organizational fanatics to having psychiatric disturbances of the obsessive-compulsive type (Klein, 1992).

Mundy's (1994) discussion of American slang and colloquialisms is particularly instructive of how common statements can be used as subtle drivers. An interesting example (particularly to teachers) is the badly overused and irritating statement "You know. /!/?" Mundy proposes that "You know" is actually a subconscious "Please me" miniscript message because it allows the speaker to not have to process thoughts, be unclear as to meaning, and trap listeners into having to assume what the speaker actually means or wants, if indeed the speaker does know.

Ways of Viewing Maladjustment

Ego State Pathology   An emotionally healthy person can choose the ego state that appears to be most useful in a given situation. One kind of ego state pathology occurs when a person's ego state boundaries break down and his or her Adult state becomes contaminated by the Child state and/or Parent state. For example, a Parent contamination occurs when the person mistakes Parent information, such as prejudices and opinions, for fact, as in "Women are no good." A Child contamination occurs when old childhood experiences are used to assess current reality inaccurately, as in "I never step on a crack because something bad will happen." A double contamination occurs when the Adult is contaminated by Parent prejudices and Child fears and beliefs at the same time. In this case, the individual may hear words from his parent (for example, "All men are evil"), respond with an Early Child conclusion ("I feel evil"), and conclude in the here and now from the contaminated Adult ("I am evil") (Woollams & Brown, 1979, pp. 35–36).

Another type of ego state pathology, *exclusion*, "occurs when one or two ego states dominate a person's behavior. When a single ego state dominates, that ego state is called *constant* or *excluding*" (Woollams & Brown, 1979, p. 36). A constant Parent may be authoritarian; a constant Adult may function like a "computer"; and a constant Child may be irresponsible.

Ego State Imbalance   Whereas the concepts of ego state contamination or exclusion and the "loser's" script relate to the "what and where" issue of maladjustment, they do not address the issues of "degree" of disturbance. Dusay and Dusay (1979) discuss the concept of the egogram (Dusay, 1972; 1977), a tool used to assess the amount of energy invested in the forces of the three ego states—the Critical Parent, Nurturing Parent, Adult, Free Child, and Adapted Child (see Figure 7.1 on page 167). A person who is well-adjusted will have an egogram in which no ego state is extremely low or particularly high (Dusay & Dusay, 1979, p. 393). The advantage of the egogram, besides its reflection of the strengths and weaknesses of an individual's personality, is that "it provides a personal map for growth and change" for the individual (Dusay & Dusay, 1979, p. 391).

Because each person has a distinct and unique personality, these five psychological forces are aligned in different amounts and balance in each individual. A bar graph may then be constructed to demonstrate to the client how much of each of these psychological forces is present and what they are doing. Egograms remain fairly fixed unless the person actively decides to change the energy balance (Dusay & Dusay, 1989, p. 409). Many TA practitioners believe this is a more effective way to view diagnosis because it suggests a direction for treatment. Individuals are considered "cured" when they are able to strengthen their "low-energy" ego states and achieve a "harmonious balance" among their ego states (Dusay & Dusay, 1979, p. 412).

Major Concepts

Transactional analysis is a humanistic, existential, dynamic theory of personality and a therapeutic modality whose practitioners believe humans are born in an "OK" state, that each person is unique, and that people ultimately are responsible for their own behavior and destinies. The following concepts, abstracted from Cassius (1980), Goldhaber and Goldhaber (1976), and Harris and Harris (1985), represent this philosophy:

1. Ego states motivate behavior patterns.
2. Ego states are energized by the experiences and feelings of childhood, the influence of parental figures, and the ability to process data and solve problems logically.
3. Ego states develop functionally to meet contingencies in the environment and may adapt in constructive or nonconstructive ways, depending on scripts and contingencies in the phenomenological field.
4. Each internal or external ego state function has positive and negative attributes.
5. Feelings associated with childhood experiences are recorded and inextricably linked to those experiences.
6. Feelings are neither good nor bad but are events, facts of our existence, real, indisputable, and part of our direct knowledge.
7. Feelings may be changed through knowledge of their origin followed by a change in behavior.
8. People's lives are dramatically represented by scripts that compel them to repeat and live out early experiences.

9. An interpersonal communication model is the basis for predicting the effectiveness of relationships.

10. Transactional analysis and analysis of rackets and games are means of examining relationships between persons and their effects on each other.

11. Change may occur through insight.

12. Change includes sorting, clarifying, interpreting, and redeciding through the Adult ego state by changing old scripts with new injunctions. This task generally requires therapeutic assistance (reparenting).

13. People in emotional difficulty are nevertheless complete, intelligent human beings.

14. All emotional difficulties are curable, given adequate knowledge and the proper approach.

THE THERAPEUTIC PROCESS

Goals

In life, individuals "write" their own scripts rather than being "scripted." In therapy, clients "rewrite" their scripts "with the help of a strong Parent that clients build for themselves rather than incorporating it from the counselor" (Goulding & Goulding, 1979, p. 42). Berne (1964) implies that the overall goal of the therapeutic process may be autonomy, which he defined as "the recovery of three capacities: awareness, spontaneity, and intimacy" (p. 178). To achieve this autonomy, clients must come to realize that they have "the power" to understand and change the early decisions they made in response to parental injunctions.

In the redecision process, clients reexperience these early-life decisions and make new, more "healthy" decisions. Some TA theorists speak of this change as adopting a "winner's script" (James & Jongeward, 1971); others believe it involves becoming "script-free" (Woollams, 1978).

The Therapist's Perspective

Transactional analysis emphasizes a therapeutic approach based on the assumption "I'm OK—You're OK," which means that everyone has a lovable part and is capable of change. This position does not mean TA therapists cannot express dissatisfaction with a client's behavior or suggest areas for change (Woollams & Brown, 1979, p. 221). Through contracting, therapist and client are made "equal partners." It is the client's job to decide what he or she wants to change and the therapist's job to lend his or her expertise to accomplish those changes (Steiner, 1968).

In accomplishing therapeutic changes, TA therapists are commonly involved in four kinds of rational analysis: structural analysis (the analysis of individual personality); transactional analysis (the analysis of what people say and do to one another); game analysis (the identification of games and the resulting racket feelings); and script analysis (the analysis of the overall life plans people follow) (James & Jongeward, 1971, p. 16).

A basic philosophic difference exists between some schools of TA theorists. According to Dusay & Dusay (1979), theorists such as Berne, Steiner, Dusay, and Karpman have suggested that change can best be accomplished when the therapist takes a strong Parent role, giving potent well-timed "counterinjunctions" to "counter" the original parental injunctions. In contrast, other theorists (Goulding & Goulding, 1979; Woollams & Brown, 1979) emphasize that clients must get in touch with their own power to redecide, rather than rely on the Parent ego state of the therapist. A key task of the therapist is to help clients get in touch with their own potency, to protect themselves, and to give themselves permission to change. Both groups agree that clients are responsible for their own actions and decisions (Goulding & Goulding, 1978; Steiner, 1968).

While working as a partner for change, the therapist also helps clients learn the language and concepts of TA so that they may apply them in analyzing their own behavior. Transactional analysis therapists are great believers in using pictures to illuminate what happens to increase understanding and demystify the therapeutic process. Concepts are not only expressed verbally but also drawn as symbols, and these graphic representations of transactions and changes in ego state energy are shown to the client (Dusay & Dusay, 1989, p. 406). Transactional analysis therapists may focus on egogram balances, game interruptions, or redecisions. The notion is that a change in one area will facilitate a corresponding change in other areas (Dusay & Dusay, 1989, p. 430).

The Client's Perspective

As Dusay and Dusay (1979, p. 408) point out, many clients enter therapy because they are in pain as a result of receiving strokes in self-destructive ways. Clients are asked by the therapist to decide specifically what they want to change. If they are unclear about this, the therapist will help them get in touch with these goals through such techniques as experiencing here and now a recent, fantasized, or early situation in which they had negative feelings like those that motivated them to seek therapy. Although the therapist assists clients in defining the contract, clients essentially make the contract with themselves while the therapist serves as a witness and facilitator (Goulding & Goulding, 1979, p. 50).

Clients must be willing to take the risk of revealing themselves and to carry out assignments the therapist might recommend. In other words, clients might be assigned to engage in some behaviors that are inconsistent with their script-reinforcing behavior but that are congruent with their overall treatment contract.

STRATEGIES FOR HELPING CLIENTS

Woollams and Brown (1979, pp. 228–233) outlined seven stages of therapy: motivation; awareness; the treatment contract; deconfusing the child; redecision; relearning; and termination. In the following sections, the strategies and techniques applicable to these stages are discussed as they apply to the case of Billie Jean Overton.

Billie Jean Overton, age forty-four, oscillates between depression and hyperactivity. She is married to John W. Overton, a successful real estate developer and insurance broker. Until recently, Billie Jean immersed herself in rearing her two daughters (Johnie Ruth, age twenty-two, and Stephanie, age nineteen), serving her church, and functioning as John's perfect wife. Billie Jean reared Johnie Ruth and Stephanie to follow in her footsteps by teaching them to be alluring and enticing princesses who achieve recognition and attention from men through skillful coquettish behavior. While the younger daughter, Stephanie, has accepted a princess role, Johnie Ruth has rebelled violently.

John Overton is extremely busy and is away from home most of the time. He has alternated between addiction to his businesses and younger women. Billie Jean knows about some of John's escapades with younger women. Sometimes she has been made so angry and jealous by John's infidelity that she has contemplated divorce. But when she consulted her own father (now deceased), she took his advice to keep a stiff upper lip, live up to her marriage vows, be a dutiful wife, remember what an excellent provider John is, and work to keep the family together—just as he did.

Billie Jean is now distressed and deeply depressed that Johnie Ruth is planning to leave the United States for the Far East to study with a guru. Billie Jean has also returned to college after a twenty-year hiatus, and is now a senior. However, she recently experienced such severe academic problems that she may not graduate. Her academic failures have shaken her to her foundations, and now she believes that her best opportunity to become her own person and move out from under John's shadow is in serious jeopardy. She vows that money and a very comfortable lifestyle mean little to her and is extremely angry when John uses financial power to control her behavior by providing her with unlimited charge accounts, vacations, servants, and a magnificent home. However, she is not willing to give up her material comforts with John even though the emotional part of their marriage has long been dead.

As Billie Jean presents herself for therapy, her body language is rigid. In contrast, her speech is disorganized, scattered, ambivalent, and replete with pleas to the therapist to "fix" things for her and help to get her life straightened out.

The TA therapist's analysis of Billie Jean's injunctions indicate that she has carried deep within her since early childhood the following "Don'ts:"

1. "Don't be important!" (You're only important in regard to how you look and what kind of social contacts you can make to enhance the importance of your husband.)
2. "Don't grow!" (As a youngster, be the ideal daughter—be daddy's perfect little girl; later, be the dutiful all-giving wife.)
3. "Don't be you!" (Be alert to sensing what others, especially male authority figures, want you to be, and strive to meet their expectations; put others' needs ahead of your own.)
4. "Don't think!" (Think what your parents thought; think what your husband thinks; don't have your own thoughts.)
5. "Don't feel!" (You may emote, but do not feel; don't manifest any of the emotions underlying feelings; don't act on feelings; either deny having feelings or ascribe them to external causes, such as your husband's wishes, social peers, God, or your children's dilemmas.)

Billie Jean's "Do" counterinjunctions, also transmitted by her parents and ingrained in her Adapted Child state, include the following:

1. "Do be perfect!" (You must always appear to be perfect in looks and behavior.)
2. "Do please me!" (Please Mommy and Daddy; please your husband; please your daughters.)
3. "Do be strong!" (Never show weakness; keep your chin up and keep a stiff upper lip, with a pleasant smile; be assured that you will be well taken care of.)

Billie Jean's principal games are IWFY and Peasant:

IWFY (If It Weren't for You). ("I could _____ if I didn't have to be at home and take care of things for John," or "I would never wear clothes like that or fix my hair like that, because he wouldn't allow that," or "Johnie Ruth might not have been so quick to follow that guru if John hadn't been so stern about cutting off her support)." IWFY (Berne, 1964, pp. 50–58, 103–104), the most common game played between married couples, typically originates in the initial choice of marriage partners. The woman associates with women who feel they are likewise victimized, and that reinforces her IWFY beliefs. She plays IWFY in her marital role, in her social life, and in her vocation. She refrains from doing things she really doesn't want to do, but pretends that she wants to do them and complains that she could do them if it weren't for her husband.

JOHN: Billie Jean, you stay here and take care of the house while I'm on my business trip to Florida.

BILLIE JEAN: I could finish my degree and get a job of my own if it weren't for you and all those trips you take.

Peasant (Berne, 1964, pp. 151–154). ("Gee, you're a wonderful _____ [husband, father, doctor, daughter, delivery person, etc.].") In Billie Jean's case, Peasant, in the form of GYWH (Gee you're a wonderful husband), is played on two levels. First, by romanticizing and praising John's attributes, Billie Jean publicly obligates him to be well-behaved socially. Second, once she has him convinced that she believes he is wonderful, she can make herself look saintly or make him look foolish. The simplest way for the GYWH player to win is to not get better.

BILLIE JEAN: (at John's office party) Look what a beautiful turquoise bracelet John brought me from Florida. I guess it was worth staying home and minding the answering machine after all. He's such a wonderful husband!

Strategies for Increasing Client Motivation and Awareness

Typically, in order for clients to enter therapy they must be in touch with their own pain enough to feel a need or desire to change. This awareness of their own unhappiness or discomfort drives the *motivation* (stage one) necessary to work toward change.

CL: (*very stiff posture; speaking dramatically*) I need help. I think I'm going to flunk out of school. It's making me a nervous wreck, and I can't sleep. I don't know what to do. I've struggled so hard to get this far and I've really tried, plus I've got a lot of other problems right now with my daughter, and my father's death on my mind. He's been gone only two years, and my husband who is gone all the time selling and we aren't getting along well. They suggested that I get psychological help at my internship site, so here I am, but I think they are wrong. They made me feel so bad, like I wasn't worth anything. What do you think?

Billie Jean's initiating behavior illuminates the verbal and nonverbal transactions that provide interpersonal communication hooks to ensnare others into her games and rackets. Her monologue is replete with disowned messages. Others make her the way she is. Indefinite pronouns and global externalized "theys" are not "I" statements of what the Child in her wants (Goulding & Goulding, 1979, pp. 5–6). Closely tied with "Don't" injunctions, received from her parents and adapted by her Little Professor, she follows the parental injunction "Don't think." She turns to external authorities, such as the therapist, an "expert" much in the model of what she believes her father was to her and what her husband has failed to be in regard to "fixing" her tremendous number of emotional needs. Even though the therapist is a woman, she will have to be very careful and aware of the strokes she delivers and what reinforcement her responses have for the client's script (Clarkson, 1992). The therapist now asks a number of here-and-now questions while listening very closely to the client's responses and carefully monitoring her body language. Throughout therapy the therapist avoids falling into the jargon of TA, because this in itself would embellish the "expert" status that the needy client seeks and also would undoubtedly play into the hands of more indirect transactions that would not facilitate awareness or change (Goulding & Goulding, 1979, p. 49).

TH: What are the feelings that go with this?

CL: I'm angry at my supervising teacher. I really did a good job.

TH: What other feelings?

CL: I'm really scared. What will happen to me if I don't graduate?

TH: What *will* happen?

CL: I don't know. I'd like to be my own person, not just somebody's wife, excepting that if he cared for me I wouldn't have to do this now. I really want a good relationship with him which I don't have now, and I can't understand that because I've tried to be everything he's ever wanted, but it's never enough.

TH: So are you saying you've had enough or you've not had enough?

CL: I keep thinking that perhaps he'll change, really come back and love me. I've devoted all my energy to him and the kids and it's all fallen apart. I need to feel like I'm somebody. I've failed with them and now it looks like I've failed with school. (*starts sobbing*)

TH: (*indicates tissues on table*) What is it you want?

The client makes a number of indirect behavioral transactions that are designed to bring the therapist to her assistance. The therapist wisely does not respond to these indirect pleas for help, but rather pushes forth very direct statements that seek to put the transactions on an Adult-to-Adult level (Goulding & Goulding, 1979, p. 28).

Once individuals are in touch with their dissatisfaction enough that they are willing to commit to change, they are ready to enter stage two of therapy—*awareness*. In the *awareness* stage, although clients may be aware that they are dissatisfied with what is occurring in their lives, they may not be clear about what exactly they want to change. So in this stage the therapist assists clients in deciding what it is, in concrete, specific terms, that they want to change through therapy.

CL: If I could get this degree it'd make me somebody. I mean I could go out and get a professional job, I wouldn't be so dependent.

TH: What do you want to change so you won't be dependent? And what are you willing to do to make that change to being independent?

CL: This degree would do it.

TH: Be factual. How would the degree change you to being "it"? I don't know what "it" means. What do you want?

CL: (*rather icily*) To be loved and appreciated and feel like I am somebody. Is that specific enough?

TH: No! How do you want to be loved, appreciated, and felt for so that you are somebody to you?

CL: (*head back, eyes deflected up to the right and away, with a sad smile*) Like my father. He was wonderful. It was perfect when he was alive. I adored him and he me.

TH: But your father is now dead.

CL: (*tears return to eyes*) Yes, and I miss him terribly, he took care of me. I don't know why my husband can't be like him, caring and loving and all that.

TH: What you are saying is that you now want to be independent and the degree would somehow do that for you. You don't want to be victimized by the whims of somebody else and you want to be your own boss. You also say that you want to be cared for just like your father did for you. Also it sounds as if you spend a lot of time rescuing or trying to "fix" things for your daughters and husband, but that hasn't worked very well either, yet you still go about doing it. How do those notions hook up with being independent?

The therapist makes this interpretation because of the drama the client plays out that keeps her at an impasse. She is operating under both injunctions and counterinjunctions. She responds to the injunctions from her father's Parent ego state ("Be nice") and Child ego state (Don't think . . . particularly angry thoughts"). Her decision then becomes, "If I show how smart I can think, I'm uppity and men will put me in my place. I can't be nice and smart at the same time and still get strokes. Therefore, I'll be nice and make myself helpless."

The client is vacillating between two points, victim and rescuer, on Karpman's (1968) drama triangle. As long as she is bound to this script pattern, it is going to be very difficult for her to assume independence. Certainly a degree by itself will no more make her her own person than being married, bearing children, or having a Mercedes. It is apparent that there are some very strong parental injunctions and counterinjunctions in her life, given the extremely strong emotional ties her dead father still has on her. However, on the positive side she has moved toward some "Dos" in her life, such as returning to college and coming to therapy.

CL: I don't know.

TH: Don't or won't?

CL: I am really trying to get my act together. I just don't know what to do. I need to get on with my life.

TH: As a result of this there seem to be a lot of "Don'ts" in your life. There also seem to be some vaguely defined "Dos." You say you need to do some things, but will you change that to a "want?" Very specifically, I'd like you to state the differences you want in your life, how far you want to go in making those changes, what the gain and loss will be, and what you will do to achieve those differences.

The therapist is setting up some clear behavioral plans for change. Whereas thinking one wants to do something is a prerequisite for change, action steps specifically put the client's Adapted Parent on notice that change is imminent and provides the concrete motivation for change (Harris & Harris, 1985, pp. 186–187).

CL: (*wistfully, wringing her hands*) If my husband could just pay attention to me. If things were like they were when we got married; he adored me then. Perhaps I could get him in here and we could both work things out. It's the same with the oldest girl. If I could just make her see the light, then she might get out of that horrible sect she's in.

TH: "Perhaps"? "If things were like they were"? "Might"? That's magical thinking. Things will never be like they were. Indeed, you, yourself propose to "change" things by going to school and becoming "independent." What do you want to change about you and not them right now, and I mean today, in this room?

Billie Jean uses a number of "cop-out" words—*might, perhaps, try,* and *work.* These qualifiers do not indicate a real commitment to risk change. They leave the person an out because one can always "try" to do something and can continue to "work" forever without changing. By saying "What do you want to change?" the therapist puts the onus squarely on the client to decide not only what she wants but also what she is willing to do (Goulding & Goulding, 1979, p. 73). The therapist catches the client's words that are based on the magical thinking she has scripted for herself and confronts her tentativeness. The therapist's confrontation is intended to disturb the client's egogram energy imbalance and cause the client to start making energy shifts toward more balanced ego states (Dusay & Dusay, 1989, p. 441).

CL: (*whining*) But I don't want to be alone. I hate that.

TH: Becoming independent does not mean going it alone. It does mean broadening your social support base, not putting all your eggs in one basket. Are you willing to do that, take a risk that goes with freedom?

While seeking to create awareness and motivation in the client, the therapist also *reparents:* she brings attention to how the client discounts the present and to the assertive action that is needed for change in the future.

CL: (*avoiding the question*) I just wish she'd listen. I just want what's best for her. I know she despises me for interfering, but . . . my husband keeps after me to take care of it and get her straightened out, and it's my Christian duty.

TH: Do you see how you have attempted to placate, even rescue, others, much as you have placated and fooled yourself by allowing others to rescue you and by giving them permission to think for you?

The therapist pushes this aspect of the client's "Don't think" injunction that she attempts to carry over from her Adapted Child into her own parental role with the daughter. While Billie Jean may sound as if she is speaking from a Nurturing Parent ego state because of her concern for her daughter, there is much in her worry over her daughter that comes from a script she wrote many years ago. Thus, it is within the Adapted Child that the redecision process must start, for it is that ego state that made the original decision (Goulding & Goulding, 1979, p. 212).

Strategies for Establishing the Therapeutic Contract

The therapeutic contract sets the focus for treatment. The client decides in terms of beliefs, emotions, and behaviors what she plans to change about herself to reach her goals (Goulding & Goulding, 1979, p. 50). A good contract should be brief, stated in words that are understandable to the Child ego state, and as behaviorally specific as possible. Although the contract is basically an Adult-Adult agreement, all of the client's and therapist's ego states need to approve and be involved in the contract and end up at an OK position (Woollams & Brown, 1979, pp. 223–224).

CL: I want to gain respect . . . like from my professors, that I'm really not a bundle of fluff.

TH: Give me an example. A recent time when you wanted respect but didn't get it. Imagine yourself in that scene and the professor there in that empty chair. What do you say to him to get respect?

CL: I feel kinda dumb doing this.

TH: "Dumb" is a judgment. Tell me how you feel when you are dumb.

CL: I felt dumb with my professor.

TH: You were making yourself dumb. How did you feel?

CL: Like I was going to come apart. I knew the material, but when I opened my mouth a bunch of nonsense spilled out and I just couldn't focus on the topic. I was angry . . . I guess at myself.

TH: What were you angry with yourself about?

CL: That I knew the answer but couldn't respond and then had to ask for help, as if I'd never had an ounce of sense. It's sort of the way I am around John.

TH: You just had an incisive insight, that you give up any wits (power) to important men in your life. So, clearly, you are not dumb. What would you then change about yourself?

CL: Stop thinking I'm dumb. Dumb people don't deserve respect and I am *not* dumb!

TH: Fantastic! That's right! So are you willing to make a contract to be smart and be respected for what you know and not how you look?

Billie Jean conveys a part of her life script ("You can't think!"). As she encounters a new, unorthodox, and risky situation she plays "dumb" with the therapist. If the therapist lets her get away with being "dumb" with her, she and Billie Jean will have made an *ulterior contract,* a pact between therapist and client to prevent the client from reaching her goals (Goulding & Goulding, 1979, p. 85). Billie Jean's acknowledgement of also acting this way with her husband indicates her "Think dumb" is at least one of the scripts in her life drama of being a victim, a script acted out in front of her family, peers, and professors.

If the contract comes only from Billie Jean's Parent ego state (for example, "I can't be angry" because of the counterinjunction "Be nice") it will be difficult to achieve because the motivation to change comes from Billie Jean's Free Child ("Oh yes, I can be angry, and I can stand up for my rights and that's tough noogies for any of you guys who try to put me down") (Woollams & Brown, 1979, p. 229). If Billie Jean had made a contract not to be dumb and not to be angry with her professor, it would not be acceptable because her Child ego state would have no investment in it (Goulding & Goulding, 1979, p. 71).

A further complication may arise if Billie Jean tries to negotiate a *contract to change others.* All too commonly, the client initially attempts to continue a game and a racket by getting others, rather than herself, to change (Goulding & Goulding, 1979, p. 75).

CL: I would like to change the way I relate to men.

TH: Be specific when you say "relate."

CL: I'd like to be able to be open enough to be myself.

TH: Are you unopened?

CL: Well, yes! Right now I am but if . . .

TH: Are you disabled?

CL: Well, ah, no.

TH: So then you are able. You are able to open, whatever that may be. Again, be specific as to what you want to change in you.

CL: I want to become so assertive that all the important men in my life will have to pay attention to me.

TH: To do that you will have to become assaultive. You cannot make others do that unless you plan to hold a .357 magnum to their heads. Is that your goal?

CL: Certainly not.

TH: Then you have not made a contract for you; you've made it for others. What will you do for you to make yourself think smart and not be dictated to in a fawning, chauvinistic way?

Billie Jean manifests the type of life script that holds another potential problem for contracting. Because she operates a great deal of the time out of a victim stance, she is a past master at playing a component of the game "Look How Hard I'm Trying." Thus, if not careful, the therapist may agree to a *forever contract*. Such a contract allows the client to work hard forever toward some nebulous goal but keep the secret goal of remaining unhappy. This game will allow the Adapted Child to continue to receive the same strokes that were achieved in childhood—working hard and suffering (Goulding & Goulding, 1979, p. 80).

CL: If men were just like my father—he was truly a wonderful man. The greatest man I have ever known. And I miss him terribly.

TH: He has been dead now for two years?

CL: Yes.

TH: So the greatest person in your life is dead. How can one compete against a dead person?

CL: (*face flushes and tears start to well up in her eyes*) I don't understand. I cherish his memory, it's still hard to cope without him.

TH: You still cherish him, not his memory, as if he were alive, which he is not. That deal you have cut about relationships is with a dead person who will be that way forever. As long as you do that no man can ever measure up and you will continue to contract relationships in the same way you did with your dead father. I will not accept a "forever" contract.

While the approach of the therapist may seem unnecessarily cruel, the client needs to accept her father's death and the unfinished business she has with him by keeping him alive (Goulding & Goulding, 1979, pp. 174–184). Under no circumstances would the therapist pursue the death of Billie Jean's father or uncover the kinds of intense emotions that underlie it unless she knew exactly how to promote a successful conclusion (Goulding & Goulding, 1979, p. 149). (One of the most vicious, and justified, criticisms of TA is that in the hands of amateurs, confrontation may be used injudiciously to strip away the defenses of the client and leave nothing in place).

If the therapist allows Billie Jean to continue to hunt for her Prince (Father) Charming, she will be allowing her to engage in a *game contract*. Game contracts are those in which the client asks the therapist's approval to do that which will continue to hurt his or her chances of redeciding and changing the game (Goulding & Goulding, 1979, p. 78).

CL: I've thought about what I would do, and a divorce seems best, to get me out on my own, but I did promise my father I'd stay with this.

TH: I am not here to affirm your decision about a divorce one way or another. I am here to say that the implicit message is that if you do that, you are a failure to a rather awesome cast of characters and most particularly to yourself. So are you building a new life by deciding to start as a failure?

CL: So you're saying that I shouldn't get a divorce?

TH: I am saying that if you do that, you will continue to perpetuate the rotten feelings you have. I would like you to look at what the best and worst possible outcomes would be given you decided to take such action, not only in terms of being "independent," but also in terms of your feelings.

Strategies for Deconfusing the Child

Woollams and Brown (1979) describe this stage as one in which clients learn to accept responsibility for their decisions and discover how they use their present behavior to maintain their scripts. The two major goals for this stage of therapy are to (1) deconfuse the client's Child ego state by helping him or her become aware of and express unmet needs and feelings; and (2) help the client "develop an internal sense of safety sufficient to make a redecision."

Some TA therapists emphasize cognitive strategies to get the answers to these sorts of questions. Such analyses may be primarily done in four areas: script analysis, structural analysis, game and racket analysis, and transactional analysis.

Other TA practitioners choose to focus primarily on affective strategies, as opposed to cognitive analysis, to help the client reach the point of readiness for a redecision. For example, the Gouldings (1976) use Gestalt techniques to help clients experience the early decisions they made in the Child ego state. To get to the here and now, the therapist asks the client to imagine a scene from his or her past, most likely from early childhood, and conduct an interview with a parent or significant other *as if it were happening in the present moment in therapy.* The goal is to uncover early injunctions and counterinjunctions that parents give to their children. It is not uncommon for the client to ignore certain contextual parts of the image to justify the old scripts (Goulding & Goulding, 1979, pp. 204–205).

TH: Billie Jean, I want you to take a little trip down memory lane. I want you to go back in time when you were with your father and felt like he was being wonderful.

CL: That's easy. It was my tenth birthday. We had a party at my house, and I was all dressed up. It was a great party. He took lots of pictures and told everybody how cute and what a precious little peach I was. He nicknamed me Peaches. He got me my first pony for my birthday. It was a pinto and I named him Scooter.

TH: I want you to bring that scene up to present time and have a conversation with your father. Tell him how wonderful he is.

CL: Daddy, you're the greatest! The party was just grand and I love Scooter to pieces. When can I ride him?

TH: Take the role of your father. What does he say?

CL: (as father) Right now, if that's what you want, Billie. There's nothing too good for Daddy's little girl. You know that, don't you, Peaches?

TH: How does that make you feel as you say that, particularly as that soft, fuzzy little fruit?

CL: My dad got me everything I wanted, and he put me on a pedestal. Looking back on it though, I was a spoiled brat, I guess.

TH: You may have been, but how do you feel as you listen to your "father" talking to you?

CL: It's odd but I somehow feel cheated, and powerless, like I was dependent on him for everything. Like I am with John.

TH: Change that first "was" to "am."

CL: "I am." I don't like that. It's like he's still doing it.

TH: How do you feel right now?

CL: I'm starting to realize that I'm an emotional midget. It would have been better if I would have got a healthy dose of independence when I was a kid. I was pretty capable, but I never got credit for it.

Strategies for Redecision

Woollams & Brown (1979) comment that redecisions involve the client changing some aspect of his or her script. Billie Jean's last sentence, stated in a benign way, is a clue to her script. No place prior to this in therapy has she mentioned having any worth other than being "cute." The therapist immediately recognizes this slight perceptual shift and probes it.

TH: How were you capable?

CL: Momma always had a bad case of nerves and I had to look after her because Daddy was gone a lot in the cotton business.

TH: Nerves?

CL: (*twisting her hair and wringing her hands*) Well . . . ah . . . actually she was . . . I guess . . . an alcoholic. And there were pills too! God! I'd mix her drinks, get dinner ready, dress my little sister Kate, pack her a lunch, and get her off to school and do the same for me. I never said a word about that. I was really the woman of the house since I was nine. (*in a muted, but hard and angry voice*) And he never said a word about that and he knew it.

TH: So things were not so wonderful as they seemed, for either you or your mom.

CL: It was like . . . I mean . . . this is terrible . . . I was like his wife! (*breaks into sobs*)

TH: So the fact of the matter is you had to be a thinking, grown-up person when you were only a child. On the one hand you were your dad's pretty little girl, but also you were his wife. I wonder if he could ever come to admit that. As a result, he discounted you and kept you little so he'd never have to come to grips with his lousy relationship with his wife.

CL: (*regains some composure*) I guess so. He couldn't have ever really handled that. Everything had to be nice and peaceful at home, but it wasn't. It was like a big secret.

The therapist immediately shifts Billie Jean back to a scene where she is taking care of her mother.

TH: Put your mother right in front of you and tell her how you feel as you do all those things she should be doing.

CL: I hate it.

TH: You can't hate an "it." Who or what precisely do you hate. Her? Yourself? Your father? Your life? Tell her specifically what you hate.

CL: I hate you for being so weak and caving in to Daddy. I also feel sorry for you and pity you for giving up. You've got no way out. You're a prisoner, and so am I!

TH: So, is your dad still wonderful?

CL: No, he isn't. I shouldn't have gotten put in the middle. He hamstrung Momma and he hamstrung me. But I didn't realize it then.

TH: Now you put yourself in the same position of being hamstrung again. A victim like your mom, and you also attempt to hamstring your daughter, only she won't allow you to do it to her. How are you different from your mother who prostituted herself to your father's checkbook just as you prostitute yourself to John's?

CL: My God! (*yelling*) *That's right!* That *is* right! They both should have been horse-whipped.

TH: Yet, it's you who gets horsewhipped now. What do you want to do about rede-ciding who gets whipped? You can decide what you want.

Transactional analysts have taken a good deal or interest in anger (Clark, 1995; Frazier, 1995; Garcia, 1995; Hyams, 1994; Joines, 1995). Anger, or the repression of it, is often an overlay or the person's true emotional state. Other negative feelings that are not being resolved undergird and support the anger. Different types of anger (Garcia, 1995; Joines, 1995) signal different ego states and developmental stages in operation and are part of the client's disowning of self. As Billie Jean interacts with the therapist in ways that were missing in childhood, she may experience what Garcia (1995) calls responsive anger. Learning how to use responsive anger will allow her to be effective in setting boundaries and making contact when others are intruding on, or alienating themselves from her, such as her wayward and controlling husband and her oppositionally defiant daughter. By understanding and learning to use her anger in productive ways rather than stuffing it in her Adapted Child, she is much more likely to solve the problems that she is now experiencing.

The client is now asked to play her father as she imagines the role to be. She may play her father as she remembers him, but as traumatic material emerges she must not change him to fit her maladaptive script or game. She may fight with him, understand him better, and change herself, but her father's role is fixed in the script (Goulding & Goulding, 1979, p. 206).

TH: See yourself alone with your father right after the birthday party. Go back to that time and tell your dad what your feelings are based on these injunctions you were given and the decisions you made. First, "Don't grow!" Be your dad!

CL: (*as her father*) I don't want you to grow up because then I'd have to admit you were the woman I love and not your mother.

CL: (*as herself as a child*) Well, I am not your wife. I am your little girl. Sometimes I have to act like your wife and I really get angry, particularly when you don't acknowledge all that I do and treat me like a little girl because of your own crap.

TH: Don't be the sex you are.

CL: (*as her father*) I treat you like a little girl, but I didn't even name you a girl. I really wanted a boy, but your mother let me down again.

CL: (*as herself*) Nobody let you down except your own chromosomes. I'll take my name, but I'm not a boy, I'm a girl, and you can't deny that. Plus I'm a very capable little girl who has to think like a woman, but always gets discounted.

TH: Don't think. Particularly about our little secret.

CL: (*as her father*) It would kill me if you really knew what was going on here.

CL: (*as herself*) Well, I do know what's going on, I deal with it every day. You're the one who won't 'fess up to it. I am not stupid. You are going to have to deal with your wife.

The therapist now moves to a recent scene to problem solve. In such scenes the client is being herself at her current age and thus may use her Adult ego state.

CL: John is telling me I've got to take care of this crazy business with Johnie Ruth and I'm trying to think but I don't know what to do.

TH: Trying . . . don't know. Bring your dad into the scene. What does he say?

CL: He's saying. "There, there . . . you need to do what John says."

TH: What in the world does he know about it? He never handled knotty problems like that.

CL: Nothing. He never, ever dealt with those tough family problems.

TH: Are you ready to fire him as your interpersonal supervisor?

CL: Yes. *"Dad, you are fired. Further, John, I'm fixing to fire you too if you don't take some responsibility. It's your kid, too."*

TH: Victory!

The use of imagery is a clear blending of TA redecision therapy's use of Gestalt approaches to resolve impasses (Gladfelter, 1995). Here, the imagery is particularly useful in bringing insight about how a past ego state applies to a present ego state and motivating the client to action. The key component of this redecision drama is having the client achieve success and not have the play end in tragedy. The therapist knows what baggage from the past the client needs to set aside and writes in some lines that will help Billie Jean expunge the maladaptive tapes transmitted to her by her father (Goulding & Goulding, 1979, pp. 211–212).

Redecision and Change

It may be necessary early in therapy to focus on the shortcomings of others, such as parents, to clarify early injunctions and decisions. Later in therapy, however, it is important for clients to realize that their parents, are, after all, only human and no longer responsible for their offsprings' mental health. Finally, for a successful redecision, it is crucial that the scene end "victoriously" for the client. To accomplish this, the therapist helps clients to recognize or find something new in the scene or, more important, to discover some hidden power in themselves (Goulding & Goulding, 1979, pp. 207–211).

Egograms

"Energy distribution action" therapists support the concept of *ego state oppositions.* Through techniques of ego state opposition, clients learn to transfer their ego state energies from those states considered too high to those considered too low. These states are graphically represented by the egogram (Dusay & Dusay, 1979). In the case of Billie Jean, she has almost no Critical Parent (others dictate to her), an extremely high Nurturing Parent (she can be smothering), little Adult (she is too boring), little Free Child (it shows up when she is close to small children or by herself, and is clearly a precious commodity), and an extremely high Adapted Child (she feels depressed and guilty and worries about what others will think) (see Figure 7.5, Billie Jean's egogram).

Dusay (1976) hypothesizes that a rule of constancy operates with the ego states: when one state increases, another must decrease in a complementary way because of the finite amount of psychic energy that may be expended (p. 65). The ideal egogram for Billie Jean would be a bell-shaped curve showing an increased Critical Parent, a greatly decreased Nurturing Parent, a greatly increased Adult, a somewhat increased Free Child, and a severely decreased Adapted Child.

Woollams and Brown (1979) comment that after the redecision process, it is important that the therapist remain available to clients to provide information and strokes for changing, as well as to confront residual script behaviors. They suggest that therapist and client may benefit from considering the following question during this stage of therapy: (1) How does the client block him- or herself from carrying our the new decisions? (2) How can the client work through these blocks? They assert that once a client is regularly carrying out the new decision, he or she is ready to decide whether to work on a different issue and establish a new therapeutic contract or terminate therapy (p. 231).

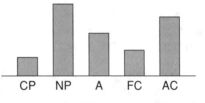

FIGURE 7.5   Billie Jean's Egogram

CONTRIBUTIONS OF TRANSACTIONAL ANALYSIS

One of the strengths of TA is its emphasis on the therapeutic contract to guide the direction of the therapeutic process (Harper, 1975). Since therapist and client work together in achieving the goals of the contract, they function more as partners than as "doctor and patient," thus lessening the power differential existing in some other therapeutic approaches. Furthermore, a contract enables both client and therapist to better assess whether the outcome of therapy has been successful.

A second strength of TA is that clients can easily understand and apply its concepts in analyzing their own interpersonal behavior. This is positive in that clients can apply this understanding to problems that arise when they are no longer in therapy.

From a dynamic viewpoint, TA has done much to demystify the psychodynamic approach to therapy. Its use of common, everyday language and metaphors to label its techniques and theoretical principles simply makes sense and is understandable to most clients. TA's view of human beings as essentially "OK" places it as one of the few theories alongside Person-centered that views the human dilemma in nonpathological terms.

Inspired by Eric Berne's focus on building a strong theoretical foundation, the International Transactional Analysis Association (ITAA) encourages contributions to TA theory and practice by publishing the *Transactional Analysis Journal*, providing advanced training for clinical certification for its ten thousand members, and holding regional, national, and international conventions (Dusay & Dusay, 1989, p. 417). Thus, TA has evolved from a pop psychology of the sixties and seventies to a dynamic, internationally recognized therapeutic modality.

SHORTCOMINGS OF TRANSACTIONAL ANALYSIS

Transactional analysis has been criticized as being "simple," "superficial," and "palliative." We disagree with this criticism. However, in some instances, TA practitioners overemphasize diagrams and "cutesy" jargon (e.g., "pig parent," "witch mother," "warm fuzzy").

A major limitation of TA applies more to possible misuses of the approach rather than to TA itself. It is quite possible that some therapists could incorporate only the jargon and the analytical cognitive components of TA into their therapeutic approaches. Therapists who do this place too much emphasis on "analyzing" and not enough emphasis on changing behavior or on the affective or relationship aspects of the therapeutic process (Goulding & Goulding, 1979).

Some of the techniques of TA such as Schiff's Reparenting approach (1970) are extremely confrontational, can strip clients of needed defenses, and create tremendous dependency on the therapist. The International Transactional Analysis Association's ethics committee has looked into the ethics of this and other techniques that might put clients at risk (Weiss, 1994). However, the fact remains that in the hands of therapists who do not have a strong ethical foundation, the ease of use of TA makes its extremely susceptible to misuse.

Because of its simple vocabulary and game approach, TA became a self-help hit in the 1970s. Many professionals in the human service field were left with a bitter taste as they saw the harm inflicted on gullible and maladjusted individuals by the psychobabble of self-appointed gurus. This acid professional view is aptly characterized by Gholson's (1973) satire "I'm OK, You're So-So" and still prevails to a great extent in professional therapeutic circles. While we see a good deal of worth in psychological self-help books and call-in therapy on radio shows, regard various components of TA as excellent therapeutic techniques, and know many excellent practitioners of TA, we are still concerned that TA is one of the most abused therapies when put into the hands of people who do not know what they are doing.

On the other hand, although the terminology is simple, there is a lot of it. Understanding "Transactionalese" is not easy for anyone not initiated into TA's vast array of metaphors. The reading required may be too time-consuming or difficult for some individuals who have not made a habit of reading.

For those with diminished mental capacity, TA may have little utility because of its reliance on cognition. The welter of crossed transactions, ego states, and energy distribution can become mind-boggling, especially if the therapist is not competent enough to keep from relying on the verbiage of TA to impress the client with his or her expertise.

TRANSACTIONAL ANALYSIS WITH DIVERSE POPULATIONS

Transactional analysis is becoming one of the world's most multicultural therapies, with rapid growth in Western and Eastern Europe, the former Soviet Union, and South America (Cassius, 1992). In a recent issue of the *Transactional Analysis Journal,* the editor spoke to the international flavor of the approach by noting that four of the six major articles were from England, South Africa, and India. Such cultural diversity provides practitioners in North America a much broader therapeutic perspective as they are increasingly exposed to clients with different cultural backgrounds (Douglass, 1992).

For many transplanted ethnic groups, reliance on and respect for one's family is a primary survival technique. Injunctions such as "Don't shame the family" and "Don't put your interests ahead of the family's" are ironclad rules for preserving the sanctity and authority of the family system—no matter how pathological or how much that system may be out of touch with what is occurring in the contemporary world around it. From cultures such as these, generational transmission of scripts make sense. Transactional analysis may be helpful in ferreting out parental messages that culturally different clients have received and that may conflict with their present living conditions.

However, for those cultures that place a great deal of respect in parental authority, delving into parental injunctions may cause problems. Confronting injunctions and scripts obtained from one's parents without respecting the client's belief system about loyalty to family can generate all kinds of guilt feelings in the client.

As an example, Cassius (1992) reports in his training of Brazilian therapists that they have enthusiastically adapted the fundamental tenets of TA to their own cultural milieu. Because of the preeminent role tight-knit families play in that culture, Brazilian therapists have placed a good deal of emphasis on Schiff's (1970) reparenting techniques. Parental injunctions are not so much seen as being malevolent, but rather reframed as statements delivered under stress. Thus, *in vivo* reparenting techniques can easily replace old script messages with newer, more adaptive ones without disparaging the family in the process.

The use in TA of simple and concrete terminology and metaphors such as "stamps," "discounts," "rackets," and "games" makes it ideally suited to work with clientele without the sophistication or desire to put up with more complex analytic or cognitive strategies. The Parent, Adult, and Child ego states can be understood by anyone. Also, TA attempts to demystify therapy by very clearly stating what it will do and how it will do it. Transactional analysis is egalitarian in that it involves the client in an equal partnership. Clients who have continuously heard, from early on in life, the injunctions and driver statements often tend to believe they are merely pawns, directed by fate. For these clients, TA debunks this external locus of control and asks them to take responsibility for who they are and what they do.

Transactional analysis simplifies the complexity of insight therapy through concrete diagrams and images that serve as a chronological history of progress and graphically demonstrate to clients what is happening in their lives, what needs to be changed, and whether that change is occurring. Its emphasis on rackets, games, and transactions strikes a responsive chord in individuals whose existence may be tied to how well they can engage in games and complete ulterior transactions—for example, prison inmates.

Transactional analysis also works well with those who are shackled to a past nonnurturing, pathological childhood, such as adult survivors of child sexual and physical abuse and adult children of alcoholics. For survivors of these dysfunctional families, unraveling the ego/genograms of family functioning may be extremely helpful in coming to grips with the past, repressed material. Thus, for people who have a pathological family genealogy, TA makes a great deal of sense.

For clients with physical disabilities, TA may play an extremely important role in helping them come to grips with problems in relationships that have resulted from early scripts they have written for themselves because of their disabilities (Champeau, 1992). From a dynamic point of view, physical disability occurring in early childhood has an adverse impact on ego development because of the severe impact it has on the family system and how that system reacts to the disabling condition. Parents may engage in overindulgence and overprotection or may neglect the child. The outcome may be a physically and emotionally disabled adult who plays passive-aggressive, dependent, and narcissistic games (Livneh & Sherwood, 1991). Unless these individuals become aware of the manipulative games they play, they will have difficulty forming equitable relationships with others.

Transactional analysis seems to work especially well for schizophrenics. Voices in the clients' minds that may say terrible things about them can be shown to be a critical parent who is sending them injunctions not to be sane. Transactional analysis can help schizophrenics to obtain a foot- and handhold on reality by showing them how to rewrite such insane scripts.

TA concepts are readily adaptable to children. "Warm pink fuzzy" and "cold grey prickly" are TA terms that would be understood in practically every elementary school in North America. TA's use of simple analogies and figural drawings to make therapy as concrete as possible for children is exemplified in *TA for Kids* (Freed & Freed, 1974a) and *TA for Tots* (Freed& Freed, 1974b).

Finally, when therapists are challenging the life scripts of ethnically distinct and culturally diverse clientele, they need to understand how those scripts differ from their own cultures. For example, the normative life script for a fifth-generation American Caucasian whose ancestors have lived on the family farm for over one hundred years may be radically different from a Vietnamese boat person disenfranchised from her homeland, a Hispanic migrant worker who lives a nomadic existence for most of the year, or a homeless African American from the inner city who was raised in an extended family with few positive male images present. To attempt to apply generic scripts to all of these individuals without understanding the environmental context within which they operate is at best, poor judgment, and at worst, unethical.

SUMMARY

Transactional analysis, originated by Eric Berne in the 1950s, is contractual and decisional in its approach to treatment. It considers emotional difficulties to be the result of inappropriate decisions made in response to early, "unhealthy" parental messages and contends that individuals have the capacity and the responsibility to make new, more appropriate decisions.

One characteristic of TA is that its concepts and the vocabulary to describe them are shared by TA practitioners. Such terms include *Parent, Adult, Child, script, game, racket, discount, stamp, stroke, contract, decisions,* and *redecision.* Transactional analysis therapists emphasize a treatment approach based on the assumption" I'm OK—You're OK."

Transactional analysis attacks maladaptive behavior by examining ego states, uncovering parental driver and injunction messages, detecting games and rackets, rewriting scripts, and redistributing energy distribution between ego states. It is an equitable therapy that involves the client as a full and contributing partner through the therapeutic contract.

Although TA has a variety of divergent international camps as far as its theory and practice are concerned, many TA theorists (Cassius, 1980; Clarkson, 1992; Dusay & Dusay, 1989) believe that TA will continue to integrate techniques from other therapeutic approaches into its constantly evolving frameworks. From that standpoint, while it still adheres to its analytic roots, its use of cognitive, behavioral, Gestalt, and rational-emotive and bioenergetic techniques makes it much more eclectic than it was early in its development.

SUGGESTIONS FOR FURTHER READING

Berne, E. (1964). *Games people play: The psychology of human relationships.* New York: Grove Press.

Clarkson, P. (1992). *Transactional analysis psychotherapy: An integrated approach.* London: Routledge.

Goulding, M., & Goulding, R. (1979). *Changing lives through redecision therapy.* New York: Brunner/Mazel.

Harris, A. B., & Harris, T. A. (1985). *Staying OK*. New York: Harper & Row.

Harris, T. A. (1969) *I'm OK—You're OK*. New York: Harper & Row.

James, M., & Jongeward, D. (1971). *Born to win: Transactional analysis with Gestalt experiments*. Reading, MA: Addison-Wesley.

Woollams, S., & Brown, M. (1979). *TA: The total handbook of transactional analysis*. Englewood Cliffs, NJ: Prentice-Hall.

REFERENCES

Bary, B. B., & Hufford, F. M. (1990). The six advantages to games and their use in treatment. *Transactional Analysis Journal, 20*(4), 214–220.

Berne, E. (1964). *Games people play: The psychology of human relationships*. New York: Grove Press.

Berne, E. (1966). *Principles of group treatment*. New York: Oxford University Press.

Berne, E. (1972). *What do you say after you say hello?* New York: Grove Press.

Cassius, J. (1980). Bodyscript release: How to use bioenergetics and transactional analysis. In J. Cassius (Ed.), *Horizons in bioenergetics: New dimensions in mind/body psychotherapy* (pp. 212–224). Memphis: Promethean.

Cassius, J. (1992). *The future of TA and the multicultural issues involved in its use* (cassette recording no. 7581-92-1). Memphis, TN: Memphis State University, Department of Counseling and Personnel Services.

Champeau, T. (1992). Transactional analysis and rehabilitation: An integrative approach to disability. *Transactional Analysis Journal, 22*(4), 234–242.

Clark, F. C. (1995). Anger and its disavowal in shame-based people. *Transactional Analysis Journal, 25*(2), 129–132.

Clarkson, P. (1992). *Transactional analysis psychotherapy: An integrated approach*. London: Routledge.

Douglass, J. (1992). Letter from the editor. *Transactional Analysis Journal, 22*, 64–65.

Dusay, J. M. (1972). Egograms and the constancy hypothesis. *Transactional Analysis Journal, 2*, 37–40.

Dusay, J. M. (1976). Egograms and the "constancy hypothesis." in G. M. Goldhaber & M. B. Goldhaber (Eds.), *Transactional analysis: Principles and applications* (pp. 62–67). Boston: Allyn & Bacon.

Dusay, J. M. (1977). The evolution of transactional analysis. In G. Barnes (Ed.), *Transactional analysis after Eric Berne* (pp. 32–52). New York: Harper's College Press.

Dusay, J. M., & Dusay, K. M. (1979). Transactional analysis. In R. J. Corsini (Ed.), *Current psychotherapies* (2nd ed.; pp. 374–427). Itasca, IL: F. E. Peacock.

Dusay, J. M., & Dusay, K. M. (1989).Transactional analysis. In R. J. Corsini & D. Wedding (Eds.), *Current Psychotherapies* (4th ed.; pp. 405–453). Itasca, IL: F. E. Peacock.

Frazier, T. (1995). Anger: Don't express it and don't repress it. *Transactional Analysis Journal, 25*(2), 123–128.

Freed, A., & Freed, M. (1974a). *TA for kids*. Sacremento, CA: Freed.

Freed, A., & Freed, M. (1974b). *TA for tots*. Sacremento, CA: Freed.

Garcia, F. N. (1995). The many faces of anger. *Transactional Analysis Journal, 25*(2), 119–122.

Gholson, B. G. (1973). I'm OK, you're so-so. *Playboy*, December, p. 213.

Gladfelter, J. (1995). Imagery in redecision therapy. *Transactional Analysis Journal, 25*(4) 319–320.

Goldhaber, G. M., and Goldhaber, M. B. (1976). *Transactional analysis: Principles and applications.* Boston: Allyn & Bacon.

Goulding, R. (1989). Teaching transactional analysis and redecision therapy. *Journal of Independent Social Work, 3*(4), 71–86.

Goulding, R., & Goulding, M. (1976). Injunctions, decisions and redecisions. *Transactional Analysis Journal, 6,* 41–47.

Goulding, R., & Goulding, M. (1978). *The power is in the patient: A TA/Gestalt approach to psychotherapy.* San Francisco: TA Press.

Goulding, R., & Goulding, M. (1979). *Changing lives through redecision therapy.* New York: Brunner/Mazel.

Harper, R. (1975). *The new psychotherapies.* Englewood Cliffs, NJ: Prentice-Hall.

Harris, A. B., & Harris, T. A. (1985). *Staying OK.* New York: Harper & Row.

Harris, T. A. (1969) *I'm OK—You're OK.* New York: Harper & Row.

Hyams, H. (1994). Shame: The enemy within. *Transactional Analysis Journal, 24*(4), 255–264.

James, M., & Jongeward, D. (1971). *Born to win: Transactional analysis with Gestalt experiments.* Reading, MA: Addison-Wesley.

Joines, V. S. (1995). A developmental approach to anger. *Transactional Analysis Journal, 25*(2), 112–118.

Kahler, T., & Capers, H. (1974). The miniscript. *Transactional Analysis Journal, 4,* 26–42.

Karpman, S. B. (1968). Fairy tales and script drama analysis. *Transactional Analysis Bulletin, 7,* 39–43.

Klein, M. (1992). The enemies of love. *Transactional Analysis Journal, 22,* 76–81.

Laing, R. D. (1971). *The politics of the family and other essays.* New York: Pantheon.

Livneh H., & Sherwood, A. (1991). Application of personality theories and counseling strategies to clients with physical disabilities. *Journal of Counseling and Development, 69,* 525–538.

McClendon, R., & Kadis, L. B. (1995). Redecision therapy: On the leading edge. *Transactional Analysis Journal, 25*(4), 339–342.

Mellor, K., & Schiff, E. (1975). Discounting. *Transactional Analysis Journal, 5,* 295–302.

Mundy, W. L. (1994). "You know": Or do you? *Transactional Analysis Journal, 24*(3), 216–219.

Novellino, M., & Moiso, C. (1990). The psychodynamic approach to transactional analysis. *Transactional Analysis Journal, 20*(3), 187–192.

Schiff, J. L., with Day, B. (1970). *All my children.* New York: Evans.

Steiner, C. M. (1967). A script checklist. *Transactional Analysis Bulletin, 6,* 38–39.

Steiner, C. M. (1968). Transactional analysis as a treatment philosophy. *Transactional Analysis Bulletin, 7,* 61–63.

Steiner, C. M. (1971). The stroke economy. *Transactional Analysis Journal, 1,* 9–15.

Steiner, C. M. (1974). *Scripts people live: Transactional analysis of life scripts.* New York: Grove Press.

Summerton, O. (1992). The game pentagon. *Transactional Analysis Journal, 22,* 66–75.

Weiss, L. (1994). The ethics of parenting and reparenting in psychotherapy. *Transactional Analysis Journal, 24*(1), 57–59.

Woollams, S. (1978). The internal stroke economy. *Transactional Analysis Journal, 8,* 194–197.

Woollams, S., & Brown, M. (1979). *TA: The total handbook of transactional analysis.* Englewood Cliffs, NJ: Prentice-Hall.

8

BEHAVIORAL COUNSELING, THERAPY, AND MODIFICATION

FUNDAMENTAL TENETS

History

The history and practice of the behavioral approach can be divided into three components. The first, *classical* or *respondent conditioning,* is based on the work of Pavlov (1960) and Hull (1943). In practice, respondent conditioning is called *behavior therapy* (Chambless & Goldstein, 1979, p. 230) and traces its human application to Watson and Rayner's (1920) and Jones's (1924) work in sensitizing and desensitizing children to small furry animals. The first large-scale clinical application of these principles occurred in the late 1950s, when Wolpe (1954; 1958; 1961) introduced systematic desensitization by reciprocal inhibition.

The second component is *operant conditioning.* It is based on the work of B. F. Skinner (1953) and in practice is called *behavior modification* (Chambless & Goldstein, 1979, p. 230). Skinner practiced behavior modification with individuals (1953) and groups (1948; 1958). While different in theory, in practice behavior therapy and behavior modification are often used in tandem and are difficult, if not impossible, to distinguish (Kaplan, 1986).

Because behaviorists find their roots in learning theory, two works are particularly important to understanding how behaviorism got out of the laboratories and into therapy. The first is *Personality and Psychotherapy,* by Dollard and Miller (1950). This book translated psychoanalytic theory and practice into learning theory terms and laid the foundation for behaviorists to enter the field of therapy. The second work is *Case Studies in Behavior Modification* by Ullmann and Krasner (1965). This book brought a variety of behavioral techniques, previously known only to the back wards of mental hospitals and a few behavioral therapists, to the forefront of psychology. Ullmann and Krasner's brilliant introduction to the book clearly stated the theory, use, and efficacy of a psychological model as opposed to the customary medical or disease model of therapy.

The third and latest component is *cognitive behavior therapy.* This therapy represents the convergence of two different streams of therapeutic thought. For all its startling appearance and promise as it came onto the therapeutic stage in the 1960s, the pure behavioral approach to treatment did not become the panacea its advocates originally thought it would be. Although rats could be conditioned to run the same way every time in a Skinner box, it soon became apparent that strict application of respondent or operant procedures would not guarantee the same results in the treatment of humans, even though the laws of conditioning would seem to dictate otherwise. Even early operant procedures, such as Wolpe's (1958) desensitization techniques, could not be called a pure behavioral approach because of the use of the client's thinking processes to modify noxious stimuli. As behaviorists struggled to come to grips with this perplexing issue, the question of cognition as a mediating variable continued to surface.

Borrowing equally from the respondent and operant precepts of Pavlovian and Skinnerian behavioral psychology and from the cognitive precepts of Ellis's (1962) rational-emotive behavior therapy (REBT), innovative theorists such as Ellis and Grieger (1977), Lazarus (1977), Beck (1976), Kazdin (1974; 1976), and Meichenbaum (1977) welded behavioral and REBT approaches into cognitive behavior therapy in the late 1970s. In the 1980s, cognitive behaviorism moved beyond the respondent and operant approaches of behaviorism and the philosophical systems of REBT and became distinctly broader than either. Therefore, cognitive behaviorism as a specific therapeutic modality is dealt with separately, in Chapter 11.

Today, behavior therapists and cognitive behaviorists deal with every facet of human events—from simple stimulus–response behaviors to the emission and control of complex cognitive patterns. Wilson (1995, pp. 197–201) describes how behavioral approaches have broadened in scope as well as in theory and application. The behavioral family is progressively becoming more "eclecticlike," more scientific, systematic, and heterogeneous in methodology. Concomitantly, the system's basic concepts characteristic of the short history of the approach "are clear and its commonalities with and differences from nonbehavioral therapeutic systems can be identified" (p. 197). Wilson (1995) further identifies the three major approaches that characterize modern behavior therapy as (1) *applied behavior analysis,* (2) *a neo-behavioristic mediational stimulus-response model,* and (3) *social-cognitive theory* (p. 198). The three approaches are described as differing in the extent that each uses cognitive concepts and procedures. Applied behavior analysis focuses exclusively on observable, measurable behavioral events and rejects all cognitive mediating processes. Social-cognitive theory, at the other end of the spectrum, relies mainly on cognitive concepts and events, while the *neo-behavioristic mediational stimulus-response model* operates largely on classical conditioning principles.

To date, behavioral approaches view the client as both the producer and the product of the environment (Kazdin, 1978), capable of imagining which behaviors are desirable (Meichenbaum, 1977) and then working to make those images a behavioral reality (Watson & Tharp, 1981; 1989). Thus runs the brief but phenomenal history of the behavioral system of counseling and psychotherapy. If one remembers that 90 percent of the work in the field has been accomplished in three decades. Its development is impressive indeed.

Overview of the Behavioral Approach

The concepts and techniques presented in this chapter demonstrate the two initial thrusts of the behavioral approach: respondent and operant. A variety of commonly used strategies are discussed, but it is beyond the purview of any one chapter or book to treat the world of behavioral counseling exhaustively. The suggestions for further reading at the end of the chapter provide a starting point for further exploration of the many facets of behavioral theory and practice.

The case study touches on the two respondent and operant processes of the behavioral approach. The chapter portrays the counselor in a personal and collaborative mode, helping the client generate corrective learning experiences. This view of the behavioral counselor refutes many of the erroneous descriptions of the approach that present it as too mechanistic and impersonal.

Theory of Personality

No single theory of personality has been exclusively identified with behaviorism. Behaviorists have given more attention to learning theory than to the development of a behavioral model of human personality. Behaviorists assume that individuals develop those consistencies known as personality through maturation and the laws of learning (Chambless & Goldstein, 1979, p. 237). Therefore, for behaviorists, what most nearly fits a personality theory is actually learning theory.

Major theorists who could be classified as behavioristic personality theorists include Bandura (1991; 1995), Dollard and Miller (1950), Eysenck (1960), Krumboltz (1966), Lundin (1961; 1972; 1977), Mowrer (1950; 1973), Skinner (1948; 1953; 1971; 1974), and Wolpe (1982; 1991). Behavioral theorists have explained human personality in a variety of ways. However, there are a few general tenets of behavioral theory and personality:

1. The *behavior* of organisms, *not mental phenomena,* determine learning, attitudes, habits, and other aspects of personal development.
2. Personality development is deterministic. That is, the environment and experiences determine how the personality develops.
3. Individual differences are derived from different experiences.
4. Dualisms such as mind–body, body–spirit, and body–soul have no scientific validity in the development, prediction, and control of human behavior.
5. Although personality development has certain genetic limitations, which are fixed, the effects of environmental and internally generated stimuli play the dominant role.

Lundin (1977) has elaborated on twelve basic Skinnerian principles that form the basis for an *operant reinforcement* view of personality development. Such a view holds, essentially, that given a specific genetic endowment limit, the personality of the organism is determined by antecedent conditions. That is, operant reinforcements shape the personality. For Skinner (1953) the concept of self represents a functionally integrated system of responses, and one's knowledge of self is a description of one's own behavior. What other theorists see as traits, Skinner sees as differences in the processes or independent variables to which persons are exposed. This concept is important because if traits are not set in stone, but are ongoing behavioral processes, then there is the possibility for treatment intervention and change (Chambless & Goldstein, 1979, p. 239). Lundin (1977) has specified eight principles of operant reinforcement that pertain to personality *development* (1–8) and four principles that pertain to personality *maintenance* (9–12):

1. In the development of a theory of personality, prediction and control of behavior are paramount. There is no such thing as free will. Environmental variables determine responses. Once the variables are known, the behavior can be predicted and controlled (p. 183).
2. All behavior can be divided into operant and respondent classes. That is, the individual responds to, or operates on, the environment. Since all behavior falls under the control of environmental stimuli, there is no such thing as voluntary behavior (p. 184).
3. One's personality is acquired through the use of reinforcers. Besides the primary positive reinforcers—food, water, and air—certain conditioned positive reinforcers, such as money and social approval, shape personality. Negative reinforcers that strengthen a behavior when a stimulus is removed also shape personality. Turning the air conditioning up to cool off and stopping at a traffic light are examples of negative primary and conditioned reinforcers that help people avoid aversive stimuli (pp. 184–185).
4. Behavior may be changed by weakening or withholding reinforcement—a process called *extinction*. An example of changing behavior by extinction is ignoring the tantruming, attention-seeking behavior of a small child. In practice such procedures may take a long time if the behavior has had a long history of reinforcement or if attempts to extinguish the behavior have been interspersed with intermittent reinforcement (p. 185).
5. Personality develops by a process of discrimination from a generalization of responding. When a response has been conditioned to a particular stimulus, other stimuli similar to the conditioned stimulus can produce the conditioned response. Discrimination occurs as differentiations are made between stimuli that closely resemble one another. Selective reinforcement, in which the presence of certain stimuli is reinforced and not others, develops discrimination (p. 186). The generalization "All professors have fossilized brains" may be discriminated to statistics professors have "fossilized brains," counseling psychology professors "have some brains," and Dr. Gilliland "is really a brain"—the selective reinforcement perhaps being an A from Dr. Gilliland and a more aversive grade from the statistics professor.
6. Personality is shaped or differentiated by the variability of responding. Differentiation also involves selective reinforcement. Initial efforts to accomplish a task or learn a skill usually have large variable-ratio schedules of reinforcement. As the individual differentiates which responses are reinforced and which are not, skill and accomplishment are gained. From learning how to talk to performing brain surgery, differentiation and shaping of responses to obtain less variability is the end goal. However, even in tasks well learned there is some variability, otherwise all individuals would be B. F. Skinners, Arnold Palmers, or Katharine Hepburns (p. 187).

7. Modeling develops many aspects of personality. Behavior is acquired by watching significant others and is reinforced the more the behavior approximates that of the significant others. The use of role playing to teach assertiveness is modeling (p. 187).

8. Besides positive reinforcement, personality is controlled by aversive stimuli that can result in escape, avoidance, punishment, or anxiety (p. 188). (This assertion is dealt with at length in the section on maladjustment.)

9. Personality is maintained by a series of conditioned reinforcers. Conditioned reinforcers start out as neutral stimuli, but by pairing with primary reinforcers they can later strengthen behavior in their own right. Some conditioned reinforcers are specific to individuals; others are general to all people. Approval and affection are examples of intrinsic conditioned reinforcers, and tokens in the form of money are extrinsic conditioned reinforcers. If conditioned reinforcers are not paired with primary reinforcers from time to time they lose their power. If money, even gold, could not be exchanged for other primary or conditioned reinforcers, it would soon lose its potency as a reinforcer (p. 190).

10. Behavior can be maintained by reinforcers delivered regularly or intermittently. Regular or continuous reinforcement means every response is followed by reinforcement. Taken to the extreme, continuous reinforcement causes satiation and loses its power. Intermittent reinforcement means behavior is reinforced on schedules. Intermittent reinforcement schedules develop strong behavior. There are four types of schedules:

    a. *Fixed-interval reinforcement* occurs at regular intervals, such as receiving a weekly paycheck.
    b. *Variable-interval reinforcement* occurs on a time schedule that varies but averages out to a specified time. The automatic change makers at convenience stores are set up on this schedule to foil robbery attempts.
    c. *Fixed-ratio reinforcements* are delivered at a specified rate that depends on how many responses are made. Being paid by the number of "widgets" turned out on an assembly line exemplifies this schedule.
    d. *Variable-ratio reinforcements* are obtained irregularly but average out to a given figure. Duck hunting in miserable weather and shoving quarters into slot machines are outstanding examples of how powerful this schedule can be (pp. 190–191).

11. Depriving or satiating an individual with some kind of reinforcement is a *motivator*. Deprivation of primary reinforcers affects all people in about the same way. People who are deprived of food become hungry. However, conditioned reinforcers may substantially alter what is considered deprivation. The absence of chocolate cake, potato chips, and ice cream to a person on a diet may constitute deprivation of the severest kind. The other side of the coin is satiation. Reinforcement occurs so often and in such quantity that a response no longer occurs. A typical example is the between-meals snacker who, to the chagrin of the cook, is not hungry when dinner is served (pp. 191–92).

12. Behavior can be maintained or altered by motivation-like operations, in which something other than deprivation or satiation affects the behavior of the individual. The most common, and addictive, examples of motivation-like operations are alcohol and cocaine (p. 192).

Throughout these twelve basic tenets is the overarching concept of overt observable responses and the identifiable stimuli that go with them. Nowhere among respondent or operant behaviorists will attempts at dynamic explanations of personality be found. For these behaviorists, behavior is the explanation of personality.

Nature of Maladjustment

Although respondent and operant theories of maladjustment will be distinguished for purposes of clarity, they are intermingled in terms of behavioral outcomes (Ullmann & Krasner, 1965, p. 22). Maladaptive behaviors, like adaptive behaviors, are learned. This being the case, they can also be unlearned (Chambless & Goldstein, 1979, p. 230). The implications of these statements are that there are few if any disease pathologies present in maladjusted individuals (Ullmann & Krasner, 1965, p. 20).

Maladjustment is specific to the culture, time, social class, and situation. What may be maladjustive in one culture may be adjustive in another. The distinction is that the individual is able to obtain reinforcement from the significant others that control reinforcement (Ullmann & Krasner, 1965, p. 20). An outstanding example is the New Guinea headhunter. In Western society such a person would be seen as a homicidal maniac who had the additional "crazy" behavior of having a trophy room filled with human heads. Yet, the more trophies the headhunter mounts, the more reinforcement he receives. An American man transplanted to a New Guinea tribe would probably find himself shunned, expelled, or made into the main course at a tribal feast! In behavioral terms, he would not live up to the expectations for one in his role, would not respond positively to all the stimuli present, and would not obtain the maximum reinforcement available to "warrior" status.

The times we live in have a great deal to do with what is construed to be maladjusted behavior, and the very nature of maladjustment may change from one generation to the next. St. Vitus' dance—the frenzied gyrations of mobs of people that occurred in Europe in the Middle Ages—might be viewed in an entirely different manner if it occurred on the main street of a midwestern town in the United States today.

Each social class has its own definition and particular ways of acting out maladjustive behavior. Myers and Roberts (1959) found considerable difference in symptoms between neurotics and psychotics from different social classes. Middle-class individuals were inhibited, self-deprecating, and guilt-ridden, whereas lower-class individuals were aggressive, rebellious, violent, self-indulgent, and lawbreaking.

Combat is an excellent example of what may be situation-adjustive or maladjustive behavior. To subject oneself voluntarily to being killed or maimed would seem to be the height of insanity. Yet, to escape such circumstances in combat may have consequences that are considered extremely maladaptive. Even if a soldier manifests combat-related psychosomatic symptoms, this may not be an acceptable maladjustment in terms of the safety needs of his or her combat unit. As a result, the "sick" soldier may suffer some very aversive consequences from his or her peer group. The major implication of these examples is that there is no discontinuity between "healthy" and "sick" behavior except in terms of what a particular society in a particular time and place perceives the malady to be.

How, then, do people become "sick"? Because behaviorists believe that people learn by either respondent or operant means, it follows that maladaptive behavior is learned to either increase positive reinforcement or decrease an aversive stimulus (Chambless & Goldstein, 1979, p. 239). The client in psychotherapy is an excellent example of the person who obtains positive reinforcement for maladaptive behavior. He or she receives treatment (attention) and causes considerable consternation (attention) among significant others. Conversely, the aversive stimuli the client encounters may play an even greater part in the development of maladjustment. By escaping or avoiding a situation, one strengthens behavior by removing the aversive stimuli. If enough aversive stimuli are presented early in the client's conditioning history, then the client's continued avoidance of those stimuli will lead to withdrawal into a fantasy world where the stimuli are not present (Lundin, 1977, p. 188).

If an individual cannot escape or avoid aversive stimuli, punishment occurs. For Skinner (1953), most emotional problems are reactions to overcontrolling, punitive environments. Fear is a conditioned outcome to punishment and elicits such environmentally conditioned emotions as guilt, depression, and anger.

Guilt and depression lead to a state of anxiety. Anxiety may be defined behaviorally as an autonomic response to noxious stimuli and is maladaptive in circumstances where objectively there is no threat (Wolpe, 1954). In respondent terms, anxiety reactions may change physiological reactions such as heart rate, blood pressure, and perspiration; from an operant standpoint they may elicit nervousness, feelings of being upset, and hyperactivity (Lundin, 1977, p. 189). Because learning leads to the ability to anticipate an event, when a real or imaginary aversive stimulus is perceived, anxiety preceding the punishing event may be worse than the punishment itself. Excessive conditioning in this manner can lead to neurotic anxiety attacks in which the individual is paralyzed with fear or panic. On the opposite end of the behavioral continuum, interpersonal relationships may be impeded by displaced aggression against persons or objects not originally responsible for the punishment (Azrin, 1966).

In respondent terms, an aversive stimulus is paired with a previously neutral stimulus. Later, after learning has occurred, the previously neutral stimulus elicits the maladaptive response prior to encounter of the situation. One of the authors experienced such learning after going on an overnight camping trip as a child. While on the camping trip (neutral stimulus), the author developed a stomachache (aversive stimulus). On subsequent camping trips he again became sick (pairing), and eventually the mere mention of camping (conditioned aversive stimulus) made him nauseous (aversive response).

A second group of maladaptive behaviors may be learned through operant conditioning. Patterns of maladaptive behaviors in operant conditioning are shaped, increased, and maintained through reinforcement. The example of the stomachache and the camping trip may be taken a step further. Suppose that the individual discovers that a stomachache offers attention through increased caring, concern, sympathy, and worry by his or her parents. Such a discovery can be put to gainful use. That is, the individual can now extricate him- or herself from an uncomfortable situation, such as going to school. By having stomachaches, one can avoid an aversive situation. The individual is now operating on the environment, changing it to meet perceived needs. Taken to the extreme, generalization may occur and any situation imagined to be threatening, unpleasant, or harmful may result in a stomachache. Why does this happen? The answer is simply that it pays off. As conditioning is ingrained, the original payoff (attention from one's parents) may be of minimal significance. In fact, such maladaptive responding may become extremely debilitating to the individual (getting sick before a graduate exam). The individual may wish to change the behavior, but because avoiding an aversive stimulus has been learned to be such a good payoff, it may be extremely difficult to extinguish "getting-sick" behavior without therapeutic intervention.

In summary, both behavior therapy and behavior modification treat maladjustive behavior directly. There are no underlying causes. Second, changing maladjustive behavior is the major focus; insight is not. As Eysenck (1959) puts it, "there is no neurosis underlying the symptom, but merely the symptom itself. Get rid of the symptom and you have eliminated the neurosis." Contemporary cognitive behaviorists, though, have come to see this premise as too simplistic. Cognitive behaviorists assume that the symptom is not the entire problem but part of the larger problem of thoughts, feelings, actions, and interactions with other people and the environment (see Chapter 11). Yet Eysenck and Martin (1987) have made a strong case to disprove the notion that the underlying tenets of conditioning and cognition are contradictory. They present considerable experimental evidence that even though conditioning and cognitive theories have oppositional aspects, a formidable body of theory undergirds both.

THE COUNSELING PROCESS

In behavioral counseling, as in any system of counseling or psychotherapy, it is essential that the counselor demonstrate accurate listening, concern, caring, acceptance, and understanding of the client as a unique person. A positive relationship between client and counselor is necessary to ensure that the counselor thoroughly understands the client's problem before intervention strategies are begun and to provide the client with enough motivation to succeed in the difficult and often complex process of acquiring adaptive behaviors. Most modern behavioral counselors approach the helping process from a much broader perspective than was the case a few years ago. Rather than viewing the counselor as the expert who scientifically develops and imposes behavior-modifying processes on the client, the modern approach strives to involve the client in the analysis, planning, process, and evaluation of his or her behavior-management program. Modern behavioral counselors seek to help the client extinguish a wide range of maladaptive behaviors and learn adaptive behaviors needed to establish and maintain targeted goals and consequences. The counselor collaborates with the client. The counselor is expected to have training and experience in human behavior modification and also to serve as consultant, teacher, adviser, reinforcer, and facilitator. The counselor even instructs and supervises noncounseling personnel (paraprofessionals, technicians, and volunteers) who function as counselor extensions and support persons. The qualities of the counselor are understanding, friendliness, caring, and being personal in the relationship. Such a description is a far cry from the earlier stereotype of the behavioral counselor as an indifferent, mechanical, manipulative technician.

In counseling or psychotherapy, the initial concern is to help the client analyze behavior, define problems, and select goals. This process is facilitated if the counselor and the client develop effective communication, trust, and cooperation. These relationship factors are also valuable throughout the client–counselor involvement. The counselor is more than a caring helper, however. He or she is skilled in applying scientific knowledge and experimental techniques in helping clients define and solve a wide range of human problems, which the client alone would not be able to do. Behavioral counseling and therapy have evolved from a mechanistic and reductionist system that viewed clients as responding to their genetic histories and to environmental influences that controlled them, toward viewing clients as agents who operate on and influence their environments. That evolution has included the active involvement of clients in every phase of counseling, from the definition of their problems through the evaluation and maintenance of their adaptive behavioral patterns (Watson & Tharp, 1989; Williams & Long, 1983; Wilson, 1995).

STRATEGIES FOR HELPING CLIENTS

Most of the strategies presented in this section are aimed at entry-level professional human services helpers. Some should be useful to professionals in developmental or preventive counseling with individuals. In the main, the strategies presented emphasize the collaborative effort of counselor and client. Since clients are both regulated by and regulators of their environments, the counselor's role as facilitator or mentor of their self-management is emphasized.

We have included eight representative strategies that are associated with *overt* behavioral change: behavioral contracting; behavioral prescribing; role playing; assertion training; aversion therapy; satiation; token economies; and self-management, self-monitoring, and self-reinforcement. Thumbnail sketches of each are provided. Readers who desire more detail are invited to begin with the suggested readings at the end of the chapter.

Behavioral Contracting

Also called *self-contracting* or simply *contracting,* this is a self-management strategy wherein the client enters into an agreement with one or more persons to perform or attain specific predetermined responses or goals. The contract usually contains specified consequences related to the time and level of performance or nonperformance. Extensive and varied use of contracting has been made in group and individual counseling to address such issues as weight management, drug and alcohol treatment, reduction in cigarette smoking, and monitoring physical fitness. The contract may serve as the primary behavior-change strategy or it may simply be an evaluative tool. Contingency contractual consequences may vary from requiring the client to deposit a considerable sum of money or an object of value to merely giving his or her word by affixing a signature to the agreement. Behavioral contracts allow for virtually unlimited flexibility and creativity. Rarely are any two alike. If a contract is to be of optimum help to the client, it should contain several basic features identified by Cormier and Cormier (1979, p. 507; 1991, pp. 320–321):

1. The contractual terms should be clear to every person involved. The behavioral goals and performance levels should be specific.
2. Rewards and sanctions should be specific and appropriate to the contracted behavior.
3. The contract should be written in a positive mode and may include a bonus clause.
4. Another person or persons should be included as positive supports. Their supportive role should be specified.
5. Commitments, through signatures at appropriate places, should be obtained from all persons involved.
6. Provision should be made for a progress chart, log, or other visible means of monitoring progress toward goal attainment, rewards, and sanctions, and if possible there should be verification by one other person.
7. An informed consent statement should contain a descriptive paragraph and a place for the date and both client and counselor signatures.

The applied behavioral principles found in contracting provide effective strategies for counseling clients in all age and social groups. Contracting has proved highly effective with many types of clients, particularly with children in school settings. The guidelines in Figures 8.1 (p. 209), 8.2 (p. 210), and 8.3 (p. 210) for using contracting with clients should prove useful to counselors interested in employing behavioral contracting to help clients attain their goals. These guidelines are based on behavioral principles and suggestions found in Alberto and Troutman (1982, pp. 188–200), Homme (1970, pp. 18–20), and Krumboltz and Krumboltz (1972).

The effectiveness of contracting depends on the particular use, user, and situation. Many clients like having something formalized, on paper, specific, and positive. A written contract appears to have some reinforcement value in itself. The contract should be a tangible symbol, for the client, of the counseling relationship and of the targeted behavioral goals. The case of Peggy Smith in this chapter contains an example of a written behavioral contract for an adult.

Behavioral Prescripting

James (1997) described how a comprehensive program of systematic behavioral prescripting and contracting can be implemented in schools to improve student learning and cope with problem behaviors. Behavioral prescripting entails an organized, systematic, and comprehensive team effort to focus on an individual student's unique problem situation. Typically, the team is comprised of teachers,

FIGURE 8.1   Contracting Guide

1. Select one or two behaviors that you want to work on first.
2. Describe those behaviors so that they can be observed and counted.
3. Identify rewards that will help provide motivation to do well. Utilize a reinforcing-event menu. Build in specific and varied contract payoffs:

   a. Rewards should be immediate.
   b. Initially, contract should reward *successive approximations*—small approximations that progress toward the target behavior.
   c. Payoffs should be frequent and in small amounts.
   d. The contract should call for and reinforce attainment rather than obedience.
   e. Payoffs should be made *after* attainment occurs.
   f. To reinforce a client with a previously ineffective reward, use the *substitution principle:* present the reward just before (or as close as possible to) the time the more effective reward is given.
   g. To stop a client from behaving in a particular way, build in the *incompatible-alternative principle:* reward an alternative action that is inconsistent with (or cannot be performed at the same time as) the desired act.
   h. To condition a client to remember to act at a specific time, use the *cueing principle:* arrange for the client to receive a cue for the correct performance immediately prior to the expected behavior rather than after the client has performed the act incorrectly.
   i. To help the client overcome fear, use the *fear-reduction principle:* gradually increase the client's exposure to the feared situation while the client is otherwise comfortable, secure, or rewarded.

4. Locate people who can help you keep track of the behaviors being performed and who can perhaps give out the rewards.
5. Write the contract so everyone can understand it and the method is used systematically.
6. Collect the data.
7. Troubleshoot the system if the data do not show an improvement.
8. Rewrite the contract if the goal is not achieved.
9. Continue to monitor, troubleshoot, and rewrite until there is improvement in the behaviors that were troublesome.
10. Select another behavior to work on.

---

parents, guidance counselors, and school administrators. Each student receiving behavioral prescripting is targeted for systematic analysis whereby team members assemble data on a format such as the following:

I. How to collect the data
   (a) Objectifying the data into countable units
   (b) Monitoring frequencies of occurrence using a behavioral grid
   (c) Using random time sampling
   (d) Assimilating and interpreting behavioral data as to frequency, time, and place
   (e) Utilizing data to indicate presence or absence of presenting problem and goal resolution

II. Resources needed:
   Data collector trained to observe, chart, compile, and analyze discrete behaviors in the school setting

FIGURE 8.2   Negotiating a Contract and Putting It on Paper

A *contract is negotiated*. Imposing a contract on a student or client will not work. Imposed agreements are not contracts because one party has not had the freedom to determine the terms and may have been forced to sign or accept it. The exact form of the contract is not very important if you include these items:

1. Date the agreement begins, ends, or is renegotiated
2. Behavior targeted for change (must be clear, honest, positive)
3. Amount and kind of rewards or reinforcers to be used
4. Schedule of delivery of reinforcers
5. Signatures of all parties involved
6. Schedule for review of progress (optional, but strongly suggested)
7. Bonus clause for sustained or exceptional performance
8. Statement of the penalties that will be imposed if the specific behavior is not performed

III. Training of team members:
   Approximately four two-hour sessions: training is divided into sessions of set-up, collection, and analysis of behavior

IV. Behavior modification procedure implemented

V. Functional assessment conducted

VI. References:
   Buckley and Walker (1970)
   Cormier and Cormier (1991)
   Deibert and Harmon (1972)
   Thorp and Wetzel (1969)
   Walker and Shea (1976)

FIGURE 8.3   Behavioral Contract Troubleshooting Guide

1. Was the target behavior clearly specified?
2. Did the contract provide for immediate reinforcement?
3. Did it ask for small approximations to the desired behavior?
4. Was reinforcement frequent and in small amounts?
5. Did the contract call for and reward accomplishment rather than obedience?
6. Was the performance rewarded after its occurrence?
7. Was the contract fair?
8. Was the contract honest?
9. Were the terms of the contract realistic?
10. Was the contract positive?
11. Was the contract, as a method, being used systematically?
12. Was the contract mutually negotiated?
13. Was the penalty clause too punitive?
14. Was the bonus clause motivational, reasonable, and attainable?

Each behavioral prescription is carried out following extensive groundwork and collaboration among team members. Attention is given to accurately defining and assessing the behavior to be changed, establishing a behavioral baseline using data obtained through direct observation (Cormier & Cormier, 1991, pp. 144–253; James, 1997; Wilson, 1995, p. 211), implementing reinforcement contingencies, evaluating before and after results, conducting follow-up evaluation of behavioral performance, and effecting any changes needed in the behavioral prescripting/ behavior modification process (Cormier & Cormier, 1991, pp. 254–325).

Although the behavioral prescripting approach described here has been greatly abbreviated, the full-blown comprehensive system is a "pure" behavioral approach that has been highly successful in schools (Buckley & Walker, 1970; James, 1997; Homme, 1970). Behavioral prescripting is a flexible and effective behavior modification technique that is also applicable to and adaptable for clients in nonschool settings (Cormier & Cormier, 1991; Deibert & Harmon, 1972; Kibler, Barker, & Miles, 1970; Krathwohl, Bloom, & Masis, 1964; Mayer, 1962; Thorp & Wetzel, 1969; Walker & Shea, 1976). The planning and implementation of the behavioral prescripting procedure require leadership that is skilled in behavioral principles, capable of establishing alliances among administration and providers, astute in the training of providers, and assertive in overseeing and facilitating the procedure from start to finish.

Role Playing

Role playing with clients has been used by behavioral counselors in assertiveness training, covert modeling, career counseling, rehearsal, and aversion therapy (Krumboltz & Thoresen, 1969; 1976). Role play is an excellent technique for expanding client awareness and showing the client alternative behaviors. For example, in the counseling session an incarcerated client can role play and develop effective social behaviors before having to use them alone on the streets. Another client may discover, in role play, that he or she cannot confront a strong-willed parent and must therefore learn assertion skills prior to attempting a confrontation in real life. The uses of role play are limited only by the counselor's resourcefulness and skill in using the technique and by the client's need for viewing, hearing, and experiencing a particular role in the risk-free environment of the counseling session.

Assertion Training

The fundamental goals of assertion training are (1) to empower clients actively to initiate and carry out desired choices and behaviors that do not harm other people physically or emotionally, and (2) to teach clients alternatives to passive, helpless, dependent, and stifled ways of dealing with life situations.

Many counselors find their clients need to develop assertion skills to strengthen their overall coping and problem-solving behaviors (Bellack & Hersen, 1977). Clients may lose self-esteem by allowing others to take advantage of them, may be unable to confront parents, employers, spouses, or other important persons in appropriate ways, or may elicit unwanted responses from others by using aggression instead of assertion. Assertion training is usually accomplished by role playing and modeling of passive, aggressive, and assertive situations the client faces regularly. Through problem exploration and definition, assertion goal development, repeated role play, role reversal, and progressive and successive approximation of the desired behaviors, the client learns appropriate (assertive) ways of expression. In the safety of the client-counselor encounter, the client not only forms new behaviors but also has an opportunity to participate, with the counselor, in analysis and critique of successive approximations of the behaviors the client seeks to develop. Counselors who employ both assertion training and the use of audiovisual feedback are able to provide their clients with immediate documented feedback on client progress. Clients can then try out the techniques in the real world and return for further training (Alberti & Emmons, 1978).

Aversion Therapy

Aversion therapy is a controversial technique that is infrequently used by counselors and is not recommended for most school situations with children. It is sometimes used in clinics by highly skilled therapists to help clients who want to be helped and whose maladaptive behaviors are not amenable to intervention through other strategies. Aversion therapy employs procedures such as electric shock, emetics, stimulus satiation, unpleasant mental or visual imagery, or unpleasant sounds or verbal descriptions to inhibit unwanted behaviors. Competent behavior therapists have treated difficult problems such as drug and alcohol addiction, sexual deviation, and smoking by combining aversive techniques with other behavioral procedures (Franks & Wilson, 1973, p. 193). The goal of this therapy is to get the client to "associate an undesirable behavior pattern with unpleasant stimulation or to make the unpleasant stimulation a consequence of the undesirable behavior" (Franks, 1969, p. 280).

An example of the use of aversion therapy with an alcoholic client is to encourage the client to see, smell, and drink alcoholic beverages containing an emetic drug—one that causes illness, retching, and vomiting. The treatment is continued until the client associates the smell, sight, and taste of alcoholic beverages with extreme discomfort. At the same time, the client is provided with desirable, pleasant, and comforting reinforcements for nondrinking cravings and behaviors. The counselor who seeks to use aversion therapy should be thoroughly trained and experienced in the technical, therapeutic, philosophic, and ethical issues involved in using the technique with clients (Morrison & Bellack, 1987; Poling, 1986).

Satiation

Satiation is a mild aversive technique that uses an excessive amount of reinforcement to make the undesired reinforcer lose its effectiveness. The reinforcer is emitted by the subject or given by another person in such quantities that the individual not only tires of the reinforcer but also becomes repelled by it. Smoking, eating, and acting-out behaviors have been amenable to this technique. One of the most famous uses of satiation occurred with the towel-hoarding behavior of a long-term hospital patient (Allyon, 1965). A weekly average of nineteen to twenty-nine towels were found in the patient's room despite attempts by the ward nurses to retrieve the towels. Stimulus satiation was introduced without comment by the nurses, who gave the patient seven towels daily. This rate was increased until, by the third week, the number had increased to sixty. When the total number of towels reached 625, continuing to receive towels became noxious. Verbal responses of the patient in the first week were positive. "Oh, you found it for me. Thank you." By the fourth, fifth, and sixth weeks verbal responses were extremely negative: "Get these dirty towels out of here. I can't stay up all night folding these. I can't drag any more of these out of here, I just can't do it." No more towel hoarding was reported. A major problem is that if satiation does not occur, the behavior becomes entrenched because of all the reinforcement.

Token Economies

Another widely used behavioral strategy is the token economy (Chambless & Goldstein, 1979). It is a systematic procedure in which tokens are given as immediate tangible reinforcers for appropriate behaviors. The tokens can be poker chips, script, points, or other concrete items that can be cashed in by the holder for articles of value or for privileges. Token economies have proved successful in institutional settings such as hospitals, schools, clinics, day-care units, and prisons. The procedure is amenable to almost any setting, and the options for creative employment are virtually infinite.

In an institutional setting, behavioral planners can develop token economy structures to reinforce patients or inmates for performing positive acts or to invoke penalties or loss of tokens for infraction of rules or failure to carry out assigned responsibilities. The strategy is powerful in dealing with either simple or complex behaviors; it is effective in extinguishing maladaptive behaviors or shaping adaptive ones.

One important question raised about the token economy has been, "How does it move from laboratory reinforcement to changes in the real world?" Although the strategy is amenable to wide application and creative innovation by professionals and lay personnel alike, maintenance of modified behavior may pose problems. Behavior planners can generally improve retention by:

1. Obtaining the commitment of all personnel (professionals, clients, aides, lay workers, and volunteers) to the goals and concepts of the token economy;
2. Selecting behaviors that are likely to receive natural social and environmental reinforcement;
3. Adhering to proven laboratory principles of behavior modification (for example, providing for giving out tokens in an immediate, fair, and consistent manner);
4. Ensuring that tokens maintain their reinforcement value and that clients have frequent opportunities to redeem tokens for desired payoffs;
5. Pairing material reinforcers (tokens) with social reinforcers (verbal praise), so that the value of intrinsic motivation is learned;
6. Fading out material reinforcers (tokens) and fading in social reinforcers (verbal praise) so that long-term results can be maintained solely by intrinsic motivation;
7. Focusing on behaviors that affect both long-term and short-term quality of life, thereby demonstrating to clients and staff that the program means more than simply controlling unruly behavior;

8. Ensuring that behaviors modified will transfer to client requirements outside the institution;

9. Maintaining sound assessment and feedback procedures so that necessary strategy changes can be made when problems occur (for example, when the reinforcement value of certain rewarded behaviors diminishes).

Self-Management, Self-Monitoring, and Self-Reinforcement

The terms *self-management, self-monitoring,* and *self-reinforcement* embody a trend toward expecting the client to be an active collaborator in the counseling and psychotherapeutic process (Cormier & Cormier, 1991, pp. 518–549; Watson & Tharp, 1981; 1989; Wilson, 1995, p. 211). Compared with earlier views of many theorists, the self-management/self-monitoring/self-reinforcement movement contains some notable shifts: (1) clients play an active role in every phase of counseling—they are far less passive; (2) clients augment the introspective and didactic aspects of counseling by developing specific action steps and/or action skills; (3) client thought processes are considered internal events and are dealt with in counseling; (4) clients assume greater responsibility for therapeutic outcomes; (5) clients learn self-reinforcement techniques (Bandura, 1976; Cormier & Cormier, 1991, pp. 538–547); (6) clients are called on to observe, monitor, record, self-reinforce (Cormier & Cormier, 1991, pp. 520–533), and sometimes interpret their own behavioral data; and (7) counselors and therapists take on a greater mentor and educator role and a lesser expert role. The self-management/self-monitoring/self-reinforcement strategies described by Cormier and Cormier (1991, pp. 518–549), Watson and Tharp (1981; 1989), and Williams and Long (1979; 1983), provide a framework whereby *any* of the different behavioral strategies can be used in the client's own behavioral plan. Following is an adaptation from several sources, including the above citations from self-management/self-monitoring/self-reinforcement literature, outlining five important steps and sample counselor–client dialogue for guiding the client through each successive step of generating his or her own self-management/self-monitoring/self-reinforcement plan. (The terms identified with an asterisk are defined in the next section).

Step 1: Conceptualizing and Defining the Problem and Selecting Appropriate Outcome Goals in Behavioral Terms

A. Establish one target outcome goal* at a time
B. Goal should be:

1. Understandable, important, and of value to the client
2. Measurable in objective and analyzable terms
3. Realistic and attainable
4. Positive and constructive

C. Statement of target outcome goal should include:

1. Client's desired and attainable level of performance or extinction
2. Successive approximations of projected milestones and targeted goal attainment dates

CO: So, Peggy, what you've *really decided* to do is to attain your goal of getting some weight off and then, this time, keeping it off.

CL: That's exactly right, because my health is my greatest concern.

CO: So, since you're fully committed to it and you're wanting to start work on it now, let's determine exactly how many pounds you're aiming at losing and also plan a realistic and medically safe timeline and target date for attaining that weight.

Step 2: Managing and Monitoring Target Behavior

A. Select appropriate target process goals* based on client objectives
B. Initiate baseline assessment* of targeted behaviors prior to implementing behavior-change strategies
C. Begin monitoring and recording data on behaviors related to process goals

    1. Record behavior immediately after it occurs
    2. Use paper and pencil, wrist counter, knitting–stitch counter, stopwatch, wristwatch, biofeedback monitoring device, or other appropriate recording system or technique to record or document behavioral data
    3. Do a frequency count,* time duration,* or product assessment,* or use some other accurate monitoring strategy to document the behavior

CO: Peggy, how are you going to change the way you record and monitor your behavior this time so that you make sure you stay on your timeline and achieve your desired weight on schedule?

CL: Well, I've figured out all the weights, calories, exercises, and ways to keep track of what I do each day. And I have decided on some ways to monitor my behavior so that I don't cheat on myself.

CO: You say, "Some ways to monitor." Peggy, precisely what are those procedures? I want you to have a no-fail system. I really do want you to succeed this time. I want us to go over every detail of what you're planning to do and how you're going to do it.

CL: OK, let me show you what I've written down so far.

CO: (*Looks at the list*) That's a pretty good list. Let's examine it and perhaps brainstorm together for some more specific but simple and effective monitoring devices or strategies you might employ that either of us alone might overlook.

Step 3: Changing Precipitating Conditions and Setting Events* and Generating Appropriate Action Steps

Continue recording the targeted behaviors.

A. Initially avoid environments and situations that are certain to produce undesirable or maladaptive behaviors
B. Alter environments, conditions, and situations to ensure that you:

    1. Become aware of what you're doing
    2. Limit the stimuli that evoke the "bad" behaviors
    3. Make it easy and satisfying to emit desired behaviors
    4. Specify alternatives or substitute behaviors that are incompatible with maladaptive behaviors

CO: Peggy, this is the step at which you determine what you're going to do differently. If you keep on following the previous patterns you've established for yourself it will be hard to change setting events, and you may simply keep on eating and doing the physical activities you've been used to. That will make it harder. It seems to me you've got to make some pretty drastic changes if you intend to ensure that you reach your goals.

CL: Well, I know some of the things I must do. The first thing I thought of was to prepare my low-fat, low-calorie lunch for the next day each evening before I go to bed.

CO: OK, anything else?

CL: I was thinking about figuring out some way to make sure I do my dancercises every day—maybe even every morning!

CO: Good! Now, let's together examine that and also some more ways you might change your setting events to make sure your plan succeeds this time.

Step 4: Generating Appropriate Reinforcement Contingencies* and Establishing Consequencies That Are Meaningful and Effective for the Client

Continue recording the targeted behaviors.
Continue maintenance of changing of precipitating conditions and setting events and generating appropriate action steps.

A. Identify reinforcers or consequences that would be positively reinforcing or aversively punitive to the client
B. Implement reinforcement contingencies such that:

   1. Appropriate behaviors are immediately reinforced
   2. Criteria for reinforcement are realistic and readily attainable
   3. Significant others will support attainment of desired behavioral goals
   4. A graduated (approximated) time frame is established for reinforcing behavior leading to process goals
   5. Extrinsic* as well as intrinsic* reinforcers are available and included
   6. Reinforcers have enough valence or power to be effective
   7. Reinforcements are scheduled to provide maximum—short-, medium-, and long-term incentives
   8. An accurate system for graphing, displaying, and examining behavioral data is continuously used
   9. A specific behavioral contract may be written

C. Consider use of aversive consequences if reinforcement contingencies fail to produce desired changes in behavior

   1. Write in and make commitments to penalize yourself in the event of noncompliance (perhaps contract with a support person to forfeit something of real value to you in the event of noncompliance)
   2. Use mechanically induced pain or aversive consequences
   3. Induce a state of stimulus satiation*

CO: I want your rewards to be strong enough to ensure your compliance with your plan. But I don't want to see you go off the deep end and make them unrealistically high. Nor do I want you to rely only on yourself to administer your rewards. I would like to know who will serve as support persons—persons who have a stake in your meeting your goals—to increase the chances that you will succeed.

CL: I am sure my husband will be glad to be a key support. I thought about asking my supervisor. I would trust her to be fair but firm with me. She would certainly know if I cheated at lunch, and she'd certainly call my hand on it.

CO: Good! Put those names down on your pad and let's devise a strategy whereby you can enlist them in a way that will be good for both you and them. Also, I'd like to suggest that we figure out some short-range, medium-range, and long-range rewards that will be fair, effective, and sure to work for you.

CL: OK, I want to fix it so that I definitely get this weight off this time and keep it off!

Step 5: Maintaining and Consolidating Gains

Continue recording targeted behaviors.
Continue maintenance of precipitating conditions and setting events and generating appropriate action steps.
Continue generation of appropriate reinforcement contingencies and establishing consequences that are meaningful to the client.

A. Establish an effective system of assessment/feedback to ensure that self-management/self-monitoring/self-reinforcement can be altered, redefined, or redirected to achieve and maintain target outcome goals
B. Maintain natural consequences

   1. Phase out self-recording
   2. Provide for natural, continuous self-monitoring/self-reinforcement
   3. Maintain most changes in setting or precipitating events
   4. Phase out artificial reinforcement contingencies
   5. Enlist social support
   6. Apply self-management/self-monitoring/self-reinforcement in other areas in which the client wants to effect behavioral change

CL: One thing I can do is to get my husband involved and invested in my maintaining my safe and healthy weight—once I'm on it.

CO: You think there's any chance he might somehow sabotage it and subtly reinforce your previous behavior?

CL: No way! He's as concerned about my health as I am.

CO: Then I'd certainly recommend that you use him as a maintenance support. Let's compile a list of the additional maintenance strategies and perhaps additional support persons you will use to make sure you never again have to face the task of losing this much weight and that you remain alive to enjoy the fruits of your goal attainment.

CL: OK.

CO: Also, I want to work with you as you develop your behavioral contracts. Written and signed contracts are vital to both you and your support persons. I want your contracts to be clear and specific and to accurately reflect your action goals and commitments as well as to clearly specify those behaviors your support persons have pledged to provide to help ensure your compliance and success.

Definitions of Terms in the Self-Management Behavior Model

Baseline assessment. The initial appraisal of behavior; it more clearly defines the problem and serves as a basis of comparison for assessing the effectiveness of treatment.

Extrinsic reinforcer. A reward or payoff that increases the probability of a particular response and comes from the environment, i.e., is external to the individual emitting the response.

Frequency count. Tabulating the number of times a particular behavior or event occurs, e.g., a procedure was interrupted three times.

Intrinsic reinforcer. A reward or payoff that increases the probability of a particular response and comes from within the individual emitting the response, i.e., inner thoughts and feelings.

Product assessment. Evaluating behavior in terms of its products, e.g., number of completed assignments, grade point average attained, number of cavities reported at a dental checkup.

Reinforcement contingencies. The conditions under which a schedule of reinforcers or punishers is administered, e.g., "You can have ice cream only after you clean your room."

Setting events. Stimuli in the environment that precipitate or trigger behavior, e.g., seeing a vending machine may trigger an eating binge.

Stimulus satiation. A strategy of continuously repeating a reinforcing activity until the activity becomes no longer reinforcing, e.g., eating candy until one is repulsed at the sight or taste of candy.

Target outcome goal. A statement of the aim of a behavioral plan in terms of a specific product, e.g., grades, weight, money saved, number of miles jogged per day.

Target process goal. A statement of the aim of a behavioral plan in terms of responses that either facilitate or hinder achievement of the desired outcome, i.e., the target outcome goal. For example, fifty situps per day may contribute to the desired amount of weight loss.

Time duration. A method of assessing behavior by recording the amount of time devoted to the behavior, e.g., she studies for four hours or he cried for five minutes.

Source: From Williams, Robert L. and James D. Long, *Toward a Self-managed Life Style,* Third Edition. Copyright © 1983 by Houghton Mifflin Company. Adapted with permission.

Self-management/self-monitoring/self-reinforcement not only emphasizes great responsibility on the part of the client but also places confidence and trust in the client. The behavioral model presented here is recommended as a general guide rather than a narrow prescription for solving all behavioral problems. A client often finds that completion of Steps 1 and 2 is sufficient to produce desired changes. Also, clients who experience success in using self-management/self-monitoring/ self-reinforcement often find that the successful consequences of changing one specific behavior transfers to other similar behavioral situations. Such transfers may translate into something akin to habit and thus eliminate the need to apply a comprehensive behavioral change model singularly to every debilitative problem they may encounter.

SAMPLE CASE

The case of Peggy Smith, age fifty-six, illustrates a fairly typical use of the self-management/ self-monitoring/self-reinforcing procedure. The counselor is in a *collaborative role*— working *with* the client instead of doing something *to* or *for* the client to facilitate change. Typical of the case management in behavioral systems, Peggy's counselor places a great deal of autonomy and responsibility on the client. The terms *counselor/ consultant* or *mentor* seem to accurately capture the flavor of what the counselor does.

Background

Peggy's presenting problem was her concern over her excessive weight. She saw it as a longstanding, recurring, very serious problem. The counselor worked with Peggy for several weeks in the development of her plan for losing weight. Rather than summarizing the counseling techniques used with Peggy during the sessions, we present the plan itself, written in the first person by the client.

> Baseline Statement. *Two years ago I was informed by my doctor that I had developed mild congestive heart disease. In no uncertain terms I was told to go on a salt-free diet and lose weight or suffer the consequences. Although I had lived fifty-four full and interesting years, I was not yet ready to depart this planet, so I did what I was told.*
>
> *I went on a 750-calorie low-salt diet, signed up for a class in yoga, memorized a list of low-salt foods, and learned to think thin. In four months I lost twenty-five pounds, my lungs were free of fluid, I felt and looked better, and I was on my way.*
>
> *Alas, my good intentions went awry; I changed jobs, and one of the benefits of my new job was free lunch in the employees' dining room. "Lunch" was always a full-course meal, and, being free, it was extremely hard to pass up.*
>
> *I now have more than my twenty-five pounds back, like an unwelcome guest. Thinking about it does not help; telling myself to do something about it does not help; my only recourse is to set up a behavioral plan to lose weight, with positive and negative consequences and just DO IT! Steps one through five contain a description of my behavioral plan, with attendant data-collection provisions, and a behavioral contract signed by myself and the parties involved in helping me keep my commitment.*

Self-Management/Self-Monitoring/Self-Reinforcement Plan

Losing Weight by Peggy Smith (May 23 ____)

Step 1.   *Goal selection.* I must lose weight for my health and for my own satisfactory self-image. My plan, therefore, is to lose 48 pounds in 12 months to achieve my ideal weight of 127 pounds.

Step 2.   *Monitoring target behavior*

Step 2a.   *Process goal selection*

1. I will establish a 750-calorie low-salt diet of three meals per day with low-calorie snacks.

2. I will establish a regular routine of a minimum of six exercises to be done daily, reaching a minimum of two fifteen-minute sets per day.

3. I will establish a regular routine of walking, working up to a minimum of two miles per day, rain or shine.

Step 2b.   *Baseline assessment*

1. I now weigh 175 pounds.

2. I now intake between 4,000 and 5,000 calories per day.

3. I engage in no regular exercise.

4. Since I have the money to buy clothes whenever I want, I don't worry about size.

5. I eat a large free lunch in the employee dining room every day.

Step 2c.   *Recording behavior related to process and outcome goals*

1. Weight will be recorded biweekly on a chart in graph form.

2. I will keep a daily calorie count.

3. Exercises will be done daily and when each daily series has been completed, it will be checked off on a calendar.

4. Walking will be done daily and after completion of a scheduled daily distance, it will be checked off on a calendar.

5. My supervisor will validate on her desk calendar each day I bring my diet lunch. She will praise me for compliance and criticize me for non-compliance.

Step 3.   *Changing precipitating conditions and setting events*

1. I will not go to bed until I have made my low-calorie lunch for the next day and put it in the refrigerator with a sign on the door reminding me not to forget it.

2. When I watch television or study, I will have available at my side a bowl of carrot and celery sticks to munch on.

3. I will set a timer on my stereo so that at 7:00 A.M. every morning my dancercise records will start playing.

4. Before I leave in the morning, I will set my jogging shoes in the entrance-way so that they will be the first thing I see when I come home after work.

5. In lieu of going straight to the employee dining room at lunch, I will go to my supervisor's office, where my lunch will be monitored by my supervisor.

Step 4. *Generating appropriate reinforcement contingencies and effective consequences*

1. Any month that I meet my four-pound goal, my husband will contribute another $50 to my account. Any month that I do not attain my goal, I forfeit $50 to my husband.

2. Any time that I have a bowl of carrot and celery sticks by my side, I may continue watching television or studying. If not, I will stop studying or watching television immediately. My husband has agreed to monitor this.

3. Each time I do my exercises, I will enjoy a twenty-minute warm bubble bath. Each time I do not exercise, I will take a cold shower with Lava soap.

4. Each time I complete my walking, I will take fifteen minutes to tend my flowers, an activity I thoroughly enjoy. If I do not, I will shine my husband's shoes.

5. I will bring my diet lunch to my supervisor, who will praise me publicly in the dining room. If I do not, my supervisor will criticize me publicly in the dining room.

6. If I successfully meet my target outcome goal on the specified date, I will receive my $600 plus $600 of matching funds from my husband to be used to visit a friend in California. If I do not, I forfeit all the money to my husband.

7. My husband has agreed to praise me whenever he sees me following the provisions set forth in this plan.

Step 5. *Maintaining and consolidating gains*

Step 5a. *Evaluation*

1. If at any biweekly weighing period I have not lost at least two pounds, my counselor and I will review the components of this plan and make the necessary adjustment.

2. My husband has agreed to give me feedback regarding any behaviors or events he observes that may be deterring my progress.

Step 5b. *Maintenance*

1. Upon reaching 127 pounds, I will continue to maintain a weight chart for evaluating my weight. If at any month my weight goes above 130 pounds, the full behavioral plan will be reinstated.

2. All clothes I have above a size ten will be given to Goodwill Industries.

Continued

Self-Management/Self-Monitoring/Self-Reinforcement Plan (*Continued*)

3. My husband will install a full-length mirror in our bedroom so I can appreciate my new figure.

4. I believe my new behaviors will become so much a part of my life that I will feel good when I do them and guilty when I do not.

Behavioral contracts. I, Peggy Smith, agree to carry out a weight reduction and exercise plan as outlined in the foregoing document, in which I shall lose forty-eight pounds during the twelve months from June 1 this year to June 1 next year.

I further agree to abide by all the stipulations as described in my behavioral plan and to forfeit $600 to my husband, Oscar Smith, if I fail to fulfill the terms of this contract.

_____
(Signature—Peggy Smith)

_____
(Date)

I, Oscar Smith, agree to abide by the stipulations described in the attached document. I also agree to refrain from remarking about the diet and exercise plan or referring to it in any way except in the manner described in said document.

I further agree to provide matching funds of $600 if the terms of the contract are successfully met by Peggy Smith. I agree to accept $600 from Peggy Smith if she does not fulfill the conditions of the above contract.

_____
(Signature—Oscar Smith)

_____
(Date)

I, Annie Mae Jones, Peggy's supervisor, agree to monitor Peggy's diet at lunch time. I further agree to provide praise and criticism as described in the attached document.

_____
(Signature—Annie Mae Jones)

_____
(Date)

(*Note:* Four attachments to Peggy Smith's behavior plan have been omitted: weight chart, salt-free diet, schedule of exercises, and exercise charts.)

Discussion

In behavioral counseling and behavior modification, the counselor does not look for deep underlying causes or hidden emotional disturbance. The theoretical assumption in Peggy's case was that the most direct and efficient way to help Peggy was to focus on overt behaviors and consequences.

Peggy Smith's plan was unique to her. Even though the plan was lengthy, improvements could have been made. For example, she could have strengthened her incentives by availing herself of social supports, such as a weight-management group. She might have chosen more powerful rewards and consequences. For instance, her husband might sabotage her plan if his incentive for getting money is stronger than his desire to see her lose weight. Perhaps a better plan would have allowed the husband to give the money to an organization that she deplores. Another improvement might have been for Peggy to include other people in her recording and data-keeping plan.

On the plus side, Peggy's plan was systematic, based on behavioral principles, thorough, and problem-centered. Her target goals were specific, important, measurable, attainable, realistic, and positive. She used support persons who had a stake in her success. Finally, the self-management method provided Peggy an opportunity to learn not only weight control but also a self-action strategy for similar problems.

CONTRIBUTIONS OF THE BEHAVIORAL SYSTEM

The growth of behavior therapy has been characterized by the system's movement from focusing on a few simple problems (such as phobias and obsessions) to attending to a wide "range of the most complex social neuroses and so-called existential problems" (Wolpe, 1981, p. 162). It is unique in that it is the only system of therapeutic intervention that "does what had been predicted on theoretical grounds" (Wolpe, 1981, p. 161).

Another contribution of the behavioral system is its accountability. No system is better suited for accountability. Funding sources have increasingly demanded tangible evidence that psychotherapy produces positive results (Garfield, 1981, p. 181). Behaviorism's rigorous insistence on identifying success in terms of measurable gains in objective data has given the system a great deal of credibility with funding agencies and legislatures.

Related to accountability is specificity (Cormier & Cormier, 1991), one of the most important characteristics of behavioral counseling. Other systems have adopted and attempted to adapt some of the typical behavioral methods, such as identifying and defining problems in objective terms and specifying target goals, reinforcement contingencies, outcomes, feedback, assessment, and follow-up in objective and measurable terms (Wilson, 1995, pp. 200–201).

Another strength of the behavioral system is its insistence on defining and directly attacking problems (Goldstein, Heller, & Sechrest, 1966). Clients and funding sources alike have come to appreciate the fact that everyone knows, up front, what is being worked on, what the goals are, and when and to what extent gains or changes are expected. Since the approach is centered in a specific problem there are few deep-seated mysteries within the client that require an outside "expert" to reach in, understand, analyze, interpret, prescribe, and fix without the client being aware, involved, and responsible. The behavioral system's premise that the proof is in the data (and the evidence that such proof generalizes to similar events) has given other counseling systems incentives to move from the mystical toward the scientific.

SHORTCOMINGS OF THE BEHAVIORAL SYSTEM

Behavioral counseling has received extensive criticism from proponents of other systems. Behavioral counseling may change simple, overt behavior, but it does not deal with deep-seated emotions and feelings. Further, it fails to provide the client with insights and deep understanding of the problem. Behavioral counseling focuses mainly on symptoms; as a result, when one symptom is "fixed" another appears. Behavioral counseling ignores the historical roots of present maladaptive behaviors. Behavior modification strategies are applicable only to a narrow range of anxieties and phobias, and they are too effective in that they "program" clients into rigid, manipulative behavioral responses that rob them of their autonomy and freedom of choice. Behavioral systems largely ignore the higher levels of human cognition or functioning and program clients toward minimum or tolerable levels of behaving, reinforce conformity, stifle creativity, and ignore client needs for self-fulfillment, self-actualization, and feelings of self-worth. Behavior therapy requires too much education and experience in behavior analysis to provide enough therapists to be of practical value to the multitudes needing help. Behavior modification does not really work. There may be short-term effects, such as habit changes, but no appreciable lasting changes accrue. Behavioral strategies are dangerous to society in that they take away freedom. If "control" is in the "wrong" hands, large numbers of people may be manipulated into doing things they don't really want to do (much like being subjected to unwanted brainwashing).

Practically every rival system has attacked behavior therapy, behavior modification, and behavioral counseling. The charge regarding loss of freedom has probably been the most formidable criticism.

BEHAVIORAL COUNSELING WITH DIVERSE POPULATIONS

Because behavioral counseling derives from learning theory and focuses on modification of behavior rather than feelings and self-disclosure, it has definite advantages over some of the other therapies in helping clients from diverse ethnic, cultural, lifestyle, and racial backgrounds. Because its conceptual structure is easy to understand and its application is concrete and makes sense to ordinary people in every walk of life, it enjoys wide usage and popularity by counselors with such disparate populations as special groups of children, mental health clients, prisoners, nursing home residents, and other institutionalized clients. The straightforward steps such as setting goals, changing setting events, monitoring performance, and establishing rewards have wide appeal to people who are oriented toward concrete behavioral performance as opposed to abstract symbolizing, or focusing on the personhood of the client. Whether the client's presenting concern is indicative of anxiety, phobia, or simply some maladaptive habit, the counselor is not intrusive in the client's cultural or ethnic background. Instead, the counselor targets the malady using generic laws of learning common to all people. The foundational behavioral principles, based on many years of development by researchers such as Pavlov, Skinner, Bandura, and Wolpe (Wilson, 1995, pp. 197–202), tend to be culture-free and to present a minimal threat to clients.

According to Wilson (1995, pp. 200–204), behavioral approaches offer a broad range of heterogeneous procedures with different theoretical rationales for systematically assessing and treating a wide variety of disorders. The approach's scientific method of changing behaviors and developing problem-solving skills is suited for diverse cultural populations whose members are sometimes offended by catharsis and the open expression of personal feelings and concerns. Eysenck, Eysenck, and Barrett (1995) noted that the behavioral system views and responds to client gender, age, and socioeconomic differences in unique and appropriate ways.

The objective, organized, systematic, contractual nature of the behavioral approach tends to minimize the counselor–client relationship as a factor in the equation. Much of the counseling process is a rational stimulus-response formulation that does not place blame or demand perfectionism. It is easy for anyone to understand because its "programmed-by-the-numbers" approaches provide immediate feedback and place responsibility on the client for performance. Behavioral counseling works for mentally limited clients because of its behavior modification/ management techniques that successively approximate their goals and does not rely heavily on the cognitive domain of that clientele. The approach also works for many parents and students of inner city schools and rural environments where clients are conditioned to operate on short-term contingencies and where concrete, clear, structured formats are desired. In these cases, the client is not dependent on the counselor. Progress is visible and evident because clients can tell when beds are made, cigarette consumption is diminished, pounds are lost, and money is saved. They may have real trouble discerning when they are "doing better," "thinking straight," or "improving their attitudes." Measurable goals and attainments put immediate and short-term reinforcements within the grasp of clients who can neither wait for long-term rewards nor delay gratification.

People of color as well as people from other diverse backgrounds, such as those with language disadvantages, physically disabling conditions, economic and educational disadvantages, and diverse sexual orientations often face social, political, and other environmental influences and problems that require more than one-to-one talk to resolve (Sue, 1992). The behavioral system of counseling offers many alternatives for the counselor of diverse clientele. The counselor can scientifically examine what needs to be done; involve clients in the planning, goal setting, and employing techniques needed to effect behavioral or environmental change; and guide, mentor, and teach clients how to alter both their behaviors and their environments in positive and constructive ways. Counselors can assist and empower clients from lower socioeconomic, disadvantaged, and/or disenfranchised backgrounds to obtain the services they need or attain goals that have been denied them by the dominant culture. Perhaps more important, behavioral counselors can assist clients to become more autonomous and independent by learning ways to get past dependence on artificial or nonsubstantive reinforcers.

Livneh and Sherwood (1991, pp. 534–536) describe how the behavioral approach can provide the practicing counselor with numerous concepts and strategies for helping clients with physical disabilities. The intervention strategies they cite for helping clients with physical disabilities include eliminating maladaptive behaviors and replacing them with positive, constructive, and adaptive behaviors; approximating learning new skills needed to cope with their personal limitations and environmental restrictions; strengthening their self-concept and power of positive thinking through covert conditioning and cognitive restructuring; and establishing effective self-management procedures for more independent living through systematic operant conditioning.

No one system of counseling is perfect for all clients. People who respond positively to catharsis and open disclosure of emotions may fare better under a more person-centered, humanistic, existential, or holistic type of therapy. For some, the most effective counseling, for instance, may be what Gilchrist (1992, pp. 11–13) refers to as the four primary "dimensions of being" of the holistic approach: body, mind, spirit, and emotions. For others, an empathic listener may be the preferred style of counseling to help them attain self-realization or self-actualization.

In summary, it is clear that the behavioral approach has much to commend it to counselors of diverse clientele (Livneh & Sherwood, 1991, pp. 534–536; Wilson, 1995, pp. 197–222). Structurally, behavioral counselors draw from the fundamental precepts of classical, instrumental, and operant conditioning as well as from cognitive behavior modification. Counseling strategies run the gamut from simple stimulus-response to cognitive restructuring. Since it is uniformly goal- and behavior-centered, it is personally nonthreatening to clients. That is its greatest asset in dealing with diverse clientele.

SUMMARY

Behavioral counseling is not a single system of helping. It is a family of systems, formulations, and strategies. There are no clear-cut distinctions among behavioral counseling, behavior therapy, behavior modification, operant conditioning, and so forth. Generally, one could say that the main thrust of behavioral counseling has been preventive (keeping healthy clients healthy) and that the main thrust of behavior therapy has been restorative (to make unhealthy clients healthy again). That, however, is an oversimplification.

Behavioral systems of counseling have been evolving since the days of Pavlov and Watson, making the behavioral family broader and more pragmatic each year. In both theory and strategy behavioral counseling encompasses the simple to the complex, the short-term habit and the long-term social problem, tally marks on a card and networks of computers, self-regulated breathing and sophisticated biofeedback systems, the paraprofessional who charts the number of behaviors emitted and the highly educated (and skilled) behavior analyst. Behavioral counseling offers a wide range of strategies for clients with diverse backgrounds and problems. The effectiveness of these strategies depends on many factors including the knowledge, training, and skill of the counselor and the motivation, expectation, and cooperation of the client. Behavioral counseling has progressed from a simplistic, structured, counselor-controlled activity applied to clients toward a collabora-tive, consultative, facilitative process of participating with clients in their own growth-promoting activity. The strongest thread of behaviorism remains its adher-ence to a scientific base. The "data" have become broader and more complex. Strate-gies have expanded exponentially, bringing trends such as cognitive behavior techniques, self-managed and self-directed procedures, and greater counselor–client collaboration. But the scientific base has remained at the core.

SUGGESTIONS FOR FURTHER READING

Alberto, P. A., & Troutman, A. C. (1982). *Applied behavior analysis for teachers: Influencing student performance.* Columbus, OH: Chas. E. Merrill.

Eysenck, H. J., & Martin, I. (Eds.). (1987). *Theoretical foundations of behavior therapy.* New York: Plenum.

Franks, C. M., Wilson, G. T., Kendall, P., & Brownell, K. D. (1984). *Annual review of behavior therapy: Theory and practice* (Vol. 10). New York: Guilford.

Gambrill, E. D. (1977). *Behavior modification: Handbook of assessment, intervention, and evaluation.* San Francisco: Jossey-Bass.

Goldfried, M. R., & Merbaum, M. (Eds.). (1973). *Behavior change through self-control.* New York: Holt, Rinehart & Winston.

Goldstein, A. P., & Foa, E. (Eds.). (1980). *Handbook of behavioral interventions: A clinical guide.* New York: Wiley.

Kazdin, A. E. (1978). *History of behavior modification: Experimental foundations of con-temporary research.* Baltimore: University Park Press.

Kazdin, A. E. (1980). *Behavior modification in applied settings* (rev. ed.). Homewood, IL: Dorsey.

Krumboltz, J. D., & Thoresen, C. E. (Eds.). (1976) *Counseling methods.* New York: Holt, Rinehart & Winston.

Lazarus, A. A. (1977). *In the mind's eye: The power of imagery for personal enrichment.* New York: Guilford.

Lazarus, A. A. (1989). *The practice of multimodal therapy.* Baltimore: Johns Hopkins Uni-versity Press.

Lazarus, A. A. (1995). Multimodal therapy. In R. J. Corsini & D. Wedding (Eds.), *Cur-rent psychotherapies* (5th ed.; pp. 322–355). Itasca, IL: F. E. Peacock.

Lundin, R. W. (1972). *Theories and systems of psychology.* Lexington, MA: Heath.

O'Leary, K. D., & Wilson, G. T. (1987). *Behavior therapy: Application and outcome* (2nd ed.). Englewood Cliffs, NJ: Prentice-Hall.

Skinner, B. F. (1953). *Science and human behavior.* New York: Macmillan.

Skinner, B. F. (1971). *Beyond freedom and dignity.* New York: Knopf.

Skinner, B. F. (1974). *About behaviorism.* New York: Knopf.

Watson, D. L., & Tharp, R. G. (1989). *Self-directed behavior: Self-modification for personal adjustment* (5th ed.). Pacific Grove, CA: Brooks/Cole.

Williams, R. L., & Long, J. D. (1983). *Toward a self-managed life style* (3rd ed.). Boston: Houghton Mifflin.

Wilson, G. T. (1995). Behavior therapy. In R. J. Corsini & D. Wedding (Eds.), *Current psychotherapies* (5th ed.; pp. 197–228). Itasca, IL: F. E. Peacock.

Wolpe, J. (1958). *Psychotherapy by reciprocal inhibition.* Stanford, CA: Stanford University Press.

Wolpe, J. (1981). Behavior therapy versus psychoanalysis. *American Psychologist, 36,* 159–164.

Wolpe, J. (1991). *The practice of behavior therapy* (4th ed.). Elmsford, NY: Pergamon.

REFERENCES

Alberti, R. E., & Emmons, M. L. (1978). *Your perfect right: A guide to assertive behavior* (3rd ed.). San Luis Obispo, CA: Impact.

Alberto, P. A., & Troutman, A. C. (1982). *Applied behavior analysis for teachers: Influencing student performance.* Columbus, OH: Chas. E. Merrill.

Allyon, T. (1965). Intensive treatment of psychotic behavior by stimulus satiation and food reinforcement. In L. Ullmann & L. Krasner (Eds.), *Case studies in behavior modification* (pp. 77–84). New York: Holt, Rinehart & Winston.

Azrin, N. H. (1966). Sequential effects of punishment. In T. Verhave (Ed.), *The experimental analysis of behavior* (pp. 186–189). New York: Appleton-Century-Crofts.

Bandura, A. (1976). Self-reinforcement: Theoretical and methodological considerations. *Behaviorism, 4,* 135–155.

Bandura, A. (1991). Social cognitive theory of self-regulation. [Special issue: Theories of self regulation.] *Organizational Behavior and Human Decision Processes, 50*(2), 248–287.

Bandura, A. (1995). Comments on the crusade against causal efficacy of human thought. [Special issue: Cognition, behavior and causality: A broad exchange of views stemming from the debate on the causal efficacy of human thought.] *Journal of Behavior Therapy and Experimental Psychiatry, 26*(3), 179–190.

Beck, A. T. (1976). *Cognitive therapy and the emotional disorders.* New York: International Universities Press.

Bellack, A. S., & Hersen, M. (1977). *Behavior modification: An introductory textbook.* Baltimore: Williams & Wilkins.

Buckley, N. K., & Walker, H. M. (1970). *Modifying classroom behavior.* Champaign, IL: Research Press Company.

Chambless, D. L., & Goldstein, A. J. (1979). Behavioral psychotherapy. In R. Corsini (Ed.), *Current psychotherapies* (2nd ed.; pp. 230–272). Itasca, IL: F. E. Peacock.

Cormier, W. H., & Cormier, L. S. (1979). *Interviewing strategies for helpers: A guide to assessment, treatment and evaluation.* Monterey, CA: Brooks/Cole.

Cormier, W. H., & Cormier, L. S. (1991). *Interviewing strategies for helpers: Fundamental skills and cognitive behavioral interventions* (3rd ed.). Pacific Grove, CA: Brooks/Cole.

Deibert, A. N., & Harmon, A. (1972). *New tools for changing behavior.* Champaign, IL: Research Press Company.

Dollard, J., & Miller N. E. (1950). *Personality and psychotherapy: An analysis in terms of learning, thinking, and culture.* New York: McGraw-Hill.

Ellis, A. (1962). *Reason and emotion in psychotherapy.* Secaucus, NJ: Lyle Stuart.

Ellis, A., & Grieger, R. (Eds.). (1977). *Handbook of rational-emotive therapy* (Vol. 1). New York: Springer.

Eysenck, H. J. (1959). Learning theory and behavior therapy. *Journal of Mental Science, 105,* 61–75.

Eysenck, H. J. (1960). *The structure of human personality.* London: Methuen.

Eysenck, H. J., Eysenck, S. B. G., & Barrett, P. (1995). Personality differences according to gender. *Psychological Reports, 76*(3), 711–716.

Eysenck, H. J., & Martin, I. (Eds.). (1987). *Theoretical foundations of behavior therapy.* New York: Plenum.

Franks, C. M. (1969). *Behavior therapy: Appraisal and status.* New York: McGraw-Hill.

Franks, C. M., & Wilson, G. T. (Eds.). (1973). *Annual review of behavior therapy, theory, and practice.* New York: Brunner/Mazel.

Garfield, S. L. (1981). Psychotherapy: A forty year appraisal. *American Psychologist, 36,* 174–183.

Gilchrist, R. (1992, Summer). The need for holistic counseling. *American Counselor, 1,* 10–13.

Goldstein, A. P., Heller, K., & Sechrest, L. B. (1966). *Psychotherapy and the psychology of behavior change.* New York: Wiley.

Homme, L. (1970). *How to use contingency contracting in the classroom.* Champaign, IL: Research Press.

Hull, C. L. (1943). *Principles of behavior.* New York: Appleton-Century-Crofts.

James, R. K. (1997). *Behavioral prescripting, by the numbers* (2nd ed.). (Unpublished workshop manual.) Memphis, TN: The University of Memphis, Department of Counseling, Educational Psychology and Research.

Jones, M. C. (1924). A laboratory study of fear: The case of Peter. *Pediatric Seminar, 31,* 308–315.

Kaplan, S. J. (1986). *The private practice of behavioral therapy: A guide for behavioral practitioners.* New York: Plenum.

Kazdin, A. E. (1974). Comparative effects of some variations of covert modeling. *Journal of Behavior Therapy and Experimental Psychiatry, 5,* 225–231.

Kazdin, A. E. (1976). Assessment of imagery during covert modeling of assertive behavior. *Journal of Behavior Therapy and Experimental Psychiatry, 7,* 213–219.

Kazdin, A. E. (1978). *History of behavior modification: Experimental foundations of contemporary research.* Baltimore: University Park Press.

Kibler, R. J., Barker, L. L., & Miles, D. T. (1970). *Behavioral objectives and instruction.* Boston: Allyn & Bacon.

Krathwohl, D. R., Bloom, B. S., & Masis, B. (1964). *A taxonomy of educational objectives: Handbook II, The affective domain.* New York: David Mackay Co.

Krumboltz, J. D. (1966). *Revolution in counseling: Implications of behavioral science.* Boston: Houghton Mifflin.

Krumboltz, J. D., & Krumboltz, H. B. (1972). *Changing children's behavior.* Englewood Cliffs, NJ: Prentice-Hall.

Krumboltz, J. D., & Thoresen, C. E. (Eds.). (1969). *Behavioral counseling: Cases and techniques.* New York: Holt, Rinehart & Winston.

Krumboltz, J. D., & Thoresen, C. E. (Eds.). (1976). *Counseling methods.* New York: Holt, Rinehart & Winston.

Lazarus, A. A. (1977). *In the mind's eye: The power of imagery for personal enrichment.* New York: Guilford.

Livneh, H., & Sherwood, A. (1991). Application of personality theories and counseling strategies to clients with physical disabilities. *Journal of Counseling and Development, 69,* 525–538.

Lundin, R. W. (1961). *Personality: An experimental approach.* New York: Macmillan.

Lundin, R. W. (1972). *Theories and systems of psychology.* Lexington, MA: Heath.

Lundin, R. W. (1977). Behaviorism: Operant reinforcement. In R. J. Corsini (Ed.), *Current personality theories* (pp. 177–202). Itasca, IL: F. E. Peacock.

Mayer, R. F. (1962). *Preparing objectives for programmed instruction.* San Francisco: Fearon Publishers.

Meichenbaum, D. (1977). *Cognitive-behavior modification: An integrative approach.* New York: Plenum.

Morrison, R. L., & Bellack, A. S. (Eds.). (1987). *Medical factors and psychological disorders: A handbook for psychologists.* New York: Plenum.

Mowrer, O. H. (1950). *Learning theory and personality dynamics.* New York: Ronald Press.

Mowrer, O. H. (1973). *Learning theory and behavior.* Huntington, NY: Robert Kreiger.

Myers, J. K., & Roberts, B. H. (1959). *Family and class dynamics in mental illness.* New York: Wiley.

Pavlov, I. P. (1960). *Conditioned reflexes.* New York: Dover.

Poling, A. (1986). *A primer of human behavioral pharmacology.* New York: Plenum.

Skinner, B. F. (1948). *Walden two.* New York: Macmillan.

Skinner, B. F. (1953). *Science and human behavior.* New York: Macmillan.

Skinner, B. F. (1958). Teaching machines. *Science, 128,* 969–977.

Skinner, B. F. (1971). *Beyond freedom and dignity.* New York: Knopf.

Skinner, B. F. (1974). *About behaviorism.* New York: Knopf.

Sue, D. W. (1992, Winter). The challenge of multiculturalism: The road less traveled. *American Counselor, 1,* 6–14.

Thorp, R. G., & Wetzel, P. J. (1969). *Behavior modification in the natural environment.* New York: Academic Press.

Ullmann, L. P., & Krasner, L. (1965). *Case studies in behavior modification.* New York: Holt, Rinehart, & Winston.

Walker, J. E., & Shea, T. M. (1976). *Behavior modification.* St. Louis: C. V. Mosby.

Watson, D. L., & Tharp, R. G. (1981). *Self-directed behavior: Self-modification for personal adjustment* (3rd ed.). Monterey, CA: Brooks/Cole.

Watson, D. L., & Tharp, R. G. (1989). *Self-directed behavior: Self-modification for personal adjustment* (5th ed.). Pacific Grove, CA: Brooks/Cole.

Watson, J. B., & Rayner, R. (1920). Conditioned emotional reactions. *Journal of Experimental Psychology, 3,* 1–14.

Williams, R. L., & Long, J. D. (1979). *Toward a self-managed life style* (2nd ed.). Boston: Houghton Mifflin.

Williams, R. L., & Long, J. D. (1983). *Toward a self-managed life style* (3rd ed.). Boston: Houghton Mifflin.

Wilson, G. T. (1995). Behavior therapy. In R. J. Corsini & D. Wedding (Eds.), *Current psychotherapies* (5th ed.; pp. 197–228). Itasca, IL: F. E. Peacock.

Wolpe, J. (1954). Reciprocal inhibition as the main basis of psychotherapeutic effects. *Archives of Neurological Psychiatry, 72,* 205–226.

Wolpe, J. (1958). *Psychotherapy by reciprocal inhibition.* Stanford, CA: Stanford University Press.

Wolpe, J. (1961). The systematic desensitization treatment of neuroses. *Journal of Nervous and Mental Disease, 132,* 189–203.

Wolpe, J. (1981). Behavior therapy versus psychoanalysis. *American Psychologist, 36,* 159–164.

Wolpe, J. (1982). *The practice of behavior therapy* (3rd ed.). New York: Pergamon Press.

Wolpe, J. (1991). *The practice of behavior therapy* (4th ed.). Elmsford, NY: Pergamon Press.

9

RATIONAL-EMOTIVE BEHAVIOR THERAPY

FUNDAMENTAL TENETS

History

Albert Ellis, a clinical psychologist and, at the time, a practicing psychoanalytically oriented psychotherapist, initiated the development of rational-emotive behavior therapy as a separate therapeutic system in 1955. Ellis had become disillusioned with traditional psychoanalytic therapy because clients rarely gave up their presenting symptoms or they developed new ones. This lack of progress occurred even though his clients could achieve insight by connecting the events of early childhood to their present emotional disturbances. Ellis came to realize that the problem was that clients continued actively to reindoctrinate themselves with the irrationalities they had invented and learned in childhood (Ellis, 1979a, p. 191). Influenced by behaviorists such as Watson, Ellis reacted strongly in a series of papers (1949; 1950; 1956; 1958) to the passivity and antiempirical stances of the Freudians and Rogerians. Ellis's early practice and thinking culminated in a book on the psychotherapeutic principles of REBT—*Reason and Emotion in Psychotherapy* (Ellis, 1962).

Although Ellis in his youth had no inclination toward a career in psychotherapy, he became absorbed in the philosophy of happiness and read hundreds of books on the subject (Ellis & Bernard, 1986, pp. 3–4). Ellis's early and continuing interest in philosophy pervades REBT and may be best characterized in Epictetus's words, "Men are not disturbed by things, but the view they take of them." Related to this viewpoint are the Buddhist and Taoist concepts that human emotions originate from human thinking and that to change emotions, one must change one's thinking. These ideas fit nicely into Ellis's notion of how people get into psychological trouble (Ellis, 1979a, p. 190). From a psychotherapeutic standpoint Ellis has taken much from Alfred Adler, who believed that an individual's emotional reactions were generated by his or her attitudes, beliefs, and perceptions and were therefore cognitively created (Ellis, 1970; 1971).

As REBT has developed, it has been termed *rational therapy* (RT), *semantic therapy, cognitive behavior therapy* (CBT), and *rational behavior training* (RBT) (Ellis & Harper, 1979, p. 202). For many years the name *rational-emotive therapy* (RET) was commonly used to identify the approach. Recently, however, Ellis (1995) proposed that the name be changed to *rational-emotive behavior therapy* (REBT) because behavior is and always has been an essential part of the theory.

Today *general* REBT is virtually synonymous with cognitive behavior therapy (CBT; see Chapter 11), but *preferential* or *elegant* REBT, as Ellis (1984, p. iii) calls it, seeks a deeper, philosophic change in the client and is used whenever the client is capable of profiting from it.

Ellis has maintained his empirical scientific view of psychology and therapy throughout his life and has just as enthusiastically attacked nonscientific, nonrational, "it must be taken on faith or intuition" approaches (Ellis, 1986b, 1989a). He has long taken umbrage with Freudian psychoanalytics and currently he has taken to task the transpersonalists, a somewhat amorphous collection of transcendental, mystical, "new age" therapists who may combine a good deal of religion, spirituality, and philosophy in their therapy (Keegan, 1989). Ellis has not shirked from any attacks (Walsh, 1989; Wilber, 1989) on his "cognitive constructionist" approach and has vigorously debated and counterattacked those who attack his approach as an antiquated, reductionist form of logical positivism (Ellis, 1989a; 1990).

Currently, the focal point for REBT is The Institute for Rational-Emotive Behavior Therapy in New York. It is a multifaceted not-for-profit organization that promotes REBT. The Institute is worldwide and undertakes a variety of endeavors that range from in-depth training programs, clinical fellowships, consulting services, workshops, and courses to sales of books, audio and videotapes, and even T-shirts! *The Journal of Rational-Emotive & Cognitive-Behavior Therapy* is the official institute journal that publishes articles on the research, theory, and practice of REBT and cognitive-behavior therapy. Albert Ellis is actively involved in running the organization and is still busily writing, conducting workshops, and promoting REBT.

Overview of Rational-Emotive Behavior Therapy

Rational-emotive behavior therapy is a comprehensive approach to treatment and education that employs cognitive, emotive, and behavioral approaches. It advocates a humanistic, educative model of treatment as opposed to a medical model, and "consists of a theory of personality, a system of philosophy, and a technique of psychological treatment" (Ellis, 1971; Ellis & Abrahms, 1978, p. 36).

One of the fundamental tenets of REBT is that human problems stem not from external events or situations but from people's views or beliefs about them. More specifically, people's emotions stem from their beliefs, evaluations, interpretations, and philosophies about what happens to them, not from the events themselves.

Ellis suggests that an individual's belief system may consist of both a set of rational beliefs and a set of irrational beliefs. The irrational beliefs are the principal origin of emotional disturbance, and the main therapeutic goal of REBT is to change them. Through the therapeutic process, clients develop skills that allow them to first identify and then dispute their own irrational beliefs, a process they can then apply to other problem areas in their lives. In addition, effective therapy involves teaching clients to replace their problematic thinking and behavior with vitally absorbing interests aimed at long-range fulfillment rather than short-range hedonism.

It is this concern with long-range fulfillment that demarcates elegant REBT from the general type, or CBT. Where CBT frequently concentrates on practical problem solving, REBT much more frequently focuses on solving the emotional problem about the practical problem and then, if required, helps the client with the original problem (Ellis, 1986c, p. 37). The elegant approach calls for realigning one's thinking and indeed one's philosophy about life in broad-based ways. Whereas CBT may include such comprehensive changes, in elegant REBT philosophical change is central to personality change (Ellis, 1986c, p. 37). Ellis proposes that, to be "elegant," a theory of psychotherapy should offer economy of time and effort, rapid symptom reduction, effectiveness with a large percentage of different kinds of clients, depth of solution to problems, and lasting effects. A good deal of research finds that REBT's cognitive behavioral approaches meet these tough criteria (Ellis, 1989b; Engles, Garnefski, & Diekstra, 1993; Lyons & Woods, 1991; Silverman, McCarthy, & McGovern, 1992).

Theory of Personality

Biological Basis

Rational-emotive behavior therapy, unlike most other systems of psychotherapy, suggests that there is a biological basis for human behavior (Dryden, 1994). Ellis (1976a) hypothesized that probably 80 percent of the variance of human behavior can be accounted for by biological makeup and only about 20 percent by environmental training. Rational-emotive behavior therapy proposes that humans teach themselves irrational beliefs and are biologically prone to do so, as characterized by such attributes as inertia, negativism, habituation, moodiness, comfort striving, and excitement seeking, all of which interfere with productive thinking and planning and result in errors of judgment and self-defeating behavior (Dryden, 1984, p. 2; Ellis, 1991b). Ellis (1976a) offers the following points to substantiate this controversial view:

1. Virtually all humans show evidence of major irrationalities.
2. No social or cultural group is devoid of irrational behavior.
3. Many irrationalities run counter to teaching by significant others and society at large.
4. Irrationality is not exclusive to the stupid or retarded; bright and gifted humans can act irrationally.
5. Those who may oppose irrational activity and be most aware of it may also fall prey to it.
6. People often adopt new irrationalities after giving up old ones or go back to an irrational activity after working hard to overcome it.

Summarizing this pessimistic view, Ellis suggests that "humans are born with an exceptionally strong tendency to want and to insist that everything happens for the best in their life and to soundly condemn (1) themselves, (2) others, and (3) the world when they do not immediately get what they want" (Ellis, 1979a, p. 195). In this sense humans continue to think "humanly" all their lives, and only with great effort are they able to think and behave rationally. The saving grace of this dilemma is that humans also have powerful tendencies toward growth and self-actualization. Each person has the potential to effect change by changing his or her cognitive and behavioral processes, and can do so while overcoming gigantic barriers (Dryden, 1984, pp. 2, 44). This perspective puts REBT squarely in a secular humanistic operating mode that emphasizes flexibility and scientific outlook, self-acceptance instead of self-esteem, and long-range self-satisfaction and pleasure in one's activities, flexibility and alternative-seeking behavior, individualism and sociality, and accepts nothing—particularly religious dogma—on blind faith (Ellis, 1991a; 1992).

Social Basis

People spend much of their lives attempting to live up to others' expectations. They become "other-directed" and neglect to spend time developing the interpersonal skills they need to succeed socially and develop a healthy self-concept (Ellis, 1977, p. 196). For Ellis, however, the notion that one learns from the environment is nonsense. In his view, a more appropriate term is that people *teach* themselves as they aspire to succeed socially and live comfortably (Dryden, 1984, p. 43).

Psychological Basis

People who develop healthy personalities have an internal locus of control founded on self-enhancing and efficient thinking. However, movement toward psychological growth and self-actualizing behavior is often sabotaged by self-defeating thoughts (Ellis, 1979a, p. 196). People become emotionally distraught by upsetting themselves *about* external events. Convinced that the trouble is outside themselves, they complicate matters by condemning others and the world in general. If they continue this faulty belief in an external locus of control, they eventually come to view themselves in the same despicable way (Ellis, 1977, p. 199). The way this twisted and convoluted thinking, emoting, and behaving occurs can be explained by the ABC theory (Ellis 1958; 1962).

ABC Theory

At point A there occurs an event, behavior, feeling, or attitude termed an *activating event*. For example, Dr. James, rational and mild-mannered counselor, is caught in the express lane at the supermarket behind a person who has nine items (three over the limit), who is debating the check-out clerk over the price of an item, has coupons to turn in, and wants to write a check for $3.95 though the lane clearly says "cash only." All this occurs when the good doctor is already late for a therapy appointment.

At point C there is an emotional and/or behavioral *consequence*. Dr. James turns purple, swears under his breath, has visions of carving the miscreant with a chainsaw, and slams his microwave gourmet dinner down on the check-out counter while glaring at the clerk. Because of the close proximity between the activating event (A) and the emotional consequence (C), our agitated counselor may falsely assume that A causes C and conclude, "I am righteously indignant at this cretin for holding *me* up. I'll have to speed to get to my therapy session. Further, it's my lazy, good-for-nothing wife's fault for not taking care of *me* and getting these frozen dinners in the first place!" (A subsequent speeding ticket will link A to C even more closely.)

However, REBT theory asserts that A (the hang-up in the check-out line) does not cause C (the doctor's minipsychotic break and speeding ticket). Instead it asserts B (one's *belief* about A) causes C. If Dr. James were to tell himself, "It's inconvenient I'm stuck here, but it's not the end of the world, and the next time I've got to budget my time better," then he would tend to feel disappointment, chagrin, and a bit of guilt. In reality, however, Dr. James tells himself, "Here is another example of stupidity and incompetency insinuated on *me*, and it is a major catastrophe that this jerk is now making *me* late for *my* therapy session." Indignation, anger, and outrage predominate, and Dr. James suffers some very aversive consequences that reinforce his irrational belief about what others *ought* to do to make his life easier. The result is that the bad doctor has a lousy therapy session, gets in a quarrel with his wife about who has what responsibilities, and gets slapped with a divorce decree! In this not so extreme example of irrational statements and their consequences, the individual stays so absorbed in nurturing these beliefs that he spends no time working out what contributed to the situation and constructing a more realistic schedule. If no *disputation (D)* by the doctor or some significant other takes place, then he will be doomed to repeat the process and no new cognitive or behavioral *effect (E)* will occur.

This example illustrates a key aspect of REBT: cognition, emotion, and behavior are never considered in a monolithic sense. Although the ABCs of a situation may be viewed as distinct entities, they also transact with and include one another (Ellis, 1984, p. iii). In particular, thought and emotion are not two different processes, but essentially the same thing. Like the other two basic life processes, sensing and acting, they are interrelated. Thus, if a person senses, acts, emotes, or thinks, he or she is also consciously or unconsciously involving him- or herself in the other behavioral processes (Ellis, 1962, pp. 38–39).

Components of ABC

Many times the ABC paradigm presents a semantic rat's warren of interlocking passages that are a confounding maze. To clarify and properly categorize statements, Wessler and Wessler (1980) developed the emotional episode and partitioned the ABC paradigm into eight distinct parts (Wessler, 1986, pp. 13–14). A is composed of (1) an internal or external *objective stimulus,* which starts the sequence. The person then becomes (2) *aware* of its existence and (3) *defines and describes* it. Then a cognitive (4) *interpretation* is inferred about unobservable and unknown aspects of the objective event. This inference has the potential to lead to irrational ideation because there is no factual evidence to support it.

The B component is (5) an *evaluation* of the objective stimulus as positive, negative, or neutral. Further complicating matters, Wessler (1986) proposes that there are at least four objects of evaluation—the action, its intent, the consequences of the action, and the actor. Typically, individuals do not separate these entities and make singular, all-inclusive evaluations among them. When the belief is irrational this singular evaluation becomes all-inclusively catastrophic.

The resulting C may be divided into (6) *affective* arousal and (7) overt *behavior* that may or may not follow arousal. However, for the emotionally disturbed individual, negative affective arousal and negative overt behavior are almost always guaranteed. This circular cognitive chain is completed by (8) *reinforcing consequences* that may influence and strengthen future episodes of the event (Wessler, 1986, pp. 13–14).

Belief Categories

Observations, descriptions, evaluations, inferences, and conclusions become commingled in the person's belief system and, depending on how they are cognated, have much to do with whether the individual will behave in a rational or an irrational manner. The following categories demonstrate how observations and inferences get tangled with one another and, based on the degree and kind of evaluation, lead to irrational beliefs and problem behavior (Ellis, 1984, pp. vi–vii; Ellis & Bernard, 1986, pp. 12–13):

1. *Nonevaluative observations or descriptions of what is happening:* "I see I'm going to be held up in this check-out line."
2. *Nonevaluative inferences about what is happening:* "I'm probably going to be late for my appointment because of this delay."
3. *Positive evaluative absolutistic inferences about what is happening:* "Because of this delay I'm going to be late. Since my clients are utterly dependent on me, these people should make way for me due to my importance. I will now have to speed to get to my appointment and save my client."
4. *Negative evaluative absolutistic external inferences about what is happening:* "People and events must not interfere with my life. It is wretched of these rotten swine to do so. The callous customer, the officious cop, my indignant client, and my uncaring wife all prove I am not given the due consideration I should have. I hate them and this burning feeling in my gut that *they* gave me!"
5. *Negative evaluative absolutistic internal inferences about what is happening:* "How many times will I try to cram too much in and not plan my time effectively. I am doomed to repeat this sloppy planning as long as I live. No professional would be so inefficient. I am an incompetent dirtbag!"

Consequences of Beliefs

Consequences about the foregoing ways of evaluating beliefs from an unpleasant activating event may also be partitioned according to their outcome (Ellis & Bernard, 1986).

1. *Desirable emotional consequences:* "Rats! You've once again crammed too much in and you wind up suffering the consequences." Appropriate bad feelings of frustration and irritation are manifested by the guilty doctor.
2. *Desirable behavioral consequences:* "You're just going to have to shape up and plan more effectively—particularly on Monday. Don't forget your appointment book next time!" Determination and planning to do better are self-contracted by the resolute doctor.

3. *Undesirable emotional consequences:* "If I had an Uzi submachine gun right now I'd make Rambo look like Mother Theresa and clean this #@&^*@! grocery store out!" Anger takes over the now running amok doctor.
4. *Undesirable behavioral consequences:* The Indianapolis Five Hundred doctor roars out of the grocery store and is immediately picked up for going forty-five in a thirty-mile-an-hour zone. Undesirable anger consequences are manifested in wildly inappropriate driving and a hefty fine—not to mention alimony payments to come later.

Healthy, Growth-Promoting, Self-Actualized Personalities

As may be seen from these cognitive states, people largely create their own emotional disturbances. Because people have a measure of self-determination, they can choose to indoctrinate themselves in disturbed or undisturbed ways. Rational-emotive behavior theorists believe people have the power to change their self-defeating habits, but such change requires actively working at modifying thoughts, behaviors, and feelings. Inherent in such change is a philosophy of long-range hedonism predicated on a scientific and empirical, rather than a mystical, devoutly religious, or external, locus of control (Ellis, 1986c, p. 32). Attainment of this goal calls for living rationally rather than irrationally (Dryden, 1984, p. 2). Easily said, the ABCs of living one's life profitably often become as indecipherable as hieroglyphs, and without a psychological Rosetta stone to translate one's erroneous beliefs, maladjustment is the inevitable outcome.

Nature of Maladjustment

Precursors

Although emotional disturbance is acquired through the combined influence of one's biological tendencies and one's life experiences, it is maintained by self-indoctrination. Ellis believes that children, much more than adults, lack the ability objectively to assess themselves and their environments and therefore tend to internalize the critical attitudes of their parents. Even if a child's parents are not exceptionally critical, Ellis suggests, children will tend to adopt the negative and perfectionistic attitudes from others in their surroundings, such as teachers, peers, and the media. However, children become emotionally disturbed *not only* because of parental attitudes toward them but also because of their "own tendency to take these attitudes too seriously, to internalize them, and to perpetuate them through the years" (Ellis, 1973, p. 34). It is this self-propagandizing that keeps the original irrational beliefs alive.

Psychological problems stem from the way people think about things: it is one's belief system (*B*) that leads to inappropriate emotional consequences (*C*) such as rage, depression, and extreme anxiety. This belief system (*B*) consists of two sets of beliefs. One set consists of rational beliefs (*rBs*), such as "How unfortunate it is that I have been fired, because it will be inconvenient to look for a new job." The other set of beliefs, those that lead to emotional disturbance, are irrational beliefs (*iBs*), such as "I must not be fired! How terrible and unjust! It will be catastrophic if I cannot find another job immediately! (Ellis & Abrahms, 1978, p. 14). It is this limited set of irrational beliefs and their variations that underlie most emotional disturbance. These irrational beliefs typically occur in the form of simple declarative sentences that exist on a conscious or a preconscious level and are therefore readily accessible to conscious thought.

Musturbation
Rational-emotive behavior therapy's most important and basic premises about irrational beliefs spring from unconditional "shoulds," "oughts," and "musts" people say to themselves about events. These explicitly commanding and demanding words generate what Ellis calls *musturbation.* Musturbation occurs when one moves from preferences, desires, and wishes about what is happening to absolutes and necessities about what is happening. Musturbatory thinking leads to three irrational beliefs (Ellis, 1984, p. viii):

1. *Awfulizing:* "I have no job. I'm forty-five years old. I can't get another job. My family will starve. This is not just awful, it is catastrophic."
2. *Self-damnation:* "I am no good at my job. I am no good to my family. I am no damn good for anything."
3. *I-can't-stand-it-itis:* "I will not tolerate them firing me. I am totally destroyed by this and I will get even if it's the last thing I do."

Cold, Warm, and Hot Cognitions
Cold cognitions are generally descriptions, observations, and nonevaluative inferences: "I lost my job. Tomorrow I'll have to start looking for another one." Cold cognitions are unemotional evaluations of facts. *Warm cognitions* emphasize preferences and nonpreferences rather than necessities and absolutes: "I sure don't like the fact that I lost my job after all these years. I'll have to start looking for another one. At my age, I wonder how tough that'll be." Warm cognitions may be seeded with mild or intense emotions, but as long as they indicate preference, they do not fall in the realm of emotional disturbance. *Hot cognitions* emphasize commands and demands: "I must get another job equal to what I lost. If I don't I'm a miserable failure." Hot cognitions are heavily laden emotional-demand statements that usually lead to dysfunctional behavior such as anxiety or depression (Ellis, 1984, p. vi; Zajonc, 1980). Hot cognitions may take a variety of forms—overgeneralizing, catastrophizing, magnification, non sequiturs, personalizing, labeling, and all-or-none thinking. These are all unrealistic statements because no empirical evidence exists to substantiate them (Ellis, 1984, p. ix). It is these hot cognitions with which REBT is mainly concerned.

Ego and Discomfort Anxiety
Either or both of these anxiety types are generally present in emotional disturbance. *Ego anxiety* is a dramatic, powerful feeling that is accompanied by feelings of guilt and inadequacy in regard to a person's ability to perform: "I couldn't do that; therefore I'm a bum." Thus, the person's personal worth is threatened (Ellis, 1991b). *Discomfort anxiety* is often less dramatic, but it is more common, tends to be specific to "dangerous" situations, and is inherent in most phobias: "I've got to get out of this claustrophobic room or I'll die!" It is emotional tension that occurs when one's comfort is threatened (Ellis, 1986a, pp. 105–106). When the two types commingle, emotional disturbance is exponentially more profound (Ellis, 1986a, p. 110).

Secondary Symptoms

An emotionally disturbed person will typically experience both primary and secondary symptoms. A secondary symptom occurs when the individual starts musturbating and develops irrational beliefs about the primary symptom. An ego-anxious person may start feeling depressed not only about a broken love affair but also about the depression state itself: "Oh God! I can't stand to think about that wave of depression washing over me, and even as I think of that I'm becoming depressed!" The discomfort-anxious person may feel threatened not only by the prospect of getting in a crowded elevator but also by the anxiety state itself: "Oh Jesus! When I remember how I felt, all sweaty, shaky, and queasy, those feelings start to come up again" (Ellis, 1986c, pp. 37–38).

Discomfort anxiety may become a secondary symptom of ego anxiety: "I must be comfortable about my performance around men." And ego anxiety may become a secondary symptom of discomfort anxiety: "This time I must be cool when I go out on a date; that way I won't feel like I'm in a torture chamber" (Ellis, 1984, p. xiii). Such circular, irrational thinking becomes a self-fulfilling prophecy and pulls the individual deeper and deeper into a vortex of dysfunctional behavior.

Low Frustration Tolerance

People who fail to change their problematic behavior have largely their low frustration tolerance (LFT) to blame (Ellis, 1979b). LFT is central to understanding a variety of emotional disturbances ranging from procastination to agoraphobia. The ability to tolerate discomfort, not for its own sake but so that psychological changes may be made, is a primary criterion of good mental health (Dryden, 1984, p. 8). Low frustration tolerance is a predictable consequence of a person holding on to one or more of the following ideas in the face of difficult circumstances: (1) "The world has to be arranged so that I do what I want, when I want, without hassle"; (2) "It is horrible to be presented with such difficult circumstances, and this must stop immediately"; (3) "I can't stand it when things go wrong" (Ellis, 1976b). Therefore, such people avoid short-term discomfort that may result in long-term benefit and opt for comfortable discomfort in the present and probably in the future (Ellis, 1979b).

Major Concepts

Self-Actualizing Behavior

The main purpose of humans is to stay alive, but "staying alive" is not just moving from day to day in a "veil of tears" or "do-what-feels-good" world. The idea is to maximize happiness in a long-term investment program that operates within a social context (Dryden, 1984, p. 1). Major REBT precepts for receiving large dividends from such a program include:

1. Self-interest where sacrifice may be made for others, but not in an overwhelming, martyring sense;
2. Social interest that contributes to and allows one to enjoy the benefits of living in a social group or community;
3. Self-direction that assumes responsibility for oneself and does not demand support or succor from others;

4. Tolerance of both oneself and others in accepting behavior that may be disliked, and refraining from damning such behavior;
5. Flexibility to the extent of being open to change and not imposing rigid rules for oneself or others;
6. Accepting the uncertainty of what at times seems a randomly cruel universe where probability and chance exist and absolute certainties never will;
7. Commitment to something outside oneself to the extent of having at least one powerful creative interest as well as some major human involvement that one considers so important that a good portion of one's life is structured around it;
8. Scientific thinking that allows one to act concertedly with deep feelings in a regulated, reflective, and logical manner on the consequences of behavior;
9. Unconditional self-acceptance—that is, self-acceptance that avoids absolutistic self-rating that is contingent on external achievements or what others think of them;
10. Risk taking that is adventurous, exhilarating, and exciting, but well gauged so as not to be foolhardy;
11. Long-range hedonism that seeks both the pleasures of the moment and those of the future but does not often chance future pain for present gratification;
12. A non-Utopian view that refuses to believe unrealistically in a life either full of unrelenting happiness or totally devoid of pain and lack of anxiety;
13. A high frustration tolerance that enables one to accept what cannot be changed, change those conditions that can be changed, and know the difference between the two;
14. Being responsible for one's disturbances rather than projecting blame onto others or onto environmental events;
15. Avoiding irrational thinking, self-damaging habituations, wishful thinking, and intolerance, which is frequently exacerbated by one's culture and family;
16. Knowing that almost all serious emotional problems come from magical thinking that cannot be validated and that these nonverifiable thoughts, in turn, become engrained, dogmatic, and irrational beliefs;
17. Knowing only hard work and practice will correct irrational beliefs and their negative emotional and behavioral outcomes (Ellis, 1989b, pp. 197–199; Ellis & Bernard, 1986, pp. 9–10).

Holistic Functioning

Ellis proposes that humans have four basic processes necessary to survival and happiness; perceiving or sensing; feeling or emoting; moving or acting; and reasoning or thinking. He suggests that these processes are interrelated; human beings rarely experience any one of them in isolation. Thus, human beings function holistically—perceiving, moving, thinking, and emoting simultaneously (Ellis & Harper, 1979, p. 16). For example, when a person says, "I am thinking about this test," it would be more accurate to say, "I am perceiving, moving, feeling, and thinking about this test," for when one perceives a test, one also feels (e.g., anxious), thinks ("this looks difficult"), and acts (picks up a pen and writes).

Appropriate versus Inappropriate Emotions

Feelings are necessary as well as important, because without them people would not experience such positive emotions as creativity, joy, and love—the kinds of feelings that help humans to survive "happily." Also, some negative emotions are necessary and helpful because they are based on threats to one's basic needs and thus serve to keep the person motivated to avoid danger (Ellis & Harper, 1979, p. 23).

Rational versus Irrational Thinking

Rational thinking has five main characteristics. A person who thinks rationally (1) derives thoughts from objective fact as opposed to subjective opinion; (2) will be more likely to preserve life and limb; (3) will define his or her personal goals more quickly; (4) will produce a minimum of personal conflict and turmoil; and (5) will prevent him- or herself from getting into personal conflict with significant others (Ellis & Harper, 1979, p. 73).

The three main barriers to effective thinking and emoting are (1) lack of intelligence; (2) lack of knowledge about how to think intelligently; and (3) inability, because of neurotic behavior, to put intelligence and knowledge to good use. Ellis quips that neurosis "consists of stupid behavior by nonstupid people" (Ellis & Harper, 1979, p. 37).

Comprehensive Approach

Rational-emotive behavior therapy openly employs cognitive, emotional, and behavioral approaches on the theoretical grounds that because human beings function in a holistic way, it is desirable to employ a diversity of techniques in treatment (Ellis & Abrahms, 1978, p. 39). Rational-emotive behavior therapy "assumes that people make themselves disturbed in complex ways; therefore, no simple way exists in which they can help themselves to become less disturbed" (Ellis & Abrahms, 1978, p. 14).

Humans tend to emote, think, and behave simultaneously. Thus, to understand their self-defeating behavior the therapist needs to understand how people perceive, think, emote, and act and use a comprehensive combination of perceptual-cognitive, emotive-evocative, and behavioristic-reeducative methods (Ellis, 1989b, p. 198).

Because REBT does not limit itself to a few particular disorders but takes on a wide range of clients, many of whom are, in Ellis's words, "tough customers," REBT and Ellis in particular have not been bashful about adapting techniques from other modalities to fit client needs. Thus, as long as the basic REBT framework is used, almost any effective therapeutic technique may be employed, and in this respect, REBT is perhaps the most eclectic system of all (Wessler & Wessler, 1980, p. 185).

Goals of Psychotherapy

Ellis (1979a, p. 205) has stated that the overall goal of REBT involves "minimizing the client's central self-defeating outlook and acquiring a more realistic, tolerant philosophy of life." Two other central goals are reducing the client's anxiety (self-blame) and hostility (blaming others and the world) and teaching clients a method of self-observation and self-assessment that will ensure that this improvement continues (Ellis, 1973, p. 147). Thus, a primary goal of counseling is to teach clients to detect and dispute irrational beliefs.

Another long-term goal is to assist clients in becoming involved in activities that are vitally absorbing to them. The primary job of the therapist is not to show clients what will bring happiness but to help them discover how they block themselves from pursuing happiness and how they can remove those blocks (Dryden, 1984, pp. 1–2).

Humanism

Ellis asserts that "REBT is one of the most humanistically oriented of all therapies" in that it emphasizes that humans can fully accept themselves just because they are alive, just because they exist; they do not have to prove their worth in any way. Thus, humans can create their own meaningful purposes and therefore they need neither "magic nor gods on whom to rely." Ellis contends that this humanistic-existentialist approach to life is as much a part of REBT as its rational, logical, and scientific methodology (Ellis, 1973, p. 63).

Educational Model

In essence, REBT involves teaching clients effective self-analysis. Rather than holding that its principles are the sole province of trained therapists, REBT advocates learning its principles through any available source. Therefore, within and outside of individual therapy, REBT uses a number of education-oriented techniques and resources, such as bibliotherapy, lectures, tape recordings, stories, seminars, demonstrations, and other mass presentations (Ellis & Harper, 1979, p. x).

Scientific Method

Ellis has stated that there are two kinds of psychotherapy: scientific and nonscientific. Rational-emotive behavior therapy may be viewed as scientific in two ways. First, it strongly advocates the use of controlled experiments to test its efficacy. Second, clients are taught to test their theories about themselves and others and to question their own ideas, retaining those that have beneficial results and discarding those that have self-defeating consequences (Ellis & Abrahms, 1978, p. 13).

Semantic Approach

Ellis has described REBT as a form of semantic therapy. Because individuals tell themselves both "sane" and "insane" things and because these beliefs take the form of internalized sentences, or "self-talk," one of the most powerful and elegant modalities for change consists of understanding, disputing, and acting against these internal verbalizations (Ellis & Harper, 1979, p. x).

Self-Acceptance

This central concept of REBT may be distinguished from the concepts of self-esteem and self-confidence. Rational-emotive behavior therapy contends that self-esteem and self-confidence are built on a person's accomplishment, so that when an individual performs well the result is increased self-esteem. However, if someone derives a sense of self-esteem from good performance, then that person suffers a loss of self-esteem with failure. Thus, even if the individual manages rarely to fail, there is always the possibility of future failure and along with it a decrease in self-esteem. Ellis endorses the concept of "unconditional self-acceptance," which means that "one accepts oneself—one's existence, one's aliveness, without any requirements or conditions whatever" (Ellis, 1971; Ellis & Abrahms, 1978, pp. 5–6).

Therapeutic Relationship

Although empathy and unconditional positive regard are encouraged (Ellis, 1984, p. xi), rational-emotive therapists "do not believe a warm relationship between client and therapist is a necessary or a sufficient condition for effective personality change" (Ellis, 1979a, p. 186). On the contrary, Ellis suggests, too much personal warmth and empathic understanding may foster client dependence and the need for the therapist's approval. Ellis suggests that REBT principles work "with clients who think you dislike them, who actively hate you, who feel you are only lecturing to them, who blindly follow exercises you give them, and who otherwise maintain a minimal, and often unpleasant, relationship with you" (Ellis, 1973, p. 410). If a positive therapeutic relationship is engendered, it will most likely be because of the REBT therapist's authority and confidence in the approach; the absolute certainty he or she indicates concerning the cause of problems; constant monitoring of client progress through homework assignments; and the therapist's encouragement, compliments, focus on current meaningful problems, and use of down-to-earth language (Garfield, 1995).

Insight

Ellis suggests that the kind of insight achieved by clients through psychoanalysis may mislead clients to conclude that early activating events (traumas) "cause" emotional disturbance. In contrast, REBT theory suggests it is not the events themselves that cause emotional disturbance but the way the individual interprets them (Ellis, 1979a, p. 187).

It is this type of insight that REBT therapists are interested in providing the client. The following five insights are critical to REBT and, collectively or individually, may need to be discovered by clients before progress can occur. The client (1) understands that current ideas and beliefs play an important role in causing his or her problems; (2) knows that feeling upset and disturbed today is caused by continued self-indoctrination with the irrational beliefs he or she learned in the past; (3) needs to have awareness, acknowledgement, and appreciation of his or her irrational beliefs, because awareness without acknowledgment and appreciation is nonmotivating; (4) learns to accept him- or herself without guilt, even though no one but the client has caused the problem; and (5) sees that he or she has practiced self-propagandization for so long that the irrational beliefs have become incorporated as fact and that only hard work at detecting and disputing these irrationalities will rectify the problem. Clearly, understanding the first four insights will do little good if the client does not come to understand the fifth (Grieger, 1986, pp. 207–208).

THE COUNSELING PROCESS

Overview

The REBT therapeutic process is active, direct, confrontive, and based on the use of the logicoempirical method of scientific questioning, challenging, and debating (Ellis & Grieger, 1977, p. 20). During initial sessions, therapists confront their clients with evidence of their irrational thinking and behavior. Therefore, therapists teach clients the ABC theory and other basics of REBT. To accomplish this goal of reeducation, the therapist explains, persuades, lectures, teaches, confronts, and uses humor in disputing clients' irrational beliefs. Typically, therapists do not "tread lightly" in confronting, nor do they believe it is necessary to delay interpretations to later stages of therapy (Ellis, 1973, p. 90).

Three initiating procedures are necessary in REBT intervention. First, the therapist attempts to form a bond with the rational part of the client's personality against the irrational part. By being unconditionally accepting, empathic, and genuine with the client, the therapist sets the facilitative conditions for therapy and obtains the credibility necessary to intervene directively with the irrational part of the client. This does not mean that the therapist is gullible or passive with the irrational parts. Indeed, clear differentiations are made early on between person and behavior. There is no one way to develop such bonds, and initiating procedures may range from a "familiar" to an "expert" role (Dryden, 1984, p. 17; Young, 1986b).

Second, agreement on desired outcome goals is reached. The therapist develops a problem list jointly with the client. The therapist must be careful at this juncture not only to avoid falling into the abyss of the external and environmental events (*A*s) the client believes are causing the problem, but also to avoid disputing these events so vigorously that the client has no hope of success. Thus, the therapist suggests that for the moment the client assume that external events or people are beyond his or her control, and that various options might be viewed in that light (Dryden, 1984, pp. 18–19).

Third, the therapist solicits agreement on tasks to be undertaken in pursuit of the desired goals. Throughout the endeavor, the therapist collaborates in obtaining the client's feelings and reactions to every session, being particularly sensitive to any negative reactions as both grapple with the dilemma. Periodic review of progress and renegotiation of goals are assumed, because what the client initially believes to be the problem *A*s may change dramatically as his or her *iB*s unfold.

Inherent in these three procedures is a clear and constant understanding by the client of what is occurring. Therefore, the language the therapist uses must clearly communicate what is planned—no small chore given the complexities involved in unraveling the client's *iB*s (Dryden, 1984, p. 19).

It should be clear from this overview that REBT makes no pretense about being value-free or entirely objective (Ellis & Bernard, 1986, p. 7; Young, 1986c). As a result, REBT strategies vigorously confront the twisted values and irrational belief systems of clients. The three broad categories of REBT techniques—cognitive, emotive, and behavioral—are all designed to jar the client's crooked thinking, feeling, and acting.

Cognitive REBT deals with the *shoulds* and *oughts* in clients' lives that lead them to perfectionist and absolutist thinking and behaving. It works on semantic precision in that it continuously asks clients to evaluate whether what has happened is as bad as they melodramatically make it (Ellis, 1989b, p. 213).

Emotive-evocative REBT dramatically emphasizes the difference between preferences and "musts" so clients can distinguish between the two. By use of modeling, humor, role playing, and unconditional acceptance, REBT therapists demonstrate how clients can actively dispute and distinguish between preferential and musturbatory thinking (Ellis, 1989b, p. 213).

Behavioral REBT employs various types of operant conditioning not only to change undesirable behavior and reinforce the client for more adaptive ways of behaving, but also to change the client's cognitions about the behavior. Clients may be asked to perform risk-taking activities in which they may intentionally set themselves up to fail to see that the results are not as fearsome as they imagined. They may be given hard tasks so that they can engage in tough activities and learn not to be upset or scared by them (Ellis, 1989b, p. 214).

STRATEGIES FOR HELPING CLIENTS

Rational-emotive behavior therapists view cognitive interventions as the heart of therapy. Specifically, emotional disturbance can be traced to a finite number of irrational beliefs and their corollaries. The therapist, therefore, seeks to identify any of the following irrational beliefs or their variations to which the client subscribes (Ellis & Harper, 1979):

1. The idea that you must have love or approval from all people you find significant.
2. The idea that you must prove thoroughly competent, adequate, and achieving.
3. The idea that when people act obnoxiously and unfairly, you should blame and damn them and see them as bad, wicked, or rotten.
4. The idea that you have to view things as horrible and catastrophic when you get seriously frustrated, treated unfairly, or rejected.
5. The idea that emotional misery comes from external pressures and that you have little ability to control or change your feelings.
6. The idea that if something seems dangerous or fearsome, you must preoccupy yourself with it and make yourself anxious about it.
7. The idea that you can more easily avoid facing many life difficulties and self-responsibilities than undertake more rewarding forms of self-discipline.
8. The idea that your past remains all-important and that because something once strongly influenced your life, it has to keep determining your feelings today.
9. The idea that people and things should turn out better than they do and that you must view life as awful if you don't find good solutions to its realities.
10. The idea that you can achieve maximum human happiness by inertia or inaction or by passively or uncommittedly "enjoying yourself."

Strategies for Detecting Irrational Beliefs

Education

Using examples of other clients whose problems are similar and providing analogies that the client can understand are ways of educating clients about what may occur with them and what they may expect to happen. By telling clients that therapy helps them to learn how to think differently and more sensibly about the problem, therapists can turn the unknown and anxiety-provoking thought of going into therapy into commonly understood familiar terms. Clients should also clearly understand that therapy won't cure all the problems they have but will make the burden easier to bear and will help them feel less miserable (Young, 1986b, p. 95).

Problem Exploration

A mistake often made by beginning therapists is not to gain a panoramic vision of all the things that brought the client to therapy. Boring right in to challenge the client's first irrational thought is likely to be counterproductive, even though it may be theoretically correct. Therapists need to hear the client out completely in regard to his or her ABCs, what part environmental circumstances play in them, and how the client's values contribute to his or her belief systems (Young, 1986b, p. 95).

One of the most important procedures in REBT is assessing A to the extent that a complete cognitive description of the event is obtained. Without all of the client's forecasts, predictions, assumptions, expectations, and interpretations of A, the therapist has little knowledge of the client's beliefs about and ways of prioritizing the numerous noxious stimuli within the "bad" event. Therapists new to REBT often do not spend enough time tracking the client's chain of inferences that led to the irrational beliefs and resulting emotional disturbances and negative behavioral outcomes. A simple procedure that will allow for complete exploration of A is to use two questions: "Then what?" and "Why's that?" (Moore, 1986, p. 6).

Once the client outlines the presenting problem, the therapist poses a continuous series of "Then what?" questions. Because the client will invariably mix a few B and C statements in with A, the therapist needs to respond to these statements by getting the client back on track with "Why's that?" questions. The interrogation stops when the client's inference chain of responses is exhausted. Typically the client will say, "That's all there is!" The therapist may then attack any part of the inference chain to which the client has reacted most strongly or that the therapist feels is most critical (Moore, 1986, pp. 6–12).

Subsequent sessions will begin with a request for a problem or a review of homework on a problem. Because many clients have such a constellation of problems that they cannot settle on one, the therapist may decide on one problem so that corrective measures can be started as soon as possible. Each session typically is limited to working on one or two problems. (Young, 1986b, p. 99).

Ferreting Out B

On the surface REBT seems ridiculously simple, yet digging out B in the ABC sequence drives many of our students crazy. A therapist may identify A and C but have a great deal of difficulty identifying B, and more difficulty identifying the irrational component of B. As Moore (1986, p. 3) has indicated, clients' "thoughts" are not the disturbance causing the irrational ideation. If Dr. James "thinks" he is about to have coronary arrest and has a dull burning stomachache, thinks his client will believe he is unprofessional and leave because he is late, believes his wife is an incompetent dolt and berates her for it, and flies into a rage because of the hold-up in the check-out line, none of these "thoughts" necessarily belongs in the B category.

Complicating things further, all of these "thoughts" may be valid and rational. If Dr. James's cholesterol level doesn't get within reasonable bounds he is a candidate for a heart attack—a possible C consequence. His stomachache is an immediate psychosomatic C consequence. His B belief about his wife, while unkind, may or may not be true, but it has little to do with irrationality. His rage is the resulting emotional C consequence of his hot cognitions. Further, all of these C consequences can just as reasonably do double duty as secondary effects of his original A event because they are reactions that have become chained to the original "stuck in the grocery line" event (Moore, 1986, p. 4). The irrationality of the rather long linkage of events and consequences from "stuck in the check-out line" to "appearance in divorce court" hinges not on any of the foregoing and what may be inferred or predicted from them so much as absolutes like "awful," "should," "must," and "completely worthless" that are pinned to them (Moore, 1986, p. 5).

Ellis & Grieger (1977, p. 10) have made some helpful suggestions for detecting irrational beliefs:

1. Look for "awfulizing" and ask the person, "What is awful about this situation?"
2. Look for beliefs such as "I can't stand it!" and examine what about this situation the person believes is "unbearable."
3. Look for "musturbating" thoughts and determine what "shoulds," "oughts," and/or "musts" the person is telling him- or herself about the situation.
4. Look for blaming or "damning" of self or others and ask, "What does the person view as 'damnable' or unforgivable about this behavior?"

Another simple way of detecting irrational beliefs is to look for them under one of three major "musturbating" belief systems:

1. "I am 'no good' unless I always do well and receive complete acceptance for my performance." (I *must* behave perfectly and be loved and accepted by everyone.)
2. "You are 'no good' unless you always act fairly and kindly toward me." (You *must* behave in ways that please me.)
3. "Life is 'no good' unless it always provides me what I want or what I believe I deserve." (Life *must* be the way I believe it *should* be.)

Almost all irrational beliefs are related in some way to one or more of these three irrational beliefs (Ellis, 1984, p. viii).

A third way of detecting iBs is to listen for client problems about problems. Secondary symptoms are key signals of emotional disturbance: "I get nauseous every time I even think about asking a good-looking woman out for a date, not to mention how screwed up I get on the date." These secondary symptoms have nothing to do with the primary event (going out on a date) and everything to do with feelings, thoughts, and behaviors antecedent to the event (fear, terror, inadequacy, incompetence, stomachache, etc.) (Grieger, 1986, pp. 204–205).

Strategies for Disputing Irrational Beliefs

To dispute clients' irrational beliefs once they have been identified, the therapist uses three processes: debating, discriminating, and defining (Ellis & Grieger, 1977, p. 20). Ellis and Grieger describe *debating* as asking such questions as "What evidence is there to support this belief?" or "What makes this belief so or not so—in which way does it have truth or falseness?" In debating, the therapist often plays devil's advocate by putting such rhetorical questions squarely in the path of the client's illogical inferences and absolutist evaluations about events (Grieger, 1986, p. 210).

Discriminating helps the client to distinguish clearly between wants and needs, desires and demands, rational and irrational ideas, absolute and nonabsolute values, and behavior and personhood (Grieger, 1986, p. 210).

Defining consists of helping clients to choose their terms more precisely. Therapists do this by reflecting the following logical principles: (1) just because one may act in certain ways at certain times, it does not follow that one will *always* act in this way; (2) just because one feels a certain way at a given point in time, it does not follow that one will feel that way forever; and (3) just because one has behaved in a certain way over a period of time, it does not follow that one is a failure (or any other descriptive term that attempts to define one's being or essence). The concept of being implies that one behaves this same way all the time and under all conditions both now and in the future (Ellis & Grieger, 1977, pp. 20–21).

Let's look at an example of how to challenge a client's irrational beliefs. Suppose a client who lost a job thinks, "I behaved awfully in that situation. I should never have behaved in that way. Therefore, I am a worthless clod, both now and in the future, who deserves to be punished!" In response, the REBT therapist might make the following challenges (Ellis & Grieger, 1977): First, assuming that one did behave stupidly, how can one substantiate the "awfulness" of that behavior? One cannot substantiate this because behaving badly does not mean that one behaved *totally* badly, as "awfulness" would imply. Second, viewing one's behavior as totally bad and viewing this as "awful" also implies that one lacks the capacity to do better in the future. However, poor past performance does not prove one can never make progress, which in any event is an unprovable assumption. Third, behaving "totally" badly implies that one could *not* have acted worse. This is also an invalid assumption, because no matter how badly one behaves, one could always have done worse. Fourth, assuming one "should not" have acted in this way is also unempirical, because no reason exists that one should not have acted in a certain way. Though it might have been preferable to have acted differently, it is not a necessity. By implying that one should have acted differently, one implies that there is a law of the universe that commands that one must have acted differently. This is clearly an impossibility, because if such a law existed, one would have been forced to have acted differently. Fifth, believing that one is a rotten person for behaving badly is also unprovable, because it suggests that one would forever behave rottenly in relation to everything. It is impossible to prove that one will always continue to act badly.

At the conclusion of this disputing process, the client acquires a new effect (*E*) or philosophy that enables him or her to think about self, others, and the world more rationally in the future. This effect (*E*) involves a new cognitive effect (c*E*), a new emotive effect (e*E*), and a new behavioral effect (b*E*) as well. For example, a client will begin to feel less depressed (although still concerned) about not having a job at present. Also, instead of avoiding looking for a job, the client will actively begin to seek a new one and to work on correcting whatever problems contributed to the loss of the old one (Ellis & Grieger, 1977, pp. 22–31).

Cognitive Techniques

Although its core cognitive technique is disputing irrational beliefs, REBT employs a variety of verbal procedures to enhance disputation. The following techniques demonstrate the broad array available.

Interpretation of Defenses
Unlike psychoanalysis, REBT assumes that defenses stem largely from self-condemnation. Thus, if clients condemn themselves for having a symptom they will often use various defenses to keep this symptom out of their conscious awareness (Ellis & Abrahms, 1978).

TH: Yep! It sure sounds like your wife is an interfering nag. Yet, you did marry her. You did make that choice, and I wonder if blaming her for the rotten marriage isn't a subtle way of condemning yourself for all those crummy decisions you indicate you've made.

Presentation of Alternative Choices and Actions
Clients often have many more choices than they think they have. Therefore, rational-emotive behavior therapists often help clients see their full range of alternatives (Ellis & Abrahms, 1978).

TH: You say you have to stay in the job even though you despise it. Yet I've heard at least five other things you could do that would be more fulfilling, even though you quickly add that they'd be impossible. I'd like for us to test the impossibility of those and see if that's true.

Analogies, Parables, and Metaphors
In REBT, cognitive restructuring involves altering the language and meaning that clients apply to their situations and problems so that abstract beliefs become clear and concrete. Thus metaphors, analogies, and parables can play an important role in reframing the problem so that the irrational ideation can be seen more easily (DiGiuseppe & Muran, 1992; Wessler & Wessler, 1980).

TH: So you are the little Dutch boy with his finger in the dike, courageously holding back the sea of problems for your children. But in your protecting them, I wonder if you're really Pinocchio and it's your nose and not your finger that's involved when you tell yourself that you must protect them from everything in an evil world. By telling yourself that it becomes easy to believe that you are absolutely necessary to their existence and survival. That, of course, really hinders them in becoming independent and they wind up hating you for smothering them. You, in turn, wind up feeling righteously hurt and angry over their refusal to be docile little sheep.

Paralinguistics

The therapist may dramatically emphasize the irrationality of a situation by drawing out the emotionally hot cognitions a client makes by acting both verbally and behaviorally in a flamboyant manner (Walen, DiGiuseppe, & Wessler, 1980, p. 178).

TH: (*doubling over in feigned pain*) Ohhh, my Gawwwwd! (*whining*) how hoooorible! How (*gasp*) awwwwful.

When the therapist wishes to change from a hot to a warm cognition, he or she may speak slowly and distinctly in a controlled, calm, but powerful voice.

TH: (*straight up in chair, head up, chest out*) It is unfortunate (*shifts to slumped position*) but not awwwful.

Therapeutic Markers

Before launching into an irrational diatribe, clients often make antecedent statements that activate their belief systems. The therapist may ask the client to restate such cues (Dryden, 1984, pp. 78–79).

TH: I'm going to stop the tape. I want you to hear that last statement you made, how it leads into those chiseled-in-stone evaluations you make, but first I'd like you to give it back to me with all the emotion you just put into it.

Reduction to Absurdity

The therapist appears to accept the illogical premise of the client. Then he or she carries the faulty premise to its logical extreme (Ellis, 1971).

TH: Okay! You want people to leave you alone and quit bugging you. That sounds reasonable. How could you do that and really be alone? Lock yourself up in your room? That wouldn't work very well because you'd have to get food and water and have some minimal contact with the other folks. Perhaps you could go be a survivalist and live in the Rockies. You could be alone there, grow your own food, trap, fish, and hunt. Of course, if you do that it would be important to really know what you were doing, get all the things you need so you could survive. But then come to think of it, if you did freeze to death or die of starvation, you'd really be alone then. A rather dramatic change from a condo and a stockbroker's job in Fort Lauderdale, but certainly possible.

Visual Aids

To simplify and concretize concepts, REBT makes use of visual aids such as cartoons, wall posters, labels, notecards, chalkboards, and magic markers and butcher paper to illustrate irrational ideation and how to dispute it. For example, to differentiate between categories that are merely inconvenient and those that are intolerable and to show the client that there are a great many more of the former than there are of the latter, the therapist may create columns labeled "Pain in the neck hassles" and "End of the world catastrophes." Likewise, to differentiate between events as bad and the self as bad, columns labeled "It's bad" and "I'm bad" may be used to diminish guilt-ridden behavior that issues out of self-blame (Young, 1986a, p. 106).

Bibliotherapy

Another common method of practicing and reinforcing rational cognitions is a weekly assignment of bibliotherapy—reading books, listening to tapes, and viewing slides and film presentations outlining the essential principles of REBT (Ellis & Abrahms, 1978, p. 123).

Contradiction with a Cherished Value

The therapist introduces a dissonant situation for the client by demonstrating that a particular cognition is incongruent with a valued belief or quality (Crabb, 1971).

TH: You've stated that your word is your bond. Yet do you not keep a bond with yourself? It appears not when you go back on the promises you make to yourself.

Pragmatic Disputes

One way of encouraging clients to surrender their irrational beliefs is to indicate rather dramatically their continued adherence to one such belief (Dryden, 1984, p. 79).

TH: If you continue to behave in that way, you will be miserable for the rest of your life. So have a miserable forever!

Paradoxical Intention

Here the therapist prescribes the symptom and asks the client to practice it repeatedly or to exaggerate the problem (Nardi, 1986, p. 279). Specifically, this technique may be helpful with a resistant client with whom all else has failed. However, care must be taken in its use because of its caustic and regressive nature.

TH: I can see that the anger you feel toward her is the only thing that's keeping you going. I couldn't possibly ask you to give that up since it's so important. I really understand why you'd want to bring that emotion into therapy and try it out in here.

TH: Therefore, I'd suggest you reserve some time for it. Take an hour every morning just to harp and brood on that anger. It deserves at least that much quality time.

TH: Anger has served you well in your present marriage of twenty years. So if you really are getting a divorce, that's certainly something you need to take into your next marriage to keep it going.

Humor

Almost all neurotic resistance comes from taking things too seriously. One of the antidotes to irrational thinking is a strong dose of therapeutic humor (Ellis, 1986a, p. 34). Humor helps to clarify clients' self-defeating behavior in a nonthreatening manner and to show them the absurdity, realism, hilarity, and enjoyability of life (Ellis & Abrahms, 1978, pp. 145–149). Incredulous responses and irony are typical ways REBT therapists attempt to get clients to laugh at their irrationalities and thus take responsibility for them (Ellis, 1986d, p. 264).

TH: Uh-huh! That pecan pie jumps out of the refrigerator and demands that you devour it.

TH: That's right. It's all a plot. It's the Wall Street term paper trust. They've gobbled up every good idea and have all those term papers locked up in a big vault and will only sell them for your firstborn.

TH: I have this image of you in your coffin, dead from lung cancer, the undertaker nailing the lid shut, and you rising up and asking if he couldn't stop and everybody have a cigarette break.

Semantic Precision
Rational-emotive behavior therapists pay particular attention to the language their clients use because they believe language shapes thinking and vice versa. Therefore, the REBT therapist, following the principles of general semantics founded by Alfred Korzybski, assists clients in making the following changes in their language usage (Ellis & Abrahms, 1978, pp. 133–135).

1. Instead of using "must" or "should," clients learn to use "It would be preferable" or "It would be highly desirable."
2. Instead of using "I can't" or "It's impossible," clients learn to use "I can, but I find it difficult to do so" or "So far I haven't, but that doesn't prove it is impossible."
3. Instead of using "I always do badly," clients learn to use "I usually do badly, but that does not mean it is impossible to do better."
4. Instead of saying "It would be awful or terrible if . . . ," clients learn to use "It would be disadvantageous or inconvenient if. . . ."
5. Instead of stating, "I am a bad or worthless person because . . . ," clients learn to use "I cannot legitimately rate myself on the basis of my actions."

As a result of changing the language in their thinking process, clients think and behave differently. Consequently, they also feel differently.

Emotive Techniques

This second broad category of therapeutic techniques is termed *evocative-emotive* (Ellis & Abrahms, 1978). In REBT not too much time and energy are spent trying to get the client to express feelings or the emotions surrounding them. When a client does emote, it merely means there is some concrete idea behind each outburst. The problem then becomes to find out what it is (Ellis, 1989b, p. 229). Therefore, while not a great deal of emphasis is paid to affect, it is an integral component of REBT therapeutic techniques (Morris, 1989). Uncovering affect is important for two reasons. For some clients, identifying emotions and beliefs by verbal means is extremely difficult. Other clients may be able to identify their feelings and cognitions but have trouble anchoring them to events. When this occurs, the REBT therapist can use *vivid imagery* to generate images of activating events. Focusing on such images enables the client to anchor emotions with events and gain access to cognitions below the level of awareness that might not be reached by verbal methods (Dryden, 1984, p. 60).

Negative Imagery

Ellis believes dramatic intrusion into the aversive event is much more likely to influence clients' irrational ideas than slowly desensitizing them to it (Ellis, 1986a, p. 43). In negative imagery, clients are asked to imagine one of the worst things that could happen to them, intensely imagine themselves feeling their most feared inappropriate emotions, implode these feelings, and visualize themselves changing them to appropriate feelings, such as regret or determination (Ellis, 1986d, p. 270).

Stepping Out of Character

The client identifies ways of emoting or behaving that he or she would like to adopt but that involve stepping out of character to do so. Along with the thought of *risk taking* when he or she moves out of therapy and into the real world, the client imagines what it would be like if he or she were to act in opposition to present circumstances. Often, imagining how a significant other would act in the situation is used as a model (Dryden, 1984, pp. 34–35).

Future Imaging

Extreme anxiety is often generated by forecasting negative consequences about a future event and starting to live as if the catastrophic image were occurring in the present (Dryden, 1984, p. 60). The client is asked to imagine the feared situation as if it were happening in the present. As the image occurs, the therapist processes the anxiety and the irrationality that form the basis of the fear.

A converse approach may be applied when a client is having extreme distress with what is happening in the present. The client is asked to imagine what the event would appear to be in the distant future. Events viewed as terrible in the present usually take on a less dramatic hue when seen from a chronological distance (Dryden, 1984, p. 26).

Labeling

When clients continue to generalize and assign global ratings to themselves or others, they are asked to describe some of their behaviors, attitudes, talents, interests, and so on by writing them on sticky notes and pasting them all over their bodies. Clients can thus begin to see the futility of ascribing a generic label to themselves or to others (Wessler & Wessler, 1980; Young, 1986b).

Role Playing

This technique has both dramatic-emotive and behavioral components. Rational-emotive behavior therapists use role-playing techniques in which clients act out (behaviorally rehearse) their interactions with others in order to bring out their emotions. The therapist then uses the feelings that emerge to help clients work through their underlying irrational beliefs.

A variation of role playing is *rational role reversal.* Once the client has gained some sophistication with ABC theory, the therapist takes the role of a rather naive client with a problem much the same as the client's. The client then takes on the role of the therapist and actively disputes the therapist's beliefs. This procedure gives clients excellent practice in detecting, debating, defining, and, it is hoped, inoculating themselves against their irrationalities (Kassinove & DiGiuseppe, 1975).

Emotionally Charged Language

Rational-emotive behavior therapists often use emotionally toned words, phrases, and sentences that their clients can then use with themselves. Ellis suggests that strong language often has more impact and hence is more powerful in inducing clients to change their irrational beliefs (Dryden, 1984, p. 82).

TH: You should! You should shit! Particularly every time you start into thinking, "I should be cool, this date should be perfect, he's the only guy left, I'll never get married, I'll be an old maid in a rest home with the oatmeal drooling down my chin. I'm sooo alone and I'm sooo depressed! I shouldn't be like this and absolutely shouldn't end up like that!" Every time those mental billboards run through your head, you ought to give yourself a psychological enema, run right to the bathroom and flush that crap out.

CL: I don't know. The way you say that, it's really crude and vulgar.

TH: Maybe, but all those "shoulds," those absolute ways you evaluate each relationship are pretty shitty in what they do for you. In fact, I wonder if you might not interject, in big capital letters, the word "S-H-I-T" into those statements. If the word is really that distasteful, it may just make the "shoulds" pretty distasteful too!

Behavioral Techniques

This third broad category of therapeutic techniques may also be described as *behavioral-active-directive* (Ellis & Abrahms, 1978, pp. 102–123). Indeed, REBT draws on many techniques that behavior therapists employ, although its objectives are different in that it uses behavior modification and management as means to reinforce cognitive change rather than as ends in themselves.

Homework Assignments

One of the central REBT techniques is action-oriented homework assignments. Usually, a rational-emotive behavior therapist will assign something that the client fears or finds difficult to do. Rational-emotive behavior therapy is one of the first therapeutic modalities to use homework as an effective reinforcer. Homework helps ensure that what goes on in the safe haven of therapy is carried out and taken into the "dangerous" world of the client. Homework assignments are applied directly and forcefully to the problem rather than in incremental approximations, as in behavioral approaches. The reasoning is that many clients would see setting up an elaborate incremental plan as merely creating another problem, rather than solving the original problem (Young, 1986b, p. 117).

An example of homework that a therapist might assign is as follows. For a client who wants to make friends but is fearful of initiating conversations with fellow students, the therapist might assign the client to say hello to three students during the week and follow up the hello with a self-disclosing statement and an open-ended question, such as "I find history difficult and I don't understand the last chapter. How is it going for you?"

At the next session the therapist and client could discuss how the client fared. The client might report that one student replied, "I'm not taking history this term." The client then thought, "What a goof I am to make a mistake like this!" and consequently he responded by feeling inadequate and depressed. The therapist might ask what the client could say to himself instead of "I'm a goof." In response, the client might come up with a challenge something along these lines: "So what if I made a mistake. I'm human, aren't I? At least I spoke up and deserve credit for initiating a new behavior. The world certainly isn't going to collapse because that student wasn't in my history class!"

Flooding

Whereas homework may involve a series of graduated assignments that slowly increase in difficulty, it is more likely that clients will be asked to tackle problems head on. This philosophy of aggressive proactivity ranges throughout REBT techniques and comes from Ellis's belief that graduated approaches only confirm client fears that the assignment is too risky to attempt. Sudden, repeated, and maximum effort is much more effective, not only in desensitizing clients to the pain of taking action, but also in extinguishing ideas that they can't perform the behavior and that it will destroy them if they do (Ellis, 1984, p. xiii; Ellis, 1986c, p. 43). Therefore, no matter what excuses or rationalizations clients make about not doing the fearsome behavior, REBT pushes hard to convince them they can do it.

CL: Look, I'm telling you I'll come apart. I know what happens when I walk into a crowded room with all those classy people. I become so terrified I may even throw up.

TH: That's what you did before we rolled over all those belief rocks and those slimy little irrational musturbations came crawling out. Now you've got all kinds of new armor-plated self-statements to carry you through this. Even if you did puke in front of everybody it would only be embarrassing. The coroner does not check out people who vomit. You will not die! You will have the opportunity to enjoy the hell out of yourself, and maybe even have a chance to meet an attractive person. You can harp and brood about being the consummate social ass for the rest of your life or you can start enjoying yourself right now. So you choose!

Penalization

What Ellis has to say about punishment flies in the face of what most humane therapists and behavioral researchers might accept as a legitimate therapeutic procedure. However, the low frustration tolerance of Ellis's "tough customers" invariably prompts them to go for immediate reinforcement as opposed to long-term gains. Therefore, the counterpoint to immediate gratification is often immediate and drastic penalization of a repetition of the problem behavior (Ellis, 1986c, p. 42).

TH: Okay! If you chicken out of the reception at the Peabody Hotel that the Junior League is giving for Senator Phoghorn, I'd like to propose that you immediately avail yourself of getting a date with that guy you refer to as a casting reject from the

Hunchback of Notre Dame. You know, the guy that keeps asking you out, the one with the garlic breath and industrial-grade musk ox cologne. The one that really makes you want to throw up. How about making a little contract that you'll do that?

Skill Training

Rational-emotive behavior therapy advocates training in assertiveness, social skills, and other skills. The rationale is that if people can behave more effectively (at point A), there will be less of a tendency for them to formulate irrational sentences about their performances (at point B). However, the first step in client change is to dispute the irrational belief, which might be something like "I must communicate well or I am worthless." Rational-emotive therapy suggests that without prior disputing, a client's irrational belief may interfere with learning new skills. Therefore, skill training is limited when used alone because it does not include a basic change in irrational beliefs (Ellis, 1986c, p. 43).

Practicing and Reinforcing Positive Cognitions

Like cognitive behaviorists, practitioners of elegant REBT make extensive use of rational, positive, coping statements. The REBT Self-Help Form (Sichel & Ellis, 1983) is a paper-and-pencil version of what goes on in the disputational process in therapy. The generic rational beliefs presented previously in this chapter are listed with space for the client's own irrational beliefs. The client is asked to circle each irrational belief that applies to him or her and then write a disputational statement and a corresponding rational belief next to it. For example:

> *Irrational Belief*
> I must be approved or accepted by people I find important.
>
> *Disputes* (client statements)
> Why must I? And who is to say these people are more important than I am?
>
> *Effective Rational Beliefs* (client statements)
> While it would be grand if everyone thought I was great, that's not going to happen, particularly if I'm me. And if I am me and people like me, I'll know they really like me for what I really am and not for what I pretend to be. Further, I'm only anxious about this. It isn't dangerous. It's a bit uncomfortable right now, but risk in any new situation is distressing. The only thing I have to fear is fear itself, and right now I'm a lot more excited than scared about seeing that foxy guy over there.

These statements are not only written down but also may be audio- or video-taped for the client to use at home to "rewire" his or her cognitions. The client is then given the mission of building a complete menu of the disputational and positive coping statements to introject when irrational beliefs and their attendant behavior start to crop up. It is common in such assignments to have the client carry around three-by-five notecards with such statements written on them and murmur or silently repeat these positive coping statements as he or she engages in the threatening behavior (Dryden, 1984, pp. 30–34; Meichenbaum, 1977). (This procedure is examined in extensive detail in Chapter 11.)

SAMPLE CASE

Rafael Munoz, age twenty-one, is a senior finance major in college. He is a good-looking, well-built young man with jet black hair and coal black eyes. On first appearance, he could melt the heart of any woman, but as he speaks, a quite different story unfolds in this condensed therapeutic encounter.

CL: (*looking askance*) I'm embarrassed to talk about this problem. Nobody knows about it but me. Err . . . that's not quite right . . . some other people . . . women . . . they know about it. I feel . . . well . . . inadequate . . . if you know what I mean . . . and I thought . . . ah . . . maybe I could use some help.

TH: I understand how difficult it is to come to counseling, particularly when the problem is personal, but I wonder if you could just spell it out and for right now not worry about how embarrassing it might be.

While being accepting and empathic, the therapist immediately sets the REBT stage by asking the client to hook some self-statements (beliefs) into the problem.

CL: (*gazes off into the distance*) Well, okay. I've been pretty decent with women. Not any great playboy, but holding my own while playing the field. However, the last couple of women I've been close to, I really wanted a relationship, but when we'd get serious I'd start to get really uptight. Worst of all, this last girl, Maranda, is someone I really like a lot, I mean we've even thought about maybe marriage. But a month ago, we started making out, and one thing led to another and we finally got in bed, but . . . I . . . couldn't perform. I don't know if I'm gay or what. Went to the doctor but nothing's physically wrong. Maranda probably thinks I'm some kinda weirdo. We tried a couple more times, but nothing. Now all I can do is think about getting it up, but the more I think about it the more nervous I get. I keep telling myself, "You've got to get over this, there's nothing wrong and this is the woman of your dreams," but the more I think about it the worse it gets and I'm starting to think it'll go on forever and I'm nuts or something. Maranda will get sick of this, and then what? Who'd want some eunuch?

TH: So what you now believe is, "I'm a complete wimp, I know it, and pretty soon every woman in the universe will know it too and that would be absolutely intolerable." Indeed, just thinking about it makes you uptight. Notice how your belief about this one instance gets generalized to every other relationship.

CL: Maybe not a total wimp, but for sure sexually and you're right about the intolerable. I couldn't stand that.

The therapist, while listening to the client's description of the activating event (a sexual encounter) and consequences (nonperformance), is much more concerned about his beliefs (inadequate, laughed at, worrying about future events). The therapist continues to tap the client's beliefs about the event by finding out what negative self-talk he practices when in the "intolerable" situation.

TH: Rafael, for a moment lean back, shut your eyes, and imagine you're in bed with Maranda. What are you saying to yourself?

CL: (*shuts eyes and starts to squirm and fidget*) "Oh Mother of Mary. This can't be happening again. Come on, get with it. She's so foxy. Hell! You love this woman. You've got to cut it now. Get hold of yourself, but I can't! Man, if I can't make it with her, I'll never do it. I've gotta get outta here. Look at how I'm shaking and in a cold sweat. How can this be happening?"

By setting the client in the event, the therapist now has several insane statements that the client uses to pursue his irrational beliefs and the bad consequences that issue from those beliefs. The "can'ts," "got tos," and "nevers" are all absolutistic evaluations and inferences that the therapist seeks to counter-propagandize by first showing the client what these musturbatory thoughts do to him. He does this by using warm cognitions and nonabsolutistic inferences through an analogy using the client's favorite pastime, soccer.

TH: You said you play on the soccer team. Let me make an analogy to that. Let me propose what you might say if you performed poorly and missed an easy shot. You'd probably say, "Hell, I blew that snap shot on goal. Man, I've got to get another shot." You'd feel disappointed and maybe even a bit angry and embarrassed, but you surely wouldn't say, "Because I missed this shot, I'll *never* make another." "Because I can't perform in this situation, I can't perform in any other." But that's what I hear you saying about your relationship with Maranda.

CL: That's true enough. So why is this bugging me?

TH: I'm also saying your so-called "failure" is not your real problem. It is more what you're saying to yourself and have probably been saying for a while, even before you had sexual performance anxiety. It would also appear that as you get closer and closer to really thinking about an enduring relationship now that you're about finished with school, there's anxiety about all the responsibility concerned with that. Since you can't even handle a little sex, how can you handle all the other responsibilities of a relationship? So at the least I hear these kinds of billboards flashing through your head:

1. I am a worthless person when I don't do very well (at sex) and I must be thoroughly competent and adequate.
2. My miserable feelings come from external pressures (pretty women who want to get married), and I have little ability to control my feelings (panic).
3. Because this is so fearsome, all my time has to be spent thinking about it (being potent).
4. Things (relationships) are awful and catastrophic when I get seriously frustrated (at the prospect of assuming responsibility).

The therapist uses some interpretation to propose what the client's deep, philosophical beliefs about responsibility are and how they are entangled in the problem. He then proposes the major irrationalities that drive the client into hot inferences and evaluations. This lengthy discourse is typical of the psychoeducational approach used by REBT to reprogram client thinking.

CL: I think you're right about all that performance and responsibility stuff. That sure goes through my head and I get sick thinking about both those things, but . . . I don't know, it really is awesome. I don't know if I can handle it. Doesn't make me feel like much of a man, I can tell you.

TH: You like sex? It makes you feel good?

CL: Sure. It's . . . er . . . was great.

TH: So you get pleasure from it. You like soccer too. It makes you feel good, a real man, right?

CL: Well, sure.

TH: If you blew your knee out and couldn't play any more, then what?

CL: I'd hate it. I love that game.

TH: Would you be a eunuch? Not a real man?

CL: Of course not. I mean I'd miss it, but lots of guys don't play soccer.

TH: Why then would you think yourself more inadequate if one satisfaction is taken away as opposed to another? Do you see how that self-value is generated in your head? Even if your condition of impotence were permanent—which it is not—all that would have happened is that you would be without one major satisfaction in your life. It would sure not be fun and it would certainly be a bummer, but you would be no less of a man. I mean, would you go into the women's locker room to change?

CL: (*Laughs*) That's really crazy, of course not.

TH: So you see how in the one instance a particular disappointment allows you to talk yourself into being crazy—"not a man"—while another disappointment would not.

CL: When you put it that way it makes sense, but the bigger thing you said, the relationship stuff—I don't know if I could handle that responsibility.

TH: Who told you you can't? Where is it written that Rafael is inadequate to the task of handling a meaningful relationship? Have you a crystal ball that allows you to predict the future?

The therapist directively confronts the client by engaging him in a Socratic dialogue. The client is asked to query himself as to the evidence of these irrational beliefs, for which, of course, there is none. A technique from Young (1986c, p. 154) is used that compares favorite satisfactions and asks the client to equate them to his overall self-worth. The foregoing is typical of what Young (1986c, p. 151) calls "Less Me" thinking, wherein clients believe they have some kind of inborn or built-in value, and that disappointment in the form of failure or disapproval somehow lessens that value.

CL: Well, no. I guess there isn't any real proof that I couldn't, but frankly what am I going to do about making love?

TH: Forget about the event, the sex, and concentrate on replacing all those "shoulds" and "oughts" with some sentences such as "It would be nice if we made love, but who I am sure as hell is not contingent on my being a stud. Maranda liked me before we ever tried to go to bed, so there's some little bit of me that she finds attractive. Nobody is making me do this, so if I don't really feel like making love that's just fine. It is something that I prefer to do. This is a superfine woman I'm with and she feels the same about me, and I really feel good and enjoy being with her.

By replacing the negative, self-defeating thoughts with positive, enhancing ones, the therapist promotes a way to change beliefs and subsequent maladaptive behavior. The therapist does this by replacing hot demand statements with cooler preferential statements.

CL: That all sounds fine, the power of positive thinking and all, but I don't know if I've even got the courage to face her again.

TH: You're probably right. She's probably too good for you. I wouldn't want you to have to go through that trauma. I'd propose you lower your sights on the kind of a girl you really want. That way you wouldn't have to feel so inept.

CL: Now wait, I didn't mean that. I'd just kinda like to ease back into this.

TH: If you do that, then you only give yourself more time to harp and brood and anxious yourself. By backing away from the problem you continue anxiousing yourself, which feeds into your insane ideas about what this is all about and just piles more insane thoughts onto what the wretched consequences are for you. Picture yourself as a Dagwood Bumstead sandwich, with all those beliefs packed in there, and see if you don't have some gastric distress as you keep trying to eat it.

When the client backs away from dealing with the problem, the therapist uses a bit of paradox and humor to call into question the behavior of what the client really wants. Further, the therapist uses *anxious* as a verb to demonstrate to the client that his thinking, and not a crippled libido or an exceptional woman, makes him suffer these behavioral outcomes.

TH: I am going to propose a homework assignment to you, but first I want to tape a session with you in the situation where you use all those killer statements. Then we'll shift and replace them with positive, coping thoughts. For example, "Because I didn't respond as I liked once, it doesn't necessarily mean I never will. Just because getting into a deep relationship seems scary doesn't mean it will be life-threatening. There is absolutely no evidence at all to substantiate that notion." (*turns the recorder on, relaxes the client, and then floods him with the aversive thoughts, feelings, and behaviors of the situation; sets the image up to confirm the client's worst nightmare about the event in the most noxious manner, plugging in what the client says to himself and also what he believes Maranda might be saying to herself about him*)

CL: Whew! Talk about going through a wringer. But I can see how I get myself into that state, and it really pisses me off.

TH: Well if it really pisses you off, then are you willing to use some of that angry energy to try plugging in some of those coping thoughts?

CL: All right. I'll give it a go.

The therapist now builds and enhances the coping statements as the tape is made, hammering relentlessly at each irrational statement the client makes and putting a new positive statement in its place.

TH: Indeed, now that we've got that down on tape, I want you to go home and listen to it every day for a week. Then I want you to take what you've learned and try it out on a date with Maranda.

This brief excerpt demonstrates two components of REBT. First, general REBT is used to deal with the problem—overcoming sexual impotence. Second, elegant REBT seeks to change the client's beliefs about the far deeper problem of assuming responsibility in a relationship. This second problem, if successfully resolved, will mean the client attains not only a behavioral change but a philosophical change as well, one that will have meaning across and throughout his life.

CONTRIBUTIONS OF RATIONAL-EMOTIVE BEHAVIOR THERAPY

Rational-emotive behavior therapy has made a number of valuable contributions to the helping professions. One of its most valuable contributions is that it has emphasized, as well as clarified, the relationship between human thinking and emotion. It is abundantly clear that an effective way to approach changing one's emotions is to change the content of one's thinking.

Another contribution of REBT is its comprehensive, eclectic approach to treatment that includes cognitive, behavioral, and emotive components. Thus, REBT maintains an openness about using workable approaches to treatment that are adapted from other schools of psychotherapy. In addition, REBT principles have contributed to the development of some important therapeutic innovations. For example, REBT's cognitive emotive imagery is one of the foundations of modern cognitive-behavior therapy.

A third contribution of REBT is its emphasis not on past events or traumas themselves as creating human disturbances but on one's interpretation of them. Ellis, with his ABC theory, has clearly delineated how this process might occur and how it can be changed. Thus REBT has reinforced the concept that the therapist needs to focus on clients' internal processes rather than on the situation itself in searching for the roots of clients' problems.

Another strong point of REBT is its emphasis on action-oriented homework. When clients actually behave in new and different ways, it is much more likely that therapeutic change will occur and be maintained through the formation of new behavioral patterns.

Also, REBT has made a valuable contribution by delineating the common irrational beliefs that form the basis of emotional disturbances as well as challenges to those beliefs. Whether REBT proponents or not, therapists often use these beliefs in targeting some of their clients' basic problems. What therapist has not seen clients who suffer from an inordinate desire for others' approval or who are perfectionists who blame themselves for every minor imperfection?

Another valuable aspect of REBT is its educational, preventive, "democratic" stance toward treatment. Rational-emotive behavior therapy does not insist that the therapist be the "keeper of secret knowledge" but instead advocates that people can learn and change through a variety of means, including impersonal methods such as tape recordings, films, and lectures. Rational-emotive behavior therapy proponents also favor a preventive approach as well as a remedial approach, and hence are adapting REBT principles so that they may be applied to other settings, such as the classroom.

SHORTCOMINGS OF RATIONAL-EMOTIVE BEHAVIOR THERAPY

One possible shortcoming of REBT is its de-emphasis of the therapeutic relationship as well as the therapeutic conditions of empathy and therapist–client rapport. Ellis claims that therapeutic change may occur even when the client actively dislikes the therapist. If a client feels "not understood," "not listened to," or "not cared about," it is quite possible that he or she may terminate therapy before obtaining the benefits of the REBT approach.

A related concern is REBT proponents' suggestion that it is desirable to confront clients immediately with their irrational thinking and to make interpretations in the initial sessions, despite client defensiveness. However, client readiness to listen and respond to what the therapist is trying to communicate is a critical factor.

Another limitation is the belief that it is effective for the therapist to talk, persuade, and be highly active during the initial as well as later therapeutic sessions. One danger of this approach is prematurely defining and hence "misdefining" or limiting the problem. Once the problem is erroneously defined, the therapist may convince the client that this off-target definition is indeed the root of the problem.

A possible limitation of REBT is its almost total emphasis on changing emotion by changing one's thinking to a more rational perspective. As Hendricks (1977) and other Gestalt therapists suggest, in some cases the most effective way to change emotion is by letting oneself completely experience the emotion rather than trying to block the expression of it. Sometimes more energy is expended trying to change or block the feeling, as in the case of experiencing grief, than simply letting oneself fully experience and "work through," rather than "against," the feeling.

Also, as Corey (1982, p. 812) points out, "because the REBT therapist has a large degree of power by virtue of persuasiveness and directiveness, psychological harm is more possible in REBT than in the less directive client-centered approach." Thus, it is crucial that the REBT therapist be sensitive and knowledgeable in the application of REBT techniques so as to avoid misusing REBT to browbeat clients into confused and angry individuals who feel misunderstood, frustrated, and powerless. Another possible danger is that clients may accede to the therapist's authority without really internalizing the belief system necessary for change to occur.

Although REBT may at first glance seem as simple as the *ABCs*, it is not. No theory we teach gives students a harder time when they attempt to put it into practice, with the possible exception of cognitive behaviorism, REBT's therapeutic stepchild. The reason is twofold. First, digging out belief systems is not a simple matter. The deductive form of reasoning that REBT calls for requires the ability to grasp the basic premises of the client's syllogisms (Cohen, 1987). Doing so is long, tough detective work, and time and again neophytes get tangled in the activating event or the consequences without ever nailing down the belief.

Finally, Franks (1995) questions whether Ellis's insertion of "behavior" in the theory name is valid because REBT has not consistently employed the data-before-the-fact approach that is the iron-clad rule of behavior therapy. When concrete behavioral data are not obtained before intervention, it is difficult to tell exactly what has happened, particularly when client self-report under the commanding presence of a powerful and directive REBT therapist is open to question.

RATIONAL-EMOTIVE BEHAVIOR THERAPY WITH DIVERSE POPULATIONS

Human beings are reared in social groups and spend much of their lives trying to impress, live up to the expectations of, and outdo the performances of others. Emotional disturbance is frequently associated with people caring too much about what others think and stems from their believing they can accept themselves only if others think well of them. Thus, cultural as well as family influences tend to play a significant part in bolstering people's irrational thinking (Ellis, 1989b, pp. 206–209).

As a result, REBT therapists have not shied away from diverse populations, or what Ellis has sometimes called "tough customers." Rational-emotive behavior therapy is an excellent therapeutic vehicle for incarcerated individuals who typically have had little positive guidance in the development of their belief system or little awareness that their thinking may play a substantive part in what negative behavioral outcomes occur for them. Rational-emotive behavior therapy is further appropriate because of its no-nonsense view and straightforward teaching approach, which has a good deal of appeal and makes a lot of sense to inmates who, for the first time in their lives, start to get a notion about how their thinking gets them in trouble. It also can show them how to stay out of jail if they choose to think differently. The emphasis on forming partnerships between therapist and client to isolate and crucify bad behavior, as opposed to crucifying the "bad person," has great appeal to prisoners, because for many of them the "bad person" message has been driven home since childhood.

Young's (1986a; 1986b; 1986c) work probably best depicts the REBT view of working with many diverse populations. However, the philosophy and treatment techniques Young proposes in his articles on lower-class clients, bible-belt Christians, and other tough customers are likely to raise the hackles on a variety of therapists ranging from the very liberal to the archconservative. Young makes no pretense on who is the boss and who is responsible for blowing away irrational beliefs. Put bluntly, the role of the therapist is that of a manipulator who uses the interpersonal relationship to maneuver the client to act in positive and beneficial ways.

Young's philosophy and descriptions of command and friendship power would likely horrify "client-centered" therapists. His view is that lower socioeconomic class clients expect the therapist to be an authority, provide expert advice, teach them what they need to know, and be sure of themselves while doing so. Such clients have little use for an egalitarian, self-actualized, client-centered relationship and would be uneasy with and probably view such a therapeutic approach as a sign of weakness on the therapist's part (Young, 1986b, pp. 88–89).

His command power suggestions range from conspicuously displaying diplomas and mentioning accomplishments such as articles written and working radio call-in shows to using a loud voice and definitive gestures such as finger pointing and fist clenching to make a point and assume a commanding presence (Young, 1986b, pp. 88–89). Some of his friendship power suggestions are probably even more controversial. Young believes flattery in regard to client personal attributes and preferences such as complimenting hair style, automobiles, clothes, and so on is a powerful tool in establishing interpersonal power. Further, he proposes that the most effective form of flattery is to make comparisons between the client and the therapist both in regard to accomplishing difficult tasks and, sometimes, in becoming upset and failing to solve similar problems. Finally, he may unabashedly tell clients he has enjoyed the session with them or really respects the way they have handled their problems (Young, 1986b, pp. 94–95).

On first glance, Young's approach may seem outrageous in its condescending view of clients and portrayal of effete therapists willfully manipulating disadvantaged clients like so many sheep to a psychological shearing pen. However, Young takes great pains to differentiate between authoritarian and authoritative roles. His emphasis on acknowledgment and empathy for the environmental constraints and cultural barriers that may militate against the success of lower socioeconomic class clients goes far in establishing trust and an empathic relationship. Likewise, REBT's ability to tolerate value differences in child rearing, religiosity, marital relationships, and work attitudes without subtly attaching biases and negative evaluations to values different from the therapist's enhances the therapist's credibility with such clients. Under no circumstances does the therapist assume a godlike image or start to feel omnipotent. The therapist's role is to maintain a strong position of leadership while at the same time remaining empathic and responsive to client needs (Young, 1986b, pp. 89–92). Like it or not, believe it or not, our own work in conducting groups of chemically dependent prison inmates and adolescents with behavioral problems and child-rearing classes for lower socioeconomic parents convinces us there is more than a grain of therapeutic truth in what Young is saying.

From the perspective of many Asian clients, the logical thinking, cognition as the origin of emotion, therapist as teacher, paternalism, and expertness of the therapist that are characteristic of REBT have much to recommend it and seem effective when applied with such populations (Chen, 1995; Waxer, 1989; Yang, 1992).

For gays and lesbians, Mylott (1994) believes that REBT is effective in dealing with their irrational beliefs about such issues as love, rejection, growing old alone, approval, sexuality, and issues surrounding AIDS.

From a feminist perspective, REBT is a nonexclusive theory and is a powerful therapeutic tool to depropagandize and dispute many stereotypes that female clients may believe (Shibles, 1991). Wolfe's (1995) twenty-year review of REBT women's groups provides strong evidence of its utility with females in providing powerful corrective socialization experiences and dealing with dependency, power, and risk-taking issues.

The awfulizing thinking engaged in by clients who have experienced a profoundly disabling physical condition is ideally suited for REBT (Gandy, 1995; Kelly, 1992; Sweetland, 1990). For example, while certainly a noxious event by any standard, a disabling condition such as becoming a parapalegic is not catastrophic to the extent that the individual's life is completely hopeless and useless because the person can no longer walk (Ostby, 1985). Rather, such emotions as frustration, anger, depression, and the host of other negative feelings attributed to the disability psychologically paralyze the individual even more than his or her physical immobility.

To one observing physically disabled persons mired in the debilitating cognitive and emotional phases of their adjustment to their disabling condition, the educative and confrontational techniques of REBT may on first view seem somewhat cruel and unnecessarily punitive. By demonstrating in an active and directive way how such self-defeating ideas and verbalizations are exaggerated and generalized, the therapist does not allow the client to sink further into self-deprecating talk, disparaging thinking, or despairing behavior. Rational-emotive behavior therapy pushes physically disabled clients to modify their environments, accept limitations when existing circumstances cannot be altered, and set short-term goals to compensate for social, vocational, educational, and sexual deficits (Ostby, 1985). Rational-emotive behavior therapists actively engage clients in homework assignments to reduce passivity, extinguish negative thoughts about the disability, and increase motivation to overcome obstacles and succeed at reentering the world of functional and effective living and enter the final psychological phases of acknowledgment and adjustment (Livneh & Sherwood, 1991).

SUMMARY

Rational-emotive behavior therapy advocates the application of cognitive, behavioral, and emotive approaches to treatment. Because REBT places more emphasis on cognitive and behavioral techniques, it is most often classified as a cognitive-behavioral approach to therapy. It is geared toward the use of logic and the scientific method, but it also emphasizes human values such as growth and happiness. Hence, it is humanistically as well as empirically oriented.

Rational-emotive behavior therapy theory contends that people are born with the predisposition to think distortedly and irrationally but also with the ability to reason and thus are able to transcend some of their own limitations. However, even the most rational of persons are subject to emotional overload that takes the form of hot cognitions about events. Combined with low frustration tolerance and the desire to avoid immediate discomfort at the expense of long-term gain, humans engage in crooked, illogical thinking and become emotionally disturbed.

Rational-emotive therapy theory suggests that emotional disturbance may be explained by the ABC theory. This theory states that when an unpleasant event (activating event) occurs at point *A*, an individual may react in two ways. One is to conclude, at point *B*, that this event is unfortunate and disadvantageous (a rational belief) and therefore have at point *C* (the consequence) an appropriate feeling, such as regret or annoyance. These appropriate feelings stimulate the person to do something to change the unpleasant situation. However, individuals often react to unpleasant situations in a different manner: they may conclude at point *B* that circumstances are terrible or even catastrophic and therefore should not exist (an irrational belief). As a result, at point *C* they inappropriately feel depression, anxiety, rage, or lethargy. Such feelings, instead of facilitating constructive action, often interfere with problem-solving behavior.

The main goal of REBT is to teach clients how to detect the irrational beliefs that underlie their emotional disturbance and how to dispute these beliefs, replacing them with beliefs constituting a "more rational philosophy of life." This detecting and disputing of irrational beliefs is typically done by the therapist in a very active, directive, confrontive, and didactic manner. Effective psychotherapy has two distinct parts (Ellis & Abrahms, 1978). The first and more basic part disputes irrational beliefs. The second part encourages and teaches clients how to fulfill and enjoy themselves more by helping them to find "vitally absorbing" interests aimed at long-range personality change for self-fulfillment (p. 174).

In conclusion, Ellis has observed that REBT is a psychotherapy "uniquely designed to enable the individual to observe, to understand, and to persistently attack irrational, grandiose, perfectionistic *shoulds, oughts,* and *musts*" (1979a, p. 226). As a consequence of disputing (at point *D*) their own irrational beliefs, clients initially experience new, more appropriate cognitive effects and then new, more appropriate emotional effects (at point *E*). Thus, the outcome of therapy is the acquisition of a new, more logical, and scientific approach to life so that clients learn not only to think, feel, and act differently toward their current unpleasant circumstances but also to apply these principles to other new and different situations that may occur in the future.

SUGGESTIONS FOR FURTHER READING

Dryden, W. (1984). *Rational-emotive therapy: Fundamentals and innovations.* London: Croom Helm.

Dryden, W., & Trower, P. (Eds.). (1986). *Rational-emotive therapy: Recent developments in theory and practice.* Bristol, England: Institute for RET.

Ellis, A., & Abrahms, E. (1978). *Brief psychotherapy in medical and health practice.* New York: Springer.

Ellis, A., & Grieger, R. (Eds.). (1977). *Handbook of rational-emotive therapy* (Vol. 1). New York: Springer.

Ellis, A., & Grieger, R. (Eds.). (1986). *Handbook of rational-emotive therapy* (Vol. 2). New York: Springer.

Ellis, A., & Harper, R. A. (1979). *A new guide to rational living* (rev. ed.). Englewood Cliffs, NJ: Prentice-Hall; Hollywood, CA: Wilshire Books.

REFERENCES

Chen, C. P. (1995). *Journal of Rational Emotive and Cognitive Behavior Therapy, 13*(2), 117–129.

Cohen, E. D. (1987). The use of syllogism in rational-emotive therapy. *Journal of Counseling and Development, 66,* 37–39.

Corey, G. (1982). *Theory and practice of counseling and psychotherapy* (2nd ed). Monterey, CA: Brooks/Cole.

Crabb, L. J. (1971). *Sensible psychotherapy.* Manuscript, University of Illinois, Champaign-Urbana.

DiGiuseppe, R. A., & Muran, J. C. (1992). The use of metaphor in rational-emotive therapy. *Psychotherapy in Private Practice, 10,* (1–2), 151–165.

Dryden, W. (1984). *Rational-emotive therapy: Fundamentals and innovations.* London: Croom Helm.

Dryden, W. (1994). Reason and emotion in psychotherapy: Thirty years on. *Journal of Rational Emotive and Cognitive Behavior Therapy, 12*(2), 83–89.

Ellis, A. (1949). Towards the improvement of psychoanalytic research. *Psychoanalytic Review, 36,* 123–143.

Ellis, A. (1950). *An introduction to the scientific principles of psychoanalysis.* Provincetown, MA: Journal Press.

Ellis, A. (1956). An operational reformulation of some of the basic principles of psychoanalysis. *Psychoanalytic Review, 43,* 163–180.

Ellis, A. (1958). Rational psychotherapy. *Journal of General Psychology, 59,* 35–49.

Ellis, A. (1962). *Reason and emotion in psychotherapy.* Secaucus, NJ: Lyle Stuart.

Ellis, A. (1970). Humanism, values, rationality. *Journal of Individual Psychology, 26,* 37–38.

Ellis, A. (1971). *Growth through reason.* Palo Alto, CA: Science and Behavior Books; Hollywood, CA: Wilshire Books.

Ellis, A. (1973). *Humanistic psychotherapy: The rational-emotive approach.* New York: Crown.

Ellis, A. (1976a). The biological basis of human irrationality. *Journal of Individual Psychology, 32,* 143–168.

Ellis, A. (1976b). Techniques of handling anger in marriage. *Journal of Marriage and Family Counseling, 2,* 305–315.

Ellis, A. (1977). The basic clinical theory of rational-emotive therapy. In A. Ellis & R. Grieger (Eds.), *Handbook of rational-emotive therapy* (Vol. 1, pp. 185–202). New York: Springer.

Ellis, A. (1979a). Rational-emotive therapy. In R. Corsini (Ed.), *Current psychotherapies* (2nd ed., pp. 185–229). Itasca, IL: F. E. Peacock.

Ellis, A. (1979b). The theory of rational-emotive therapy. In A. Ellis & J. M. Whiteley (Eds.), *Theoretical and empirical foundations of rational-emotive therapy* (pp. 1–27). Monterey, CA: Brooks/Cole.

Ellis, A. (1984). Foreword. In W. Dryden, *Rational-emotive therapy: Fundamentals and innovations* (pp. i–xv). London: Croom Helm.

Ellis, A. (1986a). Discomfort anxiety: A new cognitive behavioral construct. In A. Ellis & R. Grieger (Eds.), *Handbook of rational-emotive therapy* (Vol. 2, pp. 105–120). New York: Springer.

Ellis, A. (1986b). Fanaticism that may lead to a nuclear holocaust. *Journal of Counseling and Development, 65,* 146–150.

Ellis, A. (1986c). Rational-emotive therapy and cognitive behavior therapy: Similarities and differences. In A. Ellis & R. Grieger (Eds.), *Handbook of rational-emotive therapy* (Vol. 2, pp. 131–135). New York: Springer.

Ellis, A. (1986d). Rational-emotive therapy approach to overcoming resistance. In A. Ellis & R. Grieger (Eds.), *Handbook of rational-emotive therapy* (Vol. 2, pp. 246–274). New York: Springer.

Ellis, A. (1989a). Dangers of transpersonal psychology: A reply to Ken Wilber. *Journal of Counseling and Development, 67,* 336–337.

Ellis, A. (1989b). Rational-emotive therapy. In R. J. Corsini & D. Wedding (Eds.), *Current psychotherapies* (4th ed., pp. 197–238). Itasca, IL: F. E. Peacock.

Ellis, A. (1990). Is rational-emotive therapy "rationalist" or "constructivist?" *Journal of Rational-Emotive and Cognitive Behavior Therapy, 8,* 169–193.

Ellis, A. (1991a). Achieving self-actualization: The rational-emotive approach. *Journal of Social Behavior and Personality, 6,* 1–18.

Ellis, A. (1991b). The philosophical basis of rational-emotive therapy. *Psychotherapy in Private Practice, 8,* 97–106.

Ellis, A. (1992). Secular humanism and rational emotive therapy. *Humanistic Psychologist, 20*(2–3), 349–358.

Ellis, A. (1995). Changing rational-emotive therapy (RET) to rational emotive behavior therapy (REBT). *Journal of Rational Emotive and Cognitive Behavior Therapy, 13*(2), 85–89.

Ellis, A., & Abrahms, E. (1978). *Brief psychotherapy in medical and health practice.* New York: Springer.

Ellis, A., & Bernard, M. E. (1986). What is rational-emotive therapy (RET). In A. Ellis & R. Grieger (Eds.), *Handbook of rational-emotive therapy* (Vol. 2, pp. 3–31). New York: Springer.

Ellis, A., & Grieger, R. (Eds.). (1977). *Handbook of rational-emotive therapy* (Vol. 1.). New York: Springer.

Ellis, A., & Harper, R. A. (1979). *A new guide to rational living* (rev. ed.). Englewood Cliffs, NJ: Prentice-Hall; Hollywood, CA: Wilshire Books.

Engels, G. I., Garnefski, N., & Diekstra, R. F. (1993). Efficacy of rational-emotive therapy. *Journal of Consulting and Clinical Psychology, 61,* 1083–1090.

Franks, C. M. (1995). RET, REBT, and Albert Ellis. *Journal of Rational Emotive and Cognitive Behavior Therapy, 13*(2), 91–95.

Gandy, G. L. (1995). Disputing irrational beliefs in rehabilitation counseling. *Journal of Applied Rehabilitation Counseling 26*(1), 36–40.

Garfield, S. L. (1995). The client–therapist relationship in rational-emotive therapy. *Journal of Rational Emotive and Cognitive Behavior Therapy, 13,* (2), 101–116.

Grieger, R. M. (1986). The process of rational-emotive therapy. In A. Ellis & R. Grieger (Eds.), *Handbook of rational-emotive therapy* (Vol. 2, pp. 203–212). New York: Springer.

Hendricks, G. (1977). What do I do after they tell me how they feel? *Personnel and Guidance Journal, 55,* 249–252.

Kassinove, H., & DiGiuseppe, R. (1975). Rational role reversal. *Rational Living, 10,* 44–45.

Keegan, A. (1989, February). A Guidepost interview: Albert Ellis: On psychotherapy, psychology, and science. *Guidepost, 31,* 1, 4.

Kelly, L. J. (1992). Rational emotive therapy and aural rehabilitation. *Journal of the Academy of Rehabilitative Audiology, 25,* 43–50.

Livneh, H., & Sherwood, A. (1991). Application of personality theories and counseling strategies to clients with physical disabilities. *Journal of Counseling and Development, 69,* 525–538.

Lyons, L. C., & Woods, P. J. (1991). The efficacy of rational-emotive therapy: A quantitative review of the outcome research. *Clinical Psychology Review, 11*(4), 357–369.

Meichenbaum, D. (1977). *Cognitive-behavior modification: An integrative approach.* New York: Plenum.

Moore, R. H. (1986). Inference as "A" in rational-emotive therapy. In W. Dryden and P. Trower (Eds.), *Rational-emotive therapy: Recent developments in theory and practice* (pp. 2–12). Bristol, England: Institute for RET.

Morris, G. B. (1989). Affect, Albert Ellis, and rational-emotive therapy. *Canadian Journal of Counselling, 23,* 252–262.

Mylott, K. (1994). Twelve irrational ideas that drive gay men and women crazy. *Journal of Rational Emotive and Cognitive Behavior Therapy, 12*(1), 61–71.

Nardi, T. J. (1986). The use of psychodrama in REBT. In A. Ellis & R. Grieger (Eds.), *Handbook of rational-emotive therapy* (Vol. 2, pp. 275–280). New York: Springer.

Ostby, S. S. (1985). A rational-emotive perspective. *Journal of Applied Rehabilitation Counseling, 16,* 30–33.

Shibles, W. (1991). Feminism and the cognitive theory of emotion: Anger, blame and humor. *Women and Health, 17,* 57–69.

Sichel, J., & Ellis, A. (1983). *RET self-help form.* New York: Institute for Rational Living.

Silverman, M. S., McCarthy, M., McGovern, T. (1992). A review of outcome studies of rational-emotive therapy. *Journal of Rational Emotive and Cognitive Behavior Therapy, 10*(3), 111–186.

Sweetland, J. D. (1990). Cognitive behavior therapy and physical disability. *Journal of Rational Emotive and Cognitive Behavior Therapy, 8*(2), 71–78.

Walen, S., DiGiuseppe, R., & Wessler, R. L. (1980). *A practitioner's guide to rational-emotive therapy.* New York: Oxford University Press.

Walsh, R. (1989). Psychological chauvinism and nuclear holocaust: A response to Albert Ellis and defense of non-rational therapies. *Journal of Counseling and Development, 67,* 338–340.

Waxer, P. H. (1989). Cantonese versus Canadian evaluation of directive and non-directive counseling. *Canadian Journal of Counseling, 23,* 263–272.

Wessler, R. A. (1986). Value judgments and self-evaluation in rational-emotive therapy. In W. Dryden and P. Trower (Eds.), *Rational-emotive therapy: Recent developments in theory and practice* (pp. 12–23). Bristol, England: Institute for RET.

Wessler, R. A., & Wessler, R. L. (1980). *The principles and practice of rational-emotive therapy.* San Francisco: Jossey-Bass.

Wilber, K. (1989). Let's nuke the transpersonalists: A response to Albert Ellis. *Journal of Counseling and Development, 67,* 332–335.

Wolfe, J. L. (1995). Rational emotive behavior therapy women's groups: A twenty year perspective. *Journal of Rational Emotive and Cognitive Behavior Therapy, 13*(3) 153–170.

Yang, R. (1992). Rational emotive group therapy applied to sense of inferiority among university students. *Chinese Mental Health Journal, 6*(2), 74–76, 83.

Young, H. S. (1986a). Practicing RET with bible-belt Christians. In W. Dryden and P. Trower (Eds.), *Rational-emotive therapy: Recent developments in theory and practice* (pp. 122–142). Bristol, England: Institute for RET.

Young, H. S. (1986b). Practicing RET with lower-class clients. In W. Dryden and P. Trower (Eds.), *Rational-emotive therapy: Recent developments in theory and practice* (pp. 85–121). Bristol, England: Institute for RET.

Young, H. S. (1986c). Teaching rational self-value concepts to tough customers. In W. Dryden and P. Trower (Eds.), *Rational-emotive therapy: Recent developments in theory and practice* (pp. 143–170). Bristol, England: Institute for RET.

Zajonc, R. B. (1980). Feeling and thinking: Preferences need no inferences. *American Psychologist, 35,* 151–175.

10

CONTROL THEORY/REALITY THERAPY

FUNDAMENTAL TENETS

History

Doubts about the traditional psychoanalytic approach led William Glasser, under the tutelage of G. L. Harrington, to start formulating his ideas about reality therapy while completing his psychiatric residency at the University of California, Los Angeles, in 1956. Reality therapy first gained recognition for its positive therapeutic outcomes through Harrington's use of it with chronic psychotics and Glasser's use of it with delinquent adolescent girls (Glasser & Zunin, 1979, p. 309). Glasser's first book, *Mental Health or Mental Illness?* (1961), spelled out the basic tenets and application of reality therapy. The term *reality therapy* was coined in 1964 (Glasser, 1964) and resulted in the formal presentation of the approach in a book of the same name (Glasser, 1965). The book, while refining the theory and practice of the approach, also attempted to refute the basic concepts of conventional therapy and to promote a system of teaching clients how to fulfill their needs in responsible ways without the stigma of mental illness.

Following publication of *Schools without Failure* (Glasser, 1969), reality therapy's approach received an enormous amount of acceptance in school systems. The recognition and success in schools led to the establishment by Glasser's Institute for Reality Therapy of the Education Training Center (ETC) and the William Glasser LaVerne College Center, both with the purpose of eliminating academic failure and both in Los Angeles. For several years the Los Angeles–based Institute for Reality published the *Journal of Reality Therapy*. Even though the journal is no longer published, it provided a comprehensive repertoire of training programs for a diversity of human services workers in addition to its strong emphasis on schools. Glasser has continued to focus on school improvement as evidenced by his books *Control Theory in the Classroom* (1986) and *The Quality School: Managing Students without Coercion* (1990b).

With the publication of *Stations of the Mind* (Glasser, 1981) reality therapy took a new turn. Glasser launched an in-depth examination of personality called

Behavior: The Control of Perception Psychology (BCP). The basic premise of this theory is that the brain operates to gain the perception of what is wanted from the environment. To express this idea another way, people control what they perceive, not what actually exists. Building on the theory presented in *Stations of the Mind,* Glasser wrote *Taking Effective Control of Your Life* (1984), published subsequently as *Control Theory: A New Explanation of How We Control Our Lives* (1984). The advent of the publication of *Control Theory* signaled a conceptual expansion of reality therapy that eventually led to the approach's becoming "control theory/reality therapy," "control theory" for short, and the Institute for Reality Therapy being changed to The Institute for, Control Theory, Reality Therapy, and Quality Management. *Staying Together* (Glasser, 1996) not only focused the power of control theory on keeping marriages healthy, it also emphasized the overarching axiom for all human endeavors: "The only person we can control is ourself," not others (p. 8). *Control Theory* is a self-help work that expands the basic psychological needs to include survival, belonging, power, fun, and freedom. It seems to be designed to provide lay people with the tools they need to become more successful and responsible. To this end, control theory has become a prevention-oriented system with a goal of making the expert therapist unnecessary.

Overview of Control Theory

Control theory practice has grown rapidly among therapists since the mid-1980s. It is applicable to individual and group counseling, in mental health, in community agencies, and in schools. Its popularity is based on a number of positive attributes. It is understandable; nontechnical; results- and success-oriented; problem-centered; cost effective in terms of time, resources, and effort; and based on common sense. Because of its common-sense approach, control theory can be learned and used by a wide variety of responsible persons, not just highly trained specialists. It incorporates more a teaching process than a healing process; it is more a preventive method than a restorative procedure. Figures 10.1 (page 272) and 10.2 (page 273) illustrate a wide range of aspects, from an enormous number of both conceptual and applied reportings, that are characteristic of control theory.

Control theory makes sense to clients, therapist, and students because it emphasizes personal involvement, responsibility, success, positive planning, and action. Even though the therapist may be directive and confrontive, the helping process is humanistic in that it targets problem behaviors, not the person. It encourages positive growth and success; it refutes the medical or disease model of classifying behavior; and it encourages positive personal involvement with clients rather than impersonal, judgmental, or punitive behaviors.

Theory of Personality

A fundamental philosophical tenet of control theory is that people are ultimately self-determining. Internal and external psychosocial pressures may relate directly to present emotional functioning of clients, but in the long run clients are autonomous, selective, responsible people who can control their own behaviors, thinking, and destinies.

FIGURE 10.1   Diverse *Conceptual* Dimensions of Control Theory

Conceptual Aspects of Control Theory	Pertinent References
Control theory efficacy	Bassin (1993); Cockrum (1989); Edens & Smryl (1994); Glasser (1965; 1972; 1976; 1981; 1984; 1996); Glasser & Wubbolding (1995); Glasser & Zunin (1979); Scanlan & Stumph (1995); Schatz (1995); Wubbolding (1988; 1990; 1991a; 1991b; 1992)
Meaningful relationships and involvement	Billings (1994); Glasser (1961; 1965; 1981; 1984; 1996); Glasser & Wubbolding (1995); Protheroe (1992)
Attitudinal change, self-esteem, and identity formation	Glasser (1972; 1976; 1981; 1984; 1996); Glasser & Wubbolding (1995); Glasser & Zunin (1979); Parish (1989; 1991; 1992); Schaeffer & Bratter (1990); Williamson (1992)
Diversity and multicultural issues	Glasser & Wubbolding (1995); Livneh & Sherwood (1991); Mickel (1991); Sanchez & Garriga (1995)
Spirituality	Emed (1995)
Control theory use of metaphors (1989)	Glasser (1996); Hallock (1989)
Sex, sexual love, and basic needs	Glasser (1984; 1996); Glasser & Wubbolding (1995); Glasser & Zunin (1979)
Control theory applications in child foster care	Duncan (1991)
Quality world and environment	Glasser (1996); Glasser & Wubbolding (1995)

Need Fulfillment

Everything clients do is to satisfy their basic needs. In *Stations of the Mind* (1981, pp. 40–60), *Control Theory* (1984, pp. 6–9), and *The Control Theory–Reality Therapy Workbook* (1990a), Glasser presented his theory of the brain as a control system. He stated that the brain has inborn genetic instructions that drive both physiological and psychological needs. At first these inborn instructions serve physiological needs to ensure survival of the individual and the species and later begin to drive the psychological needs for belonging, power, freedom, and fun to ensure socialization. Glasser and Wubbolding (1995, pp. 299–300) view the human brain as a system that seeks to manipulate the external environment through experimentation to find need-satisfying or need-threatening people, events, objects, behaviors, situations, and choices.

In *Staying Together* (1996, pp. 14–35) Glasser succinctly describes the concept of the five basic needs that are inherent in the human genetic structure. He proposes that *the need to survive* is the most physiologic of our basic needs; *love and belonging* is our first psychological need; *power* is our second psychological need; *freedom* is our third psychological need; and *fun,* including recreation, is our fourth psychological need. Further, he points out that nothing in our genetic codes that drives our thinking, feeling, and behaving is moral or immoral (p. 15). The process is neutral.

FIGURE 10.2 Diverse *Applied* Dimensions of Control Theory

Applied Aspects of Control Theory	Pertinent References
School systems and classrooms	Chance & Chance (1987); Dempster & Raff (1989); Edens & Smryl (1994); Glasser (1969; 1986; 1989; 1990a; 1990b); Glasser & Wubbolding (1995); Schaeffer & Bratter (1990); Schatz (1995); Williamson (1992)
Changing attitudes and thinking patterns; role playing and critiquing; mentoring, teaching, and coaching	Chambers & McLaughlin, (1994); Cockrum (1993); Glasser (1961; 1965; 1972; 1976; 1984; 1989); Palmatier (1990); Scanlan & Stumph (1995); Wubbolding (1988)
Special education and cognitively diverse clients	Barbieri (1994); Chance & Chance (1987); Green & Droff (1991); Glasser (1986); Renna (1990)
Family counseling and dynamics and marriage enhancement	Glasser (1984; 1996); Glasser & Wubbolding (1995); Mickel (1993); Smadi (1991)
High-risk clients and behaviors	Comiskey (1993); Dempster & Raff (1989); Glasser & Wubbolding (1995); Green & Droff (1991); Katz (1991); Renna (1990; 1991)
Physically disabled populations	Easterbrooks (1995); Iadeluca (1991); Livneh & Sherwood (1991)
Addiction and chemical dependency issues	Glasser (1976; 1984); Honeyman (1988; 1990); Hulbert (1992); Peterson & Woodward (1994)
Physical fitness, exercise, and physical education strategies	Acevedo (1994); Clagett (1992); Edens (1993); Edens & Smryl (1994); Glasser (1976; 1984); Hart (1992)
Sexual assault, rape, and sexual offenses/offenders	Kitchen (1991); McArthur (1990); Stanton (1992)
Pain control	Glasser (1984); Iadeluca (1991)
Bereavement and grief	Stanwood (1992)
College student personnel work	Fried (1990)
Group therapy	Clagett (1992); Glasser (1965; 1984; 1996); Glasser & Wubbolding (1995); Glasser & Zunin (1979); Williamson (1992)

Choices and Discovery
Control theory states that we choose behaviors (Glasser, 1984, pp. 45–69; Glasser & Wubbolding, 1995, p. 300). When we make choices, we discover that the consequences are desirable or undesirable. We thus discover whether our behaviors are effective or ineffective in fulfilling our needs. We also determine whether particular aspects of the environment are pleasurable (need-satisfying), painful (need-aversive), or neutral. As babies we "choose" the only behaviors available to us as we strive to fulfill our physiological needs related to survival—comfort and hunger. As

growing children we develop and progressively discover (through social influence and experimentation) more complex ways to satisfy our physiological and psychological needs.

Personality Development
Glasser (1972) and Glasser and Wubbolding (1995) identify two general types of human personality: (1) people who view themselves from their own internal frames of reference, and (2) people who perceive of themselves as others see them. As we seek to accomplish our various developmental tasks and fulfill our needs we may succeed or fail. As a result, we develop a *success identity* or a *failure identity*. The latter is described by Glasser and Wubbolding (1995, p. 300) as ineffective or out-of-control behavior.

Success Identity
Success identity is characterized (Glasser, 1972; Glasser and Wubbolding, 1995; Wubbolding, 1988) as our development of health and success as evidenced through our coming to possess a willingness as well as a repertoire of skills for attaining our basic needs of belonging, power, fun, freedom, and survival in positive and constructive ways. Wubbolding's (1988) model of success identity describes the positive stages we may experience as we learn to be successful and positive. If we are fortunate enough to attain a full measure of positive addiction, we might view ourselves at *stage one* through fulfilling our needs in responsible ways without infringing on the rights of others. At *stage two* we cope with life through positive and constructive symptoms such as (1) altrustic activities; (2) effective thinking; (3) positive affect such as self-confidence, enthusiasm, and trust; and (4) effective behaviors, such as choosing a healthy diet and exercise. We reach *stage three*, the optimal stage of success identity, when we become positively addicted to life-enhancing choices and activities that are so valuable, positive, and constructive that our lives and the lives of those around us are enhanced and if we ceased doing the positively addictive activities, we would feel pain and discomfort. Glasser (1976) proposes that two examples of positively addictive behaviors are meditation and noncompetitive exercise. Examples of *pure positive addiction* identified by Glasser and Wubbolding (1995, p. 301) include such activities as travel, reading, walking, and other habitual enjoyment-related behaviors.

Failure Identity
Failure identity is synonymous with pathology or failure to attain one's needs in responsible ways. If we develop a failure identity we might seek to fulfill our needs through negative and destructive behaviors and make choices that infringe on the rights of others and, inadvertently, keep us from getting what we really want in life. The three stages of failure identity development proposed by Glasser and Wubbolding (1995, p. 300) are the following *Stage one, giving up:* We give up when we perceive that we cannot attain our needs or that something external keeps us from doing so. *Stage two, choosing negative symptoms:* As a result of having given up we may choose antisocial activities, negative thinking, debilitative feelings, and negative physiological conditions such as psychosomatic disorders. While we are engaging in these negative choices, we believe that we are doing the best we can to fulfill our needs at the moment and that we are either constrained by the environment or are not competent to make more effective choices. *Stage three, negative addictions:*

When we regress to the point at which we believe that our negative symptoms, behaviors, and choices are need-satisfying, then we have developed negative addictions. We then have the delusion that the negative, destructive, and needs-aversive activities are really positive and that such activities provide for our immediate belonging, power, fun, and freedom. Glasser and Wubbolding (1995, pp. 300–301) list several negatively addictive identifiers such as alcohol, drugs, gambling, food, and addiction to work. If we develop a failure identity we might have a distorted and momentary sense of popularity, power, excitement, enthusiasm, or liberation from stress and pain. Such distortions rob us of the ability to fulfill our needs in responsible ways; we need to learn to use remedial or restorative procedures such as control theory strategies to counteract the destructive and debilitative effects of our *failure identity* and empower us to move toward a state of *success identity.*

Development of Personality Characteristics
Glasser (1990a; 1990b; 1996) proposes a multipart behavioral system that provides us with ways to satisfy our needs. He believes people are born with a powerful motivating force that drives behavior until needs are satisfied and with the capacity to detect when a need is not met. Needs are not met when there is a difference between the input a person wants and the input the person receives. When this difference is perceived, our current behavior is not controlling perception. So in the infant, the motivational force continues to drive random behavior until the need is satisfied or until the baby exhausts itself crying.

Eventually the infant develops the capacity to behave more precisely so that a specific behavior can be selected to satisfy a specific need. The example of the baby who learns that crying will lead to satisfaction of a variety of needs applies here. The infant uses comparing abilities to either accept or reject behavior on the basis of its capacity to satisfy needs. Then the ability to allow action on the basis of current information, such as proceeding through an intersection when the light turns green, is developed. The motivational force, the ability to detect when needs are met, and the ability to process and act on new information are the sources for all we do, think, and feel (Glasser, 1981, p. 82).

Concerning the development of personality characteristics, Glasser (1972, pp. 27–54) sees the acquisition of a positive and successful personal identity as the most important occurrence in the growth of an individual. In modern Western civilization, where the *survival society* has been largely replaced by an *identity society,* the development of a psychologically healthy personality involves a struggle to find oneself as a human being. In the survival society, personal identity was tied almost exclusively to the individual's goals, aspirations, or task performance; in the identity society, identity relates more to one's search for acceptance as a person than as a performer of a task (Glasser, 1972, p. 10). The need for a success identity is a basic social force. Glasser and Zunin (1979, p. 314) state that "a person's identity defines him (or her) in relation to others. This need for involvement is an integral part of the organism and is the primary driving force governing all behavior."

A person's success identity is based on experiencing both love and worth. The two traits are integral. A person who experiences love but not worth can become constantly dependent on others for validation. A person who experiences worth but not love can become alienated, because regardless of the number of successes achieved, there is never a feeling of being cared for by significant others (Glasser & Zunin, 1979, p. 312).

Nature of Maladjustment

The maladjusted personality is equated with what Glasser (1972, pp. 72–101; Glasser & Wubbolding, 1995, pp. 299–303) calls a *failure identity.* Persons who develop failure identities tend to be lonely, self-critical, and irrational. Their behaviors are likely to be rigid and ineffective. They often exhibit weakness, irresponsibility, and lack of confidence. Failure-identity persons may be prone to giving up, exhibiting maladaptive symptoms, or even negative addiction. They may expend their energies attempting to reduce their pain by giving up, denying failure, or even finding pleasure in failure.

Control theory holds that maladjustment generally begins during the very early years of life, when the individual cannot or does not fulfill the need to experience love or self-worth. The inability to acquire or maintain self-worth comes from the absence of the experience of success or of *doing* something worthwhile. The person who does not feel worthwhile cannot give and receive love in appropriate ways. The absence of love and a feeling of worth causes disinvolvement and leads to a failure identity (Glasser, 1972, pp. 72–101).

In control theory all behavior, including maladjusted behavior, is an attempt to control perceptions. However, maladjusted behavior results in losing *effective* control over our perceptions, and consequently our lives (Glasser, 1981, p. 44). Glasser states that people choose their misery, such as depression, anxiety, or guilt, to keep anger under control, to get other people to help them, to gain control over others, and to excuse their unwillingness to do something more effective (1981, pp. 56–62). Glasser says that rather than being in a state of depression, anxiety, or guilt, people engage in "depressing, anxietying, or guilting." He uses the -*ing* form of the word to designate feeling behaviors and to show that people are *doing* something to choose their misery. A few other examples of feeling behaviors are paining, headaching, migraining, psychosing, and obsessing.

These feeling behaviors are the result of an attempt to maintain control of our lives (Glasser, 1981, pp. 154–155). Although these behaviors provide some control, they are not effective in the long run. Furthermore, the person is just as responsible for this "crazy" behavior, such as compulsive hand washing, as he or she is for a more reasonable and effective way to gain control (Glasser, 1981, p. 98).

Basic Concepts

Basic Human Needs

The need to survive and reproduce is a basic biological need. Examples of functions governed by these structures are breathing, digesting, sweating, and regulating blood pressure. These functions occur automatically and without conscious thought. Four other needs are psychological, and these drive us just as powerfully as the need to survive. The first of these is the need to *belong,* which involves the need for friends, family, and love. A second is the need for *power,* which involves self-esteem, recognition, and competition. The third need is for *fun* and involves play, laughter, learning, and recreation. The fourth is a need for *freedom* to make choices. These four psychological needs require a delicate balance of interplay if people are to be in maximum control of their lives. If one of the needs dominates, then the others will be neglected, with a resultant loss of control (Glasser, 1984; 1996).

Identity

Identity has to do with the way one sees oneself as a human being in relation to others. Glasser states, "Almost everyone is personally engaged in a search for acceptance as a person rather than as a performer of a task" (1972, p. 10). Personality identity, then, precedes performance; acceptance as a person comes before achievement of a goal or a task.

Responsibility

Responsible behavior is the goal of therapy. To behave responsibly means "to fulfill one's needs, and to do so in a way that does not deprive others of the ability to fulfill their needs" (Glasser, 1965, p. 13). The responsible person is individually autonomous and has enough internal psychological support to determine what he or she wants from life and can develop responsible plans to fulfill his or her needs and goals (Glasser & Zunin, 1979, p. 314).

Total Behavior

Control theory focuses on four aspects of the person's total behavior: acting (things you do), thinking (thoughts and what you say to yourself), feeling (anger, joy), and physiology (breathing, vomiting). Because these aspects are interrelated, if one part is changed, the whole is changed. In therapeutic work control theory focuses on the parts of the total behavior a person can choose to change: current acting and thinking (Glasser & Zunin, 1979, p. 337). Focusing on the past is avoided because past behavior cannot change; only present behaviors can be changed.

Learning

Learning occurs throughout life and is a central concept of control theory. "We are what we do, and to a great extent, we are what we learn to do, and identity becomes the integration of all learned and unlearned behavior" (Glasser & Zunin, 1979, p. 316).

THE COUNSELING PROCESS

Control theory is a cognitive-behavioral model of therapy (works with thinking and acting components of behavior) composed of two interrelated parts: (1) the counseling environment; and (2) procedures for change. Previously, these two parts were known as the eight steps of reality therapy. These steps have been incorporated into the two parts of the counseling process so that students of control theory would conceptualize control theory as a process rather than as a series of lock steps. In this process of counseling, the overall therapeutic objective is to help the client feel better. This is accomplished when the client is able to meet needs by taking effective control of his or her life (Wubbolding, 1988; 1990; 1991a; 1991b; 1992).

The Counseling Environment

The counseling environment can be characterized by authenticity, warmth, caring, acceptance, and involvement. Trust and rapport are established by listening to the client's story. This signals to the client that the therapist believes in the client's personal worth, competence, and ability to succeed and behave responsibly. In this supportive environment, the therapist focuses on present thinking and behaving, and redirects talking about the past except when a connection can be easily related to the present concern. It is necessary for the client to become aware of his or her behavior and thinking because these are the two components of the person's total behavior he or she can control (Wubbolding, 1988, pp. 10–21). In keeping with a present-oriented therapeutic focus, the therapist helps the client be aware that feelings and physiology are related to current actions and thoughts. Therefore, if the client talks about feelings as separate from action and thought, the therapist will direct the client to examine what he or she is doing and thinking to maintain his or her feeling state.

Other important characteristics of the counseling environment concern the therapist's attitude about client responsibility, consequences of behavior, and demonstrating support. The therapist accepts no excuses for irresponsible behavior, because ultimately the responsibility is the client's. Second, there is no punishment or criticism for irresponsible behavior. Allowing natural consequences of behavior to occur is a strong enough message. Finally, the therapist imparts his or her belief in the client's ability to take effective control of his or her life by never giving up. This attitude confirms to the client that the therapist cares (Wubbolding, 1988, pp. 23–28; 1991a; 1991b; 1992).

Procedures for Change

The procedures that lead to change continue to convey the supportive atmosphere of the counseling environment and are construed as integral parts of that environment. These procedures include: (1) exploring needs and perceptions; (2) exploring and evaluating total behavior; and (3) planning and commitment.

Exploring Needs and Perceptions
The focus of this procedure is to help the client become aware of what he or she wants. These wants can be as specific as obtaining material possessions or as broad as projecting a lifestyle. For most people not all needs are equal—they compete with each other—and their fulfillment involves negotiation because they often conflict (Glasser, 1984, pp. 16–18). Because of these factors, exploring needs and perceptions is critical in helping the client to sort out values and to determine priorities.

TH: You say your wife complains because you don't spend much time with your family. How do you spend your time?

CL: Well, I work long hours so I can get ahead in the company and provide more for my family. I stop off after work a few nights a week with my supervisor for happy hour, and my family has finished eating when I get home. This makes my wife mad. On weekends I like to have some time to myself to fish, hunt, and play golf. I do try to attend church with them when I don't have too much yard work.

TH: Well, tell me this. How much of a priority is your family?

CL: You may not believe this, but I've always thought they were number one. I've worked hard to give them things I didn't have. At times, I've thought my wife should be happy I'm such a good provider. On the other hand, she did say something that kind of got to me . . . that I was missing out on my kids growing up and that they wondered why I worked so much.

TH: Well, what do you think is the most important? Your work, your family, your leisure?

CL: I think it's a toss-up between family and work. I get a lot of satisfaction and recognition at work. On the other hand, my family is important because they're the closest people I have, and I don't think I could get along without them. The hobbies aren't as important, but I do need time to relax.

TH: So let's talk about what you are willing to do to have more time for your family.

Exploring and Evaluating Total Behavior

It is essential that clients evaluate their own behavior and make a value judgment about whether what they are doing is fulfilling their needs. The therapist is active and objective in helping the client openly evaluate the behavior. The client is the one who must judge the "rightness" or "wrongness" of the behavior. The therapist is not the judge or moral guide. Exploring the client's behavior can be facilitated by asking "What are you doing?" "What do you do?" and "What did you do?" questions (Wubbolding, 1988, pp. 28–38). Examples include: "What are you doing to contribute to the situation?" "What do you do when you are depressing?" "What are you doing to alleviate the situation?" "What did you do when your mother grounded you?"

These questions and others like them can be asked until the client has provided specific information about his or her behaviors. The behaviors can then be examined and evaluated by the client for their potential to fulfill his or her stated needs. Further questions are asked to help the client evaluate his or her behavior: "Is your behavior helping or hurting you?" "Is what you are doing getting you what you want?" "Does the way you talk to your mother help you to relate to her in the way you said you want to?" "Is what you are doing against the rules or illegal?" "Does it help or hurt you to look that way at the situation with your teacher?" "Is what you are doing acceptable behavior?"

Clients who have been habitually exhibiting behavior that is self-defeating do not always recognize what they are doing. They may strongly deny their problem behavior and erect valid-sounding excuses for continuing to engage in it. An example is a teacher who continues to teach even though he or she has a medical need for hospitalization. The teacher might make excuses such as "My students need me," to the detriment of his or her own health now and to the ultimate detriment of the students. It may be difficult for the client to make the value judgment "What I'm doing is really not good for me or my students." Such a value judgment is critical. It is not up to the therapist to say, "Look, what you're doing is killing you and hurting your students." If the client has difficulty evaluating the behavior objectively, the therapist can intervene with genuine, caring, but confrontive responses.

TH: How is what you're doing going to help you and the students? Can you tell me how putting off the operation that you badly need is helping you to get what you want?

CL: That's true. It's really not good for me to put off the operation.

TH: Then putting off the operation at this time is *wrong* for you; it won't get you what you want.

CL: That's right. I'm worried about what will happen to the students while I'm gone. But when I think about it, I know they will be taken care of—they'll be okay. And I'm scared for me too. But I know, too, that putting off surgery may really injure my health even more.

TH: So, you have about concluded that going ahead with the operation is the best course of action for you right now.

CL: Yes. There's no really sensible reason to put it off.

Here the therapist is forceful and facilitative by actively pursuing the client's own evaluation.

To summarize, control theory contends that clients must judge their own behavior, identify what they are doing to cause the difficulty or failure, and decide what they must *do* to begin to behave in more responsible ways (Glasser & Zunin, 1979, p. 319).

Planning and Commitment

Once the client has decided his or her behavior is not meeting needs and that he or she is willing to behave in a responsible way, the therapist helps him or her develop a realistic plan. The plan should be a positive plan of action, need-fulfilling, simple, realistic and attainable, something to do (not stop doing), dependent on the client, specific, and something the client does everyday (Wubbolding, 1988, pp. 58–73). Client ownership of the plan is vital. No matter how much the therapist wants the client to "buy into" a plan, the success of the plan must rest with the client. The action steps should be of manageable size and complexity to ensure a high probability of success. If the client wishes to develop and own a plan with little chance for success, the therapist points that out and seeks to get the client to make a more realistic plan. As an example, an overweight client who is enthusiastically anticipating a weight loss may want to lose too many pounds too fast.

CL: I'm so excited about this idea of losing weight. I figured it out last night. If I go on a 600-calorie diet, jog two miles a day, and go to aerobics class three times a week, I can lose five pounds a week. In three months that would be sixty pounds.

TH: I can see you're really enthusiastic about doing something about your weight. I've learned from experience with weight-loss programs that motivation is important, and you certainly have that. What I'd like you to consider is a more moderate approach.

CL: You don't think I should lose the weight so fast.

TH: That's right. My experience says that people such as you are more likely to stick to diet and exercise programs that are much less stressful than what you are thinking about.

CL: Well, maybe you're right. I sometimes have the tendency to jump into things full force and later burn out quickly.

A formal commitment enhances the client's motivation to carry out the plan successfully (Glasser, 1972, pp. 125–126). Commitment to the plan binds the client both to the plan and to personal involvement with the person helping him or her. Commitment encourages and reinforces the client to take action steps. The commitment stimulates the client to think and do things that the inertia of ordinary living would usually prevent. The commitment is to self, to the agreement, and to the helper. An example of a verbal commitment follows.

TH: When do you plan to get the operation?

CL: I don't know. I'll have to see my doctor about it.

TH: When can you see your doctor about it?

CL: Oh, I could call him tomorrow to set up an appointment to talk about it. He'll want to see me in his office to examine me before setting a time to go into the hospital.

TH: What time can you call him tomorrow?

CL: Oh, I guess in the morning.

TH: What time in the morning do you intend to call him?

Another way to foster commitment to the plan is to put the essential parts into written form, such as a behavioral schedule or a contract. The written plan is not only a tangible reminder, but also a symbolic shift toward an action step by the client. The very act of writing the plan becomes the first action step and ensures that the client can sense some degree of success. It also gives the therapist an opportunity to reinforce the client verbally for making the plan.

TH: What would be a more moderate version of the plan you thought up, one you think you would maintain?

CL: Well, what do you think of a 1500-calorie diet, walking two miles a day, and maybe putting off aerobics until I see how that works?

TH: That seems reasonable to me and a lot less stressful. How much would you lose a week on that plan?

CL: From all the diets I've been on, I think I would lose about two pounds a week.

TH: So it would take about seven and a half months to lose sixty pounds. Do you think you could commit to a program that long? If you do, let's put something down on paper, kind of like a contract.

For many clients, a commitment in writing is of great importance. A written contract can serve as a memory jog and a catalyst to take action not previously taken. Some clients keep a pocket-sized book containing the written plan, contract, or performance diary. Such written plans enable therapist and client to agree on specific wording of goals and actions steps and to identify target dates, times, places, and activities. The commitment also can be expressed in other ways, such as "shaking on it" and telling other people about the plan.

STRATEGIES FOR HELPING CLIENTS

Positiveness

The control theorist talks about, focuses on, and reinforces positive and constructive planning and behaving. Clients who have been exposed to other therapies may believe the therapist wants to hear about their miseries, problems, failures, disappointments, and debilitating situations over and over again. Such negative discussion leads to more depression and cannot contribute to the improvement of the client's thinking or behaving. The facilitative strategy is to accept the fact that the client truly feels miserable (or depressed, or defeated, or disappointed, or helpless) and to encourage him or her to break the negative pattern and focus on something constructive and positive in the here and now (Glasser & Zunin, 1979, pp. 317–318). For example, a client might say, "I just have this hopeless feeling about what she did to me yesterday." Instead of "She really made you feel hopeless and depressed," a better reply by the therapist would be, "What are you doing to produce this hopeless feeling in you?" The latter statement focuses on changing the client's cognition about the hopeless feeling and on responsibility for the doing aspect of the feeling. These are the two aspects of the client's total behavior that can be controlled.

Controlling Perceptions

In control theory, behavior is an attempt to control perception. That is, people act in such a way as to reduce the discrepancy between what they want and what they perceive they are getting. Positively addicting behaviors, or *meditations,* as Glasser calls them, are activities people can undertake to reduce their discrepancies and gain a feeling of control over their lives. Glasser categorizes a wide variety of behaviors as meditations, ranging from relatively weak ones, such as regularly taking a vitamin C pill, to strong ones, such as regularly running (Glasser, 1981, pp. 247–262). Other examples are transcendental meditation, biofeedback, visualization and imagery, chanting, hiking, swimming, bicycling, gardening, writing, and sewing. Glasser states that it is not the activity that is important in the meditation behavior, but that (1) the person believes in the process of meditation and that it has some value; (2) it is fulfilling in some way; and (3) it can be done easily (Glasser, 1981, p. 249).

For positive addiction to be of optimum benefit, the client must pursue the activity about an hour each day until an addictive state is achieved—that is, until the client experiences discomfort or withdrawal if the activity is omitted, just as the lack of alcohol or heroin brings on withdrawal pain in the case of negative addiction. Positive addictions enable clients to overcome their negative addictions and lead more constructive, integrated, and rewarding lives (Glasser, 1976). As a counseling strategy, prescribing or planning a regular meditation activity is consistent with the control theory concept that what a person does has the most potential for changing or establishing how he or she experiences life.

Confrontation

Because control theory emphasizes client responsibility and "no excuses," it is natural that confrontation is a necessary and effective strategy. Confronting clients in ways that are helpful yet nonpunitive requires concentration, caring, and skill in zeroing in on the client's excuses or irresponsibilities. A caring confrontation can reinforce the belief that the therapist values the client. Confronting client excuses, explanations, or rationalizations is necessary to facilitate client movement toward responsible behavior.

Glasser and Zunin (1979, pp. 325–326) emphasize the role of confrontation as an intentional strategy. Confrontation pertains to the reality of the client's current behavior, not to the therapist's personal or emotional feelings triggered by the client. Here is an example of appropriate confrontation of an excuse:

CL: I was going to face up to him, but . . . after he gave me the roses . . . and we were so rushed for time . . . well, I just didn't want to cause any hard feelings.

TH: Evelyn, I have two questions about what you've just said. When you change your mind about facing him, what are you doing? And how is this going to help you get what you want?

An inappropriate confrontation follows.

TH: Evelyn, I have two things to say to you. It bugs me to hear about you doing this to yourself again and again. Why can't you learn to say what's on your mind? It's time you grew up.

The first confrontation addresses the client's behavior, not her autonomy, integrity, or personal worth, while still ascribing to her the ability to choose and act rationally. The second example has a high probability of making the client feel bad and lacks the advantage of having her focus on her behavior.

Plans and Contracts

Setting the limits for the therapy in such matters as the number of sessions and their cost, therapist and client responsibilities, intermediate and long-term goals, and specific plans for goal attainment establishes a structural and rational process for gaining a success identity. Moreover, it is important that the plan be in writing—a contract or a self-managed behavioral plan such as the one for Peggy in the chapter on behavioral counseling. The written plan must carry the specific action steps needed to move the client toward success.

Specifying and Pinning Down

This strategy is related to confrontation in that it may prevent the client from coming up with excuses for failing to follow through with plans. Suppose the therapeutic session has begun to focus on the client's intention to apply for a job. The client has stated that he intends to put several applications on file next week. The therapist pins the client down by asking the following questions: "What day next week will you do this? What time of the day? What will you wear? How are you going to get there? Are you going to call for an appointment? What will you *do* if the interview is not successful?" The most important benefit of these questions is to cement the client's commitment to do something positive to attain a goal. With each affirmative answer to a "pinning down" question, the client moves closer and closer to doing a specific positive behavior. Each answer is a verbal commitment to the therapist and to him- or herself about what will be done. Then the therapist can reinforce each verbal commitment by saying, "So, on Wednesday at 9:00 A.M. you are going to file an application with the A & I Nut and Bolt Company. You plan to wear a sport coat, a tie, dress pants, and a pair of dress shoes. You will ride the No. 16 Metro bus and leave home at 8:00 A.M. to allow ample time to arrive before your 9:00 A.M. appointment. Is that correct?"

Resolving Conflicts

Glasser (1984, pp. 146–158) says there are two types of conflicts: true and false. The true conflict is one that develops from an attempt to change the behavior of persons who do not want to change because the condition of control does not satisfy them. The reason this is a true conflict is that no single behavior can solve it; there is no solution to it, and a major part of the stress in it comes from repeated frustrating attempts to do something to resolve it. Glasser recommends reducing the stress by doing nothing, choosing to be passive, or just waiting. In the meantime, some aspect of the conflict may change without intervention. During the interim, Glasser recommends expending energy to satisfy oneself in a nonconflict area.

If the client is the type of person who is not able to put the conflict situation on hold, a different strategy is recommended. Rather than maintain the conflict by not making a decision, the strategy is to choose one side or the other for a given period. During this time, the client behaves as if the conflict is resolved in an effort to determine whether taking one side or the other in any way changes the nature of the conflict. Depending on the feedback during this trial period, the client can then choose to stick to the original decision, opt for a trial period experiencing the other side, or choose a third alternative. Suppose a married woman wants her husband to refuse a promotion that would require their moving to a different state in three months. She wants to stay where she is so she can finish her graduate degree. He wants to move to further his career. There is no way for both of them to get what they want. If she cannot tolerate the tension of delaying a decision to see if anything changes on its own, then selecting one of the choices for a given period may bring resolution. Some of her options include finishing graduate school and joining her husband, staying in graduate school for a trial period, or moving with her husband. Making any one of these decisions may fulfill her need to do something concrete to reduce her anxiety. Once she makes a decision, other circumstances about the situation may change, such as her husband getting a better job offer where they currently live.

Glasser (1984, pp. 149–150) says that most situations that people construe as conflict are in reality false conflicts. In these situations, there is a behavior the person can do to resolve the conflict, but the person is unwilling to engage in the behavior. Glasser cites an example of the overweight person who would like to be thinner but doesn't want to diet. One solution would be to jog or exercise daily to burn calories while maintaining the same caloric intake. Although exercising may be hard work and time-consuming, it is a solution. Glasser says that doing something in these situations is necessary because hoping and complaining are not effective behaviors (1984, p. 154).

SAMPLE CASE

The case of Evelyn, age thirty-four, illustrates a control theorist working with a client in planning concrete, responsible action steps. It illustrates several important strategies typical to the application of reality therapy.

CL: I've been so unhappy lately. I've tried to talk to Bill, but it's hard to pin him down. I've been his fiancée for over four years, but we never get around to discussing our marriage or setting a date. I get the feeling he wants it that way. He's a very strong and forceful person. I guess he intimidates me. I don't want to risk losing him by pushing him. His job keeps him so tied up I rarely see him. When I do see him, we do lots of neat things. Sometimes I wonder if we'll ever get married. I feel so helpless.

TH: You say you hope to get married to Bill, but he won't discuss it or set a date. What are you doing to contribute to his not discussing it?

CL: I don't know. (*pause*) Yes, I do too. I guess I'm doing something. I'm being patient. Not pushing him. I'm being his steady girlfriend who doesn't ask questions and who doesn't nag him.

TH: Is this waiting getting you what you want? What are your present actions doing for you?

CL: (*pause*) Gosh! I hadn't thought of it that way. What's it doing for me? (*pause*) Hmmm, I don't think it's doing anything *for* me. It's certainly doing something *to* me. Making me feel low. Making me worry all the time.

TH: What do you want to see happen in the relationship?

CL: I want us to get married. I want us to get together. I want us to talk about it, to set a definite date. Oh, I'm willing to wait—a while. Even several months. As long as it's set. I want to know where I stand.

TH: What can you do to bring that about?

CL: I don't know. I don't know that *I* can make it happen. I don't know if I can confront him. He is very logical, very convincing. I'm afraid I'd just melt away.

TH: You don't think you are ready to stand up to him, then.

CL: I know I've got to. Nobody else can do it for me.

TH: You want to confront him. But are afraid you'd fail. I gather you don't think it's very realistic that you would walk right up to him right now and get an answer.

CL: I wish I could. I think if I practiced it or something maybe I could—I don't know.

TH: Would it help if we practice it now?

CL: I don't know.

TH: What have we got to lose by practicing?

CL: Okay, if it'll help. I'm willing to try practicing.

TH: To help you practice more realistically, could you tell me how he'll likely respond to you when you talk about your future plans together?

CL: Oh, he'll be calm, cool, and collected. He'll handle it just like a business deal. He'll not raise his voice—in fact, he'll lower it. He's likely to say, "Honey, I've been thinking that as soon as I wrap up these next four important business deals, I have got to sit down with you and map out some definite plans. You know you're important to me, Sugar. I know you don't mind waiting a little longer." That's about the way he would be. Except he wouldn't be meek like me.

TH: That was helpful. Are you ready to practice?

CL: I guess so. I just hope I can be strong enough.

TH: Let's talk about it a little—how do you want to be in your session with him?

CL: Well, I want to be able to be me—to command respect, and to get my ideas across without threatening him and without harming our relationship. And I want to be strong enough to do it without getting put off and without going away feeling like a helpless child.

TH: Can you rehearse with me now what you'd like to say to him if you had the opportunity and the conditions were right?

CL: I'll try.

TH: Now, I'll be Bill. We're all alone and it seems like a good time for you to bring it up.

TH: Well, Evelyn, you look like you have something important on your mind.

CL: Hmmm. Well, Bill, there's something I've been wanting to talk with you about.

TH: Okay, shoot, Sugar.

CL: It's about us—our relationship. You tell me you care about me, and I certainly care about you a whole bunch. And I'm still thrilled every time I look at my engagement ring. But every time the subject of definite planning comes up, it gets put off. I'm wondering if it's ever going to happen. Bill, I don't want you to think I'm pushy, but I really would like to know where I stand.

TH: Evelyn—dear! You know I love you. You know you're the most important thing in my life. We'll get it together, believe me! Just trust me! You know how confining my work is and how much stress I'm under. Sugar, it wouldn't be fair to you for me to try to finalize plans for us with all this unfinished business hanging over our heads. Just a few more months and things will be right for us.

CL: I . . . Oh my gosh—you're just like him. I don't know what to say.

TH: Okay, cut! You think my playing the part of Bill was too strong for you right now to be able to get your point across successfully.

CL: You were almost like he'd be, all right. I wonder if I can ever do it.

TH: Let's talk some more about what you want to do and try to figure out how you can succeed in doing it if you decide you really want to do it.

A discussion, an assertiveness training session, and more planning followed, and another rehearsal episode proved to be quite successful for Evelyn. She was able to decide what she wanted to say; she was able to hold her ground and stand up to the therapist even though the therapist was being as persuasive as possible. Evelyn was obviously pleased with herself and felt good about having taken such a definite and assertive stand. Her posture, voice, and facial expression showed confidence and a more positive outlook.

TH: Evelyn, I'm pleased with your performance in our practice session, and you are apparently feeling positive about the way you handled yourself.

CL: I felt really good about myself. I really surprised myself. I couldn't believe it was really me, saying those things.

TH: Then it is realistic to assume that you will be able to be just as strong, just as self-assured with him as you demonstrated with me.

CL: I think so. I am really a very strong person when I really want to be. Yes, I can do it.

TH: You *can* do it. Does that mean you *will* do it?

CL: Well, yes. I've got to do it. I don't intend to live the rest of my life feeling miserable.

TH: You seem quite certain about wanting to get this thing settled. When do you plan to confront him?

CL: I don't know. Soon. Before the summer's over.

TH: It's now June twenty-first. *When* this summer do you plan to do it?

CL: I won't see him again till the middle of July.

TH: What day in July will you see him?

CL: I'll be with him the weekend of the fifteenth—Friday, Saturday, and Sunday.

TH: What day will it be?

CL: Friday—Friday evening at dinner will be the best time to do it. That will give us the whole weekend.

As the session continued, the client made a written commitment to carry out her plan followed by an appointment with the therapist to discuss it after July seventeenth. The therapist gave Evelyn verbal reinforcement for her successful rehearsal and for having developed a reasonable written plan, and let her know that he would be genuinely interested in hearing how she did in the real meeting with her fiancé.

CONTRIBUTIONS OF CONTROL THEORY

Control theory has made a number of important contributions to the helping professions. It has had a significant influence in challenging the medical model of client treatment in counseling and psychotherapy. Another major contribution has been the application of its principles to a variety of educational problems. These principles have proved successful in educational settings from kindergarten through graduate school.

Control theory is both a positive and an action therapy. Helping clients acquire "positive addictions" in areas they choose for growth helps them for the rest of their lives. Control theory, by emphasizing the power and potential of positive thinking and acting, gives the therapeutic community a rationale for turning the self-fulfilling prophecy into a real benefit for clients.

As evidenced by Figures 10.1 and 10.2, control theory has grown to have conceptual and applied dimensions in a wide array of human endeavors and dilemmas. The direct, frank, realistic approach has been appealing and particularly effective with a variety of clients traditionally classified as difficult to help including delinquents, offenders, schizophrenics, drug abusers, depressed and suicidal clients, survivors of assault, grieving people, physically disabled clients, and other crisis clients.

SHORTCOMINGS OF CONTROL THEORY

Some of the underlying assumptions of control theory are questionable. For example, the assumptions that mental illness is equated with irresponsibility of the client and that a failure identity stems from lack of need fulfillment seem to be oversimplifications. Even though these assumptions may be valid in a large number of cases, their narrow view limits the full range of therapeutic intervention, especially when we consider the environmental, sociological, physiological, and biochemical precursors to human functioning in modern life. A larger view of the causes of maladaptive behavior, coupled with the use of a global, multidisciplinary helping approach, is more defensible.

Focusing on the here and now and staying away from the client's past history are appropriate in many cases. However, humans are products of their pasts, and there are instances in which helping clients to find their roots—their connectedness—may be of great importance to them in fulfilling the need to become whole. Taking stock of where we have been is at times a helpful strategy and may serve as both an instructional and a motivational impetus toward making better choices for the future.

Another shortcoming is that the simple, efficient methods employed in control theory lend themselves to surface-level, symptom-oriented problems that can be quickly attacked and show noticeable results. This may give the "fix-it-quick" therapist (especially the beginning therapist) a sense of accomplishment, but it may also permit deep-seated emotional feelings in the client to go unexamined.

Questions frequently asked in our discussions with students studying control theory include "Who decides which 'reality' is valid—the therapist, the client, or both?" "Doesn't this system encourage therapists to impose their values and moral beliefs on the client?" "Who is to say what is responsible and what is irresponsible?" "Which is right—society's norms or the individual's norms?" "How do we know that people's pasts or unconscious thoughts aren't crucial to them?" These questions are bothersome from both a practical and a philosophical point of view and have not been adequately resolved by proponents of control theory.

LaFontaine (1994, 1995) judges control theory to be lacking in information and awareness of issues related to homosexuality in general and to gay and lesbian youth in particular. She recommended a more diversified framework for control theory if the approach is to adequately serve the needs of the underserved population of clients of diverse sexual orientations.

Cunningham (1995) expresses similar concerns regarding control theory's sensitivity to the ten most frequently encountered examples of cultural bias in counseling. These assumptions (examples) of cultural bias included the supposition that normal behavior does not vary across cultures. An inferred shortcoming of control theory was that the approach places too much emphasis on Western world individualism, fragmentation by academic disciplines, dependence on abstract words, linear thinking, and neglect of the client's traditional cultural support systems. Glasser and Wubbolding (1995, pp. 302–303) counter Cunningham's criticism by pointing out that such alleged cultural bias is more a function of the *use* of control theory than a flaw of the theory. Glasser and Wubbolding point out that when using control theory with different cultures and in different parts of the world the therapy should be adjusted to meet the needs, style, experience, manner of expression, thought patterns, total behavior, and specific wants of members of various cultures. Obviously Glasser and Wubbolding view control theory as sufficiently flexible to meet the needs of diverse clients.

CONTROL THEORY WITH DIVERSE POPULATIONS

Control theory's emphasis on changing behavior to fit into the social context of the environment without passing judgment on or delving into the personal styles of its clients provides its most unique contribution for diverse populations. For people who might have trouble understanding more esoteric dynamic or process-oriented psychotherapies, control theory makes plain sense. It is admirably suited to teach people to operate on a behavioral philosophy of simple, specific, and concrete actions and to understand the positive and negative results of those actions as they apply to themselves and others.

Students, children, parolees, and other clients who cannot or will not deal with the consequences of their actions, engage in negative addicting behaviors, or otherwise have a failure identity can be given easily understood and implemented methods and techniques for changing their behavior. Its clear-cut procedures allow control theory to be easily and effectively used by parents, teachers, parole officers, and others who are not psychotherapists. In this regard, Glasser's (1984) action-oriented control theory is particularly applicable to cross-cultural counseling because of its utility and ease of implementation.

Glasser's original clinical trials with the approach at Ventura School for Girls has been followed by a long history of success in schools and correctional settings (Glasser, 1965; 1969; 1972; 1984). Nowhere else has one counseling theory been applied more successfully to such a large, diverse population than that found in the nation's school system (Chance & Chance, 1987; Dempster & Raff, 1989; Green & Droff, 1991; Renna, 1991). The reason for its success with such clients is its view of failure not as a personal defect but as a distinct component of behavior that has not been planned carefully enough to allow the behavior and, subsequently, the person to succeed. The linchpins of control theory are its principles of "no punishment," "no excuse," and "no failure," which focus the client on achieving a success identity. For many such failure-identity clients this approach may be a strange new way of thinking and behaving in direct contradiction to the punitive and repressive atmosphere in which they have existed. Many such clients, when they discover they are not condemned for their past problems, provided with understanding for failures, supported for renewed efforts, and given positive reinforcement for success, are capable of remarkable achievements through adherence to control theory principles.

Control theory has much to offer persons suffering from substance, emotional, relational, and other negative addictions (Glasser, 1984; Honeyman, 1988; 1990). When people compound their addictive behaviors by using the excuse of denial as a psychological narcotic to dull the pain of nonachievement, they push themselves farther down Glasser's negative addiction continuum. Through control theory, therapists can paint very clear and grim pictures for addictive clients of how their addictive behavior causes their personal worlds to become ever narrower and more constricted. However, Glasser's theory also provides for moving up the continuum into positive addicting behavior. Looking at behavior on an addiction/control continuum makes a great deal of sense and has a great deal of applicability to most addicted clients. Further, by not accepting excuses, control theory strikes at the very heart of the addict's denial system, which keeps the addictive behavior in operation. The focus in primary and after-care chemical dependency treatment on relating feelings to behavior, behavior to consequences, and thinking to impulse control closely match control theory.

Livneh and Sherwood (1991) have documented several aspects of how control theory concepts help counselors understand the psychological adjustment to disability and promote rehabilitation. First, the *success identity/failure identity* dichotomy is particularly applicable to clients with disabilities. A failure identity is but one variable that might interfere with the client's development of a success identity, which is considered a crucial factor in the rehabilitative process. Second, the therapy's emphasis on the needs to belong, to love and be loved, and to feel worthwhile is especially vital in clients with disabilities.

A third strength of control theory is helping clients with disabilities to focus appropriately on increasing their control over the environment by evaluating their own behavior and choosing more effective and productive behaviors. Thus, responsibility is achieved when clients are able to fulfill their needs competently and autonomously without depriving others of the means to satisfy their own needs (Livneh & Sherwood, 1991). The client's inherent limitations are not ignored, but neither are disabilities allowed to be used as excuses for personal failures and dependency. The therapeutic emphasis is on clients' attainment of personal independence and the efficient use of their assets, personal attributes, and potentialities. The client and counselor conjointly develop strategies to identify and meet the demands of the social, vocational, and recreational environments that confront people with inherent limitations. Because many physically disabled clients find their rehabilitation slow going and fraught with setbacks, control theory's no-punishment, no-excuses, and no-failure principles work well for them. Clients are not penalized for failure to carry out a rehabilitation plan. Instead, cooperative trouble-shooting of the old plan is conducted and a new plan is collaboratively developed and implemented.

One of the major shortcomings of control theory when used with minority or other socially disenfranchised clients is the notion that positive change can occur only within the moral and legal boundaries of existing institutions and society. When such institutions are seen as being not overly concerned and perhaps even punitive toward those individuals, the control theorist may have a difficult time convincing such clients to change and adapt to existing norms. As a result, therapists may be seen by such clients as little more than bureaucratic stooges charged by "the man" with keeping the status quo.

The "no-excuses" principle is also a double-edged sword. Few clients relish having their defense systems attacked. Minority and other disenfranchised clients may have extremely stout and rigid defense systems. Confrontation of these clients' most cherished defenses must be done skillfully and carefully, or clients will use those same defenses to cast the therapist as simply another member of the establishment who is attempting to control and coerce their lives.

SUMMARY

Control theory is a modern system of helping developed by William Glasser geared toward verbal clients in the technological society of the United States. The client is viewed as always behaving to achieve control by fulfilling perceived needs. When attempting to fulfill these needs, the client is always responsible for the choices made. The therapist is rational, didactic, directive, instructive, caring, empathic, and personally involved with the client. He or she reinforces the client in exhibiting responsible and positive actions and in focusing on successful behaviors (not feelings) in the here and now. The therapeutic process, comprised of the counseling environment and procedures for change, focuses on the total behavior of the client: acting, thinking, feeling, and physiology. Emphasis, however, is placed on acting and thinking behaviors, the behaviors most easily changed.

Control theory has enjoyed wide success with a variety of client populations. Its principles are applicable to preventive as well as restorative situations; to individual and group therapy; to everyday living; and to schools and institutions. The strategies of the system are not the exclusive tools of therapists. Glasser encourages everyone—teachers, parents, ministers, employers, supervisors, therapists, and others—to practice the concepts of control theory.

SUGGESTIONS FOR FURTHER READING

Glasser, W. (1965). *Reality therapy.* New York: Harper & Row.

Glasser, W. (1969). *Schools without failure.* New York: Harper & Row.

Glasser, W. (1972). *The identity society.* New York: Harper & Row.

Glasser, W. (1976). *Positive addiction.* New York: Harper & Row.

Glasser, W. (1986). *Control theory in the classroom.* Harper & Row.

Glasser, W. (1986). *The quality school.* New York: Harper & Row.

Glasser, W. (1996). *Staying together: The control theory guide to a lasting marriage.* New York: HarperCollins (Perennial paper edition).

Glasser, W., & Zunin, L. M. (1979). Reality therapy. In R. J. Corsini (Ed.), *Current psychotherapies* (2nd ed.) (pp. 302–339). Itasca, IL: F. E. Peacock.

REFERENCES

Acevedo, E. O. (1994). Reality therapy: A framework for implementing psychological skills for athletes. *Journal of Reality Therapy, 14,* 29–36.

Barbieri, P. (1994). Using meditation and RT/CT to help students with cognitive challenges be "creative" in reorganizing more effective behaviors. *Journal of Reality Therapy, 14,* 18–25.

Bassin, A. (1993). The reality therapy paradigm. *Journal of Reality Therapy, 12,* 3–13.

Billings, B. P. (1994). "The importance of involvement in counseling": Erratum. *Journal of Reality Therapy, 14,* 65.

Chambers, C. L., & McLaughlin, T. F. (1994). An evaluation of a Glasser quality classroom: No effects on achievement in mathematics but on attitude towards school. *Perceptual and Motor Skills, 78,* 478.

Chance, E. W., & Chance, P. L. (1987). Applying control theory in the gifted and talented classroom. *Journal of Reality Therapy, 7,* 36–41.

Clagett, A. F. (1992). Group-integrated reality therapy in a wilderness camp. *Journal of Offender Rehabilitation, 17,* 1–18.

Cockrum, J. R. (1989). Reality Therapy: Interviews with Dr. William Glasser. [Special issue: Counseling.] *Psychology: A Journal of Human Behavior, 26,* 13–16.

Cockrum, J. R. (1993). Teaching role playing and critiquing. *Journal of Reality Therapy, 12,* 70–75.

Comiskey, P. E. (1993). Using reality therapy group training with at-risk high school freshmen. *Journal of Reality Therapy, 12,* 59–64.

Cunningham, L. M. (1995). Control theory, reality therapy, and cultural bias. *Journal of Reality Therapy, 15,* 15–32.

Dempster, M., & Raff, O. (1989). Managing students in primary schools: A successful Australian experience. *Journal of Reality Therapy, 8,* 19–23.

Duncan, D. (1991). Reality therapy/control theory in a treatment foster care network. *Journal of Reality Therapy, 11,* 46–49.

Easterbrooks, S. R. (1995). Improving pragmatic language outcomes of a college student with hearing loss: Effects on the individual and staff. *Journal of Reality Therapy, 14,* 37–44.

Edens, R. M. (1993). Strategies for quality physical education: The Glasser approach to physical education. *Journal of Reality Therapy, 13,* 46–52.

Edens, R. M., & Smryl, T. (1994). Reducing disruptive classroom behaviors in physical education: A pilot study. *Journal of Reality Therapy, 13,* 40–44.

Emed, Y. (1995). Control theory and spirituality. *Journal of Reality Therapy, 14,* 63–66.

Fried, J. (1990). Reality and self-control: Applying reality therapy to student personnel work in higher education. *Journal of Reality Therapy, 9,* 60–64.

Glasser, W. (1961). *Mental health or mental illness?* New York: Harper & Row.

Glasser, W. (1964). Reality therapy: A realistic approach to the young offender. *Crime & Delinquency, 10,* 135–144.

Glasser, W. (1965). *Reality therapy.* New York: Harper & Row.

Glasser, W. (1969). *Schools without failure.* New York: Harper & Row.

Glasser, W. (1972). *The identity society.* New York: Harper & Row.

Glasser, W. (1976). *Positive addiction.* New York: Harper & Row.

Glasser, W. (1981). *Stations of the mind: New directions for reality therapy.* New York: Harper & Row.

Glasser, W. (1984). *Control theory: A new explanation of how we control our lives.* New York: Harper & Row.

Glasser, W. (1986). *Control theory in the classroom.* New York: Harper & Row.

Glasser, W. (1989). *Control theory in the practice of reality therapy: Case studies.* New York: Harper & Row.

Glasser, W. (1990a). *The control theory–reality therapy workbook.* Canoga Park, CA: Institute for Reality Therapy.

Glasser, W. (1990b). *The quality school: Managing students without coercion.* New York: Harper & Row.

Glasser, W. (1996). *Staying together: The control theory guide to a lasting marriage.* New York: HarperCollins (Perennial paper edition).

Glasser, W., & Wubbolding, R. E. (1995). Reality Therapy. In R. J. Corsini & D. Wedding (Eds.), *Current psychotherapies* (5th ed.; pp. 293–321). Itasca, IL: F. E. Peacock.

Glasser, W., & Zunin, L. M. (1979). Reality therapy. In R. J. Corsini (Ed.), *Current psychotherapies* (2nd ed.) (pp. 301–339). Itasca, IL: F. E. Peacock.

Green, B., & Droff, S. (1991). Quality education and at risk students. *Journal of Reality Therapy, 10,* 3–11.

Hallock, S. (1989). Making metaphors in therapeutic process. *Journal of Reality Therapy, 9,* 25–29.

Hart, E. A. (1992). Using reality therapy for exercise initiation. *Journal of Reality Therapy, 12,* 24–31.

Honeyman, A. (1988). Counseling addiction a paradoxical consistency: Powerless and control theory. *Journal of Reality Therapy, 9,* 20–24.

Honeyman, A. (1990). Perceptual changes in addicts as a consequence of reality therapy based group treatment. *Journal of Reality Therapy, 9,* 53–59.

Hulbert, R. J. (1992). The Iowa therapeutic community model of chemical dependency treatment. *Journal of Substance Abuse Treatment, 9,* 389–393.

Iadeluca, M. C. (1991). Whose back is it anyway? Use of reality therapy in back rehabilitation. *Journal of Reality Therapy, 10,* 51–54.

Katz, A. J. (1991). Renegotiation: What to do when you don't follow your plan. *Journal of Reality Therapy, 11,* 63–65.

Kitchen, C. D. (1991). Crisis intervention using reality therapy for adult sexual assault victims. *Journal of Reality Therapy, 10,* 34–39.

LaFontaine, L. (1994). Quality schools for gay and lesbian youth: Lifting the cloak of silence. *Journal of Reality Therapy, 14,* 26–28.

LaFontaine, L. (1995). Basic needs and sexuality: Is something missing in reality therapy/control theory? *Journal of Reality Therapy, 15,* 32–36.

Livneh, H., & Sherwood, A. (1991). Application of personality theories and counseling strategies to clients with physical disabilities. *Journal of Counseling and Development, 69,* 525–538.

McArthur, M. J. (1990). Reality therapy with rape victims. *Archives of Psychiatric Nursing, 4,* 360–365.

Mickel, E. (1991). Integrating the African centered perspective with reality therapy/control theory. *Journal of Reality Therapy, 11,* 66–71.

Mickel, E. (1993). Reality therapy based planning model. *Journal of Reality Therapy, 13,* 32–39.

Palmatier, L. L. (1990). Changing pictures by changing symptom patterns. *Journal of Reality Therapy, 10,* 3–25.

Parish, T. S. (1989). Ways to take effective control and enhance self-concepts. *Journal of Reality Therapy, 9,* 34–38.

Parish, T. S. (1991). The influence of attitudes and beliefs in the classroom and beyond. *Journal of Reality Therapy, 11,* 14–20.

Parish, T. S. (1992). Using quality school procedures to enhance student enthusiasm and student performance. *Journal of Instructional Psychology, 19,* 266–268.

Peterson, A. V., & Woodward, G. D. (1994). Pete's pathogram as a tool to measure the success of the CHOICE drug education program. *Journal of Reality Therapy, 14,* 88–93.

Protheroe, D. (1992). Reality therapy and the concept of cognitive developmental stages. *Journal of Reality Therapy, 12,* 37–44.

Renna, R. (1990). The use of control theory in the education of students with sensory, cognitive, and physical challenges: A public school special education collaborative approach. *Journal of Reality Therapy, 10,* 34–39.

Renna, R. (1991). The use of control and reality therapy with students who are out of control. *Journal of Reality Therapy, 11,* 3–13.

Sanchez, W., & Garriga, O. (1995). Reality therapy, control theory, and Latino activism: Towards empowerment and social change. *Journal of Reality Therapy, 15,* 3–14.

Scanlan, W., & Stumph, A. J. (1995). Bridges to Glasser: An application of reality therapy/control theory to the process by which we manage change. *Journal of Reality Therapy, 15,* 66–70.

Schaeffer, S. B., & Bratter, B. I. (1990). The uses of Glasser learning team model to evaluate the John Dewey Academy. *Journal of Reality Therapy, 10,* 46–53.

Schatz, A. M. (1995). School reform and restructuring through the use of the "quality school" philosophy. *Journal of Reality Therapy, 14,* 23–28.

Smadi, A. A. (1991). Dynamics of marriage as interpreted through control theory. *Journal of Reality Therapy, 10,* 44–50.

Stanton, D. T. (1992). Treating sexual offenders: Reality therapy as a better alternative. *Journal of Reality Therapy, 12,* 3–10.

Stanwood, D. L. (1992). Grief and the process of recovery. *Journal of Reality Therapy, 12,* 11–18.

Williamson, R. S. (1992). Using group reality therapy to raise self-esteem in adolescent girls. *Journal of Reality Therapy, 11,* 3–11.

Wubbolding, R. E. (1988). *Using reality therapy.* New York: Harper & Row.

Wubbolding, R. E. (1990). Evaluation: The cornerstone in the practice of reality therapy. *Omar Psychology Practitioner Series, 2,* 6–27.

Wubbolding, R. E. (1991a). *Understanding reality therapy.* New York: HarperCollins.

Wubbolding, R. E. (1991b). *Using reality therapy in group counseling* (videotape). Cincinnati, OH: Center for Reality Therapy.

Wubbolding, R. E. (1992). *Reality therapy training manual.* Cincinnati, OH: Center for Reality Therapy.

11

COGNITIVE THERAPY

FUNDAMENTAL TENETS

History

Cognitive therapy, as we know it today, draws on several important precursors, which taken separately would not likely be identified as contributing to the powerful, eclectic system that we will describe in this chapter. We include under the heading of cognitive therapy all systems, strategies, and techniques that in recent years have come to be recognized as belonging in the therapeutic purview of the cognitive processes. What we call *cognitive therapy* is really *cognitive therapies,* which have coalesced since about 1970 into a new formal system of counseling and psychotherapy that has experienced phenomenal growth. In a survey of influential psychotherapists who were also clinical psychologists, Warner (1991) reported that one in three respondents identified *eclecticism* as their primary theoretical orientation. A close second was *cognitive behavioral orientation,* which was strongly preferred to the third ranked *psychoanalytically oriented* theories. Warner's findings are indicative that the cognitive therapies have swiftly emerged as a family of potent treatment modalities.

As Albert Ellis (1982; 1984) has reminded us throughout his career, the concepts and principles you will find in this chapter have been handed down through many generations of helpers and philosophers. Knapp (1985) has highlighted the career of T. V. Moore, author of *Cognitive Psychology* (1939), which described many of the therapeutic perspectives that cognitive psychologists have owned as new developments in the field. Moore and other psychologists of his time, such as E. C. Tolman, recognized the centrality of perception, imagery, memory, and consciousness as topics worthy of investigation. George Kelly's (1955) "personal constructs" psychology was an early precursor to cognitive therapy. His cognitive model was among the first to emphasize the role of beliefs in the controlling and changing of thoughts, feelings, and behaviors.

Cognitive therapy has been formulated on many separate but important building blocks. No one person is credited with being the specific therapeutic architect of the distinct structure of applied cognitive psychology. Perhaps Albert Ellis (1962; 1984), Aaron Beck (1970), and Donald Meichenbaum (1977) should be considered the major contributors to what cognitive therapists refer to as the *cognitive system.* We include in that system the essential components found in cognitive behavior modification (CBM) (Meichenbaum, 1977), cognitive therapy (CT) (Beck, 1970), and cognitive behavior therapy (CBT) (Beck & Emery, 1985; Beck & Weishaar, 1995; Ellis, 1984; Ellis & Grieger, 1986).

Overview of Cognitive Therapy

Cognitive therapy is based on the formulation that how one thinks largely determines how one feels and behaves (Beck & Weishaar, 1995). Therapy is a collaborative process of empirical investigation, experimentation, reality testing, and collaborative problem solving between therapist and client. The client's maladaptive conceptions, interpretations, and conclusions are subject to scientific scrutiny and hypothesis testing. Cognitive and behavioral experiments as well as verbal techniques "are used to explore alternative interpretations and to generate contradictory evidence that supports more adaptive beliefs and leads to therapeutic change" in the client (p. 229). Cognitive therapy is used in the treatment of a number of mental disorders. Some of the best known applications have been Beck, Rush, Shaw, and Emery's (1979) treatment of depression and Beck and Emery's (1979; 1985) use of the approach in helping clients experiencing anxieties and phobias. But cognitive therapy's scope is by no means limited to these disorders. Beck and Weishaar (1995); Cormier and Cormier (1991); and Freeman, Simon, Beutler, and Arkowitz (1989) have shown that cognitive procedures have been used effectively with an array of human dilemmas. In this chapter we provide the reader only a glimpse of the vast scope of the cognitive system of therapies.

Cognitive Concepts

When we speak of cognitive behavior therapy or cognitive therapy, we include a wider scope of techniques and strategies than most cognitive therapists do. In our philosophy and practice, we include many techniques that are cognitive, even though such techniques may contain elements traditionally classified as behavioral or as belonging in some other therapeutic system (Lazarus, 1977a). For example, in our highly eclectic cognitive behavior practice we may use any one or a combination of the following under the rubric of *cognitive:* systematic desensitization with reciprocal inhibition, mental and emotive imagery, relaxation therapy, covert and/or cognitive modeling, thought stopping, cognitive restructuring, eye movement desensitization and reprocessing (EMDR) (Shapiro, 1989a; 1989b), stress inoculation, meditation, biofeedback, cognitive rehearsal, implosive therapy, flooding and satiation, aversion, hypnosuggestive techniques, and the communications theory system of cognitive mapping or processing of internal and external information called *neurolinguistic programming* (Bandler & Grinder, 1975; Grinder & Bandler, 1976).

While these techniques have operant and respondent behavioral components and also deal with affect, still the vital linchpin of all these procedures is cognition. Such a strong cognitive thrust requires that the therapist possess a sufficient level of expertise and knowledge to set up all these procedures, ferret out cognitions, and catalyze client collaboration. The therapist must be able to travel sensitively yet unobtrusively into the client's cognitive world. It is the client who must validate each cognition and be an integral part of the collaboration. It is the client who must image both dysfunctional and adaptive cognitions and erect and use the cognitive billboards needed to generate internal controls over external behaviors.

For cognitive procedures to be optimally successful, clients must be able to image situations they are seeking to improve or extinguish as if they were occurring in real time. Whether events clients wish to enhance or change are occurring now, have occurred in the past, or may occur in the future, therapeutic success requires that both therapist and client know clearly, without question, what it is the client is seeing, feeling, thinking, and saying to him- or herself internally.

Theory of Personality

Cognitive theory views personality as reflecting the individual's cognitive organization and structure, which are based on both genetic endowment and social influence (Beck & Weishaar, 1995, pp. 236–242). Cognitive therapy recognizes the centrality of cognitive processing in emotion and behavior. The emotional and behavioral responses people emit are largely determined by how they perceive, interpret, and ascribe meaning to situations and events (Beck, 1986). Core beliefs and basic assumptions called *schemas* have a substantial influence on one's cognitive operations. Schemas affect the way an individual structures reality, makes assumptions about the self, interprets past experiences, organizes vicarious learning, makes behavioral choices, and develops expectations about the future (Beck & Weishaar, 1995, pp. 236–239.)

Schemas may be either adaptive or dysfunctional, depending on how the individual's cognitive structures are formed and maintained. The person may have competing schemas, some of which are adaptive and some of which are dysfunctional. *Cognitive vulnerability* is the term Beck and Weishaar (1995, p. 237) use to describe how a person's beliefs and assumptions predispose him or her to a particular psychological distress. Thus, the ways people form, organize, and interpret their basic cognitive structures determine how they will perceive and behave.

Differences between CBT and REBT

Although the theoretical and philosophical underpinnings of cognitive behavior therapy and REBT are closely related and the two systems have more commonalities than differences, there are some noteworthy distinctions, as reported by Dryden (1984, pp. 42–49) and Beck and Weishaar (1995, pp. 236–245). The two systems are summarized in Figure 11.1 on pages 298–299.

In critically comparing cognitive behavior therapy and REBT, Dryden (1984) has argued that although REBT has a more thoroughly developed philosophical framework, CBT's strengths lie in the explicit practical guidelines it offers therapists (p. 40). In a nutshell, Beck (1970) views personality development as founded more on a progression of learned cognitions than on biological predispositions. That is why the cognitive therapies tend to be less philosophic than REBT and have more kinship with the scientific psychology of behaviorism than Ellis usually ascribes to REBT. As indicated in Figure 11.1, REBT views every individual as capable of overcoming great odds to cope with life's maladaptive obstacles, whereas the cognitive therapies propose no clear theoretical position, leaving the data concerning human dilemmas to speak for themselves.

FIGURE 11.1   Comparison of Cognitive Behavior Therapy and Rational-Emotive Behavior Therapy

Criterion	CBT	REBT
Major contributor(s)	Beck, Meichenbaum	Ellis
Development	Experimentally and academically based; reaction to psychoanalytic therapy	Therapeutically and practice-based; reaction to psychoanalytic therapy
Diagnosis	Much data retrieval through lengthy diagnostic interviews	Verbal uncovering of irrational beliefs and integrated with therapy; diagnosis per se not carried out
Client type	Clinical focus on depression and anxiety disorders	No clinical focus; broad spectrum
Therapeutic outcome	Rigorously controlled pre–post empirical studies	Minor emphasis on systematic study
Acquisition of disturbance	Premorbidity with some biological predisposition and early learning of dysfunctional assumptions	Biological predisposition engendering irrational beliefs
Potential for psychological growth	Substantial; no clear philosophy	Great, given its humanistic, positive philosophy
Nature of emotional disturbance	Cognitive; with feelings and behavior underlying cognitive structure and rooted in inferential cognitive distortions; no clear distinction between evaluation and inference	Cognitive; related with feelings and behavior underlying cognitive structure and rooted in musturbatory ideologies; clear distinction between evaluation and inference
Basic themes of emotional disturbance	Idiosyncratic processing of cognitive distortions; no clear generic processes; disturbance about disturbance in anxiety disorders only	Ego disturbance, discomfort disturbance; thematic irrationalities generic to many disturbances
Perpetuation of emotional disturbance	Cognitive schemata and faulty informational processing edit and distort problems and generate dysfunctional beliefs and maladaptive behavior	Low frustration tolerance; comfort seeking through short-term self-defeating goals
Emotionally healthy personality	Scientifically tests own hypotheses and generates functional beliefs and adaptive behaviors	Scientific and humanistic; atheistic
Psychopathology	Pathological disorders each characterized by a different set of cognitive deficits or distortions	All pathologies have a similar set of underlying irrational beliefs
Distorted client beliefs	Faulty cognitive processing that is self-corrective	Philosophically incongruent with reality

FIGURE 11.1 *Continued*

Criterion	CBT	REBT
Goal of therapy	Help individuals to identify, reality test, and correct maladjusted conceptualization and dysfunctional schema underlying cognitions; little concern with philosophic change	Profound philosophic change; work on self-enhancing life-goals, which are specified
Therapist role in change process	Force not advocated; collaborative, empiricist role; confrontation used as a last resort	Forceful and energetic; didactic, directive, confrontive
Client role in change process	Try out new behaviors in a graded fashion negotiated equal to expectations of client	Try out new behaviors by immediate maximum flooding and exposure beyond immediate expectations of client
Therapeutic strategies	1. Initial task is to identify and correct automatic thoughts 2. Tentative hypotheses developed concerning both secondary and primary assumptions underlying automatic thoughts 3. Hypotheses confirmed or rejected depending on data 4. Therapeutic process based on *induction,* since therapist does not know at outset the nature of the client's cognitions related to the disturbance	1. Determine absolutistic evaluations couched in "musts" or in grossly exaggerated negative conclusions 2. Considerable amount of freelancing 3. Go straight to evaluative thinking; therapeutic process operates on *deduction*
Therapeutic techniques	1. Uses Socratic dialogue: inductive questioning of client at length 2. Asks for evidence concerning client inferences (hypotheses), where data can be gathered from outside world to corroborate or falsify the hypotheses 3. Daily record of dysfunctional thoughts (DRDT) kept by client 4. Wide range of imagery used 5. Behavioral assignments used to test faulty inferences 6. Against flooding because it would threaten the therapeutic alliance 7. Little use of flamboyant and dramatic interventions 8. Cannot use paradox because to do so would require explanation of rationale to client 9. Pragmatic throughout 10. Graded assignments used progressively to approximate goal attainment successively	1. Uses Socratic dialogue; inductive questioning of client as long as it is fruitful 2. Often asks for evidence when the therapist knows a priori that evidence does not exist because clients may believe these irrational beliefs are facts 3. REBT self-help form kept by client 4. Variable use of imagery 5. Behavioral assignments used to change evaluations 6. Flooding used to raise levels of frustration tolerance 7. Frequent use of risk taking, humor, and a wide range of educational and social–psychological methods 8. Uses paradoxical intention 9. Pragmatic and philosophical 10. Against graded assignments because that says client can't tolerate the discomfort

Nature of Maladjustment

Beck and Weishaar (1995, pp. 231–242) maintain that maladjustment stems not so much from irrational beliefs (as RET contends), but from distorted cognitions. One of the systematic errors in cognitive reasoning they identified is selective abstraction (viewing the event or situation out of context). Beck and Weishaar take the position that a great deal of client behavioral dysfunction derives from systematic errors, distorted thinking or expectations, and/or maladaptive cognitions.

Maladaptive cognition, as described by Mahoney (1974), springs from several cognitive deficits: (1) selective inattention—ignoring relevant stimuli and attending to irrelevant stimuli; (2) misperception—mislabeling certain stimuli, both internal and external; (3) maladaptive focusing—focusing on irrelevant external events or stimuli; (4) maladaptive self-arousal—focusing on irrelevant internal cues; and (5) repertory deficiencies—limited or maladjustive behavior caused by deficiencies in cognitive (covert) and/or behavioral (overt) skills. These deficiencies go beyond traditional behavioral views because such views cannot account for vicarious learning, semantic generalization, imagined response patterns, and symbolic processes, all of which are exclusively human functions (Lazarus, 1977a).

Cognitive behavior therapy, cognitive therapy, and cognitive behavior modification are based on the assumptions that (1) maladaptive cognitions lead to maladaptive, self-defeating behaviors; (2) adaptive, self-enhancing behaviors can be induced through the client's learning to generate positive, self-enhancing thoughts; and (3) clients can be taught to shift from covert, self-defeating thoughts and attitudes to self-enhancing thoughts, attitudes, and behaviors.

THE COUNSELING PROCESS

Eclectic Leanings

Cognitive behavior therapy (Beck, 1976; Beck & Emery, 1985; Beck & Weishaar, 1995) and cognitive behavior modification (Mahoney, 1974; Meichenbaum, 1977) use a variety of procedures to assist clients in changing negative, self-defeating responses to positive, self-enhancing, successful behaviors. Cognitive behavior therapy goes beyond operant and respondent thinking in asserting that the client's negative beliefs, thoughts, attitudes, images, and self-dialogue are all generated internally. It further assumes that the therapist can gain access to these data and help initiate positive thoughts, images, and self-dialogue that promote a restructuring of the client's thinking, coping, and behaving.

Depending on the particular client situation, the therapist might operate in a variety of modes—from directive to unconditionally acceptant; from scientific to empathic; from systematic to open; from suggestive to instructive. Indeed, our view of cognitive therapy is that it is highly eclectic within the parameters of the client's thought processes. In cognitive therapy the therapist takes full advantage of everything we know about *cognitive and behavioral* psychology.

Collaborative Qualities

During the helping interview the therapist typically employs a *combination* of cognitive and behavioral strategies (Gilliland & James, 1983). Therefore, therapy incorporates the collaborative involvement (Dryden, 1984, p. 50) of both therapist and client in (1) working together hard and persistently as mentor/facilitator and student/helpee to enable the client to gain permanent cognitive and behavioral control over the presenting problem; (2) *imaging* and *observing* different models of behavior that are positive (negative) and successful (unsuccessful); (3) vicariously thinking about human emotions and behaviors and learning to convert such thoughts into action; and (4) successively practicing new cognitive and behavioral patterns until new self-enhancing thoughts and performance approximate the levels desired by the client. The entire therapeutic process is viewed not as being done *to* or *for* the client, but as being done *with* the client (Beck & Weishaar, 1995; Dryden & Trower, 1986; Gilliland & James, 1997, p. 53; Gilliland & Myer, 1985).

STRATEGIES FOR HELPING CLIENTS

A great many procedures fall within the purview of cognitive helping strategies. We will comment briefly on the following major techniques:

1. Beck's cognitive psychotherapy
2. Relaxation training and relaxation therapy
3. Systematic desensitization
4. Mental and emotive imagery
5. Cognitive and covert modeling
6. Thought stopping
7. Cognitive restructuring
8. Meditation
9. Biofeedback
10. Neurolinguistic programming
11. Eye movement desensitization and reprocessing (EMDR)

Beck's Cognitive Psychotherapy

The goals of Beck's cognitive therapy are to correct faulty information processing and help clients modify assumptions that maintain maladaptive behaviors and emotions (Beck, 1986; 1989; Beck & Emery, 1985; Beck & Weishaar, 1995). The first and most important strategy is to develop a trustful and collaborative relationship through the use of accurate empathy, warmth, and genuineness (Beck, 1986; Beck & Weishaar, 1995). A collaborative relationship enables the therapist to assess the client's expectations regarding therapeutic success (Beck, 1986; Beck & Emery, 1985; Beck & Weishaar, 1995).

Once the therapeutic relationship is established, the therapist uses collaborative empiricism, Socratic dialogue, and guided discovery in an attempt to get clients to recognize their erroneous assumptions, identify their cognitive distortions, and counteract their dysfunctional behavioral and emotional responses (Beck, 1986; 1989; Beck & Emery, 1985; Beck & Weishaar, 1995).

Collaborative Empiricism

This requires the therapist and client to become coinvestigators, scientifically examining the evidence to support or reject the client's distorted cognitions. The collaborative relationship facilitates the mutual determination of treatment goals, eliciting and providing feedback, and demystifying therapeutic change. Biased thinking is corrected and adaptive alternatives are jointly developed. Brief segments taken from the case of Myra (whom we shall follow through this chapter), a woman undergoing chemotherapy following a mastectomy, illustrate the eclectic leanings of cognitive therapy.

TH: Myra, you say you can't stand thinking about it and can't possibly face it! Yet, you've described how in the army you handled some of the toughest problems of panic at the firing range among the young soldiers in your platoon. What's the fundamental difference between facing that stress and what you're facing now?

CL: Well, I guess I knew all the soldiers were looking up to me and somehow I mustered up the strength to do it.

TH: What are some similarities between that tough situation and your ability to muster up strength in your present situation?

CL: (pause) Well, this is different, but I still have the same strengths of character that I had then. I haven't really lost that.

Socratic Dialogue

In Socratic dialogue (Beck & Young, 1985), careful questioning by the therapist promotes new learning in the client. The objectives are to catalyze the client's (1) exploration and definition of problems; (2) identification of assumptions, thoughts, and images; (3) evaluation of the meanings of situations and events; and (4) assessment of the consequences of maintaining maladaptive thoughts and behaviors (Beck & Weishaar, 1995, pp. 244–245).

CL: At a rational level, I know that this malignancy will likely be arrested and I will probably go on with my life. So far, the tests are quite encouraging. But at the emotional level, I feel robbed or cheated, especially of a very special part of my womanhood. I also realize on some level that I'm choosing to feel that way.

TH: Myra, let's explore the consequences of your continuing to think and feel that way. What will happen if you keep focusing your energy on that one aspect of yourself, as if all of your negative and erroneous assumptions are true—even though right now there is no medical evidence to support those assumptions?

Guided Discovery

This enables the client to reassess and modify maladaptive beliefs and assumptions. Through collaboration with the therapist the client is guided in designing and carrying out experiments that result in the client's discovery of new and adaptive ways of thinking that, in turn, translate into improved cognitive and behavioral choices for the client (Beck & Weishaar, 1995, p. 245).

CL: Ever since my lab tests came in this morning I've felt relieved—kind of like I've been given a new lease on life.

TH: So, what does that tell you about your previous unfounded assumptions and premature fears?

CL: Well, it says that all this worry about how bad things are liable to be is really wasted worry.

TH: Myra, it seems to me you may have identified a key ingredient in your own healing process. Now, if what you've discovered is true, let's you and me set up an experiment to test whether your assumptions and fears can be altered before you encounter your next hurdle—which, incidentally, is tomorrow morning, when your prosthesis consultation is scheduled to occur.

We have found that the therapeutic application of each of these strategies is enhanced through the use of audiotape and/or videotape techniques. Our clients consistently report that their learning and retention of the relaxation, cognitive, imagery, modeling, and practice activities engaged in during the therapy interview are greatly strengthened by either listening to the audiotapes of our sessions or watching the videotapes. They frequently report that the audio or video reviews, reexperienced as homework assignments, are more powerful and lasting than the initial therapy sessions. We believe this is true because the time lapse allows them to process mentally what went on during the sessions and because they are instructed to watch or listen to playbacks in a state of complete relaxation in their own homes, with no interruptions from the telephone, television, or any other source.

As a part of the video or audio helping strategy, we ask our clients to bring their own cassettes for use during therapy. That provides them with ownership of both the process and the media and with a repository of their own therapeutic progress. Our clients report that the audio or video enhancement is enormously valuable to them. We believe that because most people have access to standard VCR or audio equipment in their homes, the use of audio or video media is a valuable adjunct to many therapy situations. However, this strategy should be used with great care, discretion, and ethical and professional judgment. It requires a great deal of risk taking by both therapist and client.

Relaxation Training and Relaxation Therapy

The development of effective relaxation strategies has played an important role in the emergence of cognitive therapy as a viable system of helping. Some of the noteworthy contributors have been Benson (1976); Bernstein and Borkovec (1973); Carrington (1978a; 1978b); Cautela and Groden (1978); Jacobson (1964); Lehrer (1982); Lehrer, Woolfolk, Rooney, McCann, and Carrington (1983); Shapiro (1980); Southam, Agras, Taylor, and Kraemer (1982); and Woolfolk, Lehrer, McCann, and Rooney (1982).

Modern problems commonly amenable to remediation through relaxation training and relaxation therapy include stress, anxiety, physiological problems (such as headaches or other pain not traceable to organic causes), and pressures related to the workplace and the fast pace of modern lifestyles. A great number of procedures have been developed to help clients relax both mind and body, meditate, and manage their stress and the pressures of life. Beginning with Jacobson in 1929 and proceeding through the 1980s, much sophisticated work has taken place to empower therapists to use their mental and emotive talents to help clients learn to relax, meditate, and restore equilibrium to their hectic lives.

One example of the effective use of relaxation therapy would be helping a client with no organic disorders whose presenting problem is headaches and vomiting attributed to severe test anxiety. Relaxation therapy would be used to teach the client how to (1) relax all muscle groups and put the whole body in a state of complete physical relaxation, (2) relax mentally (cognitively), (3) reduce anxiety while being totally relaxed, (4) keep out extraneous background cognitions while working on the test anxiety, and (5) use self-relaxation permanently to control not only test anxiety but other debilitating stresses as well.

The theoretical principle underlying relaxation therapy is that it is not possible for the human organism to be in a state of complete physical relaxation and at the same time be emotionally anxious. Conversely, it is not possible for the organism to be totally relaxed mentally and at the same time physically uptight. Thus, the therapist applying the cognitive strategy of relaxation assumes the client is physically relaxed in a way that associates that relaxed feeling and image with being cognitively relaxed in the examination room. It is further assumed that the client will transfer that mentally relaxed state to the real testing situation.

Systematic Desensitization

Wolpe (1958; 1961; 1982) and Lazarus (1968; 1982) developed and perfected techniques for systematically using clients' internal mental processes to help them control their own adverse responses to aversive stimuli and inhibit undesirable behaviors. They used both cognitive and behavioral concepts and strategies to teach clients to desensitize themselves to debilitating phobias. Many writers classify systematic desensitization as a purely behavioral strategy. However, we believe it represents one of the earliest behavioral procedures that clearly extended traditional behavioral principles to include internal cognitive events as behavioral data to be used in therapy. Both Wolpe (1982) and Lazarus (1968) used clients' mental processes as rich sources for connecting thinking and behaving. Both called for the client mentally to generate pictures or images and to use reciprocal images to inhibit, counterbalance, or dispel anxieties. With the advent of the incorporation of emotional (emotive) images in the therapeutic process, we are even more sure that systematic desensitization belongs squarely in the cognitive camp (Cormier & Cormier, 1991, pp. 480–507).

Although systematic desensitization was originally based on the learning principles of classical conditioning, it has become the first treatment of choice for many problems—such as phobias, irrational fears, and anxieties—where there are no obvious external dangers and where the main source of the phobias is internal. An example of an appropriate use of systematic desensitization is the treatment of a client who has an irrational fear of elevators. The therapy would incorporate three basic steps: (1) muscle relaxation and relaxation therapy, (2) construction of a hierarchy representing the anxiety-producing situations the client typically faces and needs to overcome, and (3) graduated and progressive pairing through emotive imagery of the anxiety-producing situations with the relaxed state of the client (Wolpe, 1982). The desensitization sessions would be continued until the client could "stand," without debilitating anxiety, to be presented with elevator scenes and finally could go alone to an elevator and ride it without discomfort.

Mental and Emotive Imagery

Mental imagery is a process through which a person focuses on vivid mental pictures of experiences or events—past, present, or future. Mental imagery can be useful to the therapist in both the assessment of clients' problems and the therapy process. Boswell (1987) calls it *abstract imaging*. He finds it useful in (1) assessing the relationships between clients' emotional and intellectual experiences and their presenting symptoms, and (2) determining how those experiences become exaggerated and intensified in clients' minds. He uses mental imagery as a primary therapeutic strategy for helping clients forget the past and focus on the here and now (p. 175).

Emotive imagery is a procedure developed by Lazarus and Abramovitz (1962) in which the client imagines, in a covert but vivid way, the emotional sensations and feelings of an actual situation or behavior. Since the early 1960s the use of imagery as a therapeutic strategy has gained wide acceptance and use (Horan, 1976; Kazdin, 1979b; Lazarus, 1977b; 1982; Lazarus & Abramovitz, 1962; Mahoney, 1974; Maultsby, 1984; Sheikh, 1983; Shorr, Sobel-Whittington, Robin, & Connella, 1984). A mental image becomes emotive whenever the person imagines an emotional or feeling state paired with a specific image. For example, a person may clearly imagine dealing with a very abusive person and, at the same time, imagine feeling a growing sense of strength, confidence, calmness, and security.

Emotive imagery is a derivation of systematic desensitization in that it extends and expands to many other problem categories the systematic desensitization concept of maximizing the use of client-generated cognitive images and pictures to cope with phobias. In emotive imagery the client focuses on safe, positive, and pleasant images as a strategy for blocking and coping with many anxiety-provoking situations in real life (Cormier & Cormier, 1991, pp. 349–366).

The case of a practicum student who was threatened and emotionally paralyzed by a verbally abusive client vividly demonstrates emotive imagery. The student's practicum supervisor borrowed an idea from Lazarus's (1977b) use of superheroes or superheroines with children (pp. 106–107). The supervisor had previously noticed that the student always wore large bunches of bracelets on her wrists. The student was told to imagine herself as Wonder Woman and use her magic bracelets to fend off the verbal bullets of the abrasive client. Armed with her bracelets, at the next therapy session she was able to confront the client with his inappropriate behavior. The student used emotive imagery to prepare for the session by imagining herself as Wonder Woman and at the same time vividly envisioning herself exercising a strong sense of control, strength, self-confidence, and poise.

In therapy that uses any form of imagery, if the client has trouble or shows reluctance in imaging, another technique may be more appropriate. Clients who are psychotic or who have generalized anxiety neuroses are not appropriate subjects for the procedure because they may lose touch with reality or become extremely threatened.

Cognitive and Covert Modeling

Cognitive Modeling

Cognitive modeling was developed by a number of therapists (Beck, 1970; 1976; Kazdin & Mascitelli, 1982a; Mahoney, 1974; Sarason, 1973) who wanted to find ways to help clients learn what to say to themselves to ensure that they would avoid self-defeating thoughts and behaviors while performing tasks that they want to complete. Cognitive modeling (Beck, 1976) is a combination of overt and covert strategies. Therapist and client work collaboratively to change the client's beliefs, self-statements, or mental attitudes toward a task, behavior, or situation. In a structured, systematic series of modeling episodes, the therapist usually employs five steps, such as those demonstrated in the following example, to help the client learn and independently use cognitive modeling.

Consider the example of a therapist helping a male graduate student overcome the fear and intimidation that keep him from asking his advisory committee chair to step down so that he may acquire a different chair. Here, the five steps of cognitive modeling are as follows: (1) the therapist serves as a model (taking the role of the student) by performing the task of confronting the imaginary advisory committee chair while talking aloud to himself; (2) the client is instructed to perform the task (as modeled by the therapist) while the therapist instructs the client aloud; (3) the client is asked to perform the same task again while instructing himself aloud; (4) the client whispers the instructions while performing the task of confronting the imaginary advisory chair; and (5) the client performs the task while instructing himself covertly. In the final step, the student confronts his advisory chair entirely by himself and in a purely cognitive mode. He performs, under instruction of the therapist, what Cormier and Cormier (1991, p. 377) describe as cognitive modeling with cognitive self-instruction.

Covert Modeling

Covert modeling, initiated by Cautela (1971), has been used extensively to teach clients mentally to envision a model (preferably themselves performing an imaginary task) successfully accomplishing a desired goal (Bornstein & Devine, 1980; Bry & Blair, 1979; Cautela, 1971; 1976; Kazdin, 1979a; 1980; Kazdin & Mascitelli, 1982b; Watson, 1976).

Covert modeling provides a variety of effective, efficient, and creative ways to help clients visualize themselves engaging in positive and successful actions (Cautela, 1976; Kazdin, 1975). It is similar to cognitive modeling except that the client does not model or perform overtly. All the steps of the modeling, which are similar to the steps in cognitive modeling, are described aloud by the therapist, with the client relaxed and being verbally instructed to imagine the scenes the therapist presents. Covert modeling is applicable to helping clients develop assertive behaviors, reduce avoidance behaviors, treat alcoholism, and deal with obsessive-compulsive anxiety. Covert modeling has been used in combination with cognitive modeling and observational learning as an effective method of in-service training of school counselors in the use of cognitive procedures (Cormier & Cormier, 1991, pp. 354–375; Gilliland & Johnston, 1987; Johnston & Gilliland, 1987).

One example of an appropriate use of covert modeling was with a forty-five-year-old woman who complained of the fear of possible encounters with her ex-husband. In a series of covert modeling scenes, followed by audiotaped homework assignments, the client was able to (1) visualize herself feeling frightened and intimidated; (2) experience, initiate, and use appropriate assertion skills; (3) successfully confront her ex-husband at a social gathering; and (4) demonstrate positive, self-enhancing actions and feelings that she remembered from the covert modeling. While the woman was physically and mentally relaxed with her eyes closed, the therapist verbally presented to her all of the scenes, images, and cognitive and emotive descriptions of herself performing the task she had told the therapist she wanted to be able to do.

In completing her homework assignments, the client reported that her fears and apprehensions were reduced to tolerable levels and that, to her surprise, the exercises provided self-enhancing carryover in her long-term troubled relations with her mother. This report was not unusual. Covert modeling and other cognitive strategies frequently generalize to desensitize and improve the effects of client fears and anxieties that were similar to, but not the specified target of, the structured therapy program.

Thought Stopping

Thought stopping was introduced by Taylor in 1963. Since then it has been widely used to help clients control unproductive, debilitating, and self-defeating thoughts and images through both sudden and progressively systematic elimination of maladaptive thoughts and emotions (Martin, 1982; Rimm, 1973; Tryon & Pallandino, 1979; Wolpe, 1982).

Thought stopping is initially directed by the therapist. The rationale is that if unwanted thoughts are consistently interrupted whenever they occur, their occurrence will eventually be inhibited (Cormier & Cormier, 1985, pp. 385–390). Since thought stopping enables clients to inhibit unwanted and troublesome thoughts, the procedure involves instructing clients to focus on the unwanted thoughts from ten to twenty times daily for several days and shouting "Stop" to end each trial. After several days of practice the client can maintain control covertly by shouting "Stop" each time the unwanted thought occurs (Williams & Long, 1979, p. 285). As soon as the client becomes familiar enough with the strategy to exercise self-control autonomously, he or she is given homework assignments of practicing self-control through thought stopping in situations outside therapy (Cormier & Hackney, 1987, p. 155).

Cognitive Restructuring, Reframing, and Stress Inoculation

A major development in the cognitive therapy movement has been what Cormier and Cormier (1985, pp. 403–447) have described as influencing or mediating the client's cognitions through cognitive restructuring, reframing, and stress inoculation.

Cognitive Restructuring

Cognitive restructuring (Cormier & Cormier, 1991, pp. 402–415; Ellis & Grieger, 1986, pp. 286–289; Meichenbaum, 1977; Mitchell & Krumboltz, 1987) is a rapidly growing systematic strategy whereby clients are taught to replace negative, debilitating cognitions with positive, self-enhancing thoughts and actions. The strategy assumes (1) that self-defeating behaviors flow from either the development of defective cognitions or irrational thinking and/or self-defeating self-statements; and (2) that a person's defective thinking or self-defeating self-statements can be changed by altering his or her cognitions or views about them. To the extent that the therapist is actively involved in and models self-enhancing thinking and behavior appropriate to the client's stressful situation, the procedure is didactic and directive (Gilliland & Johnston, 1987). However, such a directive approach is derived from the client's unique cognitive deficits, stresses, problems, and accompanying negative self-talk. It should be clearly understood that the therapist does not impose his or her own agendas on the client.

Cormier and Cormier (1991, pp. 402–415) recommend six steps for therapists to follow in cognitive restructuring with a client: (1) verbal set, which includes the rationale (purpose and overview) of the procedure; (2) identification of client thoughts during problem situations; (3) introduction and practice of coping thoughts; (4) shifting from self-defeating thoughts to coping thoughts; (5) introduction and practice of positive or reinforcing self-statements; and (6) homework and follow-up. Typically, the therapist works collaboratively with the client through the six steps. The therapist role is that of consultant, facilitator, mentor, and coach. It is quite important that clients understand the process, that they want to change, and that they be willing to commit to a plan of action developed cooperatively by themselves and the therapist.

It is our view that cognitive restructuring represents the mainstream of cognitive behavior therapy because it makes full and appropriate use of all the cognitive strategies. In using cognitive restructuring we typically involve the client in relaxation, imagery, modeling, reframing, rehearsal, stress inoculation, and thought stopping. The case of Myra, presented in this chapter, is focused primarily in cognitive restructuring.

Reframing

The objective of reframing (also called *reformulating* or *relabeling*) is to modify or restructure a client's view or perception of a problem or behavior (Bandler & Grinder, 1982; Cormier & Cormier, 1991, pp. 415–432). Cormier and Hackney (1987) defined reframing as "the gentle art of viewing a situation differently" (p. 233). Reframing is a valuable therapeutic technique in cases where redefining, reformulating, or relabeling the problem situation, the behavior or motives of others, or the attitudes of the client changes the view or perspective of the problem so that it is more understandable, acceptable, or solvable (Borysenko, 1987, pp. 137–157).

One frequent example of the use of reframing is in counseling with persons who either are addicted to substances or are enablers or codependents for persons who are addicted. Whenever clients can reframe the problem to redefine themselves as either addicts or enablers, it sheds a different light on the whole situation by allowing them to perceive themselves as a part of the problem and solution rather than being a victim or blaming a victim.

Stress Inoculation

This technique is designed to give clients confidence and skill in dealing with future problems (Feindler & Fremouw, 1983; Meichenbaum, 1985). Stress inoculation is the process of teaching clients both cognitive and physical skills for autonomously coping with future stressful and distressing situations. It is a cognitive approach to teaching clients to (1) *discriminate* between alternative thoughts, actions, choices, and situations that lead to stress and options that lead to effective coping with stress; and (2) *use* alternative cognitive and behavioral skills to manage successfully the stresses and pressures in their lives (Cormier & Cormier, 1985, p. 423). Stress inoculation has been used since the early 1970s to prepare clients to deal with anticipated stresses, anxieties, or tensions caused by a wide variety of traumatic psychological or physical debilitation (Holcomb, 1986; Schwartz, 1986; Wells, Howard, Nowlin, & Vargas, 1986; Wertkin, 1985). Meichenbaum and Turk (1976) view stress inoculation for protection from psychological tensions as analogous to medical inoculation for defending the physical body against disease.

Cormier and Cormier (1991, pp. 421–432) recommend seven steps in the stress inoculation procedure. These steps are almost identical to those in cognitive restructuring. The main difference is that in stress inoculation the emphasis is proactive and future-oriented. The problem material, imagining scenes, cognitive and direct-action rehearsals, and homework assignments are derived explicitly from the client's descriptions of stress-evoking situations.

The application of stress inoculation is illustrated in the case of a fifty-five-year-old woman enrolled in graduate school many years after completing her bachelor's degree. Although she was quite successful in her business and family life and performed well on graduate school admissions tests, she experienced panic and periods of excessive stress and anxiety as she contemplated statistics class, performance in graduate school, and the thought of not achieving a 4.0 average. The therapy focused on teaching the woman stress inoculation so that she could (1) inoculate herself against the stress of talking to her statistics professor about her fear of statistics and need for tutoring; (2) convince herself, through inoculation, that her anxiety level could endure earning a B in the statistics course and that she would not suffer from guilt for receiving that grade; and (3) prepare herself to cope with her own negative self-evaluation and self-rejection in the event that she found schoolwork too difficult as an adult returning to the university.

Four stress inoculation sessions were recorded on audiotape. The woman was asked to listen to each session at home, in a relaxed state with no interruptions, as part of her homework. She reported that listening to the tapes at home enhanced her understanding of stress inoculation and reinforced what she learned during the therapy sessions. In a three-week follow-up contact she reported that she had had no more recurrences of panic and that her stress levels were quite tolerable. At the end of the semester she reported that her stress inoculation program was keeping her anxieties at tolerable levels and that she had made 98 on her research proposal and a 91.4 (B) for her term grade in statistics. She was quite happy with the B.

Meditation

The term *meditation* has traditionally been associated with the centuries-old mystical techniques of the Far East whereby one achieves high levels of relaxed introspection and altered states of consciousness. Examples are Zen (Zazen) breath meditation and transcendental meditation (TM) (Shapiro, 1980). Cormier and Cormier (1991, pp. 447–456) indicate that a great deal of commonality exists among the different types of meditation, self-hypnosis, and relaxation techniques such as Benson's (1976) relaxation response. They are similar in that each technique helps the client relax, sharply focus the entire mental apparatus on one important idea or thought, and keep all extraneous thoughts and/or stimuli out of the present cognition. Many kinds of meditation are used by cognitive therapists in various settings (Cormier & Cormier, 1991, pp. 447–456).

Meditation as a therapeutic technique typically helps the client concentrate on some internal or external stimulus that serves to focus the client's attention away from aversive stimuli. Borysenko (1987) characterizes meditation as "nothing more than anchoring your attention in the present" (p. 39). She recommends meditation as the method of choice for regaining control over overwhelming stress and anxiety (pp. 29–53). It is a strategy designed to help clients consciously concentrate on positive, self-enhancing thoughts as opposed to dwelling on negative, self-defeating thoughts—especially ruminations on the past (Carrington, 1978b; Shapiro, 1980). Cormier and Cormier (1985) characterize meditation strategies as useful in treating "both cognitive and physiological indexes of stress, including anxiety, anger, pain, and hypertension." They state further that the most effective use of meditation focuses on prevention as well as remediation of stress-related symptoms (p. 448).

An example of the use of meditation was in helping a thirty-five-year-old man whose job as a commodities broker made his ulcer worse and exacerbated his physical and emotional stress, which increased whenever his job pressures increased. The meditation strategy focused on helping the client learn to relax both his mind and his body, concentrate vividly and completely on the positive successes and the stress-free times at the brokerage firm, and keep job-related worries and past and future risks from intruding on his present thinking. The meditation was successful because the client was willing to learn, to use the audiotapes made during therapy sessions as homework, and to practice consistently the meditation technique.

Biofeedback

The development of *biofeedback training* (BFT) was an unprecedented event in the merging of the psychological and medical aspects of controlling one's own body (Brown, 1977). Essentially, biofeedback is a method of using technology to communicate to a person what his or her body is doing and teaching that person to use mental processes to control bodily functions (Brown, 1974). Biofeedback offered new ways to help clients control stress, anxiety, and tensions through the control of blood pressure, temperature, and other physiologic functions.

Biofeedback has been described as "simply the feedback of biological information to the person whose biology it is" (Brown, 1974, p. 4). The reasons BFT work are not clearly known. What is clear is that the mind exerts a considerably greater influence over bodily functions than many behavioral scientists formerly assumed was the case. In fact, it can be said that the human mind can exert control over any known function of the autonomic nervous system, provided it has accurate data on the level and direction of the internal physiologic events it wishes to monitor.

Some BFT clinics use sophisticated electronic equipment, such as electroencephalographs to monitor changes in the electric potential in the brain and central nervous system; electromyographs to provide audio and visual records of the electrical responses of muscle tissue to nerve stimulation; and electronic devices and technology to measure blood pressure, rate of heartbeat, galvanic skin reaction, and so forth. The essence of the therapeutic use of BFT procedures is that all involuntary bodily responses that can be accurately measured and monitored can be changed.

Used in conjunction with other techniques, BFT can be effective and efficient in helping clients with physiologically related problems such as hypertension, disorders of motor functioning, gastrointestinal difficulties, chronic pain, Raynaud's syndrome, tension headaches, and stress-related disorders (Hatch, Fisher, & Rugh, 1987). Further, BFT has been used to help athletes treat physiological deficits and improve their performance in their sport (Sandweiss & Wolf, 1985).

The range and complexity of BFT instrumentation and procedure are great. A simple indoor-outdoor thermometer can be an acceptable device for monitoring skin temperature and blood flow to the extremities. Instrument choice depends on the client's problem and the therapist's level of training and experience with BFT techniques. One relatively simple strategy, for example, was the use of a skin thermometer to help a secretary decrease her anxiety (and low score) on a civil service typing examination. The client could not perform the task because she would get "anxious" and the muscles in her arms and hands would cramp. Through BFT the secretary was taught to raise the skin temperature in her arms and hands by cognitively focusing on an appropriate image to increase the flow of warmth to that body area. After several abortive attempts to pair an image with the desired physiologic behavior (soaking in a hot tub, reclining in a warm meadow, and so on), the secretary found that she could elevate her extremity skin temperature by concentrating and imagining warm, glowing spots on the insides of her elbows. She subsequently was able to increase the blood flow to her arms and hands, relax her muscles, and remain free of cramps while she successfully passed her typing test.

Neurolinguistic Programming

Neurolinguistic programming (NLP) is the name derived from a communication theory (Bandler & Grinder, 1975; Grinder & Bandler, 1976) whereby people wield five sensory channels, referred to as *representational* (R) systems, to process information. These channels are termed (1) visual (sight), (2) auditory (hearing), (3) kinesthetic (feeling), (4) olfactory (smell), and (5) gustatory (taste). For communication and therapy purposes, the visual, auditory, and kinesthetic channels are the most important.

Neurolinguistic programming is a powerful tool for the therapist to use in effectively establishing rapport and maintaining an empathic relationship with clients. Lankton (1980) found that when the therapist can identify and utilize the sensory channel that the client predominantly uses, he or she can match or pace the client's inner experience. For example, different clients might use different predicate verbs to indicate sensory ways of communicating (mapping) their inner experience: (1) visual ("I see that . . . "); (2) auditory ("I hear that . . . "); or (3) kinesthetic ("I feel that . . . "). Lankton notes that the therapist who can match the predicates of clients "will literally be speaking the client's language" (p. 19). Cormier and Hackney (1987) describe how NLP can be effectively used to pace the client's verbal and nonverbal cues, thus allowing the therapist to understand more fully the client's internal experiencing and to mirror those cognitive experiences for the client (pp. 45–48). Pacing involves synchrony between the therapist and the client's verbal and nonverbal behavior. Cormier and Cormier (1991, p. 559) advise that timing and pacing enhance the efficiency of the interview by decreasing client resistance and enabling the therapist to avoid taking a stand prematurely.

The use of neurolinguistic programming is illustrated by a therapist doing career counseling with two different clients. One client wants to change from primary teaching to a career that affords travel; the other client cannot visualize herself as a gainfully employed person. The therapist uses visual channeling with the first client and auditory channeling with the second, having discovered that each client has different ways of mapping experiences and of processing and interpreting internal and external information. The therapist works with the first client by paying particular attention to his adjectives and adverbs and then uses sensory words to match, pace, and channel therapeutic responses to him. Thus, to program the client to examine new career choices, the therapist uses and models visual words and expressions such as *see, clear, focus, picture, view, perspective, plain, bright, colorful, glimpse, watch,* "Now look," and "Can you picture this?" Concomitantly, to program the second client to explore paid positions, the therapist employs auditory terms and expressions such as *listen, yell, tell, told, talk, hear, discuss, shout, loud, noisy, call,* "Now listen," "Sounds like," and "I can tune into this" (Cormier & Hackney, 1987, p. 47).

Eye Movement Desensitization Reprocessing (EMDR)

Eye Movement Desensitization (EMD) was developed by Francine Shapiro (1989a; 1989b) to combat posttraumatic stress disorder (PTSD). The "R" was later added by Shapiro (1991) to indicate a reprocessing of information along with changing to more positive cognitions and desensitization of the traumatic memory. EMDR has been used mainly to treat traumatic memories, but Shapiro maintains that it has utility in working with a variety of negative self-attributions that have occurred at some earlier point in time, are held in the nervous system in state-specific form (as they occurred at the time of the noxious event), and continue to plague clients (Shapiro, 1995, pp. 14, 41–42).

Although EMDR has a therapeutic basis in both psychodynamic and behavioral approaches, one of its major axioms is that a cognitive reassessment or negative thoughts needs to occur and positive new injunctions about the event and the person are incorporated by the client so that the memory is redefined (Shapiro, 1995, pp. 22–24). From that standpoint, it is our belief that EMDR most closely fits a cognitive behavioral approach, although its incorporation of a variety of techniques could place it as a self-contained eclectic or multimodal approach as well.

EMDR treats negative memories by requiring that the client maintain in awareness one or more of the following:

1. An image of the memory
2. A negative self-statement or assessment of the trauma
3. The physical anxiety response.

Shapiro (1989a; 1989b) proposes that it is best when all three conditions are held at the same time, but she acknowledges that the presence of any one is sufficient for desensitization to occur. Anxiety level is assessed by Wolpe's (1982) subjective units of discomfort scale (SUDS) (0 equals no anxiety; 10 is the highest anxiety possible). Because negative self-cognitions are also part of the disorder, shifts in the client's cognitive view of the traumatic event are also assessed by a validity of cognition (VOC) scale that Shapiro (1989a) developed (1 means the cognition is completely untrue; 7 means the cognition is completely true). The client is asked to focus on the noxious memory and then isolate the most traumatic point while he or she builds a picture of it in his or her mind's eye. The client then states which words best describe the picture and rates him- or herself on the SUDS and VOC scale, indicating the physical location of the symptoms (Shapiro 1989a; 1989b).

The client is next asked how he or she would like to feel and is told to generate a new positive self-statement that reflects the desired feeling; he or she is then asked to judge how true that new statement is (Shapiro 1989a; 1989b). Shapiro (1989b) then gives the client a standard set of instructions designed to diminish performance anxiety and performance demands. She explains the instructions are important because clients may also have difficulty accepting the initial changes they feel in themselves. Her instructions are the following:

> *What we will be doing is often a physiology check. I need to know from you exactly what is going on, with as clear feedback as possible. Sometimes things will change and sometimes they won't. I may ask you if the picture changes— sometimes it will and sometimes it won't. I may ask if something else comes up—sometimes it will and sometimes it won't. There are no "supposed to's" in this process. So just give as accurate feedback as you can as to what is happening, without judging whether it should be happening or not. Just let whatever happens, happen (p. 213).*

The client is told to generate the scene, the negative statements, and the noxious feelings, and visually follow the therapist's finger, which is moved rapidly and rhythmically back and forth about one foot in front of the client's face at a rate of approximately two back-and-forth movements per second across a sweep of about 12 inches. For clients who have trouble with this approach, Shapiro uses a slightly different format, in which the therapist's fingers are to the side of the client's field of vision and are alternately moved up and down. The movement is repeated 12 to 24 times for one set (these movements are called a *saccade,* which means a sort of a pulling or pressing movement). After each set of saccades, the client is asked to erase the scene from his or her mind and take a deep breath. The client is then told to bring up the noxious image again and ascribe an SUDS level to it. After two sets of saccades, if the image has not changed, the client is asked if the picture has changed or if anything new has come into the image. If so, the new image is desensitized before returning to the old image. Periodically, the client is asked to assess image, cognition, and memory. The answers are used to determine new insights, perceptions, or alterations.

If the cognition fails to change after two sets of eye movements, there may be a mismatch between the cognition and the image, or vice versa. In each case image and cognition must be congruent with one another. If they are not, then one or the other needs to be replaced.

The client may also be instructed to think of a physical location of anxiety in the body if the SUDS level remains high. He or she is asked to concentrate on the bodily sensation while new saccades are given. When the focal point of physical discomfort subsides, the client is asked to return to the original picture of the trauma and the standard EMDR procedure is resumed (Shapiro 1989a; 1989b).

When the SUDS level reaches 0 or 1, the client's belief in the validity of the desired cognitions is self-assessed by his or her giving a VOC rating to the original cognition. Regardless of what that rating is, the client is then asked to visualize the original picture along with the positive self-statement and another set of saccades is instituted. Shapiro (1989b) reports that it is not uncommon for different traumatic events and cognitions to be uncovered as the client moves through the procedure. When no new events or negative cognitions are elicited, the EMDR procedure is terminated.

Shapiro (1989b; 1995, pp. 328–338) reports that a 60 to 90 percent rate of removal of symptoms of one to three traumatic or negative memories can occur in as little as one session with well-selected and adequately prepared clients. This success rate is supported by other independent sources (Boudewyns, Stwertka, Hyer, Abrecht, & Sperr, 1993; Cocco & Sharpe, 1993; Forbes, Creamer, & Rycroft, 1994; Montgomery & Ayllon, 1994; Silver, Brooks, & Obenchain, 1995; Thomas & Gafner, 1993; Vaughan, Armstrong, Gold, & O'Connor, 1994; Vaughan, Wiese, Gold, & Tarrier, 1994). However, we want to caution that EMDR involves a good deal more than waving a finger in front of a client's face. As with all cognitive behavioral approaches, we urge any therapist to obtain specific and intense training for the techniques in this chapter. In unskilled hands, many of these techniques are dangerous and may create even more trauma in the client than is already present.

SAMPLE CASE

The following case study incorporates excerpts from two different sets of cognitive restructuring therapy sessions. The purpose is to provide examples of a therapist working with a client on two different presenting problems related to one major life-threatening problem. In both sets of excerpts, the client is experiencing cognitive deficits about her situation, and in both sets the therapist uses cognitive behavior therapy with primary emphasis on cognitive restructuring.

Example One

The first set of excerpts demonstrates the therapeutic use of cognitive restructuring in the case of Myra Malik, an army veteran in her early thirties who had developed the belief, following a mastectomy, that her body was unacceptably impaired and that she was destined to have a life of physical pain and emotional stress as a result. Therapy followed the six steps of cognitive restructuring.

TH: (verbal set) Myra, the main thrust of our sessions will be to assist you in identifying the self-defeating thoughts and self-talk you're giving yourself about the operation and to help you develop and learn to use self-enhancing thoughts in a way that will lead to freeing you from stress and pain. As an example of some of these negative self-thoughts you've expressed, I'm going to state what I heard you say *prior* to going into the hospital, *during your stay* there, and *after* you came out. *Before* you went in you said, "This can't be happening to me. I can't stand this horrible situation. I know I'll never be able to stand it. I can't stand to give up part of my body." *During* your stay, you said things like "Now, no man will ever want me; I know I can't stand the chemotherapy treatments; what's going to happen to me now? I'm alone and I'm scared to death." *After* you came out, your statements were something like, "Now I'm only half a woman; next time it may get me; I dread going out in public; maybe it would be better for me now if I didn't wake up so I wouldn't have to face this again."

Now let me change to positive self-talk about the same situation. I want you to imagine, as vividly as you can, saying these things *before* you went into the hospital: "This is happening to me, but I can handle it; I've been in bad situations in the army— if I could stand that, I can stand this; I may give up part of my body but I won't give up the good part—I'll only give up the diseased part." *During* the stay in the hospital, you could have said, "If no man wants me because I've had breast surgery, he isn't much of a man; if I can stand OCS basic, I can stand chemotherapy; I didn't realize I had so many friends; now I know what friendship really means." *After* you left the hospital, you could have said to yourself, "The pictures and explanations of the cosmetic surgery they showed me thrilled me; now, there's no reason why I can't live a normal, happy life; I'm young, I've got a lot to live for, and I have more friends than ever!"

TH: (identifying client thoughts in problem situations) Tell me exactly what you're thinking when you say, "I'm not going back to chemotherapy." What are those cues, ideas, et cetera, that start you off? Is it the pain? Is it fear? Is it lack of self-confidence? Lack of guts? Tell me precisely what the emotions are that make you want to behave in self-destructive ways. Imagine you have on a headset and you're hearing a very rational little announcer in your head: "The treatments are painful and inconvenient; I don't look good now; I'm sick; but the tests are coming out good, and I'm going to live; not only that, I'm going to enjoy living."

Now that you know what those negative thoughts sound like, I suggest you listen to the tape recording of this session each day for the next four days. Listen to it while you are relaxed on a couch or bed so that you've got a good idea of the difference between your negative and positive self-talk. Make a diary of the times each day you engage in both positive and negative thoughts and self-talk so we can get a handle on the length, times, and conditions in which they occur.

TH: (introduction and practice of coping thoughts) We are now going to do something that's really important to whipping this problem. We're going to replace that self-defeating, negative talk with positive, coping talk. I've already modeled what you could say in those situations that wind up being bad. You may have some other, better thoughts you can use. If so, that's fine. Either way, the idea is to conjure up some thoughts that will deal positively with the situation, plan on how to get out of the situation, relax while you're doing it, and use positive reinforcers that encourage you to keep attacking those self-defeating thoughts. Once we have those, you can go back over the tape and practice saying them to yourself.

TH: (shifting from self-defeating to coping thoughts) I'm going to demonstrate how you can shift those self-defeating thoughts around to really positive thoughts that attack the problem, so just tune that headset in and listen. Here we go! "God! I'm here in my apartment alone and that fear is just starting to sweep over me. *(anxiety)* Stop that nonsense! *(cue)* Now go over to the telephone, pick it up, and call Gayle. She said she wanted to get a pizza." *(proactive coping response)* Now that you know when those thoughts occur and how to change them, we're going to practice controlling and changing them until it's so automatic it'll be like water off a duck's back. So put yourself into that situation and let's give it a try.

TH: (introduction and practice of positive or reinforcing self-statements) Hey, Myra! You've really gotten into this and have done a super job of sticking with the game plan. You've really learned how to beat those killer statements into the ground. So why not give yourself credit where credit is due? I'd like you to add one more kind of statement to what we've already done. That is, I want you to learn how to give yourself a pay-off. Just sit back, put your earphones on and listen. "Now, I'm out here at the pizza parlor. I'm having a great time, particularly since Gayle introduced me to that cute graduate student in engineering. The way he's been giving me the eye and hanging on my every word, I really feel good! I may even decide to put some moves on that cute guy myself! Moping around at home is for dummies and wallflowers. I am a woman! I am unconquerable!" If you'll do this and really buy into it, there's no way those killer statements will get to you. So I'd like you to think up some really potent reinforcing statements, and we'll practice those until you become your own best reinforcing agent.

TH: (homework and follow-up) Myra, you've done really well implementing the techniques. I believe you're ready to go full blast! What I'd like you to do is practice it for one week without any further help from me. Keep your log up to date on your thoughts and listen to the tapes of our practice session every day. I'm sure you'll succeed at this, but if there are problems, we'll go back and troubleshoot the system.

These excerpts illustrated the therapist in a didactic mode. Of course, the client was involved along the way. The point is that this first set of excerpts gives the details of the procedures directed by the therapist toward solving one presenting problem containing clear cognitive distortions by the clients.

Example Two

Rationale and Overview
In the second set of excerpts with Myra, the therapist again demonstrated cognitive behavior therapy techniques, primarily cognitive restructuring. Myra was seen in therapy following a radical mastectomy performed in a VA hospital. The following excerpts are from audiotaped interviews with Myra at the hospital.

CL: I guess they told you how upset and depressed I get when I think about how disfigured I'm gonna be. The women from the Cancer Society are coming in tomorrow to explain the implant and prosthesis to me. I'm about to panic just thinking about their coming.

TH: Myra, I'm glad we're having this talk today! The procedure we're going to do today will help you to identify the things you're thinking when you begin to feel panicky, depressed, or anxious about dealing with the prosthesis. Before we're through, you will learn that what causes the panic and depression is simply unfounded thinking, not facts. We will begin right now to work on more realistic ways for you to think about the implant and prosthesis, and this will help you to gain control of your own unproductive and panicky emotions.

The therapist was explaining to Myra the purpose and rationale of cognitive restructuring. The therapist had noted that Myra is an educated and articulate person. She is a captain in the Army Reserve as well as a veteran of four years' active service in the U.S. Army. Therefore, the therapist's language reflects structuring the therapy according to the client's level of functioning, and the therapist's focus on the client's sensory channel of feeling and on language pacing that indicates the therapist's awareness of the value of neurolinguistic programming as practiced by Lankton (1980).

CL: I feel better already. What you've said makes sense. I hope you can help me get rid of some of this fear and panic.

TH: I sense that you're really ready to work on your thoughts. That's good! We'll do three things to help. First, we will identify the kinds of things you're thinking before, during, and following consultations about your breast implant. Second, we'll teach you how to stop a self-defeating thought about the implant situation and replace it with a positive, self-enhancing thought. Third, we will help you learn how to give yourself credit for changing your own self-defeating thoughts.

[Here the therapist was providing Myra a brief overview of the procedure.]

CL: I guess I somehow know that my anxiety and panic are caused by my exaggerated thinking, but that doesn't seem to help.

TH: That's precisely the reason it's important for us to work together on your thinking right now, Myra. You're really talking about your own self-defeating thoughts about the implant. Such self-defeating thoughts about the implant, or any other stress-producing situation, are ways you interpret the situation. But these interpretations you generate are usually negative and unproductive, like thinking that you will never be a complete woman again and this will be so awful that you cannot accept yourself, ever again. In contrast, a self-enhancing thought is a more realistic, constructive, and positive way to interpret your future life with a breast implant—like thinking, "This is not what I would want, but I am on my way to health again, and I am more than just breasts; I can live, work, be happy, marry, have a family, and do about anything I set my head to, and that's fine; I can be as strong and invincible as I can truly believe, in my mind, that I am." How does that feel to you as I say it?

The therapist was deliberate in explaining to Myra the difference between rational or self-enhancing thoughts (facts) and irrational or self-defeating thoughts (beliefs) and gave her pertinent examples.

CL: Well, I've worried myself insane over it. I've been doing exactly what you're describing, and the more I worry the worse my panic and anxiety seem to get.

TH: Myra, that's the reason it is important for you to understand that whenever you continue to be preoccupied with your inner negative thoughts and worry about the outcomes of your recovery this can affect your feelings and your behavior. Worrying about the recovery can really make you feel anxious and panicky and can actually interfere with your regaining good health. Thinking positively and using your imagination constructively can certainly help you erase your worries, help you feel more relaxed, and enable you to handle the whole implant and recovery situation more easily and effectively.

Here, the therapist was explaining the influence of irrational and self-defeating thoughts on Myra's emotions and performance.

CL: That's making a lot of sense. I'm beginning to look forward to viewing my condition more positively.

TH: So what you're wanting to do right now, Myra, is to work on developing positive mind control over your recovery. You're really wanting to use your mind to get rid of the negative emotions, such as panic, and to get on with accentuating your positive assets.

The therapist was confirming Myra's motivation to work on her own cognitive restructuring and was using a verbal set (to predispose Myra to believe that the therapy will work). What the therapist has done in these excerpts is to accomplish step one of the cognitive restructuring (rationale and overview).

Identifying Client Thoughts in Problem Situations
Now that Myra is motivated to work on her problem and accepts the therapist's rationale concerning the cognitive restructuring procedures, the next step is to identify the thoughts that are contributing to her panic and anxiety toward her impending breast implant. The therapist will want to explore both the range of situations and the specific content that Myra cognitively generates. An essential tool the therapist uses in every session with Myra is an audio tape recorder. Recorded data are valuable in helping the therapist prepare and carry out the cognitive therapy and in helping Myra, as she listens to the taped sessions, enhance her learning and awareness.

TH: Myra, think of the last time you were upset by thoughts of the implant. Describe for me what you think before you begin to feel panicky. What are you usually thinking about when conversations and consultations about the implant are presented to you?

CL: I'm thinking, "Oh my gosh, I dread this! I can't stand it! I wish they wouldn't come. I don't want to talk about this. I don't even want to think about it. I don't want to be cut on any more. I don't want any ugly scars! I just know I will look horrible by the time they're through."

TH: Good. We have that on our audiotape. Now, what are you thinking while the medical specialists are talking to you about it?

CL: By the time they get in here and crowd around my bed, I'm so upset and anxious I don't know what I'm thinking. I guess I'm thinking, "This is awful! Why don't they leave? Why are they discussing me like I'm a broken-down machine? I just know I'll end up being a defeminized person that no man would ever look at, much less love."

TH: What thoughts are going through your mind after the consultation is over?

CL: Oh Lord! I think, "I'm confused and scared. Why did this have to happen to me? My life is ruined!"

TH: All right. Now let's see which of those thoughts are actual facts about the implant situation or are positive and constructive ways to interpret it. Which thoughts are mainly your beliefs about the implant situation that are unproductive, negative, or self-defeating?

CL: I don't know. As we're talking about it right now, I get to feeling better; then I imagine the worst and just start to panic again!

TH: All right, Myra. I want you to just turn that thought off right now. Just go back, in your mind's eye, to a place of safety, relaxation, serenity, and warmth. Just relax again. Just like you did when we first started. Imagine you have lots of time. Just lots of time. So relaxed. So comfortable. Just take your time, and whenever you get completely and comfortably relaxed again, begin to tell me what you're seeing, feeling, and thinking. Just take your time. Lots of time. (*Myra relaxes; long pause*)

CL: I'm sitting on a chaise longue. I'm at the beach. I'm very comfortable. The sun is keeping me warm. The sea breezes are refreshing. I'm in my bathing suit, wearing sunglasses, with sunscreen lotion all over me. I have my music and my reading. I'm feeling relaxed and content. I'm not thinking about the hospital or my operation or anything like that. I'm thinking that the sun and the sea and the rest will make me whole again.

TH: Good. Just take lots of time. Feel yourself getting more relaxed every moment. Getting stronger and stronger. Healthier and healthier. So relaxed. Free of pressures. Free of pain. Free to think, in a very relaxed and safe place, about the power you have right there in your body—to think, to control, to emerge as a stronger you. Now, with your whole body so relaxed and in a state of pure ecstasy, I want you to begin to think about and name the thoughts you want to begin saying to yourself, whenever you begin to feel anxious and panicky. Just continue to relax, with lots of time, and whenever you begin to get a very good idea of those healthy thoughts that you most want to have and use, begin to say them . . . now.

The therapist had used relaxation many times with Myra, so she was ready and motivated to enjoy it and use it productively. The therapist was also asking Myra to recall and record specific thoughts that she could use to effect cognitive restructuring. As an additional means of identifying Myra's thoughts in the problem situation, the therapist later assigned problem-identification homework.

TH: We've made a good start on nailing down those nasty self-defeating thoughts. An additional way to help you and me identify your various thoughts about the implant situation is to keep track of your thoughts as they happen. I'm going to leave this tape recorder right here on the stand beside your bed. I want you to use it liberally. Every time you have a profound thought about your medical condition, I want you to say it into the microphone right then. If you have a positive, healing thought, say it. If you have a negative, panicky thought, say it, too. I want us to listen to the audiotape at the beginning of our next session, after supper tonight.

The therapist was using a tape recorder rather than a log. Tape recorders are often preferred to logs because clients can usually put more thoughts onto the audiotape than they can on a writing pad, and the voice helps both therapist and client to identify additional emotional content and detail about the problem.

Introduction and Practice of Coping Thoughts
The introduction and practice of coping thoughts are crucial to Myra's successful cognitive restructuring. We will briefly describe what the therapist does with Myra.

Before proceeding very far in this step, the therapist reviews the audiotape with Myra and ensures that all the negative and positive thoughts are identified. Then the therapist explains the purpose and potential use of coping thoughts and gives examples that pertain to the client's situation. Positive, self-enhancing thoughts that focus on Myra's anxiety about the implant *before* the situation are confronted and *during* conversations about the implant are collaboratively developed. Then constructive coping thoughts and behaviors are generated to equip Myra actually to deal with feeling panicky, anxious, or overwhelmed.

The therapist next directs Myra in thinking of additional coping thoughts that she could use or has used in dealing with the mastectomy, implant, or any other traumatic situation. Myra is then coached in practicing three important aspects of attaining control of her coping thoughts: (1) verbalizing the most positive and self-enhancing coping statements; (2) using the coping statements both before and during a problem situation; and (3) appropriately sequencing and mentally internalizing the meanings of her statements during rehearsal and actual problem solving.

TH: Now, Myra, let's put it all together by your imaging that you're in your room one hour before the women from the Cancer Society are coming. As you begin to feel panicky or anxious, stop and practice the coping thoughts we have been using.

TH: Myra, image, as vividly as you can, how it feels to be there and what your coping thoughts really mean to you as you picture yourself, in your mind's eye, talking with those women.

The entire session is devoted to the introduction and practice of coping thoughts that Myra and the therapist judge to have the most potential for success.

Shifting from Self-Defeating to Coping Thoughts
In this step the therapist, as a mentor, introduces Myra to the technique of rehearsing the shift from self-defeating to coping thoughts during stressful periods. The rehearsal of such shifting is done to assist Myra in using her self-defeating thoughts as cues to switch immediately to coping thoughts. Three important procedures contribute to the success of this step: (1) the therapist verbally models Myra shifting from recognizing

a self-defeating thought and stopping it to replacing it with a coping thought; (2) the therapist coaches Myra in her practice of shifting from self-defeating to coping thoughts; and (3) the therapist coaches Myra in practicing using shifting for each stressful situation until the anxiety and panic felt while practicing the situation decrease to a reasonable and negligible level and until she can carry out her own rehearsal using coping thoughts in a self-directed manner. A few examples of the therapist cognitively coaching Myra illustrate these procedures.

TH: Myra, let me demonstrate how you might shift from recognizing a self-defeating thought and stopping it to replacing it with a coping thought. First, I'm in my room, relaxed and comfortable. Suddenly it pops into my mind: "They will walk into this room with my doctor in a little over an hour! Gosh! What will I do? My hands are getting sweaty! I'm feeling both panicky and overwhelmed. I'm thinking I might just freeze up or faint. No! Stop that thought right now! I will just use my deep breathing, like we've been practicing, and I will begin to get calm, serene, and ecstatic. I will just image myself relaxed and greeting them. I will be the coolest, most relaxed person in the room."

TH: Now, Myra, let's rehearse this another way. This time you will imagine the situation and rehearse it. As soon as you begin to feel a self-defeating thought emerging, stop it. Verbalize to me the thought aloud, and command yourself to stop it. Then verbalize to yourself and to me a coping thought in place of it and vividly imagine carrying out, on your own, the coping messages you give yourself.

CL: (*long pause; relaxes*) I'm just lying here reading. Passing the time away. I look out the window. I see a car a long way off with some writing on it. Of course I can't tell what the writing is. Then I think, "Oh my gosh! What if that's them!" I'm feeling panicky and scared again. My palms and my forehead are getting sweaty. (*pause*) Then I think about my thought control! In my mind, I see that great big red stop sign! I think about what it means. I now command myself, "You stop that negative thinking this minute! You know, yourself, that you have nothing to fear and everything going for you. You have the whole VA behind you. You have your whole life in front of you. You're a strong person, both physically and intellectually. You know what you want to do in life. Open up your mind and get ready for what these experts have to tell you and to give you. You can, no, you *will*, do whatever you want to do and be whatever you want to be. You realize you need to know all that essential stuff about taking care of yourself *before* the implant operation. You need to get a thorough and professional consultation about the prosthesis, too. This is going to be a *good* day for you, Myra."

TH: Myra, I'm pleased to say that you are learning the procedure exceedingly well. I can tell that you are understanding the concepts and that you will be able to use your thought control to great advantage for yourself.

As Myra demonstrates the ability to identify, stop, and replace her self-defeating thoughts, the therapist systematically decreases the amount of coaching and mentoring. Before proceeding to the final steps of cognitive restructuring, Myra should demonstrate competence in practicing and carrying out these shifts in a completely autonomous and self-directed manner.

Introduction and Practice of Positive or
Reinforcing Self-Statements

The benefits of cognitive restructuring will not be fully available to clients until they learn how to reinforce themselves for successful coping. Clients do not automatically know the value of reinforcing self-statements and may not know that such self-statements must be learned. Typically, therapists must model and teach the art and skill of self-reinforcement. It is very important for clients to learn to reinforce themselves through self-statements because therapists can provide reinforcement only during therapy sessions. The goal of therapy is client independence, and client self-reinforcement provides a key to obtaining that goal.

The therapist follows four steps in helping Myra attain competency in using reinforcing self-statements. The first step is to explain the purposes of positive self-statements and provide verbal examples.

TH: Myra, you have made excellent progress in learning to use positive coping statements to prepare yourself for facing the implant surgery and rehabilitation. It is now time to solidify your gains by learning to reward or encourage yourself. As soon as you have coped with a panicky situation, you can pat yourself on the back for having done so by thinking a positive or rewarding thought like, "Hey! I did it!" or "I stood up to the test and passed. I can really do it!"

The second step in the introduction and practice of positive or reinforcing self-statements involves instructing Myra to think of additional appropriate self-statements and selecting some statements to practice.

TH: Myra, I want you to think of some things that would be rewarding or encouraging for you to say to yourself whenever you've accomplished your goals. Try to come up with some thoughts that will be right for you, personally.

The third step is for the therapist verbally to model application of selected positive self-statements as self-reinforcement for shifting from self-defeating to coping thoughts.

TH: Myra, this is one way you could reward yourself for having coped. You recognize the self-defeating thought. Now you're successfully using coping thoughts, and you're experiencing thoughts like "Just concentrate on drawing a deep and soothing breath, staying focused right on the task at hand, and keeping control of my thinking and my emotions." Now the consultation is concluded. You are aware that you did an excellent job using coping thoughts. You now reward yourself by thinking "I did it, and I did it well. It was really no big deal. I know how to manage my thinking."

The fourth and final step in helping Myra to practice positive or reinforcing self-statements is to instruct her to practice positive self-statements within the therapeutic interview itself; then, gradually, Myra will practice on her own in real confrontational situations. She will be taught to reward herself by giving herself positive and reinforcing self-statements during and following real situations. She will also put these self-statements on audiotape following her successes, to assist herself and her therapist in fine-tuning her self-rewarding skills.

TH: All right, Myra. As you imagine the confrontation, you're using the coping thoughts you will verbalize. Just relax and imagine your best coping thoughts. Now, imagine the confrontation is over and begin to verbalize several reinforcing thoughts for having successfully coped.

CL: Okay, I handled myself quite well. I'm improving every day. The panic I felt when they first pulled those prostheses out of the box was really nothing to dread. I handled that as well as anyone. I am really making progress, and I'm doing it myself!

Homework and Follow-Up
Even though homework is used in every step of cognitive restructuring, the ultimate goal for Myra is to use cognitive restructuring in any stressful situation in her daily life. The therapist teaches her to do her own self-pacing, monitoring, and problem solving. For a while she must practice on her own, audiotape verbalizations of her thinking patterns, and finally graduate to autonomous use of cognitive restructuring. A key concept throughout the procedure is that Myra must not emerge dependent on the therapist or anyone else.

The homework and follow-up step is the time when the therapist serves as Myra's mentor. Myra lives and demonstrates effective thinking to herself and to the therapist. She develops confidence in identifying self-defeating thoughts, stops unproductive thinking, shifts to coping thoughts, reinforces herself with positive self-statements, and uses these mechanisms effectively in her everyday life as well as in particular problem situations.

CONTRIBUTIONS OF COGNITIVE THERAPY

The foremost contribution of the cognitive movement to therapy in general and to behavioral psychology in particular is that it has firmly established internal human thought processes as data or events to be studied and used by clients in therapy.

Another contribution has been the validation of a number of relaxation techniques as legitimate procedures for use in formal therapy. Before the emergence of the cognitive strategies, little attention was paid by the therapeutic community to relaxation. Today, many kinds of therapists, inside and outside the cognitive movement, make great use of the power of relaxation to help and to heal.

The cognitive movement has enhanced the rational therapies, such as REBT. Since the emergence of the cognitive movement, more and more attention has been given to the effects of covert human beliefs and self-talk on overt behavior. That view of human functioning should prove beneficial to all the helping professions.

The two powerful cognitive perspectives—the Meichenbaum practitioner formulation and the Beck researcher base—combine to bring cognitive behavioral therapies into the forefront as a systematic scientist-practitioner model that the therapeutic community can readily understand and use. While a majority of practitioners do not necessarily validate an approach, nevertheless it appears from our vantage point that a majority of current psychotherapists use some form or degree of cognitive therapy in their work. This movement has seen a relatively rapid evolution out of operant conditioning and REBT that would not have been clearly in evidence in the 1960s and 1970s.

SHORTCOMINGS OF COGNITIVE THERAPY

One of the main shortcomings of the cognitive behavior system is that it requires a great deal of training, skill, hard work, and practice to use the various procedures available to the therapist effectively. It is almost always difficult to ferret out the cognitions that have become skewed and debilitating for the client. Not every therapist is equipped by attitude and aptitude to apply the cognitive techniques appropriately. The inertia and momentum of the medical model of therapy militate against training in and successful application of cognitive procedures. Many practitioners find it hard to believe that clients can help themselves simply by changing their thinking.

Effective cognitive practitioners must not only understand and be able to apply techniques appropriately, they must also be well grounded in behavioral techniques and learning theory. We have encountered therapists who approach cognitive techniques as no more than a "power of positive thinking" exercise, then become puzzled, frustrated, and bored when outcomes are not attained. Further, they sometimes erroneously ascribe to the cognitive approach flaws that instead are attributable to how it is applied.

A great deal of therapist discipline is essential, and there is less tolerance for error in using the cognitive approaches as compared to some of the other modalities. There is less room for freelancing and greater need to follow set procedures and guidelines. As a result, for those who are not willing to become thoroughly versed in cognitive concepts and procedures, attempting cognitive therapy may prove extremely confining and frustrating.

COGNITIVE THERAPY WITH DIVERSE POPULATIONS

Cognitive therapy is prescriptive for matching specific technique to specific problem (Cormier & Cormier, 1991) without regard to race, creed, or color. The wide diversity of techniques available is a major strength enabling the cognitive therapist, for instance, to use systematic desensitization for phobias, cognitive restructuring for depression, and thought stopping for a diversity of compulsive or habituated behaviors.

Cognitive procedures have a "sliding scale" of sophistication regarding the use of techniques, ranging on a continuum from the use of snapping a rubberband on the wrist to stop a thought to cognitive restructuring where a great deal of skill and effort is expended to enable the client to explore and modify dysfunctional interpretations.

Thomas (1992, pp. 304–310) stated that cognitive approaches are appropriate for working with minority groups. Cognitive techniques are used to engender positive expectations and examine negative expectancies, especially in African-American students and urban families. Thomas describes how she uses Beck's cognitive therapy with urban families to (1) motivate change; (2) reinforce commitment, loyalty, and trust; (3) increase behavioral expectations of love; (4) change cognitive distortions; (5) improve communication skills; (6) solve problems through management of conflict; (7) troubleshoot; and (8) deal with anger and hostility. Thomas corroborates the conclusion of Beck & Emery (1985), Beck and Weishaar (1995),

Douglas (1989), and Jacobson (1989) that one of the most widely recognized strengths of the cognitive approach is that the relationship itself can be used to promote positive changes in diverse clients.

Cognitive formulations such as systematic desensitization provide a vehicle to enable many people from lower socioeconomic classes to restore equilibrium, mobilize themselves, and engender proactive behaviors. Such clients are moved from dependence to independence by empowering them cognitively to shift from perceiving themselves to be externally controlled to putting them in the driver's seat of their thinking. Once people can change their dysfunctional thinking they can quickly see concrete results through a positive change in their own behavior.

For many people from lower socioeconomic classes who have experienced an external locus of control, the discovery that they can truly exercise autonomy over their intellectual apparatus can indeed be liberating. A wide diversity of clients can be effectively helped by cognitive therapy as long as they can recognize the relationships among thoughts, feelings, and behaviors and are able to take some responsibility for self-help (Beck & Weishaar, 1995, pp. 238–249).

The first step in the process of cognitive therapy, initiating a relationship of mutual trust (Beck & Weishaar, 1995), is that approach's greatest strength in working with a diversity of clients. DeRubeis (1990); Dolce and Thompson (1989); Lyddon (1990); Safran (1990); and Stoltenberg, Leach, and Bratt (1989) have confirmed the primacy of the cognitive therapist's relationship with the client. Cognitive therapists work effectively with diverse clientele because they actively pursue the client's point of view throughout the therapeutic process (Beck & Weishaar, 1995, pp. 243–244). By incorporating the Rogerian conditions of warmth, accurate empathy, genuineness, and acceptance, the therapist appreciates each client's personal world view. Therefore, we view the cognitive approach to be suited for use with clients from different racial and ethnic backgrounds, sexes, sexual orientations, socioeconomic statuses, and disability conditions.

Livneh and Sherwood (1991) describe the cognitive approach as having characteristics appropriate for counseling clients who are physically disabled. They cite two reasons: (1) the affect, inner self-verbalizations, and behavior of the physically disabled are largely determined by cognitive perceptions; and (2) these cognitions and self-verbalizations frequently translate into negative feelings about oneself that culminate in the client's lowered self-esteem and erroneous interpretations and conclusions.

Unlike REBT, which would likely attribute the disabled client's problem to irrational beliefs, cognitive theory emphasizes the impact of cognitive deficits or biased selection of information and distorted interpretations. Cognitive strategies and techniques are designed to deactivate such distorted cognitions and interpretations (Beck & Weishaar, 1995, p. 230) and to help the physically disabled client to shift to normal or adaptive cognitive functioning (Livneh & Sherwood, 1991, p. 532).

For clients from diverse races, religions, and national origins, cognitive therapy is similar to REBT in that it is a no-nonsense and straightforward approach that appeals to people without focusing on their origins or lifestyles. It focuses on their thinking and behavior, not on their personhood. It involves the client in every step, from problem identification through meaningful homework and follow-up. It does not view the person as being bad, flawed, or inferior; rather, it views the thinking as distorted or the behavior as debilitating. Therefore, cognitive therapy is a viable approach for helping people from diverse populations because it is adaptable to human nuance and is essentially free of threat or judgment.

SUMMARY

Cognitive therapy is new but has roots deep in the scientific psychology of behaviorism, the rational therapies, and other systems. Cognitive behavior therapy departs from traditional behavioral psychology in that it accepts the operant and respondent components but rejects the concept that only environmental factors can be rightly considered behaviors. Consequently, cognitive therapists perceive all internal thoughts and feelings, which are identifiable by clients, to be grist for study and used by therapists to help clients. We have included in our coverage of cognitive behavior therapy the work and concepts of many cognitivists, foremost among them Albert Ellis, Aaron Beck, and Donald Meichenbaum.

The vast array of procedures developed by leaders inside and outside the cognitive movement constitute an eclectic menu for helping a wide diversity of clients. Among the major procedures are (1) Beck's cognitive psychotherapy, (2) relaxation therapy, (3) systematic desensitization, (4) mental and emotive imagery, (5) cognitive and covert modeling, (6) thought stopping, (7) cognitive restructuring, (8) meditation, (9) biofeedback, (10) neurolinguistic programming, and (11) eye movement desensitization and reprocessing (EMDR).

Cognitive restructuring is probably the most representative of the cognitive procedures. We focused heavily on cognitive restructuring and presented excerpts and comments on the case of Myra to illustrate the use of cognitive strategies with a real client.

Although the cognitive movement is relatively new, it is rapidly developing and has a great many adherents. Cognitive behavior therapy shows great promise as a methodology for therapists and other helpers. It can help clients with assorted problems to use the full power and potential of their minds to gain control of their thinking, emotions, and behavior. Cognitive therapists have the opportunity to use new, creative, and exciting strategies to help clients solve their own problems by gaining control over their irrational and self-defeating thoughts and replacing them with rational self-enhancing thoughts. Cognitive strategies can be evaluated and appreciated on the basis of changes in behavior.

SUGGESTIONS FOR FURTHER READING

Bandler, R., & Grinder, J. (1975). *The structure of magic. I: A book about language and therapy.* Palo Alto, CA: Science & Behavior Books.

Beck, A. T. (1976). *Cognitive therapy and the emotional disorders.* New York: International Universities Press.

Beck, A. T., & Emery, G. (1985). *Anxiety disorders and phobias: A cognitive perspective.* New York: Basic Books.

Beck, A. T., & Weishaar, M. E. (1995). Cognitive therapy. In R. J. Corsini & D. Wedding, *Current psychotherapies* (5th ed.; pp. 229–261). Itasca, IL: F. E. Peacock.

Brown, B. B. (1974). *New mind, new body.* New York: Harper & Row.

Cormier, W. H., & Cormier, L. S. (1991). *Interviewing strategies for helpers: Fundamental skills and cognitive behavioral interventions* (3rd ed.). Pacific Grove, CA: Brooks/Cole.

Lazarus, A. A. (1977b). *In the mind's eye: The powers of imagery for personal enrichment.* New York: Guilford.

Meichenbaum, D. H. (1977). *Cognitive-behavior modification: An integrative approach.* New York: Plenum.

Meichenbaum, D. H. (1985). *Stress inoculation training.* New York: Pergamon.

Wolpe, J. (1982). *The practice of behavior therapy* (3rd ed.). New York: Pergamon.

REFERENCES

Bandler, R., & Grinder, J. (1975). *The structure of magic. I: A book about language and therapy.* Palo Alto, CA: Science & Behavior Books.

Bandler, R., & Grinder, J. (1982). *Reframing.* Moab, UT: Real People Press.

Beck, A. T. (1970). Cognitive therapy: Nature and relation to behavior therapy. *Behavior Therapy, 1,* 184–200.

Beck, A. T. (1976). *Cognitive therapy and the emotional disorders.* New York: International Universities Press.

Beck, A. T. (1986). Cognitive therapy. In E. L. Shostrom (Executive Producer), S. K. Shostrom (Producer), and H. Ratner (Director), *Three approaches to psychotherapy III* (Film no. 2, Case of Richard). Corona Del Mar, CA: Psychological and Educational Film.

Beck, A. T. (1989). An interview with a depressed and suicidal patient. In D. Wedding & R. J. Corsini (Eds.), *Case studies in psychotherapy* (pp. 124–142). Itasca, IL: F. E. Peacock.

Beck, A. T., & Emery, G. (1979). *Cognitive therapy of anxiety and phobic disorders.* Philadelphia: Center for Cognitive Therapy.

Beck, A. T., & Emery, G. (1985). *Anxiety disorders and phobias: A cognitive perspective.* New York: Basic Books.

Beck, A. T., Rush, A. J., Shaw, B. F., & Emery, G. (1979). *Cognitive therapy of depression.* New York: Guilford Press.

Beck, A. T., & Weishaar, M. E. (1995). Cognitive therapy. In R. J. Corsini & D. Wedding, *Current psychotherapies* (5th ed.; pp. 229–261). Itasca, IL: F. E. Peacock.

Beck, A. T., & Young, J. E. (1985). Cognitive therapy of depression. In D. Barlow (Ed.), *Clinical handbook of psychological disorders: A step-by-step treatment manual* (pp. 206–244). New York: Guilford.

Benson, H. (1976). *The relaxation response.* New York: Avon Books.

Bernstein, D. A., & Borkovec, T. D. (1973). *Progressive relaxation training: A manual for the helping professions.* Champaign, IL: Research Press.

Bornstein, P. H., & Devine, D. A. (1980). Covert modeling—hypnosis in the treatment of obesity. *Psychotherapy: Theory, Research, and Practice, 17,* 272–275.

Borysenko, J. (1987). *Minding the body, mending the mind.* Reading, MA: Addison-Wesley.

Boswell, L. K., Jr. (1987). Abstract imaging: Abstract imaging as a mode of personality analysis and adjustment. *Medical Hypnoanalysis Journal, 2,* 175–179.

Boudewyns, P. A., Stwertka, S. A., Hyer, L. A., Albrecht, J. W., & Sperr, E. V. (1993). Eye movement desensitization and reprocessing: A pilot study. *Behavior Therapy, 16,* 30–33.

Brown, B. B. (1974). *New mind, new body.* New York: Harper & Row.

Brown, B. B. (1977). *Stress and the art of biofeedback.* New York: Bantam.

Bry, A., & Blair, M. (1979). *Visualization: Directing the movies of your mind.* New York: Barnes & Noble.

Carrington, P. (1978a). *Clinically standardized meditation (CSM). Instructor's manual.* Kendall Park, NJ: Pace Educational Systems.

Carrington, P. (1978b). *Learning to meditate: Clinically standardized meditation (CSM). Course workbook.* Kendall Park, NJ: Pace Educational Systems.

Cautela, J. R. (1971, November). *Covert modeling.* Paper presented at the fifth annual meeting of the Association for Advancement of Behavior Therapy, Washington, DC.

Cautela, J. R. (1976). The present status of covert modeling. *Journal of Behavior Therapy and Experimental Psychiatry, 6,* 323–326.

Cautela, J. R., & Groden, J. (1978). *Relaxation: A comprehensive manual for adults, children, and children with special needs.* Champaign, IL: Research Press.

Cocco, N., & Sharpe, L. (1993). An auditory variant of eye movement desensitization in a case of childhood PTSD. *Journal of Behavior Therapy and Experimental Psychiatry, 24,* 373–377.

Cormier, L. S., & Hackney, H. (1987). *The professional counselor: A process guide to helping.* Englewood Cliffs, NJ: Prentice-Hall.

Cormier, W. H., & Cormier, L. S. (1985). *Interviewing strategies for helpers: Fundamental skills and cognitive behavioral interventions* (2nd ed.). Monterey, CA: Brooks/Cole.

Cormier, W. H., & Cormier, L. S. (1991). *Interviewing strategies for helpers: Fundamental skills and cognitive behavioral interventions* (3rd ed.). Pacific Grove, CA: Brooks/Cole.

DeRubeis, R. J. (1990). Determinants of change in cognitive therapy for depression. *Cognitive Therapy and Research, 14,* 469–482.

Dolce, J. J., & Thompson, J. K. (1989). Interdependence theory and the client–therapist relationship: A model for cognitive psychotherapy. *Journal of Cognitive Psychotherapy, 3,* 111–122.

Douglas, A. R. (1989). The limits of cognitive-behavior therapy: Can it be integrated with psychodynamic therapy? *British Journal of Psychotherapy, 5,* 390–401.

Dryden, W. (1984). *Rational-emotive therapy: Fundamentals and innovations.* London: Croom Helm.

Dryden, W., & Trower, P. (1986). *Rational-emotive therapy: Recent developments in theory and practice.* Bristol, UK: Institute for RET.

Ellis, A. E. (1962). *Reason and emotion in psychotherapy.* New York: Lyle Stuart.

Ellis, A. E. (1982). Major systems. *Personnel and Guidance Journal, 61,* 6–7.

Ellis, A. E. (1984). *Rational-emotive therapy and cognitive behavior therapy.* New York: Springer.

Ellis, A. E., & Grieger, R. M. (Eds.). (1986). *Handbook of rational-emotive therapy* (Vol. 2). New York: Springer.

Feindler, E. L., & Fremouw, W. J. (1983). Stress inoculation training for adolescent anger problems. In D. H. Meichenbaum & M. E. Jaremko (Eds.), *Stress reduction and prevention* (pp. 451–485). New York: Plenum.

Forbes, D., Creamer, M., & Rycroft, P. (1994). Eye movement desensitization and reprocessing in posttraumatic stress disorder. *Journal of Behavior Therapy and Experimental Psychiatry, 25,* 113–120.

Freeman, A., Simon, K. M., Beutler, L. E., & Arkowitz, H. (Eds.). (1989). *Comprehensive handbook of cognitive therapy.* New York: Plenum.

Gilliland, B. E., & James, R. K. (1983). Hypnotherapy and cognition: A combinatorial approach. *Medical Hypnoanalysis: Journal of the Society of Medical Hypnoanalysts, 4,* 101–113.

Gilliland, B. E., & James, R. K. (1997). *Crisis intervention strategies* (3rd ed.). Pacific Grove, CA: Brooks/Cole.

Gilliland, B. E., & Johnston, R. (1987). Human potential groups: High risk high schoolers model and rehearse for success. Memphis, TN: Memphis State University (ERIC Document Reproduction Service No. ED283084).

Gilliland, B. E., & Myer, R. (1985). Weight management and food intake control. *Medical Hypnoanalysis: Journal of the Society of Medical Hypnoanalysts, 6,* 85–90.

Grinder, J., & Bandler, R. (1976). *The structure of magic II.* Palo Alto, CA: Science & Behavior Books.

Hackney, H., & Cormier, L. S. (1988). *Counseling strategies and objectives* (3rd ed.). Englewood Cliffs, NJ: Prentice-Hall.

Hatch, J. P., Fisher, J. G., & Rugh, J. D. (Eds.). (1987). *Biofeedback: Studies in clinical efficacy.* New York: Plenum.

Holcomb, W. R. (1986). Stress inoculation therapy with anxiety and stress disorders of acute psychiatric inpatients. *Journal of Clinical Psychology, 42,* 864–872.

Horan, J. J. (1976). Coping with inescapable discomfort through in vivo emotive imagery. In J. D. Krumholtz & C. E. Thoresen (Eds.), *Counseling methods* (pp. 316–329). New York: Holt, Rinehart & Winston.

Jacobson, E. (1929). *Progressive relaxation.* Chicago: University of Chicago Press.

Jacobson, E. (1964). *Anxiety and tension control.* Philadelphia: Lippincott.

Jacobson, N. S. (1989). The therapist–client relationship in cognitive behavior therapy: Implications for treating depression. [Special issue: Client–therapist relationship and cognitive psychotherapy.] *Journal of Cognitive Psychotherapy, 3,* 85–96.

Johnston, R., & Gilliland, B. E. (1987). A program for effective interaction between school systems and consultants. *School Counselor, 35,* 110–119.

Kazdin, A. E. (1975). Covert modeling, imagery assessment, and assertive behavior. *Journal of Consulting and Clinical Psychology, 43,* 716–724.

Kazdin, A. E. (1979a). Effects of covert modeling and coding of modeled stimuli on assertive behavior. *Behaviour Research and Therapy, 17,* 53–61.

Kazdin, A. E. (1979b). Imagery elaboration and self-efficacy in covert modeling treatment of unassertive behavior. *Journal of Consulting and Clinical Psychology, 47,* 725–733.

Kazdin, A. E. (1980). Covert and overt rehearsal and elaboration during treatment in development of assertive behavior. *Behaviour Research and Therapy, 18,* 191–201.

Kazdin, A. E., & Mascitelli, S. (1982a). Behavioral rehearsal, self-instructions, and homework practice in developing assertiveness. *Behavior Therapy, 13,* 346–360.

Kazdin, A. E., & Mascitelli, S. (1982b). Covert and overt rehearsal and homework practice in developing assertiveness. *Journal of Consulting and Clinical Psychology, 50,* 250–258.

Kelly, G. (1955). *The psychology of personal constructs.* New York: Norton.

Knapp, T. J. (1985). Contributions to the history of psychology. XXXIX: T. V. Moore and his cognitive psychology of 1939. *Psychological Reports, 57,* 1311–1316.

Lankton, S. R. (1980). *Practical magic: A translation of neurolinguistic programming into clinical psychotherapy.* Cupertino, CA: Meta Publications.

Lazarus, A. A. (1968). Variations in desensitization therapy. *Psychotherapy: Theory, Research, and Practice, 5,* 50–52.

Lazarus, A. A. (1977a). Has behavior therapy outlived its usefulness? *American Psychologist, 32,* 550–554.

Lazarus, A. A. (1977b). *In the mind's eye: The powers of imagery for personal enrichment.* New York: Guilford.

Lazarus, A. A. (1982). *Personal enrichment through imagery.* Workbook (audio tape). New York: BMA Audio Cassettes.

Lazarus, A. A., & Abramovitz, A. (1962). The use of "emotive imagery" in the treatment of children's phobias. *Journal of Mental Science, 108,* 191–195.

Lehrer, P. M. (1982). How to relax and how not to relax: A reevaluation of the work of Edmund Jacobson—I. *Behaviour Research and Therapy, 20,* 417–428.

Lehrer, P. M., Woolfolk, R. L., Rooney, A. J., McCann, B., & Carrington, P. (1983). Progressive relaxation and medication: A study of psycho-physiological and therapeutic differences between two techniques. *Behaviour Research and Therapy, 21,* 651–662.

Livneh, H., & Sherwood, A. (1991). Application of personality theories and counseling strategies to clients with physical disabilities. *Journal of Counseling and Development, 69,* 525–538.

Lyddon, W. J. (1990). First and second-order change: Implications for rationalist and constructivist cognitive therapies. *Journal of Counseling and Development, 69,* 122–127.

Mahoney, M. J. (1974). *Cognition and behavior modification.* Cambridge, MA: Ballinger.

Martin, G. L. (1982). Thought-stopping and stimulus control to decrease resistant disturbing thoughts. *Journal of Behavior Therapy and Experimental Psychiatry, 13,* 215–220.

Maultsby, M. C. (1984). *Rational behavior therapy.* Englewood Cliffs, NJ: Prentice-Hall.

Meichenbaum, D. H. (1977). *Cognitive-behavior modification: An integrative approach.* New York: Plenum.

Meichenbaum, D. H. (1985). *Stress-inoculation training.* New York: Pergamon.

Meichenbaum, D. H., & Turk, D. (1976). The cognitive-behavioral management of anxiety, anger, and pain. In P. O. Davidson (Ed.), *The behavioral management of anxiety, depression, and pain* (pp. 1–35). New York: Brunner/Mazel.

Mitchell, L. K., & Krumboltz, J. D. (1987). The effects of cognitive restructuring and decision-making training on career indecision. *Journal of Counseling and Development, 66,* 171–174.

Montgomery, R. A., & Ayllon, T. (1994). Experimental desensitization across subjects: Subjective and physiological measures of treatment efficacy. *Journal of Behavior Therapy and Experimental Psychiatry, 25,* 217–230.

Moore, T. V. (1939). *Cognitive psychology.* New York: Lippincott.

Rimm, D. C. (1973). Thought stopping and covert assertion in the treatment of phobias. *Journal of Consulting and Clinical Psychology, 41,* 466–467.

Safran, J. D. (1990). Towards a refinement of cognitive therapy in light of interpersonal theory I: Theory. *Clinical Psychology Review, 10,* 87–105.

Sandweiss, J. H., & Wolf, S. L. (Eds.). (1985). *Biofeedback and sports science.* New York: Plenum.

Sarason, I. G. (1973). Test anxiety and cognitive modeling. *Journal of Personality and Social Psychology, 28,* 58–61.

Schwartz, R. M. (1986). The internal dialogue: On the asymmetry between positive and negative coping thoughts. *Cognitive Therapy and Research, 10,* 591–605.

Shapiro, D. H. (1980). *Meditation: Self-regulation strategy and altered state of consciousness.* New York: Aldine.

Shapiro, F. (1989a). Efficacy of the eye movement desensitization procedure in the treatment of traumatic memories. *Journal of Traumatic Stress, 2,* 199–223.

Shapiro, F. (1989b). Eye movement desensitization: A new treatment for post-traumatic stress disorder. *Journal of Behavior Therapy and Experimental Psychiatry, 20,* 211–217.

Shapiro, F. (1991). Eye movement desensitization and reprocessing procedure: From EMD to EMDR—a new treatment model for anxiety and related traumata. *Behavior Therapist, 14,* 128, 133–135.

Shapiro, F. (1995). *Eye movement desensitization and reprocessing.* New York: Guilford.

Sheikh, A. A. (1983). *Imagery: Current theory, research, and application.* New York: Wiley.

Shorr, J. E., Sobel-Whittington, G., Robin, P., & Connella, J. A. (Eds.). (1984). *Imagery: Theoretical and clinical applications* (Vol. 3). New York: Plenum.

Silver, S. M., Brooks, A., & Obenchain, J. (1995). Eye movement desensitization and reprocessing treatment of Vietnam veterans with PTSD: Comparative effects with biofeedback and relaxation training. *Journal of Traumatic Stress, 8,* 337–342.

Southam, M. A., Agras, W. S., Taylor, C. B., & Kraemer, H. C. (1982). Relaxation training: Blood pressure lowering during the working day. *Archives of General Psychiatry, 39,* 715–717.

Stoltenberg, C. D., Leach, M. M., & Bratt, A. (1989). The Elaboration Likelihood Model and psychotherapeutic persuasion. *Journal of Cognitive Psychotherapy, 3,* 181–199.

Taylor, J. G. (1963). A behavioral interpretation of obsessive-compulsive neurosis. *Behavior Research and Therapy, 1,* 237–244.

Thomas, M. B. (1992). *An introduction to marital and family therapy: Counseling toward healthier family systems across the lifespan.* New York: Macmillan.

Thomas, R., & Gafner, G. (1993). PTSD in an elderly male: Treatment with eye movement desensitization and reprocessing (EMDR). *Clinical Gerontologist, 14,* 57–59.

Tryon, G. S., & Pallandino, J. J. (1979). Thought stopping: A case study and observation. *Journal of Behavior Therapy and Experimental Psychiatry, 10,* 151–154.

Vaughan, K., Armstrong, M. S., Gold, R., & O'Connor, N. (1994). A trial of eye movement desensitization compared to image habituation training and applied muscle relaxation in post-traumatic stress disorder. *Journal of Behavior Therapy and Experimental Psychiatry, 25,* 283–291.

Vaughan, K., Wiese, M., Gold, R., & Tarrier, N. (1994). EMD: Symptom change in PTSD. *British Journal of Psychiatry, 154,* 533–541.

Warner, R. E. (1991). A survey of theoretical orientations of Canadian clinical psychologists. *Canadian Psychology, 32,* 525–528.

Watson, L. (1976). The effects of covert modeling and covert reinforcement on job interview skills of youth offenders. Doctoral dissertation, West Virginia University, Morgantown.

Wells, J. K., Howard, G. S., Nowlin, W. F., & Vargas, M. J. (1986). Presurgical anxiety and postsurgical pain and adjustment: Effects of a stress inoculation procedure. *Journal of Consulting and Clinical Psychology, 54,* 831–835.

Wertkin, R. A. (1985). Stress inoculation training: Principles and applications. *Social Casework, 66,* 611–616.

Williams, R. L., & Long, J. D. (1979). *Toward a self-managed life style* (2nd ed.). Boston: Houghton Mifflin.

Wolpe, J. (1958). *Psychotherapy by reciprocal inhibition.* Stanford, CA: Stanford University Press.

Wolpe, J. (1961). The systematic desensitization treatment of neuroses. *Journal of Nervous and Mental Disease, 132,* 189–203.

Wolpe, J. (1982). *The practice of behavior therapy* (3rd ed.). New York: Pergamon.

Woolfolk, R. L., Lehrer, P. M., McCann, B. S., & Rooney, A. J. (1982). Effects of progressive relaxation and meditation on cognitive and somatic manifestations of daily stress. *Behavior Research and Therapy, 20,* 461–467.

12

TRAIT-FACTOR COUNSELING/
PERSON × ENVIRONMENT FIT

History

Trait and factor, the Minnesota point of view, differentialist, directive, and *decisional* all describe a counseling approach centered in four decades of writings by Edmund Griffin Williamson and his colleagues at the University of Minnesota. The classic trait-factor approach that Donald Paterson, John Darley, and E. G. Williamson proposed in the late 1930s was a direct outcome of their investigation of a variety of settings. Going back to the late nineteenth and early twentieth centuries, they integrated Galton's empirical and systematic attempts to measure differences in individual capacities and aptitudes; investigations by Binet in France and Cattell in America of differential prediction of intelligence; and Munstenberg's utilization of such individual differences in industrial applications. They then bound these psychometric approaches to Frank Parsons's theories of vocational guidance (Williamson, 1972, pp. 137–140).

During the Great Depression, Paterson and Darley brought these concepts to the Minnesota Employment Stabilization Research Institute and used psychological tests and other assessment devices to analyze the vocational abilities of the unemployed. Case histories, staffing for diagnosis and prognosis, provision of educational and vocational training, and placement services were all used in a comprehensive attempt to place people in jobs (Williamson & Biggs, 1979, p. 92). At approximately the same time, Williamson was appointed director of the University of Minnesota Testing Bureau. The task of the bureau was to apply those guidance procedures developed by Paterson to the educational and vocational problems of students (Williamson & Biggs, 1979, p. 92).

Thus, out of a "dust bowl empiricism" of the 1930s, trait-factor counseling was born. Its practical purpose was to define human behavior by specific *traits*, such as aptitudes, achievements, personalities, and interests. These traits could then be integrated in a variety of ways to form constellations of individual characteristics called *factors*. Based on such traits and factors, a scientific problem-solving method could be employed that had statistically predictable outcomes that could be applied differently to individuals (Williamson & Biggs, 1979).

Trait-factor's heyday was in the 1940s, when it was put to maximum use in the military's selection and classification efforts during World War II and in developing student personnel services on college campuses. With the advent of Rogers's client-centered approach in the early 1950s, the trait-factor approach was heavily attacked as unreliable, dogmatic, and reductionist and began to fade from the scene as a therapeutic approach. Its impact has degenerated to the point that it is now relegated to career counseling texts, where it is often viewed as having historical significance only. The question may be immediately posed, "So why does it appear in this book?"

While it has not received a great deal of press in the academic literature in the last thirty years, and whether it is known by them as such, the fact is that most school, vocational, and rehabilitation counselors practice a trait-factor approach in some form or the other. Further, many of the aptitude, personality, and interest tests and occupational information materials formulated by the trait-factorists have steadily evolved and remain in use today. Finally, the trait-factor approach is admirably suited to computer-therapist–client interaction with computer-assisted instruction (CAI), particularly computer-assisted career guidance (CACG) programs such as DISCOVER (American College Testing Program, 1988) and SIGI PLUS (Educational Testing Service, 1988), which, whether therapists like it or not, is here and whose role will only expand (Sampson & Krumboltz, 1991).

Offshoots of the trait-factor approach may be seen in Holland's vocational theory (1985), the theory of work adjustment (Dawis & Lofquist, 1984), and the cognitive information processing approach (Peterson, Sampson, & Reardon, 1991). Finally, Chartrand (1991) makes a compelling case for its evolution to a person × environment (P × E) fit approach (Rounds & Tracey, 1990). The P × E fit approach draws heavily from differential psychology and acknowledges the utility of traits for predicting occupational behavior, but it is more interested in the dynamic interaction between persons and environments and in this way differs significantly from the classic trait-factor approach (Chartrand, 1991).

Two distinct attributes uniquely mark the trait-factor approach. First, the theory evolved from a vocational perspective. Second, it developed as a student personnel program in a university setting and later found its way into secondary schools. As such, many of its techniques and practices are based on the vocational and educational counseling of students. It continues to operate in those venues today and is clearly one of the few theoretical approaches at present that focuses on nonpathological clients who are experiencing typical developmental problems of living at the end of the twentieth century. From that standpoint it still operates on its historical principles of preventive counseling, information services, testing, and teaching.

Overview of Trait-Factor Counseling

The trait-factor approach is concerned with the total development of the individual across life stages and environments. Its short-term goal is to help the client stop irrational, nonproductive thinking and behaving and start using rational problem-solving skills for effective decision making (Lynch & Maki, 1981). The counselor–client relationship can be described as teaching, mentoring, and influencing. External measures that allow the individual to gauge personal development against society are used. The long-term goal of the counseling relationship is to provide the client with decision-making skills formulated jointly by the client and society. Counseling is a way station on the road to full development.

Basic assumptions of the trait-factor theory as it particularly applies to career counseling are:

1. Each person possesses a unique and stable pattern of traits that can be measured.
2. There is a unique pattern of traits required for successful performance of the critical tasks of each occupation.
3. It is possible to match the traits of persons with the trait requirements of occupations on a rational and actuarial basis.
4. The closer the fit between a person's traits and the trait requirements of that person's occupation, the greater the likelihood for successful job performance and personal satisfaction (Klein & Weiner, 1977).
5. Personal traits may be viewed in a context of how well they fit into the environmental system within which the person operates. Environmental systems may be viewed in a broad ecological context that includes geographical, local, cultural heritage, family background and influence, socioeconomic class, work/school setting, community setting, and economic climate.
6. In a broader context, "occupational" or "vocational" counseling may be replaced with any of the developmental tasks of living such as going to school, raising a family, or planning for retirement.

Theory of Personality

The trait-factor approach has been criticized as lacking comprehensive theories of personality and counseling (Crites, 1981; Patterson, 1966; Williamson & Biggs, 1979). It is more often seen as a set of procedures for counseling and probably best describes the behavior of school, employment, and rehabilitation counselors (Schmitt & Growick, 1985; Stefflre & Matheny, 1968). Does this mean that trait-factorists do not believe in theory or that school, employment, and rehabilitation counselors do not have any theoretical foundations on which to counsel?

If Chartrand's (1991) premise that the person × environment (P × E) fit approach has issued from trait-factor is taken as valid, then such criticisms seem unwarranted. Holland's (1985) theory of vocational fit between personalities of people and environments is probably one of the most researched and validated theories of personality. Chartrand has also drawn from Moos's (1981; 1987) extensive research on work and social environments to suggest that a complex matrix of P × E factors govern adaptation to a dynamic environment. Work content and personal preferences influence one's cognitive appraisal and coping resources, which in turn influence individual adaptation such as performance and well-being. Overlaying this matrix is another factor that includes the physical features of the environment, the policies and structure of the organization, and suprapersonality orientations like Holland's. Finally, Moos (1987) also promotes three major social climate dimensions: relationships and involvement with other people in the setting, personal growth as applied to goals in the setting, and system maintenance and openness to change in the setting.

Thus, modern trait-factor theory emphasizes the challenge of attaining a complex correspondence between one's traits and one's work environment (Dawis & Lofquist, 1984). The P × E fit approach moves beyond static, stable congruence between person and environment and assumes a more reciprocal, fluid, dynamic process with the individual shaping the environment and the environment influencing the individual in a continuing series of interactions that characterize developmental outcomes (Chartrand, 1991).

In *Vocational Counseling,* Williamson (1965) wrote at length on what an adequate theory should be and what it should do. Theory should not arbitrarily weld counselors to any one precept, but should allow openness to change as new conditions, new problems, and new environments are experienced. No theory is of much good if it prescribes blanket approaches and blanket goals, since that would be opposed to the individual's moral right to choose appropriate goals and would deny individual differences (pp. 153–175).

The philosophy of the trait-factorists is more than one of curative or remedial therapy. It is a general method of life adjustments (Williamson 1950a, p. 213) that reaches far beyond the counseling session. Trait-factorists assume humankind to be rational and capable of making satisfying choices if the necessary facts are available.

Therefore, the counselor's role in helping individuals is largely educational. The counselor not only teaches the client about the meaning of psychometric data presented (Williamson, 1950a, p. 38) but also illustrates the range of options and choices available from an analysis of the data. Client and counselor are concerned with the individual's unique abilities, aspirations, and plans within the context of the values and alternatives in society and its institutions. Thus, counseling must attend to both individual needs and social reality (Williamson & Biggs, 1975, p. 273).

Nature of Maladjustment

Because the roots of the trait-factor approach are based in educational and vocational counseling, a broad band of individuals are counseled who are generally not considered to be pathological. Therefore, maladjustment is viewed in terms of vocational and/or educational maladjustment. One must ask, "What is the relationship of vocational adjustment to adjustment in general?" If we may believe such social psychologists as Erikson (1959, p. 92), who states that "in general it is primarily the inability to settle on an occupational identity which disturbs young people," and Levinson (1978), who in *Seasons of a Man's Life* discusses composite adults whose career crises spill over into the rest of their lives, then vocational adjustment has a great deal to do with life adjustment in general. If one considers that a great portion of one's adult life is spent "on the job" and that a great many potential satisfactions or frustrations come from those moments, then trait-factor practitioners' emphasis on vocational and educational adjustment may not seem as narrow as at first glance.

Whereas personal growth is the vehicle for change in a P × E fit approach, it is relationships and system maintenance that influence commitment to a particular environment (Moos, 1987). Both people and environments have varying degrees of flexibility necessary for adjustment to one another. If one cannot adapt to the constraints of a rigid environment or the environment cannot be changed, there are likely to be serious adjustment problems (Chartrand, 1991).

Whether the environment is work, school, or family, when systems begin to malfunction and relationships subsequently deteriorate, bad things happen to personal growth. When the environment is extremely specific, little deviation from the person is acceptable. Therefore, as the environment changes, the person must stay in correspondence with it (Chartrand, 1991). A classic example is the magical thinking of a person engaged to be married to an alcoholic: "Well, after we're married, he/she will love me so much he/she won't want to drink anymore." Because of the very rigid, maladaptive environment of alcoholism that focuses on intoxication to the exclusion of all else, it is extremely unlikely the alcoholic will change. What is more likely is that if the other person stays in the marriage, he or she will aid and abet the rigid environment by adapting to it or, in the jargon of addiction, becoming an enabler. While the family system may achieve homeostasis, it will be a highly maladaptive environment.

THE COUNSELING PROCESS

Because counseling is an extension of the institution, particularly the school or community, it is educational and thus is involved in a relationship that might best be called guided learning toward self-understanding within the boundaries of the institution or community (Williamson, 1950a, pp. 209–210).

The client comes to counseling with an affective state that ranges from, at worst, crisis to, at best, nagging self-doubt about making the right decision. This feeling state is the result of irrational negative self-evaluation to the extent that normal, rational decision-making processes are paralyzed (Williamson & Biggs, 1979, p. 104). What the client must do at this point in counseling is to integrate the actuarial data presented with his or her own self-appraisal. The client compares him- or herself with new reference points provided by the counselor; generates action hypotheses to be tried; assesses the probability of success of different alternatives; and then tries those alternatives out in the real world. During this process the final judgment for evaluating and acting on the information is the client's (Rounds & Tracey, 1990; Williamson & Biggs, 1979, pp. 91–127).

To apply appropriate counseling techniques, the counselor must make a differential diagnosis of client problems. To obtain a diagnosis the counselor must work with the client to differentiate presenting problems, set priorities among goals, and assess current resources and stressors that could either foster or inhibit planning or adjustment. Based on this information alternative intervention strategies can be developed (Chartrand, 1991). Such a role calls for the counselor to be well grounded in assessment procedures and to have the ability to analyze and apply such data to each client's needs (Stefflre & Matheny, 1968, p. 30). The counselor is an action therapist who assesses and deals with issues in the client's life with the notion that what is gained from counseling will aid the client's self-development for the rest of his or her life (Hennessey, 1980). To accomplish this task the counselor (1) helps the client to understand himself or herself; (2) suggests steps to be taken by the client; (3) directly helps the client to explore his or her own assets and liabilities; and (4) refers the client to other personnel workers for special help (Williamson & Hahn, 1940, p. 213).

To accomplish these four services the counselor often functions as a mentor or teacher. The counselor not only delivers information on abilities, aptitudes, and interests, but also helps clients identify motivating forces in their lives, apprises them of the future implications such forces may have, and, when appropriate, encourages clients to substitute alternative behaviors that will help them reach desired life goals (Williamson, 1958).

In the past, trait-factorists have focused more on the quality and type of information presented than on how the information is processed or the acquisition of problem-solving skills to accomplish successful resolution. According to Rounds and Tracey (1990), the primary goal of P × E fit counseling is to facilitate decision making, planning, and adjusting through the acquisition of problem-solving skills. Their model is a four-step sequence of information processing that includes the following: obtaining information and synthesizing it; goal setting; developing plans; and acting to implement a situation. They acknowledge the effect of emotional arousal at each stage of the counseling process and believe it is important to assess and explore affect throughout the process.

It is the responsibility of the counselor, by virtue of knowledge, skill, and experience, to apprise the client of potential pathways and roadblocks to full development. Both counselor and client freely evaluate the sum and scope of the client's aspirations, frustrations, disappointments, successes, and failures in relation to how these can be synthesized into a meaningful diagnosis. Once this diagnosis is obtained, a prescription as to how the client can actualize positive potentials can be made. If the counselor has truly done a good job, the termination of counseling will be but a starting point that will result in continual self-counseling throughout the client's life (Williamson & Biggs, 1979, pp. 101–102).

Assessment Procedures

Trait-factorists make more use of actuarial measures than practitioners of other approaches because of their emphasis on problem solving. Objective and verified data allow the client greater understanding and exploration of problems (Williamson, 1972, pp. 292–293). Data may be collected by means of six analytic tools: (1) the cumulative record, case, or personnel file, (2) the interview; (3) the time distribution form, (4) the autobiography, (5) anecdotal records, and (6) psychological tests (Williamson, 1939, p. 68).

The *cumulative record, case,* or *personnel file* provides a comprehensive look at the educational, psychological, physical, and work records of the client. Grades, honors, military and criminal activities, work habits, leisure activities, previous test scores, attendance records, and physical and mental health histories are a sample of the variety of P × E components that paint a picture of how the client has performed in the past in the view of instructors, therapists, and supervisors. It is a longitudinal record that may provide insight into the individual's current problems and gives the counselor data with which to compare the client's self-perception in the interview and the facts as significant others view them.

The *interview* retrieves the individual's self-perception. A major component of the counseling process itself, it also serves to integrate the perceptions of the client with those of the counselor and, combined with the reports of others and particular test data, provides the framework within which the client's problem is painted.

The *time distribution form* was originally formulated to monitor how time was spent in wise and unwise ways. In business and industry it still has wide use. In counseling it has been replaced by the *behavior baseline,* which attempts to objectify discrete behaviors and count them in various times, places, and settings to determine how much, when, and where behaviors may need to be changed.

The *autobiography* may be used to obtain fast, poignant pictures of the salient features in one's life. This loose form of analysis lets the client free-associate without the threat of a face-to-face encounter with the counselor, which might cause the client to "repress" certain information that could prove highly significant.

Anecdotal records are specific little slices of the client's life. Usually they are constructed by observers such as family members, teachers, and supervisors who watch the client in specific situations. They may be formally or informally obtained and provide information that might never be seen through other assessment procedures. While admittedly colored by the observer's view, anecdotal records can vividly counterpoint the client's perception of the dimension of the problem. The substance abuser is a classic example of how important the anecdotal reporting of significant others can be in treatment planning.

Psychological tests are the capstone of the trait-factor practitioner's tools. Williamson has made a strong case for their use by contrasting the subjective data the client brings to the counseling session with the objective data of empirical assessment devices. Williamson (1972, pp. 151–153), has listed these advantages:

1. A mathematical analysis of objective and observable data is not possible if one deals only with subjective data.
2. At least an approximation of accuracy in the measurement and identification of client experience, aptitude, interest, and personality is possible.
3. Greater clarity of communication is possible through the use of quantifiable data, compared with the vagueness and bias of the purely subjective client self-report.
4. Through the use of massed data more than one individual can be characterized at a time.

Reliance on tests is not a be-all and end-all. Williamson made clear early in his work that to provide a differential view of people, tests could not be used in a mechanical or isolated fashion and should have diagnostic significance only in relation to individual case data (Williamson, 1939, pp. 74–75). A contemporary example is the belief that computer-generated expert analysis would provide perfect diagnoses. In reality, the single-test "cookbook" analysis has not worked well (Moreland, 1990). The use of objective data in classifying serves to highlight the individuality of the client, who does not lose his or her uniqueness even in an age of computerized data. That the counselor may not achieve 100 percent accuracy in prediction does not mean a return to self-analysis (Williamson 1972, pp. 151–155).

Case History

In their earliest writing (Paterson, Schneidler, & Williamson, 1939, pp. 27–51), the trait-factor practitioners understood that a one-shot test administration was not conducive to adequate reliability and validity in diagnosing and prognosing client problems. The case history therefore became central in ascertaining the differential aspects of clients (Williamson, 1972, pp. 293–294). While the case history concentrates on an ecology that includes family, work, school, health, social, and recreational interests (Williamson, 1939, p. 67), it also seeks to integrate these facets of the individual with test data so that a very clear diagnosis and prognosis can be made.

Rounds and Tracey (1990) indicate that the quality of assessment has more to do with the dependability and accuracy of information than the way the information is gathered. Thus, increasing the client's involvement in the assessment process is important. Assessment is based on client goals and interview data and is made in conjunction with the client (Chartrand, 1991). In P × E fit counseling, psychometric information is one way of organizing self-reported information and can be used to help clients develop a clearer cognitive structure of both themselves and their environments.

Interview

The interview between counselor and client is the boards and nails that build the complex pattern of individual abilities, interests, needs, wants, and values into a unified structure. The methodology of the interview is predicated on the counselor collecting and writing down information on (1) the client's description of, the circumstances of, and the persons associated with the problem; (2) the client's attitudes toward persons, places, and things associated with the problem; (3) the client's attitude as these are discussed; (4) the counselor's tentative estimation of the seriousness, causes, and possible developments; (5) new and additional information to be collected; and (6) suggested next steps discussed about what the counselor and the client will need to do in a cooperative program to work out a solution to the problem (Williamson & Hahn, 1940, pp. 178–179). The comprehensive recording procedure is no less than a continuing and updated game plan of the counseling process.

In conducting the interview the counselor (1) listens attentively, giving suggestions in the early stages of counseling and more specific suggestions in later stages; (2) asks questions to clarify the client's self-understanding; (3) explains the meaning of the client's interests, abilities, and personality traits; (4) outlines a stepwise progression to ultimate decision making; and (5) may serve as an adviser by making decisions as to what will stimulate the client to start taking responsibility for his or her own actions (Williamson, 1972, pp. 164–165).

Computer-Assisted Guidance Systems

The voluminous amount of information on vocational, educational, and social information available makes it impossible for the counselor to stay abreast of the information needs of every client. Counseling in the twenty-first century must take into account the complementary disciplines of sociology, economics, demography, and social psychology if it is to be effective (Otto, 1984). Understanding one's abilities, aptitudes, and interests in relation to the vast array of societal forces that impinge on the individual is critical if such an avalanche of information has any meaning in decision making. How might that be done?

A major innovation in the field of counseling has been the development of computer-assisted guidance (CAG) programs that provide everything from assessment to simulation activities (Sampson & Krumboltz, 1991). The interactive dialogue, storage and searching of data files, and assessment capabilities render the computer an excellent tool for use in counseling (Harris-Bowlsbey, 1984). Counselors may obtain highly reliable scoring, normative interpretations, and specific therapeutic recommendations through the use of computerized testing programs and can assign clients a variety of information retrieval and therapeutic activities that can be done on CAG systems.

In particular, computer-assisted career guidance systems have become one of the most widely used applications of computer technology in the counseling field. Clients may conduct their own self-assessment or work conjointly with the therapist through such occupational interest inventories and information systems as DISCOVER (American College Testing Program, 1988), which links interests and abilities to occupations and SIGI PLUS (Educational Testing Service, 1988), which links values to occupations.

Directories of computer software have identified hundreds of applications to counseling that range from personal, family, and career counseling to administrative, assessment, and research functions (Walz, Bleuer, & Maze, 1989). Computer-assisted instruction provides tutorials and real-life simulations to present concepts, describe examples, measure performance, and present feedback to the learner (Sampson, 1986). Its interactive capabilities allow the user to explore personal values, interests, abilities, and decision-making styles (Hinkle, 1992). A review of the literature indicates that clients react positively to CACG applications by expanding their knowledge of self and the world of work, specifying career and educational plans, and making confident career decisions (Garis, 1983; Sampson, 1984); it is particularly true of younger, better-educated clients who typically are more familiar with computers (Spinhoven, Labbe, & Rombouts, 1993).

The counselor of the future will have to be an information broker, mediator, and interpreter of such machine-generated data to meet the needs of clients (Schmitt & Growick, 1985). The computer, therefore, holds the promise of delivering a sophisticated occupational, social, and educational grouping and assessment model that can provide predictive validity based on sound scientific and actuarial methods.

STRATEGIES FOR HELPING CLIENTS

From a differential point of view, the steps in the counseling process are of primary importance. The following steps were first formulated by Williamson and Darley (1937) and still hold to the present:

1. *Analysis:* acquiring a comprehensive understanding, through appropriate assessment techniques, of how the client is and what he or she is likely to be
2. *Synthesis:* ordering and arranging the various parts of the client into a total picture by assessing information on strengths and weaknesses across the inter- and intrapersonal aspects of the client's life

3. *Diagnosis:* descriptively identifying the problem, discovering its causes, check- ing the logic and the client's reactions, and proposing a program of action based on the objective and subjective data presented

4. *Prognosis:* forecasting on the basis of available choices; diagnosis relates to past and present conditions, whereas prognosis attempts prediction of the future

5. *Counseling:* learning to deal in a generalized way with totality of life; guided learning and reeducation through personal assistance by a variety of tech- niques that help the client apply learning gained in counseling to all kinds of problem situations

6. *Follow-up:* reinforcing, reevaluating, and checking the client's progress in apply- ing what has been learned in counseling to daily life

Although counseling is only one of the helping strategies, it is woven through- out the fabric of the trait-factor approach, from analysis to follow-up. This con- cept of counseling as a pervasive strategy has seemed to evolve, as Williamson moved from understanding that a pure trait-factor approach is untenable to adopt- ing a more developmental point of view. Although we present the steps separately for the sake of clarity, there is a great deal of flux and flow among them. To illus- trate we have woven the component of counseling throughout the other parts of the therapeutic process in the case study of Glenn that follows shortly.

With the advent of computerized assessment, the ability of the counselor to collect, analyze, synthesize, and diagnose has grown dramatically. Structured inter- views, questionnaires, rating scales, and tests can be combined to measure symptom profiles, disabilities, and risk factors. Diagnostic interpretations and treatment plans can be generated by these "expert" programs. By using these in combina- tion with human decision making, a computer-assisted clinical approach can be highly effective in generating a treatment approach (Andrews & Wittchen, 1995; Farrell, 1991; Jager, 1991; Moreland, 1990; Smith, 1993; Warzecha, 1991).

The contemporary trait-factor approach views the client's problem in a devel- opmental and holistic sense (Chartrand 1991; Rounds & Tracey, 1990; Williamson & Biggs, 1979). Therefore, at each step in the case study we look at the counsel- ing process and the problems presented not just as a case of vocational decision making, but rather as a whole-person problem that has ramifications across the significant others and environments of the client.

Pertinent to this process are the hunches and guesses that the counselor makes. Hunches and guesses may seem completely opposed to the notion of a highly em- pirical trait-factor approach, but they may well be as valid as any statistical con- stant if based on valid and differential indicators about a client (Williamson, 1939, p. 105). Throughout his writing, Williamson has constantly promoted counselors as highly capable of making intuitive guesses and formulating tentative hypothe- ses if—and this is a big *if*—they have been well grounded in their discipline (Williamson, 1939), if they constantly engage in research to update their knowl- edge (Williamson & Biggs, 1975), and if they interface with other skilled profes- sionals (Williamson, 1972).

SAMPLE CASE

The following case data were retrieved by the intake counselor during Glenn's initial visit to the university counseling center.

Background

Glenn is a thirty-six-year-old male who is currently employed as a police officer in a large metropolitan city. He works on a tactical unit that is on constant standby to deal with extremely dangerous situations. He moonlights in real estate and referees high school sports. He maintains that the real estate work provides needed income and the referee jobs are for fun and relaxation.

Glenn is married to LaQuita, a nurse who has recently been promoted to a supervisory position in a large hospital. He describes her as a highly skilled professional who takes a great deal of pride and effort in her work and still has time to be an excellent wife and mother to their two children. The two children are Avon, age eight, and Danielle, age five. Glenn describes both children as bright, industrious, and involved in many activities.

Glenn was born to a large and poor sharecropper family. He is the oldest of seven siblings, four boys and three girls. Glenn attended a small, rural, segregated elementary school and was one of the first African-Americans to attend a community high school. He was active in sports and music in high school and parlayed his athletic ability into an athletic scholarship at a small state university, where he played football. He majored in criminal justice and saw himself as an "average student who could have done better," but football came first and what time was left was devoted to a social life.

After his eligibility expired, Glenn left school twelve hours short of a degree and enlisted in the army. He became a military police officer, saw duty in the Gulf war, and was wounded in action. He received the bronze star and a purple heart and was honorably discharged. He reported no recurring medical problems with his wound and indicated he is in excellent health except for some problems "with a nervous stomach," which he medicates.

After his discharge from the army, Glenn came to the present locale and joined the police department as a patrol officer, finished his degree in criminal justice, and met and married his wife. He indicates his family life is good and extremely important to him, although his job as a sergeant on the TACT squad exacts an extreme amount of physical and psychological stress, both in the amount of constant training and in the crisis situations in which he finds himself. He states that sometimes after a hard day he is "pretty short with the wife and kids."

Glenn is currently enrolled in his first semester of graduate school as a part-time student in counseling. On a questionnaire of what problems he thought he had, Glenn indicated "vocational—want to talk to counselor." At the time of his intake interview, Glenn completed a counseling intake questionnaire, which asks for specific demographic and ecological information in regard to his request for counseling. The following assessment data were retrieved during the course of Glenn's counseling sessions:

Undergraduate grades	Strong Interest Inventory
Graduate Record Exam	Priorities problem ranking by client
Counseling intake questionnaire	DISCOVER occupational preference
California Psychological Inventory	computer printout

Analysis

While Glenn has already provided a great deal of data through his intake interview and the open-ended assessment device given in his initial visit to the counseling center, these are basically self-analyses. Taken alone, self-analysis is likely to provide a very biased notion of the problem and any attempts at resolution. Therefore, the counselor uses this opening interview to collect, sift, evaluate, and classify data about Glenn. The counselor will continue doing so until a complete description can be obtained that will provide insight into the circumstances that brought the client in for counseling in the first place (Williamson, 1950b, p. 109). Accomplishing this task will require not only written and verbal client self-reports but also empirical information on aptitudes, interests, physical health, emotional balance, and other characteristics that facilitate or inhibit satisfactory adjustment (Williamson, 1950b, p. 158).

The counselor is also trying to determine in what manner the client approaches problems, for this will not only reveal the client's lifestyle but also will determine reactions to the analysis and diagnosis. These attitudes, in fact, are one of the most important pieces of analytic data the counselor can obtain (Williamson, 1950b, p. 146). As such, the excerpts from Glenn's interview sessions show the counselor dealing with both attitudes and data.

CO: Hello, Glenn, I'm Dr. Jimenez. I've been assigned as your counselor. I've been looking over the autobiographical material you submitted. On the part where it asked you to state your problem, I noticed you put vocational. I wonder if that's where you'd like to start.

CL: I . . . to tell you the truth I really feel kinda foolish being here, I mean thirty-six years old and enrolled in the master's program in counseling . . .

CO: It seems like whatever is bothering you, you ought to be able to figure it out, old as you are and particularly since you're in counseling as a major.

CL: That's for sure. You could say I feel stupid being here.

CO: You wonder whether you might be thought less of by me or your professors for seeking counseling?

CL: Yeah, that's right! I mean you don't want your professors to think you're crazy or can't cut it.

CO: My feeling is that it's a wise person who gets help. I can understand those feelings. I had them myself when I was a student. I think it also says something that you realize that counselors too need help at times. I also feel that your professors would respect that.

CL: Okay. I've been a police officer for a long time. It's exciting and I've enjoyed the work, but it's also dangerous and here I am thirty-six. I mean I really like dealing with people, but not always the negative side. So I started into counseling, but I don't know . . . you don't seem to get problems solved.

CO: So, on one side you like police work but the danger of it and seeing the bad side of people makes you think there are other jobs that might give you more satisfaction and security. On the other side, counseling seems kinda slow and at thirty-six you don't feel you can make mistakes career-wise.

CL: That's pretty much on target. I'm having some real questions about counseling as a profession and myself . . . both time-wise and financially.

CO: So far as time and money are both concerned, it's pretty important at least to have some odds on coming out right and getting on with your life—whatever direction it might take. You also seem to have some questions about yourself.

CL: I'm not so sure I can cut the mustard. It's been a long time since I was an undergraduate, and I wasn't a great big ball of fire then, and with working and family and all, it seems like there's never enough time. (*silence*) I just couldn't very well face flunking out . . . (*sigh*) That gets depressing . . . a lot of people looking over my shoulder; wife, she's smart as a whip. Other guys at the station wonder what I'm doing, and the damn beeper, never know when a call is coming, and trying to be a father, too. I wonder whether five guys could do it, and finally I get these gut pains . . . don't know whether I'm breeding an ulcer or what. Sounds weird, huh?

CO: What it sounds like is a lot of things going on in your life and sorting them all out is a real headache . . . or gutache, as the case may be. What do you back off of and what do you give your undivided attention to, particularly the big risk you're taking by getting into counseling and maybe changing not only careers but also a whole bunch of other things in your life?

CL: That's about it. I need to figure out a way to go and I need some help doing it.

CO: Okay. You seem really motivated to get some of this stuff rolling and that's super. Here's what I'm gonna do and here's what I want you to do. First, I'll call over to records and get your grades and your GRE scores. I'll look at those and compare them with some expectancy tables we've got that will give us a ballpark figure of what you might expect to do grade-wise. What you've said rings pretty true. It's not just your aptitude, but your interest and to some extent how your personality fits into an occupation and vice versa. There are a couple of inventories I'd like you to take so we can get a better line on some of the issues in your life right now—particularly how those issues fit with your educational, vocational, familial, and other kinds of goals. You'll need to make an appointment with testing and also go over to the career counseling center to get on the DISCOVER computer program. It's real easy to access, just ask the student helper over there. It'll ask you some questions and then give you some information back on a printout that should give you some food for thought. Bring it back with you for our next session. These inventories are not chiseled in stone. They are comparing you against samples of other people: their likes, dislikes, feelings, needs, values, motivations, and so on. I can give you my interpretation of the inventories, but in the final analysis, you're the one who decides how and what kind of meaning they have for you. Does that make sense?

CL: So what you're saying is that you believe that these inventories will help me get my head straight about a career and that while you'll tell me about them, I got the responsibility of making use of them.

CO: That's right! One other thing—I have a homework assignment I'd like you to do on your own. I'd like you to make a list of all those concerns you have right now and rank them according to what you think and feel, and I'd like you to give equal time to both the thinking and feeling parts. Once we obtain all this, we'll analyze it, and see if we can't put the pieces together.

The counselor is highly proactive in this first meeting. While the counselor listens, clarifies, and reflects the client's content in a nonjudgmental way, at times he also interprets the content to test the validity of tentative hypotheses he is proposing to himself. Data are being gathered, compiled, and sorted. "Returning student, older, not real sure of himself both academically and career-wise; feeling a time and financial press. Got lots of responsibilities—two jobs, family, wife successful. What kinds of pressure points in all this?" As the counselor processes these questions and comments, he is busy comparing his analysis to analyses of other clients who have demonstrated the same general set of problems. How does Glenn fit into this large reservoir? What specific idiosyncratic data bits make him distinct from the populations that fit Glenn's profile? What other assessment data are needed?

The counselor will do all that can be done to build rapport, particularly in the first session. The counselor reinforces the client for the decision to seek counseling. Even though Glenn may understand a good bit more about the meaning of tests because of his background, their use is still explained to get him motivated to start being a full-fledged partner in the process. Finally, the counselor uses a lot of "we" statements, setting the stage for a cooperative effort.

Synthesis

Before a diagnosis can be determined, synthesis needs to occur. The teasing out of a mass of sometimes seemingly irrelevant facts into a consistent pattern of behavior that is unique to the individual's assets and liabilities is based not only on the counselor's learning and data base, but also on other cases the counselor has worked with and the experience that comes with that work. Based on a synthesis of these diverse parts, the counselor is able to make a diagnosis and a prognosis of the pattern of the client's future adjustment to the problem (Williamson, 1950b, p. 101). Test scores, rating scales, autobiographical accounts, anecdotal reports, and grades, among other data, are summarized (Williamson & Hahn, 1940, p. 212). After the data are summarized the counselor explains to the client the "rules of evidence." That is, certain traits in combination with certain factors are admissible as rules of evidence (Williamson, 1950b, pp. 148–149). In Glenn's case, the initial session indicates an interest in the field of counseling, although the client's interest is somewhat cloudy and ill-defined. The counselor first explores that professed interest more closely, not only by empirically looking at it, but also by trying to establish how the client's interest manifests itself with his desires and the reality of life. The second problem is to explore how his interests mesh with the aptitudes needed for the work he desires. Can he do it?

CO: Good to see you again, Glenn. I've sifted through those inventories you took last week and put what came out on those with your own thoughts and feelings and the other data like grades and scholastic aptitude. What I'd like to do is explain some of the findings and then put our heads together and see where that leads us.

CL: Super. Okay, let's get at it.

CO: You took the Strong Interest Inventory and you should remember the caution that this is no occupational crystal ball. Your interests are based on what you said you liked or disliked. From time to time this may change somewhat. Further, this inventory measures interests, not abilities, so it doesn't necessarily mean you'd succeed either academically or on the job. Do you understand this?

CL: What you're saying is that there might be some slip in this—like depending on how I felt, some of the scales might go up or down and even though I might be interested in it, I might or might not be able to cut it, like assessments.

CO: Assessment's giving you some trouble?

CL: Yeah, it's the math . . . the statistics . . . a real headache; haven't had any since freshman year in college.

CO: Uh-huh, that seems to fit from your grades and scores and that's a good example of what I'm talking about. It's one thing to be interested in counseling, but quite another when you're dealing with math, something you probably thought you wouldn't deal much with in counseling.

CL: Man, is that ever the truth. Don't know if I'd have gotten into it if I'd known about that assessment course.

CO: Okay. We can look at that more closely in a little while. Let's see what your SCII has to say.

The counselor explains Glenn's Strong occupational themes and scales. Glenn has high Realistic (R), Social (S), and Enterprising (E) themes. These themes seem to fit with occupations of police officers, counselors, and sales—occupations in which Glenn has either a stated or a manifest interest.

CL: I could guess that Realistic would be high and maybe the Enterprising, 'cause I'm already into those things, but I gotta say I'm really amazed at that Social. I kinda felt like I had those interests but this makes me feel even more like that's what I ought to do.

The counselor then explains various combinations of occupational themes. For Glenn, his high theme combinations are RES and RSE—that is, combinations of Realistic, Enterprising, and Social—in that order.

CL: Yeah! That R for police officer fits. Not so high in realtor, E, and not so high in counselor, SE *(frowns)*.

CO: What about your realty work? Is there anything you don't like about it?

CL: Well . . . the nit-pick stuff . . . the paperwork . . . although I'll do it for the money. I sure don't like it much. The people, the selling; that's all very exciting.

CO: There are a lot of things in counseling like that, excitement working with different people, different problems,

CL: Doesn't look I'm much cut out to be a counselor either. I can't figure that out. I really like working with kids.

CO: You'll note that this is based on high school counselors. That profile will be flavored with some or the other scales such as Conventional because they have to push a lot of paper too. While I'm a counselor, I don't have a Strong profile that looks like that either, and frankly I don't think I have the right stuff to be a high school counselor.

What I'm saying is that there are a lot of different kinds of counselors and the personality and environmental fit may be different for them than that of a high school counselor, so don't take that as chiseled in concrete.

CL: (*sighs*) So I don't exactly look like a counselor . . . or at least a high school counselor. Well that makes the stuff I did on the computer make a little more sense. It sure didn't make much out of me being a counselor. Kinda depressing really. I don't like my job and now I'm not sure about what I'm gettin' into.

CO: I understand the frustration of feeling caught in the middle in something that means so much to you and the rest of your life. I wonder if you've talked to any counselors about what they do?

CL: Yes, and I can remember them saying there was a lot of paper shuffling, but I guess I forgot about that when they started talking about the other things. Those interests generally seem to fit, but it looks like I'm back to being a cop.

CO: What made you want to get out of it?

CL: I'm tired of hurting people, seeing people get hurt. I'm getting a hard shell and that bothers me. I like people and just don't want to have to come down on 'em anymore. Plus, with a family and all, it's dangerous work . . . the wife's not handling it so well, open season on cops and all. Sometimes I get really depressed about it and my guts hurt. Although at times it's a real high, but it seems like those are getting fewer and farther between.

CO: So if you move over into counseling, you feel like those positive strokes will come a lot faster.

CL: I don't know about that. It's just that . . . the way I feel right now I don't know if I could help anyone.

CO: Let's take a look at the way you feel about yourself in general—what the California Psychological Inventory (CPI) has to say. What the CPI will do is give us another perspective—where you are right now in regard to a number of personality measures, how those particular measures may be reflective of strong points and problem areas you have at present.

The counselor interprets the CPI. It pictures Glenn as fully functioning and well within the normal range of adjusted individuals. A comprehensive profile of Glenn indicates that he is ambitious, persistent, planful, enthusiastic, outgoing, and achievement-oriented. He is responsible, has a well-structured set of values, has good interpersonal relationships, and has insight, perceptiveness, and assertiveness balanced with sincerity and acceptance of others. He has weaknesses in self-acceptance, sense of personal well-being, and intellectual efficiency.

CL: I'd say that those scales are true. I have been pretty enthusiastic about life in general . . . but lately . . . I don't know. I've never felt guilty about anything. I mean I think things out, not rash, but if I ducked out on the assessment course I'd probably feel guilty and I sure as hell wouldn't be very accepting of me, but I sure don't want to come up a loser either. Damned if I do and damned if I don't.

CO: So really you'd feel pretty good and confident to handle about anything except for the assessment course.

CL: That's kinda the tip of the iceberg—it's the whole decision about the career field, but if I could handle that course it'd sure make me feel a whole lot better!

CO: Can those other strong characteristics you indicated be brought to bear on the problem?

CL: Most of the time for sure; it's just that I can't seem to get it together right now and it even spills over at home.

CO: I am wondering from these scores and what you said about your wife's fears, if some of the indecision about vocational choice isn't related to your deep feeling about being needed at home.

CL: (*long silence*) Well, you're right. On my list of priorities I put family way down, but I guess if I really admit it, I'm kinda paralyzed right now and a lot of it's got to do with LaQuita. She's so damn cool. Handled her master's . . . no sweat . . . working her job and raising the kids. I . . . I just don't feel like I can talk to her and I really feel guilty as hell about not being able to handle this, when she has.

CO: Makes you feel guilty and even a little angry that she could do all those things with seemingly no problem and you're questioning whether you can.

CL: Yeah, and the personality test confirms it.

CO: Hold it! You seem to have heard only part of what I said. Those below-average scales are well within normal range, and looking across the rest of the scales, I get the picture of a pretty well-integrated individual, saner than most, less neurotic than most, which is pretty good, looking at the heat you've been under—job, school, home. So look at both sides of the coin. Sure you've got some problems, but let's consider the strong points too.

The counselor reinforces Glenn's positive psychological traits as they relate to his numerous accomplishments. He also relates Glenn's feelings of intellectual inferiority to his Graduate Record Exam scores—high verbal and low quantitative—and undergraduate grades—high social science, low math and physical science.

CO: So I wonder how what I've said goes with what you might think?

CL: Frankly, I'm scared to death of assessments and research. I can picture two Cs or worse, and probably worse, and that gets all wrapped up in the way I'm feeling. (*cracks knuckles*) All the pressure I feel . . . couldn't face my wife if I flunked . . . myself either . . . just stuck. (*lowers head*) Looks like we're back to square one.

CO: Not necessarily. Recapping, what we've got are some data to back up those hunches and feelings I've had. We know that there are parts of counseling that you are interested in and seem to have the personality for. As far as scholastic aptitude is concerned, you seem to have more than enough ability verbally and your need to achieve is high, so there's both the ability and motivation to succeed. It's your math that is weak and has really gotten to the point where it goes beyond just class, and the fear of failure seems to be getting into lots of other parts of your life. That causes problems because you're doing so many things right now that it seems like if one aspect of your life gets out of kilter, it starts to snowball and affect everything else. How does all that seem to fit?

CL: Like a glove, really, but I sure don't know what to make or do with it.

CO: We've put a lot of pieces into the puzzle; let's stand back a bit and see where it leads us. I'd like you to take that problem list and reevaluate it for next time. Just pencil your prognosis alongside each problem and I'll be doing the same.

The counselor goes step by step through the various assessment devices with the client, looking at different combinations of the measures and how they seem to fit or not. A good deal of time may be taken in explaining to the client that one test does not constitute a diagnosis. The counselor makes it clear there is slippage in the scores, that they are not static. If scores are reported, we believe that the only acceptable ways are either by band scores, which show the amount of variation that surrounds the client's obtained score, or by stanines, which cover a broad enough range that scores do not become chiseled in stone.

The counselor is encouraging and motivating. The counselor reports weak areas honestly and objectively but does not dwell on them. If the client starts to brood or catastrophize, the counselor quickly apprises the client of this and accentuates the attributes in legitimate and reinforcing ways. After each piece of test information is given, an opportunity is given for the client to interpret the information. The counselor does not just wade relentlessly through test data. As thoughts and feelings surface from the client's self-analysis, the counselor reflects on these feelings and seeks to clarify them in response to the presenting problem. If more problems are uncovered, the counselor works through these with the client. What becomes known about the client's interests, achievements, aptitudes, and personality are put together in various combinations so that client and counselor try to puzzle out problems and their solutions. Once this has been done, counselor and client are ready to make a diagnosis and prognosis.

Diagnosis

Diagnosis is the cornerstone of the trait-factor approach. It is the differential classification of clients according to the distinguishing characteristics of their problems (Crites, 1976). Once these characteristics are identified, the counselor infers causes as they apply to the present problem and what the implications for future adjustment will be (Williamson, 1939, pp. 108–109). The proof of the diagnosis ties in the client's reaction to the counselor's logic and the tryout of a program of action based on a mutually agreed-on plan (Williamson, 1950b, p. 54). Diagnosis is a cooperative undertaking, with the client taking major responsibility for confirming or denying its validity (Williamson, 1950b, p. 180). Williamson (1939) felt that the complicated fabric that a client's life was woven from meant that a counselor could expect to diagnose more than one problem in the course of a usual case and that problems presented might well have cause-and-effect relationships (p. 110). As we shall see in the case of Glenn, this is indeed true.

To this point the counselor has been analyzing and synthesizing data. Several clues and facts have been presented:

1. *Family.* Glenn feels some pressure from his wife, who seems to be progressing well in her job and is earning a good salary. Comparing himself with her and being found wanting may be part of the motivating factor in Glenn's career change. There are also guilt feelings about not spending enough time with his children.
2. *Financial.* Glenn is faced with the prospect of needing to maintain the salary he currently has. A career shift to counseling at the entry level would not let him maintain his current standard of living as he sees it.
3. *Personal.* Glenn has a need to act in humane ways to people. Although his job provides some opportunity to do this, more often he has to enforce rules of society that may not always meet this need. He is frustrated because of these conflicting demands. The Strong reflects to some degree his interest in police work, but also it is highly indicative of his interest in human service work. This is a dilemma.
4. *Educational life.* Compounding deficient scores on the quantitative portion of the GRE are low grades received throughout high school and college in mathematics and science. Glenn will probably have trouble with courses related to this, such as assessment, research, and statistics. This problem is even more severe in that Glenn has little extra time to study because of his job, family, community, and educational commitments.

The encapsulated diagnosis is that Glenn's entering problem of indecision about a tentative vocational choice has roots in other problems. He has become involved in so many activities that, cognitively, he can no longer prioritize the issues. His inability to do so is causing him affective reactions that will only serve to paralyze him further. However, rather than wallow any longer in this quagmire, Glenn is self-actualized enough to seek counseling and try to get back on track. His determination, zeal, energy, humanness, physical stamina, and love of his family are all positive attributes. All of the foregoing is reported to Glenn in a straightforward but empathic and caring manner by the counselor.

CO: So generally that's what I am going on. You're covering a lot of territory just now and I wonder if that isn't the general problem—at least for the stress you feel.

CL: Really I guess I . . . just . . . never . . . stopped. . . .to think. It's like it's overwhelming . . . but yet I feel like all those are important commitments. What do you think?

CO: I think two things. I want to give you a tentative prognosis of where this might lead and some alternative prognoses if things are done a bit differently, but I want to emphasize "tentative." What I've got are some hunches. However, no two people are alike and what you do with these guesses is up to you. In the end *you* must choose. I'll help you look at all the ramifications of those choices but I won't make any judgments about your decisions. So I'd like to lay some of these out, then get your feelings about them, and then see if we couldn't come up with a game plan.

Prognosis

A prognosis projects the present situation into the future, arriving at a judgment of the probable outcome of the problem (Williamson, 1939, p. 116). The counselor's chief purpose is to see that the client moves in a positive direction toward an achievable goal. Therefore, the counselor carefully explains not only the diagnosis but also the prognosis so that the client is completely apprised of the facts and will have an adequate basis for choosing a goal (Williamson, 1939, pp. 112–115). The counselor must pose numerous subvocal questions as the data are culled. "If this, then what?" "If not this, then what?" Possible outcomes are written in specific and detailed form to be used as reference notes (Williamson, 1939, p. 116).

The general prognosis for Glenn is that if he continues operating under the stressful conditions that pervade his environment, something's going to give. Failing graduate school, job dissatisfaction, marital problems, and concomitant loss of self-esteem, depression, and psychosomatic illness are all high potential outcomes. Many of these signs are already present. There are too many stresses and not enough time or energy available to deal with them. There are, however, alternative positive prognoses:

1. If the job stress Glenn is experiencing can be reduced so that his human relations skills can be used, some form of police work might be acceptable. That way no financial loss would be suffered. What about community relations officer or hostage negotiator?
2. If he can sit down with his wife and talk about the stress he is under, he can reestablish an important support system as he strives to accomplish his goals. Can he do this himself, or does he need professional help? The suggestion should be raised that he consider meeting with the center's marriage counselor, Dr. Roberts.
3. The graduate problem is too much right now, given Glenn's deficits in mathematics. Chances are slim to none that he will pass assessment, research, or statistics. He might consider dropping assessment and going to the Educational Support Program for remedial help in mathematics. Once he is up to standards, he could reenter the graduate program.
4. While Glenn has previously made money and enjoyed real estate work, it is another stress. Given the present lack of financial incentive, would he consider getting out of it for a while?
5. The refereeing and coaching seem to be a source of avocational enjoyment to Glenn, but do they provide enough stress reduction to compensate for the fact that they require a lot of time?

These are questions the counselor has generated in his own mind and now carefully and fully goes over with Glenn.

CL: Well, I can see you've honed it down. The community relations job seems kinda bland. I think that the hostage negotiation job might be up my alley. I really don't think I'd mind the stress with that negotiation job; it's like you're really in there doing something worthwhile. Saving lives and using counseling skills.

CO: How can you find out about that?

CL: I can go to the captain and pick up an application tomorrow. Talk to him about it . . . see what he thinks.

CO: Sounds good. What about your wife?

CL: That I don't know about. I mean whether she'd go for it.

CO: How about you?

CL: Well, I'm a little uptight about it. Couldn't you do it? I don't know Dr. Roberts.

CO: Well . . . I feel Dr. Roberts would be better; that's not my specialty and she is a clinical member of the American Association of Marriage and Family Therapists. She's quite competent. Perhaps I could arrange an initial appointment for her to talk to you—kinda get the feel of it.

CL: Yes, I'd appreciate that. I'd like to know a little more about what would go on.

CO: Okay. I'll make the phone call today. What do you think of the Educational Support Program for your math problems?

CL: I don't know. I really hate to give up on something I start. I'm a little embarrassed about going in there.

CO: I can understand that, but I would want you to know from your test results that the expectancy of making a B or better in assessments is about one in ten at this point. However, ESP has helped people increase their math ability.

CL: I know it's probably the smart thing to do, but it really is tough to think of giving up on something.

CO: Why not check with your professor and see what he thinks?

CL: I'm a little scared about that, but that's about the only way to find out how I'm doing. Okay! I'll do it!

CO: When?

CL: I can see him before class this Thursday.

CO: Good. What about real estate?

CL: I haven't made any money what with school and all . . . can't spare the time. I could retire my license and activate it again when things get better.

CO: Plus when you get this schoolwork under your belt, it ought to give you some good communication skills in sales . . . at least that's what others who've got their degree in counseling say who are in real estate.

CL: I really feel better. Like I've got my priorities straightened out. That indecision was driving me crazy.

CO: We've covered a lot of ground today. I wonder if you could go back over what we've done and recap it so we're real clear as to what you'll do.

While the counselor listens closely to Glenn's concerns and is empathic with his needs, he also draws on a vast knowledge base and expertise in proposing what he thinks are the best bets and outcomes. These hypotheses are not forced on the client, but are reported. Together the client and the counselor decide what course of action to take: the counselor from the point of view of his analysis and synthesis of the data presented; the client from his perception of how these data fit his own analysis of the situation.

The counselor is not just concerned with the vocational problem initially presented—having broadened the scope of the client's presenting problem into a number of aspects of his life. Where the counselor has information, knowledge, and skill, he is not reticent about acting on the information obtained and imparting his own hunches. Where he feels that others with more expertise would be better at solving particular problems, he does not hesitate to refer the client, as in the case of the marriage counselor. The counselor drives toward commitment. The client is asked "when," "where," "what," "who," and "how." Clear game plans are developed for the agreed-on goals. Finally, the client is asked to recapitulate what has gone on in the session. By doing so the client reaffirms what will be done outside the session and the counselor is assured that the game plan is clear and the client is committed to it.

Follow-Up

Follow-up continues as long as additional assistance is needed with the client's entering problems (Williamson & Hahn, 1940, p. 214). It has the further advantage of helping uncover and deal with any new problems that may arise as the client attempts to resolve his or her original concerns. From the counselor's point of view it also helps to determine how effective counseling has been and, if ineffective, to formulate new hypotheses and solutions with the client (Williamson, 1950b, p. 101). The following encapsulated dialogue summarizes the case of Glenn.

CL: I checked that marriage counselor out and we've got an appointment next week. I was really sweating telling my wife, but when I mustered up the courage and we talked it over, she seemed pretty pleased. We're really starting to talk about some stuff that had just built up over a long time.

CO: Sounds like some positive things are starting to happen.

CL: Yes, and I talked to LaQuita about what I was gonna do with the work—I mean the hostage negotiation team. LaQuita thinks it'd be a good deal and I feel a lot better with her behind me. The captain also told me he thought I'd do well . . . the way I've handled domestic disputes when I was a patrol officer and with a master's in counseling, that'd put me high on the list of candidates. So now I've gotta get that degree.

CO: So the talk with your wife and the captain really has encouraged you to go for that job. But you're going to need the degree to have a really good chance at it. I'm interested as to what you found out from your professor.

CL: Well, I did that too, you know, and he was kinda surprised. Said I'd been doing real well in class participation. It was really hard to tell him that I really didn't know the math well. So he encouraged me to go to ESP, even said he'd send up a summary of math concepts I needed to know.

CO: I'm glad to hear you've taken those gutsy steps. I still have a question of spreading yourself too thin and getting back into those old binds.

CL: Yeah. I know. Even though the broker tried to talk me out of it, I told her I needed to retire my license. So that's already done and instead of running an open house last Sunday, I packed the kids up and we went to the state park and I got my studying done Sunday evening.

CO: Fantastic! You've really gotten hard-nosed about reordering priorities and rearranging your time.

CL: You know, I do feel better. I mean even though I'm still doing a lot, it doesn't seem all messed up anymore. I gotta tell you, though, I don't believe I can give up the refereeing. I like the travel to different schools, seeing old friends, talking. I really do need that, although I was feeling a little guilty about what you'd think.

CO: I guess I'm most concerned about what will do the best for you and allow you to reach your goals. It's your life and you're the one who leads it.

CL: That's right, and I feel like the refereeing is such a small part in time but so big as far as my personal satisfaction—I still want to keep it up.

CO: Okay. Is there anything else?

CL: Not really. Not that I can think of. I'd kinda like to check back from time to time. Kinda, you know, keep on track.

CO: Okay. How about a month from now, and we can keep it on that basis. Checking back in to see how your goals are coming.

Although closure is gained in this session, the client is still given the opportunity to seek assistance. It is up to the client to decide what is best for himself after listening to the counselor's input. Thus, when the counselor tentatively questions Glenn about still having too many stresses in his life, and Glenn responds by stating the rational reasons for those things, the counselor accepts those decisions. The refereeing is an excellent example of an activity that the counselor might not personally care for and thinks would be an additional stress for Glenn. Glenn has prioritized his problems, made decisions about how to attack them, and initiated a plan of action. It would appear that Glenn is on the track to becoming his own counselor again.

A final point should be made about why we chose Glenn as a representative subject for the trait-factor approach. Glenn represents the kind of student we encounter in urban college settings more and more. He is older, already established in a job and family. Yet in a very real sense he is still developing in all facets of his life. His multiple problems are rather typical of a midlife, returning student who has begun to question what is really important and what the rest of life will be. His time is limited and he is forthright in seeking assistance so that he can get on with his life. He may feel some trepidation and embarrassment about seeking help, but the need he feels about moving forward and his own experiential background outweigh his reticence. The differential emphasis of the trait-factor approach provides him with needed information that he can fit into his own scheme of things and help him get on with his life.

CONTRIBUTIONS OF THE TRAIT-FACTOR APPROACH

The trait-factor is an approach for individuals experiencing everyday adjustment problems—particularly in regard to education and vocation. It does this efficiently and expeditiously and, as far as sheer number of clients, few other approaches can match it. In times of crisis such as war and depression, it has been the approach of choice. Because of its strong emphasis on actuarial assessment techniques it has spurred the growth of the testing movement in the United States. The consequences can be seen in business and industry, schools, the armed services, and anywhere else that selection and placement of people is undertaken.

Another strength of the approach, and one most neophyte counselors would do well to consider, is the team approach and referral to other specialists (Williamson & Hahn, 1940). No one person has all the answers. Other professionals lend alternative views that provide a more comprehensive picture of problems. Few theories advocate referral to other specialists. In its pragmatic fashion, the trait-factor approach does.

Trait-factorists have been criticized for their "three interviews and a cloud of dust" format. Yet it seems realistic to suppose that many clients may only want information in as quick and efficient a manner as possible and then, of their own volition and through no dissatisfaction with counseling, make their own "cloud of dust" as they take responsibility for their decisions.

With increased pressure from insurance companies to move people with psychological and physical disabilities back into functional living, forms of therapy that provide pertinent and timely information and that are highly goal-focused with clear treatment plans to accomplish those goals will garner much attention and third-party payments. Trait-factor approaches fill that bill admirably.

While much time, training, and attention in the professional literature have been given to all of the psychopathologies that assail us, the trait-factor/P × E approach is mainly practiced on people who are reasonably healthy and are experiencing everyday, typical, developmental problems. Its emphasis on rational decision making and information dissemination practiced in a methodical way holds little of the appeal of dynamic interpretation or other, more intense, emotive techniques. There have been many apologists for this directive stance, but the fact is that if therapists really do have expertise in their field, then they have information that clients need, and they need to convey that information in as efficient and clear a manner as possible. In short, at times therapists need to teach people how to do things both to remediate problems and to prevent them. From that standpoint it is one of the few theories of counseling that takes an active and preventive therapeutic stance.

Trait-factor counseling has been somewhat negatively tied to career counseling and has somehow been seen as less sophisticated and worthy than other theories that deal with more "personal" problems. The fact is that we pretty much define ourselves by what we do and where we work. As it affects individuals and society, there is probably no other area of counseling that is so critical to the general well-being than career counseling.

Our society is changing from an industrial to an information-processing base, and the trait-factor approach is ideally suited to the computer and other electronic technology. "High-tech" counseling, in which a computer or other electronic medium is central to the accomplishment of client objectives, and "high-touch" counseling, in which the mode of delivery is by empathic, interpersonal interaction by a skilled professional, are not oppositional (Harris-Bowlsbey, 1984). Both in counseling and in counselor education, preliminary data indicate that clients and trainees adapt quickly to technology and feel that electronic counseling and training are helpful (Garis, 1983; Halpain, Dixon, & Glover, 1987).

With the advent of cost-effective computerized assessment, information, and simulation programs, large numbers of clients can be served with a reasonable degree of reliability and validity (Biggs & Keller, 1982; Dawes & Corrigan, 1974; Goldberg, 1970; Pressman, 1984; Sampson & Krumboltz, 1991). Whether we recognize it, believe it, or even want it, the trait-factor system coupled with high-tech counseling represents the wave of the future—and that future is not very far away.

SHORTCOMINGS OF THE TRAIT-FACTOR APPROACH

The severest critics of the trait-factor approach have found fault with the premise that values can be taught (Arbuckle, 1967). The problems in such a value-laden approach are twofold. The first problem is the assumption that the counseling process is always rational and that the client "can see the light" if the facts and consequences are marshalled against the client's irrational thinking. It is our experience that clients are not often inclined to buy into anything approaching rationality—particularly in crisis situations. Generally, it takes a good deal of time and effort, plus a cooling-off period, before a client who feels grievously wronged by significant others, an institution, or society can perceive the situation in ways that resemble rationality and objectivity.

A correlative problem occurs with the use of an external system to lead the client to the right, correct, and proper values. While many counselors are employed by institutions where trait-factor approaches are used, we are not sure how far one goes in imposing institutional values on the client. We believe that in many cases the counselor acts as ombudsman when individual and institutional values conflict. However, to act solely in the interests of the institution seems to deny the very essence of counseling. The trait-factor approach never seems to resolve this dilemma clearly.

We have not reached the ideal state in assessment, where perfectly reliable and valid instruments are available—although many counselors seem to believe in the infallibility of the instruments they use. One need examine only a few caustic test reviews in *The Twelfth Mental Measurements Yearbook* (Conoley & Impara, 1995) to see that this is far from true. Even in the well-researched area of occupational interests, there is poor predictive validity. When trying to predict job satisfaction, the degree of congruence between interests and occupations accounts for less than 10 percent of the variation in job satisfaction (Rounds, 1988), which is a pitiful showing in the world of statistics.

In the trait-factor approach a great deal of reliance is placed on the counselor's expertise. We would first question what this expertise would entail. Does everyone who would counsel need to have a Ph.D. with a concentration in assessment procedures? If that were the case, there would be few counselors in schools, employment bureaus, and rehabilitation clinics. If such expertise is not necessary, can counselors then be labeled as *experts?* How much trust, given what is known about test validity and counselor diagnostic reliability, should we have? How valid is the information the counselor disperses? What price might the consumer of such counseling services ultimately pay?

Many clients come to counseling because they cannot take responsibility for themselves and will do everything in their power to invest responsibility for their actions or inactions with the counselor. It appears to us that a format that is directive or teaching in nature runs the great risk of assuming responsibility for the client. Experience has shown us that dependent clients are all too willing to let this happen.

As the approach has evolved, more emphasis has been given to the affective components of counseling. Yet little is said about this in the counseling process. Arbuckle has been particularly severe in seeing adherents of this approach as lacking the intimate involvement necessary for counseling. Rather than being called counselors, Arbuckle maintains, some persons should be designated sensitive occupational teachers (Arbuckle, 1967, pp. 138–139).

Computer systems offer much not only in assessment and informational programs, but also in other psychoeducational and interactive computer counseling programs. However, as with commercial tests, therapists need to know which are reliable and valid (Farrell, 1991). As of yet there is not a comprehensive theory of how computer-assisted diagnosis should exist (Jager, 1991). Currently there is no designated venue in which computer-assisted counseling programs are subjected to the same scrutiny as tests (Andrews & Wittchen, 1995). As a result, therapists are pretty much left to their own devices or word of mouth to figure out which programs are reliable and valid.

Dramatic strides are being made in computer-assisted guidance, counseling, and assessment. The problem is that many practitioners make limited use of computers because they lack computer literacy, are not sure how to use the expert systems, and are unclear what programs are available to them or under what conditions they could be used (Farrell, 1991; Hinkle, 1992; Sampson & Krumboltz, 1991).

TRAIT-FACTOR COUNSELING WITH DIVERSE POPULATIONS

Because the emphasis is more on choice rather than on change, trait-factor is a nonthreatening approach to counseling (Peterson, Sampson, & Reardon, 1991, p. 55). Therefore, the therapeutic relationship may not hold as much importance as in other modes of counseling because the counselor has minimal chance of becoming too emotionally involved with the client. Although trait-factor does not denigrate counselor–client relationships or affective components of the client's experiencing, it also does not emphasize them. Cultures that place a premium on shielding emotions from public view will find a great deal of utility in the approach. The emphasis on teaching and learning tends to make trait-factor a nonthreatening approach that does not stigmatize clients as having "mental" problems. Because of its time-limited and clear-cut goals, trait-factor has intrinsic appeal to clients who are not used to long, drawn-out activities that have no short-term reinforcement or immediately discernible outcomes.

Trait-factor's strong actuarial and assessment basis may be a bane to some clients and a boon to others. A great deal of research has been conducted on the detrimental effects of culture, race, and ethnic bias in standardized, norm-referenced tests. Clearly caution should be used in interpreting any norm-referenced test to minority populations. Counseling with culturally different clients should be conducted with a great deal of awareness of on whom test scores have been normed. In particular, gender bias in interest inventories has caused much job stereotyping and educational channeling of males and females. The same is true of achievement, aptitude, and other mental abilities tests when used with minorities and other unacculturated people. Counselors who practice the trait-factor approach must be highly sensitive to both overt and hidden bias in the tests they use. Thus, they must temper normative results with an idiosyncratic analysis of each client. This differentialist, individual view is at the heart of the approach and no capable trait-factor counselor would base decision making on normative tests by themselves (Rounds & Tracey, 1990; Williamson, 1939; 1950a; Williamson & Biggs, 1979).

However, if local norms have been generated and solid, predictive validity developed for such criteria as academic and vocational success, it has been our experience that most clients, particularly parents of minority school children, appreciate the conveyance of straightforward, concrete, and understandable information about achievement and aptitude tests. When such test data are tied with specific information on what clients need to do to excel, test interpretation may serve as a great motivator or, conversely, serve to temper unrealistic expectations.

Although the kindly but paternalistic counselor that Williamson espoused is clearly part of the past (Chartrand, 1991), many minorities, particularly those who value learning, look to school counselors as experts who can provide them with guidance in areas with which they or their parents have little familiarity. However, care must be taken with students who come from cultures that have ironclad parental authority. Counselors do not want to become allied so much with parents that the students are excluded and have little to say about their futures. Further, if the counselor has not built trust with the client, this very directive approach may be seen as patronizing or even dictatorial by some minorities who may perceive such attempts to deliver information as "preachy putdowns." Then, no matter how valid the counselor's information or strategy, it will generally fall on deaf ears and the counselor will be perceived as another barrier placed in the minority client's way.

For the physically and mentally disabled, the trait-factor reliance on assessment, diagnosis, and prognosis provides meaningful data to apprise such clients and their support systems in realistic terms of their abilities, options, and limitations. The trait-factor approach, which matches a person's traits and abilities with job requirements, and the P × E fit approach, which considers the dynamic nature of person and environment interactions, is at the heart of rehabilitation counseling (Kosciulek, 1993). Rehabilitation counselors have a long history of using the treatment paradigm of the trait factor approach to provide assessment, diagnosis, intervention, and follow-up to their clients. In that regard there is probably no more successful group of therapists.

Computer-assisted guidance systems, as an adjunct to trait-factor therapy, hold much promise in regard to achieving a bias-free therapeutic role with diverse populations. The computer is an infinitely reinforcing machine that is nonbiased (or at least as bias-free as the programming is) in its response sets and is also free of language and dialect barriers. It is infinitely patient and doesn't get frustrated by abortive attempts of clients to learn new behaviors and concepts. With the growing body of interactive video disk technology, ethnicity can easily be matched between counselor and client so that clients can't say the counselor doesn't understand what's going on because of race, sex, or ethnic differences. The computer and video simulations are completely familiar and nonthreatening to most young people. No matter what their ethnic background, this electronic common denominator is the preferred choice of interaction for young people (Sampson & Krumboltz, 1991).

SUMMARY

The trait-factor approach has developed from a marriage of differential psychology's research and theories to Parson's vocational guidance concepts. The approach was born at the Minnesota Employment Stabilization Research Institute and the University of Minnesota Test Bureau as a practical response to educational and vocational adjustment problems of the unemployed and students. It is still closely identified with educational and vocational counseling. The approach has placed heavy reliance on the scientific method by attempting systematically to observe and measure individuals. Traits are categories that are used for describing individual differences in behavior, and statistical methods of factor analysis are used to ascertain how many factors are sufficient to account for similarities and differences in individuals.

Trait-factorists have relied heavily on empirical objective data for a logical problem-solving approach to client problems. Thus, the approach may be placed in the constellation of theories that are more cognitively than affectively oriented. Its basic model of analysis, synthesis, diagnosis, prognosis, counseling, and follow-up is a structured, stepwise attempt to help the client become self-counseled. The major component of the model is the integration of objective test data with client subjective data to arrive at a differential diagnosis.

As it has evolved, the trait-factor approach has become more developmental, dynamic, process-oriented, and eclectic. It has moved to a person × environment fit approach, which is seen not as static but as reciprocal and dynamic. Vocational counseling, in particular, is not seen as fixed but as a continuing experience with definable stages. The contemporary approach is eclectic in that it sees merit and utility in cognitive therapies such as the reality, rational-emotive, and behavioral approaches. The logical basis of the approach relies heavily on a mentoring and teaching role by the counselor to influence and change the irrational thinking and behavior of the client. A great deal of knowledge, experience, and expertise is assumed of the counselor. Trait-factor counseling is most commonly found in school, employment, and rehabilitation counseling.

By including a broader diagnostic scheme, more advanced information-processing concepts, and a more adaptive counseling style, the person × environment fit approach has matured beyond the old trait-factor model. The person × environment model includes these elements by organizing personal constructs, the world of work, person × environment interactions and then applying them in a problem-solving sequence. Including current concepts of problem solving, information processing, and attitude change has reinvigorated a venerable approach to career counseling (Chartrand, 1991).

SUGGESTIONS FOR FURTHER READING

Rounds, J. B., & Tracey, T. J. (1990). From trait-and-factor to person-environment fit counseling: Theory and process. In W. B. Walsh & S. H. Osipow (Eds.), *Career counseling* (pp. 1–44). Hillsdale, NJ: Erlbaum.

Walz, G. W., Bleuer, J., & Maze, M. (1989). *Counseling software guide: A resource for the guidance and human development professions.* Alexandria, VA: American Association for Counseling and Development.

Williamson, E. G. (1965). *Vocational counseling: Some historical, philosophical, and theoretical perspectives.* New York: McGraw-Hill.

Williamson, E. G., & Biggs, D. A. (1979). Trait-factor theory and individual differences. In H. M. Burks, Jr., & B. Stefflre (Eds.), *Theories of counseling* (3rd ed.; pp. 91–131). New York: McGraw-Hill.

REFERENCES

American College Testing Program. (1988). DISCOVER (computer program). Iowa City, Iowa.

Andrews, G., & Wittchen, H. U. (1995). Clinical practice, measurement, and information technology. *Psychological Medicine, 25*(3), 443–446.

Arbuckle, D. S. (1967). *Counseling and psychotherapy: An overview.* New York: McGraw-Hill.

Biggs, D. A., & Keller, K. E. (1982). A cognitive approach to using tests in counseling. *Personnel and Guidance Journal, 60,* 528–532.

Chartrand, J. M. (1991). The evolution of trait-and-factor career counseling: A person × environment fit approach. *Journal of Counseling and Development, 69,* 518–524.

Conoley, J. C., & Impara, J. C. (Eds.). (1995). *The twelfth mental measurements yearbook.* Lincoln, NE: University of Nebraska Press.

Crites, J. O. (1976). Career counseling: A comprehensive approach. *Counseling Psychologist, 6,* 2–12.

Crites, J. O. (1981). *Career counseling: Models, methods, and materials.* New York: McGraw-Hill.

Dawes, R. M., & Corrigan, B. (1974). Linear models in decision making. *Psychological Bulletin, 81,* 95–106.

Dawis, R. V., & Lofquist, L. H. (1984). *A psychological theory of work adjustment: An individual differences model and its applications.* Minneapolis, MN: University of Minnesota Press.

Educational Testing Service. (1988). SIGI PLUS (computer program). Princeton, NJ.

Erikson, E. H. (1959). Identity and the life cycle. *Psychological Issues, 1,* 1–171.

Farrell, A. D. (1991). Computers and behavioral assessment: Current applications, future possibilities, and obstacles to routine use. *Behavioral Assessment, 13*(20), 159–179.

Garis, J. W. (1983). The integration of the DISCOVER computer-based guidance system in a college counseling center: Its effect upon career planning (doctoral dissertation, Pennsylvania State University). *Dissertation Abstracts International, 43,* 2236A. (University Microfilms no. 822 8889).

Goldberg, L. R. (1970). Man versus model of man: A rationale plus evidence for a method of improving on clinical inferences. *Psychological Bulletin, 73,* 422–432.

Halpain, D. R., Dixon, D. N., & Glover, J. A. (1987). The great therapists program: Computerized learning of counseling theories. *Counselor Education and Supervision, 26,* 255–259.

Harris-Bowlsbey, J. (1984). The computer and career development. *Journal of Counseling and Development, 63,* 145–148.

Harris-Bowlsbey, J. (1992, December). Building blocks of computer based career planning systems. *CAPS Digest,* EDO-CG-92-7.

Hennessey, T. C. (1980). Introduction to the special issue, values and the counselor. *Personnel and Guidance Journal, 58,* 557–-558.

Hinkle, J. S. (1992). Computer-assisted career guidance and single-subject research: A scientific-practitioner approach to accountability. *Journal of Counseling and Development, 70,* 391–395.

Holland, J. L. (1985). *Making vocational choices: A theory of vocational personalities and environments.* Englewood Cliffs, NJ: Prentice-Hall.

Jager, E. S. (1991). Computer diagnostics—a survey: Practical applications of computerized assessment: Theoretical principles and perspectives. *Revue Européene de Psychologie Appliquée, 41*(4), 247–268.

Klein, K. L., & Weiner, Y. (1977). Interest congruence as a moderator of the relationship between job tenure and job satisfaction and mental health. *Journal of Vocational Behavior, 10,* 91—98.

Kosciulek, J. F. (1993). Advances in trait-and-factor theory: A person × environment fit approach to rehabilitation counseling. *Journal of Applied Rehabilitation Counseling 24*(2), 11–14.

Levinson, D. J., Darrow, C. N., Klein, E. B., Levinson, M. H., & McKee, B. (1978). *The seasons of a man's life.* New York: Knopf.

Lynch, R. K., & Maki, D. (1981). Searching for structure: A trait-factor approach to vocational rehabilitation. *Vocational Guidance Quarterly, 30,* 61–68.

Moos, R. H. (1981). *Work environment scale manual.* Palo Alto, CA: Consulting Psychologists Press.

Moos, R. H. (1987). Person-environment congruence in work, school, and health care settings. *Journal of Vocational Behavior, 31,* 231–247.

Moreland, K. L. (1990). Some observations on computer-assisted psychological testing. *Journal of Personality Assessment, 55*(3–4), 820–823.

Otto, L. B. (1984). Bringing parents back in. *Journal of Career Education, 10,* 255–265.

Paterson, D. G., Schneidler, G., & Williamson, E. G. (1939). *Student guidance techniques: Handbook for counselors in high schools and colleges.* New York: McGraw-Hill.

Patterson, C. H. (1966). *Theories of counseling and psychotherapy.* New York: Harper & Row.

Peterson, G. W., Sampson, J. P., Jr., & Reardon, R. C. (1991). *Career development and services: A cognitive approach.* Pacific Grove, CA: Brooks/Cole.

Pressman, R. M. (1984). *Microcomputers and the private practitioner.* Homewood, IL: Dow Jones-Irwin.

Rounds, J. B. (1988). *Meta analysis of research on the relationship of vocational interest and job satisfaction.* Paper presented at the annual convention of the American Education Research Association, New Orleans.

Rounds, J. B., & Tracey, T. J. (1990). From trait-and-factor to person-environment fit counseling: Theory and process. In W. B. Walsh & S. H. Osipow (Eds.), *Career counseling* (pp. 1–44). Hillsdale, NJ: Erlbaum.

Sampson, J. P., Jr. (1984). Maximizing the effectiveness of computer applications in counseling and human development: The role of research and implementation strategies. *Journal of Counseling and Development, 63,* 187–191.

Sampson, J. P., Jr. (1986). The use of computer assisted instruction in support of psychotherapeutic processes. *Computers in Human Behavior, 2,* 1–19.

Sampson, J. P., Jr., & Krumboltz, J. D. (1991). Computer-assisted instruction: A missing link in counseling. *Journal of Counseling and Development, 69,* 395–397.

Schmitt, P., & Growick, B. (1985). Trait-factor approach to counseling: Revisited and reapplied. *Journal of Applied Rehabilitation Counseling, 16,* 39–42.

Smith, R. O. (1993). Computer-assisted functional assessment and documentation. *American Journal of Occupational Therapy, 47*(11), 988–992.

Spinhoven, P., Labbe, M. R., & Rombouts, P. (1993). Feasibility of computerized psychological testing with psychiatric patients. *Journal of Clinical Psychology, 49*(3), 440–447.

Stefflre, B., & Matheny, K. (1968). The function of counseling therapy. In S. C. Stone & B. Shertzer (Eds.), *The guidance monograph series. II: Counseling.* Boston: Houghton Mifflin.

Walz, G. W., Bleuer, J., & Maze, M. (1989). *Counseling software guide: A resource for the guidance and human development professions.* Alexandria, VA: American Association for Counseling and Development.

Warzecha, G. (1991). The challenge to psychological assessment from modern computer technology. *Revue Européenne de Psychologie Appliquée, 41*(3), 213–220.

Williamson, E. G. (1939). *How to counsel students: A manual of techniques for clinical counselors.* New York: McGraw-Hill.

Williamson, E. G. (1950a). A concept of counseling. *Occupations, 29,* 182–189.

Williamson, E. G. (1950b). *Counseling adolescents.* New York: McGraw-Hill.

Williamson, E. G. (1958). Value orientation in counseling. *Personnel and Guidance Journal, 37,* 520–528.

Williamson, E. G. (1965). *Vocational counseling: Some historical, philosophical, and theoretical perspectives.* New York: McGraw-Hill.

Williamson, E. G. (1972). Trait-factor theory and individual differences. In B. Stefflre & W. H. Grant (Eds.), *Theories of counseling* (2nd ed.; pp. 136–176). New York: McGraw-Hill.

Williamson, E. G., & Biggs, D. A. (1975). *Student personnel work: A program of developmental relationships.* New York: Wiley.

Williamson, E. G., & Biggs, D. A. (1979). Trait-factor theory and individual differences. In H. M. Burks, Jr., & B. Stefflre (Eds.), *Theories of counseling* (3rd ed.; pp. 91–131). New York: McGraw-Hill.

Williamson, E. G., & Darley, J. G. (1937). *Student personnel work: An outline of clinical procedures.* New York: McGraw-Hill.

Williamson, E. G., & Hahn, M. E. (1940). *Introduction to high school counseling.* New York: McGraw-Hill.

13

ECLECTIC COUNSELING
AND PSYCHOTHERAPY

INTRODUCTION

Current Trends

Our view of eclecticism presented in this chapter takes into account several important but seldom discussed factors. First, as we approach the twenty-first century, we find that about half the major systems of counseling and psychotherapy in use are recent theories. Prior to 1950, three major schools predominated: (1) the psychoanalytic or insight theories (Freud, Jung, Adler); (2) trait-factor theories (Williamson, Darley); and (3) humanistic/existential theories (Maslow, Rogers). Since about 1960, the "young" theories (behavioral, cognitive, REBT, control/reality, TA, Gestalt) have emerged into prominence. They are less than fifty years old. We point this out to drive home the fact that much of the material found in this book is based on recent developments. Therefore, we are convinced that the *one true path* to effective psychotherapy has not yet emerged.

It is obvious to us that as of the present moment, no one theory can have all the answers to the wide variety of human dilemmas that clients present. One erroneous view of eclecticism is that bits and pieces from different theoretical systems of counseling and psychotherapy can be integrated into one counseling session to provide a stronger therapeutic treatment. That view is not valid even though some counselors may believe that clients with different presenting problems, learning styles, and personalities require an amalgamation or potpourri of strategies chosen arbitrarily from different theoretical systems.

Another view of eclectic practice is that at different times in the developmental progress of working with one or more clients, an appropriate system of therapy can be selected to match the particular problem or person. The counselor must be flexible enough to sense that an impasse has been reached and have a sufficient repertory of techniques at hand to get the client moving again in a positive direction. The competent counselor knows when to select another theory and

363

which system to employ. While some theorists have suggested that eclecticism is a jack-of-all-trades/master-of-none approach (Linden, 1984; Russell, 1986), eclectic counseling and psychotherapy as we propose it is *not* a nondescript, disorganized, nonsystematic modality. It is our view that a therapist who is *not* adept and proficient enough to change techniques as the therapeutic conditions require, but who espouses one dogmatic view, will usually experience frustration and failure. Sometimes adherents to one particular modality purport to have more answers for the human dilemma than the others. Many of these adherents organize their own systems of training, certification, and enfranchisement (Buie, 1988). The essence of their claims is that each one can solve client problems better than the others. Such claims are questionable.

Clearly, no one method, group, or theoretical system has all the answers. It is from this perspective that we present this chapter on eclectic counseling and psychotherapy.

Differing Views of Eclecticism

Perceptions of an eclectic system of therapy seem to be distributed roughly among proponents, opponents, and those who are neither. *Proponents,* such as Brammer, Shostrom, and Abrego (1989), Cormier and Cormier (1991), Corsini (1981), Garfield (1980), Lazarus (1987; 1989c), Norcross (1986; 1987), and Patterson (1986) recommend a broad-based, integrated system of therapy that makes systematic and appropriate use of the best of techniques from all known theories.

Opponents, such as Chessick (1985), Linden (1984), Russell (1986), and Stall (1984), tend either to diminish or seriously to question the efficacy of eclecticism. Their opposition is usually related to what they perceive as a lack of one or more foundational bases, whether historical, theoretical, conceptual, or empirical.

Individuals who support *both* pro and con positions on eclectic psychotherapy or *neither* include Berman (1985), Borgen (1984), Colapinto (1984), Ellis (1984), Eysenck (1984), Rychlak (1986), Scheidlinger (1984), and Sims and Sauser (1985). They tend to view the use of eclectic techniques as a selective matter rather than as a synthesis or a broad-based system of psychotherapy.

In summary, we advocate an eclectic system broad enough to include all the known theories, techniques, philosophies, and concepts needed by practitioners at all levels. We also believe that practitioners must be competent in scientifically selecting, integrating, and applying parts or whole theoretical systems appropriately, either to specific clients or to problem categories.

FUNDAMENTAL TENETS

History

A trend toward eclecticism in counseling and psychotherapy has been gaining ground since the middle 1940s (Smith, 1982). Frederick C. Thorne (1950) is credited with developing the first systematic position, which he called an attempt to gather "an eclectic collection and evaluation of all known methods in terms of empiric experience" (p. xiii). From 1945 until his death in 1978, Thorne made a formidable contribution integrating all psychological knowledge into a comprehensive and systematic approach to counseling and psychotherapy (Thorne, 1955; 1960; 1961; 1965; 1967; 1968). Even though few writers in the 1950s and early 1960s ventured into the arena as eclectics, eclecticism among practitioners grew at a phenomenal rate. Patterson (1980), reporting on Thorne's comments on the shifts in attitude toward eclecticism, stated that whereas in 1945 no members of the American Psychological Association's (APA) Division of Clinical Psychology identified themselves as eclectics, by 1970 more than 50 percent referred to themselves as eclectic (p. 572). In the mid-1970s Garfield and Kurtz (1975) reported that of the 733 members of the APA Division of Clinical Psychology, 470, or 64 percent, gave their orientation as eclectic.

Since Thorne's initial attempts to formulate an eclectic approach, the movement has become broad-based and multifaceted. From the late 1960s through 1977, Robert Carkhuff and his colleagues developed, tested, and researched a comprehensive, systematic, integrated, eclectic developmental model that incorporated proven relationship, problem-solving, and training skills into the scientific selection and preparation of prospective helpers (Carkhuff, 1969; Carkhuff & Berenson, 1977). Carkhuff's work was a monumental breakthrough because the skills he advocates for helpers are the same skills needed by anyone to function effectively.

Egan (1975; 1982; 1986; 1990) integrated the best-known therapeutic relationship techniques into a goal-oriented, systematic eclectic model. He drew from three major sources: systematic skills training systems, social influence theory, and behavioral and learning theory. He was successful in incorporating into his model developmental ideas and strategies, self-understanding, and action/problem-solving skills. Both the Egan model and the Carkhuff model have been used extensively in the training of counselors, psychotherapists, and other helpers.

Overview of Eclecticism

Concomitant with the pros and cons of eclecticism, all the known systems or approaches to counseling and psychotherapy appear to be evolving or changing. It appears that none of the theoretical systems are becoming more narrow or restrictive in their focus. The eclectic trend is really twofold: more and more practitioners and theorists are identifying themselves as adhering to some type of eclecticism (Brammer, Shostrom, & Abrego, 1989; Castonguay & Goldfried, 1994; Corsini & Wedding, 1995; D'Andrea & Daniels, 1994; Duncan, Parks, & Rusk, 1990; Fischer, 1995; Garfield, 1994; Lazarus, 1995a and 1995b; Norcross, 1995; Patterson, 1986; Watkins & Watts, 1995; Zook & Walton, 1989) and existing schools of therapy are moving toward a broader or more eclectic stance. Judging from Garfield and Kurtz's (1975) and Warner's (1991) surveys, which found eclecticism to be the leading theoretical orientation among clinical psychologists in both the United States and Canada, this list of citations appears to be merely the proverbial tip of the iceberg.

The objective of this chapter is to present eclectic counseling and psychotherapy in a way that will bridge the gap between theory and practice. One goal is to acquaint the reader with a variety of theoretical tenets, counseling processes, and helping strategies that eclectic counselors typically use. Another goal is to show how specific strategies, or clusters of strategies, can be put to use in an organized and consistent framework. We present a six-stage process model and ten clusters or categories of strategies for implementing the model. A sample case illustrates some of the eclectic counselor's options and behaviors. A thread that pervades the entire chapter is that the eclectic system is a broad, general system. We wish to depict the eclectic counselor as a skilled and highly competent generalist. The chapter also aims to portray eclecticism as comprehensive, organized, integrated, systematic, scientific, practical, open, evolving, developmental, consistent, unified, and intentional.

Personality

Eclectic counselors are concerned about personality theory because they recognize that the validity of an eclectic approach rests on the state of its supporting knowledge. Thorne (1970), the principal architect of eclectic theory, said that "the ultimate clinical validation of any theoretical viewpoint . . . is a function of breadth of phenomena which the system is able to clarify and explain . . . " (p. 142). The validation of eclectic counseling and psychotherapy necessarily requires a broad-spectrum view of personality to undergird a multifaceted approach to the counseling process.

Eclectic personality theory incorporates the valid elements from all theories into a framework for clarifying human behavior. But its primary source of data, according to both Thorne (1961) and Palmer (1980), is the *study of individuals* involved in day-to-day living in a constantly changing world. Thorne (1961) developed an original and comprehensive set of formulations on personality development, starting with the premise that "the Person is the basic datum and the only proper subject in the global unit of the 'person-running-the-business-of-his-life-in-the-world' " (Thorne, 1973, p. 455). He contended that personality theory should be derived inductively from the first-hand study of individual cases over a broad time frame using a person-centered approach.

The eclectic view of personality includes the concepts of integration, psychological states, dynamic change, developmental aspects of the organism, and social-cultural factors, with *integration* and *psychological states* constituting the core concepts (Thorne, 1961; 1967). Traditional views of static traits and personality structures are not considered valid predictors of behavior because they do not account for constant and rapid change. The human organism is viewed as continually striving to achieve and maintain the highest possible level of integration. Integration assumes that the human organism operates in a continuously evolving world and that the organism is itself constantly developing, changing, and experiencing different levels of integration. These varying levels of integration affect each other and change with time as the human develops. The highest order of human integration, which the individual theoretically strives toward, is self-actualization or satisfactory integration of all levels of need. The master motive is seen as personal enhancement, which we equate with self-actualization.

Psychological states rather than personality traits are another central focus in eclectic personality theory. Thorne (1973) views behavior (personality) as being in a continuous flux—always evolving and changing in a changing universe. Accordingly, the "Law of Universal Change" postulates that behavior is a result of (1) organismic status (but is not static), (2) situational status (in a changing interpersonal milieu), and (3) the human situation or condition in general. The stream of human life (or the psychological state), then, is an important source for studying behavior (personality) (Thorne, 1973, pp. 455–456).

Although most of the recognized proponents of eclectic systems of counseling and psychotherapy do not specify the personality theories that undergird their approaches, all of them are based on some global set of principles for understanding and predicting human behavior (Garfield, 1994; Watkins & Watts, 1995).

Major Concepts

Eclecticism, as such, has few major concepts. Thorne (1973, p. 451) identified several "necessary tasks" of eclecticism, which come as close to being concepts as we can find. One task is to "identify" valid elements in all systems and to integrate them into a mutually consistent whole that does justice to the behavior data to be explained. A second task is to consider "all pertinent theories, methods, and standards for evaluating and manipulating clinical data according to the most advanced knowledge of time and place." A third task is to identify with no specific theory, keep an open mind, and continually experiment with those formulations and strategies that produce valid results.

Based on the works of Carkhuff and Berenson (1977), Garfield (1980), Palmer (1980), and Thorne (1967; 1968; 1973), a number of statements can be made that summarize the concepts or descriptive positions of the eclectic movement in counseling and psychotherapy. Eclecticism assumes that the client's primary need is to achieve and maintain the highest feasible level of integration across time. It deals with the client's current psychological state within the client's emergent world and views consciousness as a central focal point. The approach is scientific, systematic, and logical without identifying with any proprietary "school." Eclectics are constantly evolving and changing to incorporate new ideas, concepts, techniques, and research findings. They do not operate on faith, guesswork, emotion, popularity, special interest, or ideological consistency as ends in themselves.

Eclecticism deals *directly with the person* in the person's rapidly changing and complex world, taking into account the person's developmental state and cultural, social, and personal values and goals (as opposed to talking *about* or theorizing *about* the person). Eclectics focus directly on the person's behaviors, goals, problems, and so on (as opposed to talking *about* behaviors, goals, or problems). They also recognize and deal with problem situations that are primarily outside the client's ability to control them, such as prejudice, poverty, handicapping environment, and cultural/ethnic diversities among helpers and clients.

Encapsulated, the foregoing list has these main thrusts: The eclectic counselor *makes the client fully aware* of the problem situation, *teaches the client consciously and intentionally to choose* to exercise control over the problem behavior, and *assists the client in developing a higher level of integration* through his or her proactive choice. To help the client understand and deal with the integrative processes, the helper may function in a variety of roles, such as counselor, psychotherapist, teacher, consultant, facilitator, mentor, adviser, or coach. According to Thorne (1967), *eclecticism is the only approach global enough in its scope to deal effectively with the broad spectrum of factors potentially influencing the integrative process.*

THE COUNSELING PROCESS

Overview

We have chosen to present one example (Gilliland, James, Roberts, & Bowman, 1984, pp. 274–277) of an eclectic counseling model, in the hope that readers will understand that eclecticism embraces many different processes. The six-stage model presented in this chapter incorporates the necessary global process requirements to qualify as a true eclectic system. No single counseling process can be truly "representative" of the whole array of possibilities available to eclectics. An eclectic viewpoint incorporates the therapeutic processes of all recognized systems. Two global process phases of psychotherapy resulting from many years of clinical judgment and study by Thorne (1950; 1968) are contained in some form in many eclectic models: (1) effective case handling involves the appropriate psychological conditions whereby the necessary relationship with the client can be established, and (2) effective case handling outcomes derive from the use of behavior-modification strategies that facilitate positive change in clients.

Focus on Client Growth in Systematic Counseling: Stages in a Systematic Counseling Model

In the systematic counseling model we draw on the theories, philosophies, tenets, constructs, relationship skills, processes, techniques, and strategies of all known theory systems or skills in counseling. We assume that: (1) no two clients or client situations are alike; (2) each client and counselor is in a constant state of flux—no person or situation in counseling is or can ever be static; (3) the effective counselor exhibits a flexible repertoire of activity—on a continuum from nondirective to directive; (4) the client is the world's greatest expert on his or her problem; (5) the counselor uses all the available personal and professional resources in the helping situation but is fully human in the relationship and cannot ultimately be responsible *for* the client; (6) counselors and the counseling process are fallible and cannot expect to observe overt or immediate success in every counseling or client situation; (7) competent counselors are aware of their own personal professional qualifications and deficits and take responsibility for ensuring that the counseling process is handled ethically and in the best interest of the client and of the public; (8) client safety takes precedence over counselor need fulfillment; (9) there are many different approaches and strategies available for conceptualizing and dealing with each problem—probably there is *no one best* approach or strategy; (10) many problems in the human dilemma appear to be insoluble (indeed for some problem situations we sometimes believe we can find no satisfactory options), but always there is a variety of alternatives, and some alternatives are better for the client than others; (11) generally, effective counseling is a process that is undertaken *with* the client rather than *to* or *for* the client.

The systematic counseling model can be represented in six stages, which we conceptualize as operating in a fluid process rather than as in a series of mechanistic, compartmentalized steps. Figure 13.1 shows the process flow for the model.

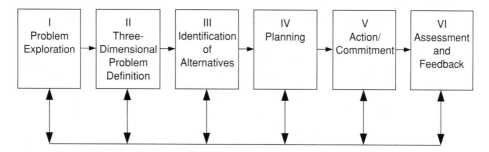

FIGURE 13.1   Stages in the Systematic Counseling Model

Stage I: Problem Exploration

Counselor's Process Goals: Establishing rapport; listening to client concerns; responding in ways that encourage client to explore concerns on a deeper level; developing mutual trust; permitting client to ventilate whenever ventilation is needed; attending to verbal as well as nonverbal behavior; attending to affect as well as content; being as genuine, real, empathic, caring, prizing, nonjudgmental, nonpossessive, and accepting as possible in the relationship (Hackney & Cormier, 1988, pp. 13–49).

Theoretical Basis: Person- or client-centered or existential therapy; use of effective relationship skills for facilitative listening and responding; Carkhuff model (1969) and Egan model (1986; 1990) are appropriate examples for counselor use during exploration stage because both models provide for a full range of helper relationship skills.

Stage II: Three-Dimensional Problem Definition

Counselor's Process Goals: Affective, cognitive, and physical aspects of client's problem(s) attended to by counselor; *thinking, feeling,* and *factual* aspects of problem(s) are verbalized until there is understanding between client and counselor (both client and counselor can agree on problem definition in precise and concrete terms); definition enables both client and counselor to ascertain the etiological base of the problem; lack of agreement on definition(s) returns the process to stage I.

Theoretical Basis: Person- or client-centered or existential therapy, same relationship skills for facilitative listening and responding as used in stage I.

Stage III: Identification of Alternatives

Counselor's Process Goals: Identification and examination of current alternatives available, including physical and emotional safety; all reasonable options should be expressed and openly examined; may make written list of alternatives during session; client encouraged to enumerate and verbalize as many viable alternatives as possible that client views as appropriate, realistic, and options he or she can "own"; counselor may use open-ended questions to clarify client's options; counselor may assist client by adding to list alternatives that client can accept as own, but does not impose alternatives on client; client may be given homework assignment to discover additional alternatives; referral resources and consultants may be used; process goal for stage III is discovery of appropriate alternatives for immediate use.

Theoretical Basis: Person-centered, control/reality, psychoanalytic, rational-emotive behavioral, trait-factor, Adlerian, Gestalt, behavioral therapy, cognitive therapy, TA, and multimodal are examples of systems used in examining alternatives available to client; elements from more than one system may be used during stage III.

Stage IV: Planning

Counselor's Process Goals: Critical evaluation of alternatives identified; plan may include rehearsal, role playing, suggestion, or emotive imagery of action steps planned by client; assisting client to decide which and how many alternatives are appropriate and realistic in view of client's past level of performance and present readiness to risk and respond; counselor may serve as teacher, mentor, or model for selected planning elements; counselor may use suggestion or didactic techniques in cases where client "needs to know," such as, not all problems can be systematically solved, some situations require time for healing, some can be only partially alleviated to minimize debilitating effects, or "we can't control what others do or think, nor can we be responsible for others"; development of a realistic, success-oriented, workable plan is a primary goal of this stage; any plan is tentative and approached pragmatically but treated as important; client ownership of realistic plan is optimum goal of planning stage.

Theoretical Basis: Person-centered, control/reality, psychoanalytic, rational-emotive behavioral, trait-factor, Adlerian, Gestalt, behavioral therapy, cognitive therapy, and TA are examples of systems used in planning client action steps; elements from more than one system may be used during planning stage.

Stage V: Action/Commitment

Counselor's Process Goals: Genuine commitment to workable *action steps* by client is primary goal; important for client to decide which action steps to undertake in terms of reality, time, emotional capability, and need fulfillment; client's commitment is specific; counselor is personally involved and genuinely supportive but cannot *do* action steps *for* client; client views action steps as viable and goal-related and shows willingness to try; nonattainment or partial attainment of goal on first trial is understood realistically by client who knows in advance that partial success on one trial is neither catastrophe, failure, nor total success; counselor role in commitment stage is clearly supportive—to help client achieve optimum success and to assist client in assessing progress and refining plan; counselor asks client to summarize plan and commitment prior to terminating interview; client's action/commitment is normally starting point for next interview.

Theoretical Basis: Person-centered, control/reality, psychoanalytic, rational-emotive behavioral, trait-factor, Adlerian, Gestalt, behavioral therapy, cognitive therapy, and TA are examples of systems that might be used in helping client make action/commitment toward successful behavior or realistic goal attainment(s) that client views as important and desirable; elements from more than one system may be used during action/commitment stage; client action deemed necessary because thinking alone may not suffice.

Stage VI: Assessment and Feedback

Counselor's Process Goals: Client usually summarizes progress made toward attainment of goal—based on action/commitment at previous session; both client and counselor review and assess level of goal attainment in terms of client's needs, feelings, and present coping level; further discussion and evaluation of plan conducted if assessment of attainment level or client's current needs so indicate; feedback and assessment data may be processed by counselor and client in light of client's desire for additional attainment or in terms of client's need to work on another problem; counselor may continue as monitor and support person, helping client on same goal (maybe more rehearsal or imagery needed, more time required, additional refinements to plan needed); systematic counseling model viewed as fluid, melding from stage I through VI, as required to respond to client needs; counselor focus may go immediately from stage VI to any other stage; collaborative assessment governs direction and focus of client-counselor interaction during each interview following initial session.

Theoretical Basis: Theoretical approaches in assessment/feedback stage selected on basis of their having developed and tested mechanisms and experienced success in a wide range of client assessment and feedback; person-centered, trait-factor, TA, behavioral, cognitive, Adlerian, rational-emotive behavioral, control/reality, and multimodal therapy are recommended as examples of systems qualifying for use with various components of the assessment and feedback stage; elements from one or more theoretical systems may be used during assessment and feedback stage.

The Process of Eclectic Counseling

Great flexibility in theory, style, and technique is inherent in the systematic model or any eclectic model. One should not infer from the considerable flexibility, however, that there is lack of organization or that this involves a hodgepodge of arbitrary, inconsistent, or contradictory assumptions and methods. The systematic model as well as every true eclectic model embodies a planned, systematic, consistent base of assumptions, formulations, and methods (Castonguay & Goldfried, 1994; Watkins & Watts, 1995).

Even though eclectic counselors are knowledgeable and skilled and have *mastered several theoretical approaches,* they do not have to be expert in every process. They are flexible, versatile, sensitive, and capable of using the best of each theoretical system in appropriate ways. Eclectics view themselves as continuous learners and accept themselves as fallible human beings. There is no place for perfectionist tendencies or parochial dogma in eclectic counseling!

STRATEGIES FOR HELPING CLIENTS

Overview

We have organized the various strategies in clusters or categories to facilitate presentation and discussion of the numerous techniques available to the eclectic counselor. The ten categories focus on relationships, interviewing, assessment, idea generation, case handling, gaining insight, behavior management, evaluation and termination, personal and professional growth, and research. We cite several representative exponents or references (from various theoretical orientations) whom we identify with each cluster of strategies. We also give a thumbnail encapsulation of the general implications and perspectives of both the counselor and the client as they experience appropriate use of the strategies.

Categories of Counseling Strategies

We have arranged the ten categories or clusters of strategies in chart form in Table 13.1 (see pages 374–377). We recognize that our arrangement contains some overlapping. For instance, several of the techniques under "case handling" could very well be placed in other categories. Also, there is overlap between "assessment" and "evaluation and termination." We preferred to make separate categories to preserve certain distinctions. We believe the cluster format of Table 13.1 serves as a concise and systematic means of portraying eclectic strategies.

The categories integrate feeling, thinking, behaving, and learning from both counselor and client perspectives. As may readily be seen, the system uses principles and techniques from a wide variety of theories.

Multimodal Therapy: A Technical Eclecticism

An alternative to the multitheory approach is the single-system multimodel of Lazarus (1981), which he promotes as *technical eclecticism* (Lazarus, 1967; Lazarus & Beutler, 1993). Lazarus proposes that multimodal therapy is a comprehensive systematic therapeutic approach to major areas of human functioning (Lazarus, 1989a, 1989b; Lazarus & Beutler, 1993). He has formulated these areas of functioning into a multimodal schema composed of seven components that he calls BASIC ID (Lazarus, 1989a; 1989b; 1989c; 1995).

Multimodal therapy is a highly comprehensive and systematic approach to behavior modification (Lazarus, 1981; 1986a; 1986b; 1987; 1989a; 1989b; 1989c; 1995b). It is pragmatically evolving and incorporating new concepts and strategies that are found to be valid through research or practice (Lazarus 1987; 1989c). Although Lazarus does not classify the system as eclectic in the usual sense, it is, in essence, a systematic approach that is a *technical eclecticism*. Lazarus himself (1989b, pp. 503–510) referred to the system as multimodal eclecticism when comparing it to the functionalism of James. Over a period of several years Lazarus (1989b; 1989c; 1995b) refined the multimodal schema into seven components that he called the BASIC ID, representing the major areas of human functioning.

B = Behavior
A = Affective responses
S = Sensations
I = Images
C = Cognitions
I = Interpersonal relationships
D = Drugs, biological functions, nutrition, and exercise

According to Lazarus (1989a; 1989b; 1989c; 1995b) effective therapy begins with a comprehensive assessment of the client's functioning on each of the seven components. No therapy is considered complete unless it assesses and treats each modality of the BASIC ID. Lazarus (1989b, p. 509) encapsulates the essence of the therapeutic treatment in the following statement.

Multimodal therapists constantly ask, "What works, for whom, and under which particular circumstances?" Thus, they take care not to attempt to fit the client to a predetermined treatment. With most practitioners, the client seems to get only what the therapist practices—which may not necessarily be what is best for the client. In multimodal therapy, there is a deliberate attempt to determine precisely what type of relationship, what type of interactive posture, each client will respond to. The multimodal orientation emphasizes therapeutic flexibility and versatility above all else. There is no unitary way to approach peoples' problems.

BASIC ID Assessment

The multimodal therapist uses assessment data to address each dimension of the BASIC ID during the course of treatment. It is a highly refined scientific therapy that defers assumptions, diagnoses, and treatment plans until the answers to pertinent questions about the client are answered. The multimodal therapist's operational assessment proceeds by ascertaining, through open questioning and written devices, the client's level of functioning on each of the seven BASIC ID components. Most open questions start with words like *what* and *how*. They are phrased to elicit from the client, in the client's own words, precisely what is being done, felt, sensed, imaged, or thought. Closed questions that elicit simple "yes" or "no" responses are usually not asked.

Behavior

Behavior may involve a wide range of psychomotor actions, from simple to complex, such as speaking, smiling, walking, writing, eating, and engaging in sexual activity. First the therapist focuses on the client's behaviors. The behavioral component targets overt, observable, measurable emitted responses, actions, reactions, habits, and patterns of performance. For assessment purposes the therapist may rely on inferences or on self-reports. The therapist pays particular attention to behavioral excesses or deficits.

TABLE 13.1 Categories of Counseling Strategies

Counseling Strategy Category	Representative Exponents or References	Implications of Strategies for Feeling, Thinking, Behaving, and Learning	
		From the Counselor's Perspectives and Behaviors/Goals	From the Client's Perspectives and Behaviors/Goals
Relationship strategies	Rogers (1951); Brammer (1985; 1990); Carkhuff (1969); Egan (1986); Hackney & Cormier (1988); Cormier & Cormier (1991)	Attending, listening, respecting, responding, caring, empathic understanding, accepting, being genuine, trusting, being open, creating a climate of unconditional positive regard; ensuring physical/ emotional safety of client	Trusting self and others; feeling understood, valued, safe, respected, worthwhile, secure, and authentic; experiencing a climate of acceptance or unconditional positive regard; getting in touch with own feelings, values, choices, and inner motives
Interviewing strategies	Thorne (1968); Ivey & Authier (1978); Cormier & Cormier (1991)	Identifying purposes of counseling: selectively responding to help client clarify problem situation and present and desired level of functioning; using summarized restatements, open-ended questions; responding to both verbal and nonverbal messages of client	Clarification of problem dimensions; discrimination among own internal/ external, emotional/behavioral functioning; recognizing desired direction and/or level of own future functioning
Assessment strategies	Lazarus (1995b); Neimeyer & Neimeyer (1990); Adler (1963); Williamson (1965); Thorne (1968); Gambrill (1977); Cormier & Cormier (1991); Gilliland & James (1997)	Problem definition, diagnosis, prognosis, goal selection, needs assessment, determination of appropriate helping resources/ techniques available; assessing coping levels of client and social/environmental implications for client; examining global and isolated, simple and complex, and long-term and short-term nature of client's situation	Problem exploration and definition; realistic goal setting and selection; surveying and understanding own attitudes, interests, abilities, problems, goals, resources, potentials, and social/environmental conditions; evaluating effects of own goals in terms of global/isolated, simple/complex, and long-term/short-term dimensions

374

Idea-generation strategies	Kelly (1995); Carkhuff (1973); Gambrill (1977); Pietrofesa et al. (1978); Williams & Long (1983); Glasser (1984, 1996)	Exploration and identification of options, alternatives, behaviors, rewards, consequences, wants, and incentives that impinge on and are appropriate to client's goals; helping client generate both overt and covert alternatives; intervening in collaborative, nondirective, or directive mode (as needed) to facilitate client recognition of viable choices and formulation of concrete list of realistic choices	Discovery of repertory of realistic options available; generation of overt and covert alternatives, both cognitive and behavioral; developing usable ideas for improving or changing own thinking, doing, and feeling patterns; expanding own awareness of the vast number of alternatives available and of own role in initiating and implementing alternatives
Case-handling strategies	Ellis (1995); Lazarus (1995b); Glasser (1965, 1984, 1996); Thorne (1968); Gambrill (1977); Cormier & Cormier (1991); Palmer (1980); Watson & Tharp (1989); Gilliland & James (1997)	Selecting and systematically using appropriate techniques, referral resources, modeling, reinforcement contingencies; facilitative responding and other helping strategies to intervene, influence, teach, lead, support, inspire, collaborate with and otherwise help client attain desired goals in positive and responsible ways; preserve client autonomy, rights, and independence during counseling	Learning to cope, adjust, change internal views, improve behavior, alter environment, make social adjustment, choose and discriminate among alternatives, gain independence, follow modeled adaptive patterns of behavior, gain confidence and self-esteem; coping with and incorporating new information and innovative adaptive choices into own lifestyle
Insight strategies	Adler (1963); Auld & Hyman (1991); Freud (1949, 1961); Lazarus (1989a; 1989b; 1989c); Perls (1969); Maslow (1976); Polster & Polster (1973); Ellis (1979); Ellis & Harper (1975); Kohut (1971, 1977, 1984)	Facilitating discovery of polar conflicts; helping client gain recognition of early life traumas that may have contributed to current problems; setting up conditions so client can discover and deal with developmental deficits; confronting client in responsible, constructive, and helpful ways; dealing with client's conscious, unconscious, and altered conscious thoughts to help client understand past cognitions and restrictive present/future conditions affecting feeling, thinking, behaving, and learning	Discovering conflicting polarities within self; recognizing that past unresolved traumas (perhaps during own childhood) are a basis for current problems; gaining a mental connectedness, from the past, of developmental deficits that may contribute to present developmental difficulties and gaining mental self-images of successful coping or acting to remediate for such deficits; confronting own biases, deficits, conflicting values, polar conflicts, and emotional disturbances in positive and constructive ways; learning to understand own inner functioning through analysis of dreams, projections, free associations, fantasies, drawings, and other methods of gaining access to the unconscious

Continued

375

TABLE 13.1 *Continued*

Counseling Strategy Category	Representative Exponents or References	Implications of Strategies for Feeling, Thinking, Behaving, and Learning	
		From the Counselor's Perspectives and Behaviors/Goals	From the Client's Perspectives and Behaviors/Goals
Behavior-management strategies	Lazarus (1989c, 1995b); Skinner (1953); Wolpe (1969); Krumboltz & Thoresen (1976); Gambrill (1977); Meichenbaum (1977); Cormier & Cormier (1985; 1991); Williams & Long (1983); Thoresen (1980); Kanfer & Goldstein (1975)	Acting and modeling in a variety of helping roles, such as counselor, therapist, teacher, mentor, consultant, facilitator, and support person; intervening in a variety of modes from directive to collaborative to nondirective; facilitating the client to change thinking and behaving from maladaptive to adaptive and to change and/or cope with a changing, complex physical and social environment; applying all known behavioral techniques in scientific approach to helping client	Implementing strategies to extinguish maladaptive thinking and behaving and to develop adaptive thinking and behaving; developing skills to change and/or cope with a changing, complex physical and social environment; learning the behavioral skills and techniques to develop ability scientifically to manage own lifestyle according to tested behavioral principles
Evaluation and termination strategies	Thorne (1973); Hansen, Stevic, & Warner (1977); Pietrofesa et al. (1978); Cormier & Cormier (1991); Palmer (1980)	Evaluating counseling effectiveness and outcomes; assessing appropriateness of concepts, assumptions, and strategies; terminating counseling sessions and counseling relationships in ways that are appropriate, helpful, professional, and ethical; providing for client to return or be referred in case further help is needed; developing effective and efficient system of follow-up	Gaining concrete understanding of outcomes of counseling; recognizing positive learning and growth steps experienced during counseling; ending each session with a knowledge of what has been accomplished; discontinuing counseling relationship in a positive mode; identifying growth steps; showing greater independence and more frequent coping behaviors than were in evidence prior to counseling; making realistic comparisons between own functioning before and after counseling and during progressive increments of counseling

Personal/ professional growth strategies	Kelly (1955); Auld & Hyman (1991); Lazarus (1989c; 1995b); Blocher (1987); Ivey (1986); Ivey, Ivey, & Simek-Downing (1987); Palmer (1980); Kell & Mueller (1966); Glasser (1984, 1996)	Continuously developing oneself as a person and as a counselor; viewing oneself as a continuous learner; discovering, creating, and implementing ways to renew one's personal and professional life; intentional improvement of counseling and relationship skills; initiating meaningful contact with colleagues, through professional/educational growth activities, and adopting training and continuous learning as a way of life; becoming sensitive and responsive to counselor accountability	Learning to grow and cope as a way of life; discovering that one has many choices and ways of implementing one's options; gaining fuller self-acceptance, self-confidence, and self-esteem; moving toward greater independence, self-sufficiency, and self-actualization; adopting prevention and proactivity as a way of life; developing life-long renewal mechanisms and strategies
Research strategies	Heppner, Kivlighan, & Wampold (1992); Huck, Cormier, & Bounds (1974); Ivey, Ivey, & Simek-Downing (1987)	Investigating accuracy and effectiveness of counseling theory and techniques; engaging in ongoing research studies and activities; supporting and sponsoring research in counseling; sharing own research findings with appropriate audiences; improving on own strategies based on research findings by self and others; making research and learning a way of life as a counselor; encouraging colleagues and students to conduct research	Whenever appropriate, participating in research in counseling; being willing to help self and others by supporting research programs/activities; developing a positive attitude toward research in counseling; returning research survey forms in a thorough and timely manner; being candid and objective in all responses involving investigative research

Affect

The affective component targets the client's emotional, feeling, and/or psychological functioning. For assessment purposes, the therapist looks for the presence or absence of particular emotions as well as hidden and/or distorted emotions.

Sensation

The sensation component is assessed to determine the adequacy of the client's sensory functioning. Sensory functioning is important because often the client's perception of personal fulfillment is connected with sensory inputs (sight, sound, smell, taste, kinesics, and so on), and may emerge, unrecognized by the client, in the form of bodily ailments such as dizziness or digestive problems. The person's total wellness and emotional adjustment may be substantially affected by such sensations.

Imagery

The imagery component targets the client's view of self in the mind's eye, including the client's imagination, dreams, daydreams, fantasies, internal pictures, meditations, memories, reminiscences, and visualizations. The therapist's assessment considers either overuse or underuse of the client's imagery, that is, the client's exaggeration of the impact or reality of a fantasy or the absence of imaging altogether.

Cognition

The cognition component targets aspects of the client's thinking processes, including evaluating, judging, valuing, theorizing, hypothesizing, and problem solving. The therapist's assessment especially considers the client's illogical or irrational cognitions.

Interpersonal Relationships

The interpersonal relationship component targets aspects of the client's interactions with other people. The therapist pays close attention to the way the client expresses and accepts feelings communicated to him or her in interpersonal exchanges. The quality of the client's social communications is also important.

Drugs/Biology

The drugs/biology component targets far more than the client's medication or substance abuse. It includes the person's nutrition, exercise, and total bodily well-being. The therapist's assessment of this component is important because neurological and biochemical factors can have a profound effect on behavior, affective responding, sensations, imagery, and cognition.

Usually the assessment data reveal that clients are troubled by multiple symptoms. Consequently, the process of psychotherapy uses a multitude of treatments. Also, because assessment is a continuous process, treatments are altered as needed as the therapy proceeds.

Constructivist Theory

Constructivist theory, formerly known as *personal construct theory,* was first developed by George A. Kelly (1955). The fundamental postulate of the theory is that personal constructs are ways of construing or categorizing people, events, and environments in the experiential world of the individual (Smith & Vetter, 1991, p. 237). Kelly embellished this basic postulate by formulating eleven corollaries, listed below that, in combination, represent an eclectic-like system that Hergen-hahn (1994, pp. 449–450) characterized as phenomenological, cognitive, existential, and humanistic.

1. *Construction corollary.* "A person anticipates events by construing their replications" (Kelly, 1955, p. 50).
2. *Individuality corollary.* "Persons differ from each other in their construction of events" (Kelly, 1955, p. 55).
3. *Organization corollary.* "Each person characteristically evolves, for his convenience in anticipating events, a construction system embracing ordinal relationships between constructs" (Kelly, 1955, p. 56).
4. *Dichotomy corollary.* "A person's construction system is composed of a finite number of dichotomous constructs" (Kelly, 1955, p. 59).
5. *Choice corollary.* "A person chooses for himself that alternative in a dichotomized construct through which he anticipates the greater possibility for extension and definition of his system" (Kelly, 1955, p. 64).
6. *Range corollary.* "A construct is convenient for the anticipation of a finite range of events only" (Kelly, 1955, p. 68).
7. *Experience corollary.* "A person's construction system varies as he successfully construes the replications of events" (Kelly, 1955, p. 72).
8. *Modulation corollary.* "The variation in a person's construction system is limited by the permeability of the constructs within whose range of convenience the variants lie" (Kelly, 1955, p. 79).
9. *Fragmentation corollary.* "A person may successively employ a variety of construction subsystems which are inferentially incompatible with each other" (Kelly, 1955, p. 83).
10. *Commonality corollary.* "To the extent that one person employs a construction of experience which is similar to that employed by another, his psychological processes are similar to the other person" (Kelly, 1955, p. 90).
11. *Sociality corollary.* "To the extent that one person construes the construction processes of another, he may play a role in a social process involving the other person" (Kelly, 1955, p. 95).

Pursuant to Hergenhahn's (1994, pp. 449–450) fourfold characterization of the constructivist system as phenomenological, cognitive, existential, and humanistic, the following assumptions, proposed by different theorists, shed interesting light on the eclectic flavor of constructivism.

> *It is phenomenological.* People perceive the world and impose their own perspectives on it from the standpoint of their own system for construing experience (Duck & Condra, 1990, p. 187).
>
> *It is cognitive.* The constructivist model views people's cognitions and behaviors as being reciprocally interrelated (Viney, 1990, pp. 119–122).
>
> *It is existential.* The constructivist system is existential in that, in the person's mind, all interpretations of the universe are subject to revision (Sechrest, 1977, p. 209).
>
> *It is humanistic.* Kelly's fundamental postulate undergirds and each corollary fleshes out a constructivist view of what it is like to be human (Neimeyer & Neimeyer, 1987, p. 4).

Personal and Scientific Attributes

In the constructivist system of therapy both the individual and the therapist use the *personal construct* as the major thrust by which the client anticipates events and construes, interprets, explains, ascribes meaning to, and predicts personal experiences. Such a *construct* is like a miniscientific theory in that it helps the client "construct" predictions about reality (Hergenhahn, 1994, p. 451). Provided the predictions generated by a client are confirmed by experience, the theory is useful. If the predictions are not confirmed, the construct must be reexamined, revised, or abandoned. Kelly (1955, pp. 8–9) postulated that we view the world through transparent patterns or templates that we create and then attempt to fit over the realities of which that world is composed. The work of the constructivist therapist is to facilitate the client's "trying on these patterns for size."

Constructive Alternativism

Constructivist theory emphasizes that each person creates his or her own constructs for dealing with the world and that each one of us has the goal of reducing future uncertainty. Even so, we are free to construe reality any way we like. Kelly called that assumption *constructive alternativism* (Hergenhahn, 1994, p. 451). In that regard, Kelly stated that "there are always alternative constructions available to choose among in dealing with the world. No one needs to paint himself into a corner; no one needs to be completely hemmed in by circumstances; no one needs to be the victim of his own biography" (1955, p. 15).

Environmental Considerations

Although the eclectic and multimodal approaches attempt to deal in as comprehensive a manner as possible with individuals, it is still clear that people operate within their environmental contexts. To suppose that therapy could work successfully without taking the environment into consideration would be erroneous and unrealistic. As a result, any of the therapeutic modalities portrayed in this book must operate in an environmental context, whether that be the client's family, job, school, or community. In that regard, any comprehensive eclectic model should provide for environmental egress into therapy. It is from that vantage point that we incorporate a brief look at family therapy in this chapter.

Family Therapy

Although family therapy is technically not a "theoretical" counseling approach, it is eclectic in that it is integrative and draws from a broad range of systems, theories, and techniques. The focus is not on an individual client, but rather on the family as a whole. The fundamental difference between family therapy and approaches focusing only on individual clients is that in family therapy the family system is the "client" (Foley, 1989, p. 459).

Assumptions

Conceptualizing the family as a system and as the "client" implies adherence to several assumptions that differentiate family and individual therapy (Becuar & Becuar, 1988, pp. 61–70). These assumptions are as follows:

1. Family systems operate recursively, meaning that behavior is reciprocally causal.
2. Feedback is a systematic process that serves to maintain the status quo or produce change in the system.
3. A state of dynamic equilibrium that balances systemic change and stability is necessary for healthy systemic functioning.
4. Unspoken rules govern behavior, express values, and establish boundaries within and without the system.
5. The system permits or screens out information to the extent that it is open or closed.

Family Therapy Approaches

There are many theoretical approaches to family therapy. Thomas (1992, pp. 190–201) selected, described, and compared distinctive features of eight of these: experimental-humanistic, psychoanalytic, intergenerational family of origin, behavioral, structural, brief, strategic, and systemic. Each has developed its own view of healthy functioning, theoretical concepts, techniques, treatment process, and role of the therapist.

Cottone (1992, pp. 181–293) conceptualizes and organizes family therapy within the framework of two fundamental categories: the systemic-relational paradigm (with external and internal models) and the contextual paradigm. He places four theoretical approaches to family therapy in the systematic-relational paradigm: conjoint family therapy, strategic problem-solving therapy, structural family therapy, and structure-determined family therapy. His contextual paradigm contains two approaches: Milan systemic family therapy and cognitive-consensual therapy.

To describe and contrast theoretical systems of family therapy, we present four examples of different models that we believe illustrate the eclectic flavor of family therapy approaches: Satir's (1967) conjoint family therapy, Haley's (1987) strategic problem-solving therapy, Minuchin's (1974) structural family therapy, and Bowen's (1978) and Kerr and Bowen's (1988) family systems theory.

Conjoint Family Therapy   The central core of Satir's theory is self-esteem and relationships between marriage partners and among family members (Cottone, 1992, p. 197; Satir, 1967; 1972; 1975; 1982; Thomas, 1992, p. 204). The healthy family is viewed as one in which verbal and nonverbal communication nurtures in each family member equal sharing, openness, inquiry, decision making, self-worth, respect for others, diversity of opinion and style, and recognition of each others' stages of growth. The unhealthy family is characterized by blaming, threat, detraction, not sharing, keeping secrets, and rigid control (Thomas, 1992, pp. 204–207).

The process of counseling involves the facilitation of effective communication, in a relational context, with the counselor acting in roles of "official observer" of family interaction and "instructor" of communication among family members (Cottone, 1992, pp. 200–208). The conjoint family therapist focuses on both the family as a whole and individuals in the family context. The therapist is active both linguistically and physically, using a broad range of expression, touching, feeling, videotape techniques, and many innovative and traditional psychotherapeutic strategies. The outcome goals are to change the family's destructive and unhealthy patterns and communications and to facilitate emotional wellness, health, and positive self-esteem in all members of the family (Cottone, 1992, pp. 200–205; Thomas, 1992, pp. 206–207).

Strategic Problem-Solving Therapy   Haley's (1987) model is a systemic-relational therapy that is highly behavioral. Haley stated:

> *If therapy is to end properly, it must begin properly—by negotiating a solvable problem and discovering the social situation that makes the problem necessary. The act of therapy begins with the way the problem is examined. The act of intervening brings out problems and the relationship patterns that are to be changed (p. 8).*

Therapy is directed toward changing the family relational dynamics that may be supportive of unwanted or symptomatic behavior (Cottone, 1992, pp. 214–215). Some of the debilitating symptomatic patterns may be unhealthy (perverse) triangular entrenchments, pervasive double-bind situations, and power struggles within the family (Thomas, 1992, pp. 364–365). Triangular entrenchments occur when two members of the family regularly take sides in opposition to a third member, who then becomes a victim or scapegoat. A double bind occurs when a member of the family is in a position of being rejected or criticized regardless of what he or she does. The strategic therapist, in effect, joins the family, becomes a functioning entity therein, and takes on the role of "director" as in a live production. The therapist is active, directive, powerful, and persuasive in getting family members to change behaviorally the operative relationships that sustain the unhealthy symptoms and power struggles that inflict so much damage (Haley, 1987). To facilitate change, the therapist involves the whole family in examining and learning effective communication, correcting destructive triangular situations, using language and metaphor to change attitudes and behavior, and behaving ethically to prevent dysfunction, promote growth and stability, and reinforce autonomous problem solving (Haley, 1987).

According to Cottone (1992, p. 227), Haley's strategic problem-solving therapy is highly consistent with its stated formulations. Its systemic-relational mechanisms invariably focus on external relational factors as fundamental to both definition and solution of the symptomatic problems. Emphasis is on the whole family's problem, not on scapegoating or singling out any one individual. The techniques are designed to produce behavioral change and to help families themselves learn to change distressful situations.

Structural Family Therapy   Minuchin's external model of systemic-relational therapy (Colapinto, 1984; Minuchin, 1974; 1984) focuses on family structural change rather than on specific targets such as communication. In Minuchin's usage, "structure" refers to *organization* and *roles* within the family. Dysfunction or pathology is almost always synonymous with enmeshment or disengagement (Foley, 1989, p. 462). Enmeshment occurs when one person's identity is so heavily invested in that of another that he or she is unable to relate to others independently. Disengagement occurs when one is emotionally estranged from others to the extent that he or she has a total lack of affect toward them. The structural family therapist seeks either to loosen or to establish boundaries, depending on the degree of closeness or distance in the family structure. In that regard, Minuchin (1974) stated that both his theory and his technique focus on the individual within the social context of the family. Therapy is directed toward changing the organization and roles in the family: "When the structure of the family group is transformed, the positions of members in that group are altered accordingly. As a result, each individual's experiences change" (p. 2).

The structural family therapist essentially "joins" the family and enters into its interactive process as a way of accessing and changing the structure (Cottone, 1992, p. 234). According to Minuchin and Fishman (1981), such joining is more an attitude than a technique. The joining process puts the therapist in a position to understand, to be trusted, and to be perceived as working for and with the family in exploring alternatives, trying unusual experiments, and effecting change in roles and structure. Joining is the glue that binds the therapist and the family together and enables the therapist to influence and devise more adaptive roles and structure.

According to Colapinto (1982), the basic goal of structural family therapy is the restructuralization of the family's system of transactional rules in such a way that more flexible interactions among family members expands the availability of alternative ways of dealing with each other: "By releasing family members from their stereotyped positions and functions, this restructuralization enables the system to mobilize its underutilized resources and to improve its ability to cope with stress and conflict" (p. 122). Cottone (1992, p. 236) further states that positive growth occurs whenever the family organization progresses to the point where it no longer supports or tolerates debilitating behaviors. Once the whole family demonstrates its propensity for sustaining positive change in the face of family stressors, therapy is no longer needed.

Family Systems Theory   Bowen's family systems theory was developed from his research in the 1950s. He discovered that hospitalization and treatment of an entire family that contained a schizophrenic member had a positive and constructive impact on the whole family as an emotional unit (Kerr & Bowen, 1988, p. 6). This sudden and fundamentally new view of the treatment of family functioning and dysfunctioning ushered in a revision of assumptions regarding therapy with a dysfunctional family member. As a result, Bowen asserted that to change a dysfunctional family member, the entire family unit had to become involved and undergo fundamental change.

According to Bowen (1978, pp. 529–530) "The one most important goal of family systems therapy is to help family members [develop] toward a better level of 'differentiation of self'. . . . In any course of therapy it has been routine to encourage each spouse to work systematically toward the differentiation of self in the family of origin." Another important goal of therapy is to identify and control the level of chronic anxiety in individual family members. The lower a person's differentiation of self the less adaptiveness that person has to cope with stress and the higher the level of chronic anxiety becomes (Kerr & Bowen, 1988, p. 112).

One basic therapeutic strategy of a family systems therapist is to assist one or more family members to move to a higher level of self-differentiation. This is done mainly by working with couples (spouses, for example) in emotional triangles consisting of the therapist and two other family members. The therapist seeks to detriangle each family member by establishing a person-to-person working relationship with the therapist in the presence of the observing partner (Thomas, 1992, p. 264). Through the Bowenian therapeutic relationship, family members learn to communicate thoughts and feelings about the self as a separate entity from the other members of the family. Rather than gossiping about another family member the person learns to focus on self and the relationship of that self to the therapist and ultimately to the other family members.

Family evaluations are accomplished by various techniques, including interviews, incorporating the therapist into the family's problems, and examining the family's multigenerational and historical patterns. Bowen developed "genograms," which he later called "family diagrams," to demonstrate graphically to family members the importance of multigenerational influences (Kerr & Bowen, 1988, pp. 282–338). Genograms are diagrams of family trees that depict the histories, personalities, and relationships of family members. They are constructed in collaboration with family members and used as both diagnostic and therapeutic tools in family therapy.

Concluding Statement

Family therapy's concepts, techniques, and outcomes are highly eclectic. Diverse models of marital and family therapy synthesize and integrate techniques that have been found to work with diverse populations. Systemic, interdisciplinary, and cross-cultural perspectives have been incorporated into most schools of family therapy. Family therapy approaches, more than other modalities, appear to take into account the psychological, social, demographic, technological, cultural, and diverse world views that tend to generate stress and affect the functioning of individuals in the modern family unit.

SAMPLE CASE

The eclectic counselor may integrate procedures from different systems of counseling during the same interview with a client or incorporate different approaches over an extended period of time. In the case of Mary, person-centered techniques were used during the initial session. At subsequent sessions the counselor used rational-emotive behavioral, analytic, behavioral, and existential strategies. There was little combination of approaches during each session, except that the Carkhuff model of listening and responding was used to initiate each session. After Mary had had an opportunity to explore and define her concerns at the beginning of each interview, the counselor selected an approach judged to be appropriate to the case handling during the remainder of that interview.

Mary, age fifty-two, came to the counselor at the urging of her husband, George. George was a fifty-two-year-old Ph.D. who held a high-level administrative position in a large organization. Mary was a professional in the same organization. Mary and George were born and reared in the geographical region where they worked. They both attended school at state universities and had lived and worked in the same region of the state during their entire careers up to the time counseling was initiated. They had reared two children. Linda, age twenty-six, lived and worked in a large city some 150 miles away and Mark, twenty-two, had just been accepted to the state university's dental school located in the same city where Linda lived. The family was known as an "ideal" family.

Suddenly George let it be known to Mary that he wanted a divorce. Initially he told only Mary (and also the counselor) that he wished to take early retirement, move to a city some 450 miles away, take a different managerial job, and marry a younger woman. George did not want to tell anyone else about his decision, especially Linda or Mark. George met with the counselor to disclose his decision and express his concern over the possible damaging effects his actions might have on Mary. Mary agreed to see the counselor, and within a few days George retired and left town to carry out his plan. During the first interview Mary was composed but in emotional shock. She expressed disbelief, denial, self-blame, and severe depression.

Initiating Eclectic Counseling

A brief segment from the first interview with Mary gives some idea of the client's level of functioning and the eclectic counselor's initial technique.

CL: I keep wondering, "Is this really happening? What did I do to bring all this on?" I must be dreaming. This must be a nightmare. What did I do?

CO: You're finding it hard to believe that this is really happening to you. Yet, you believe that somehow *you* had some part in bringing on this disaster. But you are at a loss to explain it.

CL: I must have been living in a dream world. George has always been a perfect husband, a perfect father. It *must* be something I've done or failed to do! If I could just go to sleep (*pause*) and let the whole world just pass on by (*no tears, no emotion, no affect shown*).

CO: A part of you is blaming yourself and asking, "Why?" But another part of you says, "I just wish I could go to sleep and not wake up—just wish I could experience a painless death."

CL: Oh, I've thought about that, seriously. Right after George first exploded this bombshell. Dying really appealed to me. I contemplated it all right. (*long pause*)

CO: I'm very concerned about your thoughts about suicide. I noticed you were talking about it in the past tense, though. I'm concerned about your present danger to yourself and about the availability of your means of doing it if you should decide—maybe on impulse—to actually do it.

CL: Oh, I could do it all right. But I thought, "What would happen to Mark and Linda?" No, I couldn't do that to them. They are going to have it rough enough as it is, without me making matters worse for them.

CO: Your concern for Mark and Linda's welfare is too strong to allow you to carry out such a drastic act and complicate their lives even more.

CL: Definitely, I feel they are going to need me more than ever when they find out what George has done—and what he still plans to do.

CO: So you feel you can't abandon them now.

CL: Never. They're all I've got. And I may be all they've got. We're going to need each other more than ever now.

The counselor was concerned about Mary's safety, was attempting to assess her level of lethality and coping potential, and was using reflection to assist her in ventilating and deeply exploring the problem. By the end of the first interview the counselor felt, from observing Mary's nonverbal behavior, tone of voice, and verbal responses, that she was not in imminent danger to herself. The counselor referred her to her physician for a complete physical examination, and gave her a calling card to use in case she experienced a crisis prior to the next interview. The counselor obtained a firm commitment from Mary that she would talk with the counselor by phone immediately in the event of a crisis of such a nature as to cause her impulsively to harm herself.

Process of Multimodal Psychotherapy, Using the BASIC ID

In multimodal therapy the assessment process precedes therapy and attends to all of the BASIC ID patterns. Psychotherapy is governed fundamentally by the assessed unique needs and requirements of each client. There is no typical treatment regimen (Lazarus, 1989b, p. 521, 1995a; 1995b; pp. 337–341). Further, the multimodalist will not really decide on treatment modalities until the interview sessions begin. A preliminary modality and treatment plan is usually decided on by the start of the third session. For Mary, it was determined that the three most compelling BASIC ID areas needing therapeutic work were behavior, sensations, and images.

Processing Mary's Behavior

The multimodal therapist actively, intentionally, and directively guided Mary's attention to specific behavioral deficits uncovered through the assessment process and inferred in her interviews.

CL: I haven't had the nerve to tell Mama yet. But I did contact my friend about the possibility of leaving here and getting a job in the city where Linda lives.

CO: Well, those are perhaps important things to do. But what about your communication with George that you talked about last time? You indicated that you didn't want to make any major career decisions until you knew what financial resources you are going to have. What have you done to clarify your financial status?

CL: I was hoping he would come by to get the remainder of his clothing and that I would see him and maybe talk to him then.

CO: Will *hoping* and *what he does* get you where you want to go within the time frame you have set for yourself? You've said you want to take charge and be your own pilot. What actions do *you want to initiate* to take charge and begin to chart your own course?

CL: Hmm. . . . What I really want to do is to get some independent legal advice before I have any more discussion with him about financial or property settlement matters.

CO: So, what's the next step going to be for you?

In working on Mary's *behaviors* the multimodal therapist kept her largely in the here-and-now and guided her concentration on those behaviors that were critical to her current needs. Also typical in multimodal therapy, metaphors that were derived from Mary's own situation were used by the therapist to drive home to her what she had verbally stated she wanted to do. Multimodal therapists use metaphors to enrich, strengthen, affirm, and empower clients to take realistic and positive action steps that they themselves choose to do. Concrete behaviors designed to put control and autonomy in the hands of clients is of primary importance.

Mary's therapist might have applied a variety of other mechanisms of behavioral processing had Mary's situation warranted them. Extinction techniques (such as massed practice, response prevention, and flooding), counterconditioning (such as using incompatible response techniques), positive reinforcement, and operant procedures (such as token economies, contingent praise, timeout, and aversion strategies) are a few of the mechanisms that might be brought to bear in multimodal therapy (Lazarus, 1989b, pp. 525–526; 1995b, pp. 342–347).

Processing Mary's Sensations

In helping Mary to focus on, recognize, and validate her sensations, the therapist's objective was to enable Mary to get in touch with the pleasures, pains, and bodily sensations and responses to environmental stimuli such as sex, food, music, art, and aesthetic stimulations (Lazarus, 1989b, p. 515; 1995b, pp. 332–341).

CL: I guess I'm still in too much of a daze to fully realize what I'm doing and what I'm up against. Much of the time since George dropped this bombshell I've simply been too tense and too numb to really feel anything.

CO: Let's concentrate on your tenseness and numbness. What kinds of activities typically get you going, provide relaxation throughout your body, and stimulate your inner enjoyment and pleasure during more normal times in your life when you find yourself temporarily stressed out?

CL: Strolling in nature. Beauty in the park. The trees and the birds . . . the flower gardens in Audubon Park! Those are the kinds of things that get inside me and touch me when I'm emotionally stuck—that I have neglected by staying inside, lying in bed, and crying since this happened.

CO: Let's talk about how you can get some pleasure . . . some tension-releasing sensations back into your life.

The multimodalist placed a great deal of importance in facilitating sensory pleasuring (Lazarus, 1989b, p. 526, 1995b, pp. 332–337) in Mary's life. Such sensations may involve mechanisms such as biofeedback, relaxation training, purposeful physical exercise, positive tactile sensations, and aesthetic experiences. In Mary's case, she provided the therapist with a viable lead when she remembered her positive sensations experienced in a particular natural setting.

Processing Mary's Imagery

Mary's vivid imagination, fantasies, and daydreams constituted what amounted to negative and distorted mental pictures of herself, because she was unable to evoke positive self-images.

CO: So you can only picture yourself as a worn-out discard. Let's talk about where you got those images and then work together to change that view of yourself as some awful, despicable person.

CL: I keep thinking I must be deplorable. I see myself through his eyes, I guess, and I view myself as unacceptable, because if I were pleasant to look at and be with, he wouldn't reject me and look for another woman.

CO: That's exactly where we will start, right now. I think we can come up with what I call "coping images" that will enable you to evoke some different pictures of yourself—some pictures that will portray you to yourself as worthwhile, having self-control, and capable, competent, and deserving of respect.

The therapist recognized Mary's need for positive and constructive imaging. The therapist then began to help Mary develop a different repertoire of images—mainly through using mental and emotive imagery, positive self-talk, and visualizations that were realistic and true for her.

The multimodalist's use of the BASIC ID model with many different types of clients transcends traditional behaviorist approaches by invoking unique assessments and by working with great intensity and depth with the client in coping with presenting dilemmas. The therapist goes into specific detail in using the mechanisms that improve sensations, imagery, cognitions, and interpersonal functioning in addition to making improvements in behavior and personal physiology. A fundamental premise of multimodal therapy is that clients are usually troubled by a multitude of problems, as was Mary, and that a multitude of specific treatment mechanisms may therefore be necessary to effect positive and constructive change (Lazarus, 1989b, p. 503, 1995a, 1995b, pp. 341–342).

Continuing Eclectic Counseling with Mary

We have briefly illustrated one multimodalist technique and shall continue with the fundamental processing of Mary's case with an eclectic counselor. During her first few interviews several themes emerged: putting herself down, blaming herself for what had happened, protecting George from blame, assuming responsibility for George's continued unhappiness, focusing on her past behavior that may have caused George to reject her, and worrying about the effects of the divorce on Mark and Linda. The counselor used rational-emotive behavioral techniques to help the client sort out these issues. REBT was employed because the client appeared to be quite a cognitive person. She was quick to grasp and deal with the world of ideas, beliefs, philosophies of life, and rational decisions.

CO: Mary, you seem to be saying to yourself that there must have been something pretty awful you were doing—that you were somehow pretty bad to let all this happen. Let's examine what you're saying to yourself about what was happening to give you such a picture of yourself, now.

CL: Well, I know I've been very critical of myself—perhaps too critical. But I can't help thinking, "I must have been stupid to have neglected him—to have forced him to go looking somewhere else for his love and comfort."

CO: Look how you just devalued yourself—using the word *stupid.* You seem to have already tried and convicted yourself of some heinous crime before even analyzing what really happened. You seem to be saying, "It's all my fault, look how terrible I am," and to be protecting him at all costs. Did you *really* force him to do those things? Let's examine your "crimes" for a moment. Did you sneak around behind George's back for three or four years, having a clandestine affair with a male friend?

CL: Certainly not! I would never even think of such a thing!

CO: Was it you who took a lover with you to conventions at resort hotels and stayed several days extra, time and time again, leaving George at home to keep things going?

CL: No, he was doing that, long before I even knew anything was wrong.

CO: Was it you who allocated family funds and fabricated weekend conferences to spend time with your boyfriend, leaving George and Mark to fend for themselves, and then did you lie to them about doing it?

CL: No. (*pause*) It's true that I have done the best I could. I have never lied to George, and I've never done him wrong. I haven't been perfect, but I've certainly done nothing to deserve what I've got.

CO: So you *can* assign some of the responsibility to George.

CL: Well, I guess I just hung on to my image of him so long, I just couldn't believe (*pause*). But yes, he did do those things. (*pause*) I don't want to give you the impression that George is a terrible person. He has lots of very good qualities. It's like, he just went off his rocker—lost his sanity. That's not the George I thought I knew and trusted and loved.

CO: Sounds like you can admit that he did those things, and that you were not the cause of his doing them. But it also sounds like you are still protecting him—or your image of him—by saying that it wasn't the real George who did them; that the real George wouldn't behave like that and that maybe the real, sane George might still exist.

CL: I guess it is hard to admit to myself the raw truth. I guess it is really hard for me to realize that he has discarded me. Just cast me off like an old piece of clothing. That he prefers someone else to me. That's what hurts.

CO: I can see that you're hurting, and you have real cause to be hurt. I can also see that what you're telling yourself *about* this rejection may be at the source of some of the hurt. Let's see if we can determine what messages you're giving to yourself *about* the rejection that's resulting in your rejecting yourself, before all the facts are in. What are you saying to yourself at the moment you're feeling like an old discard?

CL: Well, I know I'm feeling like, "this is the ultimate put-down," like a curse he's put on me. But I also realize that I'm being hard on myself—maybe too hard.

CO: So, when you think about it, it may be distasteful; it may be degrading; but it isn't an absolute catastrophe—it *is* something you'll get over.

CL: Oh yes, I'll get over it. I may even be stronger—more independent—when I do. It's just such a new experience for me to suddenly have to fight and claw for every little crumb of my being—it's left such a void in my life.

CO: It seems to me you're realizing that this is going to be a tough, hard hill to climb. But it seems that you're telling yourself now that you dread it; that it is inconvenient and highly distasteful; but that you can stand it, and that you may be less dependent when it's all settled.

CL: I really have no choice. I'll have to survive, some way.

Mary was quick to grasp and deal with the exaggerations and catastrophic tendencies. Each time she returned, the counselor had to reindoctrinate her because she would lapse into her old patterns of irrational thinking between interviews. After several sessions of coaching and confronting with the rational techniques, Mary began to discard her self-blame, guilt, and awfulizing. The counselor noticed some new emotions emerging—anger directed at George, chagrin at herself for not having been a more independent person during the marriage, and puzzlement over the dynamics of her inner motives and emotions. She seemed to have achieved a plateau of sorts, where she was rational, decision-oriented, poised, and in control. Her concern now seemed to be directed toward self-understanding.

Mary resigned her job, rented the family home, moved to the city where Linda and Mark were residing, obtained another professional position, and continued seeing the counselor. She expressed great desire to achieve self-understanding. In discussing various insight techniques, Mary was resistant to most of the procedures suggested and described by the counselor. She was not personally suited to dream analysis and interpretation or Gestalt techniques. However, she had a vivid imagination and proved to be able to deal with imagery quite effectively, as was previously illustrated with the multimodal counselor. The counselor was about to conclude that working mainly on Mary's resistance was needed when the idea of analysis of her writing was mentioned as a possibility. That idea appealed to Mary and the counselor gave her an initial writing assignment as a trial strategy toward achieving insight. That strategy worked well. Mary was ideally suited to expressing her emotions on paper.

Over the course of eight months, Mary dealt with her anger, her need for assertiveness, her unfinished business from the past, and a number of other important emotional and motivational concerns. Her treatment on each topic was one of written free association. She was completely free to write anything she thought or felt on the preselected topic. Her many topics were planned, progressively, toward achieving a variety of insights. A few of her seventy-five different compositions were (1) Why do I feel despondent? (2) My hang-ups, (3) Divorce! (4) Off my pedestal, (5) Severance, (6) I must not fear life, (7) Patience and reality, (8) I'm making progress, (9) Am I crazy? (10) My pluses and minuses, and (11) I saw a sunset—I can feel again. Writing proved to be the one avenue through which Mary could experience release from her inhibitions. No emotional topic or thought was sacrosanct. She expressed her pain as well as her ecstasy; her fears as well as her hopes; her doubts as well as her convictions; her weaknesses as well as her strengths. It soon became obvious to the counselor and to Mary that she was making positive movement toward insightful handling of her defenses, fantasies, fears, and so on. A sample of Mary's free-association writing appears below (reproduced by permission of "Mary," her alias for this book).

6/9, Monday, 9:00 P.M. Tonight I'm going to try to recapture my emotions at the time of the first realization of the possibility of divorce. George never said to me until the first of last October the words, "I want a divorce." That is the only time he has actually said it to me. This realization came earlier, in August.

DIVORCE! It can't be! Not I; not us! Never! Other people, yes! But not us! Those years! All those years! A DIVORCED woman! Sylvia, yes! Peggy, yes! But Mary Jones! No! No! No! TO NO LONGER BE HIS WIFE! I can't stand it! I'd rather be dead! I will be dead! I'll kill myself first. Oh, agony, oh sick, sick, sick unto death! "Oh God! Please let me die! I want to die. AND NO ONE WILL EVER HAVE TO KNOW. Not Linda, not Mark or Mama or Mother or Daddy or anyone. Please, God please!" (I actually prayed this prayer.) MY WORLD HAS ENDED!

Now, I'm going to pick out key words or phrases to analyze. DIVORCE—the utter horror of the word. Unspeakable. The one thing I felt could never happen to me. To me. A DIVORCED WOMAN. Branded! Shamed! I didn't want to see anybody. I didn't want to talk with anyone. I was enveloped in a fog of hurt, confusion, and despair. My whole body ached! My greatest desire was to ESCAPE. Complete lethargy filled my being. TO NO LONGER BE HIS WIFE! To no longer be Mrs. George Jones; to no longer be No. 1 in his heart and mind! I couldn't bear the thought. Death would be sweet. An end. An end to the hurt, the shame, the anguish, the heartache.

KILL MYSELF! Yes, I contemplated suicide. What did I have to live for? What good was I now? Linda and Mark were old enough to take care of themselves. My brother would see after Mother and Daddy. Besides, if I killed myself, no one would ever have to know the TRUTH. Everyone would be shocked, but ultimately they would reason, "How unfortunate! Mary was that age, you know." Menopause would be blamed.

George could wait a decent time, marry; everything would be all right. . . . Oh yes, I not only contemplated suicide; I considered several methods! Gun? No! Knife? No! Automobile accident? No! Pills? Possibly! Electric shock? Maybe! Drowning—yes! It would be easy to fall over the side of the boat. I couldn't swim! Yes, that was the best—drowning! (As I write and reread this, I am struck with the thought: HOW INSANE—HOW UTTERLY INSANE! How selfish! How irrational! How cowardly! YET, the fact of suicide is still there. The emotion of it has diminished. . . .)

6/24. 9:00 P.M. Tuesday. Burl is very discreet in allowing me to find answers to my own questions. I can now answer the one concerning time: "Did you perceive that I might be wanting to rush things?" The answer is "Yes." Because I have been, in the past few weeks, inclined to want to hasten this process. HURRY to feel happy. HURRY to find answers. HURRY to heal! HURRY to get it over! HURRY! HURRY! HURRY! I must remember that I am not meeting a deadline (no pun intended). Time is on my side. This whole situation did not develop overnight. It cannot be resolved overnight. . . .

Mary filled four notebooks in eight months. Not only were the writings used during counseling sessions, but also Mary read and reread them from time to time. She still does. She reports that the written "history" helps her keep a healthy perspective.

Family Therapy in Mary's Case

Mary's total eclectic treatment program involved family therapy. She was referred to an experienced family systems therapist for two specific reasons. First, she was concerned about Mark and Linda's persistent bitterness toward their father following the divorce. Second, she was fearful that her own previous inability to sustain and preserve the marital relationship signaled some sort of intergenerational weakness that might be passed on to her offspring. She was particularly concerned about Linda, who was considering marriage to a man with characteristics and traits similar to those of her father (Mary's ex-husband). The three of them successfully pursued family therapy together.

Within a few months both Mark and Linda were able to reestablish a functional relationship with their father. The family therapist facilitated Mary, Mark, and Linda in the construction, study, and discussion of their respective family genograms. That strategy proved to be exciting, interesting, and educational for all three, and Mary reported that learning about her multigenerational dynamics enhanced her own self-confidence and self-esteem.

Finalizing Mary's Eclectic Counseling

Mary's written free-association assignments did not terminate abruptly; her writing gradually tapered off. As her goals of achieving insight were steadily fulfilled, her need for writing progressively declined. One day she made the remark, "Huh, seems like I don't need to write any more." It was like the end of a phase. Termination of counseling was discussed. "That would be O.K.," she said, "but there are some things I really need to do first." Thus began another phase of Mary's counseling. Although she was not familiar with the term *self-managed behavior model,* that is precisely what she felt the need to learn and apply to her lifestyle before she terminated the counseling relationship. She quickly learned the skills of problem identification and definition in behavioral terms, establishing measurable goals, monitoring target behaviors, changing setting events, establishing effective consequences, and consolidating gains. She was astute and conscientious about behavioral contracting. A short segment from one of the behaviorally oriented sessions between Mary and the counselor gives one example of this phase of the counseling.

CO: So you have several legal concerns that are important to you, but you've been sitting on your hands.

CL: I guess they are "legal," at that. I have just kept getting upset over them. Wondering if I should call George and confront him or write him. I don't really want to contact him, though. It's his responsibility. I've kept putting it off, but I keep worrying about it all the time.

CO: Since it's mostly legal matters relating to his breach of the written agreement, wouldn't it be wise for you to consult an attorney?

CL: Well, I have every right to. I'm not interested in punishing George. All I want is for George to meet his part of the agreement. I just don't know any attorneys—except Butch. I'm not sure that he's the one I should see. He's the one who drew up the financial and property agreements for George and me. He may consider himself George's attorney. He's a good lawyer, though, and I trust him.

CO: Sounds like you're reluctant to consult a new attorney until you can clarify whether it would be a conflict for you to retain Butch.

CL: That's right. I have an aversion to starting legal proceedings. But I can't keep up this worrying. And I can't keep ignoring George's not keeping his end of the bargain.

CO: Then it sounds like you're to the point of deciding how and when you're going to get the answers to your legal questions.

CL: Yes, there's no sense in putting it off.

CO: How do you intend to go about getting this thing off dead center and getting some peace of mind for yourself?

CL: Well, I was just thinking. (*pause*) I have to go up to that county Friday. I could call Butch's office to see if he could see me Friday afternoon or Saturday morning.

CO: When do you intend to call Butch's office to make the appointment?

CL: This afternoon.

(*Later in the interview*)

CO: Okay, Mary. We've laid out the plans of what you're contracting to do. Can you summarize so we are both clear on what you are going to do to relieve yourself from this particular financial worry?

CL: First of all, I feel good about what I've decided to do. It should relieve me of lots of stress. I plan to go back to the office today and call Butch's office and make an appointment as soon as I can—preferably this Friday afternoon or Saturday. Second, I plan to ask him if he can ethically serve as my attorney in case I decide to bring litigation against George. Third, if he says, "Yes," I will ask him for an opinion on two things: Can I require George to sign the quit claim deeds on the property, so we can sell the property and divide it evenly, as he agreed to do in the legal settlement? Next, what legal steps must I take to get George to pay his share of Mark's education and upkeep while he's in dental school? Because George has quit sending Mark his support payments, in violation of the written agreement.

CO: You've given a good summary of what you've contracted to do. Anything else?

CL: Yes, I will call you Monday morning to give you a status report.

Mary was the type of client who didn't need a written contract. The verbal agreement was sufficient. She appeared to receive a great deal of intrinsic reinforcement through completion of action steps.

The termination of Mary's case was a natural turn of events—a collaborative decision between the client and the counselor. Both she and the counselor knew that the time was near when she desired to make it on her own. She made remarks such as, "The time has come for me to launch out on my own. It's important to me to handle it myself now." The counselor, sensing her need for autonomy and privacy, left the door open for her to return or to call if, in her judgment, she needed further personal contact.

We might ask, "Why was the *eclectic* model appropriate for Mary?" Several reasons. First, *Mary came to counseling with the answers within herself.* But initially, she didn't know how to frame the questions. Second, she was *unable to find the answers* that were within herself. The eclectic counseling was versatile enough to employ whatever techniques were needed to help her ask herself the right questions and find her own answers. Third, the eclectic method *exposed her to enough strategies and alternative action steps* to enable her to find the options that were uniquely effective for her. The eclectic counselor used a wide repertoire of strategies and was able to come up with an appropriate strategy for Mary each time she needed it. This is what eclectic counseling is all about!

CONTRIBUTIONS OF THE ECLECTIC SYSTEM

Eclecticism has demonstrated that it is possible and desirable to integrate and utilize a wide variety of techniques that have proven to be of practical value. The system has been able to accommodate even opposing points of view. This has been perhaps its greatest strength. Also, eclecticism has focused on the commonalities of therapies. It has synthesized the positive points of various systems rather than treating each as separate, unrelated, or oppositional to the others.

Eclecticism has dealt with the total client situation. It has dealt with the person's *internal events* (cognitions such as motivations, emotions, and beliefs); the client's *external events* (behaviors or overt acts); and *social influences* (other persons; organizations; groups, starting with primary groups, such as the family; and the entire social structure). Eclecticism has drawn on a diversity of ideas and sources for its formulations: experimental research, clinical observation, nonscientific study, practical experience, and even an "understanding of poets, philosophers, and novelists" (Palmer, 1980, p. 4). Eclecticism has shown that the human condition is too complex to be served by a single, narrow approach. That theory serves best which is not tied to one limited set of formulations, technology, and techniques and which isn't tailored or skewed toward benefiting only a few types of people, problems, or syndromes.

SHORTCOMINGS OF THE ECLECTIC SYSTEM

The first and foremost shortcoming of the eclectic system has to do more with the practical than the theoretical. Simply, it is unrealistic to expect an individual to acquire sufficient expertise in all the therapeutic systems to become a proficient eclectic. Most aspiring counselors and psychotherapists cannot devote enough time and resources to master the theories, skills, and experiential requirements to become effective eclectic helpers. Many do not have the personality and attitudinal and interest characteristics to be compatible with the many modalities advocated for eclectics. Eclecticism might be ideal, but it is not always practical in terms of human limitations and fallibilities. A related criticism is that if eclectics must master all techniques, then they will probably be expert in none.

The second major shortcoming is that eclecticism has no unifying set of principles, philosophies, theories, tenets from which to build a rationale of operation.

Without a blueprint or map, how can we determine which way to go, make corrections during the journey, or determine when we have arrived at the desired destination?

A third criticism is that the world of clients and the techniques of counseling are changing so rapidly that it is difficult to keep up. Even those proficient in eclectic counseling soon fall behind. We live in an age of change and specialization. Often expert counselors must specialize to attain and retain competence.

As of yet, we know of no clear formulae that can be arbitrarily applied to the idiosyncratic nature of specific client problems. The clusters of therapeutic strategies proposed in this chapter are more far reaching than merely assessing and applying a generic prescription to a client problem. In that regard no eclectic has thus far been able to reduce therapy to a formula. Given the current status of affairs in therapy, we would urge caution for any beginner who would accept lock, stock, and barrel any theorist who proposes that he or she has found the one eclectic path to therapeutic truth and knowledge.

ECLECTIC COUNSELING WITH DIVERSE POPULATIONS

An integral part of the multicultural counseling movement has emerged from the impetus of professional organizations and the research and writing of a large number of counseling professionals espousing essentially eclectic counseling principles (AACD, 1988; 1989; APA, 1991; 1992; Atkinson, Morten, & Sue, 1989; Pedersen, 1988; 1989; 1990; Sue, 1991; 1992; Sue, Arredondo, & McDavis, 1992; Sue & Sue, 1990). According to Sue, Arredondo, and McDavis (1992), culturally skilled counselors have competencies in a wide variety of verbal and nonverbal techniques. They are skilled at both receiving and sending nonverbal as well as verbal communications and they *"are not tied down to only one method or approach to helping but recognize that helping styles and approaches may be culture bound"* (p. 87) (emphasis added).

Sue (1992) makes several important points in favor of the eclectic approach and against traditional theories (such as behavioral, Rogerian, REBT, and Gestalt), including statements that: (a) licensing committees that administer examinations look with suspicion on candidates who claim to be eclectic, and (b) culturally sensitive eclectic counselors recognize that cross-cultural counseling involves not only people's thinking, feeling, behaving, and social interacting but also their cultural and political orientations. The real difficulty with traditional theories is that they are culture-bound. The eclecticism that Sue advocates values, counsels, and affirms a diversity of clients and client orientations, including special concerns of the culturally different and economically and educationally disadvantaged clients that traditional therapists may not be prepared to handle. Many of the "talk therapies" are oriented toward self-disclosure, which is incompatible with the cultural values of many minority clients.

Several fundamental issues point to the validity of Sue's (1992) call for counselors to employ varied intervention strategies. For instance, the typically Euro-American belief that the "individual" is of paramount importance is not held in all cultures. A client from a culture in which the family, the clan, or the sect takes precedence over the individual may feel totally disaffected or even demeaned in the presence of a counselor who is ignorant of such values. Regarding clients from some minority backgrounds, even subtle and unconsciously held prejudices and stereotypic thinking on the part of the counselor can negatively affect the therapeutic relationship. Also, not all people have been acculturated to embrace such Euro-American ideals as rugged individualism and competition. Clearly, the sociopolitical atmosphere of which some narrowly focused traditional counselors are a part may be counter to the minority client's values, orientation, and style and may be detrimental to the client and the counseling process.

Sue, Arredondo, and McDavis (1992) reviewed the Association for Multicultural Counseling and Development's (AMCD) approved document outlining the need and rationale for a multicultural perspective in counseling. The major components of the plan call for counselors to possess the following broad cross-cultural competencies:

1. Awareness of own cultural values and biases
2. Awareness of client's world view
3. Culturally appropriate intervention strategies (pp. 84–88).

The AMCD document calls for the incorporation of the above competencies in the training and practice of counselors so that the inculcation of appropriate multicultural counselor attitudes, beliefs, knowledge, and skills may become the norm rather than the exception. Sue (1992) describes the counseling profession as being at a crossroads. On the one hand, monoculturalism/ethnocentrism, the road we have traditionally traveled, is forcing us to recognize that we are not serving the interests of the many diverse groups in our society. Multiculturalism, the alternate path, is the road less traveled. "It recognizes and values diversity. It values cultural pluralism and acknowledges our nation as a cultural mosaic rather than a melting pot. It is the road that challenges us to study multiple cultures, to develop multiple perspectives, and to teach our children how to integrate broad and conflicting bodies of information to arrive at sound judgments" (p. 8).

Sue's (1992) perspective represents an eclectic counseling theory that integrates the philosophical, theoretical, and practical elements into a cohesive and systematic system. He states that culturally, economically, and educationally disadvantaged clients may not be oriented toward "talk therapies," that self-disclosure may be incompatible with the cultural values of such populations as Asian Americans, Latinos, and Native Americans. He views therapeutic systems founded only on traditional European populations as being deficient in the world view needed by today's counselors. Sue says he once would have proudly announced that he was "behavioral in orientation," but today he is an advocate of an even broader and more flexible helping process to facilitate equal access and opportunities for all clients (p. 14).

We believe an eclectic model is appropriate and viable for a cross-cultural counseling perspective. To be an eclectic means to be adaptable in both theory and technique. Adherence to any one narrow, inflexible traditional theoretical approach is outmoded and inappropriate. If we are to do what Sue (1992) proposes, we must operate in some type of organized, consistent, systematic, and integrated eclectic system that is well-grounded in a broad array of theories, is sensitive and responsive to diversity, and is geared to the idiosyncratic and phenomenal world of each client. An eclectic system, "a road less traveled," offers a broad enough world view of clients and their inner worlds to understand, affirm, and help people in all cultures and lifestyles.

SUMMARY

Eclectic counseling and psychotherapy selectively and systematically applies all the known and valid helping procedures to assist individuals in solving their problems and maintaining stability in their lives. No one theoretical position is embraced. No one strategy or set of strategies is used or advocated exclusively. Eclectic methodology, according to Thorne (1967) and others, is a basic scientific approach to the process of selecting suitable strategies to meet the needs of specific clients.

Several eclectic models have been developed. Approaches by Thorne (1968); Brammer (1979); Brammer and Shostrom (1968); Carkhuff and Berenson (1977); Cormier and Cormier (1991); Garfield (1980); Gilliland, James, Roberts, and Bowman (1984); Ivey and Simek-Downing (1980); Lazarus (1981; 1989c); and Palmer (1980) are only a few of the many systematic models that might be called eclectic. Eclecticism utilizes strategies from several schools (analytical, Gestalt, TA, REBT, humanistic-existential, and so on) to help clients gain *insights* for understanding and controlling *internal events*. It uses techniques from other schools (behavior modification, behavior therapy, REBT, reality therapy, trait-factor, and so on) to assist clients in modifying their *behavior* for the control and maintenance of *external events*.

Although the eclectic approach has been subjected to a great deal of skepticism and criticism from proponents of various special schools of therapy, it has experienced tremendous growth in the number of self-identified followers since the mid-1940s. It is the viewpoint of eclectics that all schools have some contribution to make and that practitioners should try to learn and incorporate valid techniques that each of these schools has developed.

SUGGESTIONS FOR FURTHER READING

Brammer, L. M. (1985). *The helping relationship: Process and skills* (3rd ed.). Englewood Cliffs, NJ: Prentice-Hall.

Brammer, L. M., Shostrom, E. L., & Abrego, P. J. (1989). *Therapeutic psychology: Fundamentals of actualizing counseling and psychotherapy* (5th ed.). Englewood Cliffs, NJ: Prentice-Hall.

Cormier, W. H., & Cormier, L. S. (1991). *Interviewing strategies for helpers: Fundamental skills and cognitive behavioral interventions* (3rd ed.). Pacific Grove, CA: Brooks/Cole.

Corsini, R. J., & Wedding, D. (Eds.). (1989). *Current psychotherapies* (4th ed.). Itasca, IL: F. E. Peacock.

Egan, G. (1990). *The skilled helper: Model, skills, and methods for effective helping* (4th ed.). Pacific Grove, CA: Brooks/Cole.

Gilliland, B. E., & James, R. K. (1997). *Crisis intervention strategies* (3rd ed.). Pacific Grove, CA: Brooks/Cole.

Ivey, A. E. (1991). *Developmental strategies for helpers: Individual, family, and network interventions.* Pacific Grove, CA: Brooks/Cole.

Ivey, A. E., Ivey, M. B., & Simek-Downing, L. (1987). *Counseling and psychotherapy: Integrating skills, theory, and practice* (2nd ed.). Englewood Cliffs, NJ: Prentice-Hall.

Kelly, G. A. (1955). *The psychology of personal constructs* (Vols. 1 & 2). New York: Norton.

Lazarus, A. A. (1989). *The practice of multimodal therapy.* Baltimore: Johns Hopkins University Press.

Palmer, J. O. (1980). *A primer of eclectic psychotherapy.* Monterey, CA: Brooks/Cole.

Shostrom, E. L. (1976). *Actualizing therapy: Foundations for a scientific ethic.* San Diego: EDITS.

Thorne, F. C. (1950). *Principles of personality counseling: An eclectic viewpoint.* Brandon, VT: Journal of Clinical Psychology.

Thorne, F. C. (1968). *Psychological case handling, I: Establishing the conditions necessary for counseling and psychotherapy.* Brandon, VT: Clinical Psychology Publishing Co.

Thorne, F. C. (1973). Eclectic psychotherapy. In R. Corsini (Ed.), *Current psychotherapies* (pp. 445–486). Itasca, IL: F. E. Peacock.

REFERENCES

Adler, A. (1963). *The practice and theory of individual psychology.* Paterson, NJ: Littlefield, Adams.

American Association for Counseling and Development. (1988). *Ethical standards.* Alexandria, VA: Author.

American Association for Counseling and Development. (1989). *Bylaws.* Alexandria, VA: Author.

American Psychological Association. (1991). *Guidelines for providers of psychological services to ethnic, linguistic, and culturally diverse populations.* Washington, DC: Author.

American Psychological Association. (1992, December). Ethical principles of psychologists and code of conduct (an *American Psychologist* publication). Washington, DC: Author.

Atkinson, D., Morten, G., & Sue, D. W. (1989). *Counseling American minorities: A cross-cultural perspective* (3rd ed.). Dubuque, IA: Brown.

Auld, F., & Hyman, M. (1991). *Resolution of inner conflict: An introduction to psychoanalytic therapy.* Washington, DC: American Psychological Association.

Becuar, D., & Becuar, R. (1988). *Family therapy: A systematic integration.* Boston: Allyn & Bacon.

Berman, E. (1985). Eclecticism and its discontents. *Israel Journal of Psychiatry and Related Sciences, 22,* 51–60.

Blocher, D. H. (1987). *The professional counselor.* New York: Macmillan.

Borgen, F. H. (1984). Counseling psychology. *Annual Review of Psychology, 35,* 579–604.

Bowen, M. (1978). *Family therapy in clinical practice.* New York: Jason Aronson.

Brammer, L. M. (1979). *The helping relationship: Process and skills* (2nd ed.). Englewood Cliffs, NJ: Prentice-Hall.

Brammer, L. M. (1985). *The helping relationship: Process and skills* (3rd ed.). Englewood Cliffs, NJ: Prentice-Hall.

Brammer, L. M. (1990). *How to cope with life transitions.* New York: Hemisphere.

Brammer, L. M., & Shostrom, E. L. (1968). *Therapeutic psychology: Fundamentals of actualization counseling and psychotherapy* (2nd ed.). Englewood Cliffs, NJ: Prentice-Hall.

Brammer, L. M., Shostrom, E. L., & Abrego, P. J. (1989). *Therapeutic psychology: Fundamentals of counseling and psychotherapy* (5th ed.). Englewood Cliffs, NJ: Prentice-Hall.

Buie, J. (1988). Psychoanalysis: Lawsuit takes aim on barriers to training, practice for non-MDs. *The APA Monitor, 19,* 1–14.

Carkhuff, R. R. (1969). *Helping and human relations.* New York: Holt, Rinehart & Winston.

Carkhuff, R. R. (1973). *The art of problem-solving: A guide for developing problem-solving skills for parents, teachers, counselors, and administrators.* Amherst, MA: Human Resources Development Press.

Carkhuff, R. R., & Berenson, B. G. (1977). *Beyond counseling and therapy* (2nd ed.). New York: Holt, Rinehart & Winston.

Castonguay, L. G., & Goldfried, M. R. (1994). Psychotherapy integration: An idea whose time has come. *Applied and Preventive Psychology, 3*(3), 159–172.

Chessick, R. D. (1985). The frantic retreat from the mind to the brain: American psychiatry in mauvaise foi. *Psychoanalytic Inquiry, 5,* 369–403.

Colapinto, J. (1982). Structural family therapy. In A. Horne & M. M. Ohlsen (Eds.), *Family counseling and therapy* (pp. 112–140). Itasca, IL: F. E. Peacock.

Colapinto, J. (1984). Integration and model integrity. *Journal of Strategic and Systemic Therapies, 3,* 38–42.

Cormier, W. H., & Cormier, L. S. (1985). *Interviewing strategies for helpers: Fundamental skills and cognitive behavioral interventions* (2nd ed.). Monterey, CA: Brooks/Cole.

Cormier, W. H., & Cormier, L. S. (1991). *Interviewing strategies for helpers: Fundamental skills and cognitive behavioral interventions* (3rd ed.). Monterey, CA: Brooks/Cole.

Corsini, R. J. (Ed.). (1981). *Handbook of innovative psychotherapies.* New York: Wiley.

Corsini, R. J., & Wedding, D. (Eds.). (1995). *Current psychotherapies* (5th ed.). Itasca, IL: F. E. Peacock.

Cottone, R. R. (1992). *Theories and paradigms of counseling and psychotherapy.* Boston: Allyn & Bacon.

D'Andrea, M., & Daniels, J. (1994). Group pacing: A developmental eclectic approach to group work. *Journal of Counseling and Development, 72,* 585–590.

Duck, S., & Condra, M. (1990). To be or not to be: Anticipation, persuasion, and retrospection in personal relationships. In G. J. Neimeyer & R. A. Neimeyer (Eds.), *Advances in personal construct psychology: A research annual* (pp. 187–202). Greenwich, CT: JAI Press.

Duncan, B. L., Parks, M. B., & Rusk, G. S. (1990). Strategic eclecticism: A technical alternative to eclectic psychotherapy. *Psychotherapy, 27,* 568–577.

Egan, G. (1975). *The skilled helper: A model for systematic helping and interpersonal relating.* Monterey, CA: Brooks/Cole.

Egan, G. (1982). *The skilled helper: Model, skills, and methods for effective helping* (2nd ed.). Monterey, CA: Brooks/Cole.

Egan, G. (1986). *The skilled helper: A systematic approach to effective helping* (3rd ed.). Monterey, CA: Brooks/Cole.

Egan, G. (1990). *The skilled helper: Model, skills, and methods for effective helping* (4th ed.). Pacific Grove, CA: Brooks/Cole.

Ellis, A. (1979). Rational-emotive therapy. In R. Corsini (Ed.), *Current psychotherapies* (2nd ed.; pp. 185–229). Itasca, IL: F. E. Peacock.

Ellis, A. (1984). The use of hypnosis with rational emotive therapy (RET). *International Journal of Eclectic Psychotherapy, 3,* 15–22.

Ellis, A. (1995). Rational-emotive behavior therapy. In R. J. Corsini & D. Wedding (Eds.), *Current psychotherapies* (5th ed., pp. 162–196). Itasca, IL: F. E. Peacock.

Ellis, A., & Harper, R. (1975). *A new guide to rational living.* Hollywood, CA: Wilshire Books.

Eysenck, H. J. (1984). Personality and individual differences. *Bulletin of the British Psychological Society, 37,* 237.

Fischer, J. (1995). Uniformity myths in eclectic and integrative psychotherapy. *Journal of Psychotherapy Integration, 5*(l), 41–56.

Foley, V. D. (1989). Family therapy. In R. J. Corsini & D. Wedding (Eds.), *Current psychotherapies* (4th ed.; pp. 455–500). Itasca, IL: F. E. Peacock.

Freud, S. (1949). *An outline of psychoanalysis.* New York: Norton.

Freud, S. (1961). *The standard edition of the complete psychological works of Sigmund Freud.* (J. Strachey, Ed. and Trans.). London: Hogarth Press. (Original work published 1924)

Gambrill, E. (1977). *Behavior modification: Handbook of assessment, intervention, and evaluation.* San Francisco: Jossey-Bass.

Garfield, S. L. (1980). *Psychotherapy: An eclectic approach.* New York: Wiley.

Garfield, S. L. (1994). Eclecticism and integration in psychotherapy: Developments and issues. *Clinical Psychology Science and Practice, 1*(2), 123–137.

Garfield, S. L., & Kurtz, R. (1975). Clinical psychologists: A survey of selected attitudes and views. *The Clinical Psychologist, 28,* 4–7.

Gilliland,. B. E., & James, R. K. (1997). *Crisis intervention strategies* (3rd ed.). Pacific Grove, CA: Brooks/Cole.

Gilliland, B. E., James, R. K., Roberts, G. T., & Bowman, J. T. (1984). *Theories and strategies in counseling and psychotherapy.* Englewood Cliffs, NJ: Prentice-Hall.

Glasser, W. (1965). *Reality therapy.* New York: Harper & Row.

Glasser, W. (1984). *Control theory: A new explanation of how we control our lives.* New York: Harper & Row.

Glasser, W. (1996). *Staying together: The control theory guide to a lasting marriage.* New York: HarperCollins (Perennial paper edition).

Hackney, H., & Cormier, L. S. (1988). *Counseling strategies and interventions* (3rd ed.). Englewood Cliffs, NJ: Prentice-Hall.

Haley, J. (1987). *Problem-solving therapy.* San Francisco: Jossey-Bass.

Hansen, J. C., Stevic, R. R., & Warner, R. W., Jr. (1977). *Counseling: Theory and process.* Boston: Allyn & Bacon.

Heppner, P. P., Kivlighan, D. M., Jr., & Wampold, B. E. (1992). *Research design in counseling.* Pacific Grove, CA: Brooks/Cole.

Hergenhahn, B. R. (1994). *An introduction to theories of personality* (4th ed.). Englewood Cliffs, NJ: Prentice-Hall.

Huck, S. W., Cormier, W. H., & Bounds, W. G. (1974). *Reading statistics and research.* New York: Harper & Row.

Ivey, A. E. (1986). *Developmental therapy: Theory into practice.* San Francisco: Jossey-Bass.

Ivey, A. E., & Authier, J. (1978). *Microcounseling: Innovations in interviewing, counseling, psychotherapy, and psychoeducation* (2nd ed.). Springfield, IL: Chas. C. Thomas.

Ivey, A. E., Ivey, M. B., & Simek-Downing, L. (1987). *Counseling and psychotherapy: Integrating skills, theory, and practice* (2nd ed.). Englewood Cliffs, NJ: Prentice-Hall.

Ivey, A. E., & Simek-Downing, L. (1980). *Counseling and psychotherapy: Skills, theories, and practice.* Englewood Cliffs, NJ: Prentice-Hall.

Kanfer, F. H., & Goldstein, A. P. (Eds.). (1975). *Helping people change.* Elmsford, NY: Pergamon.

Kell, B. L., & Mueller, W. J. (1966). *Impact and change: A study of counseling relationships.* New York: Appleton-Century-Crofts.

Kelly, G. A. (1995). *The psychology of personal constructs* (Vols. 1 & 2). New York: Norton.

Kerr, M. E., & Bowen, M. (1988). *Family evaluation: An approach based on Bowen theory.* New York: Norton.

Kohut, H. (1971). *The analysis of self.* New York: International Universities Press.

Kohut, H. (1977). *The restoration of the self.* New York: International Universities Press.

Kohut, H. (1984). *Now does analysis cure?* Chicago: University of Chicago Press.

Krumboltz, J. D., & Thoresen, C. E. (Eds.). (1976). *Counseling methods.* New York: Holt, Rinehart & Winston.

Lazarus, A. A. (1967). In support of technical eclecticism. *Psychological Reports, 21,* 415–416.

Lazarus, A. A. (1981). *The practice of multimodal therapy.* New York: McGraw-Hill.

Lazarus, A. A. (1986a). Multimodal therapy. In J. C. Norcross (Ed.), *Handbook of eclectic psychotherapy* (pp. 65–93). New York: Brunner/Mazel.

Lazarus, A. A. (1986b). Multimodal therapy. In E. L. Shostrom (Executive Producer), S. K. Shostrom (Producer), & H. Ratner (Director), *Three approaches to psychotherapy II* (Film no. 2, Case of Kathy). Corona Del Mar, CA: Psychological and Educational Film.

Lazarus, A. A. (1987). The need for technical eclecticism: Science, breadth, depth, and specificity. In J. K. Zeig (Ed.), *The evolution of psychotherapy* (pp. 164–178). New York: Brunner/Mazel.

Lazarus, A. A. (1989a). The case of George. In D. Wedding & R. J. Corsini (Eds.), *Case studies in psychotherapy* (pp. 227–238). Itasca, IL: F. E. Peacock.

Lazarus, A. A. (1989b). Multimodal therapy. In R. J. Corsini & D. Wedding (Eds.), *Current psychotherapies* (4th ed.; pp. 503–544). Itasca, IL: F. E. Peacock.

Lazarus, A. A. (1989c). *The practice of multimodal therapy.* Baltimore: Johns Hopkins University Press.

Lazarus, A. A. (1995a). Different types of eclecticism and integration: Let's be aware of the dangers. *Journal of Psychotherapy Integration, 5*(l), 27–39.

Lazarus, A. A. (1995b). Multimodal therapy. In R. J. Corsini & D. Wedding (Eds.), *Current psychotherapies* (5th ed, pp. 322–355). Itasca, IL: F. E. Peacock.

Lazarus, A. A., & Beutler, L. E. (1993). On technical eclecticism. *Journal of Counseling & Development, 71,* 381–385.

Linden, G. W. (1984). Some philosophical roots of Adlerian psychology. *Individual Psychology: Journal of Adlerian Theory, Research, and Practice, 40,* 254–269.

Maslow, A. H. (1976). *The farther reaches of human nature.* New York: Penguin Books.

Meichenbaum, D. H. (1977). *Cognitive behavior modification: An integrative approach.* New York: Plenum.

Minuchin, S. (1974). *Families and family therapy.* Cambridge, MA: Harvard University Press.

Minuchin, S. (1984). *Family kaleidoscope.* Cambridge, MA: Harvard University Press.

Minuchin, S., & Fishman, H. C. (1981). *Family therapy techniques.* Cambridge, MA: Harvard University Press.

Neimeyer, G. J., & Neimeyer, R. A. (Eds.). (1990). *Advances in personal construct psychology: A research annual* (Vol 1). Greenwich, CT: JAI Press.

Neimeyer, R. A., & Neimeyer, G. J. (Eds.). (1987). *Personal construct therapy casebook.* New York: Springer.

Norcross, J. C. (Ed.). (1986). *Handbook of eclectic psychotherapy.* New York: Brunner/Mazel.

Norcross, J. C. (Ed.). (1987). *Casebook of eclectic psychotherapy.* New York: Brunner/Mazel.

Norcross, J. C. (1995). A roundtable on psychotherapy integration: Common factors, technical eclecticism, and psychotherapy research. *Journal of Psychotherapy Practice and Research, 4*(3), 248–271.

Palmer, J. O. (1980). *A primer of eclectic psychotherapy.* Monterey, CA: Brooks/Cole.

Patterson, C. H. (1980). *Theories of counseling and psychotherapy* (3rd ed.). New York: Harper & Row.

Patterson, C. H. (1986). *Theories of counseling and psychotherapy* (4th ed.). New York: Harper & Row.

Pedersen, P. B. (1988). *A handbook for development of multicultural awareness.* Alexandria, VA: American Association for Counseling and Development.

Pedersen, P. B. (1989). Developing multicultural ethical guidelines for psychology. *International Journal of Psychology, 24,* 643–652.

Pedersen, P. B. (1990). The constructs of complexity and balance in multicultural counseling theory and practice. *Journal of Counseling and Development, 68,* 550–554.

Perls, F. (1969). *Gestalt therapy verbatim.* Lafayette, CA: Real People Press.

Pietrofesa, J. J., Hoffman, A., Splete, H. H., & Pinto, D. V. (1978). *Counseling: Theory, research, and practice.* Skokie, IL: Rand McNally.

Polster, E., & Polster, M. (1973). *Gestalt therapy integrated: Contours of therapy and practice.* New York: Brunner/Mazel.

Rogers, C. R. (1951). *Client-centered therapy.* Boston: Houghton Mifflin.

Russell, R. L. (1986). The inadvisability of admixing psychoanalysis with other forms of psychotherapy. *Journal of Contemporary Psychotherapy, 16,* 76–86.

Rychlak, J. F. (1986). Eclecticism in psychological theorizing: Good and bad. *Journal of Counseling and Development, 63,* 351–353.

Satir, V. (1967). *Conjoint family therapy.* Palo Alto, CA: Science and Behavior Books.

Satir, V. (1972). *Peoplemaking.* Palo Alto, CA: Science and Behavior Books.

Satir, V. (1975). *Self-esteem.* Millbrae, CA: Celestial Arts.

Satir, V. (1982). The therapist and family therapy. In A. M. Horne and M. M. Ohlsen (Eds.), *Family counseling and therapy* (pp. 12–42). Itasca, IL: F. E. Peacock.

Scheidlinger, S. (1984). Group psychotherapy in the 1980's: Problems and prospects. *American Journal of Psychotherapy, 38,* 494–504.

Sechrest, L. (1977). *Personal constructs theory.* In R. J. Corsini (Ed.), *Current personality theories* (pp. 203–241). Itasca, IL: F. E. Peacock.

Sims, R. R., & Sauser, W. I. (1985). Guiding principles for development of competency-based business curricula. *Journal of Management Development, 4,* 51–65.

Skinner, B. F. (1953). *Science and human behavior.* New York: Macmillan.

Smith, B. D., & Vetter, H. J. (1991). *Theories of personality* (2nd ed.). Englewood Cliffs, NJ: Prentice-Hall.

Smith, D. (1982). Trends in counseling and psychotherapy. *American Psychologist, 37,* 802–809.

Stall, R. (1984). Disadvantages of eclecticism in the treatment of alcoholism: The "problem" of recidivism. *Journal of Drug Issues, 14,* 437–448.

Sue, D. W. (1991). A conceptual model for cultural diversity training. *Journal of Counseling and Development, 70,* 99–105.

Sue, D. W. (1992, Winter). The challenge of multiculturalism: The road less traveled. *American Counselor, 1,* 6–14.

Sue, D. W., Arredondo, P., & McDavis, R. J. (1992). Multicultural counseling competencies and standards: A call to the professionals. *Journal of Counseling and Development, 70,* 477–486.

Sue, D. W., & Sue, D. (1990). *Counseling the culturally different: Theory and practice.* New York: Wiley.

Thomas, M. B. (1992). *An introduction to marital and family therapy: Counseling toward healthier family systems across the lifespan.* New York: Macmillan.

Thoresen, C. E. (Ed.). (1980). *The behavior therapist.* Monterey, CA: Brooks/Cole.

Thorne, F. C. (1950). *Principles of personality counseling: An eclectic approach.* Brandon, VT: Journal of Clinical Psychology.

Thorne, F. C. (1955). *Principles of psychological examining.* Brandon, VT: Clinical Psychology Publishing Co.

Thorne, F. C. (1960). *Clinical judgment.* Brandon, VT: Clinical Psychology Publishing Co.

Thorne, F. C. (1961). *Personality.* Brandon, VT: Clinical Psychology Publishing Co.

Thorne, F. C. (1965). *How to be psychologically healthy: Tutorial counseling.* Brandon, VT: Clinical Psychology Publishing Co.

Thorne, F. C. (1967). *Integrative psychology.* Brandon, VT: Clinical Psychology Publishing Co.

Thorne, F. C. (1968). *Psychological case handling, I: Establishing the conditions necessary for counseling and psychotherapy.* Brandon, VT: Clinical Psychology Publishing Co.

Thorne, F. C. (1970). Adler's broad-spectrum concept of man, self-consistency, and unification. *Journal of Individual Psychology, 26,* 135–143.

Thorne, F. C. (1973). Eclectic psychotherapy. In R. Corsini (Ed.), *Current psychotherapies* (pp. 445–486). Itasca, IL: F. E. Peacock.

Viney, L. L. (1990). A constructivist model of psychological reactions to physical illness and injury. In G. J. Neimeyer & R. A. Neimeyer (Eds.), *Advances in personal construct psychology: A research annual* (pp. 117–151). Greenwich, CT: JAI Press.

Warner, R. E. (1991). A survey of theoretical orientations of Canadian clinical psychologists. *Canadian Psychology, 32,* 525–528.

Watkins, C. E., & Watts, R. E. (1995). Psychotherapy survey research studies: Some consistent findings and integrative conclusions. *Psychotherapy in Private Practice, 13,* 49–68.

Watson, D. L., & Tharp, R. G. (1989). *Self-directed behavior: Self-modification for personal adjustment* (5th ed.). Pacific Grove, CA: Brooks/Cole.

Williams, R. L., & Long, J. D. (1983). *Toward a self-managed lifestyle* (3rd ed.). Boston: Houghton Mifflin.

Williamson, E. G. (1965). *Vocational counseling.* New York: McGraw-Hill.

Wolpe, J. (1969). *The practice of behavior therapy.* Elmsford, NY: Pergamon.

Zook, A., II, & Walton, J. M. (1989). Theoretical orientations and work settings of clinical and counseling psychologists: A current perspective. *Professional Psychology: Research and Practice, 20,* 23–31.

14

COMPUTER-ASSISTED THERAPY

Introduction

Consider the following propositions:

1. Thinking is unique to humans. Therefore, computers cannot think.
2. Thinking is a series of symbolic operations. Therefore, computers can think. (Wagman, 1988, p. 8).

For most humanists and many psychotherapists, the idea that a computer could be a counselor that would deal in multimodal ways with a variety of client problems is anathematic. In the chapter on trait-factor therapy we examined how computers can deliver "expert" information from an assessment standpoint as well as from an information standpoint. Although those components may be critical to the process of psychotherapy, they are certainly not psychotherapy itself—at least not psychotherapy from a view toward a comprehensive meaning of life view as opposed to the atheoretical symptom/syndrome orientation that some critics believe currently drives the field (Brennis, 1994).

However, what if a computer could so closely approximate human behavior that the human being who interacted with it could not differentiate between its thinking and that of a human? Further, what if a computer system that used virtual reality could so closely approximate the event itself that the client's emotional and physiological responses were indistinguishable from those at the time of the actual event? If that were true, the philosophical question of whether computers do indeed think would be moot. All that would really matter would be that they *appear* to do so (Wagman, 1988, p. 10).

We end this fourth edition with what may be, to many, a controversial view of therapy in the next millennium—the computer counselor! By computer counselor we don't mean the typical computer assessment and information systems that are commonly used in a variety of counseling settings, previously discussed in the chapter on trait-factor therapy. What we do mean is a computer who will counsel clients about personal problems. (Please note that here we have not made a grammar mistake in using the pronoun "who," which is used to refer to people. The reason for this grammatical choice will soon become apparent. Also, we have chosen a different font to portray a computer screen in the Counseling Process section.)

Part of this chapter covers what already is and part covers what the experts believe will be (Franklin, 1995; 1997; Greist, 1995; Kirkby, 1996; Wagman, 1988). It would appear as we move into the twenty-first century that computers will act as both therapeutic assistant and primary therapeutic agent (Pardeck & Schulte, 1990). Given that, we believe we are all on the threshold of a truly astounding new field in psychotherapy.

History

The history of computer counseling is approximately three decades long. Initial attempts by Colby's (1963) Computer Simulation of a Neurotic Process and Weizenbaum's ELIZA (1965) were rudimentary, given the power of computers in the 1960s and the simplicity of programming then available. Colby was an active psychotherapist seeking to develop a computer that could counsel; Weizenbaum was attempting to develop a natural language program and became highly disconcerted about attempts to turn it into a psychotherapeutic model (1976).

Two interesting events mark early efforts in the 1960s to develop computers in the mental health field that would hint at the powerful roles computers might one day play in dealing with the human condition. As with many such discoveries, both events were serendipitous and largely accidental to the task at hand. Slack et al. (1966) discovered that the development of a computer program to allow clients to write down their own histories had a beneficial side effect. Clients reported that while inputting their histories they had learned a lot about themselves; further, they felt better after the experience just from working with the computer.

Weizenbaum (1965), in order to deal with communication difficulties brought about by the daunting task of programming human interaction, modeled ELIZA after a Rogerian person-centered mode of responding. Amazingly, when the program was first tried out, people became deeply involved with it and insisted the machine understood them despite Weizenbaum's (1976) efforts to remind them that they were in a dialogue with nothing more than a machine.

During the 1970s and 1980s probably the most significant and concentrated work was the PLATO project jointly engineered between Control Data Corporation and the University of Illinois (Wagman, 1979; 1980; 1982; 1984; 1988). PLATO is an expert system that has a highly structured set of strategies to deal with dilemmas. Clients are given instructions on the meaning of dilemmas and on how to formulate their dilemmas so the computer will understand them, and then are allowed practice in generating solutions. PLATO gives demonstrations of how possible solutions may be generated and then assigns each client the task of developing a solution for his or her own particular dilemma. Feedback and reinforcement are given by PLATO as clients move through the sequence. PLATO has today been accessed by more than 2000 sites around the world (Wagman, 1988, pp. 105–107).

Computer counseling in the 1990s has not expanded as extensively as possible. However, one significant shift in psychotherapy and three major advances in computers may be bellwethers for a major change in the delivery of mental health counseling and psychotherapy.

In counseling and psychotherapy, cognitive systems have gradually come to dominate the field. Whereas older systems of psychotherapy concentrated on personality dynamics; generalized predictions about a person; and motivation, needs, drive, global problem dimensions, and complete structural change of the personality, cognitive behaviorism emphasizes discrete categories, inferential thinking, situation-specific behavior change, and multiple cognitive mapping and programming schema to change the irrational, nonlogical thinking of maladaptive behavior (Amsel, 1992; Brennis, 1994; Wagman, 1988). This general shift has made psychotherapy much more compatible with the algorithmic, logical, and linear mathematical schema that drive computers and undergird artificial intelligence.

Three major technological advances have changed dramatically what computers are and will be able to do in providing psychotherapy and counseling. First, memory systems have increased and become more efficient. Memory now available to even a simple personal computer will allow for the vast amount of information a counseling computer needs to store to be truly interactive with a human being in multidimensional ways. What Colby (1963) struggled to do on a computer mainframe in the 1960s in writing a program to deal with depressed clients he could now do with relative ease on a personal computer, which can then be used in the privacy of one's own home (Colby, 1995). Indications are that there will be a vastly increased capability by the computer to simulate human interaction (Franklin, 1995). Thus, we believe that more efficient and sophisticated computer counselors will almost certainly become reality.

A second advance is the Internet. When the third edition of this book was being written in the early 1990s, using the Internet to provide mental health services was seen as a novelty—if considered at all—by most mental health providers. As of 1997, the Internet is changing the way mental health services are delivered. The Internet allows access to on-line chatrooms where interest groups with common mental health issues talk to one another, to Web sites that operate crisis lines, and to commercial enterprises that provide a variety of counseling and mental health services. This change will become exponentially more dramatic as sophisticated therapy programs that can be accessed from anywhere in the world go on-line. And go they will. John Greist (1995), clinical computing editor for the journal *Psychiatric Services,* suggests that the programming to provide effective computer counseling is already available—all we need to do is use it.

A third advance is virtual reality. Virtual reality is unheralded in the ways its technology can be used to provide the client *in vivo* access to role play, desensitization, covert modeling, and a variety of other techniques that allow him or her to practice coping and change behaviors while being directly or indirectly involved with the therapist (Biocca, 1992; Kirkby, 1996; Muscott & Gifford, 1994). Phobic reactions are particularly amenable to immersive virtual reality, wherein the client has a helmet placed on his or her head. The helmet provides graded auditory and visual scenarios of the feared situation; the clients can monitor and control the amount of exposure to the feared stimulus. The client may also receive a running score on how successful he or she is in closing proximity to and length of time spent facing the feared stimulus (Kirkby, 1996; Rothbaum, et al., 1995).

Finally, because this chapter is really about the future, some of the esoteric concepts that cognitive scientists like our esteemed colleague Stan Franklin (1995, pp. 12–15) are thinking and writing about need to be considered. Symbolic artificial intelligence, artificial neural networks, silicon nervous systems, computational neuroethology, subsumption architecture, and dynamic representations are various theories about representations of "mind" that will play a major role in the use of computers as they interact with humans.

Presently computers do not have minds in the human sense of the word, nor do they "feel" or "create" as humans do. However, that doesn't mean any of these are impossible tasks for computers by any means; indeed, some predict that a computer with humanlike consciousness will become a reality in about forty years (Moravac, 1988). Indeed, all of these tasks are being worked on as we write. A number of bright and capable cognitive scientists, ranging from mathematicians to psychologists to neurobiologists to computer engineers, are busily at work trying to understand and create artificial minds (Franklin, 1995). When these concepts are applied to the computer counselor, as far as its range of techniques is concerned, it may well equal—and perhaps exceed—the typical human therapist. Whether the future counseling computer can stand alone or will serve as an adjunct to the human therapist is an interesting question. Whether it will do as well or even better than the human therapist is another interesting question.

Theory of Personality

It should be abundantly clear that a counseling computer per se has no distinct theory of personality other than what is programmed into it. Given the current state of technology, there are limits to what that programmed theory of personality might be. Cognitive behavioral approaches are currently the most amenable to programming, in contrast to psychoanalytic approaches, which call for deep personal understanding of the client (Finkel, 1990; Kenardy & Adams, 1993; Wagman, 1988, p. 102).

Nature of Maladjustment

Presently, maladjustment is probably most limited by current programming's ability to deal with initial relationship exploration, adjustment problems that can be handled with psychoeducational techniques, and situation-specific cognitive-based problems such as phobias and depression (Colby, 1995; Kirkby, 1996). Although virtual reality is capable of being adapted to such issues it cannot, at present, generate more complex psychodynamic scenarios such as individually building the client's own personal psychodrama or role playing (Franklin, 1997).

Major Concepts

Integrating Metaphorical Systems

The language of psychotherapy and other systems is best represented in metaphors. Wagman's (1988) analysis of different types of metaphors as representative of different types of systems of psychotherapy is instructive from the standpoint of the intersection of type of therapeutic relationship and type of problem. That is, psychoanalysis has classical literary metaphors; behaviorism has physiological, mechanistic metaphors; humanistic therapies have personal and idealistic metaphors; and cognitive therapies have logical and educative metaphors.

These therapeutic systems and their metaphors can be put in contrast to one another in a dimensional analysis. On an X–Y axis the four quadrants would contrast affective and cognitive relationships (X) and focal and diffuse problems (Y). Virtually every therapeutic modality in this book could be placed in one of the quadrants, depending on how much affective (person-centered) or cognitive (cognitive-behaviorism) emphasis is placed on the therapeutic relationship and how focal (phobia; clarification of values) or diffuse (generalized, chronic depression; anxiety neurosis) the problem is (Wagman, 1988, pp. 12–14).

On the other hand, artificial intelligence has as its basis computational and schematic metaphors that Wagman in 1988 believed tended to put its metaphorical representation at cross purposes with the major therapeutic systems (p. 13). Nine years later, Franklin (1997) stated that was no longer so and that, in principle, any of the psychotherapeutic metaphors could be programmed or developed.

The Computer as Mind

The concepts of *mind* and *intelligent mind* need to be thought of in new and different ways. Franklin's (1995) work on artificial minds wrestles extensively with this problem. Suffice it to say that what he deals with in this arena goes far beyond the scope of this book. Yet the advent of attempting to make "intelligent" computers calls for divergent thinking about what *mind* is. Traditional mind–body theories fall into three categories. *The mentalist* theory holds that the mind is everything and that it produces the material world as sensation such that the mind is a spiritual entity. The *materialist* theory holds that mind is only a physical process, but that this physical process can become very sophisticated, up to and including the exotic physics of quantum mechanics. The *dualist* theory holds that the mental and the physical have existences of their own and that the mind is subject to completely different principles of operation than the body (Franklin, 1995, pp. 25–26). To get at the business of an artificial mind, Franklin proposes a workable hypothesis that considers minds in a functionalist-physicalist sense. That is, minds are the software and brains are the hardware that make the software run. In that regard, mind could certainly run on some type of hardware other than a human being's neurological system. In fact, it might just as well run on a computer (p. 28).

Computers That Can Learn

Mind, to some degree, can be implemented on machines (Franklin, 1995, p. 18). The question becomes to what degree. A truly humanlike computer counselor ought to have a mind of its own that could create, store, and modify information. It could make inferences and deductions based on that information and extrapolate it in bigger and better ways as new and different situations enter its environment. It ought to be able to hop between the quadrants of therapeutic modalities and problem specificity, described by Wagman (1988), without going into default mode. In short, it ought to be able to learn from its experience.

How much a counseling computer needs to learn is certainly open to question. For specific information the client could immediately put to use, the narrow parameters of what a computer counseling system needs to learn to effectively interact with a client is now in existence. How to engage a client in multiple and creative dynamic interactions that would be necessary in unraveling the subconscious mind that so intrigues the analytical theories remains in the future (Franklin, 1997).

The Need for Faster, Cheaper, More Effective Psychotherapy

The adherents of practically every therapeutic modality in this book—with the possible exception of the Jungians—are scurrying to provide "brief" therapies for their systems. The stark truth of this rapid movement toward brief therapies is that managed care demands fast, efficient, and effective delivery of services or it won't pay the bill. The movement toward cost containment and the necessity to provide universal mental health care to the masses—not just the affluent—has enormous economic, political, and social implications, and those who can't adapt will be left behind. It is clear that whoever uses the counseling computer most effectively will have a tremendous advantage over the competition.

THE COUNSELING PROCESS

Before you burn this book because you are now paranoid enough to believe that a counseling computer with an empathic, cheerful-looking virtual reality therapist will replace you before you even get to be one, consider the following propositions from the computer counselor's critic's and purponents.

Therapy requires a human therapist. If that were so, then there would be no crisis lines or self-help audio and video tapes. Colby (1995) believes that when clients use his computer counselor, Overcoming Depression, they are communicating with him, except they are one step removed. The bottom line is that if computer therapy can be made available for individuals who could not access human help because it was half a world away or could not afford it, then it would be highly unethical to not provide computer counseling. Let us introduce you to Lucy, who is currently undergoing therapy for treatment of depression.

CL: (Lucy in Brisbane, Australia, more than 200 miles from her home, a cattle station in Queensland, Australia, talking to Dr. Lovehaight, a psychologist). Look, I know I need the therapy, I guess I'm pretty depressed, but I'm an over-the-air school teacher, don't make much money, and live over 200 miles from here.

CO: I've got something I'd like you to try. I see by your intake form you have access to a computer and the Net. I'm hooked up to Website; it's a computer counseling system that works with depression. I've also got a computer program on depression that I'll give you on a diskette that I think will help. Would you be willing to do that and have the computer keep me informed of your progress and I would check with you or vice versa every two weeks or on an as-needed basis? The counseling computer is $20 per session and you can pay by credit card. You can access it any time. If you agree, I'll set you up on a trial basis.

The computer counselor is always accessible. Twenty-four hours a day, 365 days a year, and particularly on Christmas when you are all alone and really feeling blue. Unlike the fifty-minute counseling hour and a therapist who will not be there "this evening"—and certainly not on Christmas eve—the computer is always accessible (Colby, 1995; Zarr, 1994). The advent of the Internet and Web sites makes the computer counselor available to anyone any time, any place.

```
CL: (Christmas eve, alone on the Gipsy Plains cat-
tle station near ClonCurry, Queensland, Australia,
typing: "http:www.EnergizedHal.com")

COM: (Energized Hal on-line computer of WorldWide
Therapy Incorporated, Seattle, Washington, United
States, responding) Please enter your access code
and credit card number.

CL: (typing: "Downunder")

COM: Hello, Lucy. What would you like to talk about
this evening?
```

Use of stand-alone counseling computers is dangerous and unethical. As with all science, computers have the capacity for good and evil. (We certainly are not thrilled, for example, by the extremely violent and bloody computer action games in arcades). However, there is no reason to suppose that computers cannot be programmed, like a doctor, to "do no harm." The computer could easily determine when its skill boundaries had been reached and would then make a referral to other resources, which is not always the case with some human therapists.

```
COM: Lucy, my limits are exceeded by your current
problem. I am going to give you the E-mail address
of a marriage and family therapist in Grenada, Mis-
sissippi, USA. Dr. Sharon Latham. She is capable of
dealing with this issue. She is available for an
appointment at 11 A.M. tomorrow, your time. Would
you like me to log you into her appointment book?
The fee is a copayment of $20 Australian per hour,
which you may pay by credit card. I am also worried
that you might be thinking of harming yourself.
Thus, I have sent Dr. Lovehaight a pager call in
Brisbane. He should be contacting you immediately
by telephone. I want you to be sure and stay on-
line with me until you get his call, OK?
```

Computers also would not be prone to some of the interpersonal relationship problems that plague human therapists that prompt many of the ethical complaints that reach boards of review. Computers are not likely to have sexual harassment charges made against them.

Both the American Psychological Association and the American Counseling Association have sections in their ethical codes that deal with the use of computers.

These codes specifically consider the intellectual, emotional, and physical capabilities of the client to use computers; the client's specific needs as they fit computer capabilities; the client's understanding of what the computer program is designed to do and its limitations; and the need for adequate follow-up by the therapist to ensure appropriate use and assess subsequent client needs.

The computer counselor is unable to experience feelings. That's true as of now. However, that doesn't mean the client is unable to project his or her feelings onto the computer. In fact, the computer counselor is eminently capable of being projected on by clients (Weizenbaum, 1976). The computer is quickly anthropomorphized into a living person—both good and bad. As a result, it is the rare person indeed who doesn't experience feelings generated at the computer counselor and by the computer counselor. We are hard-pressed to see how that is very different than a human counselor.

CL: One thing I like about you, Hal, is that you never get on me about messing up. My controlling boyfriend could take a lesson!

COM: It's pretty important to let you alone to make your own mistakes, Lucy, and that includes your boyfriend not trying to tell you what to do.

CL: You don't understand how important this guy is to me Hal. I really love him . . . and hate him. About like you sometimes, you stupid machine!

COM: So you have ambivalent feelings about both your boyfriend and me. Can you tell me more about that?

From a psychoanalytic view, creating transference is critical to catharsis, insight, and resolution of the problem. This example indicates how both positive and negative transference from client to the computer counselor can occur, and how the computer counselor will respond in much the same manner as a human therapist who recognizes the phenomenon and doesn't get sucked into it.

The computer counselor is infinitely patient. The computer counselor will engage in practicing the desired behavior over and over and over again with just as much patience as the first time, perhaps unlike the human counselor, who may get tired and frustrated with the client's attempts to take therapy out into the real world. As Colby (1995) indicates, high percentages of clients have relapses of depression. Catching the slide into relapse quickly and doing something about it is as easy as turning the computer on.

CL: I have practiced and practiced being assertive. Sure it's fine when I do it with you, but boy, when I try that on him, I always wimp out. I can't do this anymore. I give up!

COM: You have practiced quite a lot, Lucy, and done very well with me. Perhaps we could try this again?

CL: Not only NO, but HELL NO.

COM: That's great! You certainly showed some assertiveness with me just now. I understand your frustration; perhaps we can try a new routine later on this evening and you could use that assertiveness on your boyfriend Schroeder the next time he tells you what to do.

The computer will not engage in countertransference. Countertransference is common when the client is frustrated and projects his or her failures onto the therapist and the therapist, equally frustrated, retaliates (Wagman, 1988, p. 16). In short, the computer counselor will not start to see the client as, for instance, a whining, parasitic sister-in-law who she tries to avoid as much as possible at family gatherings.

CL: You son-of-a-bitch. It's always back to my screwy thinking. Well he's the one that's screwy, you motherboard, and so are you for that matter.

COM: It sounds like you're angry with both him and me for questioning you.

CL: You bet your hard drive ass I am.

COM: Anger is a different emotion than you have ever expressed with me before. Want to tell me what's different now?

CL: You are, you're just like him.

COM: So we both frustrate you and make you feel overwhelmed, but now you feel safe in getting angry with me. I'm glad you feel safe enough to lose control with me. Can you catch the thought or the feeling, or even a behavior that happened right before that? It would be a good cue when Schroeder starts to do that to you.

The counseling computer is an "expert." The counseling computer may make rookie mistakes to begin with, but as the computer programmers and psychotherapists engineer the glitches out, it will make fewer and fewer—at least as far as the "experts" who programmed it are able to. A process called expert engineering that teams computer programmers with experts in the field would enable the responses of any therapeutic guru to be programmed into the counseling computer along with the necessary treatment plan to go with it (Franklin, 1997; Stout, 1992; Wagman, 1988, pp. 71–81). The computer counselor who has been programmed by these experts will be just as "expert" and most likely will not make the therapeutic errors a less experienced counselor might.

Therapeutic technique is target specific. Indeed, as therapy has evolved and cognitive therapies have come to the forefront, global personality change has become secondary to identification and reduction of specific symptoms. As such, therapy has taken on a much more educational and technological approach and has become more prescriptive in nature. The contemporary therapist has become more of an instructor, guide, and advisor, and this is exactly where the computer counselor is in its element (Colby, 1995; Wagman, 1988, p. 18)

COM: Lucy, from the issues you have presented, I am going to suggest that this problem can best be taken care of by a procedure called covert modeling. Now let me explain what we are going to do. Please feel free to ask me questions if you are unsure of my explanation.

The counseling computer is cheap mental health help. As with other technological fields, the computer is much less expensive to operate than a human being and doesn't need an insurance plan, retirement benefits, or vacation or sick leave. For the price of a monthly subscriber fee a client may have unlimited access to a multiplicity of programs that will assess, diagnose, prescribe, and refer the client for medication or other specialized help (Colby, 1995; Zarr, 1994).

COM: Lucy, it seems to me you are depressed enough to need some medication. If you agree, I will send your MMPI personality test results and symptoms to Dr. Rex Adapuss, a psychiatrist in Brisbane. He will want to talk with you and perhaps prescribe some medicine for you.

Hal sends a complete printout about Lucy to Dr. Adapuss along with an "expert" diagnosis of the problem and treatment suggestions. Indeed, programs are now available that not only diagnose but also prescribe treatment procedures for specific maladies (Hile, Ghobary, & Campbell, 1995; Warzecha, 1991) and provide specific test results and drug information for the client (Colby, 1995).

COM: Lucy I'd like you to take a brief test for depression. I'll score it and send it to Dr. Adapuss and Dr. Lovehaight. I'll also give you the interpretation and tell you whether or not it seems that an antidepressant is indicated. I'll also tell you, if you want, what your drug options are and what they can and cannot do for you. You can then check these out with your doctors.

Counseling computers don't understand subtlety. While this may be true now, there is no reason to believe that it will remain so. Voice-activated and responsive computers that respond through natural language are in the not-too-distant future (Kirkby, 1996). One has only to look at the evolution of video games to see the unlimited potential of the computer. Like the advance from the simplistic ping pong games of the seventies to the immersed virtual reality of the nineties, the potential of the computer to interact with its human counterparts has multiplied exponentially in twenty years. As we have seen with cognitive scientists, there is reason to believe that this advance will continue and that therefore, counseling computers will be able to understand the subtlest nuances of the client.

Computer therapy is currently too mechanistic. The computer counselor is presently bound to the limits of the machine's program, but it can achieve the precision of a human therapist and probably perform even better. The advent and progress of computer therapy demands that therapeutic systems finely hone techniques and construct precise language to fit the decision rules of a computer. Computer counseling is likely to force therapy to become more efficient and problem specific (Wagman, 1988, p. 29). In an age of managed care, it is hard to imagine that cost-conscious health-care providers would not embrace such precision and behaviorally targeted therapy wholeheartedly (Greist, 1995).

A computer can't understand nonverbal communication. The computer and its peripherals are admirably suited to continuous monitoring, measuring, and recording of a number of physiological responses in the client that may directly relate to what is going on in therapy (Kirkby, 1996).

COM: Lucy, so I can get a better idea of what's going on with you physically when you start to get those frustrated feelings, I'd like for you to put that skin temperature monitor on your index finger.

Some people would be turned off by a computer. A great deal of research has pointed to the therapeutic relationship as more critical than method, technique, theory, or particular therapist in predicting a successful outcome (Cormier & Cormier, 1991; Corsini & Wedding, 1995; Eysenck, 1952; 1965; Garfield, 1980; Menniger & Holzman, 1973; Patterson, 1994). Technologically, perhaps if you are over a certain age and believe that electric typewriters are "new fangled contraptions," then an inability to form a relationship with a counseling computer may be a problem. However, for the members of Generation X, the computer is as natural a part of life as eating (Colby, 1995).

In the early 1970s the wife of one of the authors, then a school counselor in a rural school district in Illinois, was asked to institute a very rudimentary version of a computer career counseling program in her high school. An experiment was conducted to determine which mode of career information accessing the students preferred—the computer or the counselor. A statistical analysis showed no significant difference in preference for the counselor or the computer. This preference ratio is not uncommon and has also been found with the widely used PLATO personal counseling program (Wagman, 1988, p. 129). Clients are often more willing to reveal personal information to a computer than to a therapist because they know the computer will not think any less of them (Plutchik & Karasu, 1991).

CL: (somewhat shyly) Hal, I . . . well . . . I'm not as sophisticated and worldly as I make out.

COM: How is that Lucy?

CL: I'm 23 years old and I'm still a virgin.

COM: Tell me what goes through your mind to make you think that being a virgin is unsophisticated.

Although the computer counselor may not consummate a "traditional" therapeutic relationship with a client, it is the client's perception and receptivity of the relationship that really counts. For the mounting numbers of people who are becoming familiar and at ease with computers, the question of "relationship" may become a moot point.

The computer is locked into its own program and can't adapt. At present, computers are hard pressed to adapt to any degree beyond what they are programmed to do. Yet computers that are adaptable in every sense of the word are currently being constructed (Franklin, 1997). To the contrary, being "locked" into a particular approach may be a positive attribute. Computers can standardize treatment without the vagaries, personal issues, therapeutic biases, or other incompetencies that can plague human therapists (Stout, 1992). In assessment terminology, the computer counselor would be highly reliable. The truth is that although particular therapeutic techniques are known to be the most effective approaches for a particular problem, they do not always get used (Greist, 1995). If a computer is counseling, the most efficacious and efficient treatment commonly employed for the problem will be used—without hesitation.

CONTRIBUTIONS OF COMPUTER COUNSELING

The possible contributions of computer counseling are manifold and a look into the future of artificial intelligence as it might apply to psychotherapy is truly staggering. We have already mentioned many of the benefits that a counseling computer could provide a client. Let us now look at what it could do for a therapist. First and foremost, it could do what computers now do best—that is, relieve the therapist of such tedious and mind numbing chores as history taking, diagnostic work-ups, and case following. It can provide the therapist with "best bet" diagnoses, therapeutic approaches, and access to expert advice at the touch of the keyboard (Hile, Ghobary, & Campbell, 1995). It can also deal quite nicely with the time-consuming trenchwork of less freewheeling and creative therapeutic techniques such as repetitious desensitization procedures or data gathering prior to cognitive restructuring. It is capable of handling any number of clients at one time. Depending on the number of terminals and the size of the server system, the computer counselor could relieve the severe understaffing that plagues so many mental health clinics. The counseling computer could also give the therapist Christmas off—for the most part. As in our dialogue with Lucy, the counseling computer could field crisis calls at any time and have a "dangerous" mode that would trigger a call to a therapist, to 911, or to anywhere else it might need to seek help.

The counseling computer can also help therapists become more proficient when its role is reversed and it becomes the computer client. A variety of computer programs have been developed to model client behavior. Colby and Gilbert (1964) developed a program to model a neurotic woman who had been in psychoanalytic therapy for a long time. Colby (1975) also developed PARRY, which becomes progressively more paranoid the longer the therapist interacts with it. This program was so effective that it fooled a group of psychiatrists who were interacting with it into believing that PARRY was a real person.

Taxi driver is a program modeled after the psychopathology of Travis Bickle, a character in the film *Taxi Driver,* and is designed to allow students to perform a full mental status examination. It is capable of analyzing and giving feedback on very complicated responses the students make while conducting the examination (Hyler & Bujold, 1994).

CLIENT 1 is a behavioral simulation of an initial exploratory session. The objective for the trainee is to ease the client's threat level about certain topics by getting him to talk in less general terms and become able to speak of his more threatening problems in more precise and explicit terms. The client, a thirtysomething businessman, adjusts his level of trust in relation to the counselor's ability to use reflection and interpretation. If the reflective and interpretive statements are off the mark, the client's threat level will continue to elevate. Continued ineptitude on the therapist's part can lead to termination of the session (Hummel, Lichtenberg, & Shaffer, 1975; Lichtenberg, Hummel, & Shaffer, 1984).

In the form of virtual reality, the computer could become one of the most powerful tools a therapist has in projecting clients into a feared situation safely while at the same time providing valuable data through peripheral biofeedback devices on how the client is responding to the situation. Because of the computer counselor's replicability it would allow for very precise measures of the treatment process (Kirkby, 1996). Its efficiency to do all of the foregoing could allow harried therapists in a managed care world to deal with more clients and more complex cases, and to provide those clients with more quality therapy time (Colby, 1995). A virtual reality therapist could also become the therapist's best friend by dealing interactively with tough cases and then lending an empathic electronic ear to woes of how ungrateful clients are, the slow pay of intransigent insurance companies, long hours, emergency phone calls in the middle of the night, and how callously the therapist's boss and significant other treat him or her.

SHORTCOMINGS OF COMPUTER COUNSELING

A major area of concern in computer counseling has to do with ethics in regard to both the social effects and the moral dimensions of computerization (Behar, 1993). There are at least three major ethical problems that critics might propose for computer counseling. The first major issue is confidentiality. There is no guarantee at present that what goes out over the airwaves does not become fodder for public consumption. However, this problem is very near a solution, and there is good reason to believe that clients will soon have little to fear in imparting personal information to a computer (Franklin, 1997).

The second issue is program validity. The assessment movement has a long and sometimes sad history of promising much and providing little in the way of valid tests. There is no reason to suppose that commercial computer counseling programs would be any better. Whereas the *Mental Measurements Yearbook* (Conoley & Impara, 1995) does an excellent job of casting a critical eye on commercial tests, there is no such vehicle for computer counseling programs. Consumers need to be aware of just how well such programs do what they promise to—although the same could surely be said of human therapists.

The field of psychotherapy has had its own long and sad history of self-styled gurus and charlatans who promise much and deliver nothing, at best, or who are dangerous to clients, at worst. From the various larcenies and other felonies already being perpetrated over the Net, it is not to hard to imagine that a number of electronic snake oil salespeople will be in the business of trying to fleece individuals with mental health issues. The Net is clearly a caveat emptor world, particularly when the snake oil charlatan is operating half a world away.

Even if programs for computer counseling are valid, a troubling treatment issue at present is their nomenthetic nature. That is, a program for depression would be based on a standardized normative treatment procedure. Such a nomenthetic approach is not necessarily bad, given that a treatment regimen such as cognitive restructuring for treatment of depression for almost every depressed client is justified. Although computer counseling can engage in a good deal of variety now, it is not presently at the stage that true idiographic treatment procedures are available that see individuals as phenomenological entities with their own specific issues. That is, while you and I may be depressed, we are certainly not depressed in the same way. Nor is anyone else depressed quite like either one of us. Therefore, although we both may benefit from cognitive restructuring, we still need to be approached in an idiosyncratic way as distinctive individuals who just happen to have depression in common. Presently, the technology would seem to mandate that human therapists be part of the treatment procedure to ensure that therapy doesn't become an assembly line approach. Whether this will be true in the future as computers become more adaptable is an interesting question.

The third issue for concern is accessibility and usability. Until the advent of voice-activated computers, a client must have a modicum of knowledge about computers and the skill to type and input data. While this may not be a problem for most college students, it certainly would be for some portion of the world population. The simple fact is that while computers may be "cool" for the younger generation, they may not be for the older generation or the economically disenfranchised, who may have little or no knowledge of or trust in computers.

Unless a virtual reality therapist or a counseling robot can engender tactile sensation, the sense of physical touch that is often important in therapy is certainly missing with the computer counselor. Although many clients maintain that touch is the last thing they want, and fear of sexual harassment charges has certainly limited touching in the contemporary world of therapy, it is our strong belief that many clients need what they avoid most—direct human contact. Some of our most poignant, moving, and productive moments have come by touching or holding someone in therapy.

Finally, therapists themselves may be a shortcoming. For many therapists, coming to grips with a counseling computer may be as thrilling as having the Ebola virus sitting in the room. Greist (1965) states quite well the case of therapists who rigidly resist the computer by quoting the noted physicist Max Planck (1969) on the problem of scientific revolutions and paradigm shifts:

> *A new scientific truth does not triumph by convincing its opponents and making them see the light, but rather because its opponents eventually die, and a new generation grows up that is familiar with it.*

Any change is difficult, but this is one of the most dramatic changes in mental health provision since Freud decided to have a patient lie down on a couch. We hope that the profession itself has the flexibility and adaptability it extols for its clients to meet the coming shift in how therapy with a computer may be accomplished.

COMPUTER COUNSELING WITH DIVERSE POPULATIONS

As seen with our fictitious client from the Outback, computer counseling has tremendous advantages for those who live in remote geographical areas where psychotherapy is not readily available. For those who are physically disabled or otherwise unable to travel to a therapist, the counseling computer certainly would be a valuable asset. We also see the applicability of the computer counselor in crisis line work, much of which is done by volunteers. There is a constant struggle to keep enough staff available to operate phone lines twenty-four hours a day, 365 days a year; the counseling computer would seem well equipped to do such a job.

The counseling computer also has the capability of providing counseling to many people who could not otherwise afford therapy. It is well suited to communities and states strapped for funds in providing at least adjunctive mental health care to the indigent.

For people who are shy and have trouble finding the right words to express themselves, the computer is not only infinitely patient, it is nonthreatening as well. Further, the counseling computer would seem particularly appropriate for people who may believe their problems are so socially unacceptable that they would be too ashamed to talk about them. As in the case of adult survivors of childhood sexual abuse, who may feel shame and culpability in the abuse inflicted on them, the computer counselor is absolutely accepting and nonjudgmental in hearing the most intimate details of a person's life.

SUMMARY

Computers as an informational and assessment component to psychotherapy have been integral to the profession for over twenty years, but their role is changing. With the advent of more powerful memory, home computers, the Internet, and virtual reality, the computer as counselor has arrived on the therapeutic scene. Although the computer is not presently widely used as a direct service provider, that scenario is changing. The promise of easy and inexpensive accessibility has extrinsic appeal in a world of managed care that is attempting to get the most "bang for its buck." Computers that feel, create, adapt, and learn are in the works. There is no reason to suppose that these cannot be adapted to psychotherapy. As we move into the next millennium, it would appear that the counseling computer is going to be inextricably linked to the human therapist.

SUGGESTED READINGS

Franklin, S. (1995). *Artificial minds*. Cambridge, MA: MIT Press.
Wagman, M. (1988). *Computer psychotherapy systems: Theory and research foundations*. New York: Gordon and Breach Science Publishers.

REFERENCES

Amsel, A. (1992). Confessions of a neobehavioralist. *Integrative Physiological and Behavioral Science, 27*(4), 336–346.

Behar, J. (1993). Computer ethics: Moral philosophy or professional propaganda? *Computers in Human Services, 9*(3–4), 441–453.

Biocca, F. (1992). Virtual reality technology: A tutorial. *Journal of Communication, 42*(4), 23–72.

Brennis, B. C. (1994). The skewing of psychiatry. *Academic Psychiatry, 18*(2), 71–80.

Colby, K. M. (1963). Computer simulation of a neurotic process. In S. S. Tomkins & S. Messick (Eds.), *Computer simulation of personality: Frontiers of psychological research* (pp. 165–180). New York: Wiley.

Colby, K. M. (1975). *Artificial paranoia: A computer simulation of paranoid processes.* New York: Pergamon.

Colby, K. M. (1995). A computer program using cognitive therapy to treat depressed patients. *Psychiatric Services, 46*, 1223–1225.

Colby, K. M., & Gilbert, J. P. (1964). Programming a computer model of neurosis. *Journal of Mathematical Psychology, 1*, 220–227.

Conoley, J. C., & Impara, J. C. (Eds.). (1995). *The twelfth mental measurements yearbook.* Lincoln, NE: University of Nebraska Press.

Cormier, W. H., & Cormier, L. S. (1991). *Interviewing strategies for helpers: Fundamental skill and cognitive behavioral interventions* (3rd ed.). Pacific Grove: Brooks/Cole.

Corsini, R. J., & Wedding, D. (1995). *Current psychotherapies* (5th ed.). Itasca, IL: F. E. Peacock.

Erdman, H. R., Klein, M. H., & Greist, J. H. (1985). Direct patient computer interviewing. *Journal of Consulting and Clinical Psychology, 53*, 760–773.

Eysenck, H. J. (1952). *The scientific study of personality.* New York: Macmillan.

Eysenck, H. J. (1965). *Fact and fiction in psychology.* Harmondsworth, UK: Penguin Books.

Finkel, S. J. (1990). Psychotherapy, technology, and aging. *International Journal of Technology and Aging, 3*(l), 57–61.

Franklin, S. (1995). *Artificial minds.* Cambridge, MA: MIT Press.

Franklin, S. (1997). The present and future of artificial intelligence in psychotherapy. Cassette recording #9701. Institute for Intelligent Systems. Memphis, TN: University of Memphis.

Garfield, S. L. (1980). *Psychotherapy: An eclectic approach.* New York: Wiley.

Greist, J. H. (1995). Computers and psychiatry. *Psychiatric Services, 46*, 989–991.

Hile, M. G., Ghobary, B. B., & Campbell, D. M. (1995). Source of expert advice: A comparison of peer-reviewed advice from the literature with that from an automated performance support system. *Behavior Research Methods, Instruments, and Computers, 27*(2), 272–276.

Hummel, T. J., Lichtenberg, J. W., & Shaffer W. F. (1975). CLIENT 1: A computer program which simulates client behavior in an initial interview. *Journal of Counseling Psychology, 26*, 279–284.

Hyler, S. E. & Bujold, A. E. (1994). Computers and psychiatric education: The "Taxi Driver" mental status examination. *Psychiatric Annals, 21*(1), 13–19.

Kenardy, J., & Adams, C. (1993). Computers in cognitive behavior therapy. *Australian Psychologist, 28*(3), 189–194.

Kirkby, K. C. (1996). Computer assisted treatment of phobias. *Psychiatric Services, 47,* 139–142.

Lichtenberg, J. W., Hummel, T. J., & Shaffer, W. F. (1984). CLIENT 1: A computer simulation for use in counselor education and research. *Counselor Education and Supervision, 24,* 155–167.

Menniger, K. A., & Holzman, P. S. (1973). *Theory of psychoanalytic techniques* (2nd ed.). New York: Basic Books.

Moravec, H. (1988). *Mind children.* Cambridge, MA: Harvard University Press.

Muscott, H. S., & Gifford, T. (1994). Virtual reality and social skills training for students with behavioral disorders: Applications, challenges and promising practices. *Education and Treatment of Children, 17*(4), 417–434.

Pardeck, J. T., & Schulte, R. S. (1990). Computers in social intervention: Implications for professional social work practice and education. *Family Therapy, 17*(2), 109–121.

Patterson, C. H. (1994). *Theories of counseling and psychotherapy* (5th ed.). New York: Harper and Row.

Planck, M. (1968). *Scientific autobiography and other papers* (F. Gaynor, Trans.). Westport, CO: Greenwood Press. (Original work published 1949)

Plutchik, R., & Karasu, T. B. (1991). Computers in psychotherapy: An overview. *Computers in Human Behavior, 7*(1–2), 33–44.

Rothbaum, O., Hodges, L. F., Kooper, R., Opdyke, D., Williford, J. S., & North, M. (1995). Effectiveness of computer generated virtual reality graded exposure in the treatment of acrophobia. *American Journal of Psychiatry, 152,* 626–628.

Slack, W. V., Hicks, G. P., Reed, C. Z., & VanCura, L. J. (1966). A computer based medical history system. *New England Journal of Medicine, 274,* 194–198.

Stout, C. E. (1992). An automated method of psychiatric treatment planning. *Behavior Research Methods, Instruments, and Computers, 24*(2), 326–327.

Wagman, M. (1979). Systematic dilemma counseling: Theory, method, research. *Psychological Reports, 44,* 55–72.

Wagman, M. (1980). PLATO DCS. An interactive computer system for personal counseling. *Journal of Counseling Psychology, 27,* 16–30.

Wagman, M. (1982). A computer method for solving dilemmas. *Psychological Reports, 50,* 291–298.

Wagman, M. (1984). *The dilemma and the computer: Theory, research, and applications to counseling psychology.* New York: Praeger.

Wagman, M. (1988). *Computer psychotherapy systems: Theory and research foundations.* New York: Gordon and Breach Science Publishers.

Warzecha, G. (1991). The challenge to psychological assessment from modern computer technology. *European Review of Applied Psychology, 41*(3), 213–220.

Weizenbaum, J. (1965). ELIZA—A computer program for the study of natural language communication between man and machine. *Communication of the Association for Computing Machinery, 9,* 36–45.

Weizenbaum, J. (1976). *Computer power and human reason: From judgment to calculation.* San Francisco: Freeman.

Zarr, M. (1994). Computer-aided psychotherapy: Machine helping therapist. *Psychiatric Annals, 24*(l), 42–46

INDEX

Note: Italicized letters *f* and *t* following page references indicate figures and tables, respectively.

ABC theory, 234–236
  components of, 235–236
  identifying B in, 246–248
  problem exploration in, 246
Abraham, Karl, 11
Abstract imaging, 305
Absurdity, reduction to, rational-emotive behavior therapy and, 250
Accountability, and behaviorism, 223
Acting as if, in Adlerian therapy, 61
Action, in rational-emotive behavior therapy, 249
Activating event, in ABC theory, 234–235
Actualizing tendency, 113
Adaptation, mistakes of, 49
Adapted Child state, 167
Addiction(s)
  Adlerian view of, 50
  control theory/reality therapy for, 274–275, 282–283, 288, 290
  negative, 274–275
  positive, 274, 282–283, 288
  reframing for, 308–309
Adler, Alfred, 11, 42, 231
Adlerian therapy, 42–75
  contributions of, 70
  with diverse populations, 71–72
  fundamental tenets of, 42–51

history of, 42–43
overview of, 2*t*, 4, 43–44
process of, 52–57
sample case in, 64–69
shortcomings of, 70
techniques in, 57–64
Adult ego state, 165, 168
Affect, BASIC ID assessment of, 378
African Americans, cognitive therapy with, 324
Aggression, in Gestalt therapy, 138–139
Alcoholism, covert modeling for, 306
AMCD. *See* Association for Multicultural Counseling and Development
American Counseling Association, on computer-assisted therapy, 410–411
American Psychological Association (APA)
  on computer-assisted therapy, 410–411
  Division of Clinical Psychology, 365
Amplification, in dream interpretation, 92, 93
Anal stage, 16
Analogies, in rational-emotive behavior therapy, 249–250
Analysis, in trait-factor counseling, 340, 353–354
Analytical psychotherapy. *See* Jungian therapy
Anecdotal records, in trait-factor counseling, 338
Anger, in transactional analysis, 190
Anima/animus, 80
  and transformation, 86

Narcissistic identification, 19
Needs, in control theory/reality therapy, 272, 276, 278–279
Negative addictions, 274–275
Negative imagery, in rational-emotive behavior therapy, 253
Negative reinforcement, 202
Neo-behavioristic mediational stimulus-response model, 200
Neo-Freudians, 11
Neurolinguistic programming (NLP), 296, 311–312
Neurosis
    Adler's theory of, 48–51
    Freud's theory of, 12, 17–18
    Gestalt theory of, 139–141
    Jung's theory of, 82
    person-centered theory of, 113
Nomothetic principles, 46
Nonverbal behavior
    in Adlerian therapy, 53, 58
    in Gestalt therapy, 137, 147
Nonverbal communication, computer-assisted therapy and, 414
NTPS. *See* Nystul Turning Point Survey
Nurturing Parent, 167
    messages of, 170
Nystul Turning Point Survey (NTPS), 53

Objective level, of dream interpretation, 92
Objective stimulus, in ABC theory, 235
Object-loss identification, 19
Object-relations psychology, 26–27
    with diverse populations, 34–35
    techniques in, 29
Observation, and beliefs, 236
Obsessive-compulsive anxiety, covert modeling for, 306
Obsessive-compulsive person, Adler's view of, 48
Occupation, life task of, 45
Oedipus complex, 16
Operant conditioning, 199
    and maladaptive behavior, 205–206
Operant reinforcement, personality theory of, 201–203
Oppositional balancing, in Jungian theory, 83
Oppositions, ego state, 192
Oral stage, 15–16
Organ dialect, 53
Organismic self-regulation, 137

Organismic valuing process, 111–112, 114
Organization corollary, constructivist theory, 379
Origin of Species (Darwin), 10

P × E. *See* Person × environment fit
Parables, in rational-emotive behavior therapy, 249–250
Paradoxical intention
    in Adlerian therapy, 60
    in rational-emotive behavior therapy, 251
Paralinguistics, in rational-emotive behavior therapy, 250
Parent ego state, 165, 168
PARRY, 415–416
Parsons, Frank, 332
Paterson, Donald, 332. *See also* Trait-factor counseling
Peasant game, 181
Penalization, in rational-emotive behavior therapy, 255–256
Penis envy, 16
Perception(s)
    behavior as function of, 48
    in control theory/reality therapy, 278–279, 282–283
Perls, Frederick S. (Fritz), 136–137
Perls, Laura, 136–137
Person × environment (P × E) fit, 333. *See also* Trait-factor counseling
    assessment procedures in, 337–338
    case history in, 339
    counseling process in, 337
    nature of maladjustment in, 335–336
Persona, in Jungian theory, 79
Personal construct theory. *See* Constructivist theory
Personal constructs psychology, 295
Personal growth. *See* Growth
Personal unconscious, 78, 79, 80
Personality
    Adlerian theory of, 44–48
    behavioral theory of, 201–204
    biological basis of, 233–234
    cognitive therapy theory of, 297
    computer-assisted therapy theory of, 407
    control theory/reality therapy and, 271–275
    eclecticism theory of, 366–367
    Freudian theory of, 13–15
    Gestalt theory of, 138–139
    Jungian theory of, 78–82, 84–85